Getting Money for College

Scholarships
for
Hispanic
Students

THOMSON
★
PETERSON'S ™

Australia • Canada • Mexico • Singapore • Spain • United Kingdom • United States

THOMSON
™
PETERSON'S

About The Thomson Corporation and Peterson's

The Thomson Corporation, with 2002 revenues of US$7.8 billion, is a global leader in providing integrated information solutions to business and professional customers. The Corporation's common shares are listed on the Toronto and New York stock exchanges (TSX: TOC; NYSE: TOC). Its learning businesses and brands serve the needs of individuals, learning institutions, corporations, and government agencies with products and services for both traditional and distributed learning. Peterson's (www.petersons.com) is a leading provider of education information and advice, with books and online resources focusing on education search, test preparation, and financial aid. Its Web site offers searchable databases and interactive tools for contacting educational institutions, online practice tests and instruction, and planning tools for securing financial aid. Peterson's serves 110 million education consumers annually.

For more information, contact Peterson's, 2000 Lenox Drive, Lawrenceville, NJ 08648; 800-338-3282; or find us on the World Wide Web at www.petersons.com/about.

ISBN 0-7689-1358-6

Printed in Canada

10 9 8 7 6 5 4 3 2 1   05 04 03

First Edition

Contents

Introduction v

The System and How It Works: The ABCs of Paying for College

How Can You Pay for College? 3
Where Can You Find Help? 23
Scholarship Scams: What They Are and What to
    Watch Out For 27
How to Use This Book 31

Profiles

Academic Fields/Career Goals 36
Nonacademic/Noncareer Criteria 243
Miscellaneous Criteria 318

Indexes

Award Name Index 334
Sponsor Index 342
Academic Fields/Career Goals Index 347
Civic, Professional, Social, or Union Affiliation
    Index 362
Employment Experience Index 364
Impairment Index 365
Military Service Index 366
Religious Affiliation Index 367
State of Residence Index 368
Talent Index 372

Introduction

By Richard Woodland
Director of Financial Aid
Rutgers University—Camden

A s the Hispanic population continues to increase, education remains a key issue. According to a new report issued by the *National Center for Education Statistics*, more Hispanics are attending college today than 20 years ago. Researchers found that in 2000, 22 percent of 18- to 24-year-old Hispanics were enrolled in colleges and universities, up from 16 percent in 1980.

Although Hispanic students are achieving educational excellence, reports from the U.S. Census Bureau reveal a startling discrepancy in the educational attainment of Hispanics compared to other groups. Studies show that parents of Hispanic students place an enormous emphasis on higher education. However, compared to other ethnic groups, Hispanics are much less likely to earn a college degree.[1] Hispanic students often either choose not to attend college or settle for a lower cost institution because they do not understand the financial aid opportunities available to them or do not think they will qualify for enough aid to make college possible.

That is why Peterson's is working to help Hispanic students understand the financial aid process. For those who know how to apply for the billions of dollars of scholarships and grants available each year, the dream of attending a prestigious private or state university is within reach. For the rest of you, we will provide the key that unlocks the door to the billions of dollars of financial aid.

SOURCES OF AID

Basically, there are four sources of financial aid. The largest provider is the federal government, followed by the various state programs, colleges and universities, and private sources.

The federal government offers a wide range of programs to help students pay for college. The Pell Grant program, for example, offers billions of dollars each year and is supplemented by other federal student aid programs. Likewise, state governments offer similar grant programs to residents of their states. There is extensive information available on all of these programs. Peterson's offers a number of reference books and articles about these programs at www.petersons.com/finaid. In addition, the federal government provides an excellent resource, *The Student*

---

[1] *National Center for Public Policy and Higher Education Public Agenda*, "With Diploma in Hand," June, 2003.

Guide, which is available at any college financial aid office and online at http://studentaid.ed.gov/students/publications/student_guide/index.html.

To apply for these federal and state aid programs, you must file the Free Application for Federal Student Aid (FAFSA). You can complete the FAFSA online at www.fafsa.ed.gov, print it from the site, or get an application from either your high school guidance counselor or any college or university financial aid office. Another excellent resource for parents and students is the National Association of Student Financial Aid Officers, which can be accessed at www.nasfaa.org/ParentsStudents.asp?Tab=ParentsStudents.

SCHOOL-BASED AID PROGRAMS

The best source of aid targeted toward Hispanic students comes directly from colleges and universities. Many institutions have made a commitment to opening the doors to a college education to minority students and realize that scholarship and grant programs are an important part of this effort. Further, these programs often extend beyond just financial assistance to include mentoring and academic assistance programs.

So what is the best way to maximize your chances of receiving financial aid from colleges and universities? Here are some tips:

- **Research**
  Early during your junior year of high school, meet with your guidance counselor to review your course work and to prepare for the standardized tests you will need to take. Your guidance counselor should be able to direct you toward a number of colleges and universities. If you have already graduated from high school or you feel that the guidance office is not able to help you, call your local college and speak with an admissions officer. These professionals are always available and are willing to help students plan for college. Also, keep your eyes open for college nights in your area and make every effort to attend.

- **Network**
  Seek advice from neighbors, friends, and relatives who have attended college, or turn to community resources like city and county outreach programs. Two great Web sites are www.ed.gov/offices/OPE/thinkcollege/index.html and www.mapping-your-future.org.

- **Apply Early**
  During your senior year of high school, apply for admission as early as possible, preferably in October or November. Don't limit yourself to local, low-cost colleges. Remember that after financial aid is factored in, what was once a high-priced $35,000 per year school may turn out to be much less expensive—possibly even free!

- **File Your FAFSA**
  Complete the FAFSA as soon as possible after January 1 of your senior year. For all of the colleges and universities to which you are applying, make a list of the forms required and the deadlines for submission. Most schools only

require the FAFSA, but some may require other financial aid applications, such as the PROFILE®. Check with your high school guidance office or the college financial aid office for more information on which financial aid applications you will need to fill out. Meeting the published deadlines is critical to ensure that you qualify for the maximum amount of financial aid.

ROLE OF ACADEMICS

To improve your chances for merit-based scholarships and grants, it is important to know how you measure up to the academic requirements at the schools in which you are interested. You will need to have the rank in class and standardized test scores that will make you eligible for scholarships. For example, if the college or university you are considering generally admits students with an average SAT score of 1100, you need to work toward this goal. If your score is 1025, will you be eligible for scholarships and grants? Conversely, many schools heavily discount the importance of SAT scores for Hispanic students. Rather, they focus more on overall high school performance. Contact the admissions office at the college or university you are considering, speak frankly about your record, and find out if your academic credentials are good enough to be considered for grants and scholarships.

PRIVATE SOURCES OF FINANCIAL AID

All students should check for private sources of funds from both local and national sources. On the local level, Hispanic students should contact their local ASPIRA chapter. ASPIRA is a national nonprofit organization devoted to the education and leadership development of Hispanic youth.

In addition to ASPIRA, local churches and community organizations provide scholarship assistance to students from the community. Students and parents should contact local institutions about these opportunities. Also, parents should check with their employers to see if they offer scholarship opportunities to their employees' children.

On the national level, a free scholarship search database is the first place to start looking: You'll want to check out www.petersons.com/finaid as well as www.finaid.org. When you conduct your search, you will find links to other sources of aid including:

- **Hispanic Association of Colleges and Universities (HACU)**
  www.buscapique.com/latinusa/buscafile/sud/hacu.htm

  The Hispanic Association of Colleges and Universities is a national association representing the accredited colleges and universities in the United States where Hispanic students constitute at least 25 percent of the total student enrollment. HACU's goal is to bring together colleges and universities, corporations, government agencies, and individuals to establish partnerships for:

    - promoting the development of Hispanic-serving colleges and universities;

- improving access to and the quality of postsecondary education for Hispanic students; and

- meeting the needs of business, industry, and government through the development and sharing of resources, information, and expertise.

- **Hispanic Scholarship Fund (HSF)**
  www.hsf.net/about/index.htm

  The Hispanic Scholarship Fund is the nation's leading organization supporting Hispanic higher education. HSF was founded in 1975 with a vision to strengthen the country by advancing college education among Hispanic Americans. In support of its mission, HSF provides the Hispanic community with college scholarships and educational outreach support. HSF has awarded more than 54,000 scholarships, totaling nearly $89 million, to deserving students studying at more than 1,300 colleges and universities throughout the United States, Puerto Rico, and the U.S. Virgin Islands.

- **Scholarships for Hispanics**
  www.scholarshipsforhispanics.org

  Sponsored by the National Education Association, this Web site makes more than 1,000 sources of financial aid easily accessible to Hispanic students. The site includes application guidelines, an alumni section, and a database of scholarships fully searchable by a variety of categories, including state, college, and field of interest.

- **Hispanic College Fund (HCF)**
  www.hispanicfund.org

  The Hispanic College Fund is a private nonprofit organization founded in 1993 to develop the next generation of Hispanic business leaders in America by awarding scholarships to deserving Hispanic students. HCF accomplishes its mission by securing the funds needed to award financial assistance to students seeking higher education in academic disciplines leading to careers in business.

- **The Gates Millennium Scholars (GMS)**
  www.gmsp.org/flash.htm

  The Gates Millennium Scholars, funded by a grant from the Bill & Melinda Gates Foundation, was established in 1999 to provide outstanding African-American, American-Indian/Alaskan Natives, Asian-Pacific Islander Americans, and Hispanic-American students with an opportunity to complete an undergraduate college education, in all discipline areas and a graduate education for those students pursuing studies in mathematics, science, engineering, education, or library science. The goal of the GMS is to promote academic excellence and to provide an opportunity for thousands of outstanding students with significant financial need to reach their fullest potential.

HISPANIC-SERVING INSTITUTIONS

The federal government provides significant financial assistance to colleges dedicated to providing opportunities to Hispanic students. These institutions are known as "Hispanic-serving institutions." While the federal government does not provide specific scholarship support to Hispanic students at these schools, Hispanic students can expect to find an environment that offers excellent opportunities, including specialized financial assistance. Grants are awarded to assist eligible Hispanic-serving institutions expand their capacity to serve Hispanic and low-income students. Five-year development grants and one-year planning grants may be awarded. For more information, go to www.ed.gov/offices/OPE/HEP/idues/hsi.html.

It is important to remember that there is an abundance of financial aid opportunities available to Hispanic students. By applying yourself in high school, studying for standardized tests, and doing your homework to seek out supplemental aid to traditional state and federal programs, you will be able to attend the college or university of your choice.

The System
and How It Works:
The ABCs of Paying
for College

How Can You Pay for College? 3

Where Can You Find Help?.................... 23

Scholarship Scams: What They Are and What to
Watch Out For................................ 27

How to Use This Book 31

How Can You Pay for College?

There are four basic sources of funds you can use to pay for college:

1. Family resources, including income, savings, and borrowing
2. A student's contribution from savings, loans, and jobs
3. Need-based scholarships or grants
4. Aid that is based on factors other than financial need

Loans are borrowed money that must be repaid (either after graduation or while attending college); the amount you have to pay back is the total you have borrowed plus interest.

Scholarships and grants are outright gifts and do not have to be repaid.

A student's contribution (other than a loan) usually takes the form of student employment, or work-study, which is a job arranged for a student during the academic year.

Colleges are the primary contact point for most student financial aid. The college's financial aid office, using information submitted by you on the Free Application for Federal Student Aid (FAFSA), constructs an aid "package" that is awarded after the family contribution has been determined. In most cases, this package consists of a combination of grants, scholarships, loans, and work-study.

ESTIMATING COLLEGE COSTS

The starting point for organizing a plan to pay for your college education is to make a good estimate of the yearly cost. You can use the College Cost Worksheet on the next page to do this. Most colleges publish annual tuition and room and board charges in their catalogs and often include an estimate of how much a student can expect to spend for books and incidentals. Any college should be able to provide you with figures for the current year's tuition and mandatory fee charges, as well as estimates for room and board and other expenses. Peterson's publishes a number of comprehensive guides, including Peterson's *Four-Year Colleges*, Peterson's *Two-Year Colleges*, and Peterson's *College Money Handbook*, that are one-stop resources for college cost information. You can find these in bookstores, libraries, and high school guidance offices.

To estimate your college costs for 2004–05, use 2003–04 tuition and fees and room and board figures, and inflate the numbers by 5 percent (or, if it is available, use the college's estimate for 2004–05 expenses). Add $750 for books and $1300 for personal expenses. If you will commute from your home, use $2000 instead of the college's given room and board charges and $900 for transportation. Finally, estimate the cost of two round trips if your home is more than a few hundred miles from the college. Add the items to calculate the total budget. You should now have a reasonably good estimate of college costs for 2004–05. (To determine the costs for later years, add 5 percent per year for a fairly accurate estimate.)

The next step is to evaluate whether or not you are likely to qualify for financial aid based on need. This step is critical, since more than 90 percent of the yearly total of $74.4 billion in student aid is awarded only after a determination is made that the family lacks sufficient financial resources to pay the full cost of college on its own. To judge your chance of receiving need-based aid, it is necessary to estimate an Expected Family Contribution (EFC) according to a government formula known as the Federal Methodology (FM). You can do so by referring to the Expected Family Contribution Table.

College Cost Worksheet

	College 1	College 2	College 3	Commuter College
Tuition and Fees......				
Room and Board......				$2000
Books	$ 750	$ 750	$ 750	$ 750
Personal Expenses....	$1300	$1300	$1300	$1300
Travel				$ 900
Total Budget..........				

How Aid Matches Need

	College X	College Y
Cost of Attendance	$10,000	$ 24,000
− Expected Family Contribution	−5500	−5500
= Financial Need.................	$ 4500	$ 18,500
Financial Need....................	$ 4500	$ 18,500
− Grant Aid Awarded.............	−675	−14,575
− Campus Job (Work-Study) Awarded	−1400	−1300
− Student Loan Awarded	−2425	−2625
= Unmet Need....................	—0—	—0—

Expected Family Contribution Table

Consult the following expected family contribution table using estimated 2003 income and likely asset holdings as of December 31, 2003. First, locate the approximate parental contribution in the table. If more than one family member will be in college at least half-time during 2004–05, divide the parental contribution by the number in college. If your child has savings, add 35 percent of that amount. If your child earned in excess of $2300 in 2003, include 50 percent of the amount over $2300 in the income figure. To see whether or not you might qualify for need-based aid, subtract the family contribution from each college's budget. If the family contribution is only a few thousand dollars over the budget, it is still worthwhile to apply for aid since this procedure is only intended to give you a preliminary estimate of college costs and your family contribution.

Table Used to Approximate Expected Family Contribution for 2004–05

ASSETS	INCOME BEFORE TAXES								
	$ 20,000	30,000	40,000	50,000	60,000	70,000	80,000	90,000	100,000
$ 20,000									
FAMILY SIZE 3	$ 0	950	2,550	4,500	7,300	10,100	12,800	18,300	21,300
4	0	160	1,750	3,450	5,800	8,600	11,350	16,800	19,800
5	0	0	1,000	2,600	4,600	7,200	10,000	15,400	18,500
6	0	0	200	1,800	3,500	5,700	8,400	13,800	16,900
$30,000									
FAMILY SIZE 3	$ 0	950	2,550	4,500	7,300	10,100	12,800	18,300	21,300
4	0	160	1,750	3,450	5,800	8,600	11,350	16,800	19,800
5	0	0	1,000	2,600	4,600	7,200	10,000	15,400	18,500
6	0	0	200	1,800	3,500	5,700	8,400	13,800	16,900
$40,000									
FAMILY SIZE 3	$ 0	950	2,550	4,500	7,300	10,100	12,800	18,300	21,300
4	0	160	1,750	3,450	5,800	8,600	11,350	16,800	19,800
5	0	0	1,000	2,600	4,600	7,200	10,000	15,400	18,500
6	0	0	200	1,800	3,500	5,700	8,400	13,800	16,900
$50,000									
FAMILY SIZE 3	$ 0	950	2,550	4,800	7,700	10,500	13,300	18,700	21,800
4	0	160	1,750	3,700	6,200	9,000	11,800	17,200	20,300
5	0	0	1,000	2,800	4,900	7,600	10,400	15,800	18,900
6	0	0	200	2,000	3,800	6,100	8,800	14,200	17,300
$60,000									
FAMILY SIZE 3	$ 0	950	2,550	5,200	8,300	11,100	13,800	19,300	22,300
4	0	160	1,750	4,100	6,700	9,600	12,400	17,800	20,900
5	0	0	1,000	3,100	5,400	8,200	11,000	16,400	19,500
6	0	0	200	2,300	4,100	6,600	9,400	14,800	17,900

		INCOME BEFORE TAXES								
	ASSETS	**$ 20,000**	**30,000**	**40,000**	**50,000**	**60,000**	**70,000**	**80,000**	**90,000**	**100,000**
	$80,000									
FAMILY SIZE	3	$ 0	950	2,550	6,200	9,400	12,200	15,000	20,400	23,500
	4	0	160	1,750	4,800	7,800	10,700	13,500	18,900	22,000
	5	0	0	1,000	3,800	6,300	9,300	12,100	17,500	20,600
	6	0	0	200	2,800	4,900	7,700	10,500	15,900	19,000
	$100,000									
FAMILY SIZE	3	$ 0	950	2,550	7,200	10,500	13,300	16,100	21,500	24,600
	4	0	160	1,750	5,700	9,000	11,800	14,600	20,000	23,100
	5	0	0	1,000	4,500	7,400	10,500	13,200	18,600	21,700
	6	0	0	200	3,400	5,800	8,800	11,600	17,000	20,100
	$120,000									
FAMILY SIZE	3	$ 0	950	2,550	8,300	11,600	14,400	17,200	22,600	25,700
	4	0	160	1,750	6,700	10,100	12,900	15,700	21,100	24,200
	5	0	0	1,000	5,400	8,500	11,600	14,300	19,800	22,800
	6	0	0	200	4,100	6,800	10,000	12,800	18,200	21,300
	$140,000									
FAMILY SIZE	3	$ 0	950	2,550	9,500	12,800	15,600	18,400	23,800	26,800
	4	0	160	1,750	7,800	11,200	14,100	16,900	22,300	25,400
	5	0	0	1,000	6,300	9,700	12,700	15,500	20,900	24,000
	6	0	0	200	4,900	7,900	11,100	13,900	19,300	22,400

Assumptions: Two-parent family, age of older parent is 45, lower-income families will file the 1040A or 1040EZ tax form, student income is less than $2300, no student assets, one family member in college. All figures are estimates and may vary when the complete FAFSA and PROFILE® are submitted.

SCHOLARSHIPS

What Are Scholarships? What Importance Should You Give Them?

The word "scholarship" can cause confusion. Precise usage limits the use of scholarship to "free money" given to students to help cover educational costs. However, many people, including college financial aid officials and program sponsors, use the word generically to refer to all forms of student gift aid, including fellowships and grants, especially if a program covers both undergraduate and graduate levels of study. In the profiles of scholarship programs in this book, we use whatever term the sponsor uses.

However, so that you are aware of the differences in meaning when you encounter the terms, here are further definitions:

- *Scholarships:* Undergraduate gift aid that is used to pay educational costs.

- *Need-Based Scholarships:* Gift aid based on demonstrated need. Need, as defined by colleges and the federal government, is the difference between the cost of attending a college and the EFC, which is determined by a federal and/or institutional formula.

- *Merit-Based Scholarships:* Financial aid based on criteria other than financial need, including academic major, career goals, grades, test scores, athletic ability, hobbies, talents, place of residence or birth, ethnic identity, religious affiliation, your own or your parents' military or public safety service, disability, union membership, employment history, community service, or club affiliations. The preponderance of scholarship programs described in this book are merit based, although many also use need to set the size of the award.

- *Grants:* Graduate or postdoctoral awards to support specific research or other projects. Grants cover expenses directly related to carrying out the proposed research (e.g., materials, interview costs, or computer time). Sometimes a grant includes allowances for travel and living expenses incurred while conducting research away from the home institution. Usually, living expenses at the home university are not covered. (NOTE: The word grant is also used to refer to undergraduate gift aid, for example, the Federal Pell Grant.)

- *Fellowships:* Graduate- and postgraduate-level awards to individuals to cover their living expenses while they take advanced courses, carry out research, or work on a project. Some fellowships include a tuition waiver.

- *Prizes:* Money given in recognition of an outstanding achievement. Prizes often are awarded to winners of competitions.

- *Internships:* A defined period of time working in the intern's field of interest with and under the supervision of the professional staff of a host organization. Often the intern works part-time or during the summer. Some internships offer stipends in the form of an hourly wage or fixed allowance.

- *Assistantships:* Graduate-level awards, usually waiving all or some tuition, plus an allowance for living expenses. In return, the recipient works at teaching or research facilities. Teaching assistants teach in their field of study. Research assistants often work on projects related to their dissertation or thesis.

- *Work-Study:* When capitalized, Work-Study refers to a federally supported program that provides students with part-time employment during the school year. The federal government pays part of the student's salary. Employers are usually college departments. Local agencies also can participate in the program. Eligibility for Federal Work-Study is based on demonstrated need. Work-study (not capitalized) is used to describe any student job in an aid package.

Sources of financial aid include private agencies, foundations, corporations, clubs, fraternal and service organizations, civic associations, unions, and religious groups. These sponsors provide grants, scholarships, and low-interest loans. Some employers also provide tuition reimbursement benefits for employees and their dependents.

It is always worthwhile to look into scholarships that can be found beyond the college financial aid office's network. For a family that does not qualify for need-based aid, these "outside" scholarships and merit scholarships available from colleges are the only form of gift aid available. No matter what your situation regarding need-based aid, scholarships from noninstitutional sources (those not administered by colleges or the U.S. Department of Education) are almost always useful. Be aware that the amounts received from "outside" scholarships to pay tuition and expenses may be deducted from the amount of aid offered in your college financial aid package. An "outside" scholarship may prove most useful in reducing the loan and work-study components of the college-offered package.

Use the following checklist when investigating merit scholarships:

- Take advantage of any scholarships for which you are automatically eligible based on employer benefits, military service, association or church membership, other affiliations, or student or parent attributes (ethnic background, nationality, etc.). Company or union tuition remissions are the most common examples of these awards.

- Look for other awards for which you might be eligible based on the characteristics and affiliations indicated above, but where there is a selection process and an application required. Peterson's *Scholarship Almanac* provides information about the largest scholarship programs, but there are thousands of smaller programs that may be right for you. Scholarship directories, such as Peterson's *Scholarships, Grants & Prizes*, which details more than 3,000 scholarship programs, are useful resources.

- See if your state has a merit scholarship program. Also, check to see if the state scholarships are "portable," meaning they can be used in other states or must be used at in-state institutions.

- Look into national scholarship competitions. High school guidance counselors usually know about these scholarships. Examples of these awards are the National Merit Scholarship, Coca-Cola Scholarship, Aid Association for Lutherans, Intel Science Talent Search, and the U.S. Senate Youth Program.

- ROTC (Reserve Officers' Training Corps) scholarships are offered by the Army, Navy, Marines, and Air Force. A full ROTC scholarship covers all tuition, fees, and textbook costs. Acceptance of an ROTC scholarship entails a commitment to take military science courses and to serve as an officer in the sponsoring branch of the service. Competition is heavy, and preference may be given to students in certain fields of study, such as engineering science. Application procedures vary by service. Contact an armed services recruiter or your high school guidance counselor for further information.

- Investigate community scholarships. High school guidance counselors usually have a list of these awards, and announcements are published in the town newspaper. Most common are awards given by service organizations such as the American Legion, Rotary International, and the local women's club.

- If you are strong academically (for example, a National Merit Commended Scholar or better), or very talented in fields such as athletics or performing/creative arts, you may want to consider colleges that offer their own merit awards to gifted students they wish to enroll.

Federal Scholarship Programs

The federal government is the single largest source of financial aid for students, accounting for about $62 billion annually. At the present time there are two federal grant programs—the Federal Pell Grant and the Federal Supplemental Educational Opportunity Grant (FSEOG); three loan programs—the Federal Perkins Loan, the Direct Loan, and the Stafford Loan; and a job program that helps colleges provide jobs for students—Federal Work-Study (FWS).

The application and need evaluation process is controlled by Congress and the U.S. Department of Education. The application is the FAFSA. In addition, nearly every state that offers student assistance uses the federal government's system to award its own aid. By completing the FAFSA, you automatically apply for state aid. However, you should check with your state higher education agency or high school guidance counselor for any other forms that may be required in addition to the FAFSA. (NOTE: In addition to the FAFSA, some colleges also ask the family to complete the PROFILE® application.)

The FAFSA is your "passport" to receiving your share of the billions of dollars awarded annually in need-based aid. If the College Cost Worksheet shows that you might qualify for aid, pick up a FAFSA from your high school guidance office after mid-November. The form will ask for your current year's financial data, and it should be filed after January 1, in time to meet the earliest college or state scholarship deadline. Online application can be made by accessing the FAFSA Web site at www.fafsa.ed.gov/. Both the student and at least one parent should apply for a federal PIN number at www.pin.ed.gov. The PIN serves as your electronic signature when applying for aid on the Web. Within two to four weeks after you submit the form, you will receive a summary of the FAFSA information, which is called the Student Aid Report (SAR). The SAR will give you your EFC and also allow you to make corrections to the data you submitted.

Federal Pell Grant

The Federal Pell Grant is the largest grant program: more than 4.3 million students receive awards annually. This grant is intended to be the starting point of assistance for lower-income families. Eligibility for a Federal Pell Grant depends on your EFC. The amount you receive will depend on your EFC and the cost of education at the college you will attend. The highest award depends on how much the program is funded. The maximum for the 2002–03 school year ranged from $400 to $4000. The maximum for 2003–04 is $4050.

To give you some idea of your possible eligibility for a Federal Pell Grant, the following table may be helpful. The amounts shown are based on a family size of 4, with 1 in college, no emergency expenses, no contribution from student income or assets, and college costs of at least $4000 per year.

Table Used to Estimate Federal Pell Grants for 2003–04

Adjusted Gross Income	Family Assets							
	$50,000	$55,000	$60,000	$65,000	$70,000	$75,000	$80,000	$85,000
$ 5000	$ 4000	$ 4000	$ 4000	$ 4000	$ 4000	$ 4000	$ 4000	$ 4000
$10,000	4000	4000	4000	4000	4000	4000	4000	4000
$15,000	4000	4000	4000	4000	4000	3950	3750	3650
$20,000	3650	3450	3250	3150	3050	2950	2850	2750
$25,000	2750	2550	2450	2350	2150	2050	1950	1750
$30,000	1750	1650	1550	1450	1350	1250	950	650
$35,000	1250	1150	950	750	450	400	—	—

Note: Based on family of four, one child enrolled in college, oldest parent age 41.

Federal Supplemental Educational Opportunity Grant (FSEOG)

As its name implies, the Federal Supplemental Educational Opportunity Grant provides additional need-based federal grant money to supplement the Federal Pell Grant. Each participating college is given funds to award to especially needy students. The maximum award is $4000 per year, but the amount you receive depends on the college's policy, the availability of FSEOG funds, the total cost of education, and the amount of other aid awarded.

Federal Financial Aid Programs

Name of Program	Type of Program	Maximum Award Per Year
Federal Pell Grant...........	Need-based grant	$4000
Federal Supplemental Educational Opportunity Grant.....................	Need-based grant	$4000
Federal Work-Study.........	Need-based part-time job	no maximum
Federal Perkins Loan	Need-based loan	$4000
Subsidized Stafford Direct Loan.....................	Need-based student loan	$2625 (first year)
Unsubsidized Stafford Direct Loan	Non-need-based student loan	$2625 (first year, dependent student)
PLUS Loan	Non-need-based parent loan	Up to the cost of education

Note: Both Direct and Stafford Loans have higher maximums after the freshman year. Students who meet the federal qualifications for independent status are eligible for increased loan limits in these programs.

College-Based Gift Aid

Next to the federal government, colleges provide the largest amount of financial aid to students. In addition, they control most of the money channeled to students from the federal government.

College need-based scholarships frequently are figured into students' financial aid packages. Most colleges award both need- and merit-based scholarships, although a small number of colleges (most notably the Ivy League) offer only need-based scholarships. Colleges may offer merit-based scholarships to freshmen with specific academic strengths, talents in the creative or performing arts, special achievements or activities, and a wide variety of particular circumstances. Some of these circumstances are parents in specific professions; residents of particular geographic areas; spouses, children, and siblings of other students; and students with disabilities.

A college's financial aid office can inform you about the need-based scholarships available from that college. Usually, the admissions office is the primary source to get information about any merit-based scholarships the college offers. Some colleges have information about their scholarships on their Web sites. Peterson's *College Money Handbook* is a one-stop reference guide to the financial aid programs at more than 2,100 four-year colleges and universities. You may notice that private colleges usually have larger financial aid programs, but public colleges are usually less expensive, especially for in-state students.

Colleges have different requirements regarding necessary financial aid application forms. Be prepared to check early with the colleges you are interested in about which forms they need. All colleges require the FAFSA for students applying for federal aid. The other most commonly required form is PROFILE®, the College Scholarship Service's financial aid form. To see if the college you are applying to requires PROFILE®, read the financial aid section of the admission material.

Athletic Scholarships

Some scholarships for athletic ability or participation are available from various noninstitutional sources, but the great preponderance comes directly from the colleges themselves. Athletic scholarships may be the most widely used single category of merit scholarship, and certainly they are the most widely known and sought by students. Athletic scholarships are controlled by the coaches in the athletic department of a college.

Most financial aid provided on the basis of athletic ability or achievement is in the form of scholarship aid. Loans for athletic participation are uncommon. Some coaches may describe the aid that they are offering to athletes as scholarships, when the aid really is in the form of a loan. If you believe that you are being offered a scholarship (that is money *given* to you based on need or athletic ability), insist that it be confirmed in writing and that it is not a loan or "indebtedness." Remember, scholarship money is *given* to you, while loans must be repaid. Be sure you are clear about which type of aid a coach may be offering.

Athletes who are good enough even to consider competing at the collegiate level frequently dream of being awarded an athletic scholarship, whether or not their family can afford to pay for their education. Potential college athletes want to be "on scholarship" because it is a reward, an honor, a status symbol. An athletic scholarship is a reward for hard work and success in high school or junior college.

According to current national athletic association guidelines and practices, athletic scholarships are given on a one-year, renewable basis. While your coach may have "sold" you on his or her college with the promise of having your entire education paid by an athletic scholarship, the money and free tuition could disappear at the end of any year, leaving you to search for some other way to pay for the rest of your education. Worse, if you then want to transfer to another college, you lose a season of eligibility for athletics. The chances of getting another athletic scholarship elsewhere are much less if the coach at your new school will not be able to use your talents until the following year.

So, if you are eligible to be a scholarship athlete, the primary question you must decide is whether you want *and* need an athletic scholarship or whether you just want one. The status and honor that may come with an athletic scholarship can be enjoyable, but is it worth the cost? While some coaches feel more of a commitment to athletes who are their "employees," other coaches will appreciate it if you get funds for college in some other way, freeing up a scholarship for them to offer to another athlete.

In any case, the availability of an athletic scholarship should not be your primary reason for selecting one college over another. There are too many nonathletic sources of financial aid available for you to let the offer of an athletic scholarship determine which school you attend.

Who Gets Scholarship Offers?

Most athletic scholarships at schools with top-level teams are reserved for the best high school and junior college athletes, the ones who have established a reputation in their sport. Especially in football and men's basketball, college coaches do much of their hunting for talent with the help of computer-based scouting services, which keep records of the statistics of the nation's best prospects. Athletes at that level—"blue-chip" prospects—do not have to search for athletic scholarships; recruiters come knocking at *their* door (sometimes knocking *down* the door). Occasionally an unrecruited athlete in those sports (a "walk-on") may be given a partial or full scholarship after proving him- or herself under fire.

Virtually all NCAA Division I schools (except for the Ivy League and Patriot League colleges) offer athletic scholarships, and in most sports the coach does his or her own scouting rather than using computerized scouting services. The same is true at Division II schools, a lower level of athletic competition. These schools are allowed fewer scholarships, and many of these cover only part of the educational costs. Division III NCAA schools—the lowest level—are not allowed to offer scholarships directly for athletic talent, yet most of them still scout high school and junior college prospects.

NCAA colleges may compete at a particular level in one sport and at another level in other sports. For example, a school with a Division II basketball team (athletic scholarships allowed) may field a Division III soccer team (no athletic scholarships). While this may be confusing, you only need to be concerned about the level at which they field a team in *your* sport.

Many colleges affiliated with the NAIA (National Association for Intercollegiate Athletics) also offer scholarships. These schools are among the smaller and lesser known, so they generally do not have as much money to put into athletic scholarships. A number of junior colleges, or community colleges, also offer athletic scholarships. As at NCAA Division II schools, NAIA and junior college scholarships are more likely to be partial (i.e., quarter, half, or tuition-only) rather than "full rides."

Athletic scholarships for women have increased tremendously in recent years. In large part, this is a result of Title IX (part of a federal law called the Education Amendments of 1972). Within this law, colleges must provide athletic scholarship aid to female and male athletes in proportion to their enrollment. Also, all resources, support, and opportunities to compete in athletics must be shared equitably by men and women. Title IX was reinforced in 1997 by a Supreme Court ruling in a case filed by women student-athletes against Brown University.

Despite these advances, the opportunities women have for obtaining athletic scholarships at some schools still may lag behind the financial aid offered to men. Once you are in college and can see what types and amounts of aid are available to female athletes as compared to male athletes, you will be in a better position to determine whether female athletes are being discriminated against at that school. Contact the campus affirmative action office and ask its staff to look into the situation if you think that female athletes are not getting their fair share. You may be considered a troublemaker by some people in the athletic department, but you deserve what the law allows and should be allowed to stand up for your rights.

How to Generate an Offer

While colleges at all levels of athletic competition scout and recruit athletes, those at levels *below* Division I of the NCAA are more likely to consider information submitted by an individual student seeking an athletic scholarship. The amount of scholarship money available each year in any given sport varies greatly, and even if recruiters have not been knocking down your door, you still may have the chance to get a scholarship offer if you follow the approach described below:

1. Draw up a preliminary list of colleges that meet the criteria that are important to you, such as location, size, overall cost, type of academic environment, availability of particular academic programs or majors, and sports opportunities. (You should check on whether the school has a junior varsity team in case you do not make the varsity your first year.)

2. Find out the name of the head coach in your sport at the colleges on your list. Starting with the top contenders on your preliminary list (three to six colleges), write a letter to the head coach at each school. In the letter describe several important reasons why you want to attend his or her college. Explain that you are interested in competing on the team and that you would like to know what sources of financial aid are available for athletes. Don't be shy about telling the coach of your athletic strengths, including statistics (true ones!), that might generate the coach's interest in you. Include copies of newspaper write-ups and action photos, if you have

them. A videotape of you in competition can also help in selling yourself to the coach. That is what you are really doing, *selling yourself*. There is absolutely no shame in that. In fact, it is good practice for when you graduate and have to sell an employer on your qualifications and accomplishments.

3. If you do not receive encouragement from the first group of head coaches you write to, work down your list of college choices. There are no guarantees, but using this process certainly is more likely to result in finding athletic-related financial aid than doing nothing.

4. Ask your current or former coach to write a letter on your behalf to specific coaches on your list. A letter to a specific, named coach carries more weight than a generic letter to any coach (i.e., "Dear Coach"). The letter of recommendation should stress how much of an asset you have been to your team and would be on that coach's team. Letters from two coaches are better than one, three are better than two, etc.

Seldom will a coach offer financial aid to an athlete sight unseen. Since most coaches operate with a tight recruiting budget, you may have to pay your own travel expenses to see a coach who shows some interest. If you are then offered financial aid—full or partial scholarship, loans, work-study, or some combination—your efforts have paid off *and* that coach knows you as more than just another "wanna-be." He or she knows that you are hungry to compete on that team and that you are an aggressive seeker of success, a trait all coaches want in their athletes. But beware when a coach promises financial aid in the future, if things work out. The coach may come through for you, but do not bank on such promises because they are "written on air."

Even if, after all that effort, you receive no athletics-related financial aid, you are likely to be in a better position to be accepted by the school and to be considered for other types of aid not directly tied to athletics. Students who have special talents—i.e., those who are "well-rounded" and take the initiative to make these talents known—are often more desired by schools than those who present only academic credentials. If you get only a partial athletic scholarship or none at all—like the majority of college athletes—you may be eligible for financial aid based on need.

Great athletes and good ones are sometimes tempted to accept—or even to ask for—money or other financial benefits beyond the amount for which the rules allow. It is not worth whatever "extra" you might get, since there are penalties and other liabilities. For example, in 1997, the University of Massachusetts men's basketball team forfeited its "Final Four" standing (achieved a few years before) and had to return $151,000 because one of its players took money that he should not have. Why compromise friendships, your teammates' goals, your own ethics, possibly your athletic career, and even your chance at the aid you deserve by trying to take more than you should?

State and Local Scholarships

Each state government has established one or more financial aid programs for qualified students. Usually, only legal residents of the state are eligible to benefit from such programs. However, some are available to out-of-state students attending colleges within the state. In addition to residential status, other qualifications frequently exist. States may also offer internship or work-study programs, graduate fellowships and grants, or low-interest loans in addition to grant and forgivable loan programs.

If you are interested in learning more about state-sponsored programs, the state higher education office should be able to provide information. Information brochures and application forms for state scholarship programs are usually available in your high school guidance office or from a college financial aid office in your state.

Increasingly, state government agencies are putting state scholarship information on their Web sites. The financial aid page of state-administered college or university sites frequently has a list of state-sponsored scholarships and financial aid programs. You can access college and university Web sites easily through Peterson's Education Center (www.petersons.com).

Businesses, community service clubs, and local organizations often sponsor scholarship programs for residents of a specific town or county. These can be attractive to a scholarship seeker because the odds of winning can be higher than they would be for scholarships that draw from a wider pool of applicants. However, because the information network at the local level is spotty, it is often difficult to find information about their existence. Some of the best sources of information about these local programs are high school guidance offices, community college financial aid offices, high school district administrative offices, and public libraries. In addition, you may want to check with the local offices of organizations that traditionally sponsor scholarships, such as the International Kiwanis Club, the Benevolent and Protective Order of Elks, the Lions Club International, or the National Association of American Business Clubs (AMBUCS).

Private Aid

Billions of dollars are given every year by private donors to students and their families to help with the expenses of a college education. Last year, noninstitutional and nongovernment sponsors gave more than $3 billion in financial aid to help undergraduate students pay for college costs.

Foundations, fraternal and ethnic organizations, community service clubs, churches and religious groups, philanthropies, companies and industry groups, labor unions and public employees' associations, veterans' groups, and trusts and bequests all make up a large network of possible sources.

It is always worthwhile for any prospective student to look into these scholarships, but they are especially important to students who do not qualify for need-based financial aid, to students and families who wish to supplement the aid being given by governmental or university sources, and to students who possess special abilities, achievements, or personal qualifications (e.g., memberships in church or civic organizations, specific ethnic backgrounds, parents who served in the armed forces, etc.) that fit the criteria of one or more of the various private scholarship sponsors.

Some factors that can affect eligibility for these awards, such as ethnic heritage and parental status, are beyond a student's control. Other criteria, such as academic, scientific, technological, athletic, artistic, or creative merit, are not easily or quickly met unless one has previously committed himself or herself to a particular endeavor. However, eligibility for many programs is within your control, especially if you plan ahead. For example, you can start or keep up current membership in a church or civic organization, participate in volunteer service efforts, or pursue an interest, from amateur radio to golf to raising animals to writing and more. Any of these actions might give you an edge for a particular scholarship or grant.

The eligibility criteria for private scholarships, grants, and prizes are a real mosaic; they vary widely and include financial need as well as personal characteristics and merit. The number and amounts of the awards available from individual sponsors can vary each year depending upon the number of grantees, fund contributions, and other factors. However, practically anyone can find awards to fit his or her individual circumstances.

Peterson's *Scholarship Almanac* was created to provide students and their families access to the biggest and most lucrative private financial aid programs. In this publication you will find detailed information about the top 500 scholarship/grant programs and prize sources. Peterson's *Scholarships, Grants & Prizes* is a comprehensive guide to the more than 3,000 scholarship/grant programs and prize sources that will provide more than 1.6 million financial awards to undergraduates in the 2004–05 school year.

SOURCES OF COLLEGE FINANCING OTHER THAN SCHOLARSHIPS

Financing strategies are important because the high cost of a college education today often requires families, whether or not they receive aid, to think about stretching the payment for college beyond the four-year period of enrollment. For high-cost colleges it is not unreasonable to think about a 10-4-10 plan: ten years of saving; four years of paying college bills out of current income, savings, and borrowing; and ten years to repay a parental loan.

Family Savings

Although saving for college is always a good idea, many families are unclear about its advantages. Families do not save for two reasons. First, after expenses have been covered, many families do not have much money to set aside. An affordable but regular savings plan through a payroll deduction is usually the answer to the problem of spending your entire paycheck every month.

The second reason that saving for college is not a high priority is the belief that the financial aid system penalizes a family by lowering aid eligibility. The Federal Methodology determination is very kind to savers. In fact, savings are ignored completely for families that earn less than $50,000 and who are eligible to file a short form federal tax return (1040A or EZ). Savings in the form of home equity and retirement plans are excluded from the calculation. And even when savings are counted, a maximum of 5.6 percent of the total is expected each year. In other words, if a family has $40,000 in savings after an asset protection allowance is considered, the contribution is no greater than $2240, an amount very close to the yearly interest that is accumulated. Therefore, it is possible for a family to meet its savings contribution without depleting the face value of its investments.

A sensible savings plan is important because of the financial advantage of saving compared to borrowing. The amount of money students borrow for college is now greater than the amount they receive in grants and scholarships. With loans becoming so widespread, savings should be carefully considered as an alternative to borrowing. Your incentive for saving is that a dollar saved is a dollar not borrowed.

Several state governments are enacting new programs to help families save for college education. There are two basic categories of these programs. Under a prepaid or guaranteed tuition program, in exchange for early tuition purchase (usually in installments), a tuition rate is locked in at the plan's participating colleges or universities, almost always public institutions. In a college savings plan trust program, participants save money in a special college savings account on behalf of a prospective student. These accounts usually have a guaranteed minimum return and offer favorable treatment for state and federal taxes. In many cases, the interest earned in these programs will result in no tax liability. You should check with your state's higher education agency for more details.

Work-Study and Jobs

Federal Work-Study
The Federal Work-Study program provides jobs for students who need financial aid to pay for their educational expenses. Funds from the federal government and the college (or the employer) pay the salary. The student works on an hourly basis on or off campus and must be paid at least the federal minimum wage. Students may earn only up to the amount awarded, which depends on the calculated financial need and the total amount of money available to the college.

Many colleges, after assigning jobs to students who qualify for Federal Work-Study (FWS), offer other part-time positions to nonqualifying students from regular college funds. In fact, at many colleges, the ratio is about 50-50, meaning half are employed under the FWS program while the other half are paid directly by the college. Students who qualify for FWS are usually assigned jobs through the student employment office. Other students should contact the Career Planning Office, or check with individual offices and departments for possible openings. In addition, there are usually off-campus employment opportunities available to everyone.

AmeriCorps
AmeriCorps is a national umbrella group of service programs for a limited number of students. Participants work in a public or private nonprofit agency providing service to the community in one of four priority areas: education, human services, the environment, and public safety. In exchange, they earn a stipend of $7400 to

$14,800 a year for living expenses and up to $4725 for two years to apply toward college expenses. Students can work either before, during, or after they go to college and can use the funds to either pay current educational expenses or repay federal student loans. Speak to a college financial aid officer for more details about this program and any other new initiatives available to students.

Cooperative Education Programs

Co-op programs, also known as cooperative education, are special programs usually administered at the departmental level. A formal arrangement with off-campus employers allows students to combine work and study, either at the same time or in alternating terms. Generally, these programs begin at the end of the sophomore year and add a year or a semester to the length of the degree program. Co-op programs enable students to earn regular marketplace wages while gaining experience, often specifically related to the field they are studying. The National Commission for Cooperative Education, 360 Huntington Avenue, Boston, Massachusetts 02115-5096, 617-373-3770, is a central source of information about these programs.

Loans

In addition to scholarships and work-study, there are loan opportunities available for all students. The federal loan programs are called the Stafford and Direct. Student and parent loans are provided by both programs. Some of the organizations that sponsor scholarships, such as the Air Force Aid Society, also provide loans.

For those students who demonstrate need, the interest on the loans is paid by the federal government during the time the student is in school. If you do not demonstrate financial need, or your need has been met with other forms of aid, you can apply for the unsubsidized Stafford or Direct Loan. Unsubsidized loans begin to accrue interest as soon as the money is received.

Federal Perkins Loan

This loan is a low-interest (5 percent) loan for students with exceptional financial need. Federal Perkins Loans are made through the college's financial aid office with the college as the lender. Students may borrow a maximum of $4000 per year for up to five years of undergraduate study. They may take up to ten years to repay the loan, beginning nine months after they graduate, leave school, or drop below half-time status. No interest accrues while they are in school and, under certain conditions (e.g., they teach in low-income areas, work in law enforcement, are full-time nurses or medical technicians, serve as Peace Corps or VISTA volunteers, etc.), some or all of the loan can be canceled or payments deferred.

Stafford and Direct Loans

Stafford and Direct Loans have the same interest rates, loan maximums, deferments, and cancellation benefits. A Stafford Loan may be borrowed from a commercial lender such as a bank or credit union. A Direct Loan is borrowed directly from the

U.S. Department of Education. Once you have decided on the college you plan to attend, the financial aid office will inform you of the program it participates in and advise you on all application procedures.

The interest rate varies annually up to a maximum of 8.25 percent. If you qualify for a need-based subsidized Stafford Loan, the interest is paid by the federal government while you are enrolled in college. There is also an unsubsidized Stafford Loan that is not based on need, for which you are eligible regardless of your family income.

The maximum amount dependent students may borrow in any one year is $2625 for freshmen, $3500 for sophomores, and $5500 for juniors and seniors, with a maximum of $23,000 for the total undergraduate program. The maximum amount independent students can borrow is $6625 for freshmen (of which no more than $2625 can be subsidized), $7500 for sophomores (of which no more than $3500 can be subsidized), and $10,500 for juniors and seniors (of which no more than $5500 can be subsidized). Borrowers must pay a fee of up to 4 percent of the loan, which is deducted from the loan proceeds.

To apply for a Stafford Loan, you must first complete a FAFSA to determine eligibility for a subsidized loan followed by a separate loan application that is submitted to a lender. The financial aid office can help in selecting a lender, or you can contact your state department of higher education to find a participating lender. The lender will send a promissory note indicating that you have agreed to repay the loan. The proceeds of the loan, less the origination fee, will be sent to your college to be either credited to your account or released to you. Longer term repayment plans may be available depending on your overall debt level, income, and other factors.

If you qualify for a subsidized Stafford Loan, you do not have to pay interest while in school. For an unsubsidized Stafford Loan, you will be responsible for paying the interest from the time the loan is established. However, some lenders will permit borrowers to delay making payments and will add the interest to the loan. Once the repayment period starts, borrowers of both subsidized and unsubsidized Stafford Loans will have to pay a combination of interest and principal monthly for up to ten years.

PLUS Loans

PLUS is for parents of dependent students to help families who may not have the cash available to pay their share of the charges. There is no needs test to qualify. The loan has a variable interest rate that cannot exceed 9 percent. There is no yearly limit; you can borrow up to the cost of your education less other financial aid received. Repayment begins sixty days after the money is advanced. A fee of up to 4 percent of the loan is subtracted from the proceeds. Parent borrowers must generally have a good credit record to qualify. Parents are urged to contact the financial aid office to determine if the PLUS program is the best source of alternative loan funds. Many schools have arranged other private loan programs that may offer better loan terms. Some programs administered by the state higher education agency may have parental loan programs with better terms and conditions.

Famous Scholarship Programs

The two most famous and prestigious scholarship programs are the Fulbright and Rhodes scholarships. Here is a quick overview of the programs.

The Fulbright Scholarship Program

The Fulbright Scholarship Program is the U.S. government's premier scholarship program available for international study. The Fulbright Program sponsors study, research, or teaching by American graduate scholars and artists in more than 100 host countries and by graduate-level students, teachers, or researchers from more than 125 countries at U.S. universities. In its fifty-seven years of operation, the Fulbright program has sponsored nearly 200,000 scholars. The program was established in 1946 to foster mutual understanding through educational and cultural exchanges of persons, knowledge, and skills between the United States and other countries. It is named for Senator J. William Fulbright, who sponsored the legislation in the United States Senate as a step toward constructing alternatives to armed conflict. The program's primary source of funding is the United States Information Agency (USIA).

The U.S. Student Program is designed to give recent baccalaureate-level graduates, master's and doctoral candidates, and beginning professionals and artists an opportunity for personal development and international experience. Recipients plan their own programs. Projects may include course-related work, library or field research, classes in music or art, research projects in the sciences or social sciences, or various hybrid projects. The Fulbright Scholar Program is designed to provide senior teachers and professionals the opportunity to conduct research, teach, or study abroad and to make a major contribution to global understanding.

There are five basic types of Fulbright grants open to U.S. citizens:

- *Fulbright Full Grants:* Provide round-trip transportation; language or orientation courses; tuition, in some cases; book and research allowances; maintenance for the academic year, based on living costs in the host country; and supplemental health and accident insurance. Fulbright Full Grants are payable in local currency or U.S. dollars, depending on the country of assignment.

- *Fulbright Travel Grants:* Available only to Germany, Hungary, Italy, or Korea. They are available to supplement a student's own funds or an award from a non-Fulbright source that does not provide funds for travel or to supplement study. Travel grants provide round-trip transportation to the country where the student will pursue studies for an academic year, supplemental health and accident insurance, and the cost of an orientation course abroad, if applicable.

- *Foreign and Private Grants:* Offered by international governments, universities, and private donors in specific host countries. The benefits and special requirements of the grants are determined by the sponsoring agency. If the awards do not cover the entire expense of international study, candidates are expected to cover the additional costs from their own funds, although some international grants may be supplemented by Fulbright travel grants.

- *Teaching Opportunities:* Belgium/Luxembourg, France, Germany, Hungary, Korea, Taiwan, and Turkey offer assistantships for teaching English in secondary schools, middle schools, or higher educational institutions.

- *Fulbright Scholar Program:* Offers grants for college and university faculty and administrators, professionals (lawyers, government officials, journalists, research scientists, and others), artists, and independent scholars to conduct research, teach, or study abroad.

Fulbright recipients are selected on the basis of their academic or professional record, language preparation, the feasibility of the proposed project, and personal qualifications. The decision-making procedure involves review of the application by three groups: a National Screening Committee of the Institute for International Education that consists of specialists in various fields and area studies, the supervising agency (the USIS post at the American Embassy or a special binational Fulbright Commission in the host country), and the J. William Fulbright Foreign Scholarship Board.

An application form is available from the Fulbright Program Advisor at the graduate's campus or from the Institute of International Education, 809 United Nations Plaza, New York, NY 10017-3580. Applications should be submitted between May 1 and mid-October. Check with the Fulbright Program Advisor or the Institute of International Education for the specific year's deadline.

The Rhodes Scholarship

Cecil Rhodes, a remarkable public figure of late Victorian Britain, made a fortune in diamond mining in South Africa and forcefully advocated a single world international government. On his death in 1902 at the age of 49, he left his fortune to Oxford University to establish the Rhodes scholarship program. The aim of the Rhodes scholarship is to bring from throughout the world young men and women of proven intellectual and academic achievement, integrity of character, interest in and respect for their fellow beings, the ability to lead, and the energy to use their talents to make an effective contribution to the world around them.

Because of a long history of prominent individuals who have been Rhodes scholars and the extreme selectivity of the award, the Rhodes scholarship is regarded in academe as an extremely high honor. Colleges and universities take great pride in their students who go on to win Rhodes scholarships and view the cultivation of a Rhodes scholar to be a great status symbol.

The Rhodes scholarship provides payment of all tuition and related fees in any field of study at Oxford plus a stipend for living expenses. The Rhodes trustees assist successful applicants with their travel expenses to and from Oxford.

Appointment to a Rhodes scholarship is made for two years with a possible third year if the scholar's plan of study and record at Oxford warrant extension of the award. An American Rhodes scholar with a degree from an approved American university or college is entitled to Senior Status. Subject to the consent of their college, Senior Status entitles students to read for the Oxford B.A. in any of the Final Honour Schools. If qualified by previous training and with the consent of their colleges and relevant faculty, Rhodes scholars may be admitted to read for a higher degree.

Candidates must be citizens, between the ages of 18 and 23 as of October 1 of the year of their application, and have sufficient credits to ensure completion of a bachelor's degree before the October 1 following application. Selection is made on four criteria: scholarship, character, leadership, and physical vigor. Participation in varsity sports is a usual way to demonstrate physical vigor, but it is not essential if applicants are able to demonstrate physical vigor in other ways.

Each of the world's nations is assigned a number of Rhodes scholarship slots that they may fill each year. The United States of America selects 32 Rhodes scholars annually. Applications are made through the Office of the Institutional Representative for the Rhodes scholarships at the candidate's college or university. A campus committee evaluates applicants and sends the evaluations to a state Committee of Selection. In each state a Committee of Selection may nominate 2 or 3 applicants to appear before the District Committee (the U.S. is organized into eight districts of six or seven states each). The Rhodes trustees will pay round-trip transportation of applicants nominated by State Committees to the place of the District Committee meeting. Applicants must pay their own lodging, food, and other expenses when appearing before State Committees. The names of scholarship winners are announced at the close of the District Committee meetings in December.

After selection of the scholars, the Rhodes scholarship authorities in Oxford seek places for them in Oxford colleges, following the electees' preferences, if possible. Because the colleges make their own admissions, there is no guarantee of a place. Two samples of written work, approximately 2,000 words each, are required for college placement. The award of the scholarship is not confirmed by the Rhodes Trustees until the scholar-elect has been accepted for admission by a college. Rhodes scholars are expected to be full-time students at Oxford for the duration of their degree programs. Scholars-elect enter Oxford University in October following their election. Deferment of the scholarship is not allowed except for medical internships.

Prospective applicants should study the academic system of Oxford University to determine if their plan of study is one that is feasible at Oxford. The best sources of information are the current issues of the *University of Oxford Undergraduate Prospectus* and *Graduate Studies Prospectus*, published by the Oxford University Press and available in the offices of Institutional Representatives for the Rhodes scholarships in colleges and universities. In addition, the *Oxford University Examination Decrees* is available for a charge from the Oxford University Press Bookshop, 116 High Street, Oxford OXl 4BZ, England. Copies of a brochure, *Oxford and the Rhodes Scholarships*, giving information about the scholarships and life and study at Oxford, may be obtained from Institutional Representatives at each campus as well as from the Office of the American Secretary. Students who wish further information or have difficulty in obtaining application forms should write to: Office of the American Secretary, The Rhodes Scholarship Trust, PO Box 7490, McLean, Virginia 22106-7490.

Where Can You Find Help?

THE COLLEGE FINANCIAL AID OFFICE

The cost of education at a private college likely will fall in the range of $12,000 to $35,000 annually for tuition, room, and board. Public college education is about half this amount. Your actual cost, though, depends upon your financial aid award. No matter what your family's income level or your academic record, you are likely to be eligible for some form of financial aid. Whether through scholarships, awards, grants, loans, or student employment, most colleges endeavor to provide financial assistance to admitted freshmen that will enable these students to enroll at their institution. That's why it is important to look beyond the "sticker price" of attending the college of your choice and apply for financial aid before ruling out a college based on cost.

Most financial aid is based on financial need. However, whether you demonstrate 100 percent financial need or hardly any, you can look to the financial aid office of the college that has accepted you to work with you to create a financial aid package that addresses your unique situation and makes your college education an investment that you can afford. The primary purpose of the financial aid office is to remove financial barriers to student enrollment and ensure that any qualified student can obtain sufficient resources to attend college. The essential job of the financial aid administrator is to help students who would otherwise be unable to attend college seek, obtain, and make the best use of all financial resources available.

The financial aid office in any college or university will guide you to the financial aid options available from a variety of sources—state and federal government programs, friends of the college, alumni, and the college itself. The actual amount of a financial aid package is determined not only by the evaluation of your personal financial situation but also by the unique financial resources, policies, and practices of each institution.

Financial aid packages vary significantly from school to school. Moreover, the amount of aid available from each institution can fluctuate from year to year, depending on the number of applicants, the amount of need to be met, and the financial resources and policies of the college.

After you have narrowed down the colleges in which you are interested based on academic and personal criteria, we recommend that you contact the college's financial aid office. Here are just a few questions you might want to ask the financial aid officers at the colleges you are seriously considering:

- What are the types and sources of aid provided to freshmen at your school?

- What factors are considered in determining whether a financial aid applicant is qualified for its need-based aid programs?

- How does your institution determine the combination of types of aid that make up an individual's package?

- How are non-need awards treated—as a part of the aid package or as a part of the parental/family contribution?

- Doyou "guarantee" financial aid and, if so, how is your policy implemented? Guaranteed aid means that, by policy, 100 percent of need is met for all students judged to have need. Implementation determines *how* need is met and varies widely from school to school. For example, grade point average may determine the proportioning of scholarship, loan, and work-study aid. Rules for freshmen may be different than those for upperclass students.

- To what degree is the admission process "need-blind"? Need-blind means that admission decisions are made without regard to the student's need for financial aid.

- What are the norms and practices for upperclass student aid? A college might offer a wonderful package for the freshman year, then leave you relatively on your own to fund the remaining three years. Or the school may provide a higher proportion of scholarship money to freshmen, then rebalance its aid packages to contain more self-help aid (loans and work-study) in upperclass years. There is an assumption that, all other factors being equal, students who have settled into the pattern of college time management can handle more work-study hours than freshmen. Grade point average, tuition increases, changes in parental financial circumstances, and other factors may also affect the redistribution. If you feel your financial situation warrants additional review, the financial aid office is always willing to work with you to help you find solutions.

THE HIGH SCHOOL GUIDANCE OFFICE

The high school guidance office is often the first source of information that students and parents have to learn about their college options, including financing. High school guidance counselors work to educate students and their parents about college options and the college admission and financial aid process. They counsel individual students about their postsecondary career and educational choices.

Many guidance offices are well equipped for this task, with libraries of college catalogs, college guides, interactive career or college selection software. Many high school students have access to a first-rate college and career information center and a counselor who has great knowledge about specific colleges, college selection, admissions processes, and student financial aid options and can work with students as they make the transition from high school to postsecondary education. Thousands of high schools are fortunate to have this type of resource.

Resources devoted to college advisement vary tremendously from district to district. Guidance counselors sometimes have an overwhelming number of students to counsel and urgent responsibilities in other areas that demand a greater share of their time, energy, and expertise. They often cannot find the time to provide personalized consultation to individual students about their college options. It is always necessary for parents to assess the situation at their child's particular high school. If college counseling resources at your high school are limited, it may be necessary to fill in, either by yourself or, if you can afford it, with an independent college advisement counselor.

With respect to financial aid, any high school guidance office should be able to provide you with the current FAFSA, forms for state-sponsored financial aid programs, and information about locally-sponsored scholarship programs.

College fairs are a worthwhile resource available to many parents and students. There are college fairs sponsored by school districts as well as a program of National College Fairs sponsored by the National Association for College Admission Counseling (NACAC). These usually offer exhibits and presentations by individual colleges and universities. Students and parents are able to meet with admissions representatives of different colleges; view their information presentations; take home a range of informative brochures, periodicals, and other products; and attend information sessions on college admissions and financing. Many high schools allow time off during the school day for students to attend a college fair.

NACAC's National College Fair program probably draws the greatest number of college representatives. NACAC sponsors thirty-six fairs in different parts of the country, which attract more than 300,000 students each year. Contact them at National Association for College Admission Counseling, 1631 Prince Street, Alexandria, Virginia 22314-2818; telephone: 703-836-2222; fax: 703-836-8015; or look at their Web site (www.nacac.com/) to receive an up-to-date list of college fairs.

Scholarship Scams: What They Are and What to Watch Out For

S everal hundred thousand students seek and find scholarships every year. Most require some outside help to pay for tuition costs. Although most of this outside help, in the form of grants, scholarships, low-interest loans, and work-study programs, comes from either the federal government or the colleges themselves, scholarships from private sources are an extremely important component of this network. An award from a private source can tilt the scales with respect to a student's ability to attend a specific college during a particular year. Unfortunately for prospective scholarship seekers, the private aid sector is virtually without patterns or rules. It has, over many years, developed as a haphazard conglomeration of individual programs, each with its own award criteria, timetables, application procedures, and decision-making processes. Considerable effort is required to understand and effectively benefit from private scholarships. Regrettably, the combination of a sharp urgency to locate money, limited time, and this complex and bewildering system has created opportunities for fraud. For every 10 students who receive a legitimate scholarship, 1 is victimized by a fraudulent scheme or scam that poses as a legitimate foundation, scholarship sponsor, or scholarship search service.

These fraudulent businesses advertise in campus newspapers, distribute flyers, mail letters and postcards, provide toll-free phone numbers, and even have sites on the World Wide Web. The most obvious frauds operate as scholarship search services or scholarship clearinghouses. Another quieter segment sets up as a scholarship sponsor, pockets the money from the fees and charges that are paid by thousands of hopeful scholarship seekers, and returns little, if anything, in proportion to the amounts it collects. A few of these frauds inflict great harm by gaining access to individuals' credit or checking accounts with the intent to extort funds.

A typical mode of operation is for a fraudulent firm to send out a huge mailing (more than a million postcards each year for some outfits) to college and high school students, claiming that the company has either a scholarship or a scholarship list for the students. These companies often provide toll-free numbers. When recipients call, they are told by high-pressure telemarketers that the company has unclaimed scholarships and that for fees ranging from $10 to $400 the callers get back at least $1000 in scholarship money or the fee will be refunded. Customers who pay, if they receive anything at all, are mailed a list of sources of financial aid that are no better than, and are in many cases inferior to, what can be found in any major scholarship guide available in bookstores or libraries. The "lucky" recipients have to apply on their own for the scholarships. Many of the programs are contests, loans, or work-study programs rather than gift aid. Some are no longer in existence, have expired deadlines, or demand eligibility requirements that the students cannot meet. Customers who seek refunds have to demonstrate that they have applied in writing to each source on the list and received a rejection letter from each of them. Frequently, even when customers can provide this almost-impossible-to-obtain proof, refunds are not made. In the worst cases, the companies ask for consumers' checking account or credit card numbers and take funds without authorization.

The Federal Trade Commission (FTC) warns students to be wary of fraudulent search services that promise to do all the work for you. "Bogus scholarship search services are just a variation on the 'you have won' prize-promotion scam, targeted to a particular audience—students and their parents who are anxious about paying for college," says Jodie Bernstein, former director of the FTC's Bureau of Consumer Protection. "They guarantee students free scholarship money . . . all they have to do to claim it is pay an up-front fee."

There are legitimate scholarship search services. However, a scholarship search service cannot truthfully guarantee that a student will receive a scholarship, and students almost always will fare as well or better by using a reliable scholarship information source than by wasting money, and sometimes more importantly, time, with a search service that promises a scholarship.

The FTC warns scholarship seekers to be alert for these seven warning signs of a scam:

1. **"This scholarship is guaranteed or your money back."**

   No service can guarantee that it will get you a grant or scholarship. Refund guarantees often have impossible conditions attached. Review a service's refund policies in writing before you pay a fee. Typically, fraudulent scholarship search services require that applicants show rejection letters from each of the sponsors on the list they provide. If a sponsor no longer exists, if it really does not provide scholarships, or if it has a rolling application deadline, letters of rejection are almost impossible to obtain.

2. **"The scholarship service will do all the work."**

   Unfortunately, nobody else can fill out the personal information forms, write the essays, and supply the references that many scholarships may require.

3. **"The scholarship will cost some money."**

   Be wary of any charges related to scholarship information services or individual scholarship applications, especially in significant amounts. Some legitimate scholarship sponsors charge fees to defray their processing expenses. True scholarship sponsors, however, should give out money, not make it from application fees. Before you send money to apply for a scholarship, investigate the sponsor.

4. **"You can't get this information anywhere else."**

   In addition to Peterson's, scholarship directories from other publishers are available in any large bookstore, public library, or high school guidance office. Additional information on private scholarship programs, including scams, can be found at www.finaid.org.

5. **"You are a finalist" in a contest you never entered, or "You have been selected by a national foundation to receive a scholarship."**

   Most legitimate scholarship programs almost never seek particular applicants. Most scholarship sponsors will only contact you in response to an inquiry. Most lack the budget and mandate to do anything more than this. Should you think that there is any real possibility that you may have been selected to receive a scholarship, before you send any money investigate first to be sure that the sponsor or program is legitimate.

6. **"The scholarship service needs your credit card or checking account number in advance."**

   Never provide your credit card or bank account number over the telephone to the representative of an organization that you do not know. A legitimate need-based scholarship program will not ask for your checking account number. Get information in writing first. An unscrupulous operation does not need your signature on a check. It schemes to set up situations that allow it to drain a victim's account with unauthorized withdrawals.

7. **"You are invited to a free seminar (or interview) with a trained financial aid consultant who will unlock the secrets on how to make yourself eligible for more financial aid."**

   Sometimes these consultants offer some good tips on preparing for college, but often they are trying to get you to sign up for a long-term contract for services you don't need. Often these "consultants" are trying to sell you other financial products, such as annuities, life insurance, or other services that have little to do with financial aid. By doing your own research, using the Web, working with your high school guidance office and the college financial aid office, you will get all the help you need to ensure you have done a thorough job in preparing for the financing of your college education.

In addition to the FTC's seven signs, here are some other points to keep in mind when considering a scholarship program:

- Fraudulent scholarship operations often use official-sounding names containing words such as *federal*, *national*, *administration*, *division*, *federation*, and *foundation*. Their names often are a slight variation of the name of a legitimate government or private organization. Do not be fooled by a name that seems reputable or official, looks like an official-looking seal, or has a Washington, D.C. address.

- If you win a scholarship, you will receive official written notification by mail not by telephone. If the sponsor calls to inform you, it will follow up with a letter in the mail. If a request for money is made over the phone, the operation is probably fraudulent.

- Be wary if an organization's address is a post office box number or a residential address. If a bona fide scholarship program uses a post office box number, it usually will include a street address and telephone number on its stationery.

- Beware of telephone numbers with a 900 area code. These may charge you a fee of several dollars a minute for a call that could be a long recording that provides only a list of addresses or names.

- A dishonest operation may put pressure on an applicant by saying that awards are on a first-come, first-served basis. Some scholarship programs give preference to the earlier qualified applications. However, if you are told, especially over the telephone, that you must respond quickly, but you will not hear about the results for several months, there may be a problem.

- Be wary of endorsements. Fraudulent operations claim endorsements by groups with names similar to well-known private or government organizations. The Better Business Bureau (BBB) and government agencies do not endorse businesses.

If an organization requires you to pay money for a scholarship and you have never heard of it before and cannot verify that it is a legitimate operation, the best advice is not to pay anything. If you have already paid money to such an organization and find reason to doubt its legitimacy, call your bank to stop payment on your check, if possible, or call your credit card company and tell it that you think you were the victim of a consumer fraud.

To find out how to recognize, report, and stop a scholarship scam, contact the Federal Trade Commission at 600 Pennsylvania Avenue, N.W., Washington, D.C. 20580 or go online to www.ftc.gov or the National Fraud Information Center at www.fraud.org. The National Fraud Information Center also can be contacted by calling 800-876-7060 (toll-free). The Better Business Bureau maintains files of businesses about which it has received complaints. You should call both your local BBB office and the BBB office in the area of the organization in question; each local BBB has different records. Call 703-276-0100 to get the telephone number of your local BBB or look at http://www.bbb.org for a directory of local BBBs and downloadable BBB complaint forms. The national address is The Council of Better Business Bureaus, 4200 Wilson Boulevard, Suite 800, Arlington, Virginia 22203-1838.

There are many wonderful scholarships available to qualified students who spend the time and effort to locate and apply for them. We advise you to exercise caution in using scholarship search services and, when you must pay money, to practice careful judgment in considering a scholarship program's sponsor. We hope that you take full advantage of the many real opportunities that have been opened to college students and their families by the many organizations, foundations, and businesses that have organized to help you with the burden of college expenses.

How to Use This Book

HOW TO UNDERSTAND THE PROFILES

The scholarships described in this book are organized into categories that represent the major factors used to determine eligibility for scholarship awards and prizes. To find a basic list of scholarships available to you, look under the specific category or categories that fit your particular academic goals, skills or background.

The categories are divided into two broad classes: *Academic Fields/Career Goals* and *Nonacademic/Noncareer Criteria*.

Because your major academic field of study and/or career goal has central importance in college planning, the *Academic Fields/Career Goals* section appears first. The *Academic Fields/Career Goals* category is subdivided into individual subject areas that are organized alphabetically.

These are:

- Accounting
- Agribusiness
- Agriculture
- Animal/Veterinary Sciences
- Applied Sciences
- Archaeology
- Architecture
- Area/Ethnic Studies
- Art History
- Arts
- Aviation/Aerospace
- Biology
- Business/Consumer Services
- Chemical Engineering
- Civil Engineering
- Communications
- Computer Science/Data Processing
- Criminal Justice/Criminology
- Dental Health/Services
- Drafting
- Earth Science
- Economics
- Education

- Electrical Engineering/Electronics
- Engineering-Related Technologies
- Engineering/Technology
- Fashion Design
- Filmmaking/Video
- Food Science/Nutrition
- Food Service/Hospitality
- Foreign Language
- Geography
- Graphics/Graphic Arts/Printing
- Health Administration
- Health and Medical Sciences
- Health Information Management/Technology
- History
- Home Economics
- Horticulture/Floriculture
- Hospitality Management
- Humanities
- Interior Design
- International Migration
- International Studies
- Journalism

- Landscape Architecture
- Law Enforcement/Police Administration
- Law/Legal Services
- Library and Information Sciences
- Literature/English/Writing
- Materials Science, Engineering, and Metallurgy
- Mechanical Engineering
- Meteorology/Atmospheric Science
- Museum Studies
- Music
- Natural Resources
- Natural Sciences
- Nuclear Science
- Nursing
- Peace and Conflict Studies
- Performing Arts
- Photojournalism/Photography
- Physical Sciences and Math
- Political Science
- Real Estate
- Religion/Theology
- Science, Technology, and Society
- Social Sciences
- Social Services
- Special Education
- Sports-Related
- Surveying; Surveying Technology, Cartography, or Geographic Information Science
- Therapy/Rehabilitation
- Trade/Technical Specialties
- Transportation
- TV/Radio Broadcasting

The second class of awards, *Nonacademic/Noncareer Criteria*, are those that are primarily based on a personal characteristic of the award recipient. We have organized these criteria into categories:

- Civic, Professional, Social, or Union Affiliation
- Employment Experience
- Impairment
- Military Service
- Nationality or Ethnic Heritage
- Religious Affiliation
- State of Residence
- Talent

Full descriptive profiles of scholarship awards are sequentially numbered from 1 through 546. This number appears in the upper right-hand corner of the profile with a bullet in front of it. (It is this profile number, not the page number on which the award appears, that is referenced in the indexes.) A full profile of an award appears in only one location in the book. Most awards have more than one criterion that needs to be met before a student can be eligible. Cross-references by name and sequential number are made to the full program description from the other relevant criteria categories under which the award might also have been listed if one of its multiple criteria had not come earlier in the alphabet. The full description appears in the first relevant location, the cross-references in the latter ones.

Cross-references are not provided from the *Nonacademic/Noncareer Criteria* section to programs in the *Academic Fields/Career Goals* section. You will be able to locate relevant awards in this section by any personal qualifying criteria through the indexes in the back of the book.

WHAT IS IN THE DESCRIPTIVE PROFILES?

Here are the elements of a full descriptive profile:

1. Name of the sponsoring organization

2. Award name and sequence number

3. Brief description of the award

4. Academic/Career Areas (this is only in the *Academic Fields/Career Goals* Section

5. Award descriptors (Is it a scholarship? A prize for winning a competition? A forgivable loan? An internship? For what years of college can it be used? Is it renewable or is it only for one year? How many awards are given? For what amounts?)

6. Eligibility Requirements

7. Application Requirements

8. Sponsoring organization's Web address

9. Contact name, address, phone and fax numbers, and e-mail address

WHERE OUR INFORMATION COMES FROM

Between January and April of each year, Peterson's conducts a survey of more than 5,000 organizations and agencies in the U.S. and Canada that sponsor scholarships, prizes, fellowships, grants, and forgivable loans for undergraduate- and graduate-level students.

The information is constructed from Peterson's questionnaires that went to the sponsoring bodies in December 2002. The information was verified and correct as of April 2003. The number of awards, funding amounts, and procedures can change at any time. There is no way to guarantee that the number of awards or dollar amounts reported by a sponsor will be duplicated in a new year. You should request written descriptive materials for the program in which you are interested directly from the sponsor.

Profiles

Academic Fields/Career Goals 36

Nonacademic/Noncareer Criteria 243

Miscellaneous Criteria 318

ACADEMIC FIELDS/CAREER GOALS

ACCOUNTING

AMERICAN INSTITUTE OF CERTIFIED PUBLIC ACCOUNTANTS

FELLOWSHIPS FOR MINORITY DOCTORAL STUDENTS   • 1

Fellowships are available to minority students enrolled in a doctoral program with a concentration in accounting. Must have earned a master's degree and/or completed a minimum of three years full-time experience in the practice of accounting. Recipients of the fellowship will attend school on a full-time basis.

Academic Fields/Career Goals Accounting. *Award* Fellowship for use in graduate years; renewable. *Amount:* up to $12,000.

Eligibility Requirements Applicant must be American Indian/Alaska Native, Asian/Pacific Islander, Black (non-Hispanic), or Hispanic and enrolled or expecting to enroll full-time at an institution or university. Available to U.S. citizens.

Application Requirements Application, references, transcript. *Deadline:* April 1.

World Wide Web: http://www.aicpa.org

Contact: Scholarship Coordinator
American Institute of Certified Public Accountants
1211 Avenue of the Americas
New York, NY 10036-8775
Phone: 212-596-6270
E-mail: educat@aicpa.org

SCHOLARSHIPS FOR MINORITY ACCOUNTING STUDENTS   • 2

Scholarships are given to minority students who are declared accounting majors with an overall and major GPA of 3.3. Must be a minority student who has satisfactorily completed at least 30 semester hours (or equivalent) including at least six semester hours in accounting. Must be enrolled as a full-time undergraduate or graduate student at an accredited college or university.

Academic Fields/Career Goals Accounting. *Award* Scholarship for use in junior, senior, or graduate years; not renewable. *Amount:* up to $5000.

Eligibility Requirements Applicant must be American Indian/Alaska Native, Asian/Pacific Islander, Black (non-Hispanic), or Hispanic and enrolled or expecting to enroll full-time at a four-year institution or university. Available to U.S. citizens.

Application Requirements Application, essay, financial need analysis, references, transcript. *Deadline:* July 1.

World Wide Web: http://www.aicpa.org

Contact: Scholarship Coordinator
American Institute of Certified Public Accountants
1211 Avenue of the Americas
New York, NY 10036-8775
Phone: 212-596-6270
E-mail: educat@aicpa.org

ASSOCIATION OF LATINO PROFESSIONALS IN FINANCE AND ACCOUNTING

HSF-ALPFA SCHOLARSHIPS • 3

One-time award to undergraduate and graduate Latino students pursuing degrees in accounting, finance and related majors based on financial need and academic performance. Must be enrolled full-time at a U.S. college or university. Minimum 3.0 GPA required. Must be U.S. citizen or legal permanent resident.

Academic Fields/Career Goals Accounting; Business/Consumer Services. *Award* Scholarship for use in freshman, sophomore, junior, senior, or graduate years; not renewable. *Amount:* $1250–$5000.

Eligibility Requirements Applicant must be Hispanic and enrolled or expecting to enroll full-time at a two-year or four-year institution or university. Applicant must have 3.0 GPA or higher. Available to U.S. citizens.

Application Requirements Application, essay, financial need analysis, references, transcript. *Deadline:* April 15.

World Wide Web: http://www.alpfa.org

Contact: Lisa Lopez, Executive Director
Association of Latino Professionals in Finance and Accounting
510 West Sixth Street
Suite 400
Los Angeles, CA 90014
Phone: 213-243-0004
Fax: 213-243-0006
E-mail: scholarships@national.alpfa.org

COLORADO SOCIETY OF CERTIFIED PUBLIC ACCOUNTANTS EDUCATIONAL FOUNDATION

ETHNIC DIVERSITY COLLEGE AND UNIVERSITY SCHOLARSHIPS • 4

Award of $1000 for declared accounting major at a Colorado college or university. Must be African-American, Hispanic, Asian-American, American-Indian, or Pacific Islander and have completed at least 8 semester hours of accounting courses. Scholarship is awarded for the fall semester. Must be Colorado resident. Minimum 3.0 GPA required.

Academic Fields/Career Goals Accounting. *Award* Scholarship for use in sophomore, junior, senior, graduate, or postgraduate years; not renewable. *Number:* 2. *Amount:* $1000.

Eligibility Requirements Applicant must be American Indian/Alaska Native, Asian/Pacific Islander, Black (non-Hispanic), or Hispanic; enrolled or expecting to enroll full or part-time at a four-year institution or university; resident of Colorado and studying in Colorado. Applicant must have 3.0 GPA or higher. Available to U.S. citizens.

Application Requirements Application, transcript. *Deadline:* June 30.

World Wide Web: http://www.cocpa.org

Contact: Gena Mantz, Membership Coordinator
Colorado Society of Certified Public Accountants Educational Foundation
7979 East Tufts Avenue, Suite 500
Denver, CO 80237-2845
Phone: 303-741-8613
Fax: 303-773-2877
E-mail: gmantz@cocpa.org

COMMUNITY FOUNDATION FOR PALM BEACH AND MARTIN COUNTIES, INC.

KIM LOVE SATORY SCHOLARSHIP
• 5

For female graduating senior from a Palm Beach or Martin County public or private high school interested in banking and finance. Must provide evidence of strong commitment to community service and involvement. Must demonstrate financial need.

Academic Fields/Career Goals Accounting. *Award* Scholarship for use in freshman year; not renewable. *Number:* 1. *Amount:* $750–$2500.

Eligibility Requirements Applicant must be high school student; planning to enroll or expecting to enroll full-time at a four-year institution or university; female; resident of Florida and must have an interest in English language or leadership. Available to U.S. citizens.

Application Requirements Application, financial need analysis. *Deadline:* March 1.

World Wide Web: http://www.cfpbmc.org

Contact: Carolyn Jenco, Grants Manager/Scholarship Coordinator
Community Foundation for Palm Beach and Martin Counties, Inc.
700 South Dixie Highway
Suite 200
West Palm Beach, FL 33401

EDUCATIONAL FOUNDATION FOR WOMEN IN ACCOUNTING (EFWA)

LAURELS FUND
• 6

One-year academic scholarship for women pursuing advanced degrees in accounting. Applicants must have completed at least one full year of a doctoral program. Must be a U.S. citizen.

Academic Fields/Career Goals Accounting. *Award* Scholarship for use in postgraduate years; not renewable. *Amount:* $1500–$5000.

Eligibility Requirements Applicant must be enrolled or expecting to enroll at an institution or university and female. Available to U.S. citizens.

Application Requirements Application, autobiography, essay, financial need analysis, references, test scores, transcript. *Deadline:* March 15.

World Wide Web: http://www.efwa.org

Contact: Cynthia Hires, Administrator
Educational Foundation for Women in Accounting (EFWA)
PO Box 1925
Southeastern, PA 19399-1925
Phone: 610-407-9229
Fax: 610-644-3713
E-mail: info@efwa.org

WOMEN IN NEED SCHOLARSHIP
• 7

Scholarship awarded to single women returning to school to earn a bachelor's degree in accounting. Women in Need scholarship awards $2000 for up to two years and is directed towards incoming, current or re-entry juniors. Contact for definition of women in need.

Academic Fields/Career Goals Accounting. *Award* Scholarship for use in junior or senior years; renewable. *Number:* 1. *Amount:* $2000–$4000.

Eligibility Requirements Applicant must be enrolled or expecting to enroll full-time at a four-year institution or university and single female. Available to U.S. citizens.

Application Requirements Application, autobiography, essay, financial need analysis, references, test scores, transcript. *Deadline:* April 15.

World Wide Web: http://www.efwa.org

Contact: Cynthia Hires, Administrator
Educational Foundation for Women in Accounting (EFWA)
PO Box 1925
Southeastern, PA 19399-1925
Phone: 610-407-9229
Fax: 610-644-3713
E-mail: info@efwa.org

WOMEN IN TRANSITION/WOMEN IN NEED SCHOLARSHIP • 8

Scholarship awarded to single women returning to school to earn a bachelor's degree in accounting. Women in Transition scholarship awards up to $4000 for up to four years and is directed towards incoming and current freshmen. Contact for definitions of women in transition.

Academic Fields/Career Goals Accounting. *Award* Scholarship for use in freshman, sophomore, junior, or senior years; renewable. *Number:* 1. *Amount:* $4000.

Eligibility Requirements Applicant must be enrolled or expecting to enroll full-time at a four-year institution or university and single female. Available to U.S. citizens.

Application Requirements Application, autobiography, essay, financial need analysis, references, test scores, transcript. *Deadline:* April 15.

World Wide Web: http://www.efwa.org

Contact: Cynthia Hires, Administrator
Educational Foundation for Women in Accounting (EFWA)
PO Box 1925
Southeastern, PA 19399-1925
Phone: 610-407-9229
Fax: 610-644-3713
E-mail: info@efwa.org

GOVERNMENT FINANCE OFFICERS ASSOCIATION

MINORITIES IN GOVERNMENT FINANCE SCHOLARSHIP • 9

Award given to upper-division undergraduate or graduate student of public administration, governmental accounting, finance, political science, economics, or business administration to recognize outstanding performance by minority student preparing for career in state and local government finance. Application deadline is February 7.

Academic Fields/Career Goals Accounting; Business/Consumer Services; Economics; Political Science. *Award* Scholarship for use in junior, senior, or graduate years; not renewable. *Number:* 1. *Amount:* $5000.

Eligibility Requirements Applicant must be American Indian/Alaska Native, Asian/Pacific Islander, Black (non-Hispanic), or Hispanic and enrolled or expecting to enroll full or part-time at a four-year institution or university. Available to U.S. and Canadian citizens.

Application Requirements Application, essay, resume, references, transcript. *Deadline:* February 7.

World Wide Web: http://www.GFOA.org

Contact: Jake Lorentz, Assistant Director
Government Finance Officers Association
Scholarship Committee
203 North LaSalle Street, Suite 2700
Chicago, IL 60601
Phone: 312-977-9700 Ext. 267
Fax: 312-977-4806
E-mail: jlorentz@gfoa.org

HISPANIC COLLEGE FUND, INC.

ALLFIRST/ HISPANIC COLLEGE FUND SCHOLARSHIP PROGRAM • 10

One-time scholarship open to full-time undergraduates of Hispanic descent pursuing a degree in business, accounting, economics, or finance. Must be a U.S. citizen residing in Maryland, Pennsylvania, or northern Virginia and have a minimum 3.0 GPA. Eligible students who have applied to the Hispanic College Fund need not re-apply.

Academic Fields/Career Goals Accounting; Business/Consumer Services; Computer Science/Data Processing; Economics; Engineering/Technology; Engineering-Related Technologies. *Award* Scholarship for use in freshman, sophomore, junior, or senior years; not renewable. *Number:* 5–10. *Amount:* $1000–$5000.

Eligibility Requirements Applicant must be of Hispanic, Latin American/Caribbean, Mexican, Nicaraguan, or Spanish heritage; enrolled or expecting to enroll full-time at a two-year or four-year institution or university and resident of Maryland, Pennsylvania, or Virginia. Applicant must have 3.0 GPA or higher. Available to U.S. citizens.

Application Requirements Application, essay, financial need analysis, resume, references, test scores, transcript, college acceptance letter, copy of taxes, copy of SAR. *Deadline:* April 15.

World Wide Web: http://www.hispanicfund.org

Contact: Stina Augustsson, Program Manager
Hispanic College Fund, Inc.
1717 Pennsylvania Avenue, NW, Suite 460
Washington, DC 20006
Phone: 202-296-5400
Fax: 202-296-3774
E-mail: hispaniccollegefund@earthlink.net

BURLINGTON NORTHERN SANTA FE FOUNDATION/HISPANIC COLLEGE FUND SCHOLARSHIP PROGRAM • 11

Scholarships ranging from $500 to $2500 are available for high school graduates of Hispanic origin who reside in any of the following Burlington Northern Santa Fe-served states: Arizona, Colorado, Illinois, Missouri, New Mexico, California and Texas. Must be pursuing a bachelor's degree in accounting, economics, engineering, finance, information systems, marketing or a related major.

Academic Fields/Career Goals Accounting; Business/Consumer Services; Engineering/Technology. *Award* Scholarship for use in freshman year; not renewable. *Number:* 10. *Amount:* $500–$2500.

Eligibility Requirements Applicant must be Hispanic; high school student; planning to enroll or expecting to enroll at an institution or university and resident of Arizona, California, Colorado, Illinois, Missouri, New Mexico, or Texas. Available to U.S. citizens.

Application Requirements Application. *Deadline:* April 15.

World Wide Web: http://www.hispanicfund.org

Contact: Stina Augustsson, Program Manager
Hispanic College Fund, Inc.
1717 Pennsylvania Avenue, NW, Suite 460
Washington, DC 20006
Phone: 202-296-5400
Fax: 202-296-3774
E-mail: hispaniccollegefund@earthlink.net

DENNY'S/HISPANIC COLLEGE FUND SCHOLARSHIP • 12

One-time scholarship award open to full-time undergraduates of Hispanic descent pursuing a degree in business or a business-related major with a GPA of 3.0 or better. Eligible students who have applied to the Hispanic College Fund need not re-apply.

Academic Fields/Career Goals Accounting; Architecture; Business/Consumer Services; Chemical Engineering; Communications; Computer Science/Data Processing; Economics; Electrical Engineering/Electronics; Engineering/Technology; Engineering-Related Technologies; Graphics/Graphic Arts/Printing; Hospitality Management. *Award* Scholarship for use in freshman, sophomore, junior, or senior years; not renewable. *Number:* 80–100. *Amount:* $1000.

Eligibility Requirements Applicant must be Hispanic and enrolled or expecting to enroll full-time at a two-year or four-year institution or university. Applicant must have 3.0 GPA or higher. Available to U.S. citizens.

Application Requirements Application, essay, financial need analysis, resume, references, test scores, transcript, college acceptance letter, copy of taxes, copy of SAR. *Deadline:* April 15.

World Wide Web: http://www.hispanicfund.org

Contact: Stina Augustsson, Program Manager
Hispanic College Fund, Inc.
1717 Pennsylvania Avenue, NW, Suite 460
Washington, DC 20006
Phone: 202-296-5400
Fax: 202-296-3774
E-mail: hispaniccollegefund@earthlink.net

INSTITUTE OF MANAGEMENT ACCOUNTANTS

INSTITUTE OF MANAGEMENT ACCOUNTANTS MEMORIAL EDUCATION FUND DIVERSITY SCHOLARSHIPS • 13

One-time award for students of American-Indian/Alaska Native, Asian/Pacific Islander, Black (non-Hispanic), and Hispanic heritage, as well as students with physical disabilities. Must be IMA student member pursuing a career in management accounting, financial management and information technology. Must be U.S. or Canadian citizen. Application deadline is February 15.

Academic Fields/Career Goals Accounting. *Award* Scholarship for use in junior, senior, graduate, or postgraduate years; not renewable. *Amount:* $3000.

Eligibility Requirements Applicant must be enrolled or expecting to enroll full or part-time at a four-year institution or university. Applicant must have 3.0 GPA or higher. Available to U.S. and Canadian citizens.

Application Requirements Application, essay, resume, references, transcript. *Deadline:* February 15.

World Wide Web: http://www.imanet.org

Contact: Susan Bender, Chapter and Council Services
Institute of Management Accountants
10 Paragon Drive
Montvale, NJ 07645-1760
Phone: 800-638-4427 Ext. 1543
Fax: 201-474-1602
E-mail: sbender@imanet.org

KPMG FOUNDATION

KPMG MINORITY ACCOUNTING DOCTORAL SCHOLARSHIP • 14

Renewable award for African-American, Hispanic-American, and Native-Americans who will be in full-time accounting doctoral program in September of the year application is made. It is suggested that the university will waive tuition and fees, and provide stipend and teaching assistantship opportunities. Applications are available at Web site http://www.kpmgfoundation.org.

Academic Fields/Career Goals Accounting. *Award* Scholarship for use in graduate years; renewable. *Number:* 15. *Amount:* $10,000.

Eligibility Requirements Applicant must be American Indian/Alaska Native, Black (non-Hispanic), or Hispanic and enrolled or expecting to enroll full-time at an institution or university. Available to U.S. citizens.

Application Requirements Application, transcript. *Deadline:* May 1.

World Wide Web: http://www.kpmgfoundation.org

Contact: Fiona Rose, KPMG Foundation Program Manager
KPMG Foundation
3 Chestnut Ridge Road
Montvale, NJ 07645-0435
Phone: 201-307-7628
Fax: 201-307-7093
E-mail: fionarose@kpmg.com

VIRGINIA SOCIETY OF CERTIFIED PUBLIC ACCOUNTANTS EDUCATION FOUNDATION

VIRGINIA SOCIETY OF CPAS EDUCATIONAL FOUNDATION MINORITY UNDERGRADUATE SCHOLARSHIP • 15

One-time award for a student currently enrolled in a Virginia college or university undergraduate program with the intent to pursue accounting. Applicant must have at least six hours of accounting and be currently registered for at least 3 more accounting credit hours. Applicant must be a member of one of the VSCPA-defined minority groups (African-American, Hispanic-American, Native-Americans or Asian Pacific American). Minimum overall and accounting GPA of 3.0 is required.

Academic Fields/Career Goals Accounting. *Award* Scholarship for use in sophomore, junior, or senior years; not renewable. *Number:* 3. *Amount:* $1200.

Eligibility Requirements Applicant must be American Indian/Alaska Native, Asian/Pacific Islander, Black (non-Hispanic), or Hispanic; enrolled or expecting to enroll at a two-year or four-year institution or university and studying in Virginia. Applicant must have 3.0 GPA or higher. Available to U.S. citizens.

Application Requirements Application, essay, resume, references, transcript. *Deadline:* April 15.

World Wide Web: http://www.vscpa.com

Contact: Tracey Zink, Public Relations Coordinator
Virginia Society of Certified Public Accountants Education Foundation
PO Box 4620
Glen Allen, VA 23058-4620
Phone: 800-733-8272
Fax: 804-273-1741
E-mail: tzink@vscpa.com

WASHINGTON SOCIETY OF CERTIFIED PUBLIC ACCOUNTANTS

WSCPA FIFTH-YEAR ACCOUNTING SCHOLARSHIPS • 16

These scholarships will be awarded to economically disadvantaged accounting students pursuing the 150-hour requirement to sit for the CPA exam. Students must be enrolled in a program that will qualify them to sit for the CPA exam. Deadline is April 15.

Academic Fields/Career Goals Accounting; Business/Consumer Services. *Award* Scholarship for use in junior, senior, or graduate years; not renewable. *Number:* up to 10. *Amount:* up to $2750.

Eligibility Requirements Applicant must be enrolled or expecting to enroll full or part-time at a four-year institution or university and studying in Washington. Applicant must have 2.5 GPA or higher. Available to U.S. citizens.

Application Requirements Application, essay, financial need analysis, resume, references, transcript. *Deadline:* April 15.

World Wide Web: http://www.wscpa.org

Contact: Lisa Downs, Academic and Student Relations Administrator
Washington Society of Certified Public Accountants
902 140th Avenue, NE
Bellevue, WA 98005-3480
Phone: 425-644-4800
Fax: 425-586-1119
E-mail: accountingcareers@wscpa.org

WSCPA SCHOLARSHIPS FOR MINORITY ACCOUNTING MAJORS • 17

$3500 scholarship is available to a minority accounting student who will have completed his/her sophomore year by fall of the year at an accredited four-year institution in Washington state. Deadline is April 15. Minimum 3.0 GPA required.

Academic Fields/Career Goals Accounting. *Award* Scholarship for use in junior or senior years; not renewable. *Number:* 1. *Amount:* $3500.

Eligibility Requirements Applicant must be American Indian/Alaska Native, Asian/Pacific Islander, Black (non-Hispanic), or Hispanic; enrolled or expecting to enroll full or part-time at a four-year institution or university and studying in Washington. Applicant must have 3.0 GPA or higher. Available to U.S. citizens.

Application Requirements Application, essay, resume, references, transcript. *Deadline:* April 15.

World Wide Web: http://www.wscpa.org

Contact: Lisa Downs, Academic and Student Relations Administrator
Washington Society of Certified Public Accountants
902 140th Avenue, NE
Bellevue, WA 98005-3480
Phone: 425-644-4800
Fax: 425-586-1119
E-mail: accountingcareers@wscpa.org

AGRIBUSINESS

AMERICAN AGRICULTURAL ECONOMICS ASSOCIATION FOUNDATION

SYLVIA LANE MENTOR RESEARCH FELLOWSHIP FUND • 18

Award for female graduate and post-graduate students in agricultural economics. Submit curriculum vitae, budget, research statement, and letter of intent from mentor with application. Write for more information. One-time award of $2000-$4000.

Sylvia Lane Mentor Research Fellowship Fund (continued)

Academic Fields/Career Goals Agribusiness; Agriculture; Economics; Natural Resources; Science, Technology and Society; Social Sciences. *Award* Fellowship for use in graduate, or postgraduate years; not renewable. *Number:* 1–3. *Amount:* $2000–$4000.

Eligibility Requirements Applicant must be enrolled or expecting to enroll full-time at a four-year institution or university and female. Available to U.S. and non-U.S. citizens.

Application Requirements Application, references. *Deadline:* Continuous.

World Wide Web: http://www.aaea.org

Contact: Ms. Donna Dunn, Executive Director
American Agricultural Economics Association Foundation
415 South Duff, Suite C
Ames, IA 50010-6600
Phone: 515-233-3202
Fax: 515-233-3101
E-mail: donna@aaea.org

HISPANIC COLLEGE FUND, INC.

FIRST IN MY FAMILY SCHOLARSHIP PROGRAM • 19

One-time scholarship open to full-time undergraduates of Hispanic descent pursuing a degree in business- or technology-related major. Must be a U.S. citizen residing in the United States and have a minimum 3.0 GPA. Eligible students who have applied to the Hispanic College Fund need not re-apply. Must be first in the family to attend college.

Academic Fields/Career Goals Agribusiness; Business/Consumer Services; Chemical Engineering; Communications; Computer Science/Data Processing; Drafting; Economics; Electrical Engineering/Electronics; Engineering/Technology; Engineering-Related Technologies; Graphics/Graphic Arts/Printing; Mechanical Engineering. *Award* Scholarship for use in freshman, sophomore, junior, or senior years; not renewable. *Number:* 30–60. *Amount:* $1000–$5000.

Eligibility Requirements Applicant must be of Hispanic, Latin American/Caribbean, Mexican, Nicaraguan, or Spanish heritage and enrolled or expecting to enroll full-time at a two-year or four-year institution or university. Applicant must have 3.0 GPA or higher. Available to U.S. citizens.

Application Requirements Application, essay, financial need analysis, resume, references, test scores, transcript, college acceptance letter, copy of taxes, copy of SAR. *Deadline:* April 15.

World Wide Web: http://www.hispanicfund.org

Contact: Stina Augustsson, Program Manager
Hispanic College Fund, Inc.
1717 Pennsylvania Avenue, NW, Suite 460
Washington, DC 20006
Phone: 202-296-5400
Fax: 202-296-3774
E-mail: hispaniccollegefund@earthlink.net

HISPANIC COLLEGE FUND SCHOLARSHIP PROGRAM • 20

This program awards scholarships to full-time students of Hispanic origin who have demonstrated academic excellence, leadership skills and financial need to pursue an undergraduate degree in a business or technology-related field.

Academic Fields/Career Goals Agribusiness; Business/Consumer Services; Chemical Engineering; Communications; Computer Science/Data Processing; Drafting; Economics;

Electrical Engineering/Electronics; Engineering/Technology; Engineering-Related Technologies; Graphics/Graphic Arts/Printing; Mechanical Engineering. *Award* Scholarship for use in freshman, sophomore, junior, or senior years; not renewable. *Number:* 400–600. *Amount:* $1000–$5000.

Eligibility Requirements Applicant must be of Hispanic, Latin American/Caribbean, Mexican, Nicaraguan, or Spanish heritage and enrolled or expecting to enroll full-time at a two-year or four-year institution or university. Applicant must have 3.0 GPA or higher. Available to U.S. citizens.

Application Requirements Application, essay, financial need analysis, resume, references, test scores, transcript, college acceptance letter, copy of taxes, copy of SAR. *Deadline:* April 15.

World Wide Web: http://www.hispanicfund.org

Contact: Stina Augustsson, Program Manager
Hispanic College Fund, Inc.
1717 Pennsylvania Avenue, NW, Suite 460
Washington, DC 20006
Phone: 202-296-5400
Fax: 202-296-3774
E-mail: hispaniccollegefund@earthlink.net

AGRICULTURE

AMERICAN AGRICULTURAL ECONOMICS ASSOCIATION FOUNDATION

SYLVIA LANE MENTOR RESEARCH FELLOWSHIP FUND   see number 18

CANADIAN FEDERATION OF UNIVERSITY WOMEN

CANADIAN FEDERATION OF UNIVERSITY WOMEN MEMORIAL FELLOWSHIP   • 21

One fellowship available to Canadian women who are enrolled in a master's degree program in science, mathematics, or engineering. Applicants may be studying abroad. One-time award of CAN$5,000. Must be Canadian citizen, or have held landed immigrant status for at least one year. Application fee is CAN$35.

Academic Fields/Career Goals Agriculture; Applied Sciences; Biology; Chemical Engineering; Civil Engineering; Computer Science/Data Processing; Earth Science; Health and Medical Sciences; Meteorology/Atmospheric Science; Physical Sciences and Math. *Award* Fellowship for use in graduate years; not renewable. *Number:* 1. *Amount:* $5000.

Eligibility Requirements Applicant must be Canadian citizenship; enrolled or expecting to enroll full or part-time at an institution or university and female.

Application Requirements Application, autobiography, essay, references, transcript. *Fee:* $35. *Deadline:* November 1.

World Wide Web: http://www.cfuw.org

Contact: Betty Dunlop, Fellowships Program Manager
Canadian Federation of University Women
251 Bank Street, Suite 600
Ottawa, ON K2P 1X3
Canada
Phone: 613-234-2732
E-mail: cfuwfls@rogers.com

GEM CONSORTIUM

GEM MS ENGINEERING FELLOWSHIP • 22

Renewable award for U.S. citizen who is a junior, senior, undergraduate, or baccalaureate degree recipient in an accredited engineering discipline. Must be American-Indian, Black American, Hispanic-American, or Mexican-American. Master's degree must be in same engineering discipline as bachelor's degree. Includes summer internship. Minimum 2.8 GPA required for master's students.

Academic Fields/Career Goals Agriculture; Architecture; Biology; Civil Engineering; Computer Science/Data Processing; Earth Science; Electrical Engineering/Electronics; Engineering/Technology; Materials Science, Engineering and Metallurgy; Mechanical Engineering; Nuclear Science. *Award* Fellowship for use in junior, senior, or graduate years; renewable. *Number:* 200. *Amount:* $20,000–$40,000.

Eligibility Requirements Applicant must be American Indian/Alaska Native, Black (non-Hispanic), or Hispanic and enrolled or expecting to enroll full-time at a four-year institution or university. Available to U.S. citizens.

Application Requirements Application, resume, references, transcript, statement of purpose. *Deadline:* December 1.

World Wide Web: http://www.gemfellowship.org

Contact: Saundra D. Johnson, Executive Director
GEM Consortium
PO Box 537
Notre Dame, IN 46556-0537
Phone: 574-631-7771
Fax: 574-287-1486
E-mail: gem.1@nd.edu

GEM PHD ENGINEERING FELLOWSHIP • 23

Renewable award for U.S. citizen who has attained or is in process of attaining master's degree in engineering. Minimum 3.0 GPA required. Must be American-Indian, Black American, or Hispanic-American. Must attend GEM PhD fellowship program member university. May major in any discipline within engineering. Includes summer internship.

Academic Fields/Career Goals Agriculture; Architecture; Biology; Civil Engineering; Computer Science/Data Processing; Earth Science; Electrical Engineering/Electronics; Engineering/Technology; Materials Science, Engineering and Metallurgy; Mechanical Engineering; Nuclear Science. *Award* Fellowship for use in graduate years; renewable. *Number:* 20–30. *Amount:* $60,000.

Eligibility Requirements Applicant must be American Indian/Alaska Native, Black (non-Hispanic), or Hispanic and enrolled or expecting to enroll full-time at an institution or university. Applicant must have 3.0 GPA or higher. Available to U.S. citizens.

Application Requirements Application, resume, references, transcript, statement of purpose. *Deadline:* December 1.

World Wide Web: http://www.gemfellowship.org

Contact: Saundra D. Johnson, Executive Director
GEM Consortium
PO Box 537
Notre Dame, IN 46556-0537
Phone: 574-631-7771
Fax: 574-287-1486
E-mail: gem.1@nd.edu

WOMAN'S NATIONAL FARM AND GARDEN ASSOCIATION

SARAH BRADLEY TYSON MEMORIAL FELLOWSHIP • 24

Fellowship available to a female student for graduate study in agriculture, horticulture, and related fields. Write for information and application.

Academic Fields/Career Goals Agriculture; Earth Science; Horticulture/Floriculture. *Award* Fellowship for use in graduate, or postgraduate years; renewable. *Number:* 4. *Amount:* $1000.

Eligibility Requirements Applicant must be enrolled or expecting to enroll full-time at a four-year institution or university and female. Available to U.S. citizens.

Application Requirements Application. *Deadline:* March 31.

World Wide Web: http://www.wnfga.org

Contact: Mrs. Hal Matan
Woman's National Farm and Garden Association
3801 Riverview Terrace South
East China Township, MI 48054

ANIMAL/VETERINARY SCIENCES⎯⎯⎯⎯⎯⎯

AMERICAN PHYSIOLOGICAL SOCIETY

AMERICAN PHYSIOLOGICAL SOCIETY MINORITY TRAVEL FELLOWSHIPS • 25

Travel award for physiology students from minority groups to attend Experimental Biology meeting or American Physiological Society conference. Available to advanced undergraduate and graduate students as well as to postdoctoral faculty from eligible institutions. Contact American Physiological Society or check APS Web site for deadlines. Submit curriculum vitae or resume.

Academic Fields/Career Goals Animal/Veterinary Sciences; Biology; Health and Medical Sciences; Physical Sciences and Math. *Award* Fellowship for use in freshman, sophomore, junior, senior, graduate, or postgraduate years; not renewable. *Number:* 30-40. *Amount:* $1000-$1500.

Eligibility Requirements Applicant must be American Indian/Alaska Native, Black (non-Hispanic), or Hispanic and enrolled or expecting to enroll full-time at a two-year or four-year institution or university. Applicant or parent of applicant must be member of American Physiological Society. Available to U.S. citizens.

Application Requirements Application, resume, references.

World Wide Web: http://www.the-aps.org

Contact: Mrs. Brooke Bruthers, Award Coordinator
American Physiological Society
9650 Rockville Pike
Bethesda, MD 20814-3991
Phone: 301-634-7132
Fax: 301-634-7098
E-mail: bbruthers@the-aps.org

ASSOCIATION FOR WOMEN IN SCIENCE EDUCATIONAL FOUNDATION

ASSOCIATION FOR WOMEN IN SCIENCE UNDERGRADUATE AWARD • 26

The Undergraduate Award is for women who plan a career in science as a researcher and/or teacher. Applicants must be high school seniors with a GPA of 3.75 or higher and SAT scores of at least 1200. The program is highly competitive, with a success rate of about 3. Open to U.S. citizens only.

Academic Fields/Career Goals Animal/Veterinary Sciences; Biology; Chemical Engineering; Computer Science/Data Processing; Earth Science; Engineering/Technology; Materials Science, Engineering and Metallurgy; Mechanical Engineering; Meteorology/Atmospheric Science; Natural Sciences; Nuclear Science; Physical Sciences and Math. *Award* Scholarship for use in freshman year; not renewable. *Number:* 2–15. *Amount:* $100–$1000.

Eligibility Requirements Applicant must be high school student; planning to enroll or expecting to enroll full-time at a four-year institution or university and female. Available to U.S. citizens.

Application Requirements Application, essay, references, test scores, transcript. *Deadline:* January 17.

World Wide Web: http://www.awis.org/ed_foundation.html

Contact: Barbara Filner, President
Association for Women in Science Educational Foundation
7008 Richard Drive
Bethesda, MD 20817-4838
E-mail: awisedfd@awis.org

UNITED NEGRO COLLEGE FUND

UNCF/PFIZER CORPORATE SCHOLARS PROGRAM • 27

Open to minority students enrolled in UNCF schools and other HBCU's. Minimum 3.0 GPA required and major in business, finance, chemistry, microbiology, human resources, law, pre-veterinary medicine, animal science, supply chain management, or organizational development. Must be rising college junior, senior, graduate student, or first-year law student. Must complete internship at Pfizer location. Prospective applicants should complete the Student Profile found at Web site: http://www.uncf.org.

Academic Fields/Career Goals Animal/Veterinary Sciences; Biology; Business/Consumer Services; Chemical Engineering; Law/Legal Services. *Award* Scholarship for use in sophomore, junior, or graduate years; not renewable. *Amount:* up to $15,000.

Eligibility Requirements Applicant must be American Indian/Alaska Native, Asian/Pacific Islander, Black (non-Hispanic), or Hispanic; enrolled or expecting to enroll full-time at a four-year institution or university and resident of Connecticut, Michigan, New Jersey, or New York. Applicant must have 3.0 GPA or higher.

Application Requirements Application, financial need analysis. *Deadline:* January 1.

World Wide Web: http://www.uncf.org

Contact: Program Services Department
United Negro College Fund
8260 Willow Oaks Corporate Drive
Fairfax, VA 22031

APPLIED SCIENCES

AMERICAN VACUUM SOCIETY

NELLIE YEOH WHETTEN AWARD • 28

One-time award for outstanding female graduate student in sciences and technologies of interest to the AVS. Nominee must be registered graduate student in an accredited academic institution in North America.

Academic Fields/Career Goals Applied Sciences; Engineering/Technology; Physical Sciences and Math. *Award* Scholarship for use in graduate years; not renewable. *Number:* 1. *Amount:* $1500.

Eligibility Requirements Applicant must be enrolled or expecting to enroll at a four-year institution or university and female. Available to U.S. citizens.

Application Requirements Application, references, transcript. *Deadline:* March 31.

World Wide Web: http://www.avs.org

Contact: Ms. Angela Mulligan, Member Services Coordinator
American Vacuum Society
120 Wall Street, 32nd Floor
New York, NY 10005-3993
Phone: 212-248-0200
Fax: 212-248-0245

AMERICAN WATER WORKS ASSOCIATION

HOLLY A. CORNELL SCHOLARSHIP • 29

One scholarship for female and/or minority students researching water supply and treatment. Applicant must submit GRE scores, proposed curriculum of studies, and career objectives. One-time award of $5000 for master's degree study.

Academic Fields/Career Goals Applied Sciences; Biology; Engineering/Technology; Natural Resources. *Award* Scholarship for use in graduate years; not renewable. *Number:* 1. *Amount:* $5000.

Eligibility Requirements Applicant must be enrolled or expecting to enroll at an institution or university. Available to U.S. and non-U.S. citizens.

Application Requirements Application, references, test scores, transcript, proposed curriculum of study, career objectives. *Deadline:* January 15.

World Wide Web: http://www.awwa.org

Contact: Annette Carabetta, Scholarship Coordinator
American Water Works Association
6666 Quincy Avenue
Denver, CO 80235
Phone: 303-347-6206
Fax: 303-794-6303
E-mail: acarabetta@awwa.org

CANADIAN FEDERATION OF UNIVERSITY WOMEN

CANADIAN FEDERATION OF UNIVERSITY WOMEN MEMORIAL FELLOWSHIP

see number 21

CENTER FOR THE ADVANCEMENT OF HISPANICS IN SCIENCE AND ENGINEERING EDUCATION (CAHSEE)

CAHSEE FELLOWSHIP: YOUNG EDUCATORS PROGRAM • 30

Graduate students, advanced seniors, and other undergraduate students travel to Washington, D.C. for teaching and leadership seminars, then teach a five-week college-level class to motivated Latino pre-college students at the Center for Advancement of Hispanics in Science and Engineering's STEM Institutes (Science, Technology, and Mathematics) at designated universities. Housing and air travel is paid, plus stipend of $2750-$3000. Must be Native-Americans, Latino, or African-American to apply.

Academic Fields/Career Goals Applied Sciences; Aviation/Aerospace; Biology; Chemical Engineering; Civil Engineering; Computer Science/Data Processing; Electrical Engineering/Electronics; Engineering/Technology; Engineering-Related Technologies; Mechanical Engineering; Meteorology/Atmospheric Science; Physical Sciences and Math. *Award* Fellowship for use in sophomore, junior, senior, or graduate years; not renewable. *Number:* up to 40. *Amount:* $2500-$3500.

Eligibility Requirements Applicant must be American Indian/Alaska Native, Black (non-Hispanic), or Hispanic and enrolled or expecting to enroll full-time at a four-year institution or university. Applicant must have 3.0 GPA or higher. Available to U.S. citizens.

Application Requirements Application, interview, resume, references, transcript. *Deadline:* Continuous.

World Wide Web: http://www.cahsee.org

Contact: Michael Barboza, Programs Director
Center for the Advancement of Hispanics in Science and Engineering Education (CAHSEE)
PO Box 34102
Washington, DC 20043-4102
Phone: 202-835-3600 Ext. 120
Fax: 202-835-3613
E-mail: mbarboza@cahsee.org

HISPANIC COLLEGE FUND, INC.

NATIONAL HISPANIC EXPLORERS SCHOLARSHIP PROGRAM • 31

One-time scholarship award open to full-time undergraduates of Hispanic descent pursuing a degree in science, math, engineering, or NASA-related major. Must be a U.S. resident or U.S. citizen and have a minimum of a 3.0 GPA.

Academic Fields/Career Goals Applied Sciences; Aviation/Aerospace; Biology; Chemical Engineering; Civil Engineering; Communications; Computer Science/Data Processing; Earth Science; Electrical Engineering/Electronics; Engineering/Technology; Engineering-Related Technologies; Food Science/Nutrition. *Award* Scholarship for use in freshman, sophomore, junior, or senior years; not renewable. *Number:* 125-150. *Amount:* $2000-$3000.

Eligibility Requirements Applicant must be Hispanic and enrolled or expecting to enroll full-time at a two-year or four-year institution or university. Applicant must have 3.0 GPA or higher. Available to U.S. and non-Canadian citizens.

Application Requirements Application, essay, financial need analysis, resume, references, test scores, transcript, college acceptance letter, copy of taxes, proof of US citizenship or residency. *Deadline:* April 15.

World Wide Web: http://www.hispanicfund.org

Contact: Stina Augustsson, Program Manager
Hispanic College Fund, Inc.
1717 Pennsylvania Avenue, NW, Suite 460
Washington, DC 20006
Phone: 202-296-5400
Fax: 202-296-3774
E-mail: hispaniccollegefund@earthlink.net

ARCHAEOLOGY

ASSOCIATION FOR WOMEN IN SCIENCE EDUCATIONAL FOUNDATION

ASSOCIATION FOR WOMEN IN SCIENCE PRE-DOCTORAL FELLOWSHIP • 32

The Pre-doctoral Fellowship is for women completing a PhD in the natural or social sciences or engineering. Applicants must have passed their qualifying exam and be within two years of completion of the PhD. U.S. citizens may study anywhere; others only in the U.S. The success rate is about 10

Academic Fields/Career Goals Archaeology; Biology; Computer Science/Data Processing; Earth Science; Engineering/Technology; Geography; Materials Science, Engineering and Metallurgy; Meteorology/Atmospheric Science; Natural Sciences; Physical Sciences and Math; Political Science; Social Sciences. *Award* Fellowship for use in graduate years; not renewable. *Number:* 5–15. *Amount:* $100–$1000.

Eligibility Requirements Applicant must be enrolled or expecting to enroll full-time at an institution or university and female. Available to U.S. and non-U.S. citizens.

Application Requirements Application, essay, resume, references, transcript. *Deadline:* January 28.

World Wide Web: http://www.awis.org/ed_foundation.html

Contact: Barbara Filner, President
Association for Women in Science Educational Foundation
7008 Richard Drive
Bethesda, MD 20817-4838
E-mail: awisedfd@awis.org

PHI BETA KAPPA SOCIETY

MARY ISABEL SIBLEY FELLOWSHIP FOR GREEK AND FRENCH STUDIES • 33

Awarded alternately in the fields of Greek and French on an annual basis. Must be used for the study of Greek language, literature, history, or archaeology; or of French language and literature. Must be single female ages 25-35 in doctoral or postdoctoral study program. Submit project description and plans for work. Application is available on Web site: http://www.pbk.org/scholarships/sibley.htm.

Academic Fields/Career Goals Archaeology; Area/Ethnic Studies; Art History; Arts; Foreign Language; History; Humanities; Literature/English/Writing; Religion/Theology; Social Sciences. *Award* Fellowship for use in graduate, or postgraduate years; not renewable. *Number:* 1. *Amount:* $20,000.

Eligibility Requirements Applicant must be age 25-35; enrolled or expecting to enroll full-time at a four-year institution or university; single female and must have an interest in French language or Greek language. Available to U.S. and non-U.S. citizens.

Mary Isabel Sibley Fellowship for Greek and French Studies (continued)

Application Requirements Application, references, transcript, project statement and plans for future work. *Deadline:* January 15.

World Wide Web: http://www.pbk.org/scholarships/sibley.htm

Contact: Ms. Cameron Curtis, Program Officer
Phi Beta Kappa Society
1785 Massachusetts Avenue NW, 4th Floor
Washington, DC 20036
Phone: 202-265-3808
Fax: 202-986-1601
E-mail: ccurtis@pbk.org

ARCHITECTURE

ADELANTE! U.S. EDUCATION LEADERSHIP FUND

ADELANTE U.S. EDUCATION LEADERSHIP FUND • 34

Renewable award for college juniors or seniors of Hispanic descent. Award primarily created to enhance the leadership qualities of the recipients for transition into postgraduate education, business and/or corporate America. Financial need is a factor for this award. Minimum 3.0 GPA required.

Academic Fields/Career Goals Architecture. *Award* Scholarship for use in senior year; renewable. *Number:* 20–30. *Amount:* $3000.

Eligibility Requirements Applicant must be Hispanic and enrolled or expecting to enroll full-time at a four-year institution or university. Applicant must have 3.0 GPA or higher. Available to U.S. citizens.

Application Requirements Application, essay, financial need analysis, references, transcript. *Deadline:* Continuous.

Contact: Jan Angelini, Executive Director
Adelante! U.S. Education Leadership Fund
8415 Datapoint Drive
Suite 400
San Antonio, TX 78229
Phone: 210-692-1971
Fax: 210-692-1951
E-mail: jangelini@dcci.com

AMERICAN ARCHITECTURAL FOUNDATION

AMERICAN INSTITUTE OF ARCHITECTS MINORITY/DISADVANTAGED SCHOLARSHIP • 35

Renewable award for high school seniors and college freshmen who are entering an architecture degree program. Must be nominated by architect firm, teacher, dean, civic organization director by December. Must include drawing. Deadline for nominations: December 6. Deadline for applications: January 15. Co-sponsored by AIA and AAF.

Academic Fields/Career Goals Architecture. *Award* Scholarship for use in freshman year; renewable. *Number:* 20. *Amount:* $500–$2500.

Eligibility Requirements Applicant must be American Indian/Alaska Native, Asian/Pacific Islander, Black (non-Hispanic), or Hispanic and enrolled or expecting to enroll full-time at a four-year institution or university. Available to U.S. citizens.

Application Requirements Application, financial need analysis, references, test scores, transcript, drawing.

World Wide Web: http://www.archfoundation.org

Contact: Mary Felber, Director of Scholarship Programs
American Architectural Foundation
1735 New York Avenue, NW
Washington, DC 20006-5292
Phone: 202-626-7511
Fax: 202-626-7509
E-mail: mfelber@archfoundation.org

AMERICAN ASSOCIATION OF UNIVERSITY WOMEN (AAUW) EDUCATIONAL FOUNDATION

AAUW EDUCATIONAL FOUNDATION SELECTED PROFESSIONS FELLOWSHIPS   • 36

One-time award for women pursuing full-time graduate degrees in one of the designated degree programs where women's participation traditionally has been low. Must be U.S. citizens or permanent residents. Application fee: $25-$30.

Academic Fields/Career Goals Architecture; Business/Consumer Services; Computer Science/Data Processing; Electrical Engineering/Electronics; Engineering/Technology; Engineering-Related Technologies; Health and Medical Sciences; Law/Legal Services; Physical Sciences and Math. *Award* Fellowship for use in graduate years; not renewable. *Number:* 35–45. *Amount:* $5000–$20,000.

Eligibility Requirements Applicant must be enrolled or expecting to enroll full-time at a four-year institution or university and female. Available to U.S. citizens.

Application Requirements Application, autobiography, essay, resume, references, test scores, transcript. *Fee:* $30. *Deadline:* January 10.

World Wide Web: http://www.aauw.org

Contact: Customer Service
American Association of University Women (AAUW) Educational Foundation
2201 North Dodge Street
Iowa City, IA 52243-4030
Phone: 319-337-1716
E-mail: aauw@act.org

AMERICAN INSTITUTE OF ARCHITECTS

AMERICAN INSTITUTE OF ARCHITECTS/AMERICAN ARCHITECTURAL FOUNDATION MINORITY/DISADVANTAGED SCHOLARSHIPS   • 37

Award to aid high school seniors and college freshmen from minority or disadvantaged backgrounds who are planning to study architecture in an NAAB accredited program. Twenty awards per year, renewable for two additional years. Amounts based on financial need. Must be nominated by either a high school guidance counselor, AIA component, architect, or other individual who is aware of the student's interest and aptitude. Nomination deadline is early December; applications will be mailed to eligible students. Application deadline is mid-January.

American Institute of Architects/American Architectural Foundation Minority/Disadvantaged Scholarships (continued)

Academic Fields/Career Goals Architecture. *Award* Scholarship for use in freshman, sophomore, junior, or senior years; renewable. *Amount:* $500–$2500.

Eligibility Requirements Applicant must be enrolled or expecting to enroll at a four-year institution or university. Available to U.S. citizens.

Application Requirements Application, essay, references, transcript, statement of disadvantaged circumstances, a drawing. *Deadline:* January 15.

World Wide Web: http://www.aia.org

Contact: Mary Felber, Scholarship Chair
American Institute of Architects
1735 New York Avenue, NW
Washington, DC 20006-5292
Phone: 202-626-7511
Fax: 202-626-7509
E-mail: mfelber@aia.org

ASSOCIATION FOR WOMEN IN ARCHITECTURE FOUNDATION

ASSOCIATION FOR WOMEN IN ARCHITECTURE SCHOLARSHIP • 38

Must be a California resident or nonresident attending school in California. Must major in architecture or a related field and have completed 1 year (18 units) of schooling. Recipients may reapply. Open to women only. Interview in Los Angeles required. Application deadline is April 24. Applications available the beginning of February.

Academic Fields/Career Goals Architecture; Interior Design; Landscape Architecture. *Award* Scholarship for use in sophomore, junior, senior, or graduate years; not renewable. *Number:* 3. *Amount:* $1000–$2500.

Eligibility Requirements Applicant must be enrolled or expecting to enroll full-time at a two-year or four-year or technical institution or university and female. Available to U.S. and non-U.S. citizens.

Application Requirements Application, essay, financial need analysis, interview, references, self-addressed stamped envelope, transcript. *Deadline:* April 24.

World Wide Web: http://www.awa-la.org

Contact: Scholarship Chair
Association for Women in Architecture Foundation
386 Beech Avenue Unit B4
Torrance, CA 90501-6203
Phone: 310-222-6282
E-mail: mlrbloom@aol.com

COMMUNITY FOUNDATION FOR PALM BEACH AND MARTIN COUNTIES, INC.

MARBY M. NOXON SCHOLARSHIP FUND • 39

Graduating female high school senior attending public or private school in Palm Beach or Martin Counties. Must pursue a degree in business. Based on financial need.

Academic Fields/Career Goals Architecture; Business/Consumer Services. *Award* Scholarship for use in freshman year; not renewable. *Amount:* $750–$2500.

Eligibility Requirements Applicant must be high school student; planning to enroll or expecting to enroll full-time at a two-year or four-year or technical institution or university; female and resident of Florida. Available to U.S. citizens.

Application Requirements Application, financial need analysis. *Deadline:* March 1.

World Wide Web: http://www.cfpbmc.org

Contact: Carolyn Jenco, Grants Manager/Scholarship Coordinator
Community Foundation for Palm Beach and Martin Counties, Inc.
700 South Dixie Highway
Suite 200
West Palm Beach, FL 33401

COMTO-BOSTON CHAPTER

COMTO BOSTON/GARRETT A. MORGAN SCHOLARSHIP • 40

The COMTO-Boston scholarship program is designed to help youth maximize their educational potential in the transportation industry. We offer five corporate-sponsored scholarships specifically for engineering students and five chapter scholarships for graduating high school seniors pursuing careers in both transportation and non-transportation related fields.

Academic Fields/Career Goals Architecture; Civil Engineering; Drafting; Education; Electrical Engineering/Electronics; Engineering/Technology; Engineering-Related Technologies; Mechanical Engineering; Surveying; Surveying Technology, Cartography, or Geographic Information Science; Transportation. *Award* Scholarship for use in freshman or sophomore years; not renewable. *Number:* up to 10. *Amount:* $1000–$5000.

Eligibility Requirements Applicant must be American Indian/Alaska Native, Asian/Pacific Islander, Black (non-Hispanic), or Hispanic and enrolled or expecting to enroll full-time at a four-year or technical institution or university. Applicant must have 2.5 GPA or higher. Available to U.S. citizens.

Application Requirements Application, essay, references, transcript. *Deadline:* March 31.

World Wide Web: http://www.comto.org/local_boston.htm

Contact: Virginia Turner, Scholarship Chairperson
COMTO-Boston Chapter
Scholarship Program
PO Box 1173
Boston, MA 02117-1173
Phone: 617-248-2878
Fax: 617-248-2904
E-mail: virginia.turner@state.ma.us

GEM CONSORTIUM

GEM MS ENGINEERING FELLOWSHIP
see number 22

GEM PHD ENGINEERING FELLOWSHIP
see number 23

HISPANIC COLLEGE FUND, INC.

DENNY'S/HISPANIC COLLEGE FUND SCHOLARSHIP
see number 12

OSCAR B. CINTAS FOUNDATION, INC.

CINTAS FELLOWSHIPS PROGRAM • 41

Program is for artists of Cuban citizenship or direct lineage, not resident in Cuba, and working in the fields of architecture, literature, music composition, or visual arts and photography. The fellowships do not support academic study or work, or performance art. Eligible fields change from year to year.

Academic Fields/Career Goals Architecture; Arts; Literature/English/Writing. *Award* Fellowship for use in ; not renewable. *Number:* 2–3. *Amount:* $10,000.

Eligibility Requirements Applicant must be of Latin American/Caribbean heritage; Hispanic; enrolled or expecting to enroll at an institution or university and must have an interest in art, music, photography/photogrammetry/filmmaking, or writing. Available to U.S. and non-U.S. citizens.

Application Requirements Application, autobiography, essay, portfolio, references, self-addressed stamped envelope. *Deadline:* April 1.

World Wide Web: http://www.iie.org/fulbright/cintas

Contact: Ms. Jody Dudderar, Program Officer/U.S. Student Programs
Oscar B. Cintas Foundation, Inc.
809 United Nations Plaza
New York, NY 10017-3580
Phone: 212-984-5565
Fax: 212-984-5325
E-mail: cintas@iie.org

WORLDSTUDIO FOUNDATION

WORLDSTUDIO FOUNDATION SCHOLARSHIP PROGRAM • 42

Worldstudio Foundation provides scholarships to minority and economically disadvantaged students who are studying the design/architecture/arts disciplines in American colleges and universities. Among the foundation's primary aims are to increase diversity in the creative professions and to foster social and environmental responsibility in the artists, designers, and studios of tomorrow. To this end, scholarship recipients are selected not only for their ability and their need, but also for their demonstrated commitment to giving back to the larger community through their work.

Academic Fields/Career Goals Architecture; Arts; Fashion Design; Filmmaking/Video; Graphics/Graphic Arts/Printing; Interior Design. *Award* Scholarship for use in freshman, sophomore, junior, senior, graduate, or postgraduate years; not renewable. *Number:* 30–50. *Amount:* $1000–$5000.

Eligibility Requirements Applicant must be enrolled or expecting to enroll full-time at a two-year or four-year or technical institution or university. Applicant must have 2.5 GPA or higher. Available to U.S. and non-U.S. citizens.

Application Requirements Application, essay, financial need analysis, photo, portfolio, references, self-addressed stamped envelope, transcript. *Deadline:* February 14.

World Wide Web: http://www.worldstudio.org

Contact: Scholarship Coordinator
Worldstudio Foundation
200 Varick Street, Suite 507
New York, NY 10014
Phone: 212-366-1317 Ext. 18
Fax: 212-807-0024
E-mail: scholarships@worldstudio.org

AREA/ETHNIC STUDIES_____

HISPANIC DIVISION, LIBRARY OF CONGRESS

HISPANIC DIVISION FELLOWSHIPS • 43

One-time award for bibliographical research in the Hispanic Division of the Library of Congress. Applicants must be enrolled at the junior or senior undergraduate level, at the graduate level, or have just completed their degree at an accredited college or university. Thorough knowledge of Spanish is required. Applications from women, minorities and persons with disabilities are encouraged. Application deadline is April 18.

Academic Fields/Career Goals Area/Ethnic Studies; Foreign Language; Geography; History; Humanities; International Migration; International Studies; Library and Information Sciences; Political Science. *Award* Fellowship for use in junior, senior, graduate, or postgraduate years; not renewable. *Number:* 2. *Amount:* $2400.

Eligibility Requirements Applicant must be enrolled or expecting to enroll full or part-time at a four-year institution or university and studying in District of Columbia. Available to U.S. and non-U.S. citizens.

Application Requirements Application, interview, resume, references, transcript. *Deadline:* April 18.

Contact: Tracy North, Assistant Editor
Hispanic Division, Library of Congress
101 Independence Avenue, SE
Washington, DC 20540-4850
Phone: 202-707-5400
Fax: 202-707-2005
E-mail: tnor@loc.gov

INSTITUTE FOR INTERNATIONAL PUBLIC POLICY (IIPP)

INSTITUTE FOR INTERNATIONAL PUBLIC POLICY FELLOWSHIP PROGRAM • 44

Through a comprehensive program of summer policy institutes, study abroad, intensive language training, internships, graduate study, mentoring and career development, the IIPP Fellowship Program provides underrepresented minority students with the education and training needed to successfully enter, advance and lead in international affairs careers. Must have 3.2 GPA.

Academic Fields/Career Goals Area/Ethnic Studies; Economics; Foreign Language; Humanities; International Studies; Peace and Conflict Studies; Political Science; Social Sciences. *Award* Fellowship for use in sophomore year; not renewable. *Number:* 20–30. *Amount:* $35,000–$50,000.

Eligibility Requirements Applicant must be American Indian/Alaska Native, Asian/Pacific Islander, Black (non-Hispanic), or Hispanic and enrolled or expecting to enroll full-time at a four-year institution or university. Available to U.S. and non-U.S. citizens.

Application Requirements Application, essay, financial need analysis, resume, references, transcript, institutional nomination, proof of citizenship or permanent residency. *Deadline:* March 1.

World Wide Web: http://161.58.87.106/content/apply.cfm

Institute for International Public Policy Fellowship Program (continued)

Contact: Helen Ezenwa, Program Manager
Institute for International Public Policy (IIPP)
2750 Prosperity Avenue
Suite 600
Fairfax, VA 22031
Fax: 703-205-7645
E-mail: helen.ezenwa@uncfsp.org

INSTITUTE OF CHINA STUDIES
INSTITUTE OF CHINESE STUDIES AWARDS • 45
Renewable award for minority students already in college. Must major in China studies including Mandarin, history or other related studies. Minimum 3.0 GPA required. Students who have completed 30 hours and 15 hours of studies are eligible for $1000 award and $500 award, respectively.

Academic Fields/Career Goals Area/Ethnic Studies. *Award* Scholarship for use in freshman, sophomore, junior, or senior years; renewable. *Number:* 10. *Amount:* up to $1000.
Eligibility Requirements Applicant must be American Indian/Alaska Native, Asian/Pacific Islander, Black (non-Hispanic), or Hispanic and enrolled or expecting to enroll full-time at a four-year institution or university. Applicant must have 3.0 GPA or higher. Available to U.S. citizens.
Application Requirements Photo, transcript, birth certificate. *Deadline:* Continuous.
Contact: Dr. Harry Kiang, President
Institute of China Studies
7341 North Kolmar Street
Lincolnwood, IL 60712
Phone: 847-677-0982

PHI BETA KAPPA SOCIETY
MARY ISABEL SIBLEY FELLOWSHIP FOR GREEK AND FRENCH STUDIES
see number 33

UNITED STATES INSTITUTE OF PEACE
JENNINGS RANDOLPH SENIOR FELLOW AWARD • 46
Awards to scholars and practitioners from a variety of professions, including college and university faculty, journalists, diplomats, writers, educators, military officers, international negotiators, lawyers. Funds projects related to preventive diplomacy, ethnic and regional conflicts, peacekeeping and peace operations, peace settlements, post-conflict reconstruction and reconciliation, democratization and the rule of law, cross-cultural negotiations, U.S. foreign policy in the 21st century, and related topics. Projects which demonstrate relevance to current policy debates will be highly competitive. Open to citizens of all nations. Women and members of minorities are especially encouraged to apply. Deadline: September 17.

Academic Fields/Career Goals Area/Ethnic Studies; Economics; History; International Migration; International Studies; Journalism; Law/Legal Services; Peace and Conflict Studies; Political Science; Science, Technology and Society; Social Sciences. *Award* Fellowship for use in graduate, or postgraduate years; not renewable. *Number:* 10-13. *Amount:* $60,000-$80,000.

Eligibility Requirements Applicant must be enrolled or expecting to enroll full-time at an institution or university. Available to U.S. and non-U.S. citizens.

Application Requirements Application, references. *Deadline:* September 17.

World Wide Web: http://www.usip.org

Contact: United States Institute of Peace
1200 17th Street, NW, Suite 200
Washington, DC 20036-3011
Phone: 202-429-3886
Fax: 202-429-6063
E-mail: jrprogram@usip.org

ART HISTORY_____

PHI BETA KAPPA SOCIETY

MARY ISABEL SIBLEY FELLOWSHIP FOR GREEK AND FRENCH STUDIES
see number 33

WELLESLEY COLLEGE

HARRIET A. SHAW FELLOWSHIP • 47

One-time award for graduates of Wellesley College to study or research music, art, or allied subjects, in the U.S. or abroad. Preference given to music candidates; undergraduate work in art history is required of other candidates. Submit resume. Award based on merit and need.

Academic Fields/Career Goals Art History; Arts; Museum Studies. *Award* Fellowship for use in graduate years; not renewable. *Amount:* up to $11,000.

Eligibility Requirements Applicant must be enrolled or expecting to enroll at an institution or university and female. Available to U.S. citizens.

Application Requirements Application, financial need analysis, resume, references, test scores, transcript. *Deadline:* January 6.

World Wide Web: http://www.wellesley.edu/CWS/

Contact: Mary Beth Callery, Secretary to the Committee on Graduate Fellowships
Wellesley College
106 Central Avenue, Green Hall 441
Wellesley, MA 02481-8200
Phone: 781-283-3525
Fax: 781-283-3674
E-mail: cws-fellowships@wellesley.edu

ARTS_____

NATIONAL LEAGUE OF AMERICAN PEN WOMEN, INC.

NLAPW VIRGINIA LIEBELER BIENNIAL GRANTS FOR MATURE WOMEN (ARTS) • 48

One-time award given in even-numbered years to female artists ages 35 and older who are U.S. citizens to be used to further creative purpose of applicant. Submit three 4x6 or bigger color

NLAPW Virginia Liebeler Biennial Grants for Mature Women (Arts) (continued)

prints (no slides) of work in any media. For photography, submit three 4x6 prints in color or black and white. All applicants submit statements of background, purpose of grant, and how applicant learned of grant. Application fee of $8. Send self-addressed stamped envelope for further requirements. Deadline for entry is October 1 of odd-numbered year.

Academic Fields/Career Goals Arts. *Award* Grant for use in freshman, sophomore, junior, senior, graduate, or postgraduate years; not renewable. *Number:* 1. *Amount:* $1000.

Eligibility Requirements Applicant must be age 35; enrolled or expecting to enroll at an institution or university; female and must have an interest in art or photography/photogrammetry/filmmaking. Available to U.S. citizens.

Application Requirements Applicant must enter a contest, self-addressed stamped envelope, proof of U.S. citizenship. *Fee:* $8. *Deadline:* October 1.

Contact: Mary Jane Hillery, National Scholarship Chair
National League of American Pen Women, Inc.
66 Willow Road
Sudbury, MA 01776-2663
Phone: 978-443-2165
Fax: 978-443-2165
E-mail: nlapw1@juno.com

NATIONAL OPERA ASSOCIATION

NOA VOCAL COMPETITION/ LEGACY AWARD PROGRAM • 49

Awards granted based on competitive audition to support study and career development. Singers compete in Scholarship and Artist Division. Legacy Awards are granted for study and career development in any opera-related career to those who further NOA's goal of increased minority participation in the profession.

Academic Fields/Career Goals Arts; Performing Arts. *Award* Prize for use in freshman, sophomore, junior, senior, graduate, or postgraduate years; not renewable. *Number:* 3–8. *Amount:* $250–$1000.

Eligibility Requirements Applicant must be age 18-24; enrolled or expecting to enroll full or part-time at a two-year or four-year or technical institution or university and must have an interest in music or music/singing. Available to U.S. and non-U.S. citizens.

Application Requirements Application, applicant must enter a contest, autobiography, photo, references, audition tape/proposal. *Fee:* $20. *Deadline:* November 1.

World Wide Web: http://www.noa.org

Contact: Robert Hansen, Executive Secretary
National Opera Association
PO Box 60869
Canyon, TX 79016-0869
Phone: 806-651-2857
Fax: 806-651-2958
E-mail: hansen@mail.wtamu.edu

OSCAR B. CINTAS FOUNDATION, INC.

CINTAS FELLOWSHIPS PROGRAM see number 41

PHI BETA KAPPA SOCIETY

MARY ISABEL SIBLEY FELLOWSHIP FOR GREEK AND FRENCH STUDIES
see number 33

WATERBURY FOUNDATION

LOIS MCMILLEN MEMORIAL SCHOLARSHIP FUND   • 50

Scholarships to women who are actively pursuing or who wold like to pursue an artistic career. Must reside in the Foundation's service area, which is the greater Waterbury area of Connecticut. Awarded for the purpose of attending an accredited college or university or a qualified artists-in-residence program in a chosen artistic field. Preference will be given to artists in the visual arts of painting and design.

Academic Fields/Career Goals Arts. *Award* Scholarship for use in freshman, sophomore, junior, senior, or graduate years; not renewable. *Amount:* $500–$4000.

Eligibility Requirements Applicant must be enrolled or expecting to enroll at a four-year institution or university; female and resident of Connecticut.

Application Requirements Application, essay, references. *Deadline:* April 1.

World Wide Web: http://www.waterburyfoundation.org

Contact: Jill Stone, Program Officer
Waterbury Foundation
81 West Main Street
Waterbury, CT 06702-1216
Phone: 203-753-1315
Fax: 203-756-3054
E-mail: jstone@waterburyfoundation.org

WELLESLEY COLLEGE

HARRIET A. SHAW FELLOWSHIP   see number 47

WORLDSTUDIO FOUNDATION

WORLDSTUDIO FOUNDATION SCHOLARSHIP PROGRAM   see number 42

AVIATION/AEROSPACE

CENTER FOR THE ADVANCEMENT OF HISPANICS IN SCIENCE AND ENGINEERING EDUCATION (CAHSEE)

CAHSEE FELLOWSHIP: YOUNG EDUCATORS PROGRAM   see number 30

HISPANIC COLLEGE FUND, INC.

NATIONAL HISPANIC EXPLORERS SCHOLARSHIP PROGRAM   see number 31

HISPANIC ENGINEER NATIONAL ACHIEVEMENT AWARDS CORPORATION (HENAAC)

HISPANIC ENGINEER NATIONAL ACHIEVEMENT AWARDS CORPORATION SCHOLARSHIP PROGRAM   • 51

Scholarships available to Hispanic students maintaining a 3.0 GPA. Must be studying an engineering or science related field. For more details and an application go to Web site: http://www.henaac.org

Hispanic Engineer National Achievement Awards Corporation Scholarship Program (continued)

Academic Fields/Career Goals Aviation/Aerospace; Biology; Chemical Engineering; Civil Engineering; Computer Science/Data Processing; Electrical Engineering/Electronics; Engineering/Technology; Materials Science, Engineering and Metallurgy; Mechanical Engineering; Nuclear Science. *Award* Scholarship for use in freshman, sophomore, junior, senior, or graduate years; not renewable. *Number:* 12–20. *Amount:* $2000–$5000.

Eligibility Requirements Applicant must be of Hispanic heritage and enrolled or expecting to enroll full-time at a four-year institution or university. Applicant must have 3.0 GPA or higher. Available to U.S. and Canadian citizens.

Application Requirements Application, essay, resume, references, transcript. *Deadline:* April 21.

World Wide Web: http://www.henaac.org

Contact: application available at Web site

INTERNATIONAL SOCIETY OF WOMEN AIRLINE PILOTS (ISA+21)

INTERNATIONAL SOCIETY OF WOMEN AIRLINE PILOTS AIRLINE SCHOLARSHIPS
• 52

Scholarship available to ISA members and nonmembers. Program disburses cash awards toward pilot certificates, ratings and type ratings to qualifying women. Each year the number and type of these awards vary. All applicants must meet FAA medical requirements for a CLASS I Medical certificate. Visit Web site at http://www.iswap.org for additional information and deadlines.

Academic Fields/Career Goals Aviation/Aerospace. *Award* Scholarship for use in ; not renewable. *Number:* up to 5.

Eligibility Requirements Applicant must be age 21; enrolled or expecting to enroll at an institution or university and female. Applicant must have 3.5 GPA or higher. Available to U.S. and non-U.S. citizens.

Application Requirements Application, autobiography, financial need analysis, interview, resume, references, transcript.

World Wide Web: http://www.iswap.org

Contact: application available at Web site

INTERNATIONAL SOCIETY OF WOMEN AIRLINE PILOTS CAREER SCHOLARSHIP
• 53

Scholarship available to ISA members and nonmembers. Program disburses cash awards towards pilot certificates, ratings and type ratings to qualifying women. This award is used solely for advanced pilot ratings. All applicants must meet FAA Medical requirements for CLASS I Medical certificate. Visit Web site at http://www.iswap.org for additional information and deadlines.

Academic Fields/Career Goals Aviation/Aerospace. *Award* Scholarship for use in ; not renewable.

Eligibility Requirements Applicant must be age 21; enrolled or expecting to enroll at an institution or university and female. Applicant must have 3.5 GPA or higher. Available to U.S. and non-U.S. citizens.

Application Requirements Application, autobiography, financial need analysis, interview, resume, references, transcript.

World Wide Web: http://www.iswap.org

Contact: application available at Web site

INTERNATIONAL SOCIETY OF WOMEN AIRLINE PILOTS FIORENZA DE BERNARDI MERIT SCHOLARSHIP ● 54

Scholarship available to ISA members and nonmembers. Program disburses cash awards towards pilot certificates, ratings and type ratings to qualifying women. Award for applicants that do not meet the requirements for the Career Scholarship. All applicants must meet FAA Medical requirements for CLASS I Medical certificate. Visit Web site at http://www.iswap.org for additional information and deadlines.

Academic Fields/Career Goals Aviation/Aerospace. *Award* Scholarship for use in ; not renewable.

Eligibility Requirements Applicant must be age 21; enrolled or expecting to enroll at an institution or university and female. Applicant must have 3.5 GPA or higher. Available to U.S. and non-U.S. citizens.

Application Requirements Application, autobiography, financial need analysis, interview, resume, references, transcript.

World Wide Web: http://www.iswap.org

Contact: application available at Web site

INTERNATIONAL SOCIETY OF WOMEN AIRLINE PILOTS GRACE MCADAMS HARRIS SCHOLARSHIP ● 55

Scholarship available to ISA members. Program disburses cash awards towards pilot certificates, ratings and type ratings to qualifying women. This award may fund any ISA scholarship if the applicant has demonstrated exceptional spirit and attitude under difficult circumstances as it pertains to the field of aviation. All applicants must meet FAA Medical requirements for CLASS I Medical certificate. Visit Web site at http://www.iswap.org for additional information and deadlines.

Academic Fields/Career Goals Aviation/Aerospace. *Award* Scholarship for use in ; not renewable.

Eligibility Requirements Applicant must be age 21; enrolled or expecting to enroll at an institution or university and female. Applicant must have 3.5 GPA or higher. Available to U.S. and non-U.S. citizens.

Application Requirements Application, autobiography, financial need analysis, interview, references, transcript.

World Wide Web: http://www.iswap.org

Contact: application available at Web site

INTERNATIONAL SOCIETY OF WOMEN AIRLINE PILOTS HOLLY MULLENS MEMORIAL SCHOLARSHIP ● 56

Scholarship available to ISA members and nonmembers. Program disburses cash awards towards pilot certificates, ratings and type ratings to qualifying women. Award for single mother applicants. All applicants must meet FAA Medical requirements for CLASS I Medical certificate. Visit Web site at http://www.iswap.org for additional information and deadlines.

Academic Fields/Career Goals Aviation/Aerospace. *Award* Scholarship for use in ; not renewable.

Eligibility Requirements Applicant must be age 21; enrolled or expecting to enroll at an institution or university and single female. Applicant must have 3.5 GPA or higher. Available to U.S. and non-U.S. citizens.

Application Requirements Application, autobiography, financial need analysis, interview, references, transcript.

World Wide Web: http://www.iswap.org

Contact: application available at Web site

INTERNATIONAL SOCIETY OF WOMEN AIRLINE PILOTS NORTH CAROLINA CAREER SCHOLARSHIP • 57

Scholarship available to ISA members and nonmembers. Program disburses cash awards towards pilot certificates, ratings and type ratings to qualifying women. Must be a North Carolina resident interested in a career with the airline industry. All applicants must meet FAA Medical requirements for CLASS I Medical certificate. Visit Web site at http://www.iswap.org for additional information and deadlines.

Academic Fields/Career Goals Aviation/Aerospace. *Award* Scholarship for use in ; not renewable.

Eligibility Requirements Applicant must be age 21; enrolled or expecting to enroll at an institution or university; female and resident of North Carolina. Applicant must have 3.5 GPA or higher. Available to U.S. and non-U.S. citizens.

Application Requirements Application, autobiography, financial need analysis, interview, resume, references, transcript.

World Wide Web: http://www.iswap.org

Contact: application available at Web site

NAMEPA NATIONAL SCHOLARSHIP FOUNDATION

NATIONAL ASSOCIATION OF MINORITY ENGINEERING PROGRAM ADMINISTRATORS NATIONAL SCHOLARSHIP FUND • 58

NAMEPA offers one-time scholarships for African-American, Hispanic, and American-Indian students who have demonstrated potential and interest in pursuing an undergraduate degree in engineering. Must have a minimum 3.0 GPA. Must have a score above 25 on ACT, or above 1000 on SAT. Visit Web site at http://www.namepa.org for application materials and further details.

Academic Fields/Career Goals Aviation/Aerospace; Chemical Engineering; Civil Engineering; Computer Science/Data Processing; Electrical Engineering/Electronics; Engineering/Technology; Engineering-Related Technologies; Materials Science, Engineering and Metallurgy; Mechanical Engineering. *Award* Scholarship for use in freshman or junior years; not renewable. *Number:* 10–50. *Amount:* $1000–$5000.

Eligibility Requirements Applicant must be American Indian/Alaska Native, Black (non-Hispanic), or Hispanic and enrolled or expecting to enroll full-time at a two-year or four-year institution or university. Applicant must have 3.0 GPA or higher. Available to U.S. and non-U.S. citizens.

Application Requirements Application, essay, resume, references, test scores, transcript. *Deadline:* March 30.

World Wide Web: http://www.namepa.org

Contact: Latisha Moore, Administrative Assistant
NAMEPA National Scholarship Foundation
1133 West Morse Boulevard, Suite 201
Winter Park, FL 32789
Phone: 407-647-8839
Fax: 407-629-2502
E-mail: namepa@namepa.org

SOCIETY OF WOMEN ENGINEERS

JUDITH RESNIK MEMORIAL SCHOLARSHIP • 59

One-time award available to aerospace or astronautical engineering major at the sophomore, junior or senior level. Must be a member of the Society of Women Engineers. Minimum 3.0 GPA required. Deadline: February 1.

Academic Fields/Career Goals Aviation/Aerospace; Engineering/Technology. *Award* Scholarship for use in sophomore, junior, or senior years; not renewable. *Number:* 1. *Amount:* $2500.

Eligibility Requirements Applicant must be enrolled or expecting to enroll at a four-year institution or university and female. Applicant or parent of applicant must be member of Society of Women Engineers. Applicant must have 3.0 GPA or higher. Available to U.S. citizens.

Application Requirements Application, references, self-addressed stamped envelope, transcript. *Deadline:* February 1.

World Wide Web: http://www.swe.org

Contact: Program Coordinator
Society of Women Engineers
230 East Ohio Street, Suite 400
Chicago, IL 60611-3265
Phone: 312-596-5223
Fax: 312-644-8557
E-mail: hq@swe.org

TRANSPORTATION CLUBS INTERNATIONAL

TRANSPORTATION CLUBS INTERNATIONAL GINGER AND FRED DEINES MEXICO SCHOLARSHIP • 60

Scholarship for a student of Mexican nationality/residency who is enrolled at an institution in Mexico or the U.S. Must be preparing for a career in transportation. Must have completed at least one year of study. Submit photo and three references.

Academic Fields/Career Goals Aviation/Aerospace; Transportation. *Award* Scholarship for use in sophomore, junior, senior, graduate, or postgraduate years; not renewable. *Number:* 1. *Amount:* $1500.

Eligibility Requirements Applicant must be of Mexican heritage; Hispanic and enrolled or expecting to enroll full or part-time at a two-year or four-year or technical institution or university.

Application Requirements Application, essay, photo, references, transcript. *Deadline:* April 30.

World Wide Web: http://www.transportationclubsinternational.com

Contact: Gay Fielding, Traffic Manager
Transportation Clubs International
7031 Manchester Street
New Orleans, LA 70126-1751
Phone: 504-243-9825

WHIRLY-GIRLS, INC., INTERNATIONAL WOMEN HELICOPTER PILOTS

WHIRLY GIRLS SCHOLARSHIP FUND • 61

Several scholarships for add-on helicopter and advanced helicopter ratings for women pilots only. Scholarship amount varies. Application fee of $25. Deadline is October 1. See Web site for additional information and to download application.

Academic Fields/Career Goals Aviation/Aerospace. *Award* Scholarship for use in ; not renewable. *Number:* 8.

Eligibility Requirements Applicant must be enrolled or expecting to enroll part-time at an institution or university and female. Available to U.S. and non-U.S. citizens.

Whirly Girls Scholarship Fund (continued)

Application Requirements Application, financial need analysis, photo, references, pilot's certificate, medical certificate. *Fee:* $25. *Deadline:* October 1.

World Wide Web: http://www.whirlygirls.org

Contact: Catherine Adams, Vice President, Scholarships
Whirly-Girls, Inc., International Women Helicopter Pilots
7 Hastings Lane
Williamsburg, VA 23188
Phone: 757-564-7864
E-mail: scholarships@whirlygirls.org

ZONTA INTERNATIONAL FOUNDATION

AMELIA EARHART FELLOWSHIP AWARDS • 62

Awards for female graduate students with a BS in science or engineering in an aerospace-related field. Must have completed one year of graduate study, senior research project or publication, and be pursuing an advanced degree in aerospace-related studies. One-time award of $6000. Application is available at Web site http://www.zonta.org.

Academic Fields/Career Goals Aviation/Aerospace. *Award* Fellowship for use in graduate years; not renewable. *Number:* 35. *Amount:* $6000.

Eligibility Requirements Applicant must be enrolled or expecting to enroll at an institution or university and female.

Application Requirements Application, essay, photo, references, transcript, proof of acceptance or enrollment in graduate program. *Deadline:* November 15.

World Wide Web: http://www.zonta.org

Contact: Ms. Ana Ubides, Foundation Assistant
Zonta International Foundation
557 West Randolph Street
Chicago, IL 60661-2206
Phone: 312-930-5848 Ext. 629
Fax: 312-930-0951
E-mail: zontafdtn@zonta.org

BIOLOGY

AMERICAN FISHERIES SOCIETY

J. FRANCES ALLEN SCHOLARSHIP AWARD • 63

The qualified applicant must be a female PhD student who was an AFS member as of December of the preceding year. The applicant must be conducting aquatic research in line with AFS objectives, which include all branches of fisheries science, including but not limited to aquatic biology, engineering, fish culture, limnology, oceanography, and sociology.

Academic Fields/Career Goals Biology; Natural Resources; Natural Sciences. *Award* Scholarship for use in postgraduate years; not renewable. *Number:* 1. *Amount:* $2500.

Eligibility Requirements Applicant must be enrolled or expecting to enroll full-time at a four-year institution or university and female. Available to U.S. and non-U.S. citizens.

Application Requirements Application, references, transcript, publications, presentations, professional experience history, AFS participating history, dissertation proposal. *Deadline:* March 7.

World Wide Web: http://www.fisheries.org

Contact: Carolina Franco, Unit Services Coordinator
American Fisheries Society
5410 Grosvenor Lane
Bethesda, MD 20814-8096
Phone: 301-897-8616 Ext. 201
Fax: 301-897-8096
E-mail: cfranco@fisheries.org

AMERICAN PHYSIOLOGICAL SOCIETY

AMERICAN PHYSIOLOGICAL SOCIETY MINORITY TRAVEL FELLOWSHIPS
see number 25

PORTER PHYSIOLOGY FELLOWSHIPS • 64

Award for students pursuing careers in physiology. Must be Hispanic, Native-Americans, African-American, Pacific Islander, or Native Alaskan. Submit application, transcript, and references. Application deadlines are January 15 and June 15.

Academic Fields/Career Goals Biology; Health and Medical Sciences; Physical Sciences and Math. *Award* Fellowship for use in graduate years; not renewable. *Number:* 6–8. *Amount:* $18,000.

Eligibility Requirements Applicant must be American Indian/Alaska Native, Asian/Pacific Islander, Black (non-Hispanic), or Hispanic and enrolled or expecting to enroll full-time at a four-year institution or university. Available to U.S. citizens.

Application Requirements Application, references, transcript.

World Wide Web: http://www.the-aps.org

Contact: Dr. Marsha Matyas, Education Officer
American Physiological Society
9650 Rockville Pike
Bethesda, MD 20814-3991
Phone: 301-634-7132
Fax: 301-634-7098
E-mail: education@the-aps.org

AMERICAN PSYCHOLOGICAL ASSOCIATION

MINORITY FELLOWSHIP FOR NEUROSCIENCE TRAINING • 65

Renewable award for U.S. citizen or permanent resident enrolled in a full-time doctoral program in the area of neuroscience. An important goal of the program is to increase the representation of underrepresented students within neuroscience. Based on academic research ability. Students from all disciplines related to neuroscience may apply. Application available at Web site.

Academic Fields/Career Goals Biology; Health and Medical Sciences. *Award* Fellowship for use in graduate, or postgraduate years; renewable. *Number:* 11. *Amount:* $18,156.

Eligibility Requirements Applicant must be enrolled or expecting to enroll full-time at an institution or university. Available to U.S. citizens.

Application Requirements Application, essay, financial need analysis, references, transcript. *Deadline:* January 15.

Minority Fellowship for Neuroscience Training (continued)

World Wide Web: http://www.apa.org/mfp
Contact: Candace D. Davis, Program Coordinator
American Psychological Association
750 First Street, NE
Washington, DC 20002-4242
Phone: 202-336-6027
Fax: 202-336-6012
E-mail: cddavis@apa.org

AMERICAN SOCIETY FOR MICROBIOLOGY

ASM MINORITY UNDERGRADUATE RESEARCH FELLOWSHIP • 66

Summer research laboratory experience available at sites for students majoring in microbiology science. Must be U.S. citizens or permanent residents belonging to an underrepresented ethnic minority group. Write for details. Award includes $2500 stipend and travel, lodging and supplies expenses.

Academic Fields/Career Goals Biology. *Award* Fellowship for use in freshman, sophomore, junior, or senior years; not renewable. *Number:* up to 16. *Amount:* up to $4000.

Eligibility Requirements Applicant must be American Indian/Alaska Native, Asian/Pacific Islander, Black (non-Hispanic), or Hispanic and enrolled or expecting to enroll full-time at a four-year institution or university. Available to U.S. citizens.

Application Requirements Application, essay, references, transcript. *Deadline:* February 1.

World Wide Web: http://www.asmusa.org/
Contact: American Society for Microbiology
1752 N Street, NW
Washington, DC 20036
Phone: 202-942-9283
Fax: 202-942-9329

ROBERT D. WATKINS MINORITY GRADUATE RESEARCH FELLOWSHIP • 67

Award for formally admitted doctoral student who has successfully completed first year as doctoral candidate in the microbiology sciences at an accredited U.S. institution. Must be an ASM member and have an approved research project, and be a member of an underrepresented minority group. Program lasts three years. Must be U.S. citizen.

Academic Fields/Career Goals Biology. *Award* Fellowship for use in graduate years; not renewable. *Number:* 1. *Amount:* $15,000.

Eligibility Requirements Applicant must be American Indian/Alaska Native, Asian/Pacific Islander, Black (non-Hispanic), or Hispanic and enrolled or expecting to enroll at an institution or university. Applicant or parent of applicant must be member of American Society for Microbiology. Available to U.S. citizens.

Application Requirements Application, essay, references, transcript. *Deadline:* May 1.

World Wide Web: http://www.asmusa.org/
Contact: American Society for Microbiology
1752 N Street, NW
Washington, DC 20036
Phone: 202-942-9283
Fax: 202-942-9329

AMERICAN WATER WORKS ASSOCIATION

HOLLY A. CORNELL SCHOLARSHIP
see number 29

ASSOCIATION FOR WOMEN IN SCIENCE EDUCATIONAL FOUNDATION

ASSOCIATION FOR WOMEN IN SCIENCE PRE-DOCTORAL FELLOWSHIP

see number 32

ASSOCIATION FOR WOMEN IN SCIENCE UNDERGRADUATE AWARD   see number 26

BUSINESS AND PROFESSIONAL WOMEN'S FOUNDATION

BPW CAREER ADVANCEMENT SCHOLARSHIP PROGRAM FOR WOMEN   • 68

Scholarships ranging from $1000-$5000 each are awarded for full-or part-time study. Applicant must be studying in one of the following fields: biological sciences, teacher education certification, engineering, social science, paralegal studies, humanities, business studies, mathematics, computer science, physical sciences, or for a professional degree (JD, MD, DDS). The Career Advancement Scholarship Program was established to assist women seeking the education necessary for entry or re-entry into the work force, or advancement within a career field. Must be 25 or over. Send self-addressed double-stamped envelope between January 1 and April 1 for application.

Academic Fields/Career Goals Biology; Computer Science/Data Processing; Dental Health/Services; Education; Engineering/Technology; Engineering-Related Technologies; Health and Medical Sciences; Humanities; Law/Legal Services; Physical Sciences and Math; Social Sciences. *Award* Scholarship for use in junior, senior, or graduate years; not renewable. *Number:* up to 100. *Amount:* $1000–$5000.

Eligibility Requirements Applicant must be age 25; enrolled or expecting to enroll full or part-time at a two-year or four-year or technical institution or university and female. Applicant must have 2.5 GPA or higher. Available to U.S. citizens.

Application Requirements Application, essay, financial need analysis, references, self-addressed stamped envelope, transcript. *Deadline:* April 15.

World Wide Web: http://www.bpwusa.org

Contact: Diane Thurston Frye, Development and Scholarship Manager
Business and Professional Women's Foundation
1900 M Street, NW, Suite 310
Washington, DC 20036
Phone: 202-293-1100 Ext. 182
Fax: 202-861-0298

CANADIAN FEDERATION OF UNIVERSITY WOMEN

CANADIAN FEDERATION OF UNIVERSITY WOMEN MEMORIAL FELLOWSHIP

see number 21

CENTER FOR THE ADVANCEMENT OF HISPANICS IN SCIENCE AND ENGINEERING EDUCATION (CAHSEE)

CAHSEE FELLOWSHIP: YOUNG EDUCATORS PROGRAM   see number 30

ENTOMOLOGICAL FOUNDATION

STAN BECK FELLOWSHIP • 69

Fellowship to assist needy undergraduate or graduate students. Need may be based on physical limitations or economic, minority, or environmental conditions. Must be nominated. Application deadline is July 1.

Academic Fields/Career Goals Biology. *Award* Fellowship for use in freshman, sophomore, junior, senior, or graduate years; not renewable. *Amount:* $2000.

Eligibility Requirements Applicant must be enrolled or expecting to enroll at an institution or university.

Application Requirements Application, essay, financial need analysis, references, transcript. *Deadline:* July 1.

World Wide Web: http://www.entfdn.org

Contact: Entomological Foundation
9332 Annapolis Road
Suite 210
Lanham, MD 20706

GEM CONSORTIUM

GEM MS ENGINEERING FELLOWSHIP see number 22

GEM PHD ENGINEERING FELLOWSHIP see number 23

GEM PHD SCIENCE FELLOWSHIP • 70

Renewable award for U.S. citizen who is junior, senior, undergraduate, or baccalaureate degree recipient in accredited engineering or science discipline. Minimum 3.0 GPA required. Must be American-Indian, Black American, or Hispanic-American. Must attend GEM PhD fellowship program member university. May major in any discipline within natural sciences. Includes summer internship.

Academic Fields/Career Goals Biology; Earth Science; Meteorology/Atmospheric Science; Physical Sciences and Math. *Award* Fellowship for use in junior, senior, or graduate years; renewable. *Number:* 20–30. *Amount:* $60,000.

Eligibility Requirements Applicant must be American Indian/Alaska Native, Black (non-Hispanic), or Hispanic and enrolled or expecting to enroll full-time at a four-year institution or university. Applicant must have 3.0 GPA or higher. Available to U.S. citizens.

Application Requirements Application, resume, references, transcript, statement of purpose. *Deadline:* December 1.

World Wide Web: http://www.gemfellowship.org

Contact: Saundra D. Johnson, Executive Director
GEM Consortium
PO Box 537
Notre Dame, IN 46556-0537
Phone: 574-631-7771
Fax: 574-287-1486
E-mail: gem.1@nd.edu

HISPANIC COLLEGE FUND, INC.

NATIONAL HISPANIC EXPLORERS SCHOLARSHIP PROGRAM see number 31

HISPANIC ENGINEER NATIONAL ACHIEVEMENT AWARDS CORPORATION (HENAAC)

HISPANIC ENGINEER NATIONAL ACHIEVEMENT AWARDS CORPORATION SCHOLARSHIP PROGRAM
see number 51

NATIONAL INSTITUTES OF HEALTH

NIH UNDERGRADUATE SCHOLARSHIP PROGRAM FOR STUDENTS FROM DISADVANTAGED BACKGROUNDS • 71

The NIH Undergraduate Scholarship Program offers competitive scholarships to exceptional students from disadvantaged backgrounds who are committed to biomedical, behavioral and social science research careers at the NIH. Applicants must be U.S. citizens, nationals, or qualified permanent residents.

Academic Fields/Career Goals Biology; Health and Medical Sciences; Social Sciences. *Award* Scholarship for use in freshman, sophomore, junior, or senior years; renewable. *Number:* 10–20. *Amount:* up to $20,000.

Eligibility Requirements Applicant must be enrolled or expecting to enroll full-time at a four-year institution or university. Available to U.S. citizens.

Application Requirements Application, essay, financial need analysis, references, transcript. *Deadline:* February 28.

World Wide Web: http://ugsp.info.nih.gov

Contact: NIH Undergraduate Scholarship Program Director
National Institutes of Health
2 Center Drive, Room 2E30, MSC 0230
Bethesda, MD 20892-0230
Phone: 800-528-7689
Fax: 301-480-5481
E-mail: ugsp@nih.gov

SOCIETY OF TOXICOLOGY

MINORITY UNDERGRADUATE STUDENT AWARDS • 72

Travel funds are provided for members of groups underrepresented in the sciences to attend a special program at the Society of Toxicology Annual Meeting. Must have a 3.0 GPA. The deadline is October 9.

Academic Fields/Career Goals Biology; Health and Medical Sciences. *Award* Grant for use in freshman, sophomore, junior, or senior years; not renewable. *Number:* 20–50. *Amount:* $1000–$1500.

Eligibility Requirements Applicant must be American Indian/Alaska Native, Black (non-Hispanic), or Hispanic and enrolled or expecting to enroll full-time at a two-year or four-year institution or university. Applicant must have 3.0 GPA or higher. Available to U.S. citizens.

Application Requirements Application, essay, references, transcript. *Deadline:* October 9.

World Wide Web: http://www.toxicology.org

Contact: Nichelle Sankey, Program Coordinator
Society of Toxicology
1767 Business Center Drive, Suite 302
Reston, VA 20190
Phone: 703-438-3115
Fax: 703-438-3113
E-mail: nichelle@toxicology.org

UNITED NEGRO COLLEGE FUND

UNCF/PFIZER CORPORATE SCHOLARS PROGRAM see number 27

UNITED STATES DEPARTMENT OF HEALTH AND HUMAN SERVICES

NIH UNDERGRADUATE SCHOLARSHIP FOR INDIVIDUALS FROM DISADVANTAGED BACKGROUNDS • 73

Renewable awards of up to $20,000 per year for individuals from disadvantaged backgrounds to pursue degrees in physical and life sciences (including chemistry). Must complete one year of National Institutes of Health employment for each year of scholarship plus ten weeks during each year of scholarship. Minimum 3.5 GPA required.

Academic Fields/Career Goals Biology; Health and Medical Sciences; Physical Sciences and Math. *Award* Scholarship for use in freshman, sophomore, junior, or senior years; renewable. *Number:* 15–20. *Amount:* up to $20,000.

Eligibility Requirements Applicant must be enrolled or expecting to enroll full-time at a four-year institution or university. Applicant must have 3.5 GPA or higher.

Application Requirements Application, essay, financial need analysis, references, transcript. *Deadline:* March 31.

World Wide Web: http://helix.nih.gov:8001/oe/student/ugsp.html

Contact: Dr. Alfred C. Johnson, Director of Undergraduate Scholarship Program
United States Department of Health and Human Services
2 Center Drive, Room 2E30
Bethesda, MD 20892-0230
Phone: 800-528-7689
Fax: 301-402-8098
E-mail: ugsp@nih.gov

VIRGINIA BUSINESS AND PROFESSIONAL WOMEN'S FOUNDATION

WOMEN IN SCIENCE AND TECHNOLOGY SCHOLARSHIP • 74

One-time award offered to women completing a bachelor's, master's or doctoral degree within two years who are majoring in actuarial science, biology, bio-engineering, chemistry, computer science, dentistry, engineering, mathematics, medicine, physics or similar field. The award may be used for tuition, fees, books, transportation, living expenses, or dependent care. Must be a Virginia resident studying in Virginia.

Academic Fields/Career Goals Biology; Computer Science/Data Processing; Dental Health/Services; Engineering/Technology; Health and Medical Sciences; Physical Sciences and Math; Science, Technology and Society. *Award* Scholarship for use in junior, senior, graduate, or postgraduate years; not renewable. *Number:* 1–5. *Amount:* $500–$1000.

Eligibility Requirements Applicant must be age 18; enrolled or expecting to enroll full or part-time at a four-year institution or university; female; resident of Virginia and studying in Virginia. Available to U.S. citizens.

Application Requirements Application, essay, financial need analysis, references, transcript. *Deadline:* April 1.

World Wide Web: http://www.bpwva.advocate.net/foundation.htm

Contact: Scholarship Chair
Virginia Business and Professional Women's Foundation
PO Box 4842
McLean, VA 22103-4842
E-mail: bpwva@advocate.net

BUSINESS/CONSUMER SERVICES_____

AMERICAN ASSOCIATION OF UNIVERSITY WOMEN (AAUW) EDUCATIONAL FOUNDATION

AAUW EDUCATIONAL FOUNDATION SELECTED PROFESSIONS FELLOWSHIPS
see number 36

ASSOCIATION OF LATINO PROFESSIONALS IN FINANCE AND ACCOUNTING

HSF-ALPFA SCHOLARSHIPS
see number 3

CASUALTY ACTUARIAL SOCIETY/SOCIETY OF ACTUARIES JOINT COMMITTEE ON MINORITY RECRUITING

ACTUARIAL SCHOLARSHIPS FOR MINORITY STUDENTS ● 75
Award for underrepresented minority students planning careers in actuarial science or mathematics. Applicants should have taken the ACT Assessment or the SAT. Number and amount of awards vary with merit and financial need. Must be a U.S. citizen or permanent resident. All scholarship information including application is available online. Do not send award inquiries to address.

Academic Fields/Career Goals Business/Consumer Services. *Award* Scholarship for use in freshman, sophomore, junior, senior, or graduate years; not renewable. *Number:* 20–40. *Amount:* $500–$3000.

Eligibility Requirements Applicant must be American Indian/Alaska Native, Black (non-Hispanic), or Hispanic and enrolled or expecting to enroll full or part-time at a two-year or four-year institution or university. Available to U.S. citizens.

Application Requirements Application, financial need analysis, references, test scores, transcript. *Deadline:* May 1.

World Wide Web: http://www.BeAnActuary.org

Contact: Frank Lupo, Minority Scholarship Coordinator
Casualty Actuarial Society/Society of Actuaries Joint Committee on Minority
    Recruiting
475 North Martingale Road, Suite 800
Schaumburg, IL 60173-2226
Phone: 703-276-3100
E-mail: flupo@casact.org

CHARLOTTE OBSERVER

CHARLOTTE OBSERVER MINORITY SCHOLARSHIPS • 76

Scholarship is available for minority high school students who are interested in the newspaper business, either in the newsroom or business operations. Applicants must send in samples of their work along with the application. Deadline for submitting application is in December. Must be resident of North Carolina or South Carolina.

Academic Fields/Career Goals Business/Consumer Services; Journalism. *Award* Scholarship for use in freshman year; not renewable. *Number:* 2. *Amount:* $1000.

Eligibility Requirements Applicant must be American Indian/Alaska Native, Asian/Pacific Islander, Black (non-Hispanic), or Hispanic; high school student; planning to enroll or expecting to enroll full-time at a four-year institution or university and resident of North Carolina or South Carolina. Available to U.S. citizens.

Application Requirements Application, essay, interview, resume, references, transcript. *Deadline:* December 27.

Contact: Zaira Goodman, Human Resources Manager
Charlotte Observer
600 South Tryon Street
Charlotte, NC 28202
Phone: 704-358-5715
E-mail: zgoodman@charlotteobserver.com

COMMUNITY FOUNDATION FOR PALM BEACH AND MARTIN COUNTIES, INC.

BANK OF AMERICA MINORITY SCHOLARSHIP • 77

Student member of minority community attending Palm Beach County public or private high school intending to major in business. Must have "C" average or better, financial need, be enrolled in an accredited four year college or university.

Academic Fields/Career Goals Business/Consumer Services. *Award* Scholarship for use in freshman year; not renewable. *Number:* 1. *Amount:* $750–$2500.

Eligibility Requirements Applicant must be American Indian/Alaska Native, Asian/Pacific Islander, Black (non-Hispanic), or Hispanic; high school student; planning to enroll or expecting to enroll full-time at a four-year institution or university and resident of Florida. Available to U.S. citizens.

Application Requirements Application, financial need analysis, transcript. *Deadline:* March 1.

World Wide Web: http://www.cfpbmc.org

Contact: Carolyn Jenco, Grants Manager/Scholarship Coordinator
Community Foundation for Palm Beach and Martin Counties, Inc.
700 South Dixie Highway
Suite 200
West Palm Beach, FL 33401

GINA AUDITORE BONER MEMORIAL SCHOLARSHIP FUND • 78

Palm Beach or Martin County female graduating high school student interested in pursuing career in advertising, journalism, marketing, or graphic design. Based on financial need as makes extracurricular activities related to this field.

Academic Fields/Career Goals Business/Consumer Services; Graphics/Graphic Arts/Printing; Journalism. *Award* Scholarship for use in freshman year; not renewable. *Amount:* $750–$2500.

Eligibility Requirements Applicant must be high school student; planning to enroll or expecting to enroll full-time at a two-year or four-year or technical institution or university; female; resident of Florida and must have an interest in English language. Available to U.S. citizens.

Application Requirements Application, financial need analysis. *Deadline:* March 1.

World Wide Web: http://www.cfpbmc.org

Contact: Carolyn Jenco, Grants Manager/Scholarship Coordinator
Community Foundation for Palm Beach and Martin Counties, Inc.
700 South Dixie Highway
Suite 200
West Palm Beach, FL 33401

MARBY M. NOXON SCHOLARSHIP FUND
see number 39

CONSORTIUM FOR GRADUATE STUDY IN MANAGEMENT

CONSORTIUM FELLOWSHIP
• 79

Fellowship pays full tuition for minority applicant at one of 14 consortium member schools. Must be a U.S. citizen. Application fee of $120 and up. Early application deadline: December 1. Regular application deadline: January 15.

Academic Fields/Career Goals Business/Consumer Services. *Award* Fellowship for use in graduate years; renewable. *Number:* 250–300.

Eligibility Requirements Applicant must be American Indian/Alaska Native, Black (non-Hispanic), or Hispanic and enrolled or expecting to enroll full-time at an institution or university. Available to U.S. citizens.

Application Requirements Application, essay, interview, photo, resume, references, test scores, transcript. *Fee:* $120. *Deadline:* January 15.

World Wide Web: http://www.cgsm.org

Contact: Erica Reddick, Receptionist
Consortium for Graduate Study in Management
5585 Pershing Avenue #240
St. Louis, MO 63112
Phone: 314-877-5500
Fax: 314-877-5505
E-mail: frontdesk@cgsm.org

CUBAN AMERICAN NATIONAL FOUNDATION

MAS FAMILY SCHOLARSHIPS
• 80

Graduate and undergraduate scholarships in the fields of engineering, business, international relations, economics, communications, and journalism. Applicants must be Cuban-American and have graduated in the top 10
of high school class or have minimum 3.5 college GPA. Selection based on need, academic performance, leadership. Those who have already received awards and maintained high level of performance are given preference over new applicants.

Academic Fields/Career Goals Business/Consumer Services; Chemical Engineering; Communications; Economics; Electrical Engineering/Electronics; Engineering/Technology; Engineering-Related Technologies; Journalism; Mechanical Engineering; Political Science. *Award* Scholarship for use in freshman, sophomore, junior, or senior years; renewable. *Number:* 10–15. *Amount:* $1000–$10,000.

Mas Family Scholarships (continued)

Eligibility Requirements Applicant must be of Latin American/Caribbean heritage; enrolled or expecting to enroll full-time at a two-year or four-year institution or university and must have an interest in leadership. Applicant must have 3.5 GPA or higher. Available to U.S. citizens.

Application Requirements Application, autobiography, essay, financial need analysis, references, test scores, transcript. *Deadline:* March 31.

Contact: Director
Cuban American National Foundation
Mas Family Scholarships
1312 SW 27th Avenue, 3rd Floor
Miami, FL 33145
Phone: 305-592-7768
Fax: 305-592-7889

GOVERNMENT FINANCE OFFICERS ASSOCIATION

MINORITIES IN GOVERNMENT FINANCE SCHOLARSHIP   see number 9

GOVERNOR'S OFFICE

GOVERNOR'S OPPORTUNITY SCHOLARSHIP   • 81

A $5,000 scholarship will be awarded in each of the following categories: business, education, nursing, health care, law enforcement/public service, and science. Must be applied and will be mailed directly to a related academic or work program in an accredited California institution. Scholarship winners must attend the Governor's conference for Women to receive the award. Minimum 3.3 GPA. Contact for further information and application deadline.

Academic Fields/Career Goals Business/Consumer Services; Education; Health and Medical Sciences; Law Enforcement/Police Administration; Nursing; Political Science; Science, Technology and Society. *Award* Scholarship for use in junior, senior, graduate, or postgraduate years; not renewable. *Number:* 6. *Amount:* $5000.

Eligibility Requirements Applicant must be enrolled or expecting to enroll full or part-time at a two-year or four-year or technical institution or university; female; resident of California and studying in California. Available to U.S. citizens.

Application Requirements Application, applicant must enter a contest, autobiography, essay, references, self-addressed stamped envelope, transcript.

Contact: Ms. Crystal Clark, Scholarship Coordinator
Governor's Office
State Capitol Building
Sacramento, CA 95814
Phone: 916-445-7097

HISPANIC COLLEGE FUND, INC.

ALLFIRST/ HISPANIC COLLEGE FUND SCHOLARSHIP PROGRAM   see number 10

BURLINGTON NORTHERN SANTA FE FOUNDATION/HISPANIC COLLEGE FUND SCHOLARSHIP PROGRAM   see number 11

DENNY'S/HISPANIC COLLEGE FUND SCHOLARSHIP   see number 12

FIRST IN MY FAMILY SCHOLARSHIP PROGRAM   see number 19

HISPANIC COLLEGE FUND SCHOLARSHIP PROGRAM see number 20

HISPANIC COLLEGE FUND/INROADS/SPRINT SCHOLARSHIP PROGRAM • 82

One-time award open to undergraduates of Hispanic descent pursuing a degree in a business- or technology-related major. Must be a U.S. citizen and have a minimum 3.0 GPA. Recipients will participate in INROADS Leadership Development Training while interning at Sprint during the summer.

Academic Fields/Career Goals Business/Consumer Services; Communications; Computer Science/Data Processing; Economics; Electrical Engineering/Electronics; Engineering/ Technology; Engineering-Related Technologies; Mechanical Engineering. *Award* Scholarship for use in freshman, sophomore, junior, or senior years; not renewable. *Number:* 10–20. *Amount:* $1000–$5000.

Eligibility Requirements Applicant must be of Hispanic, Latin American/Caribbean, Mexican, Nicaraguan, or Spanish heritage and enrolled or expecting to enroll full-time at a two-year or four-year institution or university. Applicant must have 3.0 GPA or higher. Available to U.S. citizens.

Application Requirements Application, essay, financial need analysis, resume, references, test scores, transcript, college acceptance letter, copy of taxes, copy of SAR. *Deadline:* April 15.

World Wide Web: http://www.hispanicfund.org

Contact: Stina Augustsson, Program Manager
Hispanic College Fund, Inc.
1717 Pennsylvania Avenue, NW, Suite 460
Washington, DC 20006
Phone: 202-296-5400
Fax: 202-296-3774
E-mail: hispaniccollegefund@earthlink.net

HISPANIC SCHOLARSHIP FUND

HSF/GENERAL MOTORS SCHOLARSHIP • 83

Scholarships are available to Hispanic students pursuing a degree in business or engineering at an accredited U.S. four-year college. For more details, deadlines and an application see Web site: http://www.hsf.net.

Academic Fields/Career Goals Business/Consumer Services; Chemical Engineering; Civil Engineering; Electrical Engineering/Electronics; Engineering/Technology; Engineering-Related Technologies; Mechanical Engineering. *Award* Scholarship for use in freshman, sophomore, junior, or senior years; not renewable. *Number:* 83. *Amount:* $2500.

Eligibility Requirements Applicant must be Hispanic and enrolled or expecting to enroll full-time at a four-year institution or university. Applicant must have 3.0 GPA or higher. Available to U.S. citizens.

Application Requirements Application.

World Wide Web: http://www.hsf.net

Contact: application available at Web site

HSF/NATIONAL SOCIETY OF HISPANIC MBA'S SCHOLARSHIP PROGRAM • 84

Scholarships are available to Hispanic students pursuing Master's degrees in management/ business at an accredited U.S. college. For more details, deadlines and an application see Web site: http://www.hsf.net.

Academic Fields/Career Goals Business/Consumer Services. *Award* Scholarship for use in graduate years; not renewable. *Amount:* $2000–$5000.

Eligibility Requirements Applicant must be Hispanic and enrolled or expecting to enroll full or part-time at a four-year institution or university. Applicant must have 3.0 GPA or higher. Available to U.S. citizens.

Application Requirements Application.

World Wide Web: http://www.hsf.net

Contact: application available at Web site

JORGE MAS CANOSA FREEDOM FOUNDATION

MAS FAMILY SCHOLARSHIP AWARD • 85

Scholarship up to $10,000 per year to any financially needy, Cuban American student who is direct descendant of those who left Cuba or was born in Cuba. Minimum 3.5 GPA in college. Scholarships available only in the fields of engineering, business, international relations, economics, communications and journalism. Deadline is March 31. Write for application.

Academic Fields/Career Goals Business/Consumer Services; Chemical Engineering; Civil Engineering; Communications; Economics; Electrical Engineering/Electronics; Engineering-Related Technologies; Journalism; Materials Science, Engineering and Metallurgy; Mechanical Engineering. *Award* Scholarship for use in freshman, sophomore, junior, or senior years; renewable. *Amount:* up to $10,000.

Eligibility Requirements Applicant must be of Latin American/Caribbean heritage; Hispanic and enrolled or expecting to enroll at an institution or university. Applicant must have 3.5 GPA or higher. Available to U.S. citizens.

Application Requirements Application, autobiography, essay, financial need analysis, test scores, transcript, proof of Cuban descent. *Deadline:* March 31.

Contact: Jorge Mas Canosa Freedom Foundation
Cuban American National Foundation, 1312 Southwest 27th Avenue
Miami, FL 33145

KNIGHT RIDDER

KNIGHT RIDDER MINORITY SCHOLARSHIP PROGRAM • 86

Four $40,000 scholarships are given to graduating minority high school seniors who have plans of pursuing business or journalism as a college major and eventually as a career. Funds are given out over a four year period: $5,000 is given the first and second years, $15,000 is given out the third and fourth years. Recipients must work as an intern for a Knight-Ridder Company and maintain a 3.0 GPA. Must be sponsored by local Knight Ridder newspaper. Contact local Knight-Ridder Company for further information and deadlines.

Academic Fields/Career Goals Business/Consumer Services; Graphics/Graphic Arts/Printing; Journalism. *Award* Scholarship for use in freshman, sophomore, junior, or senior years; renewable. *Number:* 4. *Amount:* $5000–$15,000.

Eligibility Requirements Applicant must be American Indian/Alaska Native, Asian/Pacific Islander, Black (non-Hispanic), or Hispanic; high school student and planning to enroll or expecting to enroll full-time at a two-year or four-year institution or university. Applicant must have 3.0 GPA or higher. Available to U.S. citizens.

Application Requirements Autobiography, essay, interview, references, test scores, transcript.

World Wide Web: http://www.kri.com

Contact: Larry Olmstead, Vice President, HR/Diversity and Development
Knight Ridder
50 West San Fernando Street, Suite 1200
San Jose, CA 95113-2413
Phone: 408-938-0335
Fax: 408-938-0205
E-mail: lolmstead@knightridder.com

LEAGUE OF UNITED LATIN AMERICAN CITIZENS NATIONAL EDUCATIONAL SERVICE CENTERS, INC.

GE/LULAC SCHOLARSHIP • 87

Renewable award for minority students who are enrolled as business or engineering majors at accredited colleges or universities in the United States and who will be entering their sophomore year. Must maintain a minimum 3.0 GPA. Selection is based in part on the likelihood of pursuing a career in business or engineering. Application deadline is July 15.

Academic Fields/Career Goals Business/Consumer Services; Engineering/Technology. *Award* Scholarship for use in sophomore year; renewable. *Number:* 2. *Amount:* $5000.

Eligibility Requirements Applicant must be Hispanic and enrolled or expecting to enroll full-time at a four-year institution or university. Applicant must have 3.0 GPA or higher. Available to U.S. citizens.

Application Requirements Application, references, transcript. *Deadline:* July 15.

World Wide Web: http://www.lnesc.org

Contact: Scholarship Administrator
League of United Latin American Citizens National Educational Service Centers, Inc.
2000 L Street, NW
Suite 610
Washington, DC 20036

LEXINGTON HERALD-LEADER

LEXINGTON HERALD-LEADER/KNIGHT RIDDER MINORITY SCHOLARSHIPS • 88

One-time award for any minority senior attending high school in specific Kentucky counties. Must plan to attend a four-year college and major in journalism or business-related field. May qualify for the national Knight Ridder Minority Scholarship. Application deadline is January 6.

Academic Fields/Career Goals Business/Consumer Services; Journalism. *Award* Scholarship for use in freshman year; not renewable. *Number:* 2. *Amount:* $1000.

Eligibility Requirements Applicant must be American Indian/Alaska Native, Asian/Pacific Islander, Black (non-Hispanic), or Hispanic; high school student; planning to enroll or expecting to enroll full-time at a four-year institution or university and resident of Kentucky. Applicant must have 2.5 GPA or higher. Available to U.S. citizens.

Application Requirements Application, essay, interview, references, test scores, transcript. *Deadline:* January 6.

Contact: Kathy Aldridge, Executive Assistant
Lexington Herald-Leader
100 Midland Avenue
Lexington, KY 40508
Phone: 859-231-3104
Fax: 859-231-3584
E-mail: kaldridge@herald-leader.com

NATIONAL ASSOCIATION FOR THE ADVANCEMENT OF COLORED PEOPLE

EARL G. GRAVES NAACP SCHOLARSHIP • 89

One-time award of $5,000 to a full-time minority student. Must be an enrolled junior or senior at an accredited college or university in the United States as a declared business major, or a graduate student enrolled or accepted in a masters or doctoral program within a business school at an accredited university. Must demonstrate financial need.

Academic Fields/Career Goals Business/Consumer Services. *Award* Scholarship for use in junior, senior, or graduate years; not renewable. *Number:* 1. *Amount:* $5000.

Eligibility Requirements Applicant must be American Indian/Alaska Native, Asian/Pacific Islander, Black (non-Hispanic), or Hispanic and enrolled or expecting to enroll full-time at a four-year institution or university. Applicant must have 2.5 GPA or higher. Available to U.S. citizens.

Application Requirements Application, financial need analysis, references, transcript. *Deadline:* March 28.

World Wide Web: http://www.naacp.org

Contact: Education Department, Scholarship Request
National Association for the Advancement of Colored People
4805 Mt. Hope Drive
Baltimore, MD 21215-3297

SOCIAL SCIENCE RESEARCH COUNCIL

PHILANTHROPHY AND THE NONPROFIT SECTOR DISSERTATION FELLOWSHIP • 90

Fellowships provide support for dissertation research on the history, behavior and role of nonprofit and/or philanthropic organizations in the U.S. Must be enrolled in a doctoral program in the U.S. Applications from women and persons of color are especially encouraged. Applications available on Web site: http://www.ssrc.org/fellowships. Applications must be submitted by regular mail.

Academic Fields/Career Goals Business/Consumer Services; History. *Award* Fellowship for use in graduate years; not renewable. *Number:* up to 7. *Amount:* up to $18,000.

Eligibility Requirements Applicant must be enrolled or expecting to enroll full-time at an institution or university. Available to U.S. and non-U.S. citizens.

Application Requirements Application.

World Wide Web: http://www.ssrc.org

Contact: Heloisa Griggs, Program Assistant
Social Science Research Council
810 Seventh Avenue
New York, NY 10019
Phone: 212-377-2700
Fax: 212-377-2727
E-mail: phil-np@ssrc.org

UNITED DAUGHTERS OF THE CONFEDERACY

WALTER REED SMITH SCHOLARSHIP • 91

Award for full-time female undergraduate student who is a descendant of a Confederate soldier, studying nutrition, home economics, nursing, business administration, or computer science. Must carry a minimum of 12 credit hours each semester and have a minimum 3.0 GPA. Submit letter of endorsement from sponsoring chapter of the United Daughters of the Confederacy.

Academic Fields/Career Goals Business/Consumer Services; Computer Science/Data Processing; Food Science/Nutrition; Home Economics; Nursing. *Award* Scholarship for use in freshman, sophomore, junior, or senior years; renewable. *Number:* 1–2. *Amount:* $800–$1000.

Eligibility Requirements Applicant must be enrolled or expecting to enroll full-time at a four-year institution or university and female. Applicant or parent of applicant must be member of United Daughters of the Confederacy. Applicant must have 3.0 GPA or higher. Available to U.S. citizens.

Application Requirements Application, essay, financial need analysis, photo, references, self-addressed stamped envelope, transcript. *Deadline:* February 15.

World Wide Web: http://www.hqudc.org

Contact: Second Vice President General
United Daughters of the Confederacy
328 North Boulevard
Richmond, VA 23220-4057
Phone: 804-355-1636

UNITED NEGRO COLLEGE FUND

COLLEGE FUND/COCA COLA CORPORATE INTERN PROGRAM • 92

Provides educational opportunities for minority students. Must be rising college juniors with a minimum GPA of 3.0. Scholarship based on successful internship performance. Open to majors in engineering, business, finance, information technology, chemistry, communications, and human resources. Prospective applicants should complete the Student Profile found at Web site: http://www.uncf.org.

Academic Fields/Career Goals Business/Consumer Services; Communications; Computer Science/Data Processing; Engineering/Technology. *Award* Scholarship for use in junior year; not renewable. *Number:* up to 50. *Amount:* $10,000.

Eligibility Requirements Applicant must be American Indian/Alaska Native, Asian/Pacific Islander, Black (non-Hispanic), or Hispanic and enrolled or expecting to enroll full-time at a four-year institution or university. Applicant must have 3.0 GPA or higher.

Application Requirements Application, references, transcript. *Deadline:* December 16.

World Wide Web: http://www.uncf.org

Contact: Program Services Department
United Negro College Fund
8260 Willow Oaks Corporate Drive
Fairfax, VA 22031

HOUSEHOLD INTERNATIONAL CORPORATE SCHOLARS • 93

Scholarship provides opportunities for minority sophomores and juniors majoring in business, finance, accounting, marketing, computer science or human resources. Must attend a UNCF member college or university or a selected historically black college or university. Minimum 3.0 GPA required. Prospective applicants should complete the Student Profile found at Web site: http://www.uncf.org.

Academic Fields/Career Goals Business/Consumer Services; Computer Science/Data Processing. *Award* Scholarship for use in sophomore or junior years; not renewable. *Number:* up to 30. *Amount:* up to $10,000.

Household International Corporate Scholars (continued)

Eligibility Requirements Applicant must be American Indian/Alaska Native, Asian/Pacific Islander, Black (non-Hispanic), or Hispanic and enrolled or expecting to enroll at a four-year institution or university. Applicant must have 3.0 GPA or higher.

Application Requirements Application, financial need analysis. *Deadline:* March 1.

World Wide Web: http://www.uncf.org

Contact: Program Services Department
United Negro College Fund
8260 Willow Oaks Corporate Drive
Fairfax, VA 22031

UNCF/PFIZER CORPORATE SCHOLARS PROGRAM   see number 27

WASHINGTON SOCIETY OF CERTIFIED PUBLIC ACCOUNTANTS

WSCPA FIFTH-YEAR ACCOUNTING SCHOLARSHIPS   see number 16

CHEMICAL ENGINEERING_____

AMERICAN CHEMICAL SOCIETY

AMERICAN CHEMICAL SOCIETY SCHOLARS PROGRAM   • 94

Renewable award for minority students pursuing studies in chemistry, biochemistry, chemical technology, chemical engineering or any chemical sciences. Must be U.S. citizen or permanent resident and have minimum 3.0 GPA. Must be Native-Americans, African-American, or Hispanic. Scholarship amount for freshmen is up to $2500, and up to $3000 for sophomores, juniors and seniors.

Academic Fields/Career Goals Chemical Engineering; Materials Science, Engineering and Metallurgy; Natural Sciences. *Award* Scholarship for use in freshman, sophomore, or junior years; renewable. *Number:* 100–200. *Amount:* up to $3000.

Eligibility Requirements Applicant must be American Indian/Alaska Native, Black (non-Hispanic), or Hispanic and enrolled or expecting to enroll full-time at a two-year or four-year or technical institution or university. Applicant must have 3.0 GPA or higher. Available to U.S. citizens.

Application Requirements Application, financial need analysis, references, test scores, transcript. *Deadline:* February 15.

World Wide Web: http://www.chemistry.org

Contact: Robert Hughes, Manager
American Chemical Society
1155 16th Street, NW
Washington, DC 20036
Phone: 202-872-6048
Fax: 202-776-8003
E-mail: scholars@acs.org

AMERICAN INSTITUTE OF CHEMICAL ENGINEERS

MINORITY AFFAIRS COMMITTEE AWARD FOR OUTSTANDING SCHOLASTIC ACHIEVEMENT • 95

Award recognizing the outstanding achievements of a chemical engineering student who serves as a role model for minority students. $1000 award plus $500 travel allowance to attend AICHE meeting. Must be nominated.

Academic Fields/Career Goals Chemical Engineering. *Award* Scholarship for use in freshman, sophomore, junior, senior, or graduate years; not renewable. *Amount:* $1500.

Eligibility Requirements Applicant must be American Indian/Alaska Native, Asian/Pacific Islander, Black (non-Hispanic), or Hispanic and enrolled or expecting to enroll at an institution or university.

Application Requirements Application. *Deadline:* April 15.

World Wide Web: http://www.aiche.org

Contact: Awards Administrator
American Institute of Chemical Engineers
Three Park Avenue
New York, NY 10016-5991
Phone: 212-591-7478
Fax: 212-591-8882
E-mail: awards@aiche.org

MINORITY SCHOLARSHIP AWARDS FOR COLLEGE STUDENTS • 96

One-time award for college undergraduates who are studying chemical engineering. Must be a member of a minority group that is underrepresented in chemical engineering. Must be nominated. Must be an AICHE national student member at the time of application.

Academic Fields/Career Goals Chemical Engineering. *Award* Scholarship for use in freshman, sophomore, junior, or senior years; not renewable. *Number:* up to 10. *Amount:* $1000.

Eligibility Requirements Applicant must be American Indian/Alaska Native, Asian/Pacific Islander, Black (non-Hispanic), or Hispanic and enrolled or expecting to enroll at a four-year institution or university.

Application Requirements Application, financial need analysis. *Deadline:* April 15.

World Wide Web: http://www.aiche.org

Contact: Awards Administrator
American Institute of Chemical Engineers
Three Park Avenue
New York, NY 10016-5991
Phone: 212-591-7478
Fax: 212-591-8882
E-mail: awards@aiche.org

MINORITY SCHOLARSHIP AWARDS FOR INCOMING COLLEGE FRESHMEN • 97

Up to ten awards of $1000 for high school graduates who are members of a minority group that is underrepresented in chemical engineering. Must plan to study courses leading to a chemical engineering degree. Must be nominated.

Academic Fields/Career Goals Chemical Engineering. *Award* Scholarship for use in freshman year; not renewable. *Number:* up to 10. *Amount:* $1000.

Eligibility Requirements Applicant must be American Indian/Alaska Native, Asian/Pacific Islander, Black (non-Hispanic), or Hispanic; high school student and planning to enroll or expecting to enroll at an institution or university.

Minority Scholarship Awards for Incoming College Freshmen (continued)

Application Requirements Application, financial need analysis. *Deadline:* April 15.
World Wide Web: http://www.aiche.org
Contact: Awards Administrator
American Institute of Chemical Engineers
Three Park Avenue
New York, NY 10016-5991
Phone: 212-591-7478
Fax: 212-591-8882
E-mail: awards@aiche.org

AMERICAN SOCIETY FOR ENGINEERING EDUCATION

NATIONAL DEFENSE SCIENCE AND ENGINEERING GRADUATE FELLOWSHIP PROGRAM • 98

Three-year fellowships available to students at or near the beginning of their studies towards a PhD in an engineering or science-related field. Must be citizen or national or the U.S. Must enroll at an accredited institution of higher education in the U.S. offering PhD degrees in science and engineering. Applications encouraged from women, underrepresented minorities, and persons with disabilities. For more details and deadlines see Web site: http://www.onr.navy.mil or http://www.asee.org/ndseg

Academic Fields/Career Goals Chemical Engineering; Civil Engineering; Electrical Engineering/Electronics; Engineering/Technology; Engineering-Related Technologies; Materials Science, Engineering and Metallurgy; Mechanical Engineering; Nuclear Science; Physical Sciences and Math. *Award* Fellowship for use in graduate years; not renewable. *Number:* 150–300. *Amount:* $120,000–$140,000.

Eligibility Requirements Applicant must be enrolled or expecting to enroll full-time at an institution or university. Available to U.S. citizens.

Application Requirements Application, essay, references, test scores, transcript. *Deadline:* January 6.
World Wide Web: http://www.asee.org/ndseg/
Contact: applications available at Web site

ASSOCIATION FOR WOMEN IN SCIENCE EDUCATIONAL FOUNDATION

ASSOCIATION FOR WOMEN IN SCIENCE UNDERGRADUATE AWARD   see number 26

CANADIAN FEDERATION OF UNIVERSITY WOMEN

CANADIAN FEDERATION OF UNIVERSITY WOMEN MEMORIAL FELLOWSHIP
see number 21

CENTER FOR THE ADVANCEMENT OF HISPANICS IN SCIENCE AND ENGINEERING EDUCATION (CAHSEE)

CAHSEE FELLOWSHIP: YOUNG EDUCATORS PROGRAM   see number 30

CUBAN AMERICAN NATIONAL FOUNDATION

MAS FAMILY SCHOLARSHIPS
see number 80

EAST LOS ANGELES COMMUNITY UNION (TELACU) EDUCATION FOUNDATION

TELACU ENGINEERING AWARD
• 99

Scholarships available to low-income applicants from the Greater East Side of Los Angeles. Must be U.S. citizen or permanent resident with Hispanic heritage. Must be a resident of one of the following communities: East Los Angeles, Bell Gardens, Commerce, Huntington Park, Montebello, Monterey Park, Pico Rivera, Santa Ana, South Gate, and the City of Los Angeles. Must be the first generation in their family to achieve a college degree. Must have a record of community service. For Sophomores, Juniors and Seniors only who have completed 12 credits or more of engineering course work at the time of application.

Academic Fields/Career Goals Chemical Engineering; Computer Science/Data Processing; Electrical Engineering/Electronics; Engineering/Technology; Engineering-Related Technologies; Mechanical Engineering. *Award* Scholarship for use in sophomore, junior, or senior years; not renewable. *Number:* 1–3. *Amount:* $2500–$5000.

Eligibility Requirements Applicant must be of Hispanic heritage; enrolled or expecting to enroll full-time at a four-year institution or university and resident of California. Applicant must have 3.0 GPA or higher. Available to U.S. citizens.

Application Requirements Application, autobiography, essay, financial need analysis, interview, references, self-addressed stamped envelope, transcript. *Deadline:* April 5.

Contact: Mr. Michael A. Alvarado, Director
East Los Angeles Community Union (TELACU) Education Foundation
5400 East Olympic Boulevard, #300
Los Angeles, CA 90022
Phone: 323-721-1655 Ext. 403
Fax: 323-724-3372
E-mail: malvarado@telacu.com

HISPANIC COLLEGE FUND, INC.

DENNY'S/HISPANIC COLLEGE FUND SCHOLARSHIP
see number 12

FIRST IN MY FAMILY SCHOLARSHIP PROGRAM
see number 19

HISPANIC COLLEGE FUND SCHOLARSHIP PROGRAM
see number 20

NATIONAL HISPANIC EXPLORERS SCHOLARSHIP PROGRAM
see number 31

HISPANIC ENGINEER NATIONAL ACHIEVEMENT AWARDS CORPORATION (HENAAC)

HISPANIC ENGINEER NATIONAL ACHIEVEMENT AWARDS CORPORATION SCHOLARSHIP PROGRAM
see number 51

HISPANIC SCHOLARSHIP FUND

HSF/GENERAL MOTORS SCHOLARSHIP
see number 83

JORGE MAS CANOSA FREEDOM FOUNDATION

MAS FAMILY SCHOLARSHIP AWARD
see number 85

LOS ANGELES COUNCIL OF BLACK PROFESSIONAL ENGINEERS

AL-BEN SCHOLARSHIP FOR ACADEMIC INCENTIVE
• 100

Scholarships will be granted for notable academic achievements, interests in engineering, math or science, and demonstrated desire and commitment to succeed in technical fields. Must be from a minority group that has traditionally been underrepresented in these areas. For more details or an application see Web site: http://www.lablackengineers.org.

Academic Fields/Career Goals Chemical Engineering; Civil Engineering; Computer Science/Data Processing; Electrical Engineering/Electronics; Engineering/Technology; Engineering-Related Technologies; Materials Science, Engineering and Metallurgy; Mechanical Engineering; Physical Sciences and Math. *Award* Scholarship for use in freshman, sophomore, junior, or senior years; not renewable. *Amount:* $500–$1000.

Eligibility Requirements Applicant must be American Indian/Alaska Native, Asian/Pacific Islander, Black (non-Hispanic), or Hispanic and enrolled or expecting to enroll at an institution or university. Available to U.S. citizens.

Application Requirements Application, essay, references, transcript. *Deadline:* April 5.

World Wide Web: http://www.lablackengineers.org/scholarships.html

Contact: application available at Web site

AL-BEN SCHOLARSHIP FOR PROFESSIONAL MERIT
• 101

Scholarships will be granted for exemplary actions in campus organizations or community activities while maintaining an excellent GPA. Must be from a minority group. For more details or an application see Web site: http://www.lablackengineers.org.

Academic Fields/Career Goals Chemical Engineering; Civil Engineering; Computer Science/Data Processing; Electrical Engineering/Electronics; Engineering/Technology; Engineering-Related Technologies; Materials Science, Engineering and Metallurgy; Mechanical Engineering; Physical Sciences and Math. *Award* Scholarship for use in freshman, sophomore, junior, or senior years; not renewable. *Amount:* $500–$1000.

Eligibility Requirements Applicant must be American Indian/Alaska Native, Asian/Pacific Islander, Black (non-Hispanic), or Hispanic and enrolled or expecting to enroll at an institution or university. Available to U.S. citizens.

Application Requirements Application, essay, references, transcript. *Deadline:* April 5.

World Wide Web: http://www.lablackengineers.org/scholarships.html

Contact: application available at Web site

AL-BEN SCHOLARSHIP FOR SCHOLASTIC ACHIEVEMENT
• 102

Scholarships will be granted for superlative scholastic achievements in the academic pursuits of engineering, math, computer or scientific studies. Must be from a minority group that has traditionally been underrepresented in these areas. For more details or an application see Web site: http://www.lablackengineers.org.

Academic Fields/Career Goals Chemical Engineering; Civil Engineering; Computer Science/Data Processing; Electrical Engineering/Electronics; Engineering/Technology; Engineering-Related Technologies; Materials Science, Engineering and Metallurgy; Mechanical Engineering; Physical Sciences and Math. *Award* Scholarship for use in freshman, sophomore, junior, or senior years; not renewable. *Amount:* $500–$1000.

Eligibility Requirements Applicant must be American Indian/Alaska Native, Asian/Pacific Islander, Black (non-Hispanic), or Hispanic and enrolled or expecting to enroll at a four-year institution or university. Available to U.S. citizens.
Application Requirements Application, essay, references, transcript. *Deadline:* April 5.
World Wide Web: http://www.lablackengineers.org/scholarships.html
Contact: application available at Web site

NAMEPA NATIONAL SCHOLARSHIP FOUNDATION

NATIONAL ASSOCIATION OF MINORITY ENGINEERING PROGRAM ADMINISTRATORS NATIONAL SCHOLARSHIP FUND
see number 58

NATIONAL ACTION COUNCIL FOR MINORITIES IN ENGINEERING-NACME, INC.

ENGINEERING VANGUARD PROGRAM • 103
Renewable award for minority high school seniors (African-American, American-Indian, Latino). Must demonstrate desire and potential to succeed in engineering. Must be accepted at a university participating in the Vanguard Program and enrolled in an approved major. Visit Web site for list of universities and majors, http://www.nacme.org.

Academic Fields/Career Goals Chemical Engineering; Civil Engineering; Computer Science/Data Processing; Electrical Engineering/Electronics; Engineering/Technology; Engineering-Related Technologies; Materials Science, Engineering and Metallurgy; Meteorology/Atmospheric Science; Nuclear Science; Physical Sciences and Math; Science, Technology and Society. *Award* Grant for use in freshman, sophomore, junior, or senior years; renewable.
Eligibility Requirements Applicant must be American Indian/Alaska Native, Black (non-Hispanic), or Hispanic; high school student; planning to enroll or expecting to enroll full-time at a four-year institution or university and studying in Colorado, District of Columbia, New Jersey, New York, or Pennsylvania. Applicant must have 2.5 GPA or higher. Available to U.S. citizens.
Application Requirements Application, financial need analysis, test scores. *Deadline:* October 25.
World Wide Web: http://www.nacme.org
Contact: National Action Council for Minorities in Engineering-NACME, Inc.
The Empire State Building, 350 Fifth Avenue, Suite 2212
New York, NY 10118-2299
E-mail: scholarships@nacme.org

SLOAN PHD PROGRAM • 104
Award available to minority scholars pursuing PhD in mathematical, scientific, or engineering doctoral program. Applicant must apply and be accepted to one of the 30 institutions supported by the Sloan Foundation. For additional information and to see a list of institutions, visit Web site: http://www.nacme.org

Academic Fields/Career Goals Chemical Engineering; Civil Engineering; Computer Science/Data Processing; Economics; Electrical Engineering/Electronics; Engineering/Technology; Engineering-Related Technologies; Materials Science, Engineering and Metallurgy; Meteorology/Atmospheric Science; Nuclear Science; Physical Sciences and Math; Science, Technology and Society. *Award* Grant for use in graduate years; renewable.
Eligibility Requirements Applicant must be American Indian/Alaska Native, Black (non-Hispanic), or Hispanic and enrolled or expecting to enroll full-time at an institution or university. Available to U.S. citizens.

Sloan PhD Program (continued)

Application Requirements Application, financial need analysis, references. *Deadline:* Continuous.

World Wide Web: http://www.nacme.org

Contact: National Action Council for Minorities in Engineering-NACME, Inc.
The Empire State Building, 350 Fifth Avenue, Suite 2212
New York, NY 10118-2299
E-mail: scholarships@nacme.org

NATIONAL PHYSICAL SCIENCE CONSORTIUM

NATIONAL PHYSICAL SCIENCE CONSORTIUM GRADUATE FELLOWSHIPS IN THE PHYSICAL SCIENCES • 105

Fellowship renewable for duration of six-year doctoral program. Emphasis on recruitment of underrepresented minorities and females. Must be college senior with at least a 3.0 GPA or in first year of a doctoral program, who has the ability to pursue graduate work at a National Physical Science Consortium member institution. Minimum award is $200,000.

Academic Fields/Career Goals Chemical Engineering; Computer Science/Data Processing; Earth Science; Electrical Engineering/Electronics; Materials Science, Engineering and Metallurgy; Mechanical Engineering; Meteorology/Atmospheric Science; Physical Sciences and Math. *Award* Fellowship for use in graduate years; renewable. *Number:* 20–25. *Amount:* $200,000.

Eligibility Requirements Applicant must be enrolled or expecting to enroll full-time at an institution or university. Applicant must have 3.0 GPA or higher. Available to U.S. citizens.

Application Requirements Application, references, test scores, transcript. *Deadline:* November 5.

World Wide Web: http://www.npsc.org

Contact: Dr. James Powell, Executive Director
National Physical Science Consortium
University Village
Suite E212, 33 South Hoover Street
Los Angeles, CA 90007-8001
Phone: 800-854-NPSC
Fax: 213-821-2410
E-mail: npschq@npsc.org

NEW YORK STATE SOCIETY OF PROFESSIONAL ENGINEERS

NSPE AUXILIARY SCHOLARSHIP • 106

Scholarship for a female student in the amount of $1000 for two years. Based on academic achievement. May attend any university, providing the engineering curriculum selected is accredited by the Accreditation Board for Engineering and Technology (ABET). A scholarship renewal report will be required for second year payment. GPA of 3.6 or higher.

Academic Fields/Career Goals Chemical Engineering; Civil Engineering; Electrical Engineering/Electronics; Engineering/Technology; Engineering-Related Technologies; Materials Science, Engineering and Metallurgy; Mechanical Engineering. *Award* Scholarship for use in freshman or sophomore years; renewable. *Amount:* $1000.

Eligibility Requirements Applicant must be high school student; planning to enroll or expecting to enroll at an institution or university and female.

Application Requirements Application, essay, references, test scores, transcript. *Deadline:* December 1.
World Wide Web: http://www.nysspe.org
Contact: NSPE Headquarters
New York State Society of Professional Engineers
Education Services, 1420 King Street
Alexandria, VA 22314-2794

NSPE-VIRGINIA D. HENRY MEMORIAL SCHOLARSHIP • 107

Scholarship will be awarded to female student in the amount of $1000 for her freshman year. Based on academic achievement. May attend any university, providing the engineering curriculum selected is accredited by the Accreditation Board for Engineering and Technology (ABET). GPA of 3.6 or higher.

Academic Fields/Career Goals Chemical Engineering; Civil Engineering; Electrical Engineering/Electronics; Engineering/Technology; Engineering-Related Technologies; Materials Science, Engineering and Metallurgy; Mechanical Engineering. *Award* Scholarship for use in freshman year; not renewable. *Amount:* $1000.

Eligibility Requirements Applicant must be high school student; planning to enroll or expecting to enroll at an institution or university and female.

Application Requirements Application, essay, references, test scores, transcript. *Deadline:* December 1.
World Wide Web: http://www.nysspe.org
Contact: NSPE Headquarters
New York State Society of Professional Engineers
Education Services, 1420 King Street
Alexandria, VA 22314-2794

OFFICE OF NAVAL RESEARCH

HISTORICALLY BLACK COLLEGES AND UNIVERSITIES FUTURE ENGINEERING FACULTY FELLOWSHIP • 108

Fellowships are awarded to women, underrepresented minorities and persons with disabilities who are pursuing a doctoral degree in an engineering related field. Fellows receive a stipend, full tuition and fees. For more details see Web site: http://www.onr.navy.mil.

Academic Fields/Career Goals Chemical Engineering; Civil Engineering; Engineering/Technology; Engineering-Related Technologies; Materials Science, Engineering and Metallurgy. *Award* Fellowship for use in graduate years; not renewable.

Eligibility Requirements Applicant must be enrolled or expecting to enroll at an institution or university. Available to U.S. citizens.

Application Requirements Application, references. *Deadline:* March 3.
World Wide Web: http://www.onr.navy.mil
Contact: application available at Web site

SOCIETY OF HISPANIC PROFESSIONAL ENGINEERS FOUNDATION

SOCIETY OF HISPANIC PROFESSIONAL ENGINEERS FOUNDATION • 109

Scholarships awarded to Hispanic engineering and science students throughout the U.S. Scholarships are awarded at the beginning of every academic year based upon academic achievement, financial need, involvement in campus and community activities, career goals and counselor recommendations.

Society of Hispanic Professional Engineers Foundation (continued)

Academic Fields/Career Goals Chemical Engineering; Civil Engineering; Electrical Engineering/Electronics; Engineering/Technology; Engineering-Related Technologies; Materials Science, Engineering and Metallurgy; Mechanical Engineering; Natural Sciences; Nuclear Science; Science, Technology and Society. *Award* Scholarship for use in freshman, sophomore, junior, senior, or graduate years; not renewable. *Amount:* $500–$7000.

Eligibility Requirements Applicant must be Hispanic and enrolled or expecting to enroll full-time at an institution or university. Available to U.S. citizens.

Application Requirements Application, financial need analysis, resume, references. *Deadline:* May 15.

World Wide Web: http://www.shpefoundation.org

Contact: Kathy Borunda, Director, Educational Programs
Society of Hispanic Professional Engineers Foundation
55 Second Street
15th Floor
Los Angeles, CA 94105
E-mail: kathy@shpefoundation.org

SOCIETY OF MEXICAN AMERICAN ENGINEERS AND SCIENTISTS

GRE AND GRADUATE APPLICATIONS WAIVER • 110

Grant serves as a fee waiver for the cost of testing for and applying to graduate school. Must be Mexican-American and a member of the Society of Mexican-American Engineers and Scientists, Inc. (MAES). Minimum GPA of 2.75 required. For more details and an application go to Web site: http://www.maes-natl.org.

Academic Fields/Career Goals Chemical Engineering; Civil Engineering; Engineering/Technology; Engineering-Related Technologies; Science, Technology and Society. *Award* Grant for use in senior year; not renewable.

Eligibility Requirements Applicant must be of Mexican heritage; Hispanic and enrolled or expecting to enroll at an institution or university.

Application Requirements Application, essay, resume.

World Wide Web: http://www.maes-natl.org

Contact: application available at Web site

SOCIETY OF WOMEN ENGINEERS

CHEVRON TEXACO CORPORATION SCHOLARSHIPS • 111

Eight awards open to women who are sophomores or juniors majoring in civil, chemical, mechanical, or petroleum engineering. One-time award of $2000. Must be active SWE student member. Deadline: February 1.

Academic Fields/Career Goals Chemical Engineering; Civil Engineering; Engineering/Technology; Mechanical Engineering. *Award* Scholarship for use in sophomore or junior years; not renewable. *Number:* 8. *Amount:* $2000.

Eligibility Requirements Applicant must be enrolled or expecting to enroll full-time at a four-year institution or university and female. Applicant or parent of applicant must be member of Society of Women Engineers. Available to U.S. and non-U.S. citizens.

Application Requirements Application, essay, references, self-addressed stamped envelope, test scores, transcript. *Deadline:* February 1.

World Wide Web: http://www.swe.org

Contact: Program Coordinator
Society of Women Engineers
230 East Ohio Street, Suite 400
Chicago, IL 60611-3265
Phone: 312-596-5223
Fax: 312-644-8557
E-mail: hq@swe.org

DUPONT COMPANY SCHOLARSHIPS • 112

Seven one-time award available to female undergraduate students majoring in chemical or mechanical engineering: two are for incoming freshmen. Minimum 3.0 GPA required. Limited to schools in the eastern U.S. Deadline: May 15 for freshman award; February 1 for sophomore, junior, and senior awards.

Academic Fields/Career Goals Chemical Engineering; Mechanical Engineering. *Award* Scholarship for use in freshman, sophomore, junior, or senior years; not renewable. *Number:* 7. *Amount:* $2000.

Eligibility Requirements Applicant must be enrolled or expecting to enroll full-time at a four-year institution or university and female. Applicant must have 3.0 GPA or higher.

Application Requirements Application, references, self-addressed stamped envelope, test scores, transcript.

World Wide Web: http://www.swe.org

Contact: Program Coordinator
Society of Women Engineers
230 East Ohio Street, Suite 400
Chicago, IL 60611-3265
Phone: 312-596-5223
Fax: 312-644-8557
E-mail: hq@swe.org

GENERAL MOTORS FOUNDATION GRADUATE SCHOLARSHIP • 113

One award for a first-year female graduate student who has demonstrated previous leadership role and career interest in engineering technology or mechanical, chemical, industrial, automotive, materials science, or manufacturing engineering. Send self-addressed stamped envelope for application. One-time award of $1000. Includes $500 travel grant for SWE National Conference. Deadline: February 1.

Academic Fields/Career Goals Chemical Engineering; Engineering/Technology; Materials Science, Engineering and Metallurgy; Mechanical Engineering; Trade/Technical Specialties. *Award* Scholarship for use in graduate years; not renewable. *Number:* 1. *Amount:* $1000.

Eligibility Requirements Applicant must be enrolled or expecting to enroll full-time at a four-year institution or university; female and must have an interest in leadership. Applicant must have 3.5 GPA or higher.

Application Requirements Application, essay, references, self-addressed stamped envelope, test scores, transcript. *Deadline:* February 1.

World Wide Web: http://www.swe.org

Contact: Program Coordinator
Society of Women Engineers
230 East Ohio Street, Suite 400
Chicago, IL 60611-3265
Phone: 312-596-5223
Fax: 312-644-8557
E-mail: hq@swe.org

GENERAL MOTORS FOUNDATION UNDERGRADUATE SCHOLARSHIPS • 114

Renewable award for female student entering junior year who is interested in automotive/manufacturing career. Must hold a leadership position in a student organization. Send self-addressed stamped envelope for application. Includes $500 travel grant for SWE National Conference. Must have a 3.5 GPA. Deadline: February 1.

Academic Fields/Career Goals Chemical Engineering; Electrical Engineering/Electronics; Engineering/Technology; Engineering-Related Technologies; Mechanical Engineering. *Award* Scholarship for use in junior year; renewable. *Number:* 2. *Amount:* $1000.

Eligibility Requirements Applicant must be enrolled or expecting to enroll full-time at a four-year institution or university; female and must have an interest in leadership. Applicant must have 3.5 GPA or higher.

Application Requirements Application, essay, references, self-addressed stamped envelope, test scores, transcript. *Deadline:* February 1.

World Wide Web: http://www.swe.org

Contact: Program Coordinator
Society of Women Engineers
230 East Ohio Street, Suite 400
Chicago, IL 60611-3265
Phone: 312-596-5223
Fax: 312-644-8557
E-mail: hq@swe.org

UNITED NEGRO COLLEGE FUND

UNCF/PFIZER CORPORATE SCHOLARS PROGRAM
see number 27

XEROX

TECHNICAL MINORITY SCHOLARSHIP • 115

One-time award for minority students enrolled full time in a technical science or engineering discipline. Must be studying at a four-year institution and have a GPA of 3.0 or higher. Available to U.S. citizens and individuals with permanent resident visas. Further information is available at Web site http://www.xerox.com.

Academic Fields/Career Goals Chemical Engineering; Computer Science/Data Processing; Electrical Engineering/Electronics; Engineering/Technology; Engineering-Related Technologies; Materials Science, Engineering and Metallurgy; Mechanical Engineering. *Award* Scholarship for use in freshman, sophomore, junior, senior, graduate, or postgraduate years; not renewable. *Amount:* $1000.

Eligibility Requirements Applicant must be American Indian/Alaska Native, Asian/Pacific Islander, Black (non-Hispanic), or Hispanic and enrolled or expecting to enroll full-time at a four-year institution or university. Applicant must have 3.0 GPA or higher. Available to U.S. citizens.

Application Requirements Application, resume, transcript. *Deadline:* September 15.

World Wide Web: http://xerox.com/scholarship

Contact: application available at Web site

CIVIL ENGINEERING

AMERICAN SOCIETY FOR ENGINEERING EDUCATION

NATIONAL DEFENSE SCIENCE AND ENGINEERING GRADUATE FELLOWSHIP PROGRAM
see number 98

CANADIAN FEDERATION OF UNIVERSITY WOMEN
CANADIAN FEDERATION OF UNIVERSITY WOMEN MEMORIAL FELLOWSHIP
see number 21

CENTER FOR THE ADVANCEMENT OF HISPANICS IN SCIENCE AND ENGINEERING EDUCATION (CAHSEE)
CAHSEE FELLOWSHIP: YOUNG EDUCATORS PROGRAM
see number 30

COMTO-BOSTON CHAPTER
COMTO BOSTON/GARRETT A. MORGAN SCHOLARSHIP
see number 40

GEM CONSORTIUM
GEM MS ENGINEERING FELLOWSHIP
see number 22

GEM PHD ENGINEERING FELLOWSHIP
see number 23

HISPANIC COLLEGE FUND, INC.
NATIONAL HISPANIC EXPLORERS SCHOLARSHIP PROGRAM
see number 31

HISPANIC ENGINEER NATIONAL ACHIEVEMENT AWARDS CORPORATION (HENAAC)
HISPANIC ENGINEER NATIONAL ACHIEVEMENT AWARDS CORPORATION SCHOLARSHIP PROGRAM
see number 51

HISPANIC SCHOLARSHIP FUND
HSF/GENERAL MOTORS SCHOLARSHIP
see number 83

JORGE MAS CANOSA FREEDOM FOUNDATION
MAS FAMILY SCHOLARSHIP AWARD
see number 85

LOS ANGELES COUNCIL OF BLACK PROFESSIONAL ENGINEERS
AL-BEN SCHOLARSHIP FOR ACADEMIC INCENTIVE
see number 100

AL-BEN SCHOLARSHIP FOR PROFESSIONAL MERIT
see number 101

AL-BEN SCHOLARSHIP FOR SCHOLASTIC ACHIEVEMENT
see number 102

NAMEPA NATIONAL SCHOLARSHIP FOUNDATION

NATIONAL ASSOCIATION OF MINORITY ENGINEERING PROGRAM ADMINISTRATORS NATIONAL SCHOLARSHIP FUND
see number 58

NATIONAL ACTION COUNCIL FOR MINORITIES IN ENGINEERING-NACME, INC.

ENGINEERING VANGUARD PROGRAM
see number 103

SLOAN PHD PROGRAM
see number 104

NEW YORK STATE SOCIETY OF PROFESSIONAL ENGINEERS

NSPE AUXILIARY SCHOLARSHIP
see number 106

NSPE-VIRGINIA D. HENRY MEMORIAL SCHOLARSHIP
see number 107

OFFICE OF NAVAL RESEARCH

HISTORICALLY BLACK COLLEGES AND UNIVERSITIES FUTURE ENGINEERING FACULTY FELLOWSHIP
see number 108

SOCIETY OF HISPANIC PROFESSIONAL ENGINEERS FOUNDATION

SOCIETY OF HISPANIC PROFESSIONAL ENGINEERS FOUNDATION
see number 109

SOCIETY OF MEXICAN AMERICAN ENGINEERS AND SCIENTISTS

GRE AND GRADUATE APPLICATIONS WAIVER
see number 110

SOCIETY OF WOMEN ENGINEERS

BECHTEL CORPORATION SCHOLARSHIP
• 116

Must major in either architectural, civil, electrical, environmental or mechanical engineering. Must be a member of the Society of Women Engineers. Minimum 3.0 GPA required. Open to sophomores, juniors and seniors. Deadline: February 1.

Academic Fields/Career Goals Civil Engineering; Electrical Engineering/Electronics; Engineering/Technology; Mechanical Engineering. *Award* Scholarship for use in sophomore, junior, or senior years; not renewable. *Number:* 2. *Amount:* $1400.

Eligibility Requirements Applicant must be enrolled or expecting to enroll at a four-year institution or university and female. Applicant or parent of applicant must be member of Society of Women Engineers. Applicant must have 3.0 GPA or higher. Available to U.S. citizens.

Application Requirements Application, references, self-addressed stamped envelope, transcript. *Deadline:* February 1.

World Wide Web: http://www.swe.org

Contact: Program Coordinator
Society of Women Engineers
230 East Ohio Street, Suite 400
Chicago, IL 60611-3265
Phone: 312-596-5223
Fax: 312-644-8557
E-mail: hq@swe.org

CHEVRON TEXACO CORPORATION SCHOLARSHIPS
see number 111

COMMUNICATIONS

AMERICAN SPEECH-LANGUAGE-HEARING FOUNDATION

ASHF GRADUATE STUDENT SCHOLARSHIP FOR MINORITY STUDENTS • 117

One award for racial/ethnic minority students who are U.S. citizens. Must be accepted for graduate study in audiology or speech-language pathology. See Web site at http://www.ashfoundation.org for further details. Application deadline is June 13.

Academic Fields/Career Goals Communications; Health and Medical Sciences; Social Services; Therapy/Rehabilitation. *Award* Scholarship for use in graduate, or postgraduate years; not renewable. *Number:* 1. *Amount:* $2000–$4000.

Eligibility Requirements Applicant must be American Indian/Alaska Native, Asian/Pacific Islander, Black (non-Hispanic), or Hispanic and enrolled or expecting to enroll full-time at an institution or university. Available to U.S. citizens.

Application Requirements Application, essay, references, transcript. *Deadline:* June 13.

World Wide Web: http://www.ashfoundation.org

Contact: Ms. Barbara Zvirblis, Program Associate
American Speech-Language-Hearing Foundation
10801 Rockville Pike
Rockville, MD 20853
Phone: 301-897-5700 Ext. 4314
Fax: 301-571-0457
E-mail: foundation@asha.org

KALA SINGH GRADUATE SCHOLARSHIP FOR INTERNATIONAL/MINORITY STUDENTS • 118

One award for a full-time international/minority graduate students who have demonstrated outstanding academic achievement. Must be studying communications sciences and disorders at a U.S. institution. See Web site at http://www.ashfoundation.org for further details. Application deadline is June 13.

Academic Fields/Career Goals Communications; Health and Medical Sciences; Social Services; Therapy/Rehabilitation. *Award* Scholarship for use in graduate years; not renewable. *Number:* 1. *Amount:* $2000–$4000.

Eligibility Requirements Applicant must be enrolled or expecting to enroll full-time at an institution or university. Available to Canadian and non-U.S. citizens.

Application Requirements Application, essay, references, transcript. *Deadline:* June 13.

World Wide Web: http://www.ashfoundation.org

Kala Singh Graduate Scholarship for International/Minority Students (continued)

Contact: Ms. Barbara Zvirblis, Program Associate
American Speech-Language-Hearing Foundation
10801 Rockville Pike
Rockville, MD 20853
Phone: 301-897-5700 Ext. 4314
Fax: 301-571-0457
E-mail: foundation@asha.org

ASIAN AMERICAN JOURNALISTS ASSOCIATION— SEATTLE CHAPTER

NORTHWEST JOURNALISTS OF COLOR SCHOLARSHIP • 119

Award is available to minority students from Washington state who aspire to careers in journalism. Must be undergraduates enrolled in an accredited college or university (not necessarily in Washington state). Minimum 2.5 GPA required.

Academic Fields/Career Goals Communications; Computer Science/Data Processing; Journalism; Photojournalism/Photography; TV/Radio Broadcasting. *Award* Scholarship for use in freshman, sophomore, junior, or senior years; not renewable. *Number:* 1–5. *Amount:* $500–$1000.

Eligibility Requirements Applicant must be American Indian/Alaska Native, Asian/Pacific Islander, Black (non-Hispanic), or Hispanic; enrolled or expecting to enroll full or part-time at a two-year or four-year institution or university and resident of Washington. Applicant must have 2.5 GPA or higher. Available to U.S. citizens.

Application Requirements Application, autobiography, essay, financial need analysis, references, transcript. *Deadline:* May 1.

World Wide Web: http://www.aajaseattle.org

Contact: Lori Matsukawa, Scholarship Coordinator
Asian American Journalists Association—Seattle Chapter
333 Dexter Avenue North
Seattle, WA 98109
Phone: 206-448-3853
Fax: 206-448-4525
E-mail: lmatsukawa@kings.com

CALIFORNIA CHICANO NEWS MEDIA ASSOCIATION (CCNMA)

JOEL GARCIA MEMORIAL SCHOLARSHIP • 120

Scholarships for Latinos interested in pursuing a career in journalism. Awards based on scholastic achievement, financial need, and community awareness. Submit sample of work. Award for California residents or those attending school in California. Deadline is first Friday of April.

Academic Fields/Career Goals Communications; Journalism; Photojournalism/ Photography; TV/Radio Broadcasting. *Award* Scholarship for use in freshman, sophomore, junior, senior, or graduate years; not renewable. *Number:* 10–20. *Amount:* $500–$2000.

Eligibility Requirements Applicant must be of Latin American/Caribbean heritage; Hispanic; enrolled or expecting to enroll full-time at a two-year or four-year institution or university; resident of California and studying in California. Available to U.S. and non-U.S. citizens.

Application Requirements Application, autobiography, essay, financial need analysis, interview, references, transcript, work samples.

World Wide Web: http://www.ccnma.org

Contact: Julio Moran, Executive Director
California Chicano News Media Association (CCNMA)
USC Annenberg School of Journalism
3800 South Figueroa Street
Los Angeles, CA 90037-1206
Phone: 213-743-4960
Fax: 213-743-4989
E-mail: ccnmainfo@ccnma.org

CUBAN AMERICAN NATIONAL FOUNDATION

MAS FAMILY SCHOLARSHIPS   see number 80

DALLAS-FORT WORTH ASSOCIATION OF BLACK COMMUNICATORS

FUTURE JOURNALISTS SCHOLARSHIP PROGRAM   • 121

Scholarships are available to minority high school seniors and college students pursuing careers in broadcast or print journalism, advertising, public relations, photojournalism, and graphic arts and have permanent residence in Dallas, Tarrant, Denton, Hunt, Collin or Ellis county, TX.

Academic Fields/Career Goals Communications; Graphics/Graphic Arts/Printing; Journalism; Photojournalism/Photography; TV/Radio Broadcasting. *Award* Scholarship for use in freshman, sophomore, junior, senior, or graduate years; not renewable. *Number:* 12–15. *Amount:* $500–$1500.

Eligibility Requirements Applicant must be American Indian/Alaska Native, Asian/Pacific Islander, Black (non-Hispanic), or Hispanic; enrolled or expecting to enroll full-time at a four-year institution or university and resident of Texas. Available to U.S. citizens.

Application Requirements Application, autobiography, essay, photo, portfolio, references. *Deadline:* February 1.

Contact: Dallas-Ft. Worth Association of Black Communicators
Dallas-Fort Worth Association of Black Communicators
A.H. Belo Building Lock Box 11
Dallas, TX 75265
E-mail: ayproductn@aol.com

FISHER BROADCASTING COMPANY

FISHER BROADCASTING, INC., SCHOLARSHIP FOR MINORITIES   • 122

Award for minority students enrolled in a broadcast, journalism, or marketing curriculum. For residents of Washington, Oregon, Montana, Idaho and Georgia attending schools in or out-of-state, or for out-of-state students attending institutions in Washington, Oregon, Montana, Idaho, or Georgia. Deadline: April 30.

Academic Fields/Career Goals Communications; Engineering/Technology; Journalism; Photojournalism/Photography; TV/Radio Broadcasting. *Award* Scholarship for use in sophomore, junior, or senior years; not renewable. *Number:* 2–4. *Amount:* $1000–$10,000.

Fisher Broadcasting, Inc., Scholarship for Minorities (continued)

Eligibility Requirements Applicant must be American Indian/Alaska Native, Asian/Pacific Islander, Black (non-Hispanic), or Hispanic and enrolled or expecting to enroll full-time at a two-year or four-year or technical institution or university. Applicant must have 2.5 GPA or higher. Available to U.S. citizens.

Application Requirements Application, essay, financial need analysis, interview, references, transcript. *Deadline:* April 30.

World Wide Web: http://www.fisherbroadcasting.com/

Contact: Laura Boyd, Vice President, Human Resources
Fisher Broadcasting Company
600 University Street
Suite 1525
Seattle, WA 98101-3185
Phone: 206-404-7000
Fax: 206-404-6811
E-mail: laurab@fsci.com

HISPANIC COLLEGE FUND, INC.

DENNY'S/HISPANIC COLLEGE FUND SCHOLARSHIP   see number 12

FIRST IN MY FAMILY SCHOLARSHIP PROGRAM   see number 19

HISPANIC COLLEGE FUND SCHOLARSHIP PROGRAM   see number 20

HISPANIC COLLEGE FUND/INROADS/SPRINT SCHOLARSHIP PROGRAM
     see number 82

NATIONAL HISPANIC EXPLORERS SCHOLARSHIP PROGRAM   see number 31

JORGE MAS CANOSA FREEDOM FOUNDATION

MAS FAMILY SCHOLARSHIP AWARD   see number 85

KATU THOMAS R. DARGAN MINORITY SCHOLARSHIP

THOMAS R. DARGAN MINORITY SCHOLARSHIP   • 123

Up to four awards for minority students who are citizens of the U.S. pursuing broadcast or communications studies. Must be a resident of Oregon or Washington attending an out-of-state institution or be enrolled at a four-year college or university in Oregon or Washington. Minimum 3.0 GPA required. Deadline: April 30.

Academic Fields/Career Goals Communications; TV/Radio Broadcasting. *Award* Scholarship for use in sophomore, junior, or senior years; not renewable. *Number:* 1–4. *Amount:* $4000.

Eligibility Requirements Applicant must be American Indian/Alaska Native, Asian/Pacific Islander, Black (non-Hispanic), or Hispanic and enrolled or expecting to enroll full-time at a four-year institution or university. Applicant must have 3.0 GPA or higher. Available to U.S. citizens.

Application Requirements Application, essay, financial need analysis, interview, references, transcript. *Deadline:* April 30.

World Wide Web: http://www.katu.com

Contact: Rolonda Stoudamire, Human Resources Coordinator
KATU Thomas R. Dargan Minority Scholarship
PO Box 2
Portland, OR 97207-0002
Phone: 503-231-4275
E-mail: rolandas@katu.com

NATIONAL ASSOCIATION OF HISPANIC JOURNALISTS (NAHJ)

NATIONAL ASSOCIATION OF HISPANIC JOURNALISTS SCHOLARSHIP • 124

One-time award for high school seniors, college undergraduates, and first-year graduate students who are pursuing careers in English- or Spanish-language print, photo, broadcast, or online journalism. Students may major or plan to major in any subject, but must demonstrate a sincere desire to pursue a career in journalism. Must submit resume and work samples. Applications must be postmarked on or before the final Friday in January of each year. Applications available only on Web site: http://www.nahj.org.

Academic Fields/Career Goals Communications; Journalism; Photojournalism/Photography; TV/Radio Broadcasting. *Award* Scholarship for use in freshman, sophomore, junior, senior, or graduate years; not renewable. *Number:* 20. *Amount:* $1000–$2000.

Eligibility Requirements Applicant must be enrolled or expecting to enroll full-time at a two-year or four-year institution or university and must have an interest in photography/photogrammetry/filmmaking or writing. Available to U.S. citizens.

Application Requirements Application, essay, financial need analysis, resume, references, transcript, work samples.

World Wide Web: http://www.nahj.org

Contact: Kevin Olivas, Educational Programs Manager
National Association of Hispanic Journalists (NAHJ)
529 14th Street, NW
Suite 1000
Washington, DC 20045-2001
Phone: 202-662-7145
Fax: 202-662-7144
E-mail: nahj@nahj.org

NATIONAL RESEARCH COUNCIL

FORD FOUNDATION DISSERTATION FELLOWSHIPS FOR MINORITIES • 125

Forty dissertation completion fellowships for the final year of dissertation writing. Intended for underrepresented minorities in research-based fields of study. Must be U.S. citizen of the following: Native-Americans, Alaskan Native, Native Pacific Islander, African-American, Mexican-American or Puerto Rican. Further information and application available at Web site http://www.nationalacademies.org.

Academic Fields/Career Goals Communications; Engineering-Related Technologies; Foreign Language; History; Literature/English/Writing; Physical Sciences and Math; Political Science; Religion/Theology; Social Sciences. *Award* Fellowship for use in graduate years; not renewable. *Number:* 40. *Amount:* $24,000.

Eligibility Requirements Applicant must be American Indian/Alaska Native, Asian/Pacific Islander, Black (non-Hispanic), or Hispanic and enrolled or expecting to enroll full-time at an institution or university. Available to U.S. citizens.

Ford Foundation Dissertation Fellowships for Minorities (continued)

Application Requirements Application, essay, resume, references, transcript. *Deadline:* December 3.

World Wide Web: http://www.nationalacademies.org/fellowships/

Contact: Fellowship Office
National Research Council
Fellowship Office, GR 346A
500 Fifth Street NW
Washington, DC 20001
Phone: 202-334-2872
E-mail: infofell@nas.edu

FORD FOUNDATION POSTDOCTORAL FELLOWSHIP FOR MINORITIES • 126

One-year fellowship for PhD/ScD recipients to help his/her academic career. Intended for underrepresented minorities in research-based fields of study. Stipend of $35,000 and $7500 in travel and research allowances. Must be U.S. citizen and one of the following: Native-Americans, Alaskan Native, African-American, Native Pacific Islander, Mexican-American or Puerto Rican. Further information and application available at Web site http://www.nationalacademies.org.

Academic Fields/Career Goals Communications; Engineering-Related Technologies; Foreign Language; History; Literature/English/Writing; Physical Sciences and Math; Political Science; Religion/Theology; Social Sciences. *Award* Fellowship for use in postgraduate years; not renewable. *Number:* 30. *Amount:* $35,000.

Eligibility Requirements Applicant must be American Indian/Alaska Native, Asian/Pacific Islander, Black (non-Hispanic), or Hispanic and enrolled or expecting to enroll full-time at an institution or university. Available to U.S. citizens.

Application Requirements Application, essay, resume, references, transcript. *Deadline:* January 7.

World Wide Web: http://www.nationalacademies.org/fellowships/

Contact: Fellowship Office
National Research Council
Fellowship Office, GR 346A
500 Fifth Street NW
Washington, DC 20001
Phone: 202-334-2872
E-mail: infofell@nas.edu

FORD FOUNDATION PRE-DOCTORAL FELLOWSHIPS FOR MINORITIES • 127

Sixty renewable awards to individuals near the beginning of graduate work toward a PhD or ScD in research-based fields of study. Intended for underrepresented minority groups. Must be U.S. citizen and one of the following: Native-Americans, Native Alaskan, Native Pacific Islander, African-American, Mexican-American or Puerto Rican. Deadline is November 19. Further information and application available at Web site http://www.nationalacademies.org.

Academic Fields/Career Goals Communications; Computer Science/Data Processing; Engineering-Related Technologies; Foreign Language; History; Literature/English/Writing; Physical Sciences and Math; Political Science; Religion/Theology; Social Sciences. *Award* Fellowship for use in graduate years; renewable. *Number:* 60. *Amount:* $16,000.

Eligibility Requirements Applicant must be American Indian/Alaska Native, Asian/Pacific Islander, Black (non-Hispanic), or Hispanic and enrolled or expecting to enroll full-time at an institution or university. Available to U.S. citizens.

Application Requirements Application, essay, resume, references, test scores, transcript. *Deadline:* November 19.

World Wide Web: http://www.nationalacademies.org/fellowships/

Contact: Fellowship Office
National Research Council
Fellowship Office, GR 346A
500 Fifth Street NW
Washington, DC 20001
Phone: 202-334-2872
E-mail: infofell@nas.edu

PUBLIC RELATIONS STUDENT SOCIETY OF AMERICA

MULTICULTURAL AFFAIRS SCHOLARSHIP   • 128

One-time award for members of principal minority group who are in their junior or senior year at an accredited four-year college or university. Must have at least a 3.0 GPA and be preparing for career in public relations or communications. Two scholarships at $1500 each. Must be a full-time student and U.S. citizen. Application deadline is April 12.

Academic Fields/Career Goals Communications. *Award* Scholarship for use in junior or senior years; not renewable. *Number:* 2. *Amount:* $1500.

Eligibility Requirements Applicant must be American Indian/Alaska Native, Asian/Pacific Islander, Black (non-Hispanic), or Hispanic and enrolled or expecting to enroll full-time at a four-year institution or university. Applicant must have 3.0 GPA or higher. Available to U.S. citizens.

Application Requirements Application, essay, financial need analysis, references, transcript. *Deadline:* April 12.

World Wide Web: http://www.prssa.org

Contact: Jeneen Garcia, Program Coordinator
Public Relations Student Society of America
33 Irving Place
New York, NY 10003-2376
Phone: 212-460-1474
Fax: 212-995-0757
E-mail: prssa@prsa.org

RADIO-TELEVISION NEWS DIRECTORS ASSOCIATION AND FOUNDATION

CAROLE SIMPSON SCHOLARSHIP   • 129

Award for minority sophomore, junior, or senior undergraduate student enrolled in an electronic journalism program. Submit one to three examples of reporting or producing skills on audiocassette tape or videotape, totaling 15 minutes or less, with scripts. One-time award of $2000.

Academic Fields/Career Goals Communications; Journalism; TV/Radio Broadcasting. *Award* Scholarship for use in sophomore, junior, senior, or graduate years; not renewable. *Number:* 1. *Amount:* $2000.

Eligibility Requirements Applicant must be American Indian/Alaska Native, Asian/Pacific Islander, Black (non-Hispanic), or Hispanic; enrolled or expecting to enroll full-time at a four-year institution or university and must have an interest in photography/photogrammetry/ filmmaking or writing. Available to U.S. and non-U.S. citizens.

Carole Simpson Scholarship (continued)

Application Requirements Application, essay, resume, references, video or audio tape of work. *Deadline:* May 5.

World Wide Web: http://www.rtndf.org

Contact: Karen Jackson-Buillitt, Project Coordinator
Radio-Television News Directors Association and Foundation
1600 K Street, NW, Suite 700
Washington, DC 20006
Phone: 202-467-5218
Fax: 202-223-4007
E-mail: karenb@rtndf.org

ED BRADLEY SCHOLARSHIP • 130

One-time award for minority sophomore, junior, or senior undergraduate student enrolled in an electronic journalism program. Submit one to three examples of reporting or producing skills on audiocassette tape or videotape, totaling 15 minutes or less, with scripts.

Academic Fields/Career Goals Communications; Journalism; TV/Radio Broadcasting. *Award* Scholarship for use in sophomore, junior, senior, or graduate years; not renewable. *Number:* 1. *Amount:* $10,000.

Eligibility Requirements Applicant must be American Indian/Alaska Native, Asian/Pacific Islander, Black (non-Hispanic), or Hispanic and enrolled or expecting to enroll full-time at a four-year institution or university. Available to U.S. and non-U.S. citizens.

Application Requirements Application, essay, resume, references, video or audio tape of work. *Deadline:* May 5.

World Wide Web: http://www.rtndf.org

Contact: Awards and Events Assistant
Radio-Television News Directors Association and Foundation
1600 K Street, NW, Suite 700
Washington, DC 20006
Phone: 202-467-5218
Fax: 202-223-4007

KEN KASHIWAHARA SCHOLARSHIP • 131

One-time award of $2500 for minority sophomore, junior, or senior whose career objective is electronic journalism. Submit one to three examples showing reporting or producing skills on audiocassette or VHS, with scripts. Deadline: May 5.

Academic Fields/Career Goals Communications; Journalism; TV/Radio Broadcasting. *Award* Scholarship for use in sophomore, junior, senior, or graduate years; not renewable. *Number:* 1. *Amount:* $2500.

Eligibility Requirements Applicant must be American Indian/Alaska Native, Asian/Pacific Islander, Black (non-Hispanic), or Hispanic and enrolled or expecting to enroll full-time at a four-year institution or university. Available to U.S. and non-U.S. citizens.

Application Requirements Application, essay, resume, references, video or audio tape of work. *Deadline:* May 5.

World Wide Web: http://www.rtndf.org

Contact: Awards and Events Assistant
Radio-Television News Directors Association and Foundation
1600 K Street, NW, Suite 700
Washington, DC 20006
Phone: 202-467-5218
Fax: 202-223-4007

MICHELE CLARK FELLOWSHIP • 132

One-time $1000 award for young, promising minority professionals in television or radio news with ten years or less experience. Must submit script and audiocassette or videotape, not to exceed 15 minutes. Deadline: May 5.

Academic Fields/Career Goals Communications; Journalism; TV/Radio Broadcasting. *Award* Fellowship for use in graduate years; not renewable. *Number:* 1. *Amount:* $1000.

Eligibility Requirements Applicant must be American Indian/Alaska Native, Asian/Pacific Islander, Black (non-Hispanic), or Hispanic and enrolled or expecting to enroll full-time at an institution or university. Applicant or parent of applicant must have employment or volunteer experience in designated career field or journalism.

Application Requirements Application, references. *Deadline:* May 5.

World Wide Web: http://www.rtndf.org

Contact: Awards and Events Assistant
Radio-Television News Directors Association and Foundation
1600 K Street, NW, Suite 700
Washington, DC 20006
Phone: 202-467-5218

MIKE REYNOLDS $1,000 SCHOLARSHIP • 133

Preference given to minority undergraduate student demonstrating need for financial assistance. Must include on resume jobs held related to media. Applicant must explain contribution he or she has made toward funding own education.

Academic Fields/Career Goals Communications; Journalism; TV/Radio Broadcasting. *Award* Scholarship for use in sophomore, junior, senior, or graduate years; not renewable. *Number:* 1. *Amount:* $1000.

Eligibility Requirements Applicant must be American Indian/Alaska Native, Asian/Pacific Islander, Black (non-Hispanic), or Hispanic and enrolled or expecting to enroll full-time at a four-year institution or university. Available to U.S. and non-U.S. citizens.

Application Requirements Application, essay, financial need analysis, resume, references, video or audio tape of work. *Deadline:* May 5.

World Wide Web: http://www.rtndf.org

Contact: Awards and Events Assistant
Radio-Television News Directors Association and Foundation
1600 K Street, NW, Suite 700
Washington, DC 20006
Phone: 202-467-5218
Fax: 202-223-4007

N.S. BIENSTOCK FELLOWSHIP • 134

One-time $2500 award for promising minority journalist in radio or television news management. Deadline: May 5.

Academic Fields/Career Goals Communications; Journalism; TV/Radio Broadcasting. *Award* Fellowship for use in freshman, sophomore, junior, senior, or graduate years; not renewable. *Number:* 1. *Amount:* $2500.

Eligibility Requirements Applicant must be American Indian/Alaska Native, Asian/Pacific Islander, Black (non-Hispanic), or Hispanic and enrolled or expecting to enroll at a four-year institution or university.

Application Requirements Application, references, video or audio of work. *Deadline:* May 5.

World Wide Web: http://www.rtndf.org

N.S. Bienstock Fellowship (continued)

Contact: Awards and Events Assistant
Radio-Television News Directors Association and Foundation
1600 K Street, NW, Suite 700
Washington, DC 20006
Phone: 202-467-5218
Fax: 202-223-4007

RHODE ISLAND FOUNDATION

RDW GROUP, INC. MINORITY SCHOLARSHIP FOR COMMUNICATIONS • 135

One-time award to provide support to minority students who wish to pursue a course of study in communications at the undergraduate or graduate level. Must be a Rhode Island resident.

Academic Fields/Career Goals Communications. *Award* Scholarship for use in freshman, sophomore, junior, senior, or graduate years; not renewable. *Number:* 1. *Amount:* $2000.

Eligibility Requirements Applicant must be American Indian/Alaska Native, Asian/Pacific Islander, Black (non-Hispanic), or Hispanic; enrolled or expecting to enroll at an institution or university and resident of Rhode Island.

Application Requirements Application, essay, self-addressed stamped envelope, transcript. *Deadline:* June 13.

World Wide Web: http://www.rifoundation.org

Contact: Libby Monahan, Scholarship Coordinator
Rhode Island Foundation
One Union Station
Providence, RI 02903
Phone: 401-274-4564
Fax: 401-272-1359
E-mail: libbym@rifoundation.org

SOCIETY OF PROFESSIONAL JOURNALISTS-SOUTH FLORIDA CHAPTER

GARTH REEVES, JR. MEMORIAL SCHOLARSHIPS • 136

Scholarships for senior high school students, undergraduate, and graduate minority students preparing for a news career. Must be a South Florida resident. Amount is determined by need; minimum award is $500. One-time award, renewable upon application. Application deadline April 1. Academic performance and quality of work for student or professional news media is considered. For additional information and application go to Web site: http://www.netrox.net/~dali/spj/contest.htm.

Academic Fields/Career Goals Communications; Journalism. *Award* Scholarship for use in freshman, sophomore, junior, senior, or graduate years; not renewable. *Number:* 1–3. *Amount:* $500–$1000.

Eligibility Requirements Applicant must be American Indian/Alaska Native, Asian/Pacific Islander, Black (non-Hispanic), or Hispanic; enrolled or expecting to enroll full or part-time at a two-year or four-year institution; resident of Florida and must have an interest in designated field specified by sponsor. Available to U.S. citizens.

Application Requirements Application, financial need analysis, references, self-addressed stamped envelope, transcript, examples of applicant's journalism. *Deadline:* April 1.

World Wide Web: http://www.netrox.net/~dali/spj-news.htm

Contact: Oline Cogdill, Chair, Scholarship Committee
Society of Professional Journalists-South Florida Chapter
200 East Las Olas Boulevard
Ft. Lauderdale, FL 33301
Phone: 954-356-4513
Fax: 954-356-4559
E-mail: ocogdill@sun-sentinel.com

UNITED METHODIST COMMUNICATIONS

JUDITH L. WEIDMAN RACIAL ETHNICITY MINORITY FELLOWSHIP • 137

$30,000 fellowship is available to a United Methodist of racial ethnic minority heritage who is a recent college or seminary graduate who has broad communication training including an understanding of effective public relations.

Academic Fields/Career Goals Communications; Journalism; Photojournalism/Photography; Religion/Theology; TV/Radio Broadcasting. *Award* Fellowship for use in graduate years; not renewable. *Amount:* $30,000.

Eligibility Requirements Applicant must be American Indian/Alaska Native, Asian/Pacific Islander, Black (non-Hispanic), or Hispanic and enrolled or expecting to enroll full-time at an institution or university. Available to U.S. and non-U.S. citizens.

Application Requirements Application, essay, photo, references, transcript. *Deadline:* March 17.

World Wide Web: http://www.umcom.org/scholarships

Contact: REM Fellowship Committee, c/o UMCom/Communications
United Methodist Communications
Resourcing Team, PO Box 320
Nashville, TN 37202-0320
Phone: 888-CRT-4UMC
E-mail: REM@umcom.org

LEONARD M. PERRYMAN COMMUNICATIONS SCHOLARSHIP FOR ETHNIC MINORITY STUDENTS • 138

One-time award to assist ethnic minority students who are college juniors or seniors intending to pursue careers in religious communications. Submit examples of work. Contact for complete information.

Academic Fields/Career Goals Communications; Journalism; Photojournalism/Photography; Religion/Theology; TV/Radio Broadcasting. *Award* Scholarship for use in junior or senior years; not renewable. *Number:* 2. *Amount:* $2500.

Eligibility Requirements Applicant must be American Indian/Alaska Native, Asian/Pacific Islander, Black (non-Hispanic), or Hispanic and enrolled or expecting to enroll full-time at a four-year institution or university. Available to U.S. and non-U.S. citizens.

Application Requirements Application, essay, photo, references, transcript. *Deadline:* March 7.

World Wide Web: http://www.umcom.org/scholarships

Contact: Ms. Amelia Tucker-Shaw, Administrator
United Methodist Communications
810 12th Avenue, South
Nashville, TN 37202-4744
Phone: 888-278-4862
E-mail: atucker-shaw@umcom.org

UNITED NEGRO COLLEGE FUND

COLLEGE FUND/COCA COLA CORPORATE INTERN PROGRAM
see number 92

WOMEN'S BASKETBALL COACHES ASSOCIATION

ROBIN ROBERTS/WBCA SPORTS COMMUNICATIONS SCHOLARSHIP
AWARD
• 139

One-time award for female student athletes who have completed their eligibility and plan to go to graduate school. Must major in communications. Must be nominated by the head coach of women's basketball who is a member of the WBCA.

Academic Fields/Career Goals Communications. *Award* Scholarship for use in graduate, or postgraduate years; not renewable. *Number:* 1. *Amount:* $2000.

Eligibility Requirements Applicant must be enrolled or expecting to enroll full or part-time at a four-year institution or university; female and must have an interest in athletics/sports. Available to U.S. and non-U.S. citizens.

Application Requirements Application, references, statistics. *Deadline:* February 7.

World Wide Web: http://www.wbca.org

Contact: Kristen Miller, Manager of Office Administration and Awards
Women's Basketball Coaches Association
4646 Lawrenceville Highway
Lilburn, GA 30247-3620
Phone: 770-279-8027 Ext. 102
Fax: 770-279-6290
E-mail: kmiller@wbca.org

COMPUTER SCIENCE/DATA PROCESSING

AMERICAN ASSOCIATION OF UNIVERSITY WOMEN (AAUW) EDUCATIONAL FOUNDATION

AAUW EDUCATIONAL FOUNDATION SELECTED PROFESSIONS FELLOWSHIPS
see number 36

ARMED FORCES COMMUNICATIONS AND ELECTRONICS ASSOCIATION, EDUCATIONAL FOUNDATION

ARMED FORCES COMMUNICATIONS AND ELECTRONICS ASSOCIATION RALPH W. SHRADER SCHOLARSHIPS
• 140

One-time awards for students working towards master's degrees in electrical, electronic, or communications engineering; physics; math; computer science; or information management at an accredited college or university in the United States. Provided eligibility criteria are met, at least one scholarship will be awarded to a woman or minority student. Must be U.S. citizen.

Academic Fields/Career Goals Computer Science/Data Processing; Electrical Engineering/Electronics; Engineering/Technology; Physical Sciences and Math. *Award* Scholarship for use in graduate years; not renewable. *Amount:* $3000.

Eligibility Requirements Applicant must be enrolled or expecting to enroll full-time at an institution or university. Available to U.S. citizens.
Application Requirements Application, references, transcript. *Deadline:* February 1.
World Wide Web: http://www.afcea.org
Contact: Armed Forces Communications and Electronics Association, Educational
  Foundation
  4400 Fair Lakes Court
  Fairfax, VA 22033-3899
  E-mail: scholarship@afcea.org

ASIAN AMERICAN JOURNALISTS ASSOCIATION— SEATTLE CHAPTER

NORTHWEST JOURNALISTS OF COLOR SCHOLARSHIP   see number 119

ASSOCIATION FOR WOMEN IN SCIENCE EDUCATIONAL FOUNDATION

ASSOCIATION FOR WOMEN IN SCIENCE PRE-DOCTORAL FELLOWSHIP
                                                    see number 32

ASSOCIATION FOR WOMEN IN SCIENCE UNDERGRADUATE AWARD   see number 26

BUSINESS AND PROFESSIONAL WOMEN'S FOUNDATION

BPW CAREER ADVANCEMENT SCHOLARSHIP PROGRAM FOR WOMEN
                                                    see number 68

CANADIAN FEDERATION OF UNIVERSITY WOMEN

CANADIAN FEDERATION OF UNIVERSITY WOMEN MEMORIAL FELLOWSHIP
                                                    see number 21

CENTER FOR THE ADVANCEMENT OF HISPANICS IN SCIENCE AND ENGINEERING EDUCATION (CAHSEE)

CAHSEE FELLOWSHIP: YOUNG EDUCATORS PROGRAM   see number 30

EAST LOS ANGELES COMMUNITY UNION (TELACU) EDUCATION FOUNDATION

TELACU ENGINEERING AWARD   see number 99

EATON CORPORATION

EATON CORPORATION MULTICULTURAL SCHOLARS PROGRAM   • 141
Renewable award of up to $3000. Award for minorities who are full-time students in freshman or sophomore year at a four-year college or university. Applicant must be studying computer science, electrical/mechanical engineering or related engineering field. Minimum 3.0 GPA required.

Eaton Corporation Multicultural Scholars Program (continued)

Academic Fields/Career Goals Computer Science/Data Processing; Electrical Engineering/ Electronics; Engineering/Technology; Engineering-Related Technologies; Mechanical Engineering. *Award* Scholarship for use in freshman or sophomore years; renewable. *Number:* up to 50. *Amount:* $500–$3000.

Eligibility Requirements Applicant must be American Indian/Alaska Native, Asian/Pacific Islander, Black (non-Hispanic), or Hispanic and enrolled or expecting to enroll at an institution or university. Applicant must have 3.0 GPA or higher.

Application Requirements Application, essay, financial need analysis, interview, test scores. *Deadline:* December 31.

World Wide Web: http://www.eaton.com

Contact: Mildred Neumann, Scholarship Coordinator
Eaton Corporation
Eaton Center
1111 Superior Avenue
Cleveland, OH 44114
Phone: 216-523-4354
Fax: 216-479-7354
E-mail: mildredneumann@eaton.com

GEM CONSORTIUM

GEM MS ENGINEERING FELLOWSHIP	see number 22
GEM PHD ENGINEERING FELLOWSHIP	see number 23

HISPANIC COLLEGE FUND, INC.

ALLFIRST/ HISPANIC COLLEGE FUND SCHOLARSHIP PROGRAM	see number 10
DENNY'S/HISPANIC COLLEGE FUND SCHOLARSHIP	see number 12
FIRST IN MY FAMILY SCHOLARSHIP PROGRAM	see number 19
HISPANIC COLLEGE FUND SCHOLARSHIP PROGRAM	see number 20
HISPANIC COLLEGE FUND/INROADS/SPRINT SCHOLARSHIP PROGRAM	see number 82
NATIONAL HISPANIC EXPLORERS SCHOLARSHIP PROGRAM	see number 31

HISPANIC ENGINEER NATIONAL ACHIEVEMENT AWARDS CORPORATION (HENAAC)

HISPANIC ENGINEER NATIONAL ACHIEVEMENT AWARDS CORPORATION SCHOLARSHIP PROGRAM	see number 51

IMGIP/ICEOP

ILLINOIS MINORITY GRADUATE INCENTIVE PROGRAM FELLOWSHIP • 142

Purpose is to increase the number of underrepresented faculty and professional staff at Illinois institutions of higher education and higher education governing boards. Minimum GPA of

2.75 in the last sixty hours of undergraduate work or over a 3.2 in at least 9 hours of graduate study. Award restricted to applicants studying one or more of the following: electrical engineering/electronics, engineering/technology, engineering-related technologies, physical sciences and math, or science, technology and society.

Academic Fields/Career Goals Computer Science/Data Processing; Electrical Engineering/ Electronics; Engineering/Technology; Engineering-Related Technologies; Physical Sciences and Math; Science, Technology and Society. *Award* Grant for use in graduate years; renewable. *Number:* 30. *Amount:* $17,500.

Eligibility Requirements Applicant must be American Indian/Alaska Native, Black (non-Hispanic), or Hispanic; enrolled or expecting to enroll full-time at an institution or university and studying in Illinois. Available to U.S. citizens.

Application Requirements Application, essay, references, test scores, transcript. *Deadline:* February 15.

World Wide Web: http://www.imgip.siu.edu

Contact: Ms. Jane Meuth, IMGIP/ICEOP Administrator
IMGIP/ICEOP
Woody Hall C-224, Southern Illinois University
Carbondale, IL 62901-4723
Phone: 618-453-4558
Fax: 618-453-1800
E-mail: fellows@siu.edu

LOS ANGELES COUNCIL OF BLACK PROFESSIONAL ENGINEERS

AL-BEN SCHOLARSHIP FOR ACADEMIC INCENTIVE see number 100

AL-BEN SCHOLARSHIP FOR PROFESSIONAL MERIT see number 101

AL-BEN SCHOLARSHIP FOR SCHOLASTIC ACHIEVEMENT see number 102

NAMEPA NATIONAL SCHOLARSHIP FOUNDATION

NATIONAL ASSOCIATION OF MINORITY ENGINEERING PROGRAM ADMINISTRATORS NATIONAL SCHOLARSHIP FUND see number 58

NATIONAL ACTION COUNCIL FOR MINORITIES IN ENGINEERING-NACME, INC.

ENGINEERING VANGUARD PROGRAM see number 103

SLOAN PHD PROGRAM see number 104

NATIONAL PHYSICAL SCIENCE CONSORTIUM

NATIONAL PHYSICAL SCIENCE CONSORTIUM GRADUATE FELLOWSHIPS IN THE PHYSICAL SCIENCES see number 105

NATIONAL RESEARCH COUNCIL

FORD FOUNDATION PRE-DOCTORAL FELLOWSHIPS FOR MINORITIES
see number 127

OREGON STUDENT ASSISTANCE COMMISSION

MENTOR GRAPHICS SCHOLARSHIP • 143

One-time award for computer science, computer engineering, or electrical engineering majors entering junior or senior year at a four-year institution. Preference for one award to female, African-American, Native-Americans, or Hispanic applicant.

Academic Fields/Career Goals Computer Science/Data Processing; Electrical Engineering/ Electronics. *Award* Scholarship for use in junior or senior years; not renewable. *Number:* 4. *Amount:* $2000.

Eligibility Requirements Applicant must be enrolled or expecting to enroll at a four-year institution and resident of Oregon. Available to U.S. citizens.

Application Requirements Application, essay, financial need analysis, references, transcript, activity chart. *Deadline:* March 1.

World Wide Web: http://www.osac.state.or.us

Contact: Director of Grant Programs
Oregon Student Assistance Commission
1500 Valley River Drive, Suite 100
Eugene, OR 97401-7020
Phone: 800-452-8807 Ext. 7395
E-mail: awardinfo@mercury.osac.state.or.us

SOCIETY OF WOMEN ENGINEERS

COMPAQ COMPUTER SCHOLARSHIP • 144

Scholarship awarded to an incoming female freshman with plans of majoring in engineering or computer science. Deadline: May 15. Minimum 3.5 GPA required.

Academic Fields/Career Goals Computer Science/Data Processing; Engineering/ Technology; Engineering-Related Technologies. *Award* Scholarship for use in freshman year; not renewable. *Number:* 1. *Amount:* $1825.

Eligibility Requirements Applicant must be high school student; planning to enroll or expecting to enroll full-time at an institution or university and female. Applicant must have 3.5 GPA or higher.

Application Requirements Application, essay, references, self-addressed stamped envelope, test scores, transcript. *Deadline:* May 15.

World Wide Web: http://www.swe.org

Contact: Program Coordinator
Society of Women Engineers
230 East Ohio Street, Suite 400
Chicago, IL 60611-3265
Phone: 312-596-5223
Fax: 312-644-8557
E-mail: hq@swe.org

DAVID SARNOFF RESEARCH CENTER SCHOLARSHIP • 145

One-time award for female engineering or computer science major. Must be in junior year and have a minimum 3.5 GPA. Deadline: February 1.

Academic Fields/Career Goals Computer Science/Data Processing; Engineering/ Technology. *Award* Scholarship for use in junior year; not renewable. *Number:* 1. *Amount:* $1500.

Eligibility Requirements Applicant must be enrolled or expecting to enroll at a four-year institution or university and female. Applicant must have 3.5 GPA or higher. Available to U.S. citizens.

Application Requirements Application, references, self-addressed stamped envelope, transcript. *Deadline:* February 1.

World Wide Web: http://www.swe.org

Contact: Program Coordinator
Society of Women Engineers
230 East Ohio Street, Suite 400
Chicago, IL 60611-3265
Phone: 312-596-5223
Fax: 312-644-8557
E-mail: hq@swe.org

DELL COMPUTER CORPORATION SCHOLARSHIPS • 146

Awarded to entering female juniors and seniors majoring in computer science, computer engineering, electrical engineering or mechanical engineering who demonstrate financial need and maintain a minimum 3.0 GPA. Deadline: February 1.

Academic Fields/Career Goals Computer Science/Data Processing; Electrical Engineering/ Electronics; Engineering/Technology; Mechanical Engineering. *Award* Scholarship for use in junior or senior years; not renewable. *Number:* 4. *Amount:* $2000.

Eligibility Requirements Applicant must be enrolled or expecting to enroll at a four-year institution or university and female. Applicant must have 3.0 GPA or higher. Available to U.S. and non-U.S. citizens.

Application Requirements Application, essay, financial need analysis, references, self-addressed stamped envelope, test scores, transcript. *Deadline:* February 1.

World Wide Web: http://www.swe.org

Contact: *le;1Program Coordinator*
Society of Women Engineers
230 East Ohio Street, Suite 400
Chicago, IL 60611-3265
Phone: 312-596-5223
Fax: 312-644-8557
E-mail: hq@swe.org

LYDIA I. PICKUP MEMORIAL SCHOLARSHIP • 147

Available to female student entering the first year of a master's degree program. For graduate education to advance applicant's career in engineering or computer science. Minimum 3.0 GPA required. Deadline: February 1.

Academic Fields/Career Goals Computer Science/Data Processing; Engineering/Technology. *Award* Scholarship for use in graduate years; not renewable. *Number:* 1. *Amount:* $2000.

Eligibility Requirements Applicant must be enrolled or expecting to enroll at an institution or university and female. Applicant must have 3.0 GPA or higher. Available to U.S. citizens.

Application Requirements Application, references, self-addressed stamped envelope, transcript. *Deadline:* February 1.

World Wide Web: http://www.swe.org

Contact: Program Coordinator
Society of Women Engineers
230 East Ohio Street, Suite 400
Chicago, IL 60611-3265
Phone: 312-596-5223
Fax: 312-644-8557
E-mail: hq@swe.org

MICROSOFT CORPORATION SCHOLARSHIPS • 148

Scholarships for female computer engineering or computer science students in sophomore, junior, senior year, or first year master's degree students. Must exhibit career interest in the field of computer software. Minimum 3.5 GPA required. Deadline: February 1.

Academic Fields/Career Goals Computer Science/Data Processing. *Award* Scholarship for use in sophomore, junior, senior, or graduate years; renewable. *Number:* 2. *Amount:* $2500.

Eligibility Requirements Applicant must be enrolled or expecting to enroll at a four-year institution or university and female. Applicant must have 3.5 GPA or higher.

Application Requirements Application, essay, references, self-addressed stamped envelope, test scores, transcript. *Deadline:* February 1.

World Wide Web: http://www.swe.org

Contact: Program Coordinator
Society of Women Engineers
230 East Ohio Street, Suite 400
Chicago, IL 60611-3265
Phone: 312-596-5223
Fax: 312-644-8557
E-mail: hq@swe.org

SOCIETY OF WOMEN ENGINEERS-ROCKY MOUNTAIN SECTION

SOCIETY OF WOMEN ENGINEERS-ROCKY MOUNTAIN SECTION SCHOLARSHIP PROGRAM • 149

One-time award for female high school seniors in Colorado and Wyoming who intend to enroll in engineering or computer science at an ABET-accredited college or university in those states. Female college students who have already completed at least 3 semesters or 4 quarters of study in those programs may also apply. For more information visit http://www.swe.org and look for local scholarships.

Academic Fields/Career Goals Computer Science/Data Processing; Engineering/Technology. *Award* Scholarship for use in freshman, junior, senior, or graduate years; not renewable. *Number:* 3–5. *Amount:* $500–$1000.

Eligibility Requirements Applicant must be enrolled or expecting to enroll full-time at a four-year institution or university; female; resident of Colorado or Wyoming and studying in Colorado or Wyoming. Applicant must have 3.5 GPA or higher. Available to U.S. and non-U.S. citizens.

Application Requirements Application, essay, resume, references, test scores, transcript. *Deadline:* March 1.

World Wide Web: http://www.swe.org

Contact: Barbara Kontogiannis, Scholarship Chair
Society of Women Engineers-Rocky Mountain Section
Attn: Scholarship Committee Chair
PO Box 260692
Lakewood, CO 80226-0692
Phone: 303-971-5213
E-mail: barbekon@stanfordalumni.org

UNITED DAUGHTERS OF THE CONFEDERACY

WALTER REED SMITH SCHOLARSHIP see number 91

UNITED NEGRO COLLEGE FUND

COLLEGE FUND/COCA COLA CORPORATE INTERN PROGRAM	see number 92
HOUSEHOLD INTERNATIONAL CORPORATE SCHOLARS	see number 93

VIRGINIA BUSINESS AND PROFESSIONAL WOMEN'S FOUNDATION

WOMEN IN SCIENCE AND TECHNOLOGY SCHOLARSHIP	see number 74

XEROX

TECHNICAL MINORITY SCHOLARSHIP	see number 115

CRIMINAL JUSTICE/CRIMINOLOGY_____

AMERICAN CORRECTIONAL ASSOCIATION

MARTIN LUTHER KING, JR. SCHOLARSHIP AWARD • 150

One-time award given to a minority who is a full-time student pursuing a degree in criminal justice. Applicants must submit an essay along with their application and transcript.

Academic Fields/Career Goals Criminal Justice/Criminology. *Award* Scholarship for use in freshman, sophomore, junior, senior, graduate, or postgraduate years; not renewable. *Number:* 1. *Amount:* $1000.

Eligibility Requirements Applicant must be American Indian/Alaska Native, Asian/Pacific Islander, Black (non-Hispanic), or Hispanic and enrolled or expecting to enroll full-time at a four-year institution or university. Available to U.S. and non-U.S. citizens.

Application Requirements Application, essay, financial need analysis, resume, transcript. *Deadline:* June 1.

World Wide Web: http://www.aca.org

Contact: Debbi Seeger, Administrative Manager
American Correctional Association
4380 Forbes Boulevard
Lanham, MD 20706-4322
Phone: 301-918-1800
Fax: 301-918-1900
E-mail: debbis@aca.org

DENTAL HEALTH/SERVICES_____

AMERICAN DENTAL ASSOCIATION (ADA) FOUNDATION

AMERICAN DENTAL ASSOCIATION FOUNDATION MINORITY DENTAL STUDENT SCHOLARSHIP PROGRAM • 151

For second year students of a minority group that are underrepresented in dental school enrollment. Based on financial need and academic achievement. Must be U.S. citizen and

American Dental Association Foundation Minority Dental Student Scholarship Program (continued)

full-time-student, minimum twelve hours. Must have minimum 3.0 GPA on a 4.0 scale. Applicant must be enrolled in a dental school accredited by the Commission on Dental Accreditation.

Academic Fields/Career Goals Dental Health/Services. *Award* Scholarship for use in graduate years; not renewable. *Number:* 25. *Amount:* $2500.

Eligibility Requirements Applicant must be American Indian/Alaska Native, Black (non-Hispanic), or Hispanic and enrolled or expecting to enroll full-time at a four-year institution or university. Applicant must have 3.0 GPA or higher. Available to U.S. citizens.

Application Requirements Application, autobiography, essay, financial need analysis, references. *Deadline:* July 31.

World Wide Web: http://www.adafoundation.org

Contact: Marsha L. Mountz
American Dental Association (ADA) Foundation
211 East Chicago Avenue, Suite 820
Chicago, IL 60611

AMERICAN DENTAL HYGIENISTS' ASSOCIATION (ADHA) INSTITUTE

AMERICAN DENTAL HYGIENISTS' ASSOCIATION INSTITUTE MINORITY SCHOLARSHIP • 152

Nonrenewable awards for member of minority groups currently underrepresented in dental hygiene, including males. Must have a minimum 3.0 GPA, have completed one year of a dental hygiene curriculum, and show financial need of at least $1500. ADHA of SADHA membership required. Must be a U.S. citizen.

Academic Fields/Career Goals Dental Health/Services. *Award* Scholarship for use in sophomore, junior, senior, or graduate years; not renewable. *Number:* 2. *Amount:* $1500–$2000.

Eligibility Requirements Applicant must be American Indian/Alaska Native, Asian/Pacific Islander, Black (non-Hispanic), or Hispanic; enrolled or expecting to enroll full-time at a two-year or four-year institution or university and male. Applicant or parent of applicant must be member of American Dental Hygienist's Association. Applicant must have 3.0 GPA or higher. Available to U.S. citizens.

Application Requirements Application, financial need analysis, references. *Deadline:* June 1.

World Wide Web: http://www.adha.org

Contact: Scholarship Information
American Dental Hygienists' Association (ADHA) Institute
444 North Michigan Avenue, Suite 3400
Chicago, IL 60611

COLGATE "BRIGHT SMILES, BRIGHT FUTURES" MINORITY SCHOLARSHIP • 153

One-time award to a member of a minority group currently underrepresented in dental hygiene programs, including men. Minimum 3.0 GPA required. For use after first year of study. ADHA or SADHA membership required. Must be a U.S. citizen.

Academic Fields/Career Goals Dental Health/Services. *Award* Scholarship for use in sophomore, junior, or senior years; not renewable. *Number:* 2. *Amount:* $1500.

Eligibility Requirements Applicant must be American Indian/Alaska Native, Asian/Pacific Islander, Black (non-Hispanic), or Hispanic; enrolled or expecting to enroll full-time at a two-year or four-year institution or university and male. Applicant or parent of applicant must be member of American Dental Hygienist's Association. Applicant must have 3.0 GPA or higher. Available to U.S. citizens.

Application Requirements Application, financial need analysis, references. *Deadline:* June 1.

World Wide Web: http://www.adha.org

Contact: Scholarship Information
American Dental Hygienists' Association (ADHA) Institute
444 North Michigan Avenue, Suite 3400
Chicago, IL 60611

BECA FOUNDATION, INC.

ALICE NEWELL JOSLYN MEDICAL FUND • 154

Scholarships to full-time Latino students entering the medical/health care profession and living or attending college in San Diego County. Financial need, scholastic determination, and community/cultural awareness are considered. Awarded for four years annually contingent on scholastic progress.

Academic Fields/Career Goals Dental Health/Services; Health and Medical Sciences; Nursing; Therapy/Rehabilitation. *Award* Scholarship for use in freshman, sophomore, junior, senior, or graduate years; renewable. *Amount:* $1000–$2000.

Eligibility Requirements Applicant must be of Hispanic heritage and enrolled or expecting to enroll full-time at a four-year institution or university. Applicant must have 2.5 GPA or higher. Available to U.S. citizens.

Application Requirements Application, essay, financial need analysis, references, transcript. *Deadline:* March 1.

Contact: Ana Garcia, Operations Manager
BECA Foundation, Inc.
830 East Grand Avenue
Suite B
Escondido, CA 92025
Phone: 760-741-8246

BUSINESS AND PROFESSIONAL WOMEN'S FOUNDATION

BPW CAREER ADVANCEMENT SCHOLARSHIP PROGRAM FOR WOMEN

see number 68

HISPANIC DENTAL ASSOCIATION

DR. JUAN D. VILLARREAL/ HISPANIC DENTAL ASSOCIATION FOUNDATION • 155

Scholarship offered to Hispanic U.S. students who have been accepted into or are currently enrolled in an accredited dental or dental hygiene program in the state of Texas. The awarding of these scholarships will obligate the grantees to complete the current year of their dental or dental hygiene program. Scholastic achievement, leadership skills, community service, and commitment to improving the health of the Hispanic community will all be considered. Deadlines are July 1 for dental students and July 15 for dental hygiene students.

Academic Fields/Career Goals Dental Health/Services. *Award* Scholarship for use in freshman, sophomore, junior, or senior years; not renewable. *Amount:* $500–$1000.

Dr. Juan D. Villarreal/ Hispanic Dental Association Foundation (continued)

Eligibility Requirements Applicant must be of Hispanic heritage; enrolled or expecting to enroll full-time at a two-year or four-year institution; resident of Texas and studying in Texas. Available to U.S. citizens.

Application Requirements Application, transcript.

World Wide Web: http://www.hdassoc.org

Contact: Liz Valdivia, Office Manager
Hispanic Dental Association
188 West Randolph Street, Suite 415
Chicago, IL 60601
Phone: 312-577-4013
Fax: 312-577-0052
E-mail: lizvaldivia-hda@qwest.net

MARIN EDUCATION FUND

GOLDMAN FAMILY FUND, NEW LEADER SCHOLARSHIP • 156

Applicant for scholarship must attend one of the Bay Area public universities (California State University, Howard; San Francisco State University; San Jose State University; Sonoma State University; University of California at Berkeley). Must be studying social sciences, human services, health-related fields, or public service and have completed at least 30 hours at that university. Must be upper division student, demonstrate financial need and high academic achievement. Preference given to women, recent immigrants, and students of color. Minimum 3.2 GPA required.

Academic Fields/Career Goals Dental Health/Services; Food Science/Nutrition; Health Administration; Health and Medical Sciences; Health Information Management/Technology; Nursing; Social Sciences; Social Services; Therapy/Rehabilitation. *Award* Scholarship for use in junior or senior years; renewable. *Amount:* $5000.

Eligibility Requirements Applicant must be enrolled or expecting to enroll full or part-time at an institution or university and studying in California. Available to U.S. and non-U.S. citizens.

Application Requirements Application, financial need analysis, interview, transcript, proof of enrollment. *Deadline:* March 15.

World Wide Web: http://www.marineducationfund.org

Contact: Marin Education Fund
1010 B Street, Suite 300
San Rafael, CA 94901
Phone: 415-459-4240
Fax: 415-459-0527
E-mail: info@marineducationfund.org

UNIVERSITY OF MEDICINE AND DENTISTRY OF NJ SCHOOL OF OSTEOPATHIC MEDICINE

MARTIN LUTHER KING PHYSICIAN/DENTIST SCHOLARSHIPS • 157

Renewable award available to New Jersey residents enrolled full-time in a medical or dental program. Several scholarships are available. Dollar amount varies. Must be a former or current EOF recipient, a minority or from a disadvantaged background. Applicant must attend a New Jersey institution and apply for financial aid.

Academic Fields/Career Goals Dental Health/Services; Health and Medical Sciences. *Award* Scholarship for use in graduate years; renewable.

Eligibility Requirements Applicant must be enrolled or expecting to enroll full-time at an institution or university; resident of New Jersey and studying in New Jersey. Available to U.S. citizens.

Application Requirements Application, financial need analysis. *Deadline:* Continuous.

World Wide Web: http://www.umdnj.edu

Contact: Sandra Rollins, Associate Director of Financial Aid
University of Medicine and Dentistry of NJ School of Osteopathic Medicine
40 East Laurel Road
Primary Care Center 119
Stratford, NJ 08084
Phone: 856-566-6008
Fax: 856-566-6015
E-mail: rollins@umdnj.edu

NEW JERSEY EDUCATIONAL OPPORTUNITY FUND GRANTS • 158

Grants up to $4150 per year. Must be a New Jersey resident for at least twelve consecutive months and attend a New Jersey institution. Must be from a disadvantaged background as defined by EOF guidelines. EOF grant applicants must also apply for financial aid. EOF recipients may qualify for the Martin Luther King Physician/Dentistry Scholarships for graduate study at a professional institution.

Academic Fields/Career Goals Dental Health/Services; Health and Medical Sciences. *Award* Grant for use in freshman, sophomore, junior, senior, or graduate years; renewable. *Amount:* up to $4150.

Eligibility Requirements Applicant must be enrolled or expecting to enroll full-time at a four-year institution or university; resident of New Jersey and studying in New Jersey. Available to U.S. citizens.

Application Requirements Application, financial need analysis.

World Wide Web: http://www.umdnj.edu

Contact: Sandra Rollins, Associate Director of Financial Aid
University of Medicine and Dentistry of NJ School of Osteopathic Medicine
40 East Laurel Road, Primary Care Center 119
Stratford, NJ 08084
Phone: 856-566-6008
Fax: 856-566-6015
E-mail: rollins@umdnj.edu

VIRGINIA BUSINESS AND PROFESSIONAL WOMEN'S FOUNDATION

WOMEN IN SCIENCE AND TECHNOLOGY SCHOLARSHIP
see number 74

DRAFTING

COMTO-BOSTON CHAPTER

COMTO BOSTON/GARRETT A. MORGAN SCHOLARSHIP
see number 40

HISPANIC COLLEGE FUND, INC.

FIRST IN MY FAMILY SCHOLARSHIP PROGRAM see number 19

HISPANIC COLLEGE FUND SCHOLARSHIP PROGRAM see number 20

EARTH SCIENCE

ASSOCIATION FOR WOMEN GEOSCIENTISTS, PUGET SOUND CHAPTER

PUGET SOUND CHAPTER SCHOLARSHIP • **159**

Scholarship for undergraduate women committed to completing a bachelor's degree and pursuing a career or graduate work in the geosciences, including geology, environmental/engineering geology, geochemistry, geophysics, and hydrology. Must be sophomore, junior or senior women enrolled in a university or 2-year college in western Washington State west of the Columbia and Okanogan Rivers.

Academic Fields/Career Goals Earth Science; Physical Sciences and Math. *Award* Scholarship for use in sophomore, junior, or senior years; not renewable. *Number:* 1. *Amount:* $1000.

Eligibility Requirements Applicant must be enrolled or expecting to enroll full-time at a two-year or four-year institution or university; female and studying in Washington. Available to U.S. citizens.

Application Requirements Application, financial need analysis, references, transcript. *Deadline:* April 15.

World Wide Web: http://www.awg.org/

Contact: Lynn Hultgrien, Geologist, Scholarship Committee Chair
Association for Women Geoscientists, Puget Sound Chapter
PO Box 4229
Kent, WA 98032
Phone: 206-543-9024
E-mail: awg_ps@yahoo.com

ASSOCIATION FOR WOMEN IN SCIENCE EDUCATIONAL FOUNDATION

ASSOCIATION FOR WOMEN IN SCIENCE PRE-DOCTORAL FELLOWSHIP
see number 32

ASSOCIATION FOR WOMEN IN SCIENCE UNDERGRADUATE AWARD see number 26

CANADIAN FEDERATION OF UNIVERSITY WOMEN

CANADIAN FEDERATION OF UNIVERSITY WOMEN MEMORIAL FELLOWSHIP
see number 21

GEM CONSORTIUM

GEM MS ENGINEERING FELLOWSHIP see number 22

GEM PHD ENGINEERING FELLOWSHIP	see number 23
GEM PHD SCIENCE FELLOWSHIP	see number 70

GEOLOGICAL SOCIETY OF AMERICA

GRETCHEN L. BLECHSCHMIDT AWARD • 160

One-time awards for women interested in achieving a PhD in the geological sciences and a career in academic research. Only members of the Geological Society of America are eligible. Please visit Web site (http://www.geosociety.org) for more information.

Academic Fields/Career Goals Earth Science. *Award* Grant for use in graduate years; not renewable. *Number:* 1. *Amount:* $1300.

Eligibility Requirements Applicant must be enrolled or expecting to enroll full-time at an institution or university and female. Applicant or parent of applicant must be member of Geological Society of America. Available to U.S. and non-U.S. citizens.

Application Requirements Application, references. *Deadline:* February 1.

World Wide Web: http://www.geosociety.org

Contact: Ms. Leah Carter, Program Officer, Grants, Awards and Medals
Geological Society of America
3300 Penrose Place, PO Box 9140
Boulder, CO 80301-9140
Phone: 303-357-1037
Fax: 303-357-1074
E-mail: lcarter@geosociety.org

HISPANIC COLLEGE FUND, INC.

NATIONAL HISPANIC EXPLORERS SCHOLARSHIP PROGRAM	see number 31

NASA NEW HAMPSHIRE SPACE GRANT CONSORTIUM

GRADUATE FELLOWSHIPS • 161

Fellowships award 12 months of tuition support and stipends for Master's or Doctoral degree candidates and are not renewable. Must be U.S. citizen. Must be currently enrolled or be candidate for admission to University of New Hampshire graduate program in a space-related discipline. Women and minority applicants are especially encouraged.

Academic Fields/Career Goals Earth Science; Engineering/Technology; Geography; Meteorology/Atmospheric Science; Natural Sciences; Physical Sciences and Math; Surveying; Surveying Technology, Cartography, or Geographic Information Science. *Award* Fellowship for use in graduate years; not renewable. *Number:* 3–4.

Eligibility Requirements Applicant must be enrolled or expecting to enroll full-time at an institution or university and studying in New Hampshire. Available to U.S. citizens.

Application Requirements Application, essay, references, test scores, transcript. *Deadline:* March 14.

World Wide Web: http://www.nhsgc.sr.unh.edu

Contact: Dr. David S. Bartlett, Director
NASA New Hampshire Space Grant Consortium
University of New Hampshire, Morse Hall, 39 College Road
Durham, NH 03824
Phone: 603-862-0094

NATIONAL PHYSICAL SCIENCE CONSORTIUM

NATIONAL PHYSICAL SCIENCE CONSORTIUM GRADUATE FELLOWSHIPS IN THE PHYSICAL SCIENCES
see number 105

WELLESLEY COLLEGE

PROFESSOR ELIZABETH F. FISHER FELLOWSHIP
• 162

One or more fellowships available for research or further study in geology or geography, including urban, environment or ecological studies. Preference given to geology and geography. Must be graduate of Wellesley College. Based on merit and need. E-mail inquiries to cws-fellowships@wellesley.edu

Academic Fields/Career Goals Earth Science. *Award* Fellowship for use in graduate years; not renewable. *Amount:* up to $2500.

Eligibility Requirements Applicant must be enrolled or expecting to enroll full-time at an institution or university and female. Available to U.S. citizens.

Application Requirements Application, essay, financial need analysis, resume, transcript. *Deadline:* January 6.

World Wide Web: http://www.wellesley.edu/CWS/

Contact: Mary Beth Callery, Secretary to the Committee on Graduate Fellowships
Wellesley College
106 Central Avenue, Green Hall 441
Wellesley, MA 02481-8200
Phone: 781-283-3525
Fax: 781-283-3674
E-mail: cws-fellowships@wellesley.edu

WOMAN'S NATIONAL FARM AND GARDEN ASSOCIATION

SARAH BRADLEY TYSON MEMORIAL FELLOWSHIP
see number 24

ECONOMICS

AMERICAN AGRICULTURAL ECONOMICS ASSOCIATION FOUNDATION

SYLVIA LANE MENTOR RESEARCH FELLOWSHIP FUND
see number 18

CUBAN AMERICAN NATIONAL FOUNDATION

MAS FAMILY SCHOLARSHIPS
see number 80

GOVERNMENT FINANCE OFFICERS ASSOCIATION

MINORITIES IN GOVERNMENT FINANCE SCHOLARSHIP
see number 9

HISPANIC COLLEGE FUND, INC.

ALLFIRST/ HISPANIC COLLEGE FUND SCHOLARSHIP PROGRAM   see number 10

DENNY'S/HISPANIC COLLEGE FUND SCHOLARSHIP   see number 12

FIRST IN MY FAMILY SCHOLARSHIP PROGRAM   see number 19

HISPANIC COLLEGE FUND SCHOLARSHIP PROGRAM   see number 20

HISPANIC COLLEGE FUND/INROADS/SPRINT SCHOLARSHIP PROGRAM

see number 82

INSTITUTE FOR INTERNATIONAL PUBLIC POLICY (IIPP)

INSTITUTE FOR INTERNATIONAL PUBLIC POLICY FELLOWSHIP PROGRAM

see number 44

JORGE MAS CANOSA FREEDOM FOUNDATION

MAS FAMILY SCHOLARSHIP AWARD   see number 85

KARLA SCHERER FOUNDATION

KARLA SCHERER FOUNDATION SCHOLARSHIPS   • 163

Scholarships only for women pursuing undergraduate or graduate degrees in finance or economics in preparation for careers in the private manufacturing-based sector. To request application, must provide college or university name; major; a detailed statement of career plans; and a stamped self-addressed envelope. Deadline for application request is March 1; for completed application, May 1.

Academic Fields/Career Goals Economics. *Award* Scholarship for use in freshman, sophomore, junior, senior, or graduate years; not renewable.

Eligibility Requirements Applicant must be enrolled or expecting to enroll full-time at a four-year institution or university and female. Available to U.S. and non-U.S. citizens.

Application Requirements Application, autobiography, essay, financial need analysis, interview, photo, references, self-addressed stamped envelope, test scores, transcript. *Deadline:* May 1.

World Wide Web: http://www.comnet.org/kschererf

Contact: Ms. Katherine Ross, Executive Director
        Karla Scherer Foundation
        737 North Michigan Avenue, #2330
        Chicago, IL 60611
        Phone: 312-943-9191

NATIONAL ACTION COUNCIL FOR MINORITIES IN ENGINEERING-NACME, INC.

SLOAN PHD PROGRAM   see number 104

UNITED STATES INSTITUTE OF PEACE

JENNINGS RANDOLPH SENIOR FELLOW AWARD   see number 46

WELLESLEY COLLEGE

PEGGY HOWARD FELLOWSHIP IN ECONOMICS • 164

One or more fellowships in economics to provide financial aid for Wellesley students or alumnae continuing their study of economics. The application and supporting material should be returned in early April. Based on merit and need.

Academic Fields/Career Goals Economics. *Award* Fellowship for use in graduate years; not renewable.

Eligibility Requirements Applicant must be enrolled or expecting to enroll full-time at an institution or university and female. Available to U.S. citizens.

Application Requirements Application, essay, financial need analysis, resume, references, transcript.

World Wide Web: http://www.wellesley.edu/CWS/

Contact: Economics Department
Wellesley College
106 Central Street
Wellesley, MA 02481-8260

EDUCATION

ALPHA DELTA KAPPA FOUNDATION

INTERNATIONAL TEACHER EDUCATION SCHOLARSHIP • 165

Enables women from foreign countries to study for their master's degree in the United States. Applicants must be single with no dependents, age 20-35, non-U.S. citizens residing outside the U.S., have at least one year of college completed, and plan to enter the teaching profession.

Academic Fields/Career Goals Education. *Award* Scholarship for use in sophomore, junior, senior, or graduate years; renewable. *Number:* up to 7. *Amount:* up to $10,000.

Eligibility Requirements Applicant must be age 20-35; enrolled or expecting to enroll full-time at a four-year institution or university and single female. Applicant must have 3.5 GPA or higher. Available to Canadian and non-U.S. citizens.

Application Requirements Application, autobiography, financial need analysis, photo, references, test scores, transcript, certificates of health from physician and dentist, TOEFL scores, college acceptance. *Deadline:* January 1.

World Wide Web: http://www.alphadeltakappa.org

Contact: Dee Frost, Scholarships and Grants Coordinator
Alpha Delta Kappa Foundation
1615 West 92nd Street
Kansas City, MO 64114-3296
Phone: 816-363-5525
Fax: 816-363-4010
E-mail: dfrost@www.alphadeltakappa.org

AMERICAN ASSOCIATION OF UNIVERSITY WOMEN (AAUW) EDUCATIONAL FOUNDATION

ELEANOR ROOSEVELT TEACHER FELLOWSHIPS • 166

Fellowships are open to all public school K-12 women teachers who are U.S. citizens or permanent residents, and who have taught for at least three years. Supports professional development.

Academic Fields/Career Goals Education; Physical Sciences and Math; Science, Technology and Society. *Award* Fellowship for use in graduate years; not renewable. *Number:* 20. *Amount:* $5000.

Eligibility Requirements Applicant must be enrolled or expecting to enroll at an institution or university and female. Applicant or parent of applicant must have employment or volunteer experience in teaching. Available to U.S. citizens.

Application Requirements Application, references. *Deadline:* January 10.

World Wide Web: http://www.aauw.org

Contact: Customer Service Center
American Association of University Women (AAUW) Educational Foundation
2201 North Dodge Street
Iowa City, IA 52245-4030
Phone: 319-337-1716
E-mail: aauw@act.org

ARKANSAS DEPARTMENT OF HIGHER EDUCATION

ARKANSAS MINORITY TEACHER SCHOLARS PROGRAM • 167

Renewable award for Native-Americans, African-American, Hispanic and Asian-American students who have completed at least 60 semester hours and are enrolled full-time in a teacher education program in Arkansas. Award may be renewed for one year. Must be Arkansas resident with minimum 2.5 GPA. Must teach for three to five years in Arkansas to repay scholarship funds received. Must pass PPST exam.

Academic Fields/Career Goals Education. *Award* Forgivable loan for use in junior or senior years; renewable. *Number:* up to 100. *Amount:* up to $5000.

Eligibility Requirements Applicant must be American Indian/Alaska Native, Asian/Pacific Islander, Black (non-Hispanic), or Hispanic; enrolled or expecting to enroll full-time at a four-year institution or university; resident of Arkansas and studying in Arkansas. Applicant must have 2.5 GPA or higher. Available to U.S. citizens.

Application Requirements Application, transcript. *Deadline:* June 1.

World Wide Web: http://www.arscholarships.com

Contact: Lillian Williams, Assistant Coordinator
Arkansas Department of Higher Education
114 East Capitol
Little Rock, AR 72201
Phone: 501-371-2050
Fax: 501-371-2001

MINORITY MASTER'S FELLOWS PROGRAM • 168

Renewable award for graduate students who are African-Americans, Native-Americans, Hispanics, or Asian-Americans, enrolled in full-time teacher certification program in math, science, or foreign language. Must be Arkansas resident and have 2.75 minimum GPA. Must teach two years following certification or repay scholarship. Recipients must have received Arkansas Minority Teachers' Scholarship as an undergraduate. Must attend Arkansas graduate school.

Academic Fields/Career Goals Education; Foreign Language; Physical Sciences and Math; Science, Technology and Society. *Award* Forgivable loan for use in graduate years; renewable. *Amount:* up to $7500.

Eligibility Requirements Applicant must be American Indian/Alaska Native, Asian/Pacific Islander, Black (non-Hispanic), or Hispanic; enrolled or expecting to enroll full-time at an institution or university; resident of Arkansas and studying in Arkansas. Available to U.S. citizens.

Minority Master's Fellows Program (continued)

Application Requirements Application, transcript. *Deadline:* June 1.

World Wide Web: http://www.arscholarships.com

Contact: Lillian Williams, Assistant Coordinator
Arkansas Department of Higher Education
114 East Capitol
Little Rock, AR 72201
Phone: 501-371-2050
Fax: 501-371-2001
E-mail: lillianw@adhe.arknet.edu

BROWN FOUNDATION FOR EDUCATIONAL EQUITY, EXCELLENCE, AND RESEARCH

BROWN SCHOLAR • 169

Renewable scholarship award to college student entering junior year who is admitted to teacher education program at a four-year college or university. Applicants must be minority student. Minimum 3.0 GPA required.

Academic Fields/Career Goals Education. *Award* Scholarship for use in junior or senior years; renewable.

Eligibility Requirements Applicant must be American Indian/Alaska Native, Asian/Pacific Islander, Black (non-Hispanic), or Hispanic and enrolled or expecting to enroll full or part-time at a four-year institution or university. Applicant must have 3.0 GPA or higher. Available to U.S. citizens.

Application Requirements Application, essay, photo, transcript. *Deadline:* April 1.

World Wide Web: http://brownvboard.org/foundatn/sclrbroc.htm

Contact: Chelsey Smith, Staff/Administrative Assistant
Brown Foundation for Educational Equity, Excellence, and Research
PO Box 4862
Topeka, KS 66604
Phone: 785-235-3939
Fax: 785-235-1001
E-mail: brownfound@juno.com

LUCINDA TODD BOOK SCHOLARSHIP • 170

Renewable book award of $300 to graduating high school senior planning to pursue teacher education at four-year college or university. Applicants must be minority student. Minimum 3.0 GPA required.

Academic Fields/Career Goals Education. *Award* Scholarship for use in freshman year; renewable. *Amount:* $300.

Eligibility Requirements Applicant must be American Indian/Alaska Native, Asian/Pacific Islander, Black (non-Hispanic), or Hispanic; high school student and planning to enroll or expecting to enroll full or part-time at a four-year institution or university. Applicant must have 3.0 GPA or higher. Available to U.S. citizens.

Application Requirements Application, essay, photo, transcript. *Deadline:* April 7.

World Wide Web: http://brownvboard.org/foundatn/sclrbroc.htm

Contact: Chelsey Smith, Staff/Administrative Assistant
Brown Foundation for Educational Equity, Excellence, and Research
PO Box 4862
Topeka, KS 66604
Phone: 785-235-3939
Fax: 785-235-1001
E-mail: brownfound@juno.com

BUSINESS AND PROFESSIONAL WOMEN'S FOUNDATION

BPW CAREER ADVANCEMENT SCHOLARSHIP PROGRAM FOR WOMEN
see number 68

CALIFORNIA TEACHERS ASSOCIATION (CTA)

MARTIN LUTHER KING, JR. MEMORIAL SCHOLARSHIP • 171
For ethnic minority members of the California Teachers Association, their dependent children, and ethnic minority members of Student California Teachers Association who want to pursue degrees or credentials in public education. Applications available in January and due March 15.

Academic Fields/Career Goals Education. *Award* Scholarship for use in freshman, sophomore, junior, senior, or graduate years; not renewable. *Amount:* $500–$5000.

Eligibility Requirements Applicant must be American Indian/Alaska Native, Asian/Pacific Islander, Black (non-Hispanic), or Hispanic and enrolled or expecting to enroll full-time at a two-year or four-year institution or university. Applicant or parent of applicant must be member of California Teachers Association. Available to U.S. and non-U.S. citizens.

Application Requirements Application, essay, financial need analysis, references. *Deadline:* March 15.

World Wide Web: http://www.cta.org
Contact: Human Rights Department
California Teachers Association (CTA)
PO Box 921
Burlingame, CA 94011-0921
Phone: 650-697-1400
E-mail: scholarships@cta.org

COMTO-BOSTON CHAPTER

COMTO BOSTON/GARRETT A. MORGAN SCHOLARSHIP
see number 40

GOVERNOR'S OFFICE

GOVERNOR'S OPPORTUNITY SCHOLARSHIP
see number 81

HOSTESS COMMITTEE SCHOLARSHIPS/MISS AMERICA PAGEANT

ALBERT A. MARKS, JR. SCHOLARSHIP FOR TEACHER EDUCATION • 172
Scholarship for Miss America contestants pursuing degree in education. Award available to women who have competed within the Miss America system on the local, state, or national

Albert A. Marks, Jr. Scholarship for Teacher Education (continued)

level from 1992 to the present, regardless of whether title was won. One or more scholarships will be awarded annually, depending on the qualifications of the applicants. A new application must be submitted each year, previous applicants may apply. Applications must be received by June 30. Late or incomplete applications are not accepted.

Academic Fields/Career Goals Education. *Award* Grant for use in freshman, sophomore, junior, senior, or graduate years; not renewable. *Number:* 1.

Eligibility Requirements Applicant must be enrolled or expecting to enroll at a four-year institution or university; female and must have an interest in beauty pageant. Available to U.S. citizens.

Application Requirements Application, essay, financial need analysis, references, transcript. *Deadline:* June 30.

World Wide Web: http://www.missamerica.org

Contact: Hostess Committee Scholarships/Miss America Pageant
Two Miss America Way, Suite 1000
Atlantic City, NJ 08401

ILLINOIS STUDENT ASSISTANCE COMMISSION (ISAC)

MINORITY TEACHERS OF ILLINOIS SCHOLARSHIP PROGRAM • 173

Award for minority students planning to teach at an approved Illinois preschool, elementary, or secondary school. Deadline: May 1. Must be Illinois resident.

Academic Fields/Career Goals Education; Special Education. *Award* Forgivable loan for use in freshman, sophomore, junior, senior, graduate, or postgraduate years; renewable. *Number:* 450–550. *Amount:* $4000–$5000.

Eligibility Requirements Applicant must be American Indian/Alaska Native, Asian/Pacific Islander, Black (non-Hispanic), or Hispanic; enrolled or expecting to enroll full-time at a two-year or four-year institution or university; resident of Illinois and studying in Illinois. Applicant must have 2.5 GPA or higher. Available to U.S. and non-U.S. citizens.

Application Requirements Application. *Deadline:* May 1.

World Wide Web: http://www.isac-online.org

Contact: David Barinholtz, Client Information
Illinois Student Assistance Commission (ISAC)
1755 Lake Cook Road
Deerfield, IL 60015-5209
Phone: 847-948-8500 Ext. 2385
E-mail: cssupport@isac.org

MISSOURI DEPARTMENT OF ELEMENTARY AND SECONDARY EDUCATION

MISSOURI MINORITY TEACHING SCHOLARSHIP • 174

Award may be used any year up to four years at an approved, participating Missouri institution. Scholarship is for minority Missouri residents in teaching programs. Recipients must commit to teach for five years in a Missouri public elementary or secondary school. Graduate students must teach math or science. Otherwise, award must be repaid.

Academic Fields/Career Goals Education. *Award* Scholarship for use in freshman, sophomore, junior, senior, or graduate years; renewable. *Number:* 100. *Amount:* $3000.

Eligibility Requirements Applicant must be of African, Chinese, Hispanic, Indian, or Japanese heritage; American Indian/Alaska Native, Asian/Pacific Islander, or Black (non-

Hispanic); enrolled or expecting to enroll full-time at a two-year or four-year institution or university; resident of Missouri and studying in Missouri. Applicant must have 3.5 GPA or higher. Available to U.S. citizens.

Application Requirements Application, essay, financial need analysis, references, test scores, transcript. *Deadline:* February 15.

World Wide Web: http://www.dese.state.mo.us

Contact: Laura Harrison, Administrative Assistant II
Missouri Department of Elementary and Secondary Education
PO Box 480
Jefferson City, MO 65102-0480
Phone: 573-751-1668
Fax: 573-526-3580
E-mail: lharriso@mail.dese.state.mo.us

OREGON STUDENT ASSISTANCE COMMISSION

JAMES CARLSON SCHOLARSHIP PROGRAM • 175

One-time award for elementary or secondary education majors entering senior or fifth year or graduate students in fifth year for elementary or secondary certificate. Priority given to African-American, Asian, Hispanic, Native-Americans ethnic groups; dependents of Oregon Education Association members, and others committed to teaching autistic children.

Academic Fields/Career Goals Education; Special Education. *Award* Scholarship for use in senior, or graduate years; not renewable. *Number:* 3. *Amount:* $1300.

Eligibility Requirements Applicant must be enrolled or expecting to enroll at a four-year institution and resident of Oregon. Available to U.S. citizens.

Application Requirements Application, essay, financial need analysis, test scores, transcript, activity chart. *Deadline:* March 1.

World Wide Web: http://www.osac.state.or.us

Contact: Director of Grant Programs
Oregon Student Assistance Commission
1500 Valley River Drive, Suite 100
Eugene, OR 97401-7020
Phone: 800-452-8807 Ext. 7395
E-mail: awardinfo@mercury.osac.state.or.us

SIGMA ALPHA IOTA PHILANTHROPIES, INC.

GRADUATE SCHOLARSHIP IN MUSIC EDUCATION • 176

One-time award offered yearly to members of SAI who are accepted into a graduate program leading to master's or doctoral degree in music education. Submit videotape of work. Contact local chapter for further information. Application fee: $25.

Academic Fields/Career Goals Education; Music; Performing Arts. *Award* Scholarship for use in graduate years; not renewable. *Number:* 1. *Amount:* $1500.

Eligibility Requirements Applicant must be enrolled or expecting to enroll full or part-time at a four-year institution or university; female and must have an interest in music/singing. Available to U.S. and non-U.S. citizens.

Application Requirements Application, essay, references, transcript, videotape of work. *Fee:* $25. *Deadline:* April 15.

World Wide Web: http://www.sai-national.org

Graduate Scholarship in Music Education (continued)

Contact: Ms. Ruth Sieber Johnson, Executive Director of SAI
Sigma Alpha Iota Philanthropies, Inc.
34 Wall Street, Suite 515
Asheville, NC 28801-2710
Phone: 828-251-0606
Fax: 828-251-0644
E-mail: nh@sai-national.org

SIGMA ALPHA IOTA DOCTORAL GRANT • 177

One-time award offered triennially to SAI member who is enrolled in a doctoral program in music education, music therapy, musicology, ethnomusicology, theory, psychology of music, or applied music degree programs. Submit dissertation or other required written materials outline. Contact local chapter for further information. Application fee: $25.

Academic Fields/Career Goals Education; Music; Performing Arts; Therapy/Rehabilitation. *Award* Grant for use in graduate years; not renewable. *Number:* 1. *Amount:* $2500.

Eligibility Requirements Applicant must be enrolled or expecting to enroll at an institution or university; female and must have an interest in music/singing. Available to U.S. and non-U.S. citizens.

Application Requirements Application, essay, references, transcript, dissertation outline. *Fee:* $25. *Deadline:* April 15.

World Wide Web: http://www.sai-national.org

Contact: Ms. Ruth Sieber Johnson, Executive Director of SAI
Sigma Alpha Iota Philanthropies, Inc.
34 Wall Street, Suite 515
Asheville, NC 28801-2710
Phone: 828-251-0606
Fax: 828-251-0644
E-mail: nh@sai-national.org

SIGMA ALPHA IOTA PHILANTHROPIES UNDERGRADUATE SCHOLARSHIPS • 178

One-time award to undergraduate members of SAI who are freshman, sophomores or juniors. For use in sophomore, junior, or senior year. Must be female over 18 years of age studying performing arts or performing arts education. Contact local chapter for further details. Ten scholarships of $1000 each.

Academic Fields/Career Goals Education; Performing Arts. *Award* Scholarship for use in freshman, sophomore, or junior years; not renewable. *Number:* 10. *Amount:* $1000.

Eligibility Requirements Applicant must be age 19; enrolled or expecting to enroll full-time at a four-year institution or university; female and must have an interest in music/singing. Available to U.S. and non-U.S. citizens.

Application Requirements Application, essay, financial need analysis, references, transcript. *Deadline:* April 15.

World Wide Web: http://www.sai-national.org

Contact: Ms. Ruth Sieber Johnson, Executive Director of SAI
Sigma Alpha Iota Philanthropies, Inc.
34 Wall Street, Suite 515
Asheville, NC 28801-2710
Phone: 828-251-0606
Fax: 828-251-0644
E-mail: nh@sai-national.org

SIGMA ALPHA IOTA VISUALLY IMPAIRED SCHOLARSHIP   • 179

One-time award offered triennially for member of SAI who is visually impaired, and a member of a college or alumnae chapter. Submit fifteen-minute tape or evidence of work in composition, musicology, or research. One scholarship of $1000. Application fee: $25.

Academic Fields/Career Goals Education; Music; Performing Arts. *Award* Scholarship for use in freshman, sophomore, junior, senior, or graduate years; not renewable. *Number:* 1. *Amount:* $1000.

Eligibility Requirements Applicant must be enrolled or expecting to enroll at a four-year institution or university; female and must have an interest in music/singing. Applicant must be visually impaired. Available to U.S. and non-U.S. citizens.

Application Requirements Application, essay, references, transcript, tape. *Fee:* $25. *Deadline:* April 15.

World Wide Web: http://www.sai-national.org

Contact: Ms. Ruth Sieber Johnson, Executive Director of SAI
Sigma Alpha Iota Philanthropies, Inc.
34 Wall Street, Suite 515
Asheville, NC 28801-2710
Phone: 828-251-0606
Fax: 828-251-0644
E-mail: nh@sai-national.org

STATE STUDENT ASSISTANCE COMMISSION OF INDIANA (SSACI)

INDIANA MINORITY TEACHER AND SPECIAL EDUCATION SERVICES SCHOLARSHIP PROGRAM   • 180

For Black or Hispanic students seeking teaching certification or for students seeking special education teaching certification or occupational or physical therapy certification. Must be a U.S. citizen and Indiana resident enrolled full-time at an eligible Indiana institution. Must teach in an Indiana-accredited elementary or secondary school after graduation. Contact institution for application and deadline. Minimum 2.0 GPA required.

Academic Fields/Career Goals Education; Special Education; Therapy/Rehabilitation. *Award* Scholarship for use in freshman, sophomore, junior, or senior years; not renewable. *Number:* 330–370. *Amount:* $1000–$4000.

Eligibility Requirements Applicant must be Black (non-Hispanic) or Hispanic; enrolled or expecting to enroll full-time at a four-year institution or university; resident of Indiana and studying in Indiana. Available to U.S. citizens.

Application Requirements Application, financial need analysis. *Deadline:* Continuous.

World Wide Web: http://www.ssaci.in.gov

Contact: Ms. Yvonne Heflin, Director, Special Programs
State Student Assistance Commission of Indiana (SSACI)
150 West Market Street, Suite 500
Indianapolis, IN 46204-2805
Phone: 317-232-2350
Fax: 317-232-3260
E-mail: grants@ssaci.state.un.is

TENNESSEE EDUCATION ASSOCIATION

TEA DON SAHLI-KATHY WOODALL MINORITY SCHOLARSHIP   • 181

This scholarship is available to a minority high school senior planning to major in education and planning to enroll in a Tennessee college. Application must be made by an FTA Chapter, or by the student with the recommendation of an active TEA member.

Academic Fields/Career Goals Education. *Award* Scholarship for use in freshman year; not renewable. *Number:* 1. *Amount:* $1000.

Eligibility Requirements Applicant must be American Indian/Alaska Native, Asian/Pacific Islander, Black (non-Hispanic), or Hispanic; high school student; planning to enroll or expecting to enroll full-time at a four-year institution or university; resident of Tennessee and studying in Tennessee. Applicant must have 3.0 GPA or higher. Available to U.S. citizens.

Application Requirements Application, essay, financial need analysis, references, transcript, statement of income. *Deadline:* March 1.

World Wide Web: http://www.teateachers.org

Contact: Jeanette DeMain, Administrative Assistant
Tennessee Education Association
801 Second Avenue North
Nashville, TN 37201-1099
Phone: 615-242-8392
Fax: 615-259-4581

TENNESSEE STUDENT ASSISTANCE CORPORATION

MINORITY TEACHING FELLOWS PROGRAM/TENNESSEE   • 182

Forgivable loan for minority Tennessee residents pursuing teaching careers. High school applicant minimum 2.75 GPA. Must be in the top quarter of the class or score an 18 on ACT. College applicant minimum 2.50 GPA. Submit statement of intent, test scores, and transcripts with application and two letters of recommendation. Must teach one year per year of award or repay as a loan.

Academic Fields/Career Goals Education; Special Education. *Award* Forgivable loan for use in freshman, sophomore, junior, or senior years; renewable. *Number:* 19–29. *Amount:* $5000.

Eligibility Requirements Applicant must be American Indian/Alaska Native, Asian/Pacific Islander, Black (non-Hispanic), or Hispanic; enrolled or expecting to enroll full-time at a two-year or four-year institution or university; resident of Tennessee and studying in Tennessee. Available to U.S. citizens.

Application Requirements Application, essay, references, test scores, transcript. *Deadline:* April 15.

World Wide Web: http://www.state.tn.us/tsac

Contact: Kathy Stripling, Scholarship Coordinator
Tennessee Student Assistance Corporation
404 James Robertson Parkway, Suite 1950, Parkway Towers
Nashville, TN 37243-0820
Phone: 615-741-1346
Fax: 615-741-6101
E-mail: kathy.stripling@state.tn.us

WOMEN BAND DIRECTORS INTERNATIONAL

GLADYS STONE WRIGHT SCHOLARSHIP • 183

One-time award for women instrumental music majors enrolled in a four-year institution. Applicants must be working toward a degree in music education with the intention of becoming a band director. Merit-based.

Academic Fields/Career Goals Education; Music; Performing Arts. *Award* Scholarship for use in freshman, sophomore, junior, or senior years; not renewable. *Number:* 1. *Amount:* $300.

Eligibility Requirements Applicant must be enrolled or expecting to enroll full-time at a four-year institution or university; female and must have an interest in music/singing. Applicant must have 3.0 GPA or higher. Available to U.S. and non-U.S. citizens.

Application Requirements Application, essay, financial need analysis, photo, resume, references, self-addressed stamped envelope, transcript. *Deadline:* December 1.

World Wide Web: http://womenbanddirectors.org

Contact: Linda Moorhouse, Associate Director of Bands
Women Band Directors International
292 Band Hall-Louisiana State University
Baton Rouge, LA 70803
Phone: 225-578-2384
Fax: 225-578-4693
E-mail: moorhous@lsu.edu

HELEN MAY BULTER MEMORIAL SCHOLARSHIP • 184

One-time award for women instrumental music majors enrolled in a four-year institution. Applicants must be working toward a degree in music education with the intention of becoming a band director. Merit-based.

Academic Fields/Career Goals Education; Music; Performing Arts. *Award* Scholarship for use in freshman, sophomore, junior, or senior years; not renewable. *Number:* 1. *Amount:* $300.

Eligibility Requirements Applicant must be enrolled or expecting to enroll full-time at a four-year institution or university; female and must have an interest in music/singing. Applicant must have 3.0 GPA or higher. Available to U.S. and non-U.S. citizens.

Application Requirements Application, essay, financial need analysis, photo, resume, references, self-addressed stamped envelope, transcript. *Deadline:* December 1.

World Wide Web: http://womenbanddirectors.org

Contact: Linda Moorhouse, Associate Director of Bands
Women Band Directors International
292 Band Hall-Louisiana State University
Baton Rouge, LA 70803
Phone: 225-578-2384
Fax: 225-578-4693
E-mail: moorhous@lsu.edu

MARTHA ANN STARK MEMORIAL SCHOLARSHIP • 185

One-time award for a woman college student who demonstrates outstanding contributions to bands and band music. Must be pursuing a major in music education and plan to become a band director. Merit-based. Must have a 3.0 GPA.

Academic Fields/Career Goals Education; Music; Performing Arts. *Award* Scholarship for use in freshman, sophomore, junior, or senior years; not renewable. *Number:* 1. *Amount:* $300.

Martha Ann Stark Memorial Scholarship (continued)

Eligibility Requirements Applicant must be enrolled or expecting to enroll full-time at a four-year institution or university; female and must have an interest in music/singing. Applicant must have 3.0 GPA or higher. Available to U.S. and non-U.S. citizens.

Application Requirements Application, essay, financial need analysis, photo, resume, references, self-addressed stamped envelope, transcript. *Deadline:* December 1.

World Wide Web: http://womenbanddirectors.org

Contact: Linda Moorhouse, Associate Director of Bands
Women Band Directors International
292 Band Hall-Louisiana State University
Baton Rouge, LA 70803
Phone: 225-578-2384
Fax: 225-578-4693
E-mail: moorhous@lsu.edu

MUSIC TECHNOLOGY SCHOLARSHIP • 186

One-time award of $500. Student must be able to demonstrate the use of incorporation of music technology. Applicants must be working toward a degree in music education with the intention of becoming a band director.

Academic Fields/Career Goals Education; Music; Performing Arts. *Award* Scholarship for use in freshman, sophomore, junior, or senior years; not renewable. *Number:* 1. *Amount:* $500.

Eligibility Requirements Applicant must be enrolled or expecting to enroll full-time at a four-year institution or university; female and must have an interest in music/singing. Applicant must have 3.0 GPA or higher. Available to U.S. and non-U.S. citizens.

Application Requirements Application, essay, financial need analysis, photo, resume, references, self-addressed stamped envelope, transcript. *Deadline:* December 1.

World Wide Web: http://womenbanddirectors.org

Contact: Linda Moorhouse, Associate Director of Bands
Women Band Directors International
292 Band Hall-Louisiana State University
Baton Rouge, LA 70803
Phone: 225-578-2384
Fax: 225-578-4693
E-mail: moorhous@lsu.edu

VOLKWEIN MEMORIAL SCHOLARSHIP • 187

One-time award for women instrumental music majors enrolled in a four-year institution. Applicants must be working toward a degree in music education with the intention of becoming a band director. Merit-based. Must have a 3.0 GPA.

Academic Fields/Career Goals Education; Music; Performing Arts. *Award* Scholarship for use in freshman, sophomore, junior, or senior years; not renewable. *Number:* 1. *Amount:* $300.

Eligibility Requirements Applicant must be enrolled or expecting to enroll full-time at a four-year institution or university; female and must have an interest in music/singing. Applicant must have 3.0 GPA or higher. Available to U.S. and non-U.S. citizens.

Application Requirements Application, essay, financial need analysis, photo, resume, references, self-addressed stamped envelope, transcript. *Deadline:* December 1.

World Wide Web: http://womenbanddirectors.org

Contact: Linda Moorhouse, Associate Director of Bands
Women Band Directors International
292 Band Hall-Louisiana State University
Baton Rouge, LA 70803
Phone: 225-578-2384
Fax: 225-578-4693
E-mail: moorhous@lsu.edu

ELECTRICAL ENGINEERING/ELECTRONICS____

AMERICAN ASSOCIATION OF UNIVERSITY WOMEN (AAUW) EDUCATIONAL FOUNDATION

AAUW EDUCATIONAL FOUNDATION SELECTED PROFESSIONS FELLOWSHIPS
see number 36

AMERICAN SOCIETY FOR ENGINEERING EDUCATION

NATIONAL DEFENSE SCIENCE AND ENGINEERING GRADUATE FELLOWSHIP PROGRAM
see number 98

ARMED FORCES COMMUNICATIONS AND ELECTRON-ICS ASSOCIATION, EDUCATIONAL FOUNDATION

ARMED FORCES COMMUNICATIONS AND ELECTRONICS ASSOCIATION RALPH W. SHRADER SCHOLARSHIPS
see number 140

CENTER FOR THE ADVANCEMENT OF HISPANICS IN SCIENCE AND ENGINEERING EDUCATION (CAHSEE)

CAHSEE FELLOWSHIP: YOUNG EDUCATORS PROGRAM
see number 30

COMTO-BOSTON CHAPTER

COMTO BOSTON/GARRETT A. MORGAN SCHOLARSHIP
see number 40

CUBAN AMERICAN NATIONAL FOUNDATION

MAS FAMILY SCHOLARSHIPS
see number 80

EAST LOS ANGELES COMMUNITY UNION (TELACU) EDUCATION FOUNDATION

TELACU ENGINEERING AWARD
see number 99

EATON CORPORATION

EATON CORPORATION MULTICULTURAL SCHOLARS PROGRAM   see number 141

GEM CONSORTIUM

GEM MS ENGINEERING FELLOWSHIP   see number 22

GEM PHD ENGINEERING FELLOWSHIP   see number 23

HISPANIC COLLEGE FUND, INC.

DENNY'S/HISPANIC COLLEGE FUND SCHOLARSHIP   see number 12

FIRST IN MY FAMILY SCHOLARSHIP PROGRAM   see number 19

HISPANIC COLLEGE FUND SCHOLARSHIP PROGRAM   see number 20

HISPANIC COLLEGE FUND/INROADS/SPRINT SCHOLARSHIP PROGRAM
   see number 82

NATIONAL HISPANIC EXPLORERS SCHOLARSHIP PROGRAM   see number 31

HISPANIC ENGINEER NATIONAL ACHIEVEMENT AWARDS CORPORATION (HENAAC)

HISPANIC ENGINEER NATIONAL ACHIEVEMENT AWARDS CORPORATION
SCHOLARSHIP PROGRAM   see number 51

HISPANIC SCHOLARSHIP FUND

HSF/GENERAL MOTORS SCHOLARSHIP   see number 83

IMGIP/ICEOP

ILLINOIS MINORITY GRADUATE INCENTIVE PROGRAM FELLOWSHIP
   see number 142

JORGE MAS CANOSA FREEDOM FOUNDATION

MAS FAMILY SCHOLARSHIP AWARD   see number 85

LOS ANGELES COUNCIL OF BLACK PROFESSIONAL ENGINEERS

AL-BEN SCHOLARSHIP FOR ACADEMIC INCENTIVE   see number 100

AL-BEN SCHOLARSHIP FOR PROFESSIONAL MERIT   see number 101

AL-BEN SCHOLARSHIP FOR SCHOLASTIC ACHIEVEMENT   see number 102

NAMEPA NATIONAL SCHOLARSHIP FOUNDATION

NATIONAL ASSOCIATION OF MINORITY ENGINEERING PROGRAM
ADMINISTRATORS NATIONAL SCHOLARSHIP FUND   see number 58

NATIONAL ACTION COUNCIL FOR MINORITIES IN ENGINEERING-NACME, INC.

ENGINEERING VANGUARD PROGRAM   see number 103

SLOAN PHD PROGRAM   see number 104

NATIONAL PHYSICAL SCIENCE CONSORTIUM

NATIONAL PHYSICAL SCIENCE CONSORTIUM GRADUATE FELLOWSHIPS IN THE PHYSICAL SCIENCES   see number 105

NEW YORK STATE SOCIETY OF PROFESSIONAL ENGINEERS

NSPE AUXILIARY SCHOLARSHIP   see number 106

NSPE-VIRGINIA D. HENRY MEMORIAL SCHOLARSHIP   see number 107

OREGON STUDENT ASSISTANCE COMMISSION

MENTOR GRAPHICS SCHOLARSHIP   see number 143

SOCIETY OF HISPANIC PROFESSIONAL ENGINEERS FOUNDATION

SOCIETY OF HISPANIC PROFESSIONAL ENGINEERS FOUNDATION   see number 109

SOCIETY OF WOMEN ENGINEERS

BECHTEL CORPORATION SCHOLARSHIP   see number 116

DAIMLER CHRYSLER CORPORATION SCHOLARSHIP   • 188

Renewable award for entering female sophomore majoring in mechanical or electrical engineering at an accredited school. Applicants must have minimum 3.0 GPA. Must be active contributor to and supporter of Society of Women Engineers. Must be U.S. citizen. Deadline: February 1.

Academic Fields/Career Goals Electrical Engineering/Electronics; Mechanical Engineering. *Award* Scholarship for use in sophomore year; renewable. *Number:* 1. *Amount:* $2000.

Eligibility Requirements Applicant must be enrolled or expecting to enroll full-time at a four-year institution and female. Applicant or parent of applicant must be member of Society of Women Engineers. Applicant must have 3.0 GPA or higher. Available to U.S. citizens.

Application Requirements Application, essay, references, self-addressed stamped envelope, test scores, transcript. *Deadline:* February 1.

World Wide Web: http://www.swe.org

Contact: Program Coordinator
Society of Women Engineers
230 East Ohio Street, Suite 400
Chicago, IL 60611-3265
Phone: 312-596-5223
Fax: 312-644-8557
E-mail: hq@swe.org

DELL COMPUTER CORPORATION SCHOLARSHIPS
see number 146

GENERAL MOTORS FOUNDATION UNDERGRADUATE SCHOLARSHIPS
see number 114

LOCKHEED AERONAUTICS COMPANY SCHOLARSHIPS • 189

Two $1000 scholarships for entering female juniors majoring in electrical or mechanical engineering. One scholarship for each major. Minimum 3.5 GPA required. Application deadline is February 1.

Academic Fields/Career Goals Electrical Engineering/Electronics; Mechanical Engineering. *Award* Scholarship for use in junior year; not renewable. *Number:* 2. *Amount:* $1000.

Eligibility Requirements Applicant must be enrolled or expecting to enroll full-time at a four-year institution or university and female. Applicant must have 3.5 GPA or higher. Available to U.S. and non-U.S. citizens.

Application Requirements Application, essay, references, self-addressed stamped envelope, test scores, transcript. *Deadline:* February 1.

World Wide Web: http://www.swe.org

Contact: Program Coordinator
Society of Women Engineers
230 East Ohio Street, Suite 400
Chicago, IL 60611-3265
Phone: 312-596-5223
Fax: 312-644-8557
E-mail: hq@swe.org

XEROX

TECHNICAL MINORITY SCHOLARSHIP
see number 115

ENGINEERING-RELATED TECHNOLOGIES

AMERICAN ASSOCIATION OF UNIVERSITY WOMEN (AAUW) EDUCATIONAL FOUNDATION

AAUW EDUCATIONAL FOUNDATION SELECTED PROFESSIONS FELLOWSHIPS
see number 36

AMERICAN SOCIETY FOR ENGINEERING EDUCATION

NATIONAL DEFENSE SCIENCE AND ENGINEERING GRADUATE FELLOWSHIP PROGRAM
see number 98

BUSINESS AND PROFESSIONAL WOMEN'S FOUNDATION

BPW CAREER ADVANCEMENT SCHOLARSHIP PROGRAM FOR WOMEN
see number 68

CENTER FOR THE ADVANCEMENT OF HISPANICS IN SCIENCE AND ENGINEERING EDUCATION (CAHSEE)

CAHSEE FELLOWSHIP: YOUNG EDUCATORS PROGRAM   see number 30

COMTO-BOSTON CHAPTER

COMTO BOSTON/GARRETT A. MORGAN SCHOLARSHIP   see number 40

CUBAN AMERICAN NATIONAL FOUNDATION

MAS FAMILY SCHOLARSHIPS   see number 80

EAST LOS ANGELES COMMUNITY UNION (TELACU) EDUCATION FOUNDATION

TELACU ENGINEERING AWARD   see number 99

EATON CORPORATION

EATON CORPORATION MULTICULTURAL SCHOLARS PROGRAM   see number 141

HISPANIC COLLEGE FUND, INC.

ALLFIRST/ HISPANIC COLLEGE FUND SCHOLARSHIP PROGRAM   see number 10

DENNY'S/HISPANIC COLLEGE FUND SCHOLARSHIP   see number 12

FIRST IN MY FAMILY SCHOLARSHIP PROGRAM   see number 19

HISPANIC COLLEGE FUND SCHOLARSHIP PROGRAM   see number 20

HISPANIC COLLEGE FUND/INROADS/SPRINT SCHOLARSHIP PROGRAM

see number 82

NATIONAL HISPANIC EXPLORERS SCHOLARSHIP PROGRAM   see number 31

HISPANIC SCHOLARSHIP FUND

HSF/GENERAL MOTORS SCHOLARSHIP   see number 83

IMGIP/ICEOP

ILLINOIS MINORITY GRADUATE INCENTIVE PROGRAM FELLOWSHIP

see number 142

JORGE MAS CANOSA FREEDOM FOUNDATION

MAS FAMILY SCHOLARSHIP AWARD   see number 85

LOS ANGELES COUNCIL OF BLACK PROFESSIONAL ENGINEERS

AL-BEN SCHOLARSHIP FOR ACADEMIC INCENTIVE — see number 100

AL-BEN SCHOLARSHIP FOR PROFESSIONAL MERIT — see number 101

AL-BEN SCHOLARSHIP FOR SCHOLASTIC ACHIEVEMENT — see number 102

NAMEPA NATIONAL SCHOLARSHIP FOUNDATION

NATIONAL ASSOCIATION OF MINORITY ENGINEERING PROGRAM ADMINISTRATORS NATIONAL SCHOLARSHIP FUND — see number 58

NATIONAL ACTION COUNCIL FOR MINORITIES IN ENGINEERING-NACME, INC.

ENGINEERING VANGUARD PROGRAM — see number 103

SLOAN PHD PROGRAM — see number 104

NATIONAL RESEARCH COUNCIL

FORD FOUNDATION DISSERTATION FELLOWSHIPS FOR MINORITIES — see number 125

FORD FOUNDATION POSTDOCTORAL FELLOWSHIP FOR MINORITIES — see number 126

FORD FOUNDATION PRE-DOCTORAL FELLOWSHIPS FOR MINORITIES — see number 127

NEW YORK STATE SOCIETY OF PROFESSIONAL ENGINEERS

NSPE AUXILIARY SCHOLARSHIP — see number 106

NSPE-VIRGINIA D. HENRY MEMORIAL SCHOLARSHIP — see number 107

OFFICE OF NAVAL RESEARCH

HISTORICALLY BLACK COLLEGES AND UNIVERSITIES FUTURE ENGINEERING FACULTY FELLOWSHIP — see number 108

SOCIETY OF HISPANIC PROFESSIONAL ENGINEERS FOUNDATION

SOCIETY OF HISPANIC PROFESSIONAL ENGINEERS FOUNDATION — see number 109

SOCIETY OF MEXICAN AMERICAN ENGINEERS AND SCIENTISTS

GRE AND GRADUATE APPLICATIONS WAIVER   see number 110

SOCIETY OF WOMEN ENGINEERS

ABB LUMMIS GLOBAL   • 190
Scholarship available to incoming female freshman, sophomore or junior who has demonstrated community involvement/volunteerism. Must have a minimum 3.0 GPA and be a resident of TX, NC, OH, PA, CA or GA. Must be majoring in an engineering related field. The deadline is February 1 for sophomores and juniors and May 15 for freshmen.

Academic Fields/Career Goals Engineering/Technology; Engineering-Related Technologies. *Award* Scholarship for use in freshman, sophomore, or junior years; not renewable. *Number:* 1. *Amount:* $1000.

Eligibility Requirements Applicant must be enrolled or expecting to enroll full-time at a four-year institution or university; female and resident of California, Georgia, North Carolina, Ohio, Pennsylvania, or Texas. Applicant must have 3.0 GPA or higher. Available to U.S. citizens.

Application Requirements Application, essay, references, self-addressed stamped envelope, test scores, transcript.

World Wide Web: http://www.swe.org

Contact: Program Coordinator
Society of Women Engineers
230 East Ohio Street, Suite 400
Chicago, IL 60611-3265
Phone: 312-596-5223
Fax: 312-644-8557
E-mail: hq@swe.org

ARIZONA SECTION SCHOLARSHIP   • 191
Two scholarships given to freshmen who are either residents of Arizona or attending a school in that state. Must be studying an engineering related field. Deadline: May 15. Minimum 3.5 GPA required.

Academic Fields/Career Goals Engineering/Technology; Engineering-Related Technologies. *Award* Scholarship for use in freshman year; not renewable. *Number:* 2. *Amount:* $1000.

Eligibility Requirements Applicant must be high school student; planning to enroll or expecting to enroll full-time at a two-year or four-year institution or university and female. Applicant must have 3.5 GPA or higher.

Application Requirements Application, essay, references, self-addressed stamped envelope, test scores, transcript. *Deadline:* May 15.

World Wide Web: http://www.swe.org

Contact: Program Coordinator
Society of Women Engineers
230 East Ohio Street, Suite 400
Chicago, IL 60611-3265
Phone: 312-596-5223
Fax: 312-644-8557
E-mail: hq@swe.org

COMPAQ COMPUTER SCHOLARSHIP   see number 144

GENERAL MOTORS FOUNDATION UNDERGRADUATE SCHOLARSHIPS
see number 114

XEROX
TECHNICAL MINORITY SCHOLARSHIP
see number 115

ENGINEERING/TECHNOLOGY_____

AMERICAN ASSOCIATION OF UNIVERSITY WOMEN (AAUW) EDUCATIONAL FOUNDATION
AAUW EDUCATIONAL FOUNDATION SELECTED PROFESSIONS FELLOWSHIPS
see number 36

AMERICAN NUCLEAR SOCIETY
DELAYED EDUCATION FOR WOMEN SCHOLARSHIPS • 192
One-time award is to enable mature women whose formal studies in nuclear science, nuclear engineering, or related fields have been delayed or interrupted at least one year. Must be U.S. citizen or permanent resident in a four-year program. Application available at Web site.

Academic Fields/Career Goals Engineering/Technology; Nuclear Science. *Award* Scholarship for use in freshman, sophomore, junior, or senior years; not renewable. *Number:* 1. *Amount:* $3500.

Eligibility Requirements Applicant must be enrolled or expecting to enroll full-time at a four-year institution and female. Applicant must have 2.5 GPA or higher. Available to U.S. citizens.

Application Requirements Application, financial need analysis, references, transcript. *Deadline:* February 1.

World Wide Web: http://www.ans.org

Contact: Scholarship Coordinator
American Nuclear Society
555 North Kensington Avenue
La Grange Park, IL 60526
Phone: 708-352-6611
Fax: 708-352-0499
E-mail: outreach@ans.org

AMERICAN SOCIETY FOR ENGINEERING EDUCATION
NATIONAL DEFENSE SCIENCE AND ENGINEERING GRADUATE FELLOWSHIP PROGRAM
see number 98

AMERICAN VACUUM SOCIETY
NELLIE YEOH WHETTEN AWARD
see number 28

AMERICAN WATER WORKS ASSOCIATION

HOLLY A. CORNELL SCHOLARSHIP   see number 29

ARMED FORCES COMMUNICATIONS AND ELECTRONICS ASSOCIATION, EDUCATIONAL FOUNDATION

ARMED FORCES COMMUNICATIONS AND ELECTRONICS ASSOCIATION RALPH W. SHRADER SCHOLARSHIPS   see number 140

ASSOCIATION FOR WOMEN IN SCIENCE EDUCATIONAL FOUNDATION

ASSOCIATION FOR WOMEN IN SCIENCE PRE-DOCTORAL FELLOWSHIP
                    see number 32

ASSOCIATION FOR WOMEN IN SCIENCE UNDERGRADUATE AWARD   see number 26

BUSINESS AND PROFESSIONAL WOMEN'S FOUNDATION

BPW CAREER ADVANCEMENT SCHOLARSHIP PROGRAM FOR WOMEN
                    see number 68

CENTER FOR THE ADVANCEMENT OF HISPANICS IN SCIENCE AND ENGINEERING EDUCATION (CAHSEE)

CAHSEE FELLOWSHIP: YOUNG EDUCATORS PROGRAM   see number 30

COMTO-BOSTON CHAPTER

COMTO BOSTON/GARRETT A. MORGAN SCHOLARSHIP   see number 40

CUBAN AMERICAN NATIONAL FOUNDATION

MAS FAMILY SCHOLARSHIPS   see number 80

EAST LOS ANGELES COMMUNITY UNION (TELACU) EDUCATION FOUNDATION

TELACU ENGINEERING AWARD   see number 99

EATON CORPORATION

EATON CORPORATION MULTICULTURAL SCHOLARS PROGRAM   see number 141

FISHER BROADCASTING COMPANY

FISHER BROADCASTING, INC., SCHOLARSHIP FOR MINORITIES   see number 122

GEM CONSORTIUM

GEM MS ENGINEERING FELLOWSHIP   see number 22

GEM PHD ENGINEERING FELLOWSHIP   see number 23

HISPANIC COLLEGE FUND, INC.

ALLFIRST/ HISPANIC COLLEGE FUND SCHOLARSHIP PROGRAM   see number 10

BURLINGTON NORTHERN SANTA FE FOUNDATION/HISPANIC COLLEGE FUND SCHOLARSHIP PROGRAM   see number 11

DENNY'S/HISPANIC COLLEGE FUND SCHOLARSHIP   see number 12

FIRST IN MY FAMILY SCHOLARSHIP PROGRAM   see number 19

HISPANIC COLLEGE FUND SCHOLARSHIP PROGRAM   see number 20

HISPANIC COLLEGE FUND/INROADS/SPRINT SCHOLARSHIP PROGRAM

see number 82

NATIONAL HISPANIC EXPLORERS SCHOLARSHIP PROGRAM   see number 31

HISPANIC ENGINEER NATIONAL ACHIEVEMENT AWARDS CORPORATION (HENAAC)

HISPANIC ENGINEER NATIONAL ACHIEVEMENT AWARDS CORPORATION SCHOLARSHIP PROGRAM   see number 51

HISPANIC SCHOLARSHIP FUND

HSF/GENERAL MOTORS SCHOLARSHIP   see number 83

IMGIP/ICEOP

ILLINOIS MINORITY GRADUATE INCENTIVE PROGRAM FELLOWSHIP

see number 142

INSTITUTE OF INDUSTRIAL ENGINEERS

UPS SCHOLARSHIP FOR FEMALE STUDENTS   • 193

One-time award for female undergraduate students enrolled at any school in the U.S., Canada, or Mexico in an industrial engineering program. Must be a member of Institute of Industrial Engineers, have a minimum GPA of 3.4, and be nominated by a department head.

Academic Fields/Career Goals Engineering/Technology. *Award* Scholarship for use in freshman, sophomore, junior, or senior years; not renewable. *Number:* 1. *Amount:* $4000.

Eligibility Requirements Applicant must be enrolled or expecting to enroll full-time at a four-year institution or university and female. Applicant or parent of applicant must be member of Institute of Industrial Engineers. Available to U.S. and non-U.S. citizens.

Application Requirements Application, references, transcript, nomination. *Deadline:* November 15.

World Wide Web: http://www.iienet.org

Contact: Sherry Richards, Chapter Operations Assistant
Institute of Industrial Engineers
25 Technology Park
Norcross, GA 30092-2988
Phone: 770-449-0461 Ext. 118
Fax: 770-263-8532
E-mail: srichards@iienet.org

UPS SCHOLARSHIP FOR MINORITY STUDENTS • 194

One-time award for minority undergraduate students enrolled at any school in the U.S., Canada, or Mexico in an industrial engineering program. Must be a member of Institute of Industrial Engineers, have minimum GPA of 3.4, and be nominated by a department head.

Academic Fields/Career Goals Engineering/Technology. *Award* Scholarship for use in freshman, sophomore, junior, or senior years; not renewable. *Number:* 1. *Amount:* $4000.

Eligibility Requirements Applicant must be American Indian/Alaska Native, Asian/Pacific Islander, Black (non-Hispanic), or Hispanic and enrolled or expecting to enroll at a four-year institution or university. Applicant or parent of applicant must be member of Institute of Industrial Engineers. Available to U.S. and non-U.S. citizens.

Application Requirements Application, references, transcript, nomination. *Deadline:* November 15.

World Wide Web: http://www.iienet.org

Contact: Sherry Richards, Chapter Operations Assistant
Institute of Industrial Engineers
25 Technology Park
Norcross, GA 30092-2988
Phone: 770-449-0461 Ext. 118
Fax: 770-263-8532
E-mail: srichards@iienet.org

LEAGUE OF UNITED LATIN AMERICAN CITIZENS NATIONAL EDUCATIONAL SERVICE CENTERS, INC.

GE/LULAC SCHOLARSHIP   see number 87

GM/LULAC SCHOLARSHIP • 195

Renewable award for minority students who are pursuing an undergraduate degree in engineering at an accredited college or university. Must maintain a minimum 3.0 GPA. Selection is based in part on the likelihood of pursuing a successful career in engineering. Application deadline is July 15.

Academic Fields/Career Goals Engineering/Technology. *Award* Scholarship for use in freshman, sophomore, junior, or senior years; renewable. *Number:* 20. *Amount:* $2000.

Eligibility Requirements Applicant must be Hispanic and enrolled or expecting to enroll full-time at a four-year institution or university. Applicant must have 3.0 GPA or higher.

Application Requirements Application, references, transcript. *Deadline:* July 15.

World Wide Web: http://www.lnesc.org

GM/LULAC Scholarship (continued)

Contact: Scholarship Administrator
League of United Latin American Citizens National Educational Service Centers, Inc.
2000 L Street, NW
Suite 610
Washington, DC 20036

LOS ANGELES COUNCIL OF BLACK PROFESSIONAL ENGINEERS

AL-BEN SCHOLARSHIP FOR ACADEMIC INCENTIVE
see number 100

AL-BEN SCHOLARSHIP FOR PROFESSIONAL MERIT
see number 101

AL-BEN SCHOLARSHIP FOR SCHOLASTIC ACHIEVEMENT
see number 102

NAMEPA NATIONAL SCHOLARSHIP FOUNDATION

NATIONAL ASSOCIATION OF MINORITY ENGINEERING PROGRAM ADMINISTRATORS NATIONAL SCHOLARSHIP FUND
see number 58

NASA NEW HAMPSHIRE SPACE GRANT CONSORTIUM

GRADUATE FELLOWSHIPS
see number 161

NATIONAL ACTION COUNCIL FOR MINORITIES IN ENGINEERING-NACME, INC.

ENGINEERING VANGUARD PROGRAM
see number 103

NACME SCHOLARS PROGRAM
• 196

Renewable award for African-American, American-Indian, or Latino student enrolled in a baccalaureate engineering program. Must attend an ABET-accredited institution full-time and completed one semester with a minimum 2.7 GPA. Must be a U.S. citizen.

Academic Fields/Career Goals Engineering/Technology. *Award* Scholarship for use in freshman, sophomore, junior, or senior years; renewable. *Amount:* $3000.

Eligibility Requirements Applicant must be American Indian/Alaska Native, Black (non-Hispanic), or Hispanic and enrolled or expecting to enroll full-time at a four-year institution or university. Available to U.S. citizens.

Application Requirements Application, financial need analysis, references. *Deadline:* Continuous.

World Wide Web: http://www.nacme.org

Contact: National Action Council for Minorities in Engineering-NACME, Inc.
The Empire State Building, 350 Fifth Avenue, Suite 2212
New York, NY 10118-2299
E-mail: scholarships@nacme.org

SLOAN PHD PROGRAM
see number 104

NEW YORK STATE SOCIETY OF PROFESSIONAL ENGINEERS

NSPE AUXILIARY SCHOLARSHIP
see number 106

NSPE-VIRGINIA D. HENRY MEMORIAL SCHOLARSHIP
see number 107

OFFICE OF NAVAL RESEARCH

HISTORICALLY BLACK COLLEGES AND UNIVERSITIES FUTURE ENGINEERING FACULTY FELLOWSHIP
see number 108

SOCIETY OF AUTOMOTIVE ENGINEERS

INFORMATION HANDLING SERVICES, INC./SAE WOMEN ENGINEERS COMMITTEE SCHOLARSHIP • 197

One-time award for women accepted into an accredited engineering program. Scholarship is for freshman year only and applicants must have a minimum 3.0 GPA.

Academic Fields/Career Goals Engineering/Technology. *Award* Scholarship for use in freshman year; not renewable. *Number:* 1. *Amount:* $1500.

Eligibility Requirements Applicant must be high school student; planning to enroll or expecting to enroll at a four-year institution and female. Applicant must have 3.0 GPA or higher.

Application Requirements *Fee:* $5. *Deadline:* December 1.

World Wide Web: http://www.sae.org/students/stuschol.htm

Contact: Connie Harnish, Scholarship and Loan Coordinator
Society of Automotive Engineers
400 Commonwealth Drive
Warrendale, PA 15096-0001
Phone: 724-772-4047
Fax: 724-776-0890
E-mail: connie@sae.org

SOCIETY OF HISPANIC PROFESSIONAL ENGINEERS FOUNDATION

SOCIETY OF HISPANIC PROFESSIONAL ENGINEERS FOUNDATION
see number 109

SOCIETY OF MANUFACTURING ENGINEERS EDUCATION FOUNDATION

CATERPILLAR SCHOLARS AWARD FUND • 198

Supports five one-time scholarships of $2000 each for full-time students enrolled in a manufacturing engineering program. Minority applicants may apply as incoming freshmen. Applicants must have an overall minimum GPA of 3.0 on a 4.0 scale.

Academic Fields/Career Goals Engineering/Technology. *Award* Scholarship for use in freshman, sophomore, junior, or senior years; not renewable. *Number:* 5. *Amount:* $2000.

Eligibility Requirements Applicant must be enrolled or expecting to enroll full-time at a four-year institution or university. Applicant must have 3.0 GPA or higher.

Caterpillar Scholars Award Fund (continued)

Application Requirements Application, essay, references, transcript. *Deadline:* February 1.

World Wide Web: http://www.sme.org/foundation

Contact: Cindy Monzon, Program Coordinator
Society of Manufacturing Engineers Education Foundation
One SME Drive
PO Box 930
Dearborn, MI 48121-0930
Phone: 313-271-1500 Ext. 1707
Fax: 313-240-6095
E-mail: monzcyn@sme.org

EDWARD S. ROTH MANUFACTURING ENGINEERING SCHOLARSHIP   • 199

Awarded to a graduating high school senior, a current full time undergraduate or graduate student enrolled in an accredited four-year degree program in manufacturing engineering at a sponsored ABET accredited school. Minimum GPA of 3.0 and be a U.S. citizen. Preferences will be given to students demonstrating financial need, minority students and students participating in a Co-Op program. The top three applications will be sent to Mr. and Mrs. Roth for final selection.

Academic Fields/Career Goals Engineering/Technology. *Award* Scholarship for use in freshman, sophomore, junior, senior, or graduate years; not renewable. *Number:* 1. *Amount:* $2500.

Eligibility Requirements Applicant must be enrolled or expecting to enroll full-time at a four-year institution or university and studying in California, Florida, Illinois, Massachusetts, Minnesota, Ohio, Texas, or Utah. Applicant must have 3.0 GPA or higher. Available to U.S. citizens.

Application Requirements Application, interview. *Deadline:* February 1.

World Wide Web: http://www.sme.org/foundation

Contact: Cindy Monzon, Program Coordinator
Society of Manufacturing Engineers Education Foundation
One SME Drive
PO Box 930
Dearborn, MI 48121-0930
Phone: 313-271-1500 Ext. 1707
Fax: 313-240-6095
E-mail: monzcyn@sme.org

LUCILLE B. KAUFMAN WOMEN'S SCHOLARSHIP FUND   • 200

One-time award of $1000 for a female student enrolled full-time at an accredited college or university and studying manufacturing engineering or manufacturing engineering technology. Minimum GPA of 3.5 required and must have completed a minimum of 30 college credit hours.

Academic Fields/Career Goals Engineering/Technology. *Award* Scholarship for use in sophomore, junior, or senior years; not renewable. *Number:* 1. *Amount:* $1000.

Eligibility Requirements Applicant must be enrolled or expecting to enroll full-time at a four-year institution or university and female. Applicant must have 3.5 GPA or higher. Available to U.S. and non-U.S. citizens.

Application Requirements Application, essay, references, transcript. *Deadline:* February 1.

World Wide Web: http://www.sme.org/foundation

Contact: Cindy Monzon, Program Coordinator
Society of Manufacturing Engineers Education Foundation
One SME Drive
PO Box 930
Dearborn, MI 48121-0930
Phone: 313-271-1500 Ext. 1707
Fax: 313-240-6095
E-mail: monzcyn@sme.org

SOCIETY OF MEXICAN AMERICAN ENGINEERS AND SCIENTISTS

GRE AND GRADUATE APPLICATIONS WAIVER   see number 110

SOCIETY OF WOMEN ENGINEERS

ABB LUMMIS GLOBAL   see number 190

ADMIRAL GRACE MURRAY HOPPER MEMORIAL SCHOLARSHIP   • 201
Scholarships for female freshmen entering the study of engineering in a four-year program. Must attend an ABET-accredited or SWE-approved school and have minimum GPA of 3.5. Five one-time awards of $1000 each. Deadline: May 15.

Academic Fields/Career Goals Engineering/Technology. *Award* Scholarship for use in freshman year; not renewable. *Number:* 5. *Amount:* $1000.

Eligibility Requirements Applicant must be high school student; planning to enroll or expecting to enroll full-time at a four-year institution or university and female. Applicant must have 3.5 GPA or higher. Available to U.S. and non-U.S. citizens.

Application Requirements Application, essay, self-addressed stamped envelope, test scores, transcript. *Deadline:* May 15.

World Wide Web: http://www.swe.org

Contact: Program Coordinator
Society of Women Engineers
230 East Ohio Street, Suite 400
Chicago, IL 60611-3265
Phone: 312-596-5223
Fax: 312-644-8557
E-mail: hq@swe.org

ADOBE SYSTEMS COMPUTER SCIENCE SCHOLARSHIP   • 202
Two scholarships available to female engineering students in junior or senior year. Must have 3.0 GPA. Preference given to students attending selected schools in the San Francisco Bay area.

Academic Fields/Career Goals Engineering/Technology. *Award* Scholarship for use in junior or senior years. *Number:* 2. *Amount:* $1500–$2000.

Eligibility Requirements Applicant must be enrolled or expecting to enroll at a four-year institution or university and female. Applicant must have 3.0 GPA or higher. Available to U.S. citizens.

Application Requirements Application, references, self-addressed stamped envelope, transcript. *Deadline:* February 1.

World Wide Web: http://www.swe.org

Adobe Systems Computer Science Scholarship (continued)

Contact: Program Coordinator
Society of Women Engineers
230 East Ohio Street, Suite 400
Chicago, IL 60611-3265
Phone: 312-596-5223
Fax: 312-644-8557
E-mail: hq@swe.org

ANNE MAUREEN WHITNEY BARROW MEMORIAL SCHOLARSHIP • 203

One award for a female undergraduate entering an engineering or engineering technology degree program. Must have a minimum 3.5 GPA. Send self-addressed stamped envelope for application. Renewable award of $5000. Deadline: May 15 for freshman and February 1 for sophomores, juniors and seniors.

Academic Fields/Career Goals Engineering/Technology. *Award* Scholarship for use in freshman, sophomore, junior, or senior years; renewable. *Number:* 1. *Amount:* $5000.

Eligibility Requirements Applicant must be enrolled or expecting to enroll full-time at a four-year institution or university and female. Applicant must have 3.5 GPA or higher. Available to U.S. and non-U.S. citizens.

Application Requirements Application, essay, references, self-addressed stamped envelope, test scores, transcript.

World Wide Web: http://www.swe.org

Contact: Program Coordinator
Society of Women Engineers
230 East Ohio Street, Suite 400
Chicago, IL 60611-3265
Phone: 312-596-5223
Fax: 312-644-8557
E-mail: hq@swe.org

ARIZONA SECTION SCHOLARSHIP see number 191

B.J. HARROD SCHOLARSHIP • 204

Two $1000 awards made to an incoming female freshman majoring in engineering. Deadline for application is May 15.

Academic Fields/Career Goals Engineering/Technology. *Award* Scholarship for use in freshman year; not renewable. *Number:* 2. *Amount:* $1500.

Eligibility Requirements Applicant must be high school student; planning to enroll or expecting to enroll full-time at a two-year or four-year institution or university and female. Applicant must have 3.5 GPA or higher. Available to U.S. and non-U.S. citizens.

Application Requirements Application, essay, references, self-addressed stamped envelope, test scores, transcript. *Deadline:* May 15.

World Wide Web: http://www.swe.org

Contact: Program Coordinator
Society of Women Engineers
230 East Ohio Street, Suite 400
Chicago, IL 60611-3265
Phone: 312-596-5223
Fax: 312-644-8557
E-mail: hq@swe.org

B.K. KRENZER MEMORIAL REENTRY SCHOLARSHIP   • 205

Preference is given to degreed female engineers desiring to return to the workforce following a period of temporary retirement. Recipients may be entering any year of an engineering program, undergraduate or graduate, as full-time or part-time students. Applicants must have been out of the engineering job market as well as out of school for a minimum of two years. Deadline: May 15.

Academic Fields/Career Goals Engineering/Technology. *Award* Scholarship for use in freshman, sophomore, junior, senior, or graduate years; not renewable. *Number:* 1. *Amount:* $2000.

Eligibility Requirements Applicant must be enrolled or expecting to enroll at a two-year or four-year or technical institution or university and female. Applicant must have 3.0 GPA or higher. Available to U.S. and non-U.S. citizens.

Application Requirements Application, essay, references, self-addressed stamped envelope, test scores, transcript. *Deadline:* May 15.

World Wide Web: http://www.swe.org

Contact: Program Coordinator
Society of Women Engineers
230 East Ohio Street, Suite 400
Chicago, IL 60611-3265
Phone: 312-596-5223
Fax: 312-644-8557
E-mail: hq@swe.org

BECHTEL CORPORATION SCHOLARSHIP   see number 116

CHEVRON TEXACO CORPORATION SCHOLARSHIPS   see number 111

COMPAQ COMPUTER SCHOLARSHIP   see number 144

DAVID SARNOFF RESEARCH CENTER SCHOLARSHIP   see number 145

DELL COMPUTER CORPORATION SCHOLARSHIPS   see number 146

DELPHI SCHOLARSHIP   • 206

Scholarship for female engineering students in sophomore or junior year. Limited to students at Michigan State University, University of Michigan, Purdue University at West Lafayette, Kettering University, University of Dayton.

Academic Fields/Career Goals Engineering/Technology. *Award* Scholarship for use in sophomore or junior years. *Number:* 1. *Amount:* $5000.

Eligibility Requirements Applicant must be enrolled or expecting to enroll full-time at an institution or university; female and studying in Indiana, Michigan, or Ohio. Applicant must have 3.0 GPA or higher. Available to U.S. citizens.

Application Requirements Application, references, self-addressed stamped envelope, transcript. *Deadline:* February 1.

World Wide Web: http://www.swe.org

Contact: Program Coordinator
Society of Women Engineers
230 East Ohio Street, Suite 400
Chicago, IL 60611-3265
Phone: 312-596-5223
Fax: 312-644-8557
E-mail: hq@swe.org

DOROTHY LEMKE HOWARTH SCHOLARSHIPS • 207

Scholarship awarded to entering female sophomore students in engineering who are U.S. citizens attending a four-year institution. Send self-addressed stamped envelope for more information. Must have minimum 3.0 GPA. Five one-time awards of $2000 each. Deadline: February 1.

Academic Fields/Career Goals Engineering/Technology. *Award* Scholarship for use in sophomore year; not renewable. *Number:* 5. *Amount:* $2000.

Eligibility Requirements Applicant must be enrolled or expecting to enroll at a four-year institution or university and female. Applicant must have 3.0 GPA or higher. Available to U.S. citizens.

Application Requirements Application, essay, references, self-addressed stamped envelope, test scores, transcript. *Deadline:* February 1.

World Wide Web: http://www.swe.org

Contact: Program Coordinator
Society of Women Engineers
230 East Ohio Street, Suite 400
Chicago, IL 60611-3265
Phone: 312-596-5223
Fax: 312-644-8557
E-mail: hq@swe.org

DOROTHY M. AND EARL S. HOFFMAN SCHOLARSHIP • 208

Renewable 3-year scholarship for female freshman engineering students. Must have minimum 3.5 GPA. Preference given to students at Bucknell University and Rensselaer Polytechnic University.

Academic Fields/Career Goals Engineering/Technology. *Award* Scholarship for use in freshman year; renewable. *Number:* 3. *Amount:* $3000.

Eligibility Requirements Applicant must be high school student; planning to enroll or expecting to enroll full-time at a four-year institution or university and female. Applicant must have 3.5 GPA or higher. Available to U.S. citizens.

Application Requirements Application, references, self-addressed stamped envelope, transcript. *Deadline:* May 15.

World Wide Web: http://www.swe.org

Contact: Program Coordinator
Society of Women Engineers
230 East Ohio Street, Suite 400
Chicago, IL 60611-3265
Phone: 312-596-5223
Fax: 312-644-8557
E-mail: hq@swe.org

ELECTRONICS FOR IMAGING (EFI) SCHOLARSHIPS • 209

Four scholarships available to female engineering students in sophomore, junior, senior year and graduate study. Preference given to students attending selected schools in the San Francisco Bay area.

Academic Fields/Career Goals Engineering/Technology. *Award* Scholarship for use in sophomore, junior, senior, or graduate years. *Number:* 4. *Amount:* $4000.

Eligibility Requirements Applicant must be enrolled or expecting to enroll full-time at a four-year institution or university and female. Applicant must have 3.0 GPA or higher. Available to U.S. citizens.

Application Requirements Application, references, self-addressed stamped envelope, transcript. *Deadline:* February 1.
World Wide Web: http://www.swe.org
Contact: Program Coordinator
Society of Women Engineers
230 East Ohio Street, Suite 400
Chicago, IL 60611-3265
Phone: 312-596-5223
Fax: 312-644-8557
E-mail: hq@swe.org

FORD MOTOR COMPANY SCHOLARSHIP • 210

One $1000 scholarship will be awarded to a female student studying engineering. Eligible applicants will be sophomores demonstrating leadership qualities.

Academic Fields/Career Goals Engineering/Technology. *Award* Scholarship for use in sophomore year; not renewable. *Number:* 1. *Amount:* $1000.
Eligibility Requirements Applicant must be enrolled or expecting to enroll at an institution or university; female and must have an interest in leadership. Applicant must have 3.5 GPA or higher. Available to U.S. citizens.
Application Requirements Application, references, self-addressed stamped envelope, transcript. *Deadline:* February 1.
World Wide Web: http://www.swe.org
Contact: Program Coordinator
Society of Women Engineers
230 East Ohio Street, Suite 400
Chicago, IL 60611-3265
Phone: 312-596-5223
Fax: 312-644-8557
E-mail: hq@swe.org

GENERAL ELECTRIC FOUNDATION SCHOLARSHIP • 211

Renewable award for outstanding women engineering students. Renewable for three years with continued academic achievement. Send self-addressed stamped envelope for more information. Must be U.S. citizen. Three scholarships at $1000 each. Must have a minimum 3.5 GPA. Deadline: May 15.

Academic Fields/Career Goals Engineering/Technology. *Award* Scholarship for use in freshman year; renewable. *Number:* 3. *Amount:* $1000.
Eligibility Requirements Applicant must be high school student; planning to enroll or expecting to enroll at a four-year institution or university and female. Applicant must have 3.5 GPA or higher. Available to U.S. citizens.
Application Requirements Application, essay, references, self-addressed stamped envelope, test scores, transcript. *Deadline:* May 15.
World Wide Web: http://www.swe.org
Contact: Program Coordinator
Society of Women Engineers
230 East Ohio Street, Suite 400
Chicago, IL 60611-3265
Phone: 312-596-5223
Fax: 312-644-8557
E-mail: hq@swe.org

GENERAL MOTORS FOUNDATION GRADUATE SCHOLARSHIP   see number 113

GENERAL MOTORS FOUNDATION UNDERGRADUATE SCHOLARSHIPS
see number 114

IVY PARKER MEMORIAL SCHOLARSHIP   • 212

One-time award for female engineering major. Must be in junior or senior year and have a minimum 3.0 GPA. Selection also based on financial need. Deadline: February 1.

Academic Fields/Career Goals Engineering/Technology. *Award* Scholarship for use in junior or senior years; not renewable. *Number:* 1. *Amount:* $2500.

Eligibility Requirements Applicant must be enrolled or expecting to enroll at a four-year institution or university and female. Applicant must have 3.0 GPA or higher. Available to U.S. citizens.

Application Requirements Application, financial need analysis, references, self-addressed stamped envelope, transcript. *Deadline:* February 1.

World Wide Web: http://www.swe.org

Contact: Program Coordinator
Society of Women Engineers
230 East Ohio Street, Suite 400
Chicago, IL 60611-3265
Phone: 312-596-5223
Fax: 312-644-8557
E-mail: hq@swe.org

JUDITH RESNIK MEMORIAL SCHOLARSHIP   see number 59

LILIAN MOLLER GILBRETH SCHOLARSHIP   • 213

One award for college junior or senior female engineering student. Must be a U.S. citizen and possess outstanding potential demonstrated by achievement. Send self-addressed stamped envelope for application. One-time award of $6000. Must rank in upper third of class or have a minimum GPA of 3.0. Deadline: February 1.

Academic Fields/Career Goals Engineering/Technology. *Award* Scholarship for use in junior or senior years; not renewable. *Number:* 1. *Amount:* $6000.

Eligibility Requirements Applicant must be enrolled or expecting to enroll at a four-year institution or university and female. Applicant must have 3.0 GPA or higher. Available to U.S. citizens.

Application Requirements Application, essay, references, self-addressed stamped envelope, test scores, transcript. *Deadline:* February 1.

World Wide Web: http://www.swe.org

Contact: Program Coordinator
Society of Women Engineers
230 East Ohio Street, Suite 400
Chicago, IL 60611-3265
Phone: 312-596-5223
Fax: 312-644-8557
E-mail: hq@swe.org

LOCKHEED-MARTIN CORPORATION SCHOLARSHIPS   • 214

Two $3000 scholarships awarded to female incoming freshmen majoring in engineering. Minimum 3.5 GPA required. Deadline for application is May 15.

Academic Fields/Career Goals Engineering/Technology. *Award* Scholarship for use in freshman year; not renewable. *Number:* 2. *Amount:* $3000.

Eligibility Requirements Applicant must be enrolled or expecting to enroll full-time at a four-year institution or university and female. Applicant must have 3.5 GPA or higher. Available to U.S. and non-U.S. citizens.

Application Requirements Application, essay, references, self-addressed stamped envelope, test scores, transcript. *Deadline:* May 15.

World Wide Web: http://www.swe.org

Contact: Program Coordinator
Society of Women Engineers
230 East Ohio Street, Suite 400
Chicago, IL 60611-3265
Phone: 312-596-5223
Fax: 312-644-8557
E-mail: hq@swe.org

LYDIA I. PICKUP MEMORIAL SCHOLARSHIP

see number 147

MASWE MEMORIAL SCHOLARSHIP • 215

Four $2000 awards for female engineering students who are sophomores, juniors, or seniors in college. Must be U.S. citizens and have minimum 3.0 GPA. Send self-addressed stamped envelope for application. Selection also based on financial need. Deadline: February 1.

Academic Fields/Career Goals Engineering/Technology. *Award* Scholarship for use in sophomore, junior, or senior years; not renewable. *Number:* 4. *Amount:* $2000.

Eligibility Requirements Applicant must be enrolled or expecting to enroll at a four-year institution or university and female. Applicant must have 3.0 GPA or higher. Available to U.S. citizens.

Application Requirements Application, essay, financial need analysis, self-addressed stamped envelope, test scores, transcript. *Deadline:* February 1.

World Wide Web: http://www.swe.org

Contact: Program Coordinator
Society of Women Engineers
230 East Ohio Street, Suite 400
Chicago, IL 60611-3265
Phone: 312-596-5223
Fax: 312-644-8557
E-mail: hq@swe.org

MERIDITH THOMS MEMORIAL SCHOLARSHIP • 216

Renewable award available to female engineering majors. Minimum 3.0 GPA required. Must be in ABET-accredited engineering program at SWE-approved colleges and universities.

Academic Fields/Career Goals Engineering/Technology. *Award* Scholarship for use in sophomore, junior, or senior years; renewable. *Number:* 6. *Amount:* $2000.

Eligibility Requirements Applicant must be enrolled or expecting to enroll at a four-year institution or university and female. Applicant must have 3.0 GPA or higher.

Application Requirements Application, references, self-addressed stamped envelope, test scores, transcript. *Deadline:* February 1.

World Wide Web: http://www.swe.org

Meridith Thoms Memorial Scholarship (continued)

Contact: Program Coordinator
Society of Women Engineers
230 East Ohio Street, Suite 400
Chicago, IL 60611-3265
Phone: 312-596-5223
Fax: 312-644-8557
E-mail: hq@swe.org

NEW JERSEY SCHOLARSHIP   • 217

Award granted to female New Jersey resident majoring in engineering. Available to incoming freshman. Minimum 3.5 GPA required. Application deadline is May 15.

Academic Fields/Career Goals Engineering/Technology. *Award* Scholarship for use in freshman year; not renewable. *Number:* 1. *Amount:* $1500.

Eligibility Requirements Applicant must be enrolled or expecting to enroll full-time at an institution or university; female and resident of New Jersey. Applicant must have 3.5 GPA or higher. Available to U.S. citizens.

Application Requirements Application, essay, references, self-addressed stamped envelope, test scores, transcript. *Deadline:* May 15.

World Wide Web: http://www.swe.org

Contact: Program Coordinator
Society of Women Engineers
230 East Ohio Street, Suite 400
Chicago, IL 60611-3265
Phone: 312-596-5223
Fax: 312-644-8557
E-mail: hq@swe.org

OLIVE LYNN SALEMBIER SCHOLARSHIP   • 218

One $2000 award for female students entering any undergraduate or graduate year as full- or part-time students. Applicants must have been out of the engineering job market as well as out of school for a minimum of two years. Application deadline is May 15.

Academic Fields/Career Goals Engineering/Technology. *Award* Scholarship for use in freshman, sophomore, junior, senior, or graduate years; not renewable. *Number:* 1. *Amount:* $2000.

Eligibility Requirements Applicant must be enrolled or expecting to enroll full or part-time at a four-year institution or university and female.

Application Requirements Application, essay, references, self-addressed stamped envelope, test scores, transcript. *Deadline:* May 15.

World Wide Web: http://www.swe.org

Contact: Program Coordinator
Society of Women Engineers
230 East Ohio Street, Suite 400
Chicago, IL 60611-3265
Phone: 312-596-5223
Fax: 312-644-8557
E-mail: hq@swe.org

PAST PRESIDENTS SCHOLARSHIPS   • 219

Two $1500 awards offered to female undergraduate or graduate students majoring in engineering. Minimum 3.0 GPA required. Must be U.S. citizen. Deadline: February 1.

Academic Fields/Career Goals Engineering/Technology. *Award* Scholarship for use in sophomore, junior, senior, or graduate years; renewable. *Number:* 2. *Amount:* $1500.

Eligibility Requirements Applicant must be enrolled or expecting to enroll full-time at a four-year institution or university and female. Applicant must have 3.0 GPA or higher. Available to U.S. citizens.

Application Requirements Application, essay, references, self-addressed stamped envelope, test scores, transcript. *Deadline:* February 1.

World Wide Web: http://www.swe.org

Contact: Program Coordinator
Society of Women Engineers
230 East Ohio Street, Suite 400
Chicago, IL 60611-3265
Phone: 312-596-5223
Fax: 312-644-8557
E-mail: hq@swe.org

SOCIETY OF WOMEN ENGINEERS-PACIFIC NORTHWEST SECTION

MARY ELLEN RUSSELL MEMORIAL SCHOLARSHIP • 220

Scholarship for women in their junior year who are studying engineering at an ABET-accredited engineering school in Montana or Western Washington.

Academic Fields/Career Goals Engineering/Technology. *Award* Scholarship for use in junior year; not renewable. *Amount:* $1000–$1500.

Eligibility Requirements Applicant must be enrolled or expecting to enroll full-time at an institution or university; female; resident of Montana or Washington and studying in Montana or Washington. Available to U.S. citizens.

Application Requirements Application, essay, references, transcript. *Deadline:* March 1.

World Wide Web: http://www.swe-pnw.org

Contact: Mary Moloseau Goetz, Scholarship Chair
Society of Women Engineers-Pacific Northwest Section
610 West Blaine
Seattle, WA 98119-2928

SOCIETY OF WOMEN ENGINEERS-ROCKY MOUNTAIN SECTION

SOCIETY OF WOMEN ENGINEERS-ROCKY MOUNTAIN SECTION SCHOLARSHIP PROGRAM
see number 149

TRIANGLE EDUCATION FOUNDATION

SEVCIK SCHOLARSHIP • 221

One-time award for active member of the Triangle Fraternity. Must be full-time male student who has completed at least two full academic years of school. Minimum 3.0 GPA. Preference to minority students and Ohio State undergraduates who are engineering majors. Application must be postmarked by April 30. Further information available at Web site http://www.triangle.org.

Academic Fields/Career Goals Engineering/Technology. *Award* Scholarship for use in junior or senior years; not renewable. *Number:* 1. *Amount:* $6000.

Sevcik Scholarship (continued)

Eligibility Requirements Applicant must be American Indian/Alaska Native, Asian/Pacific Islander, Black (non-Hispanic), or Hispanic; enrolled or expecting to enroll full-time at a four-year institution or university and male. Applicant must have 3.0 GPA or higher.

Application Requirements Application, essay, financial need analysis, references, self-addressed stamped envelope, transcript. *Deadline:* April 30.

World Wide Web: http://www.triangle.org

Contact: Scott Bova, Chief Operating Officer
Triangle Education Foundation
120 South Center Street
Plainfield, IN 46168-1214
Phone: 317-837-9641
Fax: 317-837-9642
E-mail: sbova@triangle.org

UNITED NEGRO COLLEGE FUND

COLLEGE FUND/COCA COLA CORPORATE INTERN PROGRAM see number 92

VIRGINIA BUSINESS AND PROFESSIONAL WOMEN'S FOUNDATION

WOMEN IN SCIENCE AND TECHNOLOGY SCHOLARSHIP see number 74

XEROX

TECHNICAL MINORITY SCHOLARSHIP see number 115

FASHION DESIGN

WORLDSTUDIO FOUNDATION

WORLDSTUDIO FOUNDATION SCHOLARSHIP PROGRAM see number 42

FILMMAKING/VIDEO

WORLDSTUDIO FOUNDATION SCHOLARSHIP PROGRAM see number 42

FOOD SCIENCE/NUTRITION

AGA FOUNDATION FOR DIGESTIVE HEALTH AND NUTRITION

AMERICAN GASTROENTEROLOGICAL ASSOCIATION STUDENT RESEARCH FELLOWSHIP UNDERREPRESENTED MINORITIES AWARD • 222

Award offers financial support for underrepresented minority students to spend time performing research in the areas of digestive diseases or nutrition. For the purpose of this award, minorities have been defined as African-American, Native-Americans (American-Indian, Alaska/Hawaii native), Mexican-American and Mainland Puerto Rican. Candidates may be high school, undergraduate, medical or graduate students (not yet engaged in thesis research) at accredited U.S. or Canadian institutions. Application deadline: March 5.

Academic Fields/Career Goals Food Science/Nutrition; Health and Medical Sciences. *Award* Fellowship for use in freshman, sophomore, junior, senior, or graduate years; not renewable. *Number:* up to 7. *Amount:* $2000–$3000.

Eligibility Requirements Applicant must be American Indian/Alaska Native, Black (non-Hispanic), or Hispanic and enrolled or expecting to enroll at a two-year or four-year institution or university. Available to U.S. and Canadian citizens.

Application Requirements *Deadline:* March 5.

World Wide Web: http://www.fdhn.org

Contact: Desta Wallace, Research Awards Manager
AGA Foundation for Digestive Health and Nutrition
4930 Del Ray Avenue
Bethesda, MD 20814
Phone: 301-222-4005
Fax: 301-222-4010
E-mail: desta@gastro.org

CALIFORNIA ADOLESCENT NUTRITION AND FITNESS (CANFIT) PROGRAM

CALIFORNIA ADOLESCENT NUTRITION AND FITNESS (CANFIT) PROGRAM SCHOLARSHIP • 223

Award for undergraduate and graduate African-American, American-Indian/Alaska Native, Asian/Pacific Islander or Latino/Hispanic students who express financial need and are studying nutrition, physical fitness, or culinary arts in California. Minimum GPA of 2.5. Must be California resident. Application deadline: March 31.

Academic Fields/Career Goals Food Science/Nutrition; Food Service/Hospitality; Health and Medical Sciences; Sports-related. *Award* Scholarship for use in junior, senior, graduate, or postgraduate years; not renewable. *Number:* 10–15. *Amount:* $500–$1500.

Eligibility Requirements Applicant must be American Indian/Alaska Native, Asian/Pacific Islander, Black (non-Hispanic), or Hispanic; enrolled or expecting to enroll full or part-time at a four-year or technical institution or university; resident of California and studying in California. Applicant must have 2.5 GPA or higher. Available to U.S. citizens.

Application Requirements Application, essay, financial need analysis, photo, references, transcript, letter by applicant about themselves. *Deadline:* March 31.

World Wide Web: http://www.canfit.org

Contact: Leena Kamat, Office Manager
California Adolescent Nutrition and Fitness (CANFit) Program
2140 Shattuck Avenue, Suite 610
Berkeley, CA 94704
Phone: 510-644-1533
Fax: 510-644-1535
E-mail: info@canfit.org

HISPANIC COLLEGE FUND, INC.

NATIONAL HISPANIC EXPLORERS SCHOLARSHIP PROGRAM   see number 31

JAMES BEARD FOUNDATION, INC.

FELIPE ROJAS-LOMBARDI SCHOLARSHIPS •224

One-time scholarship towards tuition at an accredited culinary school. Applicant must be of Hispanic/Latino origin or have lived within the Hispanic community. Applicant must submit a 500-word essay demonstrating knowledge of Hispanic/Latino cultures and cuisine and expressing career goals. Candidates must demonstrate a strong commitment to the culinary arts, an exceptional academic or work record, and financial need. See Web site at http://www.jamesbeard.org for further details.

Academic Fields/Career Goals Food Science/Nutrition. *Award* Scholarship for use in freshman, sophomore, junior, senior, or graduate years; not renewable. *Amount:* $5000.

Eligibility Requirements Applicant must be enrolled or expecting to enroll at an institution or university. Available to U.S. and non-U.S. citizens.

Application Requirements Application, essay, financial need analysis, references, transcript. *Deadline:* May 1.

World Wide Web: http://www.jamesbeard.org

Contact: Caroline Stuart, Scholarship Director
James Beard Foundation, Inc.
167 West 12th Street
New York, NY 10011
Phone: 212-675-4984 Ext. 311
Fax: 212-645-1438
E-mail: jamesbeardfound@hotmail.com

MARIN EDUCATION FUND

GOLDMAN FAMILY FUND, NEW LEADER SCHOLARSHIP see number 156

UNITED DAUGHTERS OF THE CONFEDERACY

WALTER REED SMITH SCHOLARSHIP see number 91

FOOD SERVICE/HOSPITALITY_____

CALIFORNIA ADOLESCENT NUTRITION AND FITNESS (CANFIT) PROGRAM

CALIFORNIA ADOLESCENT NUTRITION AND FITNESS (CANFIT) PROGRAM SCHOLARSHIP see number 223

FOREIGN LANGUAGE_____

ARKANSAS DEPARTMENT OF HIGHER EDUCATION

MINORITY MASTER'S FELLOWS PROGRAM see number 168

HISPANIC DIVISION, LIBRARY OF CONGRESS

HISPANIC DIVISION FELLOWSHIPS   see number 43

INSTITUTE FOR INTERNATIONAL PUBLIC POLICY (IIPP)

INSTITUTE FOR INTERNATIONAL PUBLIC POLICY FELLOWSHIP PROGRAM
see number 44

NATIONAL RESEARCH COUNCIL

FORD FOUNDATION DISSERTATION FELLOWSHIPS FOR MINORITIES
see number 125

FORD FOUNDATION POSTDOCTORAL FELLOWSHIP FOR MINORITIES
see number 126

FORD FOUNDATION PRE-DOCTORAL FELLOWSHIPS FOR MINORITIES
see number 127

PHI BETA KAPPA SOCIETY

MARY ISABEL SIBLEY FELLOWSHIP FOR GREEK AND FRENCH STUDIES
see number 33

SOCIEDAD HONORARIA HISPÁNICA

JOSEPH S. ADAMS SCHOLARSHIP   **• 225**
Applicants must be members of the Sociedad Honoraria Hispánica and a high school senior. Must have major/career interest in Spanish/Portuguese. Applicants must demonstrate high academic achievement, depth of character, leadership, patriotism, seriousness of purpose. Award available to citizens of other countries as long as they are members of the Sacred Honoraria Hispánica. For information contact local sponsor of Sociedad Honoraria Hispánica. For high school students only.

Academic Fields/Career Goals Foreign Language. *Award* Scholarship for use in freshman year; not renewable. *Number:* 44. *Amount:* $1000–$2000.

Eligibility Requirements Applicant must be high school student; planning to enroll or expecting to enroll full-time at a four-year institution or university and must have an interest in Portuguese language or Spanish language. Available to U.S. and non-U.S. citizens.

World Wide Web: http://www.sociedadhonorariahispanica.org
Contact: local sponsor of SHH at high school

GEOGRAPHY

ASSOCIATION FOR WOMEN IN SCIENCE EDUCATIONAL FOUNDATION

ASSOCIATION FOR WOMEN IN SCIENCE PRE-DOCTORAL FELLOWSHIP
see number 32

HISPANIC DIVISION, LIBRARY OF CONGRESS

HISPANIC DIVISION FELLOWSHIPS   see number 43

NASA NEW HAMPSHIRE SPACE GRANT CONSORTIUM

GRADUATE FELLOWSHIPS   see number 161

GRAPHICS/GRAPHIC ARTS/PRINTING_____

COMMUNITY FOUNDATION FOR PALM BEACH AND MARTIN COUNTIES, INC.

GINA AUDITORE BONER MEMORIAL SCHOLARSHIP FUND   see number 78

DALLAS-FORT WORTH ASSOCIATION OF BLACK COMMUNICATORS

FUTURE JOURNALISTS SCHOLARSHIP PROGRAM   see number 121

HISPANIC COLLEGE FUND, INC.

DENNY'S/HISPANIC COLLEGE FUND SCHOLARSHIP   see number 12

FIRST IN MY FAMILY SCHOLARSHIP PROGRAM   see number 19

HISPANIC COLLEGE FUND SCHOLARSHIP PROGRAM   see number 20

KNIGHT RIDDER

KNIGHT RIDDER MINORITY SCHOLARSHIP PROGRAM   see number 86

WORLDSTUDIO FOUNDATION

WORLDSTUDIO FOUNDATION SCHOLARSHIP PROGRAM   see number 42

HEALTH ADMINISTRATION_____

CONGRESSIONAL BLACK CAUCUS SPOUSES PROGRAM

CONGRESSIONAL BLACK CAUCUS SPOUSES HEALTH INITIATIVE   • 226

Award made to students who reside or attend school in a congressional district represented by an African-American member of Congress. Must be full-time undergraduate enrolled in health-related program. Minimum 2.5 GPA required. Contact the congressional office in the appropriate district for information and applications. Visit http://www.cbcfinc.org for a list of district offices.

Academic Fields/Career Goals Health Administration; Health and Medical Sciences; Health Information Management/Technology. *Award* Scholarship for use in freshman, sophomore, junior, or senior years; renewable. *Number:* 200. *Amount:* $500–$4000.

Eligibility Requirements Applicant must be enrolled or expecting to enroll full-time at a two-year or four-year or technical institution or university. Applicant must have 2.5 GPA or higher. Available to U.S. citizens.

Application Requirements Application, essay, financial need analysis, interview, photo, references, transcript. *Deadline:* Continuous.

World Wide Web: http://cbcfinc.org

Contact: Appropriate Congressional District Office

FOUNDATION OF AMERICAN COLLEGE HEALTHCARE EXECUTIVES

ALBERT W. DENT GRADUATE STUDENT SCHOLARSHIP • 227

One-time award for minority student enrolled full-time in final year of a healthcare management graduate program. Must be a Student Associate of the American College of Healthcare Executives. Must demonstrate financial need. Must be U.S. or Canadian citizen. Must be recommended by program director.

Academic Fields/Career Goals Health Administration; Health Information Management/ Technology. *Award* Scholarship for use in graduate years; not renewable. *Number:* 1-6. *Amount:* $3500.

Eligibility Requirements Applicant must be American Indian/Alaska Native, Asian/Pacific Islander, Black (non-Hispanic), or Hispanic and enrolled or expecting to enroll full-time at an institution or university. Available to U.S. and Canadian citizens.

Application Requirements Application, essay, financial need analysis, resume, references, transcript. *Deadline:* March 31.

World Wide Web: http://www.ache.org

Contact: Division of Membership
Foundation of American College Healthcare Executives
1 North Franklin Street, Suite 1700
Chicago, IL 60606-3461
E-mail: ache@ache.org

MARIN EDUCATION FUND

GOLDMAN FAMILY FUND, NEW LEADER SCHOLARSHIP see number 156

NATIONAL MEDICAL FELLOWSHIPS, INC.

W.K. KELLOGG FELLOWSHIP PROGRAM IN HEALTH POLICY RESEARCH • 228

Student must be a U.S. citizen; African-American, Hispanic, Native-Americans, or Asian with a demonstrated commitment to medically underserved areas; committed to working with underserved populations upon completion of doctorate; and willing to complete relevant dissertation research. Student must also be accepted or enrolled in a doctoral program in one of the following participating schools: The Heller Graduate School at Brandeis University, the Joseph L. Mailman School of Public Health of Columbia University, the Harvard School of Public Health, the Johns Hopkins School of Hygiene and Public Health, the RAND Graduate

W.K. Kellogg Fellowship Program in Health Policy Research (continued)

School, the UCLA School of Public Health, and the University of Michigan School of Public Health. Award will provide a yearly stipend to cover tuition, fees, and living expenses for up to five years.

Academic Fields/Career Goals Health Administration; Health and Medical Sciences; Health Information Management/Technology. *Award* Fellowship for use in graduate years; not renewable. *Number:* 5.

Eligibility Requirements Applicant must be American Indian/Alaska Native, Asian/Pacific Islander, Black (non-Hispanic), or Hispanic; enrolled or expecting to enroll at an institution or university and studying in California, Maryland, Massachusetts, Michigan, or New York. Available to U.S. citizens.

Application Requirements Application, essay, resume, references, transcript, curriculum vitae. *Deadline:* July 26.

World Wide Web: http://www.nmf-online.org

Contact: Fellowship Coordinator
National Medical Fellowships, Inc.
5 Hanover Square, 15th Floor
New York, NY 10004

ROSCOE POUND INSTITUTE

ELAINE OSBORNE JACOBSON AWARD FOR WOMEN WORKING IN HEALTH CARE LAW • 229

For female law students who, through academics and career experience, demonstrate commitment to advocacy for health-care needs of women, elderly, the disabled, and children. One-time award of $3000. Must study in North America.

Academic Fields/Career Goals Health Administration; Health and Medical Sciences; Law/Legal Services. *Award* Prize for use in graduate years; not renewable. *Number:* 1. *Amount:* $3000.

Eligibility Requirements Applicant must be enrolled or expecting to enroll full-time at an institution or university and female. Available to U.S. and non-U.S. citizens.

Application Requirements Application, autobiography, essay, resume, references. *Deadline:* January 24.

World Wide Web: http://www.roscoepound.org

Contact: Mr. Alexander Harrington, Membership and Education Coordinator
Roscoe Pound Institute
1050 31st Street, NW
Washington, DC 20007-4499
Phone: 202-965-3500 Ext. 385
Fax: 202-965-0355
E-mail: alexander.harrington@atlahq.org

WOMEN OF THE EVANGELICAL LUTHERAN CHURCH IN AMERICA

HEALTH SERVICES SCHOLARSHIP FOR WOMEN STUDYING ABROAD • 230

Scholarships provided for ELCA women studying for service in health professions associated with ELCA projects abroad. Must be at least 21 years old and hold membership in the ELCA. Must have experienced an interruption in education of two or more years since the completion of high school. For more details see Web site: http://www.elca.org/wo.

Academic Fields/Career Goals Health Administration; Health and Medical Sciences; Health Information Management/Technology. *Award* Scholarship for use in freshman, sophomore, junior, senior, or graduate years; not renewable. *Number:* 3. *Amount:* up to $1200.
Eligibility Requirements Applicant must be Lutheran; age 21; enrolled or expecting to enroll at an institution or university and female. Available to U.S. citizens.
Application Requirements *Deadline:* February 15.
World Wide Web: http://www.elca.org/wo
Contact: application available at Web site

HEALTH AND MEDICAL SCIENCES_____

AGA FOUNDATION FOR DIGESTIVE HEALTH AND NUTRITION

AMERICAN GASTROENTEROLOGICAL ASSOCIATION RESEARCH SCHOLAR AWARDS FOR UNDERREPRESENTED MINORITIES • 231
Award provides support for young, underrepresented minority investigators (American-Indian/Alaska-Hawaii native, Mexican-American and Mainland Puerto Rican) working toward an independent research career in any area of gastroenterology, hepatology or related areas. Applicants must hold full-time faculty positions at U.S. or Canadian universities or professional institutes at the time of application. Must be a member of AGA. Award is $65,000 per year for three years. Deadline: September 5.
Academic Fields/Career Goals Health and Medical Sciences. *Award* Grant for use in postgraduate years; not renewable. *Number:* 1. *Amount:* $195,000.
Eligibility Requirements Applicant must be American Indian/Alaska Native, Asian/Pacific Islander, or Hispanic and enrolled or expecting to enroll at an institution or university. Applicant or parent of applicant must have employment or volunteer experience in teaching. Available to U.S. and Canadian citizens.
Application Requirements Application, autobiography, essay, references, abstract. *Deadline:* September 5.
World Wide Web: http://www.fdhn.org
Contact: Desta Wallace, Research Awards Manager
AGA Foundation for Digestive Health and Nutrition
4930 Del Ray Avenue
Bethesda, MD 20814
Phone: 301-222-4005
Fax: 301-222-4010
E-mail: desta@gastro.org

AMERICAN GASTROENTEROLOGICAL ASSOCIATION STUDENT RESEARCH FELLOWSHIP UNDERREPRESENTED MINORITIES AWARD see number 222

AMERICAN ACADEMY OF CHILD AND ADOLESCENT PSYCHIATRY (AACAP)

AACAP JEANNE SPURLOCK MINORITY MEDICAL STUDENT CLINICAL FELLOWSHIP IN CHILD AND ADOLESCENT PSYCHIATRY • 232
Awards to African-American, Asian-American, Native-Americans, Alaskan Native, Mexican-American, Hispanic, and Pacific Islander students in accredited U.S. medical schools. Up to 14

AACAP Jeanne Spurlock Minority Medical Student Clinical Fellowship in Child and Adolescent Psychiatry (continued)

$2500 awards for work during the summer with a child and adolescent psychiatrist mentor, plus five days at the AACAP Annual Meeting. Deadline: February 1. The availability of all awards is contingent on the receipt of adequate funding.

Academic Fields/Career Goals Health and Medical Sciences. *Award* Fellowship for use in graduate years; not renewable. *Number:* up to 14. *Amount:* $2500.

Eligibility Requirements Applicant must be American Indian/Alaska Native, Asian/Pacific Islander, Black (non-Hispanic), or Hispanic and enrolled or expecting to enroll at an institution or university. Available to U.S. citizens.

Application Requirements Application. *Deadline:* February 1.

World Wide Web: http://www.aacap.org

Contact: Trish Brown, Director of Research and Training
American Academy of Child and Adolescent Psychiatry (AACAP)
3615 Wisconsin Avenue, NW
Washington, DC 20016-3007
Phone: 202-966-7300 Ext. 113
Fax: 202-966-2891
E-mail: tbrown@aacap.org

AACAP JEANNE SPURLOCK RESEARCH FELLOWSHIP IN DRUG ABUSE AND ADDICTION FOR MINORITY MEDICAL STUDENTS • 233

Awards to African-American, Asian-American, Native-Americans, Alaskan Native, Mexican-American, Hispanic, and Pacific Islander students in accredited U.S. medical schools. Five $2500 awards for substance abuse-related research during the summer with a child and adolescent psychiatrist researcher-mentor, plus five days at the AACAP Annual Meeting. Deadline February 1. The availability of all awards is contingent on the receipt of adequate funding.

Academic Fields/Career Goals Health and Medical Sciences. *Award* Fellowship for use in graduate years; not renewable. *Number:* 5. *Amount:* $2500.

Eligibility Requirements Applicant must be American Indian/Alaska Native, Asian/Pacific Islander, Black (non-Hispanic), or Hispanic and enrolled or expecting to enroll full-time at an institution or university. Available to U.S. citizens.

Application Requirements Application. *Deadline:* February 1.

World Wide Web: http://www.aacap.org

Contact: Trish Brown, Director of Research and Training
American Academy of Child and Adolescent Psychiatry (AACAP)
3615 Wisconsin Avenue, NW
Washington, DC 20016-3007
Phone: 202-966-7300 Ext. 113
Fax: 202-966-2891
E-mail: tbrown@aacap.org

AMERICAN ASSOCIATION OF UNIVERSITY WOMEN (AAUW) EDUCATIONAL FOUNDATION

AAUW EDUCATIONAL FOUNDATION SELECTED PROFESSIONS FELLOWSHIPS

see number 36

AMERICAN PHYSIOLOGICAL SOCIETY

AMERICAN PHYSIOLOGICAL SOCIETY MINORITY TRAVEL FELLOWSHIPS
see number 25

PORTER PHYSIOLOGY FELLOWSHIPS
see number 64

AMERICAN PSYCHIATRIC ASSOCIATION

AMERICAN PSYCHIATRIC ASSOCIATION/CENTER FOR MENTAL HEALTH SERVICES MINORITY FELLOWSHIP PROGRAM • 234

One-time award for psychiatric residents interested in areas of psychiatry where minority groups are underrepresented. Fellows are selected on the basis of their commitment to serve underrepresented populations, their demonstrated leadership abilities, and their interest in the interrelationship between mental health or illness and transcultural factors. Must be in at least second year of postgraduate training. Must be U.S. citizen or permanent resident. Submit curriculum vitae. Number of awards varies.

Academic Fields/Career Goals Health and Medical Sciences. *Award* Fellowship for use in postgraduate years; not renewable. *Number:* 10.

Eligibility Requirements Applicant must be enrolled or expecting to enroll full-time at an institution or university. Available to U.S. citizens.

Application Requirements Application, essay, interview, references, transcript, curriculum vitae. *Deadline:* January 31.

World Wide Web: http://www.psych.org

Contact: Program Manager
American Psychiatric Association
Office of Minority/National Affairs, 1000 Wilson Boulevard, Suite 1825
Arlington, VA 22209-3901
Phone: 703-907-7300
Fax: 703-907-7322

AMERICAN PSYCHOLOGICAL ASSOCIATION

MINORITY FELLOWSHIP FOR HIV/AIDS RESEARCH TRAINING • 235

Renewable award for U.S. citizen or permanent resident enrolled full time in doctoral program in psychology. Must be an ethnic minority member or committed to a career as a research scientist on HIV/AIDS issues related to ethnic minority mental health. Application is available at Web site.

Academic Fields/Career Goals Health and Medical Sciences; Social Sciences. *Award* Fellowship for use in graduate years; renewable. *Number:* 20. *Amount:* $18,156.

Eligibility Requirements Applicant must be enrolled or expecting to enroll full-time at an institution or university. Available to U.S. citizens.

Application Requirements Application, essay, financial need analysis, references, transcript. *Deadline:* January 15.

World Wide Web: http://www.apa.org/mfp

Contact: Program Coordinator
American Psychological Association
750 First Street, NE
Washington, DC 20002-4242
Phone: 202-336-6027
Fax: 202-336-6012
E-mail: mpf@apa.org

MINORITY FELLOWSHIP FOR NEUROSCIENCE TRAINING
see number 65

MINORITY FELLOWSHIP IN MENTAL HEALTH AND SUBSTANCE ABUSE SERVICES • 236

Renewable award for U.S. citizen or permanent resident enrolled full-time in APA-accredited doctoral program in psychology. Must be ethnic minority underrepresented in field or show commitment to career in psychology related to ethnic minority populations. Application available at Web site.

Academic Fields/Career Goals Health and Medical Sciences; Social Sciences. *Award* Fellowship for use in graduate years; renewable. *Number:* 20. *Amount:* $16,500.

Eligibility Requirements Applicant must be enrolled or expecting to enroll full-time at an institution or university. Available to U.S. citizens.

Application Requirements Application, essay, financial need analysis, references, transcript. *Deadline:* January 15.

World Wide Web: http://www.apa.org/mfp

Contact: Program Coordinator
American Psychological Association
750 First Street, NE
Washington, DC 20002-4242
Phone: 202-336-6027
Fax: 202-336-6012
E-mail: cddavis@apa.org

AMERICAN RESPIRATORY CARE FOUNDATION

JIMMY A. YOUNG MEMORIAL EDUCATION RECOGNITION AWARD • 237

Award available to undergraduate minority students studying respiratory care at an American Medical Association-approved institution. Submit letters of recommendation and a paper on a respiratory care topic. Must have a minimum 3.0 GPA. One-time award of $1000.

Academic Fields/Career Goals Health and Medical Sciences; Therapy/Rehabilitation. *Award* Prize for use in freshman, sophomore, junior, or senior years; not renewable. *Number:* 1. *Amount:* $1000.

Eligibility Requirements Applicant must be American Indian/Alaska Native, Asian/Pacific Islander, Black (non-Hispanic), or Hispanic and enrolled or expecting to enroll full or part-time at a two-year or four-year or technical institution or university. Applicant must have 3.0 GPA or higher.

Application Requirements Application, references, transcript, paper on respiratory care topic. *Deadline:* May 31.

World Wide Web: http://www.arcfoundation.org

Contact: Diane Shearer, Administrative Coordinator
American Respiratory Care Foundation
11030 Ables Lane
Dallas, TX 75229-4593
Phone: 972-243-2272
Fax: 972-484-2720
E-mail: info@aarc.org

AMERICAN SOCIETY OF RADIOLOGIC TECHNOLOGISTS EDUCATION AND RESEARCH FOUNDATION

ROYCE OSBORN MINORITY STUDENT SCHOLARSHIP • 238

Minority scholarship for certificate or undergraduate students. Must have completed at least one semester in the Radiologic Sciences to apply. Financial need is a factor. Requirements include 3.0 GPA, recommendation, and 250-300 word essay.

Academic Fields/Career Goals Health and Medical Sciences. *Award* Scholarship for use in freshman, sophomore, or junior years; not renewable. *Number:* 5. *Amount:* $4000.

Eligibility Requirements Applicant must be American Indian/Alaska Native, Asian/Pacific Islander, Black (non-Hispanic), or Hispanic and enrolled or expecting to enroll full or part-time at a two-year or four-year or technical institution or university. Applicant must have 3.0 GPA or higher. Available to U.S. citizens.

Application Requirements Application, essay, financial need analysis, references, transcript. *Deadline:* February 1.

World Wide Web: http://www.asrt.org

Contact: Phelosha Collaros, Development Specialist
American Society of Radiologic Technologists Education and Research
Foundation
15000 Central Avenue, SE
Albuquerque, NM 87123-3917
Phone: 505-298-4500 Ext. 1233
Fax: 505-298-5063
E-mail: pcollaros@asrt.org

AMERICAN SOCIOLOGICAL ASSOCIATION

MINORITY FELLOWSHIP PROGRAM • 239

Annual stipend of $16,500 and tuition payment for minority students entering a doctoral program in sociology of mental illness or for those in early stages of their graduate programs. The program provides initial funding for twelve months which may be extended up to three years.

Academic Fields/Career Goals Health and Medical Sciences; Social Sciences. *Award* Fellowship for use in graduate years; renewable. *Number:* 12. *Amount:* $16,500.

Eligibility Requirements Applicant must be American Indian/Alaska Native, Asian/Pacific Islander, Black (non-Hispanic), or Hispanic and enrolled or expecting to enroll full-time at an institution or university. Applicant must have 3.0 GPA or higher. Available to U.S. citizens.

Application Requirements Application, essay, financial need analysis, resume, references, transcript. *Deadline:* January 31.

World Wide Web: http://www.asanet.org

Contact: ASA Minority Affairs Program
American Sociological Association
1307 New York Avenue, NW, Suite 700
Washington, DC 20005-4701
E-mail: minorityaffairs@asanet.org

AMERICAN SPEECH-LANGUAGE-HEARING FOUNDATION

ASHF GRADUATE STUDENT SCHOLARSHIP FOR MINORITY STUDENTS
see number 117

KALA SINGH GRADUATE SCHOLARSHIP FOR INTERNATIONAL/MINORITY STUDENTS
see number 118

BECA FOUNDATION, INC.

ALICE NEWELL JOSLYN MEDICAL FUND
see number 154

BUSINESS AND PROFESSIONAL WOMEN'S FOUNDATION

BPW CAREER ADVANCEMENT SCHOLARSHIP PROGRAM FOR WOMEN
see number 68

CALIFORNIA ADOLESCENT NUTRITION AND FITNESS (CANFIT) PROGRAM

CALIFORNIA ADOLESCENT NUTRITION AND FITNESS (CANFIT) PROGRAM SCHOLARSHIP
see number 223

CANADIAN FEDERATION OF UNIVERSITY WOMEN

CANADIAN FEDERATION OF UNIVERSITY WOMEN MEMORIAL FELLOWSHIP
see number 21

CONGRESSIONAL BLACK CAUCUS SPOUSES PROGRAM

CONGRESSIONAL BLACK CAUCUS SPOUSES HEALTH INITIATIVE
see number 226

COUNCIL ON SOCIAL WORK EDUCATION

COUNCIL ON SOCIAL WORK EDUCATION/MENTAL HEALTH MINORITY RESEARCH FELLOWSHIP
• 240

Renewable award for full-time graduate minority students with master's in social work to help obtain a doctoral degree and master research skills. Must be interested in a mental health research career. Must have minimum 3.0 GPA. Must be American citizen or have permanent resident status. Monthly stipends defray living expenses. Tuition support provided using the NIH formula. 100 up to $3000 and 60 of balance.

Academic Fields/Career Goals Health and Medical Sciences; Social Sciences; Social Services. *Award* Fellowship for use in graduate years; renewable. *Number:* 10–20. *Amount:* up to $18,100.

Eligibility Requirements Applicant must be American Indian/Alaska Native, Asian/Pacific Islander, Black (non-Hispanic), or Hispanic and enrolled or expecting to enroll full-time at an institution or university. Applicant must have 3.0 GPA or higher. Available to U.S. citizens.

Application Requirements Application, autobiography, essay, financial need analysis, references, test scores, transcript. *Deadline:* February 28.

World Wide Web: http://www.cswe.org

Contact: Dr. E. Aracelis Francis, Director Minority Fellowship Program
Council on Social Work Education
1725 Duke Street, Suite 500
Alexandria, VA 22314-3457
Phone: 703-683-8080
Fax: 703-683-8099
E-mail: eafrancis@cswe.org

DOCTORAL FELLOWSHIPS IN SOCIAL WORK FOR ETHNIC MINORITY STUDENTS PREPARING FOR LEADERSHIP ROLES IN MENTAL HEALTH AND/OR SUBSTANCE ABUSE • 241

Renewable awards for American citizens or permanent residents who have MSW and are enrolled full-time in a doctoral social work program. Recipients required to engage in clinical services in specific areas of need for a period of time equal to the length of support, within two years after termination of award.

Academic Fields/Career Goals Health and Medical Sciences; Social Sciences; Social Services. *Award* Fellowship for use in graduate years; renewable. *Number:* 10–20. *Amount:* up to $16,500.

Eligibility Requirements Applicant must be American Indian/Alaska Native, Asian/Pacific Islander, Black (non-Hispanic), or Hispanic and enrolled or expecting to enroll full-time at an institution or university. Available to U.S. citizens.

Application Requirements Application, autobiography, essay, financial need analysis, references, test scores, transcript. *Deadline:* February 28.

World Wide Web: http://www.cswe.org

Contact: Dr. E. Aracelis Francis, Director, Minority Fellowship Programs
Council on Social Work Education
1725 Duke Street, Suite 500
Alexandria, VA 22314-3457
Phone: 703-683-8080
Fax: 703-683-8099
E-mail: eafrancis@cswe.org

GOVERNOR'S OFFICE

GOVERNOR'S OPPORTUNITY SCHOLARSHIP
see number 81

HEALTH RESOURCES AND SERVICES ADMINISTRATION DIVISION OF HEALTH CAREERS DIVERSITY AND DEVELOPMENT (DHCDD)

FACULTY LOAN REPAYMENT PROGRAM • 242

Program that will repay a faculty member of an accredited health professions school up to $20,000 of outstanding educational loans per year of faculty service. Must be from disadvantaged background. Must agree to serve on a health professions faculty for a minimum of two years.

Academic Fields/Career Goals Health and Medical Sciences. *Award* Forgivable loan for use in graduate, or postgraduate years; renewable. *Amount:* up to $20,000.

Eligibility Requirements Applicant must be enrolled or expecting to enroll at a four-year institution or university. Applicant or parent of applicant must have employment or volunteer experience in teaching. Available to U.S. citizens.

Application Requirements Application, financial need analysis. *Deadline:* Continuous.

World Wide Web: http://www.hrsa.gov

Contact: Barry Dubrow, Division of Health Career Diversity and Development
Health Resources and Services Administration Division of Health Careers
Diversity and Development (DHCDD)
5600 Fishers Lane
Rockville, MD 20859
Phone: 301-443-4021
E-mail: bdubrow@hrsa.gov

HOSTESS COMMITTEE SCHOLARSHIPS/MISS AMERICA PAGEANT

DR. AND MRS. DAVID B. ALLMAN MEDICAL SCHOLARSHIPS • 243

Scholarship for Miss America contestants who wish to enter field of medicine to become medical doctors. Award available to women who have competed within the Miss America system on the local, state, or national level from 1992 to the present, regardless of whether title was won. One or more scholarships are awarded annually, depending on qualifications of applicants. A new application must be submitted each year, previous applicants may apply. Applications must be received by June 30. Late or incomplete applications are not accepted.

Academic Fields/Career Goals Health and Medical Sciences. *Award* Scholarship for use in graduate years; not renewable. *Number:* 1.

Eligibility Requirements Applicant must be enrolled or expecting to enroll at an institution or university; female and must have an interest in beauty pageant. Available to U.S. citizens.

Application Requirements Application, essay, financial need analysis, references, test scores, transcript. *Deadline:* June 30.

World Wide Web: http://www.missamerica.org

Contact: Hostess Committee Scholarships/Miss America Pageant
Two Miss America Way, Suite 1000
Atlantic City, NJ 08401

MARIN EDUCATION FUND

GOLDMAN FAMILY FUND, NEW LEADER SCHOLARSHIP see number 156

NATIONAL FOUNDATION FOR INFECTIOUS DISEASES

COLIN L. POWELL MINORITY POSTDOCTORAL FELLOWSHIP IN TROPICAL DISEASE RESEARCH • 244

Fellowships are available to encourage and assist a qualified minority researcher to become a specialist and investigator in the field of tropical diseases. For more details see Web site: http://www.nfid.org.

Academic Fields/Career Goals Health and Medical Sciences. *Award* Fellowship for use in postgraduate years; not renewable. *Amount:* $30,000.

Eligibility Requirements Applicant must be American Indian/Alaska Native, Asian/Pacific Islander, Black (non-Hispanic), or Hispanic and enrolled or expecting to enroll at an institution or university. Available to U.S. citizens.
Application Requirements Application. *Deadline:* January 7.
World Wide Web: http://www.nfid.org
Contact: application available at Web site

NATIONAL INSTITUTES OF HEALTH

NIH UNDERGRADUATE SCHOLARSHIP PROGRAM FOR STUDENTS FROM DISADVANTAGED BACKGROUNDS
see number 71

NATIONAL MEDICAL FELLOWSHIPS, INC.

BRISTOL-MYERS SQUIBB FELLOWSHIP PROGRAM IN ACADEMIC MEDICINE FOR MINORITY STUDENTS
• 245

Thirty-five fellowships available to first through third-year underrepresented minority students attending accredited U.S. medical schools' who have demonstrated academic achievement and show promise for careers in bio-medical research and academic medicine. Fellows spend eight to twelve weeks working in a major research laboratory. Must be nominated by the dean of the medical school. One-time awards of $6000 each. Applications are requested in September and the deadline for submission of documents is November 22.

Academic Fields/Career Goals Health and Medical Sciences. *Award* Fellowship for use in graduate years; not renewable. *Number:* 35. *Amount:* $6000.
Eligibility Requirements Applicant must be American Indian/Alaska Native, Black (non-Hispanic), or Hispanic and enrolled or expecting to enroll full-time at an institution or university. Available to U.S. citizens.
Application Requirements Application, essay, references, transcript. *Deadline:* November 22.
World Wide Web: http://www.nmf-online.org
Contact: Fellowship Coordinator
National Medical Fellowships, Inc.
5 Hanover Square, 15th Floor
New York, NY 10004

FELLOWSHIP PROGRAM IN AIDS CARE FOR MINORITY MEDICAL STUDENTS
• 246

Fellowships worth $7000 will be awarded to fourth-year California medical students the opportunity to become involved in innovative basic, clinical, social/behavioral and epidemiological research on HIV that is attentive to the needs of California. The medical school deans must recommend candidates. Applications are requested in September and the deadline for submission of documents is October 25. Open to traditionally underrepresented groups in HIV/AIDS clinical care.

Academic Fields/Career Goals Health and Medical Sciences. *Award* Fellowship for use in graduate years; not renewable. *Number:* 8. *Amount:* $7000.
Eligibility Requirements Applicant must be American Indian/Alaska Native, Black (non-Hispanic), or Hispanic; enrolled or expecting to enroll full-time at an institution or university; studying in California and must have an interest in leadership. Available to U.S. citizens.
Application Requirements Application, references, transcript. *Deadline:* October 25.
World Wide Web: http://www.nmf-online.org

Fellowship Program in AIDS Care for Minority Medical Students (continued)

Contact: Fellowship Coordinator
National Medical Fellowships, Inc.
5 Hanover Square, 15th Floor
New York, NY 10004

FRANKLIN C. MCLEAN AWARD   • 247

This one-time award is National Medical Fellowship's oldest and most prestigious honor, presented to a graduating underrepresented minority medical student. Students must be nominated by their medical school dean for outstanding academic achievement, leadership and community service. Nominations are requested in June and the deadline for submission of all documents is July 26.

Academic Fields/Career Goals Health and Medical Sciences. *Award* Prize for use in graduate years; not renewable. *Number:* 1. *Amount:* $3000.

Eligibility Requirements Applicant must be American Indian/Alaska Native, Black (non-Hispanic), or Hispanic; enrolled or expecting to enroll full-time at an institution or university and must have an interest in leadership. Available to U.S. citizens.

Application Requirements References, transcript. *Deadline:* July 26.

World Wide Web: http://www.nmf-online.org

Contact: Fellowship Coordinator
National Medical Fellowships, Inc.
5 Hanover Square, 15th Floor
New York, NY 10004

GERBER FELLOWSHIP IN PEDIATRIC NUTRITION   • 248

Eligibility is limited to underrepresented minority medical students attending accredited U.S. medical schools and underrepresented minority residents participating in ongoing research in the area of pediatric nutrition. Candidates must be U.S. citizens. Candidates must also demonstrate outstanding academic achievement, leadership, and the potential to make significant contributions to pediatric nutrition research. Candidates must be recommended by the medical school dean or director of graduate education. Applicant must submit curricula vitae. Nominations are requested in July and the deadline for submission of all documents is October 25.

Academic Fields/Career Goals Health and Medical Sciences. *Award* Fellowship for use in graduate years; not renewable. *Number:* 1. *Amount:* $3000.

Eligibility Requirements Applicant must be American Indian/Alaska Native, Black (non-Hispanic), or Hispanic; enrolled or expecting to enroll full-time at an institution or university and must have an interest in leadership. Available to U.S. citizens.

Application Requirements Application, references, transcript, curriculum vitae. *Deadline:* October 25.

World Wide Web: http://www.nmf-online.org

Contact: Fellowship Coordinator
National Medical Fellowships, Inc.
5 Hanover Square, 15th Floor
New York, NY 10004

HUGH J. ANDERSEN MEMORIAL SCHOLARSHIPS   • 249

One-time award is for Minnesota residents or for students attending Minnesota medical schools. Candidates must be underrepresented minority students enrolled beyond their first-year in an accredited U.S. medical school. Candidates must demonstrate outstanding leadership, community service, and financial need. Students must be nominated by medical school deans and must submit personal essays. Nominations are requested in August and the deadline date for submission of all documents is September 27.

Academic Fields/Career Goals Health and Medical Sciences. *Award* Scholarship for use in graduate years; not renewable. *Number:* up to 5. *Amount:* $2500.

Eligibility Requirements Applicant must be American Indian/Alaska Native, Black (non-Hispanic), or Hispanic; enrolled or expecting to enroll full-time at an institution or university and must have an interest in leadership. Applicant or parent of applicant must have employment or volunteer experience in community service. Available to U.S. citizens.

Application Requirements Essay, financial need analysis, references, transcript. *Deadline:* September 27.

World Wide Web: http://www.nmf-online.org

Contact: Fellowship Coordinator
National Medical Fellowships, Inc.
5 Hanover Square, 15th Floor
New York, NY 10004
Phone: 212-483-8880
Fax: 212-483-8897

IRVING GRAEF MEMORIAL SCHOLARSHIP • 250

One scholarship available to third-year, rising minority medical students who received NMF financial assistance during their second year. Candidates must be nominated by the dean for outstanding academic achievement and leadership. Applicants must submit personal essays. One renewable award of $2000 per year. Nominations requested in October and the deadline for submission of all documents is November 29

Academic Fields/Career Goals Health and Medical Sciences. *Award* Scholarship for use in graduate years; renewable. *Number:* 1. *Amount:* $2000.

Eligibility Requirements Applicant must be American Indian/Alaska Native, Black (non-Hispanic), or Hispanic; enrolled or expecting to enroll full-time at an institution or university and must have an interest in leadership. Available to U.S. citizens.

Application Requirements Application, essay, financial need analysis, references, transcript. *Deadline:* November 29.

World Wide Web: http://www.nmf-online.org

Contact: Fellowship Coordinator
National Medical Fellowships, Inc.
5 Hanover Square, 15th Floor
New York, NY 10004

JAMES H. ROBINSON M.D. MEMORIAL PRIZE IN SURGERY • 251

One award available to underrepresented minority students at accredited U.S. medical schools who will graduate during the academic year in which the award is made available. Students must be nominated by medical school deans and department of surgery chairpersons for outstanding performance in the surgical disciplines. One-time stipend of $500. Applicant must submit curriculum vitae with application. Nominations are requested in January and the deadline for submission of all documents is February 14.

Academic Fields/Career Goals Health and Medical Sciences. *Award* Prize for use in graduate years; not renewable. *Number:* 1. *Amount:* $500.

Eligibility Requirements Applicant must be American Indian/Alaska Native, Black (non-Hispanic), or Hispanic and enrolled or expecting to enroll full-time at an institution or university. Available to U.S. citizens.

Application Requirements References, transcript, curriculum vitae. *Deadline:* February 14.

World Wide Web: http://www.nmf-online.org

James H. Robinson M.D. Memorial Prize in Surgery (continued)

Contact: Fellowship Coordinator
National Medical Fellowships, Inc.
5 Hanover Square, 15th Floor
New York, NY 10004

METROPOLITAN LIFE FOUNDATION AWARDS PROGRAM FOR ACADEMIC EXCELLENCE IN MEDICINE • 252

Need-based scholarships available to second- through fourth-year underrepresented minority medical students who attend school or reside in selected cities in the following states: AZ, CA, CO, DC, FL, GA, IL, MA, NY, OH, OK, PA, RI, SC, NJ, CT and TX. Candidates must demonstrate outstanding academic achievement and leadership. Students must be nominated by medical school deans. Up to seventeen scholarships at $4000. Nominations are requested in October and the deadline for submission of all documents is November 27.

Academic Fields/Career Goals Health and Medical Sciences. *Award* Scholarship for use in graduate years; not renewable. *Number:* up to 17. *Amount:* up to $4000.

Eligibility Requirements Applicant must be American Indian/Alaska Native, Black (non-Hispanic), or Hispanic; enrolled or expecting to enroll full-time at an institution or university and resident of Arizona, California, Colorado, District of Columbia, Florida, Georgia, Illinois, Massachusetts, New York, Ohio, Oklahoma, Pennsylvania, Rhode Island, South Carolina, or Texas. Available to U.S. citizens.

Application Requirements Application, essay, financial need analysis, references, test scores, transcript. *Deadline:* November 27.

World Wide Web: http://www.nmf-online.org

Contact: Fellowship Coordinator
National Medical Fellowships, Inc.
5 Hanover Square, 15th Floor
New York, NY 10004

NATIONAL MEDICAL FELLOWSHIPS, INC. GENERAL NEED-BASED SCHOLARSHIP PROGRAMS • 253

Available to first- and second-year medical students who are either African-American, Alaskan Natives, Native Hawaiians, mainland Puerto Rican, Mexican-American, or Native-Americans and who are in programs leading to MD or DO degrees. Based on need. Must be U.S. citizen. Must include verification of citizenship.

Academic Fields/Career Goals Health and Medical Sciences. *Award* Scholarship for use in graduate years; not renewable. *Amount:* $500–$10,000.

Eligibility Requirements Applicant must be American Indian/Alaska Native, Black (non-Hispanic), or Hispanic and enrolled or expecting to enroll full-time at an institution or university. Available to U.S. citizens.

Application Requirements Application, essay, financial need analysis, references, test scores, transcript. *Deadline:* June 29.

World Wide Web: http://www.nmf-online.org

Contact: Fellowship Coordinator
National Medical Fellowships, Inc.
5 Hanover Square, 15th Floor
New York, NY 10004
Phone: 212-483-8880
Fax: 212-483-8897

RALPH W. ELLISON MEMORIAL PRIZE • 254

One-time award presented to a graduating underrepresented minority medical student. Students must be nominated by their medical school deans for specific academic and leadership accomplishments and must submit a personal statement of at least 500 words. Nominations are requested in January and the deadline for submission of all documents is February 14.

Academic Fields/Career Goals Health and Medical Sciences. *Award* Prize for use in graduate years; not renewable. *Number:* 1. *Amount:* $500.

Eligibility Requirements Applicant must be American Indian/Alaska Native, Black (non-Hispanic), or Hispanic; enrolled or expecting to enroll full-time at an institution or university and must have an interest in leadership. Available to U.S. citizens.

Application Requirements Application, essay, transcript. *Deadline:* February 14.

World Wide Web: http://www.nmf-online.org

Contact: Fellowship Coordinator
National Medical Fellowships, Inc.
5 Hanover Square, 15th Floor
New York, NY 10004

W.K. KELLOGG FELLOWSHIP PROGRAM IN HEALTH POLICY RESEARCH
see number 228

WILLIAM AND CHARLOTTE CADBURY AWARD • 255

One-time award is available to senior underrepresented minority students enrolled in accredited U.S. medical schools. Candidates must be nominated by the medical school deans for outstanding academic achievement and leadership. Nominations are requested in June and the deadline date for submission of all documents is July 29.

Academic Fields/Career Goals Health and Medical Sciences. *Award* Scholarship for use in graduate years; not renewable. *Number:* 1. *Amount:* $2000.

Eligibility Requirements Applicant must be American Indian/Alaska Native, Black (non-Hispanic), or Hispanic; enrolled or expecting to enroll full-time at an institution or university and must have an interest in leadership. Available to U.S. citizens.

Application Requirements Essay, references, transcript. *Deadline:* July 29.

World Wide Web: http://www.nmf-online.org

Contact: Fellowship Coordinator
National Medical Fellowships, Inc.
5 Hanover Square, 15th Floor
New York, NY 10004

WYETH-AYERST LABORATORIES PRIZE IN WOMEN'S HEALTH • 256

Candidates must be underrepresented minority women attending accredited medical schools in the U.S. Students must demonstrate exceptional achievement, leadership, and potential to make significant contributions in the field of women's health. Must include nominations from medical school deans, directors, or research mentor. Must submit curriculum vitae with application. Nominations are requested in January and the deadline for submission of all documents is February 14.

Academic Fields/Career Goals Health and Medical Sciences. *Award* Prize for use in graduate years; not renewable. *Number:* 2. *Amount:* $5000.

Eligibility Requirements Applicant must be American Indian/Alaska Native, Black (non-Hispanic), or Hispanic; enrolled or expecting to enroll full-time at an institution or university; female and must have an interest in leadership. Available to U.S. citizens.

Application Requirements References, transcript, curriculum vitae. *Deadline:* February 14.

Wyeth-Ayerst Laboratories Prize in Women's Health (continued)

World Wide Web: http://www.nmf-online.org
Contact: Fellowship Coordinator
National Medical Fellowships, Inc.
5 Hanover Square, 15th Floor
New York, NY 10004

ONS FOUNDATION

ONS FOUNDATION ETHNIC MINORITY RESEARCHER AND MENTORSHIP GRANTS • 257

Award to encourage oncology nursing research by ethnic minority researchers. Beginning researchers must use a mentor for consultative services. ONS Research Mentorship Program will help find mentor. One-time award of $7500 for the conduct of research and $1000 to mentor. Deadline: November 1.

Academic Fields/Career Goals Health and Medical Sciences; Nursing. *Award* Grant for use in graduate years; not renewable. *Number:* 1. *Amount:* $8500.

Eligibility Requirements Applicant must be American Indian/Alaska Native, Asian/Pacific Islander, Black (non-Hispanic), or Hispanic and enrolled or expecting to enroll at an institution or university.

Application Requirements Application. *Deadline:* November 1.
World Wide Web: http://www.ons.org
Contact: ONS Foundation
501 Holiday Drive
Pittsburgh, PA 15220

ROSCOE POUND INSTITUTE

ELAINE OSBORNE JACOBSON AWARD FOR WOMEN WORKING IN HEALTH CARE LAW
see number 229

SOCIETY OF TOXICOLOGY

MINORITY UNDERGRADUATE STUDENT AWARDS
see number 72

UNITED STATES DEPARTMENT OF HEALTH AND HUMAN SERVICES

NIH UNDERGRADUATE SCHOLARSHIP FOR INDIVIDUALS FROM DISADVANTAGED BACKGROUNDS
see number 73

UNIVERSITY OF MEDICINE AND DENTISTRY OF NJ SCHOOL OF OSTEOPATHIC MEDICINE

MARTIN LUTHER KING PHYSICIAN/DENTIST SCHOLARSHIPS
see number 157

NEW JERSEY EDUCATIONAL OPPORTUNITY FUND GRANTS
see number 158

VIRGINIA BUSINESS AND PROFESSIONAL WOMEN'S FOUNDATION

WOMEN IN SCIENCE AND TECHNOLOGY SCHOLARSHIP

see number 74

WELLESLEY COLLEGE

M.A. CARTLAND SHACKFORD MEDICAL FELLOWSHIP • 258

Fellowships are available for the study of medicine with view to general practice, not psychiatry. Open to women graduates of any American institution for graduate study for the coming year at any medical school. Based on merit and need.

Academic Fields/Career Goals Health and Medical Sciences. *Award* Fellowship for use in graduate years; not renewable. *Amount:* up to $9000.

Eligibility Requirements Applicant must be enrolled or expecting to enroll full-time at an institution or university and female. Available to U.S. citizens.

Application Requirements Application, financial need analysis, references, test scores, transcript. *Deadline:* January 6.

World Wide Web: http://www.wellesley.edu/CWS/

Contact: Mary Beth Callery, Secretary to the Committee on Graduate Fellowships
Wellesley College
106 Central Avenue, Green Hall 441
Wellesley, MA 02481
Phone: 781-283-3525
Fax: 781-283-3674
E-mail: cws-fellowships@wellesley.edu

SARAH PERRY WOOD MEDICAL FELLOWSHIP • 259

One or more awards available to alumnae of Wellesley College for the study of medicine. Deadline January 6.

Academic Fields/Career Goals Health and Medical Sciences. *Award* Fellowship for use in graduate, or postgraduate years; not renewable. *Amount:* up to $66,000.

Eligibility Requirements Applicant must be enrolled or expecting to enroll full-time at an institution or university and female. Available to U.S. citizens.

Application Requirements Application, essay, financial need analysis, resume, references, transcript. *Deadline:* January 6.

World Wide Web: http://www.wellesley.edu/CWS/

Contact: Mary Beth Callery, Secretary to the Committee on Graduate Fellowships
Wellesley College
106 Central Avenue, Green Hall 441
Wellesley, MA 02481-8200
Phone: 781-283-3525
Fax: 781-283-3674
E-mail: cws-fellowships@wellesley.edu

WOMEN OF THE EVANGELICAL LUTHERAN CHURCH IN AMERICA

HEALTH SERVICES SCHOLARSHIP FOR WOMEN STUDYING ABROAD

see number 230

HEALTH INFORMATION MANAGEMENT/ TECHNOLOGY

CONGRESSIONAL BLACK CAUCUS SPOUSES PROGRAM

CONGRESSIONAL BLACK CAUCUS SPOUSES HEALTH INITIATIVE   see number 226

FOUNDATION OF AMERICAN COLLEGE HEALTHCARE EXECUTIVES

ALBERT W. DENT GRADUATE STUDENT SCHOLARSHIP   see number 227

MARIN EDUCATION FUND

GOLDMAN FAMILY FUND, NEW LEADER SCHOLARSHIP   see number 156

NATIONAL MEDICAL FELLOWSHIPS, INC.

W.K. KELLOGG FELLOWSHIP PROGRAM IN HEALTH POLICY RESEARCH
see number 228

WOMEN OF THE EVANGELICAL LUTHERAN CHURCH IN AMERICA

HEALTH SERVICES SCHOLARSHIP FOR WOMEN STUDYING ABROAD
see number 230

HISTORY

CANADIAN FEDERATION OF UNIVERSITY WOMEN

MARGARET DALE PHILP BIENNIAL AWARD   • 260

One-time award available to Canadian citizens or those who have held landed immigrant status for at least one year who hold a bachelor's degree or equivalent. Must be a woman who has been accepted into her proposed program and place of study for the academic year. One award of CAN$3,000. Candidate must reside in Canada. Application fee is CAN$35.

Academic Fields/Career Goals History; Humanities; Social Sciences. *Award* Scholarship for use in graduate years; not renewable. *Number:* 1. *Amount:* $3000.

Eligibility Requirements Applicant must be Canadian citizenship; enrolled or expecting to enroll full or part-time at an institution or university and female.

Application Requirements Application, autobiography, essay, references, transcript. *Fee:* $35. *Deadline:* November 1.

World Wide Web: http://www.cfuw.org

Contact: Betty Dunlop, Fellowships Program Manager
Canadian Federation of University Women
251 Bank Street, Suite 600
Ottawa, ON K2P 1X3
Canada
Phone: 613-234-2732
E-mail: cfuwfls@rogers.com

GENERAL COMMISSION ON ARCHIVES AND HISTORY

ASIAN, BLACK, HISPANIC, AND NATIVE AMERICAN UNITED METHODIST HISTORY RESEARCH AWARDS • 261

One-time award promoting research and writing in the history of Asian-Americans, African-Americans, Latinos, and Native-Americans in the United Methodist Church or its antecedents. Submit biographical information, project description, and budget plan with application.

Academic Fields/Career Goals History; Religion/Theology. *Award* Prize for use in graduate years; not renewable. *Number:* 2. *Amount:* $1500.

Eligibility Requirements Applicant must be enrolled or expecting to enroll full or part-time at an institution or university. Available to U.S. and non-U.S. citizens.

Application Requirements Autobiography. *Deadline:* December 31.

World Wide Web: http://www.gcah.org

Contact: Charles Yrigoyen, Jr., General Secretary
General Commission on Archives and History
PO Box 127
Madison, NJ 07940
Phone: 973-408-3189
Fax: 973-408-3909

HISPANIC DIVISION, LIBRARY OF CONGRESS

HISPANIC DIVISION FELLOWSHIPS
see number 43

NATIONAL RESEARCH COUNCIL

FORD FOUNDATION DISSERTATION FELLOWSHIPS FOR MINORITIES
see number 125

FORD FOUNDATION POSTDOCTORAL FELLOWSHIP FOR MINORITIES
see number 126

FORD FOUNDATION PRE-DOCTORAL FELLOWSHIPS FOR MINORITIES
see number 127

PHI BETA KAPPA SOCIETY

MARY ISABEL SIBLEY FELLOWSHIP FOR GREEK AND FRENCH STUDIES
see number 33

SOCIAL SCIENCE RESEARCH COUNCIL

PHILANTHROPHY AND THE NONPROFIT SECTOR DISSERTATION FELLOWSHIP
see number 90

UNITED METHODIST CHURCH GENERAL COMMISSION ON ARCHIVES AND HISTORY

MINORITY RESEARCH AWARDS • 262

Grants to promote excellence in research and writing in the history of four groups: Asians, African-Americans, Hispanics and Native-Americans in The United Methodist Church.

Academic Fields/Career Goals History. *Award* Grant for use in freshman, sophomore, junior, or senior years; not renewable. *Amount:* up to $3000.

Eligibility Requirements Applicant must be Methodist and enrolled or expecting to enroll at an institution or university. Available to U.S. citizens.

Application Requirements Application, autobiography, essay. *Deadline:* December 31.

World Wide Web: http://www.gcah.org

Contact: General Secretary
United Methodist Church General Commission on Archives and History
PO Box 127, 36 Madison Avenue
Madison, NJ 07940
Phone: 973-408-3189
Fax: 973-408-3909

UNITED STATES INSTITUTE OF PEACE

JENNINGS RANDOLPH SENIOR FELLOW AWARD
see number 46

WELLESLEY COLLEGE

EDNA V. MOFFETT FELLOWSHIP • 263

One or more fellowships available to young alumnae of Wellesley College for a first-year study in history. Based on merit and need. For application and additional information visit the Web site at http://www.wellesley.edu/cws.

Academic Fields/Career Goals History. *Award* Fellowship for use in graduate years; not renewable. *Amount:* up to $12,000.

Eligibility Requirements Applicant must be enrolled or expecting to enroll full-time at an institution or university and female. Available to U.S. citizens.

Application Requirements Application, essay, financial need analysis, resume, references, transcript. *Deadline:* January 6.

World Wide Web: http://www.wellesley.edu/CWS/

Contact: Mary Beth Callery, Secretary to the Committee on Graduate Fellowships
Wellesley College
106 Central Avenue, Green Hall 441
Wellesley, MA 02481-8200
Phone: 781-283-3525
Fax: 781-283-3674
E-mail: cws-fellowships@wellesley.edu

EUGENE L. COX FELLOWSHIP • 264

One or more fellowships available for graduate study in medieval or renaissance history and culture abroad or in the United States. Must be a graduate of Wellesley College. Award based on merit and need. E-mail inquiries to cws-fellowships@wellesley.edu.

Academic Fields/Career Goals History. *Award* Fellowship for use in graduate years; not renewable. *Amount:* up to $7000.

Eligibility Requirements Applicant must be enrolled or expecting to enroll full-time at an institution or university and female. Available to U.S. citizens.

Application Requirements Application, essay, financial need analysis, resume, references, transcript. *Deadline:* January 6.

World Wide Web: http://www.wellesley.edu/CWS/

Contact: Mary Beth Callery, Secretary to the Committee on Graduate Fellowships
Wellesley College
106 Central Avenue, Green Hall 441
Wellesley, MA 02481-8200
Phone: 781-283-3525
Fax: 781-283-3674
E-mail: cws-fellowships@wellesley.edu

MARY MCEWEN SCHIMKE SCHOLARSHIP • 265

Supplemental one-time award for relief from household and childcare while pursuing graduate study preferably in literature and/or history, American studies. Open to women graduates over 30 years of age from any American institution. Based on need and merit.

Academic Fields/Career Goals History; Literature/English/Writing. *Award* Scholarship for use in graduate years; not renewable. *Amount:* up to $1000.

Eligibility Requirements Applicant must be age 31; enrolled or expecting to enroll full-time at an institution or university and female. Available to U.S. citizens.

Application Requirements Application, financial need analysis, references, test scores, transcript. *Deadline:* January 6.

World Wide Web: http://www.wellesley.edu/CWS/

Contact: Mary Beth Callery, Secretary to the Committee on Graduate Fellowships
Wellesley College
106 Central Avenue, Green Hall 441
Wellesley, MA 02481
Phone: 781-283-3525
Fax: 781-283-3674
E-mail: cws-fellowships@wellesley.edu

THOMAS JEFFERSON FELLOWSHIP • 266

One or more fellowships for advanced study in history. Must be Wellesley College graduate and demonstrate merit and need. More information and applications may be found at Web site http:// www.wellesley.edu/cws.

Academic Fields/Career Goals History. *Award* Fellowship for use in graduate years; not renewable. *Amount:* up to $10,000.

Eligibility Requirements Applicant must be enrolled or expecting to enroll full-time at an institution or university and female. Available to U.S. citizens.

Application Requirements Application, essay, financial need analysis, resume, references, transcript. *Deadline:* January 6.

World Wide Web: http://www.wellesley.edu/CWS/

Thomas Jefferson Fellowship (continued)

Contact: Mary Beth Callery, Secretary to the Committee on Graduate Fellowships
Wellesley College
106 Central Avenue, Green Hall 441
Wellesley, MA 02481-8200
Phone: 781-283-3525
Fax: 781-283-3674
E-mail: cws-fellowships@wellesley.edu

HOME ECONOMICS

UNITED DAUGHTERS OF THE CONFEDERACY

WALTER REED SMITH SCHOLARSHIP   see number 91

HORTICULTURE/FLORICULTURE

GOLF COURSE SUPERINTENDENTS ASSOCIATION OF AMERICA

SCOTTS COMPANY SCHOLARS PROGRAM   • 267

The Scotts Company Scholars Program was developed by the Scotts Company in cooperation with the GCSAA Foundation to offer education and employment opportunities to students interested in pursuing a career in the "green industry." Students from diverse ethnic, cultural and socioeconomic backgrounds will be considered for judging. Must be a graduating high school senior or freshman, sophomore, or junior in college. Graduating high school seniors must attach a letter of college acceptance to application.

Academic Fields/Career Goals Horticulture/Floriculture. *Award* Scholarship for use in freshman, sophomore, junior, or senior years; not renewable. *Number:* up to 7. *Amount:* $500–$2500.

Eligibility Requirements Applicant must be enrolled or expecting to enroll full-time at a two-year or four-year or technical institution or university. Available to U.S. and non-U.S. citizens.

Application Requirements Application, essay, references, transcript. *Deadline:* March 1.
World Wide Web: http://www.gcsaa.org
Contact: Pam Smith, Scholarship Manager
Golf Course Superintendents Association of America
1421 Research Park Drive
Lawrence, KS 66049-3859
Phone: 800-472-7878 Ext. 678
Fax: 785-832-3673
E-mail: psmith@gcsaa.org

WOMAN'S NATIONAL FARM AND GARDEN ASSOCIATION

SARAH BRADLEY TYSON MEMORIAL FELLOWSHIP   see number 24

WOMEN'S NATIONAL FARM AND GARDEN ASSOCIATION

SARAH BRADLEY TYSON MEMORIAL FELLOWSHIP • 268

One-time award for women pursuing an advanced degree in agriculture, horticulture, and allied subjects at an accredited U.S. institution. Must have proven ability in field. Awards have been made in recognition of leadership in cooperative extension work as well as initiative in scientific research. Application deadline is April 15.

Academic Fields/Career Goals Horticulture/Floriculture; Landscape Architecture; Natural Resources; Natural Sciences. *Award* Fellowship for use in graduate years; not renewable. *Number:* 4. *Amount:* $1000.

Eligibility Requirements Applicant must be enrolled or expecting to enroll full-time at a four-year institution or university and female. Available to U.S. and non-U.S. citizens.

Application Requirements Photo, portfolio, references, self-addressed stamped envelope, test scores, transcript. *Deadline:* April 15.

Contact: Mrs. Harold Matyn, Chairman
Women's National Farm and Garden Association
c/o Jeannette M. Matyn
3801 Riverview Terrace, South
East China, MI 48054
Phone: 810-362-0987

HOSPITALITY MANAGEMENT_____

HISPANIC COLLEGE FUND, INC.

DENNY'S/HISPANIC COLLEGE FUND SCHOLARSHIP   see number 12

HUMANITIES_____

ASPEN INSTITUTE

WILLIAM RANDOLPH HEARST ENDOWED SCHOLARSHIP FOR MINORITY STUDENTS • 269

Scholarships will be awarded to minority students who demonstrate outstanding research skills, a background in social sciences or humanities, excellent writing and communication skills, and financial need. There is no application; send a letter of interest, resume, transcript, a letter from the appropriate college or university financial aid officer certifying demonstrated financial need, and two letters of reference.

Academic Fields/Career Goals Humanities; Social Sciences. *Award* Scholarship for use in freshman, sophomore, junior, senior, or graduate years; not renewable. *Amount:* $2500–$5000.

Eligibility Requirements Applicant must be American Indian/Alaska Native, Asian/Pacific Islander, Black (non-Hispanic), or Hispanic and enrolled or expecting to enroll at an institution or university. Available to U.S. citizens.

William Randolph Hearst Endowed Scholarship for Minority Students (continued)

Application Requirements Essay, financial need analysis, resume, references, transcript. *Deadline:* March 14.
World Wide Web: http://www.nonprofitresearch.org/
Contact: Aspen Institute
One Dupont Circle, NW, Suite 700
Washington, DC 20036

BUSINESS AND PROFESSIONAL WOMEN'S FOUNDATION

BPW CAREER ADVANCEMENT SCHOLARSHIP PROGRAM FOR WOMEN
see number 68

CANADIAN FEDERATION OF UNIVERSITY WOMEN

MARGARET DALE PHILP BIENNIAL AWARD
see number 260

HISPANIC DIVISION, LIBRARY OF CONGRESS

HISPANIC DIVISION FELLOWSHIPS
see number 43

INSTITUTE FOR INTERNATIONAL PUBLIC POLICY (IIPP)

INSTITUTE FOR INTERNATIONAL PUBLIC POLICY FELLOWSHIP PROGRAM
see number 44

PHI BETA KAPPA SOCIETY

MARY ISABEL SIBLEY FELLOWSHIP FOR GREEK AND FRENCH STUDIES
see number 33

INTERIOR DESIGN

ASSOCIATION FOR WOMEN IN ARCHITECTURE FOUNDATION

ASSOCIATION FOR WOMEN IN ARCHITECTURE SCHOLARSHIP
see number 38

WORLDSTUDIO FOUNDATION

WORLDSTUDIO FOUNDATION SCHOLARSHIP PROGRAM
see number 42

INTERNATIONAL MIGRATION_____

HISPANIC DIVISION, LIBRARY OF CONGRESS
HISPANIC DIVISION FELLOWSHIPS   see number 43

UNITED STATES INSTITUTE OF PEACE
JENNINGS RANDOLPH SENIOR FELLOW AWARD   see number 46

INTERNATIONAL STUDIES_____

HISPANIC DIVISION, LIBRARY OF CONGRESS
HISPANIC DIVISION FELLOWSHIPS   see number 43

INSTITUTE FOR INTERNATIONAL PUBLIC POLICY (IIPP)
INSTITUTE FOR INTERNATIONAL PUBLIC POLICY FELLOWSHIP PROGRAM
                                                      see number 44

UNITED STATES INSTITUTE OF PEACE
JENNINGS RANDOLPH SENIOR FELLOW AWARD   see number 46

JOURNALISM_____

ASIAN AMERICAN JOURNALISTS ASSOCIATION— SEATTLE CHAPTER
NORTHWEST JOURNALISTS OF COLOR SCHOLARSHIP   see number 119

CALIFORNIA CHICANO NEWS MEDIA ASSOCIATION (CCNMA)
JOEL GARCIA MEMORIAL SCHOLARSHIP   see number 120

CHARLOTTE OBSERVER
CHARLOTTE OBSERVER MINORITY SCHOLARSHIPS   see number 76

COMMUNITY FOUNDATION FOR PALM BEACH AND MARTIN COUNTIES, INC.

GINA AUDITORE BONER MEMORIAL SCHOLARSHIP FUND see number 78

CUBAN AMERICAN NATIONAL FOUNDATION

MAS FAMILY SCHOLARSHIPS see number 80

DALLAS-FORT WORTH ASSOCIATION OF BLACK COMMUNICATORS

FUTURE JOURNALISTS SCHOLARSHIP PROGRAM see number 121

FISHER BROADCASTING COMPANY

FISHER BROADCASTING, INC., SCHOLARSHIP FOR MINORITIES see number 122

FREEDOM FORUM

CHIPS QUINN SCHOLARS PROGRAM • 270

One-time award for students of color who are college juniors, seniors, or recent graduates. Must have a definite interest in print journalism as a career. Award requires paid internship. Applicants may be nominated by their schools, by newspaper editors, or by direct application with supporting letters of endorsement. Deadline is October 15. See Web site at http://www.freedomforum.org for further information.

Academic Fields/Career Goals Journalism. *Award* Scholarship for use in junior or senior years; not renewable. *Amount:* $1000.

Eligibility Requirements Applicant must be American Indian/Alaska Native, Asian/Pacific Islander, Black (non-Hispanic), or Hispanic and enrolled or expecting to enroll at a four-year institution or university.

Application Requirements Application, essay, photo, portfolio, resume, references, transcript. *Deadline:* October 15.

Contact: Karen Catone, Director
Freedom Forum
1101 Wilson Boulevard
Arlington, VA 22209
Phone: 703-284-2863
Fax: 703-284-3543
E-mail: chipsquinnscholars@freedomforum.org

INTER AMERICAN PRESS ASSOCIATION SCHOLARSHIP FUND, INC.

INTER AMERICAN PRESS ASSOCIATION SCHOLARSHIPS • 271

The IAPA's Scholarship Fund is an exchange program for print journalists of the Americas. Latin Americans study in the United States or Canada, and U.S. and Canadian journalists study in Latin America. Fluency in English or French and in Spanish or Portuguese, respectively, is mandatory. Applicants must be natives of the Western Hemisphere.

Academic Fields/Career Goals Journalism. *Award* Scholarship for use in graduate, or postgraduate years; not renewable. *Number:* 5. *Amount:* $13,000.

Eligibility Requirements Applicant must be age 21-35; enrolled or expecting to enroll full-time at an institution or university and must have an interest in English language, French language, Portuguese language, or Spanish language. Available to U.S. and non-U.S. citizens.

Application Requirements Application, autobiography, essay, references, test scores, transcript, clips of published articles. *Deadline:* December 31.

World Wide Web: http://www.sipiapa.org

Contact: Ms. Zulay Dominguez Chirinos, Director
Inter American Press Association Scholarship Fund, Inc.
1801 SW Third Avenue
Miami, FL 33129
Phone: 305-376-3522
Fax: 305-376-8950
E-mail: zulaydominguez@aol.com

JORGE MAS CANOSA FREEDOM FOUNDATION
MAS FAMILY SCHOLARSHIP AWARD   see number 85

KNIGHT RIDDER
KNIGHT RIDDER MINORITY SCHOLARSHIP PROGRAM   see number 86

LEXINGTON HERALD-LEADER
LEXINGTON HERALD-LEADER/KNIGHT RIDDER MINORITY SCHOLARSHIPS
see number 88

NATIONAL ASSOCIATION OF HISPANIC JOURNALISTS (NAHJ)
CRISTINA SARALEGUI SCHOLARSHIP PROGRAM   • 272

Two-year scholarship program ($5000 annually) named after Spanish-language talk show host Cristina Saralegüi. Applicant must be a current college sophomore, fluent in Spanish and planning to pursue a career in broadcast journalism. The recipient is required to intern on the Cristina Saralegüi Show during the summer following his/her junior year. Applications must be postmarked on or before the final Friday in January of each year. Awards are based on commitment to journalism, awareness of the community, academic achievement, and financial need. Applications available only at Web site: http://www.nahj.org.

Academic Fields/Career Goals Journalism; TV/Radio Broadcasting. *Award* Scholarship for use in sophomore year; not renewable. *Number:* 1. *Amount:* $5000.

Eligibility Requirements Applicant must be enrolled or expecting to enroll full-time at a four-year institution and must have an interest in Spanish language. Available to U.S. citizens.

Application Requirements Application, essay, financial need analysis, resume, references, transcript, work samples.

World Wide Web: http://www.nahj.org

Cristina Saralegui Scholarship Program (continued)

Contact: Kevin Olivas, Educational Programs Manager
National Association of Hispanic Journalists (NAHJ)
529 14th Street, NW
Suite 1000
Washington, DC 20045-2001
Phone: 202-662-7145
Fax: 202-662-7144
E-mail: nahj@nahj.org

MARIA ELENA SALINAS SCHOLARSHIP • 273

One-time scholarship for high school seniors, college undergraduates, and first-year graduate students who are pursuing careers in Spanish-language broadcast (radio or TV) journalism. Students may major or plan to major in any subject, but must demonstrate a sincere desire to pursue a career in this field. Must submit essays and demo tapes (audio or video) in Spanish. Scholarship includes the opportunity to serve an internship with Univision Spanish-language television news network. Applications must be postmarked on or before the final Friday in January of each year. Applications available only at Web site: http://www.nahj.org.

Academic Fields/Career Goals Journalism; TV/Radio Broadcasting. *Award* Scholarship for use in freshman, sophomore, junior, senior, or graduate years; not renewable. *Number:* 2. *Amount:* $5000.

Eligibility Requirements Applicant must be enrolled or expecting to enroll full-time at a two-year or four-year institution or university and must have an interest in Spanish language. Available to U.S. citizens.

Application Requirements Application, autobiography, essay, financial need analysis, resume, references, transcript.

World Wide Web: http://www.nahj.org

Contact: Kevin Olivas, Educational Programs Manager
National Association of Hispanic Journalists (NAHJ)
529 14th Street, NW
Suite 1000
Washington, DC 20045-2001
Phone: 202-662-7145
Fax: 202-662-7144
E-mail: nahj@nahj.org

NATIONAL ASSOCIATION OF HISPANIC JOURNALISTS SCHOLARSHIP

see number 124

NORTHWEST JOURNALISTS OF COLOR

NORTHWEST JOURNALISTS OF COLOR SCHOLARSHIP • 274

One-time award for Washington high school and college students seeking careers in journalism. Must be an undergraduate enrolled in an accredited college or university or a senior in high school. Must be Asian-American, African-American, Native-Americans or Latino. Application deadline is May 3.

Academic Fields/Career Goals Journalism. *Award* Scholarship for use in freshman, sophomore, junior, or senior years; not renewable. *Number:* up to 6. *Amount:* $500–$1000.

Eligibility Requirements Applicant must be American Indian/Alaska Native, Asian/Pacific Islander, Black (non-Hispanic), or Hispanic; enrolled or expecting to enroll full-time at a four-year institution or university; resident of Washington and studying in Washington.

Application Requirements Application, essay, references, work samples. *Deadline:* May 3.
World Wide Web: http://www.aaja.seattle.org
Contact: Northwest Journalists of Color
c/o King TV
333 Dexter Avenue North
Seattle, WA 98109

OHIO NEWSPAPERS FOUNDATION

OHIO NEWSPAPERS FOUNDATION MINORITY SCHOLARSHIP   • 275

Three $1,500 scholarships will be awarded to minority high school seniors who plan to pursue a newspaper journalism career. Applicants must be enrolled in an accredited Ohio college or university. A minimum high school GPA of 2.5 (C+) is required. Applicants must be African-American, Hispanic, Asian-American or American-Indian.

Academic Fields/Career Goals Journalism. *Award* Scholarship for use in freshman year; not renewable. *Number:* 3. *Amount:* $1500.
Eligibility Requirements Applicant must be American Indian/Alaska Native, Asian/Pacific Islander, Black (non-Hispanic), or Hispanic; high school student; planning to enroll or expecting to enroll at an institution or university; resident of Ohio and studying in Ohio. Applicant must have 2.5 GPA or higher. Available to U.S. citizens.
Application Requirements Application, autobiography, essay, transcript. *Deadline:* March 31.
World Wide Web: http://www.ohionews.org
Contact: Kathleen Pouliot, Secretary
Ohio Newspapers Foundation
1335 Dublin Road, Suite 216-B
Columbus, OH 43215-7038
Phone: 614-486-6677
Fax: 614-486-4940
E-mail: kpouliot@ohionews.org

RADIO-TELEVISION NEWS DIRECTORS ASSOCIATION AND FOUNDATION

CAROLE SIMPSON SCHOLARSHIP   see number 129

ED BRADLEY SCHOLARSHIP   see number 130

KEN KASHIWAHARA SCHOLARSHIP   see number 131

MICHELE CLARK FELLOWSHIP   see number 132

MIKE REYNOLDS $1,000 SCHOLARSHIP   see number 133

N.S. BIENSTOCK FELLOWSHIP   see number 134

SEATTLE POST-INTELLIGENCER

BOBBY MCCALLUM MEMORIAL SCHOLARSHIP   • 276

Scholarship is available to junior and senior college women from a Washington state university who have an interest in print journalism. Submit clips of published stories with transcripts, financial need analysis, application, and two letters of recommendation. Must be a Washington resident. Submit only questions through email. Applications must be mailed.

Bobby McCallum Memorial Scholarship (continued)

Academic Fields/Career Goals Journalism. *Award* Scholarship for use in junior or senior years; not renewable. *Number:* 1. *Amount:* $1000.

Eligibility Requirements Applicant must be enrolled or expecting to enroll full or part-time at a four-year institution; female; resident of Washington and studying in Washington. Applicant must have 3.0 GPA or higher. Available to U.S. citizens.

Application Requirements Application, financial need analysis, portfolio, resume, references, transcript. *Deadline:* April 1.

World Wide Web: http://www.seattlep-i.com

Contact: Janet Grimley, Assistant Managing Editor
Seattle Post-Intelligencer
PO Box 1909
Seattle, WA 98111
Phone: 206-448-8316
Fax: 206-448-8305
E-mail: janetgrimley@seattlep-i.com

SOCIETY OF PROFESSIONAL JOURNALISTS, LOS ANGELES CHAPTER

KEN INOUYE SCHOLARSHIP • 277

Awards are available to a minority student who is either a resident of Los Angeles, Ventura or Orange counties or is enrolled at a university in one of those three California counties. Must have completed sophomore year and be enrolled in or accepted to a journalism program.

Academic Fields/Career Goals Journalism. *Award* Scholarship for use in junior, senior, or graduate years; not renewable. *Amount:* $1000.

Eligibility Requirements Applicant must be American Indian/Alaska Native, Asian/Pacific Islander, Black (non-Hispanic), or Hispanic and enrolled or expecting to enroll full-time at a four-year institution or university. Available to U.S. citizens.

Application Requirements Application, essay, resume, work samples. *Deadline:* March 15.

World Wide Web: http://www.spj.org/losangeles

Contact: Society of Professional Journalists, Los Angeles Chapter
c/o Department of Journalism, California State University, Long Beach
1250 Bellflower
Long Beach, CA 90840

SOCIETY OF PROFESSIONAL JOURNALISTS-MID-FLORIDA CHAPTER

TYLER WARD MINORITY SCHOLARSHIP • 278

Applicants should be minority students in print or broadcast journalism. Must either live or attend college in the mid-Florida area. For full-time undergraduate study.

Academic Fields/Career Goals Journalism. *Award* Scholarship for use in freshman, sophomore, junior, or senior years; not renewable. *Number:* 1. *Amount:* up to $1000.

Eligibility Requirements Applicant must be American Indian/Alaska Native, Asian/Pacific Islander, Black (non-Hispanic), or Hispanic and enrolled or expecting to enroll full-time at a two-year or four-year institution or university. Available to U.S. and non-U.S. citizens.

Application Requirements Application, essay, resume, references. *Deadline:* November 1.

World Wide Web: http://www.spj.org/midflorida

Contact: Randy Miller
Society of Professional Journalists-Mid-Florida Chapter
5502B Loblolly Court
Tampa, FL 33617
E-mail: miller@chuma.cas.usf.edu

SOCIETY OF PROFESSIONAL JOURNALISTS-SOUTH FLORIDA CHAPTER

GARTH REEVES, JR. MEMORIAL SCHOLARSHIPS   see number 136

UNITED METHODIST COMMUNICATIONS

JUDITH L. WEIDMAN RACIAL ETHNICITY MINORITY FELLOWSHIP   see number 137

LEONARD M. PERRYMAN COMMUNICATIONS SCHOLARSHIP FOR ETHNIC MINORITY STUDENTS   see number 138

UNITED STATES INSTITUTE OF PEACE

JENNINGS RANDOLPH SENIOR FELLOW AWARD   see number 46

LANDSCAPE ARCHITECTURE_____

ASSOCIATION FOR WOMEN IN ARCHITECTURE FOUNDATION

ASSOCIATION FOR WOMEN IN ARCHITECTURE SCHOLARSHIP   see number 38

WOMEN'S NATIONAL FARM AND GARDEN ASSOCIATION

SARAH BRADLEY TYSON MEMORIAL FELLOWSHIP   see number 268

LAW ENFORCEMENT/POLICE ADMINISTRATION_____

GOVERNOR'S OFFICE

GOVERNOR'S OPPORTUNITY SCHOLARSHIP   see number 81

LAW/LEGAL SERVICES

AMERICAN ASSOCIATION OF LAW LIBRARIES

AALL AND WEST GROUP GEORGE A. STRAIT MINORITY SCHOLARSHIP ENDOWMENT • 279

One-time award for minority graduate students who have library experience and are working toward an advanced degree to further law library career. Based on need.

Academic Fields/Career Goals Law/Legal Services; Library and Information Sciences. *Award* Scholarship for use in graduate years; not renewable. *Amount:* $3500.

Eligibility Requirements Applicant must be American Indian/Alaska Native, Asian/Pacific Islander, Black (non-Hispanic), or Hispanic and enrolled or expecting to enroll full or part-time at a four-year institution or university. Available to U.S. and non-U.S. citizens.

Application Requirements Application, essay, financial need analysis, references, self-addressed stamped envelope, transcript. *Deadline:* April 1.

World Wide Web: http://www.aallnet.org

Contact: Rachel Shaevel, Membership Coordinator
American Association of Law Libraries
53 West Jackson Boulevard, Suite 940
Chicago, IL 60604-3695
Phone: 312-939-4764 Ext. 10
Fax: 312-431-1097
E-mail: rshaevel@aall.org

AMERICAN ASSOCIATION OF UNIVERSITY WOMEN (AAUW) EDUCATIONAL FOUNDATION

AAUW EDUCATIONAL FOUNDATION SELECTED PROFESSIONS FELLOWSHIPS
see number 36

BUSINESS AND PROFESSIONAL WOMEN'S FOUNDATION

BPW CAREER ADVANCEMENT SCHOLARSHIP PROGRAM FOR WOMEN
see number 68

FOLEY AND LARDNER, ATTORNEYS AT LAW

FOLEY & LARDNER MINORITY SCHOLARSHIP PROGRAM • 280

Scholarship for minority students in their first year of law school at participating institutions: Duke, Florida, Georgetown, Michigan, Northwestern, Stanford, UCLA and Wisconsin. One scholarship awarded at each school. Contact financial aid office at the participating schools for application.

Academic Fields/Career Goals Law/Legal Services. *Award* Scholarship for use in graduate years; not renewable. *Number:* 8. *Amount:* $5000.

Eligibility Requirements Applicant must be American Indian/Alaska Native, Asian/Pacific Islander, Black (non-Hispanic), or Hispanic; enrolled or expecting to enroll at an institution or university and studying in California, District of Columbia, Florida, Illinois, Michigan, North Carolina, or Wisconsin.

Application Requirements Application, resume, transcript. *Deadline:* September 27.

World Wide Web: http://www.foleylardner.com

Contact: Foley and Lardner, Attorneys at Law
Firstar Center
777 East Wisconsin Avenue
Milwaukee, WI 53202-5367

FREDRIKSON AND BYRON FOUNDATION

FREDRIKSON AND BYRON FOUNDATION MINORITY SCHOLARSHIP • 281

One-time award to provide financial aid and work experience to minority law students. Must be currently enrolled in second semester of first year of law school at time of application. Based on academic performance and potential. Download applications at http://www.fredlaw.com/news.

Academic Fields/Career Goals Law/Legal Services. *Award* Scholarship for use in graduate years; not renewable. *Number:* 1–2. *Amount:* $5000.

Eligibility Requirements Applicant must be American Indian/Alaska Native, Asian/Pacific Islander, Black (non-Hispanic), or Hispanic and enrolled or expecting to enroll full or part-time at an institution or university. Available to U.S. and non-U.S. citizens.

Application Requirements Application, essay, interview, resume, references, transcript. *Deadline:* April 1.

World Wide Web: http://www.fredlawrecruiting.com

Contact: Ms. Greta Larson, Recruiting Administrator
Fredrikson and Byron Foundation
4000 Pillsbury Center, 200 South Sixth Street
Minneapolis, MN 55402-3397
Phone: 612-492-7141
Fax: 612-492-7077
E-mail: glarson@fredlaw.com

HOSTESS COMMITTEE SCHOLARSHIPS/MISS AMERICA PAGEANT

LEONARD C. HORN AWARD FOR LEGAL STUDIES • 282

Scholarship for Miss America contestants pursuing career in field of law. Award available to women who have competed within the Miss America system on the local, state, or national level from 1992 to the present, regardless of whether title was won. One or more scholarships will be awarded annually, depending on the qualifications of the applicants. A new application must be submitted each year, previous applicants may apply. Applications must be received by June 30. Late or incomplete applications are not accepted.

Academic Fields/Career Goals Law/Legal Services. *Award* Grant for use in graduate years; not renewable. *Number:* 1.

Eligibility Requirements Applicant must be enrolled or expecting to enroll at an institution or university; female and must have an interest in beauty pageant. Available to U.S. citizens.

Application Requirements Application, essay, financial need analysis, references, test scores, transcript. *Deadline:* June 30.

World Wide Web: http://www.missamerica.org

Contact: Hostess Committee Scholarships/Miss America Pageant
Two Miss America Way, Suite 1000
Atlantic City, NJ 08401

MEXICAN AMERICAN LEGAL DEFENSE AND EDUCATIONAL FUND

MALDEF LAW SCHOOL SCHOLARSHIP PROGRAM • 283

Through its scholarship program, MALDEF seeks to increase the number of Latinos in the legal profession. The scholarships are based upon three primary factors: 1. demonstrated commitment to serve the Latino community through the legal profession; 2. financial need; and 3. academic achievement.

Academic Fields/Career Goals Law/Legal Services. *Award* Scholarship for use in graduate years; renewable. *Number:* 1–10. *Amount:* $2000–$6000.

Eligibility Requirements Applicant must be Hispanic and enrolled or expecting to enroll full-time at an institution or university. Available to U.S. and non-U.S. citizens.

Application Requirements Application, autobiography, essay, financial need analysis, resume, references, test scores, transcript. *Deadline:* July 1.

World Wide Web: http://www.maldef.org

Contact: Scholarship Coordinator
Mexican American Legal Defense and Educational Fund
634 South Spring Street, 11th Floor
Los Angeles, CA 90014
Phone: 213-629-2512
Fax: 213-629-8016

PUERTO RICAN LEGAL DEFENSE AND EDUCATION FUND

PUERTO RICAN BAR ASSOCIATION SCHOLARSHIP AWARD • 284

One-time award for Latino students attending law school in the U.S. Selection is based on financial need and academic promise. Must be in a JD degree program in an ABA-approved law school.

Academic Fields/Career Goals Law/Legal Services. *Award* Scholarship for use in graduate years; not renewable. *Number:* 5. *Amount:* $2000.

Eligibility Requirements Applicant must be of Hispanic heritage and enrolled or expecting to enroll at an institution or university. Applicant must have 2.5 GPA or higher. Available to U.S. citizens.

Application Requirements Application, essay, financial need analysis, resume, references, transcript, IRS 1040 form. *Deadline:* November 15.

World Wide Web: http://www.prldef.org

Contact: Ileana Infante, Director, Education Division
Puerto Rican Legal Defense and Education Fund
99 Hudson Street, 14th Floor
New York, NY 10013
Phone: 212-739-7496
Fax: 212-431-4276
E-mail: education@prldef.org

PUERTO RICAN LEGAL DEFENSE AND EDUCATION FUND FR. JOSEPH FITZPATRICK SCHOLARSHIP PROGRAM • 285

One-time award for Latino students in their first or second year of law school. Based on academic standing, need, and demonstration of involvement in the Latino community. Applicant must be in a JD program at a law school approved by the American Bar Association.

Academic Fields/Career Goals Law/Legal Services. *Award* Scholarship for use in graduate years; not renewable. *Number:* 5. *Amount:* up to $1500.

Eligibility Requirements Applicant must be of Hispanic heritage and enrolled or expecting to enroll at an institution or university. Applicant or parent of applicant must have employment or volunteer experience in community service. Applicant must have 2.5 GPA or higher. Available to U.S. citizens.

Application Requirements Application, essay, financial need analysis, resume, references, transcript, IRS 1040 form. *Deadline:* January 1.

World Wide Web: http://www.prldef.org

Contact: Ileana Infante, Director, Education Division
Puerto Rican Legal Defense and Education Fund
99 Hudson Street, 14th Floor
New York, NY 10013
Phone: 212-739-7496
Fax: 212-431-4276
E-mail: education@prldef.org

RHODE ISLAND FOUNDATION

MARLYNNE GRABOYS WOOL SCHOLARSHIP • 286

One-time award for women with financial need who plan to attend graduate school to attain a law degree at an accredited institution. Must be a Rhode Island resident.

Academic Fields/Career Goals Law/Legal Services. *Award* Scholarship for use in graduate years; not renewable. *Number:* 1. *Amount:* $2000.

Eligibility Requirements Applicant must be enrolled or expecting to enroll at an institution or university; female and resident of Rhode Island.

Application Requirements Application, financial need analysis, self-addressed stamped envelope. *Deadline:* June 27.

World Wide Web: http://www.rifoundation.org

Contact: Libby Monahan, Scholarship Coordinator
Rhode Island Foundation
One Union Station
Providence, RI 02903
Phone: 401-274-4564
Fax: 401-272-1359
E-mail: libbym@rifoundation.org

ROSCOE POUND INSTITUTE

ELAINE OSBORNE JACOBSON AWARD FOR WOMEN WORKING IN HEALTH CARE LAW
see number 229

UNITED NEGRO COLLEGE FUND

UNCF/PFIZER CORPORATE SCHOLARS PROGRAM
see number 27

UNITED STATES INSTITUTE OF PEACE

JENNINGS RANDOLPH SENIOR FELLOW AWARD
see number 46

WELLESLEY COLLEGE

MARGARET FREEMAN BOWERS FELLOWSHIP   • 287

One or more fellowships for a first year of study in the fields of social work, law, or public policy/public administration, including MBA candidates with plans for a career in the field of social services. Preference will be given to candidates demonstrating financial need. Must be a graduate of Wellesley College.

Academic Fields/Career Goals Law/Legal Services; Social Services. *Award* Fellowship for use in graduate years; not renewable. *Amount:* up to $8000.

Eligibility Requirements Applicant must be enrolled or expecting to enroll full-time at an institution or university and female. Available to U.S. citizens.

Application Requirements Application, essay, financial need analysis, resume, references, transcript. *Deadline:* January 6.

World Wide Web: http://www.wellesley.edu/CWS/

Contact: Mary Beth Callery, Secretary to the Committee on Graduate Fellowships
Wellesley College
106 Central Avenue, Green Hall 441
Wellesley, MA 02481-8200
Phone: 781-283-3525
Fax: 781-283-3674
E-mail: cws-fellowships@wellesley.edu

WOMEN'S BASKETBALL COACHES ASSOCIATION

CHARLES T. STONER LAW SCHOLARSHIP AWARD   • 288

One-time award available to female student athletes who have completed their eligibility. Must be nominated by the head women's basketball coach who is a member of the WBCA. Minimum 2.5 GPA required. Can only be used for law school.

Academic Fields/Career Goals Law/Legal Services. *Award* Scholarship for use in graduate years; not renewable. *Number:* 1. *Amount:* $1000.

Eligibility Requirements Applicant must be enrolled or expecting to enroll full or part-time at a four-year institution or university; female and must have an interest in athletics/sports. Applicant must have 2.5 GPA or higher. Available to U.S. and non-U.S. citizens.

Application Requirements Application, references, statistics. *Deadline:* February 7.

World Wide Web: http://www.wbca.org

Contact: Kristen Miller, Manager of Office Administration and Awards
Women's Basketball Coaches Association
4646 Lawrenceville Highway
Lilburn, GA 30247-3620
Phone: 770-279-8027 Ext. 102
Fax: 770-279-6290
E-mail: kmiller@wbca.org

LIBRARY AND INFORMATION SCIENCES_____

AMERICAN ASSOCIATION OF LAW LIBRARIES

AALL AND WEST GROUP GEORGE A. STRAIT MINORITY SCHOLARSHIP ENDOWMENT
see number 279

CALIFORNIA LIBRARY ASSOCIATION

CALIFORNIA LIBRARY ASSOCIATION SCHOLARSHIP FOR MINORITY STUDENTS IN MEMORY OF EDNA YELLAND • 289

One-time award for California resident enrolled or accepted in ALA-accredited master's program in library or information science at a California institution. Must be member of a recognized minority group and a U.S. citizen or permanent resident. Award amount varies depending upon available funds and financial need of applicant.

Academic Fields/Career Goals Library and Information Sciences. *Award* Scholarship for use in graduate years; not renewable.

Eligibility Requirements Applicant must be American Indian/Alaska Native, Asian/Pacific Islander, Black (non-Hispanic), or Hispanic; enrolled or expecting to enroll at a four-year institution; resident of California and studying in California. Available to U.S. citizens.

Application Requirements Application, essay, financial need analysis, interview, references, transcript. *Deadline:* May 31.

World Wide Web: http://www.cla-net.org

Contact: Jerry Stoehr, Staff Assistant
California Library Association
717 20th Street, Suite 200
Sacramento, CA 95814-3477

CALIFORNIA SCHOOL LIBRARY ASSOCIATION

LEADERSHIP FOR DIVERSITY SCHOLARSHIP • 290

A scholarship is available to a student representing a traditionally underrepresented group who will attend a Commission on Teacher Credentialing-accredited library media teacher credential program. For more details and an application see Web site: http://www.schoolibrary.org.

Academic Fields/Career Goals Library and Information Sciences. *Award* Scholarship for use in graduate, or postgraduate years; not renewable. *Number:* 1. *Amount:* $1000.

Eligibility Requirements Applicant must be American Indian/Alaska Native, Asian/Pacific Islander, Black (non-Hispanic), or Hispanic and enrolled or expecting to enroll at an institution or university. Available to U.S. citizens.

Application Requirements Application, financial need analysis, references, transcript. *Deadline:* June 1.

World Wide Web: http://www.schoolibrary.org

Contact: application available at Web site

HISPANIC DIVISION, LIBRARY OF CONGRESS

HISPANIC DIVISION FELLOWSHIPS see number 43

LIBRARY AND INFORMATION TECHNOLOGY ASSOCIATION

LIBRARY AND INFORMATION TECHNOLOGY ASSOCIATION/LSSI MINORITY SCHOLARSHIP • 291

Award for minority students planning to follow a career in library automation. Candidate must have applied for admission to a formal degree program in library education with emphasis on

Library and Information Technology Association/LSSI Minority Scholarship (continued)

library automation leading to a master's degree. Leadership skills, work experience, and academic excellence are considered. Must submit personal statement.

Academic Fields/Career Goals Library and Information Sciences. *Award* Scholarship for use in graduate years; not renewable. *Number:* 1. *Amount:* $2500.

Eligibility Requirements Applicant must be American Indian/Alaska Native, Asian/Pacific Islander, Black (non-Hispanic), or Hispanic and enrolled or expecting to enroll full-time at an institution or university. Available to U.S. and Canadian citizens.

Application Requirements Application, essay, references, transcript. *Deadline:* March 1.

World Wide Web: http://www.lita.org

Contact: Scholarship Committee
Library and Information Technology Association
50 East Huron Street
Chicago, IL 60611-2795
Phone: 312-280-4269
E-mail: lita@ala.org

LIBRARY AND INFORMATION TECHNOLOGY ASSOCIATION/OCLC MINORITY SCHOLARSHIP • 292

Award for minority students planning to follow a career in library automation. Candidate must have applied for admission to a formal degree in library education with emphasis on library automation leading to a master's degree. Leadership skills, work experience, and academic excellence are considered. Must submit personal statement.

Academic Fields/Career Goals Library and Information Sciences. *Award* Scholarship for use in graduate years; not renewable. *Number:* 1. *Amount:* $3000.

Eligibility Requirements Applicant must be American Indian/Alaska Native, Asian/Pacific Islander, Black (non-Hispanic), or Hispanic and enrolled or expecting to enroll full-time at an institution or university. Available to U.S. and Canadian citizens.

Application Requirements Application, essay, references, transcript. *Deadline:* March 1.

World Wide Web: http://www.lita.org

Contact: Scholarship Committee
Library and Information Technology Association
50 East Huron Street
Chicago, IL 60611-2795
E-mail: lita@ala.org

MEDICAL LIBRARY ASSOCIATION

MEDICAL LIBRARY ASSOCIATION SCHOLARSHIP FOR MINORITY STUDENTS • 293

Scholarship for minority graduate students to study at an ALA-accredited school for library science. Submit transcripts from all institutions attended, essay on career objectives, and references. One-time award of $5000. Further information and an application can be found at Web site http://www.mlanet.org/awards/grants/.

Academic Fields/Career Goals Library and Information Sciences. *Award* Scholarship for use in graduate years; not renewable. *Number:* 1. *Amount:* $5000.

Eligibility Requirements Applicant must be American Indian/Alaska Native, Asian/Pacific Islander, Black (non-Hispanic), or Hispanic and enrolled or expecting to enroll full or part-time at an institution or university. Available to U.S. and Canadian citizens.

Application Requirements Application, essay, references, transcript. *Deadline:* December 1.

World Wide Web: http://www.mlanet.org

Contact: Lisa Fried, Coordinator, Credentialing and Professional Recognition
Medical Library Association
65 East Wacker Place, Suite 1900
Chicago, IL 60601-7298
Phone: 312-419-9094
Fax: 312-419-8950
E-mail: mlapd2@mlahq.org

SPECIAL LIBRARIES ASSOCIATION

SPECIAL LIBRARIES ASSOCIATION AFFIRMATIVE ACTION SCHOLARSHIP • 294

One scholarship available to graduating college seniors and master's candidates. Must be a member of a minority group and be enrolled in a library science program. May be used for tuition or any research-related costs. One-time award of $6000.

Academic Fields/Career Goals Library and Information Sciences. *Award* Scholarship for use in graduate years; not renewable. *Number:* 1. *Amount:* $6000.

Eligibility Requirements Applicant must be American Indian/Alaska Native, Asian/Pacific Islander, Black (non-Hispanic), or Hispanic and enrolled or expecting to enroll full or part-time at a four-year institution or university. Available to U.S. citizens.

Application Requirements Application, essay, financial need analysis, interview, references, test scores, transcript. *Deadline:* October 31.

World Wide Web: http://www.sla.org

Contact: Diana Gonzalez, Membership Development Program Associate
Special Libraries Association
1700 18th Street, NW
Washington, DC 20009-2514
Phone: 202-234-4700 Ext. 671
Fax: 202-265-9317

TEXAS LIBRARY ASSOCIATION

SPECTRUM SCHOLARSHIP   • 295

Applicant must be an American Library Association (ALA) Spectrum Scholar. Must also be enrolled in an ALA recognized master's degree program in library and information studies in Texas. Award restricted to Native-Americans, Asian, African-American and Hispanic applicants. Visit Web site for additional information.

Academic Fields/Career Goals Library and Information Sciences. *Award* Scholarship for use in graduate years; not renewable. *Amount:* $2000.

Eligibility Requirements Applicant must be American Indian/Alaska Native, Asian/Pacific Islander, Black (non-Hispanic), or Hispanic; enrolled or expecting to enroll full or part-time at a four-year institution or university and studying in Texas. Available to U.S. citizens.

Application Requirements Application, transcript. *Deadline:* February 15.

World Wide Web: http://www.txla.org

Contact: Catherine Lee, Director of Administration
Texas Library Association
3355 Bee Cave Road, Suite 401
Austin, TX 78746
Phone: 512-328-1518
Fax: 512-328-8852
E-mail: catherinel@txla.org

LITERATURE/ENGLISH/WRITING_____

AIM MAGAZINE SHORT STORY CONTEST

AMERICA'S INTERCULTURAL MAGAZINE (AIM) SHORT STORY CONTEST • 296

Short fiction award for a previously unpublished story that embodies our goal of furthering the brotherhood of man through the written word. Proof that people from different racial/ethnic backgrounds are more alike than they are different. Maximum length 4,000 words. Story should not moralize. August 15 is deadline.

Academic Fields/Career Goals Literature/English/Writing. *Award* Prize for use in freshman, sophomore, junior, senior, or graduate years; not renewable. *Number:* 1–2. *Amount:* $75–$100.

Eligibility Requirements Applicant must be enrolled or expecting to enroll at a two-year or four-year or technical institution or university.

Application Requirements Applicant must enter a contest. *Deadline:* August 15.

World Wide Web: http://www.aimmagazine.org

Contact: Mark Boone, Fiction Editor
Aim Magazine Short Story Contest
PO Box 1174
Maywood, IL 60153

NATIONAL RESEARCH COUNCIL

FORD FOUNDATION DISSERTATION FELLOWSHIPS FOR MINORITIES

see number 125

FORD FOUNDATION POSTDOCTORAL FELLOWSHIP FOR MINORITIES

see number 126

FORD FOUNDATION PRE-DOCTORAL FELLOWSHIPS FOR MINORITIES

see number 127

OSCAR B. CINTAS FOUNDATION, INC.

CINTAS FELLOWSHIPS PROGRAM

see number 41

PHI BETA KAPPA SOCIETY

MARY ISABEL SIBLEY FELLOWSHIP FOR GREEK AND FRENCH STUDIES

see number 33

PLAYWRIGHTS' CENTER

MANY VOICES RESIDENCY PROGRAM • 297

The Playwrights' Center's Many Voices programs enrich the American theater by offering playwriting residencies to artists of color. Must be U.S. citizen.

Academic Fields/Career Goals Literature/English/Writing. *Award* Grant for use in freshman, sophomore, junior, senior, graduate, or postgraduate years; not renewable. *Number:* 7. *Amount:* $1200–$2000.

Eligibility Requirements Applicant must be American Indian/Alaska Native, Asian/Pacific Islander, Black (non-Hispanic), or Hispanic; enrolled or expecting to enroll full or part-time at a two-year or four-year or technical institution or university; resident of Minnesota; studying in Minnesota and must have an interest in writing. Available to U.S. citizens.

Application Requirements Application. *Deadline:* July 31.

World Wide Web: http://www.pwcenter.org

Contact: Kristen Gandrow, Director of Playwright Services
Playwrights' Center
2301 Franklin Avenue, E
Minneapolis, MN 55406-1099
Phone: 612-332-7481
Fax: 612-332-6037
E-mail: info@pwcenter.org

UNITED DAUGHTERS OF THE CONFEDERACY

MILDRED RICHARDS TAYLOR MEMORIAL SCHOLARSHIP • 298

Renewable award for undergraduate female student who is a descendant of a Confederate soldier, sailor or marine. Must be enrolled in an accredited university and be in a business or related field. Minimum of 3.0 GPA required. Submit a letter of endorsement from sponsoring Chapter of the United Daughters of the Confederacy. Preference given to former Children of the Confederacy members.

Academic Fields/Career Goals Literature/English/Writing. *Award* Scholarship for use in graduate years; renewable. *Number:* 1–2. *Amount:* $800–$1000.

Eligibility Requirements Applicant must be enrolled or expecting to enroll full-time at an institution or university and female. Applicant or parent of applicant must be member of United Daughters of the Confederacy. Applicant must have 3.0 GPA or higher. Available to U.S. citizens.

Application Requirements Application, essay, financial need analysis, photo, references, self-addressed stamped envelope, transcript. *Deadline:* February 15.

World Wide Web: http://www.hqudc.org

Contact: Second Vice President General
United Daughters of the Confederacy
328 North Boulevard
Richmond, VA 23220-4057
Phone: 804-355-1636

WELLESLEY COLLEGE

MARY MCEWEN SCHIMKE SCHOLARSHIP see number 265

RUTH INGERSOLL GOLDMARK FELLOWSHIP • 299

One or more fellowships available to graduates of Wellesley College for graduate study in English literature, English composition or the Classics. Award based on need and merit. Information and applications available at Web site http://www.wellesley.edu/cws.

Academic Fields/Career Goals Literature/English/Writing. *Award* Fellowship for use in graduate years; not renewable. *Amount:* up to $2500.

Eligibility Requirements Applicant must be enrolled or expecting to enroll full-time at an institution or university and female. Available to U.S. citizens.

Application Requirements Application, essay, financial need analysis, resume, references, transcript. *Deadline:* January 6.

World Wide Web: http://www.wellesley.edu/CWS/

Ruth Ingersoll Goldmark Fellowship (continued)

Contact: Mary Beth Callery, Secretary to the Committee on Graduate Fellowships
Wellesley College
106 Central Avenue, Green Hall 441
Wellesley, MA 02481-8200
Phone: 781-283-3525
Fax: 781-283-3674
E-mail: cws-fellowships@wellesley.edu

VIDA DUTTON SCUDDER FELLOWSHIP • 300

One or more fellowships available to alumnae of Wellesley College for study in the field of social science, political science or literature. Based on need and merit. Visit our Web site at http://www.wellesley.edu/cws for guidelines and application.

Academic Fields/Career Goals Literature/English/Writing; Political Science; Social Sciences. *Award* Fellowship for use in graduate years; not renewable. *Amount:* up to $11,000.

Eligibility Requirements Applicant must be enrolled or expecting to enroll full-time at an institution or university and female. Available to U.S. citizens.

Application Requirements Application, essay, financial need analysis, resume, references, transcript. *Deadline:* January 6.

World Wide Web: http://www.wellesley.edu/CWS/

Contact: Mary Beth Callery, Secretary to the Committee on Graduate Fellowships
Wellesley College
106 Central Avenue, Green Hall 441
Wellesley, MA 02481-8200
Phone: 781-283-3525
Fax: 781-283-3674
E-mail: cws-fellowships@wellesley.edu

WILLA CATHER FOUNDATION

NORMA ROSS WALTER SCHOLARSHIP • 301

Awarded yearly to a Nebraska female high school graduate. Must major in English at any accredited college or university. Renewable based on continued eligibility. Must have a minimum 3.0 GPA. Deadline is January 31.

Academic Fields/Career Goals Literature/English/Writing. *Award* Scholarship for use in freshman year; renewable. *Number:* 1. *Amount:* $2000.

Eligibility Requirements Applicant must be enrolled or expecting to enroll full-time at a four-year institution or university; female and resident of Nebraska. Applicant must have 3.0 GPA or higher. Available to U.S. citizens.

Application Requirements Application, essay, portfolio, references, test scores, transcript. *Deadline:* January 31.

World Wide Web: http://www.willacather.org

Contact: Dr. Steven Ryan, Executive Director
Willa Cather Foundation
326 North Webster
Red Cloud, NE 68970
Phone: 402-746-2653
Fax: 402-746-2652
E-mail: sryan@gpcom.net

MATERIALS SCIENCE, ENGINEERING, AND METALLURGY

AMERICAN CHEMICAL SOCIETY

AMERICAN CHEMICAL SOCIETY SCHOLARS PROGRAM   see number 94

AMERICAN SOCIETY FOR ENGINEERING EDUCATION

NATIONAL DEFENSE SCIENCE AND ENGINEERING GRADUATE FELLOWSHIP
PROGRAM   see number 98

ASSOCIATION FOR WOMEN IN SCIENCE EDUCATIONAL FOUNDATION

ASSOCIATION FOR WOMEN IN SCIENCE PRE-DOCTORAL FELLOWSHIP
                  see number 32

ASSOCIATION FOR WOMEN IN SCIENCE UNDERGRADUATE AWARD   see number 26

GEM CONSORTIUM

GEM MS ENGINEERING FELLOWSHIP   see number 22

GEM PHD ENGINEERING FELLOWSHIP   see number 23

HISPANIC ENGINEER NATIONAL ACHIEVEMENT AWARDS CORPORATION (HENAAC)

HISPANIC ENGINEER NATIONAL ACHIEVEMENT AWARDS CORPORATION
SCHOLARSHIP PROGRAM   see number 51

JORGE MAS CANOSA FREEDOM FOUNDATION

MAS FAMILY SCHOLARSHIP AWARD   see number 85

LOS ANGELES COUNCIL OF BLACK PROFESSIONAL ENGINEERS

AL-BEN SCHOLARSHIP FOR ACADEMIC INCENTIVE   see number 100

AL-BEN SCHOLARSHIP FOR PROFESSIONAL MERIT   see number 101

AL-BEN SCHOLARSHIP FOR SCHOLASTIC ACHIEVEMENT   see number 102

NAMEPA NATIONAL SCHOLARSHIP FOUNDATION

NATIONAL ASSOCIATION OF MINORITY ENGINEERING PROGRAM ADMINISTRATORS NATIONAL SCHOLARSHIP FUND   see number 58

NATIONAL ACTION COUNCIL FOR MINORITIES IN ENGINEERING-NACME, INC.

ENGINEERING VANGUARD PROGRAM   see number 103

SLOAN PHD PROGRAM   see number 104

NATIONAL PHYSICAL SCIENCE CONSORTIUM

NATIONAL PHYSICAL SCIENCE CONSORTIUM GRADUATE FELLOWSHIPS IN THE PHYSICAL SCIENCES   see number 105

NEW YORK STATE SOCIETY OF PROFESSIONAL ENGINEERS

NSPE AUXILIARY SCHOLARSHIP   see number 106

NSPE-VIRGINIA D. HENRY MEMORIAL SCHOLARSHIP   see number 107

OFFICE OF NAVAL RESEARCH

HISTORICALLY BLACK COLLEGES AND UNIVERSITIES FUTURE ENGINEERING FACULTY FELLOWSHIP   see number 108

SOCIETY OF HISPANIC PROFESSIONAL ENGINEERS FOUNDATION

SOCIETY OF HISPANIC PROFESSIONAL ENGINEERS FOUNDATION   see number 109

SOCIETY OF WOMEN ENGINEERS

GENERAL MOTORS FOUNDATION GRADUATE SCHOLARSHIP   see number 113

XEROX

TECHNICAL MINORITY SCHOLARSHIP   see number 115

MECHANICAL ENGINEERING_____

AMERICAN SOCIETY FOR ENGINEERING EDUCATION

NATIONAL DEFENSE SCIENCE AND ENGINEERING GRADUATE FELLOWSHIP PROGRAM   see number 98

ASSOCIATION FOR WOMEN IN SCIENCE EDUCATIONAL FOUNDATION

ASSOCIATION FOR WOMEN IN SCIENCE UNDERGRADUATE AWARD   see number 26

CENTER FOR THE ADVANCEMENT OF HISPANICS IN SCIENCE AND ENGINEERING EDUCATION (CAHSEE)

CAHSEE FELLOWSHIP: YOUNG EDUCATORS PROGRAM   see number 30

COMTO-BOSTON CHAPTER

COMTO BOSTON/GARRETT A. MORGAN SCHOLARSHIP   see number 40

CUBAN AMERICAN NATIONAL FOUNDATION

MAS FAMILY SCHOLARSHIPS   see number 80

EAST LOS ANGELES COMMUNITY UNION (TELACU) EDUCATION FOUNDATION

TELACU ENGINEERING AWARD   see number 99

EATON CORPORATION

EATON CORPORATION MULTICULTURAL SCHOLARS PROGRAM   see number 141

GEM CONSORTIUM

GEM MS ENGINEERING FELLOWSHIP   see number 22

GEM PHD ENGINEERING FELLOWSHIP   see number 23

HISPANIC COLLEGE FUND, INC.

FIRST IN MY FAMILY SCHOLARSHIP PROGRAM   see number 19

HISPANIC COLLEGE FUND SCHOLARSHIP PROGRAM   see number 20

HISPANIC COLLEGE FUND/INROADS/SPRINT SCHOLARSHIP PROGRAM

see number 82

HISPANIC ENGINEER NATIONAL ACHIEVEMENT AWARDS CORPORATION (HENAAC)

HISPANIC ENGINEER NATIONAL ACHIEVEMENT AWARDS CORPORATION SCHOLARSHIP PROGRAM   see number 51

HISPANIC SCHOLARSHIP FUND

HSF/GENERAL MOTORS SCHOLARSHIP see number 83

JORGE MAS CANOSA FREEDOM FOUNDATION

MAS FAMILY SCHOLARSHIP AWARD see number 85

LOS ANGELES COUNCIL OF BLACK PROFESSIONAL ENGINEERS

AL-BEN SCHOLARSHIP FOR ACADEMIC INCENTIVE see number 100

AL-BEN SCHOLARSHIP FOR PROFESSIONAL MERIT see number 101

AL-BEN SCHOLARSHIP FOR SCHOLASTIC ACHIEVEMENT see number 102

NAMEPA NATIONAL SCHOLARSHIP FOUNDATION

NATIONAL ASSOCIATION OF MINORITY ENGINEERING PROGRAM ADMINISTRATORS NATIONAL SCHOLARSHIP FUND see number 58

NATIONAL PHYSICAL SCIENCE CONSORTIUM

NATIONAL PHYSICAL SCIENCE CONSORTIUM GRADUATE FELLOWSHIPS IN THE PHYSICAL SCIENCES see number 105

NEW YORK STATE SOCIETY OF PROFESSIONAL ENGINEERS

NSPE AUXILIARY SCHOLARSHIP see number 106

NSPE-VIRGINIA D. HENRY MEMORIAL SCHOLARSHIP see number 107

SOCIETY OF HISPANIC PROFESSIONAL ENGINEERS FOUNDATION

SOCIETY OF HISPANIC PROFESSIONAL ENGINEERS FOUNDATION see number 109

SOCIETY OF WOMEN ENGINEERS

BECHTEL CORPORATION SCHOLARSHIP see number 116

CHEVRON TEXACO CORPORATION SCHOLARSHIPS see number 111

DAIMLER CHRYSLER CORPORATION SCHOLARSHIP see number 188

DELL COMPUTER CORPORATION SCHOLARSHIPS see number 146

DUPONT COMPANY SCHOLARSHIPS see number 112

GENERAL MOTORS FOUNDATION GRADUATE SCHOLARSHIP see number 113

GENERAL MOTORS FOUNDATION UNDERGRADUATE SCHOLARSHIPS
see number 114

LOCKHEED AERONAUTICS COMPANY SCHOLARSHIPS see number 189

XEROX

TECHNICAL MINORITY SCHOLARSHIP see number 115

METEOROLOGY/ATMOSPHERIC SCIENCE_____

AMERICAN METEOROLOGICAL SOCIETY

AMERICAN METEOROLOGICAL SOCIETY/INDUSTRY MINORITY SCHOLARSHIPS • 302

Two-year scholarships of $3000 per year for minority students entering their freshman year of college. Must plan to pursue careers in the atmospheric and related oceanic and hydrologic sciences. Must be U.S. citizen or permanent resident to apply.

Academic Fields/Career Goals Meteorology/Atmospheric Science. *Award* Scholarship for use in freshman or sophomore years; not renewable. *Amount:* $3000.

Eligibility Requirements Applicant must be American Indian/Alaska Native, Asian/Pacific Islander, Black (non-Hispanic), or Hispanic; high school student and planning to enroll or expecting to enroll full-time at a four-year institution or university. Available to U.S. citizens.

Application Requirements Application, essay, references, test scores, transcript. *Deadline:* February 20.

World Wide Web: http://www.ametsoc.org/AMS

Contact: Donna Fernandez, Fellowship/Scholarship Coordinator
American Meteorological Society
45 Beacon Street
Boston, MA 02108-3693
Phone: 617-227-2426 Ext. 246
Fax: 617-742-8718
E-mail: dfernand@ametsoc.org

ASSOCIATION FOR WOMEN IN SCIENCE EDUCATIONAL FOUNDATION

ASSOCIATION FOR WOMEN IN SCIENCE PRE-DOCTORAL FELLOWSHIP
see number 32

ASSOCIATION FOR WOMEN IN SCIENCE UNDERGRADUATE AWARD see number 26

CANADIAN FEDERATION OF UNIVERSITY WOMEN

CANADIAN FEDERATION OF UNIVERSITY WOMEN MEMORIAL FELLOWSHIP
see number 21

CENTER FOR THE ADVANCEMENT OF HISPANICS IN SCIENCE AND ENGINEERING EDUCATION (CAHSEE)

CAHSEE FELLOWSHIP: YOUNG EDUCATORS PROGRAM   see number 30

GEM CONSORTIUM

GEM PHD SCIENCE FELLOWSHIP   see number 70

NASA NEW HAMPSHIRE SPACE GRANT CONSORTIUM

GRADUATE FELLOWSHIPS   see number 161

NATIONAL ACTION COUNCIL FOR MINORITIES IN ENGINEERING-NACME, INC.

ENGINEERING VANGUARD PROGRAM   see number 103

SLOAN PHD PROGRAM   see number 104

NATIONAL PHYSICAL SCIENCE CONSORTIUM

NATIONAL PHYSICAL SCIENCE CONSORTIUM GRADUATE FELLOWSHIPS IN THE PHYSICAL SCIENCES   see number 105

MUSEUM STUDIES

WELLESLEY COLLEGE

HARRIET A. SHAW FELLOWSHIP   see number 47

MUSIC

AMERICAN MUSICOLOGICAL SOCIETY

HOWARD MAYER BROWN FELLOWSHIP   • 303

Fellowship for a minority student in good standing who has completed at least one year of graduate work and intends to pursue a PhD in musicology. Awards are based on merit only. Application deadline is January 15.

Academic Fields/Career Goals Music. *Award* Fellowship for use in graduate years; not renewable. *Amount:* $14,000.

Eligibility Requirements Applicant must be American Indian/Alaska Native, Asian/Pacific Islander, Black (non-Hispanic), or Hispanic and enrolled or expecting to enroll full-time at a four-year institution or university. Available to U.S. and Canadian citizens.

Application Requirements Application, essay, resume, references, transcript, samples of work. *Deadline:* January 15.

World Wide Web: http://www.ams-net.org

Contact: Ellen T. Harris, Massachusetts Institute of Technology, 4-246
American Musicological Society
77 Massachusetts Avenue
Cambridge, MA 02139-4301
E-mail: e-harris@mit.edu

MELLON NEW ENGLAND

SUSAN GLOVER HITCHCOCK SCHOLARSHIP   • 304

Award for women who are majoring in music. Must be a Massachusetts resident. Application deadline is April 15.

Academic Fields/Career Goals Music. *Award* Scholarship for use in freshman, sophomore, junior, or senior years; not renewable.

Eligibility Requirements Applicant must be enrolled or expecting to enroll at an institution or university; female and resident of Massachusetts.

Application Requirements Application, transcript. *Deadline:* April 15.

Contact: Sandra Brown-McMullen, Vice President
Mellon New England
One Boston Place, 024-0084
Boston, MA 02108
Phone: 617-722-3891

SIGMA ALPHA IOTA PHILANTHROPIES, INC.

GRADUATE SCHOLARSHIP IN MUSIC EDUCATION   see number 176

MUSIC THERAPY SCHOLARSHIPS (SAI)   • 305

One-time award offered triennially for undergraduate and graduate members of SAI who have completed two years in music therapy training at a university approved by the American Music Therapy Association. Contact local chapter for further information. Application fee: $25.

Academic Fields/Career Goals Music; Therapy/Rehabilitation. *Award* Scholarship for use in junior, senior, or graduate years; not renewable. *Number:* 2. *Amount:* $1000.

Eligibility Requirements Applicant must be enrolled or expecting to enroll full-time at a four-year institution or university; female and must have an interest in music/singing. Available to U.S. and non-U.S. citizens.

Application Requirements Application, essay, references, transcript. *Fee:* $25. *Deadline:* April 15.

World Wide Web: http://www.sai-national.org

Contact: Ms. Ruth Sieber Johnson, Executive Director of SAI
Sigma Alpha Iota Philanthropies, Inc.
34 Wall Street, Suite 515
Asheville, NC 28801-2710
Phone: 828-251-0606
Fax: 828-251-0644
E-mail: nh@sai-national.org

SIGMA ALPHA IOTA DOCTORAL GRANT   see number 177

SIGMA ALPHA IOTA GRADUATE PERFORMANCE AWARDS • 306

One-time award offered triennially to SAI members over 20 who are pursuing graduate study in field of music performance. Winners perform at national convention. Submit tape with required repertoire. Contact chapter for details. Four awards in each category (vocal; keyboard and percussion; strings; wind and brass) ranging from $1500 to $2000. Application fee: $25.

Academic Fields/Career Goals Music; Performing Arts. *Award* Prize for use in graduate years; not renewable. *Number:* 8. *Amount:* $1500–$2000.

Eligibility Requirements Applicant must be age 21; enrolled or expecting to enroll at an institution or university; female and must have an interest in music/singing. Available to U.S. and non-U.S. citizens.

Application Requirements Application, applicant must enter a contest, essay, references, transcript, tape. *Fee:* $25. *Deadline:* April 15.

World Wide Web: http://www.sai-national.org

Contact: Ms. Ruth Sieber Johnson, Executive Director of SAI
Sigma Alpha Iota Philanthropies, Inc.
34 Wall Street, Suite 515
Asheville, NC 28801-2710
Phone: 828-251-0606
Fax: 828-251-0644
E-mail: nh@sai-national.org

SIGMA ALPHA IOTA PHILANTHROPIES UNDERGRADUATE PERFORMANCE SCHOLARSHIPS • 307

Award offered triennially for female SAI members in freshman, sophomore or junior year in voice; keyboard and percussion; strings; winds and brass. Winners perform at national convention. Must submit tape with required repertoire. Consult local chapter for details. Four one-time scholarships of $1500. Application fee: $25.

Academic Fields/Career Goals Music; Performing Arts. *Award* Scholarship for use in freshman, sophomore, or junior years; not renewable. *Number:* 4. *Amount:* $1500.

Eligibility Requirements Applicant must be enrolled or expecting to enroll full-time at a four-year institution or university; female and must have an interest in music/singing. Available to U.S. and non-U.S. citizens.

Application Requirements Application, applicant must enter a contest, essay, references, transcript, audio tape. *Fee:* $25. *Deadline:* April 15.

World Wide Web: http://www.sai-national.org

Contact: Ms. Ruth Sieber Johnson, Executive Director of SAI
Sigma Alpha Iota Philanthropies, Inc.
34 Wall Street, Suite 515
Asheville, NC 28801-2710
Phone: 828-251-0606
Fax: 828-251-0644
E-mail: nh@sai-national.org

SIGMA ALPHA IOTA SCHOLARSHIP FOR CONDUCTORS • 308

One-time award offered triennially to SAI member who is enrolled in an accredited graduate program in music with an emphasis in conducting. Submit thirty-minute videotape of work. Contact your chapter for further details. Application fee: $25.

Academic Fields/Career Goals Music; Performing Arts. *Award* Scholarship for use in graduate years; not renewable. *Number:* 1. *Amount:* $2500.

Eligibility Requirements Applicant must be enrolled or expecting to enroll at an institution or university; female and must have an interest in music/singing. Available to U.S. and non-U.S. citizens.

Application Requirements Application, essay, references, transcript, videotape. *Fee:* $25. *Deadline:* April 15.

World Wide Web: http://www.sai-national.org

Contact: Ms. Ruth Sieber Johnson, Executive Director of SAI
Sigma Alpha Iota Philanthropies, Inc.
34 Wall Street, Suite 515
Asheville, NC 28801-2710
Phone: 828-251-0606
Fax: 828-251-0644
E-mail: nh@sai-national.org

SIGMA ALPHA IOTA SUMMER MUSIC SCHOLARSHIPS IN THE U.S. OR ABROAD • 309

One-time award for use at summer music programs in the U.S. or abroad. Must be a member of SAI and accepted by the summer music program. Contact local chapter for details. Application fee: $25.

Academic Fields/Career Goals Music; Performing Arts. *Award* Scholarship for use in freshman, sophomore, junior, or senior years; not renewable. *Number:* 5. *Amount:* up to $1000.

Eligibility Requirements Applicant must be enrolled or expecting to enroll full-time at a four-year institution or university; female and must have an interest in music/singing. Available to U.S. and non-U.S. citizens.

Application Requirements Application, essay. *Fee:* $25. *Deadline:* April 15.

World Wide Web: http://www.sai-national.org

Contact: Ms. Ruth Sieber Johnson, Executive Director of SAI
Sigma Alpha Iota Philanthropies, Inc.
34 Wall Street, Suite 515
Asheville, NC 28801-2710
Phone: 828-251-0606
Fax: 828-251-0644
E-mail: nh@sai-national.org

SIGMA ALPHA IOTA VISUALLY IMPAIRED SCHOLARSHIP see number 179

VERNA ROSS ORNDORFF CAREER PERFORMANCE GRANT • 310

Award for member of SAI launching a concert career, but not under professional management. Three-year rotation: 2004, strings, woodwind and brass; 2005, keyboard and percussion; 2006, vocal. Send tape with required repertoire. Consult chapter for further details. One-time grant of $5000. Application fee: $35.

Academic Fields/Career Goals Music; Performing Arts. *Award* Grant for use in graduate, or postgraduate years; not renewable. *Number:* 1. *Amount:* $5000.

Eligibility Requirements Applicant must be enrolled or expecting to enroll at a four-year institution or university; female and must have an interest in music/singing. Available to U.S. and non-U.S. citizens.

Application Requirements Application, applicant must enter a contest, essay, references, tape. *Fee:* $35. *Deadline:* October 1.

World Wide Web: http://www.sai-national.org

Verna Ross Orndorff Career Performance Grant (continued)

Contact: Ms. Ruth Sieber Johnson, Executive Director of SAI
Sigma Alpha Iota Philanthropies, Inc.
34 Wall Street, Suite 515
Asheville, NC 28801-2710
Phone: 828-251-0606
Fax: 828-251-0644
E-mail: nh@sai-national.org

WOMEN BAND DIRECTORS INTERNATIONAL

GLADYS STONE WRIGHT SCHOLARSHIP	see number 183
HELEN MAY BULTER MEMORIAL SCHOLARSHIP	see number 184
MARTHA ANN STARK MEMORIAL SCHOLARSHIP	see number 185
MUSIC TECHNOLOGY SCHOLARSHIP	see number 186
VOLKWEIN MEMORIAL SCHOLARSHIP	see number 187

NATURAL RESOURCES

AMERICAN AGRICULTURAL ECONOMICS ASSOCIATION FOUNDATION

SYLVIA LANE MENTOR RESEARCH FELLOWSHIP FUND	see number 18

AMERICAN FISHERIES SOCIETY

J. FRANCES ALLEN SCHOLARSHIP AWARD	see number 63

AMERICAN WATER WORKS ASSOCIATION

HOLLY A. CORNELL SCHOLARSHIP	see number 29

WOMEN'S NATIONAL FARM AND GARDEN ASSOCIATION

SARAH BRADLEY TYSON MEMORIAL FELLOWSHIP	see number 268

NATURAL SCIENCES

AMERICAN CHEMICAL SOCIETY

AMERICAN CHEMICAL SOCIETY SCHOLARS PROGRAM	see number 94

AMERICAN FISHERIES SOCIETY

J. FRANCES ALLEN SCHOLARSHIP AWARD see number 63

ASSOCIATION FOR WOMEN IN SCIENCE EDUCATIONAL FOUNDATION

ASSOCIATION FOR WOMEN IN SCIENCE PRE-DOCTORAL FELLOWSHIP
see number 32

ASSOCIATION FOR WOMEN IN SCIENCE UNDERGRADUATE AWARD see number 26

NASA NEW HAMPSHIRE SPACE GRANT CONSORTIUM

GRADUATE FELLOWSHIPS see number 161

SOCIETY OF HISPANIC PROFESSIONAL ENGINEERS FOUNDATION

SOCIETY OF HISPANIC PROFESSIONAL ENGINEERS FOUNDATION see number 109

WOMEN'S NATIONAL FARM AND GARDEN ASSOCIATION

SARAH BRADLEY TYSON MEMORIAL FELLOWSHIP see number 268

NUCLEAR SCIENCE

AMERICAN NUCLEAR SOCIETY

DELAYED EDUCATION FOR WOMEN SCHOLARSHIPS see number 192

AMERICAN SOCIETY FOR ENGINEERING EDUCATION

NATIONAL DEFENSE SCIENCE AND ENGINEERING GRADUATE FELLOWSHIP PROGRAM see number 98

ASSOCIATION FOR WOMEN IN SCIENCE EDUCATIONAL FOUNDATION

ASSOCIATION FOR WOMEN IN SCIENCE UNDERGRADUATE AWARD see number 26

GEM CONSORTIUM

GEM MS ENGINEERING FELLOWSHIP see number 22

| GEM PHD ENGINEERING FELLOWSHIP | see number 23 |

HISPANIC ENGINEER NATIONAL ACHIEVEMENT AWARDS CORPORATION (HENAAC)

| HISPANIC ENGINEER NATIONAL ACHIEVEMENT AWARDS CORPORATION SCHOLARSHIP PROGRAM | see number 51 |

NATIONAL ACTION COUNCIL FOR MINORITIES IN ENGINEERING-NACME, INC.

| ENGINEERING VANGUARD PROGRAM | see number 103 |
| SLOAN PHD PROGRAM | see number 104 |

SOCIETY OF HISPANIC PROFESSIONAL ENGINEERS FOUNDATION

| SOCIETY OF HISPANIC PROFESSIONAL ENGINEERS FOUNDATION | see number 109 |

NURSING

AMERICAN LEGION AUXILIARY, DEPARTMENT OF MARYLAND

AMERICAN LEGION AUXILIARY DEPARTMENT OF MARYLAND PAST PRESIDENT'S PARLEY NURSING SCHOLARSHIP • 311

Nonrenewable scholarship for natural or stepdaughter, granddaughter, or great-granddaughter of former serviceman or woman to pursue a degree in nursing. Must be a resident of Maryland and U.S. citizen. Need recommendation from high school official, minister, or rabbi. Must apply to Maryland American Legion Auxiliary.

Academic Fields/Career Goals Nursing. *Award* Scholarship for use in freshman, sophomore, junior, or senior years; not renewable. *Number:* 1. *Amount:* $2000.

Eligibility Requirements Applicant must be high school student; planning to enroll or expecting to enroll full-time at a two-year or four-year institution or university; female and resident of Maryland. Available to U.S. citizens. Applicant or parent must meet one or more of the following requirements: general military experience; retired from active duty; disabled or killed as a result of military service; prisoner of war; or missing in action.

Application Requirements Application, essay, references, transcript. *Deadline:* May 1.

Contact: Ms. Anna Thompson, Department Secretary
American Legion Auxiliary, Department of Maryland
1589 Sulphur Spring Road, Suite 105
Baltimore, MD 21227
Phone: 410-242-9519
Fax: 410-242-9553
E-mail: anna@alamd.org

BECA FOUNDATION, INC.

ALICE NEWELL JOSLYN MEDICAL FUND
see number 154

FOUNDATION OF THE NATIONAL STUDENT NURSES' ASSOCIATION

BREAKTHROUGH TO NURSING SCHOLARSHIPS FOR RACIAL/ETHNIC MINORITIES
• 312

Available to minority students enrolled in nursing or pre-nursing programs. Awards based on need, scholarship, and health-related activities. Application fee of $10. Send self-addressed stamped envelope with two stamps along with application request. One-time award of $1000-$2000. Application available at Web site.

Academic Fields/Career Goals Nursing. *Award* Scholarship for use in freshman, sophomore, junior, or senior years; not renewable. *Number:* 5. *Amount:* $1000–$2000.

Eligibility Requirements Applicant must be American Indian/Alaska Native, Asian/Pacific Islander, Black (non-Hispanic), or Hispanic and enrolled or expecting to enroll at an institution or university. Available to U.S. citizens.

Application Requirements Application, financial need analysis, self-addressed stamped envelope, transcript. *Fee:* $10. *Deadline:* January 31.

World Wide Web: http://www.nsna.org

Contact: application available at Web site
  E-mail: receptionist@nsna.org

GOVERNOR'S OFFICE

GOVERNOR'S OPPORTUNITY SCHOLARSHIP
see number 81

MARIN EDUCATION FUND

GOLDMAN FAMILY FUND, NEW LEADER SCHOLARSHIP
see number 156

ONS FOUNDATION

ONS FOUNDATION ETHNIC MINORITY BACHELOR'S SCHOLARSHIP
• 313

Three scholarships available to registered nurses with a demonstrated interest in oncology nursing. Must be currently enrolled in an undergraduate program at an NLN-accredited school, and must currently hold a license to practice as a registered nurse. Must be minority student who has not received any BA grants previously from ONF. One-time award of $2000. Deadline: February 1.

Academic Fields/Career Goals Nursing. *Award* Scholarship for use in freshman, sophomore, junior, or senior years; not renewable. *Number:* 3. *Amount:* $2000.

Eligibility Requirements Applicant must be American Indian/Alaska Native, Asian/Pacific Islander, Black (non-Hispanic), or Hispanic and enrolled or expecting to enroll full or part-time at a four-year institution or university. Applicant or parent of applicant must have employment or volunteer experience in designated career field. Available to U.S. citizens.

Application Requirements Application, transcript. *Deadline:* February 1.

World Wide Web: http://www.ons.org

ONS Foundation Ethnic Minority Bachelor's Scholarship (continued)

Contact: ONS Foundation
501 Holiday Drive
Pittsburgh, PA 15220

ONS FOUNDATION ETHNIC MINORITY MASTER'S SCHOLARSHIP • 314

Two awards for registered nurses with demonstrated interest in oncology nursing. Must be enrolled in a graduate nursing program in an NLN-accredited school, and must currently hold a license to practice as a registered nurse. Must be a minority student and not have received an MA scholarship. One-time award of $3000.

Academic Fields/Career Goals Nursing. *Award* Scholarship for use in graduate years; not renewable. *Number:* 2. *Amount:* $3000.

Eligibility Requirements Applicant must be American Indian/Alaska Native, Asian/Pacific Islander, Black (non-Hispanic), or Hispanic and enrolled or expecting to enroll full or part-time at an institution or university. Applicant or parent of applicant must have employment or volunteer experience in designated career field.

Application Requirements Application, transcript. *Deadline:* February 1.

World Wide Web: http://www.ons.org

Contact: ONS Foundation
501 Holiday Drive
Pittsburgh, PA 15220

ONS FOUNDATION ETHNIC MINORITY RESEARCHER AND MENTORSHIP GRANTS
see number 257

UNITED DAUGHTERS OF THE CONFEDERACY

WALTER REED SMITH SCHOLARSHIP
see number 91

PEACE AND CONFLICT STUDIES_____

INSTITUTE FOR INTERNATIONAL PUBLIC POLICY (IIPP)

INSTITUTE FOR INTERNATIONAL PUBLIC POLICY FELLOWSHIP PROGRAM
see number 44

UNITED STATES INSTITUTE OF PEACE

JENNINGS RANDOLPH SENIOR FELLOW AWARD
see number 46

PERFORMING ARTS_____

CONGRESSIONAL BLACK CAUCUS SPOUSES PROGRAM

CONGRESSIONAL BLACK CAUCUS SPOUSES PERFORMING ARTS SCHOLARSHIP • 315

Award made to students who reside or attend school in a congressional district represented by an African-American member of Congress. Must be full-time student enrolled in a performing arts program. Minimum 2.5 GPA required. Contact the congressional office in the appropriate district for information and applications. See http://www.cbcfinc.org for a list of district offices.

Academic Fields/Career Goals Performing Arts. *Award* Scholarship for use in freshman, sophomore, junior, senior, graduate, or postgraduate years; not renewable. *Number:* 5. *Amount:* $3000.

Eligibility Requirements Applicant must be enrolled or expecting to enroll full-time at a two-year or four-year or technical institution or university. Applicant must have 2.5 GPA or higher. Available to U.S. citizens.

Application Requirements Application, essay, financial need analysis, interview, photo, references, transcript. *Deadline:* Continuous.

World Wide Web: http://cbcfinc.org

Contact: Appropriate Congressional District Office

HOSTESS COMMITTEE SCHOLARSHIPS/MISS AMERICA PAGEANT

EUGENIA VELLNER FISCHER AWARD FOR PERFORMING ARTS • 316

Scholarship for Miss America contestants pursuing degree in performing arts. Award available to women who have competed within the Miss America system on the local, state, or national level from 1992 to the present, regardless of whether title was won. One or more scholarships are awarded annually, depending on qualifications of applicants. Applications must be received by June 30. Late or incomplete applications are not accepted.

Academic Fields/Career Goals Performing Arts. *Award* Scholarship for use in freshman, sophomore, junior, senior, or graduate years; not renewable. *Number:* 1.

Eligibility Requirements Applicant must be enrolled or expecting to enroll at a four-year institution or university; female and must have an interest in beauty pageant. Available to U.S. citizens.

Application Requirements Application, essay, financial need analysis, references, transcript. *Deadline:* June 30.

World Wide Web: http://www.missamerica.org

Contact: Hostess Committee Scholarships/Miss America Pageant
Two Miss America Way, Suite 1000
Atlantic City, NJ 08401

NATIONAL OPERA ASSOCIATION

NOA VOCAL COMPETITION/ LEGACY AWARD PROGRAM   see number 49

SIGMA ALPHA IOTA PHILANTHROPIES, INC.

GRADUATE SCHOLARSHIP IN MUSIC EDUCATION   see number 176

SIGMA ALPHA IOTA DOCTORAL GRANT   see number 177

SIGMA ALPHA IOTA GRADUATE PERFORMANCE AWARDS   see number 306

SIGMA ALPHA IOTA PHILANTHROPIES UNDERGRADUATE PERFORMANCE SCHOLARSHIPS   see number 307

SIGMA ALPHA IOTA PHILANTHROPIES UNDERGRADUATE SCHOLARSHIPS
see number 178

SIGMA ALPHA IOTA SCHOLARSHIP FOR CONDUCTORS	see number 308
SIGMA ALPHA IOTA SUMMER MUSIC SCHOLARSHIPS IN THE U.S. OR ABROAD	see number 309
SIGMA ALPHA IOTA VISUALLY IMPAIRED SCHOLARSHIP	see number 179
VERNA ROSS ORNDORFF CAREER PERFORMANCE GRANT	see number 310

WOMEN BAND DIRECTORS INTERNATIONAL

GLADYS STONE WRIGHT SCHOLARSHIP	see number 183
HELEN MAY BULTER MEMORIAL SCHOLARSHIP	see number 184
MARTHA ANN STARK MEMORIAL SCHOLARSHIP	see number 185
MUSIC TECHNOLOGY SCHOLARSHIP	see number 186
VOLKWEIN MEMORIAL SCHOLARSHIP	see number 187

PHOTOJOURNALISM/PHOTOGRAPHY_____

ASIAN AMERICAN JOURNALISTS ASSOCIATION— SEATTLE CHAPTER

NORTHWEST JOURNALISTS OF COLOR SCHOLARSHIP	see number 119

CALIFORNIA CHICANO NEWS MEDIA ASSOCIATION (CCNMA)

JOEL GARCIA MEMORIAL SCHOLARSHIP	see number 120

DALLAS-FORT WORTH ASSOCIATION OF BLACK COMMUNICATORS

FUTURE JOURNALISTS SCHOLARSHIP PROGRAM	see number 121

FISHER BROADCASTING COMPANY

FISHER BROADCASTING, INC., SCHOLARSHIP FOR MINORITIES	see number 122

NATIONAL ASSOCIATION OF HISPANIC JOURNALISTS (NAHJ)

NATIONAL ASSOCIATION OF HISPANIC JOURNALISTS SCHOLARSHIP	
	see number 124

UNITED METHODIST COMMUNICATIONS

JUDITH L. WEIDMAN RACIAL ETHNICITY MINORITY FELLOWSHIP   see number 137

LEONARD M. PERRYMAN COMMUNICATIONS SCHOLARSHIP FOR ETHNIC MINORITY STUDENTS   see number 138

PHYSICAL SCIENCES AND MATH_____

AMERICAN ASSOCIATION OF UNIVERSITY WOMEN (AAUW) EDUCATIONAL FOUNDATION

AAUW EDUCATIONAL FOUNDATION SELECTED PROFESSIONS FELLOWSHIPS
see number 36

ELEANOR ROOSEVELT TEACHER FELLOWSHIPS   see number 166

AMERICAN PHYSICAL SOCIETY

CORPORATE SPONSORED SCHOLARSHIPS FOR MINORITY UNDERGRADUATE STUDENTS WHO MAJOR IN PHYSICS   **• 317**

One-time award for high school seniors, college freshmen and sophomores planning to major in physics. Must be African-American, Hispanic, or Native-Americans. Must be a U.S. citizen or a legal resident. Deadline is February 1.

Academic Fields/Career Goals Physical Sciences and Math. *Award* Scholarship for use in freshman or sophomore years; not renewable. *Amount:* $2000–$3000.

Eligibility Requirements Applicant must be American Indian/Alaska Native, Black (non-Hispanic), or Hispanic and enrolled or expecting to enroll full-time at a two-year or four-year institution or university. Available to U.S. citizens.

Application Requirements Application, essay, references, test scores, transcript. *Deadline:* February 1.

World Wide Web: http://www.aps.org/educ/com/index.html

Contact: Arlene Knowles, Scholarship Administrator
American Physical Society
One Physics Ellipse
College Park, MD 20740
Phone: 301-209-3232
Fax: 301-209-0865
E-mail: knowles@aps.org

AMERICAN PHYSIOLOGICAL SOCIETY

AMERICAN PHYSIOLOGICAL SOCIETY MINORITY TRAVEL FELLOWSHIPS
see number 25

PORTER PHYSIOLOGY FELLOWSHIPS   see number 64

AMERICAN SOCIETY FOR ENGINEERING EDUCATION

NATIONAL DEFENSE SCIENCE AND ENGINEERING GRADUATE FELLOWSHIP PROGRAM   see number 98

AMERICAN VACUUM SOCIETY

NELLIE YEOH WHETTEN AWARD   see number 28

ARKANSAS DEPARTMENT OF HIGHER EDUCATION

MINORITY MASTER'S FELLOWS PROGRAM   see number 168

ARMED FORCES COMMUNICATIONS AND ELECTRONICS ASSOCIATION, EDUCATIONAL FOUNDATION

ARMED FORCES COMMUNICATIONS AND ELECTRONICS ASSOCIATION RALPH W. SHRADER SCHOLARSHIPS   see number 140

ASSOCIATION FOR WOMEN GEOSCIENTISTS, PUGET SOUND CHAPTER

PUGET SOUND CHAPTER SCHOLARSHIP   see number 159

ASSOCIATION FOR WOMEN IN MATHEMATICS

ALICE T. SCHAFER MATHEMATICS PRIZE FOR EXCELLENCE IN MATHEMATICS BY AN UNDERGRADUATE WOMAN   • 318

One-time merit award for women undergraduates in the math field. Based on quality of performance in math courses and special programs, ability to work independently, interest in math, and performance in competitions. Must be nominated by professor or adviser.

Academic Fields/Career Goals Physical Sciences and Math. *Award* Prize for use in freshman, sophomore, junior, or senior years; not renewable. *Number:* 1–6. *Amount:* $250–$1000.

Eligibility Requirements Applicant must be enrolled or expecting to enroll at a four-year institution and female. Available to U.S. citizens.

Application Requirements References, transcript, nomination. *Deadline:* October 1.

World Wide Web: http://www.awm-math.org/

Contact: Dawn V. Wheeler, Director of Marketing
Association for Women in Mathematics
4114 Computer and Space Sciences Building
College Park, MD 20742-2461
E-mail: awn@math.umd.edu

ASSOCIATION FOR WOMEN IN MATHEMATICS WORKSHOP FOR GRADUATE STUDENTS AND POSTDOCTORAL MATHEMATICIANS   • 319

Award for female graduate students and recent PhDs in math to attend annual workshops. Graduate students must have begun work on thesis problem and present it at workshop. Postdoctorates present talks on research. See Web site at http://www.awm-math.org for further information and deadlines.

Academic Fields/Career Goals Physical Sciences and Math. *Award* Grant for use in graduate, or postgraduate years; not renewable. *Number:* 20-40. *Amount:* $800-$1000.
Eligibility Requirements Applicant must be enrolled or expecting to enroll at an institution or university and female.
Application Requirements Application.
World Wide Web: http://www.awm-math.org/
Contact: Dawn V. Wheeler, Director of Marketing
Association for Women in Mathematics
4114 Computer and Space Sciences Building
College Park, MD 20742-2461

TRAVEL GRANTS FOR WOMEN IN MATHEMATICS • 320
One-time award for women who recently received PhD in mathematics to provide travel expenses to attend research conferences in their field. Submit description of recent research, curriculum vitae, and budget. Deadlines: February 1, May 1, and October 1.

Academic Fields/Career Goals Physical Sciences and Math. *Award* Grant for use in postgraduate years; not renewable. *Number:* 3-6. *Amount:* $1000-$2000.
Eligibility Requirements Applicant must be enrolled or expecting to enroll at an institution or university and female.
World Wide Web: http://www.awm-math.org/
Contact: Dawn V. Wheeler, Director of Marketing
Association for Women in Mathematics
4114 Computer and Space Sciences Building
College Park, MD 20742-2461

ASSOCIATION FOR WOMEN IN SCIENCE EDUCATIONAL FOUNDATION
ASSOCIATION FOR WOMEN IN SCIENCE PRE-DOCTORAL FELLOWSHIP
see number 32

ASSOCIATION FOR WOMEN IN SCIENCE UNDERGRADUATE AWARD   see number 26

BUSINESS AND PROFESSIONAL WOMEN'S FOUNDATION
BPW CAREER ADVANCEMENT SCHOLARSHIP PROGRAM FOR WOMEN
see number 68

CANADIAN FEDERATION OF UNIVERSITY WOMEN
CANADIAN FEDERATION OF UNIVERSITY WOMEN MEMORIAL FELLOWSHIP
see number 21

CENTER FOR THE ADVANCEMENT OF HISPANICS IN SCIENCE AND ENGINEERING EDUCATION (CAHSEE)
CAHSEE FELLOWSHIP: YOUNG EDUCATORS PROGRAM   see number 30

GEM CONSORTIUM

GEM PHD SCIENCE FELLOWSHIP   see number 70

IMGIP/ICEOP

ILLINOIS MINORITY GRADUATE INCENTIVE PROGRAM FELLOWSHIP

see number 142

LOS ANGELES COUNCIL OF BLACK PROFESSIONAL ENGINEERS

AL-BEN SCHOLARSHIP FOR ACADEMIC INCENTIVE   see number 100

AL-BEN SCHOLARSHIP FOR PROFESSIONAL MERIT   see number 101

AL-BEN SCHOLARSHIP FOR SCHOLASTIC ACHIEVEMENT   see number 102

NASA NEW HAMPSHIRE SPACE GRANT CONSORTIUM

GRADUATE FELLOWSHIPS   see number 161

NATIONAL ACTION COUNCIL FOR MINORITIES IN ENGINEERING-NACME, INC.

ENGINEERING VANGUARD PROGRAM   see number 103

SLOAN PHD PROGRAM   see number 104

NATIONAL PHYSICAL SCIENCE CONSORTIUM

NATIONAL PHYSICAL SCIENCE CONSORTIUM GRADUATE FELLOWSHIPS IN THE PHYSICAL SCIENCES   see number 105

NATIONAL RESEARCH COUNCIL

FORD FOUNDATION DISSERTATION FELLOWSHIPS FOR MINORITIES

see number 125

FORD FOUNDATION POSTDOCTORAL FELLOWSHIP FOR MINORITIES

see number 126

FORD FOUNDATION PRE-DOCTORAL FELLOWSHIPS FOR MINORITIES

see number 127

UNITED STATES DEPARTMENT OF HEALTH AND HUMAN SERVICES

NIH UNDERGRADUATE SCHOLARSHIP FOR INDIVIDUALS FROM DISADVANTAGED BACKGROUNDS   see number 73

VIRGINIA BUSINESS AND PROFESSIONAL WOMEN'S FOUNDATION

WOMEN IN SCIENCE AND TECHNOLOGY SCHOLARSHIP see number 74

POLITICAL SCIENCE_____

AMERICAN POLITICAL SCIENCE ASSOCIATION

AMERICAN POLITICAL SCIENCE ASSOCIATION MINORITY FELLOWS PROGRAM • 321

One-time award for minority students entering a doctoral program in political science for the first time. Applicants must demonstrate an interest in teaching and have potential for research in political science. Must be U.S. citizen and in financial need. See Web site at http://www.apsanet.org for further details. Application deadline is November 1.

Academic Fields/Career Goals Political Science. *Award* Fellowship for use in senior, or graduate years; not renewable. *Number:* 6. *Amount:* $4000.

Eligibility Requirements Applicant must be American Indian/Alaska Native, Black (non-Hispanic), or Hispanic and enrolled or expecting to enroll at an institution or university. Applicant must have 3.0 GPA or higher. Available to U.S. citizens.

Application Requirements Application, essay, financial need analysis, references, transcript. *Deadline:* November 1.

World Wide Web: http://www.apsanet.org

Contact: Linda Lopez, Director
American Political Science Association
1527 New Hampshire Avenue, NW
Washington, DC 20036-1206
E-mail: apsa@apsanet.org

ASSOCIATION FOR WOMEN IN SCIENCE EDUCATIONAL FOUNDATION

ASSOCIATION FOR WOMEN IN SCIENCE PRE-DOCTORAL FELLOWSHIP see number 32

CUBAN AMERICAN NATIONAL FOUNDATION

MAS FAMILY SCHOLARSHIPS see number 80

GOVERNMENT FINANCE OFFICERS ASSOCIATION

MINORITIES IN GOVERNMENT FINANCE SCHOLARSHIP see number 9

GOVERNOR'S OFFICE

GOVERNOR'S OPPORTUNITY SCHOLARSHIP see number 81

HISPANIC DIVISION, LIBRARY OF CONGRESS

HISPANIC DIVISION FELLOWSHIPS   see number 43

INSTITUTE FOR INTERNATIONAL PUBLIC POLICY (IIPP)

INSTITUTE FOR INTERNATIONAL PUBLIC POLICY FELLOWSHIP PROGRAM
                                                                see number 44

NATIONAL RESEARCH COUNCIL

FORD FOUNDATION DISSERTATION FELLOWSHIPS FOR MINORITIES
                                                                see number 125

FORD FOUNDATION POSTDOCTORAL FELLOWSHIP FOR MINORITIES
                                                                see number 126

FORD FOUNDATION PRE-DOCTORAL FELLOWSHIPS FOR MINORITIES
                                                                see number 127

UNITED STATES INSTITUTE OF PEACE

JENNINGS RANDOLPH SENIOR FELLOW AWARD   see number 46

WELLESLEY COLLEGE

VIDA DUTTON SCUDDER FELLOWSHIP   see number 300

REAL ESTATE

APPRAISAL INSTITUTE

APPRAISAL INSTITUTE EDUCATIONAL SCHOLARSHIP PROGRAM   • 322

Award available to racial, ethnic and gender groups underrepresented in real estate appraisal or allied field, and to those who are disabled. Minimum 2.5 GPA required. Must be U.S. citizen and demonstrate financial need.

Academic Fields/Career Goals Real Estate. *Award* Scholarship for use in sophomore, junior, senior, or graduate years; not renewable. *Number:* up to 10. *Amount:* up to $1000.

Eligibility Requirements Applicant must be enrolled or expecting to enroll full or part-time at a two-year or four-year institution or university. Applicant must have 2.5 GPA or higher. Available to U.S. citizens.

Application Requirements Application, essay, financial need analysis, references, transcript. *Deadline:* April 15.

World Wide Web: http://www.appraisalinstitute.org

Contact: Project Coordinator
Appraisal Institute
875 North Michigan Avenue, Suite 2400
Chicago, IL 60611-1980
Phone: 312-335-4121
Fax: 312-335-4200
E-mail: sbarnes@appraisalinstitute.org

INSTITUTE OF REAL ESTATE MANAGEMENT FOUNDATION

GEORGE M. BROOKER COLLEGIATE SCHOLARSHIP FOR MINORITIES • 323

One-time award for minority college juniors, seniors, and graduate students who are U.S. citizens and are committed to a career in real estate, specifically real estate management. Must have a minimum GPA of 3.0. Deadline is March 31.

Academic Fields/Career Goals Real Estate. *Award* Scholarship for use in junior, senior, or graduate years; not renewable. *Number:* 1-2. *Amount:* $1000–$2500.

Eligibility Requirements Applicant must be American Indian/Alaska Native, Asian/Pacific Islander, Black (non-Hispanic), or Hispanic and enrolled or expecting to enroll full-time at a four-year institution or university. Applicant must have 3.0 GPA or higher. Available to U.S. citizens.

Application Requirements Application, essay, interview, references, transcript. *Deadline:* March 31.

World Wide Web: http://www.irem.org

Contact: Kimberly Holmes, Foundation Administrator
Institute of Real Estate Management Foundation
430 North Michigan Avenue, 7th Floor
Chicago, IL 60611-4090
Phone: 312-329-6008
Fax: 312-410-7908
E-mail: foundatn@irem.org

RELIGION/THEOLOGY_____

DISCIPLES OF CHRIST HOMELAND MINISTRIES

EDWIN G. AND LAURETTA M. MICHAEL SCHOLARSHIP • 324

$2000 scholarship available to ministers' wives. Must be a member of the Christian Church (Disciples of Christ), demonstrate financial need, have a C+ average, be a full-time student, and be under the care of a regional Commission on the Ministry. Application may be submitted electronically. Deadline March 15.

Academic Fields/Career Goals Religion/Theology. *Award* Scholarship for use in freshman, sophomore, junior, or senior years; not renewable. *Amount:* $2000.

Eligibility Requirements Applicant must be Disciple of Christ; enrolled or expecting to enroll full-time at a two-year or four-year institution or university and married female. Applicant must have 2.5 GPA or higher. Available to U.S. and non-U.S. citizens.

Application Requirements Application, financial need analysis, references, transcript. *Deadline:* March 15.

Edwin G. and Lauretta M. Michael Scholarship (continued)

World Wide Web: http://www.homelandministries.org

Contact: Gaetana Durham, Administrative Assistant
Disciples of Christ Homeland Ministries
PO Box 1986
Indianapolis, IN 46206-1986
Phone: 888-346-2631
Fax: 317-635-4426
E-mail: gdurham@dhm.disciples.org

KATHERINE J. SHUTZE MEMORIAL SCHOLARSHIP   • 325

$2000 scholarship available to women seminary students. Must be a member of the Christian Church (Disciples of Christ), demonstrate financial need, have a C+ average, be a full-time student, and be under the care of a regional Commission on the Ministry. Application may be submitted electronically. Deadline March 15.

Academic Fields/Career Goals Religion/Theology. *Award* Scholarship for use in freshman, sophomore, junior, or senior years; not renewable. *Amount:* $2000.

Eligibility Requirements Applicant must be Disciple of Christ; enrolled or expecting to enroll full-time at an institution or university and female. Applicant must have 2.5 GPA or higher. Available to U.S. and non-U.S. citizens.

Application Requirements Application, financial need analysis, references, transcript. *Deadline:* March 15.

World Wide Web: http://www.homelandministries.org

Contact: Gaetana Durham, Administrative Assistant
Disciples of Christ Homeland Ministries
PO Box 1986
Indianapolis, IN 46206-1986
Phone: 888-346-2631
Fax: 317-635-4426
E-mail: gdurham@dhm.disciples.org

FUND FOR THEOLOGICAL EDUCATION, INC. (FTE)

NORTH AMERICAN DOCTORAL FELLOWS PROGRAM   • 326

Fellowship for racial ethnic minority students enrolled in PhD or ThD programs in religious or theological studies. Applicants must be citizens or permanent residents of the U.S. or Canada. Award includes a stipend of up to $10,000.

Academic Fields/Career Goals Religion/Theology. *Award* Fellowship for use in graduate years; not renewable. *Number:* 10–12. *Amount:* $5000–$10,000.

Eligibility Requirements Applicant must be Christian; American Indian/Alaska Native, Asian/Pacific Islander, Black (non-Hispanic), or Hispanic and enrolled or expecting to enroll full-time at an institution or university. Available to U.S. and Canadian citizens.

Application Requirements Application, essay, financial need analysis, resume, references, transcript. *Deadline:* March 1.

World Wide Web: http://www.thefund.org

Contact: Dr. Sharon Watson Fluker, Director, Expanding Horizons Partnership and
Doctoral Programs
Fund for Theological Education, Inc. (FTE)
825 Houston Mill Road, Suite 250
Atlanta, GA 30329
Phone: 404-727-1450
Fax: 404-727-1490
E-mail: sfluker@thefund.org

GENERAL COMMISSION ON ARCHIVES AND HISTORY

ASIAN, BLACK, HISPANIC, AND NATIVE AMERICAN UNITED METHODIST HISTORY RESEARCH AWARDS
see number 261

HISPANIC THEOLOGICAL INITIATIVE

HISPANIC THEOLOGICAL INITIATIVE DISSERTATION YEAR GRANT • 327
The HTI will award nine one-year dissertation fellowships per year throughout the life of the program to applicants who are ABD (All But Dissertation). Each award will be for an average of $16,000 for a period of one academic year. It is expected that the applicant completes his/her dissertation at the end of the award year. This grant is not renewable and cannot be extended beyond the designated award year.

Academic Fields/Career Goals Religion/Theology. *Award* Grant for use in graduate years; not renewable. *Number:* 9. *Amount:* $16,000.

Eligibility Requirements Applicant must be Christian; of Hispanic heritage and enrolled or expecting to enroll full-time at an institution or university. Available to U.S. citizens.

Application Requirements Application, interview, portfolio, resume, references, dissertation proposal, approval and timeline. *Deadline:* January 11.

World Wide Web: http://www.htiprogram.org

Contact: Joanne Rodriguez, Associate Director
Hispanic Theological Initiative
12 Library Place
Princeton, NJ 08540
Phone: 609-252-1721
Fax: 609-252-1738
E-mail: hti@ptsem.edu

HISPANIC THEOLOGICAL INITIATIVE DOCTORAL GRANT • 328
The HTI will award nine outstanding Latino doctoral students a $13,000 grant each year during the life of the program. This award is for full-time doctoral students (PhD, EdD, ThD or equivalent only) and requires that the student's institution partners with HTI in providing the student with a tuition scholarship.

Academic Fields/Career Goals Religion/Theology. *Award* Grant for use in graduate years; renewable. *Number:* 9. *Amount:* $13,000.

Eligibility Requirements Applicant must be Christian; of Hispanic heritage and enrolled or expecting to enroll full-time at an institution or university. Available to U.S. citizens.

Application Requirements Application, autobiography, essay, interview, resume, references, test scores, transcript, list of publications in print. *Deadline:* December 7.

World Wide Web: http://www.htiprogram.org

Hispanic Theological Initiative Doctoral Grant (continued)

Contact: Joanne Rodriguez, Associate Director
Hispanic Theological Initiative
12 Library Place
Princeton, NJ 08540
Phone: 609-252-1721
Fax: 609-252-1738
E-mail: hti@ptsem.edu

HISPANIC THEOLOGICAL INITIATIVE SPECIAL MENTORING GRANT • 329

Provides six awardees with a mentor each for one year and with $1,000 networking funds that are set aside for networking activities. It is offered when students have finished all of their PhD course work and are preparing for exams or when students have been awarded a stipend which will be withdrawn or diminished if the student receives other funds.

Academic Fields/Career Goals Religion/Theology. *Award* Grant for use in graduate years; not renewable. *Number:* 6. *Amount:* $5000.

Eligibility Requirements Applicant must be Christian; of Hispanic heritage and enrolled or expecting to enroll full-time at an institution or university. Available to U.S. citizens.

Application Requirements Application, references, transcript. *Deadline:* January 11.

World Wide Web: http://www.htiprogram.org

Contact: Joanne Rodriguez, Associate Director
Hispanic Theological Initiative
12 Library Place
Princeton, NJ 08540
Phone: 609-252-1721
Fax: 609-252-1738
E-mail: hti@ptsem.edu

NATIONAL RESEARCH COUNCIL

FORD FOUNDATION DISSERTATION FELLOWSHIPS FOR MINORITIES

see number 125

FORD FOUNDATION POSTDOCTORAL FELLOWSHIP FOR MINORITIES

see number 126

FORD FOUNDATION PRE-DOCTORAL FELLOWSHIPS FOR MINORITIES

see number 127

PHI BETA KAPPA SOCIETY

MARY ISABEL SIBLEY FELLOWSHIP FOR GREEK AND FRENCH STUDIES

see number 33

PRESBYTERIAN CHURCH (USA)

RACIAL ETHNIC SUPPLEMENTAL GRANT • 330

Award for minority member of Presbyterian Church (U.S.A.) preparing for professional church occupation. Must be recommended by financial aid officer at theological institution. Must be U.S. citizen. Inquire for eligibility. Must rank in upper half of class or have a minimum 2.5 GPA.

Academic Fields/Career Goals Religion/Theology. *Award* Grant for use in graduate years; not renewable. *Number:* up to 100. *Amount:* $500–$1500.

Eligibility Requirements Applicant must be Presbyterian; American Indian/Alaska Native, Asian/Pacific Islander, Black (non-Hispanic), or Hispanic and enrolled or expecting to enroll full-time at an institution or university. Applicant must have 2.5 GPA or higher. Available to U.S. citizens.

Application Requirements Application, financial need analysis, references, transcript. *Deadline:* September 30.

World Wide Web: http://www.pcusa.org/financialaid

Contact: Laura Bryan, Program Associate
Presbyterian Church (USA)
100 Witherspoon Street
Louisville, KY 40202-1396
Phone: 888-728-7228 Ext. 5735
Fax: 502-569-8766
E-mail: lbryan@ctr.pcusa.org

UNITED METHODIST CHURCH

GEORGIA HARKNESS SCHOLARSHIPS • 331

One-time award for female preparing for ordained ministry as an elder in the United Methodist Church. Must be 35 or older and enrolled in an accredited school of theology and working toward a basic seminary degree. Must study full-time.

Academic Fields/Career Goals Religion/Theology. *Award* Scholarship for use in graduate years; not renewable. *Amount:* $500–$1500.

Eligibility Requirements Applicant must be Methodist; age 35; enrolled or expecting to enroll full-time at an institution or university and female. Available to U.S. citizens.

Application Requirements Application, essay, references, transcript. *Deadline:* March 1.

World Wide Web: http://www.umc.org/

Contact: Sandy Walker, Coordinator for Continuing Education in Ministry
United Methodist Church
PO Box 340007
Nashville, TN 37203-0007
Phone: 615-340-7409
E-mail: swalker@gbhem.org

UNITED METHODIST CHURCH-IOWA ANNUAL CONFERENCE

UNITED METHODIST CHURCH ETHNIC MINORITY SCHOLARSHIP • 332

Scholarship for minority students enrolled in program of religious studies, who are from the Iowa Conference of the United Methodist Church. Must attend an approved seminary of the United Methodist Church. Application deadline is January 15. Must be an Iowa resident. Minimum 2.5 GPA required.

Academic Fields/Career Goals Religion/Theology. *Award* Scholarship for use in graduate years; renewable.

Eligibility Requirements Applicant must be Methodist; American Indian/Alaska Native, Asian/Pacific Islander, Black (non-Hispanic), or Hispanic; enrolled or expecting to enroll full-time at an institution or university and resident of Iowa. Applicant must have 2.5 GPA or higher. Available to U.S. citizens.

United Methodist Church Ethnic Minority Scholarship (continued)

Application Requirements Application, financial need analysis, references. *Deadline:* January 15.

Contact: Melvin Ammon, Grants Coordinator
United Methodist Church-Iowa Annual Conference
838 North 25th Street
Fort Dodge, IA 50501
Phone: 515-573-3514
Fax: 515-955-7426
E-mail: trinityumc.pastor@frontiernet.net

UNITED METHODIST COMMUNICATIONS

JUDITH L. WEIDMAN RACIAL ETHNICITY MINORITY FELLOWSHIP   see number 137

LEONARD M. PERRYMAN COMMUNICATIONS SCHOLARSHIP FOR ETHNIC MINORITY STUDENTS   see number 138

WOMEN OF THE EVANGELICAL LUTHERAN CHURCH IN AMERICA

CHRISTIAN SERVICES GRADUATE STUDY SCHOLARSHIPS FOR WOMEN • 333

Named scholarships provided for ELCA women in graduate courses of study preparing for occupations in Christian services. Must be at least 21 years old and hold membership in the ELCA. Must have experienced an interruption in education of two or more years since the completion of high school. For more details see Web site: http://www.elca.org/wo.

Academic Fields/Career Goals Religion/Theology. *Award* Scholarship for use in graduate years; not renewable. *Number:* 2. *Amount:* up to $1200.

Eligibility Requirements Applicant must be Lutheran; age 21; enrolled or expecting to enroll at a four-year institution or university and female. Available to U.S. citizens.

Application Requirements *Deadline:* February 15.

World Wide Web: http://www.elca.org/wo

Contact: application available at Web site

HERBERT W. AND CORINNE CHILSTROM SCHOLARSHIP • 334

Scholarship provides assistance to Lutheran women who are second career students during their final year of an ELCA seminary. Must be preparing for an ordained ministry in the ELCA. For more details see Web site: http://www.elca.org/wo.

Academic Fields/Career Goals Religion/Theology. *Award* Scholarship for use in graduate years; not renewable. *Amount:* up to $2000.

Eligibility Requirements Applicant must be Lutheran; enrolled or expecting to enroll at an institution or university and female. Available to U.S. citizens.

Application Requirements *Deadline:* February 15.

World Wide Web: http://www.elca.org/wo

Contact: application available at Web site

SCIENCE, TECHNOLOGY, AND SOCIETY_____

AMERICAN AGRICULTURAL ECONOMICS ASSOCIATION FOUNDATION

SYLVIA LANE MENTOR RESEARCH FELLOWSHIP FUND   see number 18

AMERICAN ASSOCIATION OF UNIVERSITY WOMEN (AAUW) EDUCATIONAL FOUNDATION

ELEANOR ROOSEVELT TEACHER FELLOWSHIPS   see number 166

ARKANSAS DEPARTMENT OF HIGHER EDUCATION

MINORITY MASTER'S FELLOWS PROGRAM   see number 168

GOVERNOR'S OFFICE

GOVERNOR'S OPPORTUNITY SCHOLARSHIP   see number 81

IMGIP/ICEOP

ILLINOIS MINORITY GRADUATE INCENTIVE PROGRAM FELLOWSHIP
see number 142

NATIONAL ACTION COUNCIL FOR MINORITIES IN ENGINEERING-NACME, INC.

ENGINEERING VANGUARD PROGRAM   see number 103

SLOAN PHD PROGRAM   see number 104

SOCIETY OF HISPANIC PROFESSIONAL ENGINEERS FOUNDATION

SOCIETY OF HISPANIC PROFESSIONAL ENGINEERS FOUNDATION   see number 109

SOCIETY OF MEXICAN AMERICAN ENGINEERS AND SCIENTISTS

GRE AND GRADUATE APPLICATIONS WAIVER   see number 110

UNITED STATES INSTITUTE OF PEACE

JENNINGS RANDOLPH SENIOR FELLOW AWARD   see number 46

VIRGINIA BUSINESS AND PROFESSIONAL WOMEN'S FOUNDATION

WOMEN IN SCIENCE AND TECHNOLOGY SCHOLARSHIP   see number 74

SOCIAL SCIENCES_____

AMERICAN AGRICULTURAL ECONOMICS ASSOCIATION FOUNDATION

SYLVIA LANE MENTOR RESEARCH FELLOWSHIP FUND   see number 18

AMERICAN PSYCHOLOGICAL ASSOCIATION

MINORITY FELLOWSHIP FOR HIV/AIDS RESEARCH TRAINING   see number 235

MINORITY FELLOWSHIP IN MENTAL HEALTH AND SUBSTANCE ABUSE
SERVICES   see number 236

AMERICAN SOCIOLOGICAL ASSOCIATION

MINORITY FELLOWSHIP PROGRAM   see number 239

ASPEN INSTITUTE

WILLIAM RANDOLPH HEARST ENDOWED SCHOLARSHIP FOR MINORITY
STUDENTS   see number 269

ASSOCIATION FOR WOMEN IN SCIENCE EDUCATIONAL FOUNDATION

ASSOCIATION FOR WOMEN IN SCIENCE PRE-DOCTORAL FELLOWSHIP
          see number 32

BUSINESS AND PROFESSIONAL WOMEN'S FOUNDATION

BPW CAREER ADVANCEMENT SCHOLARSHIP PROGRAM FOR WOMEN
          see number 68

CANADIAN FEDERATION OF UNIVERSITY WOMEN

MARGARET DALE PHILP BIENNIAL AWARD   see number 260

COUNCIL ON SOCIAL WORK EDUCATION

COUNCIL ON SOCIAL WORK EDUCATION/MENTAL HEALTH MINORITY RESEARCH FELLOWSHIP   see number 240

DOCTORAL FELLOWSHIPS IN SOCIAL WORK FOR ETHNIC MINORITY STUDENTS PREPARING FOR LEADERSHIP ROLES IN MENTAL HEALTH AND/OR SUBSTANCE ABUSE   see number 241

INSTITUTE FOR INTERNATIONAL PUBLIC POLICY (IIPP)

INSTITUTE FOR INTERNATIONAL PUBLIC POLICY FELLOWSHIP PROGRAM
see number 44

MARIN EDUCATION FUND

GOLDMAN FAMILY FUND, NEW LEADER SCHOLARSHIP   see number 156

NATIONAL INSTITUTES OF HEALTH

NIH UNDERGRADUATE SCHOLARSHIP PROGRAM FOR STUDENTS FROM DISADVANTAGED BACKGROUNDS   see number 71

NATIONAL RESEARCH COUNCIL

FORD FOUNDATION DISSERTATION FELLOWSHIPS FOR MINORITIES
see number 125

FORD FOUNDATION POSTDOCTORAL FELLOWSHIP FOR MINORITIES
see number 126

FORD FOUNDATION PRE-DOCTORAL FELLOWSHIPS FOR MINORITIES
see number 127

PHI BETA KAPPA SOCIETY

MARY ISABEL SIBLEY FELLOWSHIP FOR GREEK AND FRENCH STUDIES
see number 33

RADCLIFFE INSTITUTE FOR ADVANCED STUDY-MURRAY RESEARCH CENTER

BLOCK DISSERTATION AWARD   • 335

Grants to support women graduate students studying the psychological development of girls or women. Proposals should focus on sex and gender differences or some developmental issue of particular concern to American females. Priority given to projects that draw on data resources of Murray Research Center. See http://www.radcliffe.edu for details.

Block Dissertation Award (continued)

Academic Fields/Career Goals Social Sciences. *Award* Grant for use in graduate years; not renewable. *Number:* 1. *Amount:* up to $5000.

Eligibility Requirements Applicant must be enrolled or expecting to enroll full or part-time at an institution or university and female. Available to U.S. and non-U.S. citizens.

Application Requirements Application, references, 5 copies of: proposal, timetable, budget, curriculum vitae, cover page, application to use center's data. *Deadline:* April 1.

World Wide Web: http://www.radcliffe.edu/murray

Contact: Grants Administrator
Radcliffe Institute for Advanced Study-Murray Research Center
10 Garden Street
Cambridge, MA 02138
Phone: 617-495-8140
E-mail: mrc@radcliffe.edu

SOCIAL SCIENCE RESEARCH COUNCIL

SEXUALITY RESEARCH FELLOWSHIP PROGRAM • 336

Fellowship provides dissertation and postdoctoral support for social and behavioral research on sexuality, conducted in the U.S. Must be joint application from applicant and research advisor or associate who will function in a mentoring capacity. Women and members of minority groups are especially encouraged to apply. Application deadline is December 16. For further information email: srfp@ssrc.org

Academic Fields/Career Goals Social Sciences. *Award* Fellowship for use in graduate, or postgraduate years; not renewable. *Number:* 15–17. *Amount:* $28,000–$38,000.

Eligibility Requirements Applicant must be enrolled or expecting to enroll full-time at an institution or university. Available to U.S. and non-U.S. citizens.

Application Requirements Application, essay, references, transcript. *Deadline:* December 16.

World Wide Web: http://www.ssrc.org

Contact: Diane di Mauro, Program Director
Social Science Research Council
810 Seventh Avenue, 31st floor
New York, NY 10019
Phone: 212-377-2700 Ext. 519
Fax: 212-377-2727
E-mail: srfp@ssrc.org

UNITED STATES INSTITUTE OF PEACE

JENNINGS RANDOLPH SENIOR FELLOW AWARD see number 46

WELLESLEY COLLEGE

VIDA DUTTON SCUDDER FELLOWSHIP see number 300

SOCIAL SERVICES_____

AMERICAN SPEECH-LANGUAGE-HEARING FOUNDATION

ASHF GRADUATE STUDENT SCHOLARSHIP FOR MINORITY STUDENTS
see number 117

KALA SINGH GRADUATE SCHOLARSHIP FOR INTERNATIONAL/MINORITY STUDENTS
see number 118

COUNCIL ON SOCIAL WORK EDUCATION

COUNCIL ON SOCIAL WORK EDUCATION/MENTAL HEALTH MINORITY RESEARCH FELLOWSHIP
see number 240

DOCTORAL FELLOWSHIPS IN SOCIAL WORK FOR ETHNIC MINORITY STUDENTS PREPARING FOR LEADERSHIP ROLES IN MENTAL HEALTH AND/OR SUBSTANCE ABUSE
see number 241

MARIN EDUCATION FUND

GOLDMAN FAMILY FUND, NEW LEADER SCHOLARSHIP
see number 156

WELLESLEY COLLEGE

MARGARET FREEMAN BOWERS FELLOWSHIP
see number 287

SPECIAL EDUCATION_____

CONNECTICUT DEPARTMENT OF HIGHER EDUCATION

CONNECTICUT SPECIAL EDUCATION TEACHER INCENTIVE GRANT • 337

Renewable award for upper-level undergraduates or graduate students in special education programs. Must be in a program at a Connecticut college or university, or be a Connecticut resident enrolled in an approved out-of-state program. Priority is placed on minority and bilingual candidates. Application deadline is October 1. Must be nominated by the education dean of institution attended.

Academic Fields/Career Goals Special Education. *Award* Grant for use in junior, senior, or graduate years; renewable. *Amount:* $2000–$5000.
Eligibility Requirements Applicant must be enrolled or expecting to enroll full or part-time at a four-year institution or university.
Application Requirements Application. *Deadline:* October 1.
World Wide Web: http://www.ctdhe.org

Connecticut Special Education Teacher Incentive Grant (continued)

Contact: John Siegrist, Financial Aid Office
Connecticut Department of Higher Education
61 Woodland Street
Hartford, CT 06105-2326
Phone: 860-947-1855
Fax: 860-947-1311

COUNCIL FOR EXCEPTIONAL CHILDREN

STUDENT COUNCIL FOR EXCEPTIONAL CHILDREN ETHNIC DIVERSITY AWARD • 338

Scholarship awarded to a CEC student member who is from an ethnic background and pursuing a degree in special education. Must have a 2.5 GPA.

Academic Fields/Career Goals Special Education. *Award* Scholarship for use in junior, senior, or graduate years; not renewable. *Number:* 1. *Amount:* $500.

Eligibility Requirements Applicant must be American Indian/Alaska Native, Asian/Pacific Islander, Black (non-Hispanic), or Hispanic and enrolled or expecting to enroll at a four-year institution or university. Applicant must have 2.5 GPA or higher. Available to U.S. and Canadian citizens.

Application Requirements Application, autobiography, essay, references, transcript. *Deadline:* November 5.

World Wide Web: http://www.cec.sped.org

Contact: Council for Exceptional Children
1110 North Glebe Road
Suite 300
Arlington, VA 22201

ILLINOIS STUDENT ASSISTANCE COMMISSION (ISAC)

MINORITY TEACHERS OF ILLINOIS SCHOLARSHIP PROGRAM   see number 173

OREGON STUDENT ASSISTANCE COMMISSION

JAMES CARLSON SCHOLARSHIP PROGRAM   see number 175

STATE STUDENT ASSISTANCE COMMISSION OF INDIANA (SSACI)

INDIANA MINORITY TEACHER AND SPECIAL EDUCATION SERVICES SCHOLARSHIP PROGRAM   see number 180

TENNESSEE STUDENT ASSISTANCE CORPORATION

MINORITY TEACHING FELLOWS PROGRAM/TENNESSEE   see number 182

SPORTS-RELATED_____

CALIFORNIA ADOLESCENT NUTRITION AND FITNESS (CANFIT) PROGRAM

CALIFORNIA ADOLESCENT NUTRITION AND FITNESS (CANFIT) PROGRAM SCHOLARSHIP
see number 223

NATIONAL COLLEGIATE ATHLETIC ASSOCIATION

ETHNIC MINORITY AND WOMEN'S ENHANCEMENT SCHOLARSHIP • 339
One-time awards to ethnic minorities and to women are available annually to college graduates who will be entering into the first year of their initial postgraduate studies. The applicant must be seeking admission or have been accepted into a sports administration or related program that will assist in obtaining a career in intercollegiate athletics (athletics administrator, coach, athletic trainer or other career that provides a direct service to intercollegiate athletics).

Academic Fields/Career Goals Sports-related. *Award* Scholarship for use in graduate years; not renewable. *Number:* 32. *Amount:* $6000.

Eligibility Requirements Applicant must be enrolled or expecting to enroll full-time at a four-year institution or university and must have an interest in athletics/sports. Available to U.S. citizens.

Application Requirements Application, essay, resume, references, transcript. *Deadline:* December 20.

World Wide Web: http://www.ncaa.org

Contact: Arthur Hightower, Assistant Director of Professional Development
National Collegiate Athletic Association
700 West Washington Avenue
PO Box 6222
Indianapolis, IN 46206-6222
Phone: 317-917-6222
Fax: 317-917-6336
E-mail: ahightower@ncaa.org

WOMEN'S SPORTS FOUNDATION

DOROTHY HARRIS SCHOLARSHIP • 340
One-time award to provide support to female graduate students in physical education, sport management, sport psychology, or sport sociology. Must be a U.S. citizen.

Academic Fields/Career Goals Sports-related. *Award* Scholarship for use in graduate years; not renewable. *Number:* 1–3. *Amount:* $1500.

Eligibility Requirements Applicant must be enrolled or expecting to enroll full-time at a four-year institution or university and female. Available to U.S. citizens.

Application Requirements Application, references, transcript. *Deadline:* December 31.

World Wide Web: http://www.womenssportsfoundation.org

Contact: Women's Sports Foundation
Eisenhower Park
East Meadow, NY 11554
Phone: 800-227-3988
E-mail: wosport@aol.com

Getting Money for College: Scholarships for Hispanic Students   www.petersons.com   **237**

LINDA RIDDLE/SGMA SCHOLARSHIP • 341

One-time award for female high school seniors entering a two- or four-year college. Provides female athletes of limited financial means the opportunity to pursue their sport in addition to their college studies. Minimum GPA 3.5. Must be a U.S. citizen.

Academic Fields/Career Goals Sports-related. *Award* Scholarship for use in freshman year; not renewable. *Number:* 1–10. *Amount:* $1500.

Eligibility Requirements Applicant must be high school student; planning to enroll or expecting to enroll full-time at a two-year or four-year institution or university; female and must have an interest in athletics/sports. Applicant must have 3.5 GPA or higher. Available to U.S. citizens.

Application Requirements Application, essay, financial need analysis, references, transcript. *Deadline:* December 1.

World Wide Web: http://www.womenssportsfoundation.org

Contact: Women's Sports Foundation
Eisenhower Park
East Meadow, NY 11554
Phone: 800-227-3988
E-mail: wosport@aol.com

SURVEYING; SURVEYING TECHNOLOGY, CARTOGRAPHY, OR GEOGRAPHIC INFORMATION SCIENCE

AMERICAN CONGRESS ON SURVEYING AND MAPPING

CADY MCDONNELL MEMORIAL SCHOLARSHIP • 342

Award of $1000 for female surveying student. Must be a resident of one of the following western states: Alaska, Arizona, California, Colorado, Hawaii, Idaho, Montana, Nevada, New Mexico, Oregon, Utah, Washington, and Wyoming. Must provide proof of legal home residence and be a member of the American Congress on Surveying and Mapping.

Academic Fields/Career Goals Surveying; Surveying Technology, Cartography, or Geographic Information Science. *Award* Scholarship for use in freshman, sophomore, junior, or senior years; not renewable. *Number:* 1. *Amount:* $1000.

Eligibility Requirements Applicant must be enrolled or expecting to enroll full or part-time at a two-year or four-year institution or university; female and resident of Alaska, Arizona, California, Colorado, Hawaii, Idaho, Montana, Nevada, New Mexico, Oregon, Utah, Washington, or Wyoming. Applicant or parent of applicant must be member of American Congress on Surveying and Mapping.

Application Requirements Application, essay, references, transcript. *Deadline:* December 1.

World Wide Web: http://www.acsm.net

Contact: Scholarship Information
American Congress on Surveying and Mapping
6 Montgomery Village Avenue
Suite 403
Gaithersburg, MD 20879

NATIONAL SOCIETY OF PROFESSIONAL SURVEYORS FOR EQUAL OPPORTUNITY/MARY FEINDT SCHOLARSHIP • 343

Award available to female members of ACSM. Applicants must be enrolled in a four-year degree program in a surveying and mapping curriculum in the U.S.

Academic Fields/Career Goals Surveying; Surveying Technology, Cartography, or Geographic Information Science. *Award* Scholarship for use in freshman, sophomore, junior, or senior years; not renewable. *Amount:* $1000.

Eligibility Requirements Applicant must be enrolled or expecting to enroll at a four-year institution or university and female. Applicant or parent of applicant must be member of American Congress on Surveying and Mapping.

Application Requirements Application, essay, references, transcript. *Deadline:* December 1.

World Wide Web: http://www.acsm.net

Contact: Scholarship Information
American Congress on Surveying and Mapping
6 Montgomery Village Avenue
Suite 403
Gaithersburg, MD 20879

COMTO-BOSTON CHAPTER

COMTO BOSTON/GARRETT A. MORGAN SCHOLARSHIP   see number 40

NASA NEW HAMPSHIRE SPACE GRANT CONSORTIUM

GRADUATE FELLOWSHIPS   see number 161

THERAPY/REHABILITATION_____

AMERICAN RESPIRATORY CARE FOUNDATION

JIMMY A. YOUNG MEMORIAL EDUCATION RECOGNITION AWARD   see number 237

AMERICAN SPEECH-LANGUAGE-HEARING FOUNDATION

ASHF GRADUATE STUDENT SCHOLARSHIP FOR MINORITY STUDENTS
see number 117

KALA SINGH GRADUATE SCHOLARSHIP FOR INTERNATIONAL/MINORITY STUDENTS   see number 118

BECA FOUNDATION, INC.

ALICE NEWELL JOSLYN MEDICAL FUND   see number 154

MARIN EDUCATION FUND

GOLDMAN FAMILY FUND, NEW LEADER SCHOLARSHIP see number 156

SIGMA ALPHA IOTA PHILANTHROPIES, INC.

MUSIC THERAPY SCHOLARSHIPS (SAI) see number 305

SIGMA ALPHA IOTA DOCTORAL GRANT see number 177

STATE STUDENT ASSISTANCE COMMISSION OF INDIANA (SSACI)

INDIANA MINORITY TEACHER AND SPECIAL EDUCATION SERVICES SCHOLARSHIP PROGRAM see number 180

TRADE/TECHNICAL SPECIALTIES

SOCIETY OF WOMEN ENGINEERS

GENERAL MOTORS FOUNDATION GRADUATE SCHOLARSHIP see number 113

WOMEN'S JEWELRY ASSOCIATION

WOMEN'S JEWELRY ASSOCIATION SCHOLARSHIP PROGRAM • **344**

Program is designed to encourage talented female students and help support their studies in the jewelry field.

Academic Fields/Career Goals Trade/Technical Specialties. *Award* Scholarship for use in freshman, sophomore, junior, senior, graduate, or postgraduate years; not renewable. *Number:* 5–15. *Amount:* $500–$5000.

Eligibility Requirements Applicant must be enrolled or expecting to enroll full or part-time at a two-year or four-year or technical institution or university; female and must have an interest in designated field specified by sponsor. Available to U.S. citizens.

Application Requirements Application, essay, portfolio, references, transcript. *Deadline:* June 1.

World Wide Web: http://www.womensjewelry.org

Contact: Gillian Schultz, Scholarship Committee
Women's Jewelry Association
333 Route 46 West, B-201
Fairfield, NJ 07004
Phone: 973-575-7190
Fax: 973-575-1445
E-mail: info@womensjewelry.org

TRANSPORTATION

COMTO-BOSTON CHAPTER

COMTO BOSTON/GARRETT A. MORGAN SCHOLARSHIP see number 40

TRANSPORTATION CLUBS INTERNATIONAL

TRANSPORTATION CLUBS INTERNATIONAL GINGER AND FRED DEINES MEXICO SCHOLARSHIP
see number 60

TV/RADIO BROADCASTING_____

ASIAN AMERICAN JOURNALISTS ASSOCIATION— SEATTLE CHAPTER

NORTHWEST JOURNALISTS OF COLOR SCHOLARSHIP
see number 119

BOWEN FOUNDATION

EMMA L. BOWEN FOUNDATION FOR MINORITY INTERESTS IN MEDIA • 345

The Foundation's program is unlike other intern programs in that students work for a partner company during summers and school breaks from the end of their junior year in high school until they graduate from college. During that five-year period, students learn many aspects of corporate operations and develop company-specific skills. Corporations guide and develop minority students with the option of permanent placement upon completion of their college degree. Students in the program receive an hourly wage, as well as matching compensation to help pay for college tuition and expenses. Mentoring from selected staff in the sponsoring company is also a key element of the program.

Academic Fields/Career Goals TV/Radio Broadcasting. *Award* Scholarship for use in freshman, sophomore, junior, or senior years; renewable.

Eligibility Requirements Applicant must be American Indian/Alaska Native, Asian/Pacific Islander, Black (non-Hispanic), or Hispanic; age 16-20 and enrolled or expecting to enroll full-time at a four-year institution or university. Applicant must have 3.0 GPA or higher. Available to U.S. citizens.

Application Requirements Application, essay, interview, photo, resume, references, test scores, transcript. *Deadline:* December 31.

World Wide Web: http://www.emmabowenfoundation.com

Contact: Sandra Rice, Vice President, Eastern Division
Bowen Foundation
825 Seventh Avenue, 2nd Floor
New York, NY 10019
Phone: 212-456-1720
Fax: 212-456-1997
E-mail: sandra.d.rice@abc.com

CALIFORNIA CHICANO NEWS MEDIA ASSOCIATION (CCNMA)

JOEL GARCIA MEMORIAL SCHOLARSHIP
see number 120

DALLAS-FORT WORTH ASSOCIATION OF BLACK COMMUNICATORS

FUTURE JOURNALISTS SCHOLARSHIP PROGRAM
see number 121

FISHER BROADCASTING COMPANY

FISHER BROADCASTING, INC., SCHOLARSHIP FOR MINORITIES   see number 122

KATU THOMAS R. DARGAN MINORITY SCHOLARSHIP

THOMAS R. DARGAN MINORITY SCHOLARSHIP   see number 123

NATIONAL ASSOCIATION OF HISPANIC JOURNALISTS (NAHJ)

CRISTINA SARALEGUI SCHOLARSHIP PROGRAM   see number 272

MARIA ELENA SALINAS SCHOLARSHIP   see number 273

NATIONAL ASSOCIATION OF HISPANIC JOURNALISTS SCHOLARSHIP
see number 124

RADIO-TELEVISION NEWS DIRECTORS ASSOCIATION AND FOUNDATION

CAROLE SIMPSON SCHOLARSHIP   see number 129

ED BRADLEY SCHOLARSHIP   see number 130

KEN KASHIWAHARA SCHOLARSHIP   see number 131

MICHELE CLARK FELLOWSHIP   see number 132

MIKE REYNOLDS $1,000 SCHOLARSHIP   see number 133

N.S. BIENSTOCK FELLOWSHIP   see number 134

UNITED METHODIST COMMUNICATIONS

JUDITH L. WEIDMAN RACIAL ETHNICITY MINORITY FELLOWSHIP   see number 137

LEONARD M. PERRYMAN COMMUNICATIONS SCHOLARSHIP FOR ETHNIC MINORITY STUDENTS   see number 138

CIVIC, PROFESSIONAL, SOCIAL, OR UNION AFFILIATION

AMERICAN LEGION AUXILIARY, DEPARTMENT OF COLORADO

AMERICAN LEGION AUXILIARY DEPARTMENT OF COLORADO DEPARTMENT PRESIDENT'S SCHOLARSHIP FOR JUNIOR MEMBERS • 346

One-time award for members of the American Legion Junior Auxiliary who are residents of Colorado. Contact for more information. *Award* Scholarship for use in freshman year; not renewable. *Number:* 1. *Amount:* $500.

Eligibility Requirements Applicant must be high school student; planning to enroll or expecting to enroll full-time at a two-year or four-year institution or university; female and resident of Colorado. Applicant or parent of applicant must be member of American Legion or Auxiliary. Available to U.S. citizens. Applicant must have general military experience.

Application Requirements Application, essay, references, test scores, transcript.

Contact: Department Secretary/Treasurer
American Legion Auxiliary, Department of Colorado
7465 East First Avenue, Suite D
Denver, CO 80230
Phone: 303-367-5388

AMERICAN LEGION AUXILIARY, DEPARTMENT OF FLORIDA

AMERICAN LEGION AUXILIARY DEPARTMENT OF FLORIDA MEMORIAL SCHOLARSHIP • 347

Scholarship for a member, daughter or granddaughter of a member of Florida American Legion Auxiliary with minimum three years membership. Award for Florida resident for undergraduate study in Florida school. Minimum GPA 2.5. *Award* Scholarship for use in freshman, sophomore, junior, or senior years; renewable. *Amount:* $500–$1000.

Eligibility Requirements Applicant must be enrolled or expecting to enroll full-time at a two-year or four-year or technical institution or university; female; resident of Florida and studying in Florida. Applicant or parent of applicant must be member of American Legion or Auxiliary. Applicant must have 2.5 GPA or higher. Available to U.S. citizens.

Application Requirements Application, financial need analysis, references, transcript. *Deadline:* January 1.

American Legion Auxiliary Department of Florida Memorial Scholarship (continued)

Contact: Ms. Marie Mahoney, Department Secretary and Treasurer
American Legion Auxiliary, Department of Florida
PO Box 547917
Orlando, FL 32854-7917
Phone: 407-293-7411
Fax: 407-299-6522
E-mail: alaflorida@aol.com

AMERICAN LEGION AUXILIARY, DEPARTMENT OF KENTUCKY

MARY BARRETT MARSHALL SCHOLARSHIP • 348

Must be high school or GED graduate. Must attend school in Kentucky and visit Auxiliary Unit to request scholarship. Must be five-year resident of Kentucky. Must be female relative of veteran eligible for American Legion membership. *Award* Scholarship for use in freshman, sophomore, junior, or senior years; renewable. *Number:* 1. *Amount:* $500.

Eligibility Requirements Applicant must be enrolled or expecting to enroll full or part-time at a two-year or four-year or technical institution or university; female; resident of Kentucky and studying in Kentucky. Applicant or parent of applicant must be member of American Legion or Auxiliary. Available to U.S. citizens. Applicant or parent must meet one or more of the following requirements: general military experience; retired from active duty; disabled or killed as a result of military service; prisoner of war; or missing in action.

Application Requirements Application, financial need analysis, interview, references, test scores, transcript. *Deadline:* April 1.

Contact: Velma Greenleaf, Scholarship Chairman
American Legion Auxiliary, Department of Kentucky
1448 Leafdale Road
Hodgenville, KY 42748
Phone: 270-358-3341

AMERICAN LEGION AUXILIARY, DEPARTMENT OF MISSOURI

LELA MURPHY SCHOLARSHIP • 349

$500 scholarship for high school graduate. $250 will be awarded each semester. Applicant must be Missouri resident and the granddaughter or great-granddaughter of a living or deceased Auxiliary member. Sponsoring Unit and Department must validate application. *Award* Scholarship for use in freshman year; renewable. *Number:* 1. *Amount:* $500.

Eligibility Requirements Applicant must be high school student; planning to enroll or expecting to enroll at a two-year or four-year or technical institution or university; female and resident of Missouri. Applicant or parent of applicant must be member of American Legion or Auxiliary. Available to U.S. citizens. Applicant or parent must meet one or more of the following requirements: general military experience; retired from active duty; disabled or killed as a result of military service; prisoner of war; or missing in action.

Application Requirements Application. *Deadline:* March 15.

Contact: Kim Merchant, Department Secretary/Treasurer
American Legion Auxiliary, Department of Missouri
600 Ellis Boulevard
Jefferson City, MO 65101-1615
Phone: 573-636-9133
Fax: 573-635-3467
E-mail: dptmoala@socket.net

AMERICAN LEGION AUXILIARY, DEPARTMENT OF NEBRASKA

AMERICAN LEGION AUXILIARY DEPARTMENT OF NEBRASKA PRESIDENT'S SCHOLARSHIP FOR JUNIOR MEMBERS • 350

One-time prize for female resident of Nebraska who has been entered into the National President's Scholarship for Junior Members and does not win at the national level. Must be in grades 9-12. Must rank in upper third of class or have a minimum 3.0 GPA. *Award* Prize for use in freshman year; not renewable. *Number:* 3. *Amount:* up to $200.

Eligibility Requirements Applicant must be high school student; planning to enroll or expecting to enroll full-time at a two-year or four-year or technical institution or university; female and resident of Nebraska. Applicant or parent of applicant must be member of American Legion or Auxiliary. Applicant must have 3.0 GPA or higher.

Application Requirements Application, applicant must enter a contest, financial need analysis, references, transcript. *Deadline:* April 1.

Contact: Terry Walker, Department Secretary
American Legion Auxiliary, Department of Nebraska
PO Box 5227
Lincoln, NE 68505
Phone: 402-466-1808
Fax: 402-466-0182
E-mail: neaux@alltel.net

AMERICAN LEGION AUXILIARY, DEPARTMENT OF OREGON

AMERICAN LEGION AUXILIARY DEPARTMENT OF OREGON SPIRIT OF YOUTH SCHOLARSHIP • 351

One-time award available to Oregon high school seniors. Must be a female current junior member of the American Legion Auxiliary with a three-year membership history. Apply through local units. $1000 if won on National level. *Award* Scholarship for use in freshman year; not renewable. *Number:* 1. *Amount:* $300–$1000.

Eligibility Requirements Applicant must be high school student; planning to enroll or expecting to enroll at an institution or university; female and resident of Oregon. Applicant or parent of applicant must be member of American Legion or Auxiliary. Available to U.S. citizens. Applicant or parent must meet one or more of the following requirements: general military experience; retired from active duty; disabled or killed as a result of military service; prisoner of war; or missing in action.

Application Requirements Application, essay, financial need analysis, interview, references, transcript. *Deadline:* March 1.

Contact: Pat Calhoun-Floren, Secretary
American Legion Auxiliary, Department of Oregon
PO Box 1730
Wilsonville, OR 97070
Phone: 503-682-3162
Fax: 503-685-5008

AMERICAN LEGION AUXILIARY, DEPARTMENT OF SOUTH DAKOTA

AMERICAN LEGION AUXILIARY DEPARTMENT OF SOUTH DAKOTA THELMA FOSTER SCHOLARSHIP FOR SENIOR AUXILIARY MEMBERS • 352

One award for a current senior member of the South Dakota American Legion Auxiliary who has been a member for three years. Applicant may be a high school senior or older and must be female. One-time award of $300 must be used within twelve months. *Award* Scholarship for use in freshman year; not renewable. *Number:* 1. *Amount:* $300.

Eligibility Requirements Applicant must be enrolled or expecting to enroll at an institution or university; female and resident of South Dakota. Applicant or parent of applicant must be member of American Legion or Auxiliary. Applicant or parent must meet one or more of the following requirements: general military experience; retired from active duty; disabled or killed as a result of military service; prisoner of war; or missing in action.

Application Requirements Application, essay, financial need analysis, references. *Deadline:* March 1.

Contact: Patricia Coyle, Executive Secretary
American Legion Auxiliary, Department of South Dakota
PO Box 117
Huron, SD 57350
Phone: 605-353-1793
Fax: 605-352-0336

AMERICAN LEGION AUXILIARY DEPARTMENT OF SOUTH DAKOTA THELMA FOSTER SCHOLARSHIPS FOR JUNIOR AUXILIARY MEMBERS • 353

One award for junior member of the South Dakota American Legion Auxiliary who has held membership for the past three years and holds a membership card for the current year. Must be a senior in high school. One-time award of $300. *Award* Scholarship for use in freshman year; not renewable. *Number:* 1. *Amount:* $300.

Eligibility Requirements Applicant must be high school student; planning to enroll or expecting to enroll at an institution or university; female and resident of South Dakota. Applicant or parent of applicant must be member of American Legion or Auxiliary. Applicant or parent must meet one or more of the following requirements: general military experience; retired from active duty; disabled or killed as a result of military service; prisoner of war; or missing in action.

Application Requirements Application, essay, financial need analysis, references, transcript. *Deadline:* March 1.

Contact: Patricia Coyle, Executive Secretary
American Legion Auxiliary, Department of South Dakota
PO Box 117
Huron, SD 57350
Phone: 605-353-1793
Fax: 605-352-0336

AMERICAN LEGION AUXILIARY, DEPARTMENT OF SOUTH DAKOTA SENIOR SCHOLARSHIP • 354

Award for current senior member of South Dakota American Legion Auxiliary who has been a member for three years. $400 award, based on financial need. *Award* Scholarship for use in freshman year; not renewable. *Number:* 1. *Amount:* $400.

Eligibility Requirements Applicant must be enrolled or expecting to enroll at a two-year or four-year or technical institution; female and resident of South Dakota. Applicant or parent of applicant must be member of American Legion or Auxiliary. Applicant or parent must meet one or more of the following requirements: general military experience; retired from active duty; disabled or killed as a result of military service; prisoner of war; or missing in action.

Application Requirements Application, essay, financial need analysis, references, transcript. *Deadline:* March 1.

Contact: Patricia Coyle, Executive Secretary
American Legion Auxiliary, Department of South Dakota
PO Box 117
Huron, SD 57350
Phone: 605-353-1793
Fax: 605-352-0336

AMERICAN LEGION AUXILIARY, NATIONAL HEADQUARTERS

AMERICAN LEGION AUXILIARY GIRL SCOUT ACHIEVEMENT AWARD • 355

One scholarship available to recipients of Girl Scout Gold Award. Must be active in religious institution and have received appropriate religious emblem, Cadet or Senior Scout level. Must show practical citizenship in religious institution, community, and school. One-time award of $1000. *Award* Scholarship for use in freshman year; not renewable. *Number:* 1. *Amount:* $1000.

Eligibility Requirements Applicant must be high school student; planning to enroll or expecting to enroll full-time at a two-year or four-year institution or university and female. Applicant or parent of applicant must be member of Girl Scouts. Applicant or parent of applicant must have employment or volunteer experience in community service. Available to U.S. and non-U.S. citizens.

Application Requirements Application, applicant must enter a contest, essay, references, self-addressed stamped envelope, test scores, transcript. *Deadline:* February 13.

World Wide Web: http://www.legion-aux.org

Contact: Department Secretary
American Legion Auxiliary, National Headquarters
777 North Meridian Street, 3rd Floor
Indianapolis, IN 46204-1189
Phone: 317-955-3845
Fax: 317-955-3884
E-mail: youthprog@legion-aux.org

AMERICAN LEGION AUXILIARY SPIRIT OF YOUTH SCHOLARSHIPS FOR JUNIOR MEMBERS • 356

Renewable awards available to graduating high school seniors. Must be women and current junior members of the American Legion Auxiliary, with a three-year membership history. Students should apply through local chapter. Leadership considered. *Award* Scholarship for use in freshman, sophomore, junior, or senior years; renewable. *Number:* 5. *Amount:* $1000.

American Legion Auxiliary Spirit of Youth Scholarships for Junior Members (continued)

Eligibility Requirements Applicant must be high school student; planning to enroll or expecting to enroll full-time at a four-year institution or university and female. Applicant or parent of applicant must be member of American Legion or Auxiliary. Available to U.S. and non-U.S. citizens.

Application Requirements Application, essay, references, self-addressed stamped envelope, test scores, transcript. *Deadline:* March 10.

World Wide Web: http://www.legion-aux.org

Contact: Department Secretary
American Legion Auxiliary, National Headquarters
777 North Meridian Street, 3rd Floor
Indianapolis, IN 46204-1189
Phone: 317-955-3853
Fax: 317-955-3884
E-mail: aef@legion-aux.org

DELTA DELTA DELTA FOUNDATION

DELTA DELTA DELTA GRADUATE SCHOLARSHIP • 357

Scholarship awarded to alumnae members attending graduate school. All scholarship winners must complete application materials provided by the Foundation. All applicants must be highly involved in TriDelta and in their communities, they must also have achieved academic excellence. *Award* Scholarship for use in graduate years; not renewable. *Number:* 8. *Amount:* $3000.

Eligibility Requirements Applicant must be enrolled or expecting to enroll full-time at an institution or university and female. Applicant or parent of applicant must have employment or volunteer experience in community service. Available to U.S. citizens.

Application Requirements Application, references, transcript. *Deadline:* February 1.

World Wide Web: http://www.tridelta.org

Contact: Joyce Allen, Foundation Coordinator of Scholarships and Financial Services
Delta Delta Delta Foundation
PO Box 5987
Arlington, TX 76005
Phone: 817-633-8001
Fax: 817-652-0212
E-mail: jallen@trideltaeo.org

DELTA DELTA DELTA UNDERGRADUATE SCHOLARSHIP • 358

One-time award based on academic achievement, campus, chapter, and community involvement. Any initiated sophomore or junior member-in-good-standing of Delta Delta Delta may apply. Application and information available at Web site http://www.tridelta.org. *Award* Scholarship for use in junior or senior years; not renewable. *Number:* 48-50. *Amount:* $500-$2000.

Eligibility Requirements Applicant must be enrolled or expecting to enroll full-time at a four-year institution or university and single female. Applicant or parent of applicant must have employment or volunteer experience in community service.

Application Requirements Application, references, transcript. *Deadline:* February 1.

World Wide Web: http://www.tridelta.org

Contact: Joyce Allen, Foundation Coordinator of Scholarships and Financial Services
Delta Delta Delta Foundation
PO Box 5987
Arlington, TX 76005
Phone: 817-633-8001
Fax: 817-652-0212
E-mail: jallen@trideltaeo.org

DELTA GAMMA FOUNDATION

DELTA GAMMA FOUNDATION FELLOWSHIPS • 359

One-time awards for graduate and postgraduate study. Candidates must be female and members of Delta Gamma Fraternity. Deadline: April 1. *Award* Fellowship for use in graduate, or postgraduate years; not renewable. *Amount:* $2500.

Eligibility Requirements Applicant must be enrolled or expecting to enroll full-time at a four-year institution or university and female. Available to U.S. and Canadian citizens.

Application Requirements Application, autobiography, essay, photo, references, self-addressed stamped envelope, transcript. *Deadline:* April 1.

World Wide Web: http://www.deltagamma.org

Contact: Debbie Sayre, Assistant to the Development Director
Delta Gamma Foundation
3250 Riverside Drive, PO Box 21397
Columbus, OH 43221-0397
Phone: 614-481-8169
Fax: 614-481-0133
E-mail: debbie@deltagamma.org

DELTA GAMMA FOUNDATION SCHOLARSHIPS • 360

Award for members of the Delta Gamma Fraternity. Must be female. Applicants must have completed three semesters or five quarters of college with a minimum 3.0 GPA. Must be active in campus, community, and chapter activities. Freshmen are ineligible. One-time award of $1000. *Award* Scholarship for use in sophomore, junior, or senior years; not renewable. *Number:* 35. *Amount:* $1000.

Eligibility Requirements Applicant must be enrolled or expecting to enroll full-time at a four-year institution or university and female. Applicant must have 3.0 GPA or higher. Available to U.S. and Canadian citizens.

Application Requirements Application, autobiography, essay, photo, references, self-addressed stamped envelope, transcript. *Deadline:* February 1.

World Wide Web: http://www.deltagamma.org

Contact: Debbie Sayre, Assistant to the Development Director
Delta Gamma Foundation
3250 Riverside Drive, PO Box 21397
Columbus, OH 43221-0397
Phone: 614-481-8169
Fax: 614-481-0133
E-mail: debbie@deltagamma.org

ELKS GOLD AWARD SCHOLARSHIPS/GIRL SCOUTS OF THE USA

ELKS NATIONAL FOUNDATION GOLD AWARD SCHOLARSHIPS • 361

Eight awards given annually to Gold Award recipients selected by the Girl Scouts of America. One girl from each Girl Scout Service area will receive a $6000 scholarship ($1500 per year). Must be a high school senior planning full-time undergraduate study. Contact the Girl Scout Council or visit Web site: http://www.girlscouts.org for information and applications. Deadlines vary per Council. *Award* Scholarship for use in freshman, sophomore, junior, or senior years; renewable. *Number:* 8. *Amount:* $6000.

Eligibility Requirements Applicant must be high school student; planning to enroll or expecting to enroll full-time at a two-year or four-year institution or university and female. Applicant or parent of applicant must be member of Girl Scouts. Available to U.S. citizens.

World Wide Web: http://www.gsusa.org

Contact: Elks Gold Award Scholarships/Girl Scouts of the USA
420 Fifth Avenue
New York, NY 10018

GENERAL FEDERATION OF WOMEN'S CLUBS IN WYOMING

MARY N. BROOKS DAUGHTER/GRANDDAUGHTER SCHOLARSHIP • 362

Award given yearly to a female high school graduate whose mother and/or grandmother is an active member in the General Federation of Women's Clubs in Wyoming. Must be a resident of Wyoming and preparing to attend any school of higher learning in the state of Wyoming. Award is based on scholarship, community/school involvement, and financial need. Minimum 3.0 GPA required. *Award* Scholarship for use in freshman, sophomore, junior, or senior years; not renewable. *Number:* 1. *Amount:* $500.

Eligibility Requirements Applicant must be enrolled or expecting to enroll full-time at a two-year or four-year or technical institution or university; female; resident of Wyoming and studying in Wyoming. Applicant or parent of applicant must be member of General Federation of Women's Clubs in Wyoming. Applicant must have 3.0 GPA or higher. Available to U.S. citizens.

Application Requirements Application, autobiography, financial need analysis, resume, references, transcript. *Deadline:* March 15.

Contact: Mrs. Norine Samuelson, Custodian, Scholarship Funds
General Federation of Women's Clubs in Wyoming
2005 Eagle Drive
Cheyenne, WY 82009
Phone: 307-638-9443
Fax: 307-433-1020
E-mail: samuelson63291@msn.com

GIRL SCOUTS OF GULFCOAST FLORIDA, INC.

GULFCOAST COLLEGE SCHOLARSHIP AWARD • 363

Scholarships are provided for graduating high school seniors who are members of the Girl Scouts of Gulfcoast, Florida Senior Girl Scouts. Must have five years of continuous membership. Must be a resident of Florida. *Award* Scholarship for use in freshman year; not renewable. *Number:* up to 8. *Amount:* $500–$1000.

Eligibility Requirements Applicant must be high school student; planning to enroll or expecting to enroll full-time at a two-year or four-year institution or university; single female and resident of Florida. Applicant or parent of applicant must be member of Girl Scouts. Applicant must have 3.0 GPA or higher. Available to U.S. citizens.

Application Requirements Application, autobiography, references, transcript. *Deadline:* February 15.

World Wide Web: http://www.girlscoutsgulfcoastfl.org

Contact: Sue Zimmerman, Director of Administrative Services
Girl Scouts of Gulfcoast Florida, Inc.
2909 Olympic Street
Sarasota, FL 34231
Phone: 941-921-5358
Fax: 941-923-5241
E-mail: suez@girlscoutsguldcoastfl.org

KAPPA ALPHA THETA FOUNDATION

KAPPA ALPHA THETA FOUNDATION MERIT BASED SCHOLARSHIP PROGRAM • 364

Foundation scholarships are awarded to either graduate or undergraduate members of Kappa Alpha Theta. All scholarships are merit-based. Application postmark date is February 1. Applications may be downloaded from the Web site or may be obtained by calling 1-888-526-1870 ext. 336. *Award* Scholarship for use in sophomore, junior, senior, graduate, or postgraduate years; not renewable. *Number:* 120–140. *Amount:* $1000–$8000.

Eligibility Requirements Applicant must be enrolled or expecting to enroll full or part-time at a four-year institution or university and female. Available to U.S. and non-U.S. citizens.

Application Requirements Application, resume, references, transcript. *Deadline:* February 1.

World Wide Web: http://www.kappaalphatheta.org

Contact: Mrs. Jeni Hilgedag, Director of Programs
Kappa Alpha Theta Foundation
8740 Founders Road
Indianapolis, IN 46268
Phone: 317-876-1870 Ext. 110
Fax: 317-876-1925
E-mail: info@kappaalphatheta.org

KAPPA ALPHA THETA FOUNDATION NAMED TRUST GRANT PROGRAM • 365

The Kappa Alpha Theta Foundation named Trust Grant program was established to provide monies for undergraduate and alumna members of the Fraternity for leadership training and non-degree educational opportunities. Applications may be downloaded from the Web site. Application is due 90 days prior to event, workshop or program. *Award* Grant for use in freshman, sophomore, junior, or senior years; not renewable. *Number:* up to 50. *Amount:* $100–$5000.

Eligibility Requirements Applicant must be enrolled or expecting to enroll at an institution or university and female. Available to U.S. and non-U.S. citizens.

Application Requirements Application, resume, references, budget, proposal, narrative. *Deadline:* Continuous.

World Wide Web: http://www.kappaalphatheta.org

Kappa Alpha Theta Foundation Named Trust Grant Program (continued)

Contact: Mrs. Jeni Hilgedag, Director of Programs
Kappa Alpha Theta Foundation
8740 Founders Road
Indianapolis, IN 46268
Phone: 317-876-1870 Ext. 110
Fax: 317-876-1925
E-mail: info@kappaalphatheta.org

KAPPA KAPPA GAMMA FOUNDATION

KAPPA KAPPA GAMMA FOUNDATION GRADUATE SCHOLARSHIPS • 366

Kappa Kappa Gamma Foundation Scholarships are available only to members of Kappa Kappa Gamma. For complete information and application materials, send self-addressed stamped envelope. Please note chapter membership on request. Must have a minimum 3.0 GPA. Deadline: February 1. *Award* Scholarship for use in graduate years; not renewable. *Number:* 40–50. *Amount:* $3000.

Eligibility Requirements Applicant must be enrolled or expecting to enroll full-time at an institution or university and female. Applicant must have 3.0 GPA or higher. Available to U.S. and Canadian citizens.

Application Requirements Application, autobiography, essay, financial need analysis, references, self-addressed stamped envelope, transcript. *Deadline:* February 1.

World Wide Web: http://www.kappakappagamma.org

Contact: Judy Parker, Administrative Director
Kappa Kappa Gamma Foundation
PO Box 38
Columbus, OH 43216-0038
Phone: 614-228-6515
Fax: 614-228-6303

KAPPA KAPPA GAMMA FOUNDATION UNDERGRADUATE SCHOLARSHIP • 367

Scholarships are available only to members of Kappa Kappa Gamma. For complete information and application materials, send self-addressed stamped envelope. Please note chapter membership on request. Must have minimum 3.0 GPA. Deadline: February 1. *Award* Scholarship for use in freshman, sophomore, junior, or senior years; not renewable. *Amount:* $3000.

Eligibility Requirements Applicant must be enrolled or expecting to enroll full-time at an institution or university and female. Applicant must have 3.0 GPA or higher. Available to U.S. and Canadian citizens.

Application Requirements Application, applicant must enter a contest, autobiography, essay, financial need analysis, references, self-addressed stamped envelope, transcript. *Deadline:* February 1.

World Wide Web: http://www.kappakappagamma.org

Contact: Judy Parker, Administrative Director
Kappa Kappa Gamma Foundation
PO Box 38
Columbus, OH 43216-0038
Phone: 614-228-6515
Fax: 614-228-6303

LADIES AUXILIARY OF THE FLEET RESERVE ASSOCIATION

LADIES AUXILIARY OF THE FLEET RESERVE ASSOCIATION SCHOLARSHIP • 368

Scholarships are given to the daughters/granddaughters of U.S. Navy, Marine Corps, and Coast Guard personnel, active Fleet Reserve, Fleet Marine Corps Reserve, and Coast Guard Reserve, retired with pay or deceased. Deadline is April 15. Selections are based on financial need, academic standing, character and leadership qualities. Must be sponsored by a FRA member in good standing. *Award* Scholarship for use in freshman, sophomore, junior, or senior years; not renewable. *Amount:* $2500.

Eligibility Requirements Applicant must be enrolled or expecting to enroll at an institution or university and female. Applicant or parent of applicant must be member of Fleet Reserve Association/Auxiliary. Available to U.S. citizens. Applicant or parent must meet one or more of the following requirements: Coast Guard, Marine Corp, or Navy experience; retired from active duty; disabled or killed as a result of military service; prisoner of war; or missing in action.

Application Requirements Application, transcript. *Deadline:* April 15.

World Wide Web: http://www.la-fra.org

Contact: Scholarship Administrator
Ladies Auxiliary of the Fleet Reserve Association
125 North West Street
Alexandria, VA 22314-2754

LADIES AUXILIARY TO THE VETERANS OF FOREIGN WARS

JUNIOR GIRLS SCHOLARSHIP PROGRAM • 369

High school awards available to girls under 17 who have been members of Junior Girls Unit of Ladies Auxiliary for one year. Awards based on scholastic aptitude, participation in Junior Girls Unit, and school activities. Two one-time scholarships at $5000 and $10,000. *Award* Scholarship for use in freshman, sophomore, junior, or senior years; not renewable. *Number:* 2. *Amount:* $5000–$10,000.

Eligibility Requirements Applicant must be high school student; age 13-16; planning to enroll or expecting to enroll full-time at a two-year or four-year or technical institution; single female and must have an interest in leadership. Applicant or parent of applicant must be member of Veterans of Foreign Wars or Auxiliary. Applicant must have 3.0 GPA or higher. Available to U.S. citizens.

Application Requirements Application, applicant must enter a contest, references, transcript. *Deadline:* March 12.

World Wide Web: http://www.ladiesauxvfw.com

Contact: Judy Millick, Administrator of Programs
Ladies Auxiliary to the Veterans of Foreign Wars
406 West 34th Street
Kansas City, MO 64111
Phone: 816-561-8655
Fax: 816-931-4753
E-mail: info@ladiesauxvfw.com

WOMEN'S INTERNATIONAL BOWLING CONGRESS

ALBERTA E. CROWE STAR OF TOMORROW AWARD   • 370

Renewable award for a U.S. or Canadian female high school or college student who competes in the sport of bowling. Must be a current YABA or WIBC member in good standing. Must be younger than 22 years old. Minimum 2.5 GPA required. Deadline is October 15. *Award* Scholarship for use in freshman, sophomore, junior, or senior years; renewable. *Number:* 1. *Amount:* $1500.

Eligibility Requirements Applicant must be age 21 or under; enrolled or expecting to enroll at an institution or university; female and must have an interest in bowling. Applicant or parent of applicant must be member of Young American Bowling Alliance. Applicant must have 2.5 GPA or higher. Available to U.S. and Canadian citizens.

Application Requirements Application, essay, references, transcript. *Deadline:* October 15.

World Wide Web: http://www.bowl.com

Contact: Women's International Bowling Congress
       5301 South 76th Street
       Greendale, WI 53129-1192
       Fax: 414-421-3013
       E-mail: pr@bowlinginc.com

EMPLOYMENT EXPERIENCE_____

AMERICAN LEGION AUXILIARY, NATIONAL HEADQUARTERS

AMERICAN LEGION AUXILIARY GIRL SCOUT ACHIEVEMENT AWARD
see number 355

DELTA DELTA DELTA FOUNDATION

DELTA DELTA DELTA GRADUATE SCHOLARSHIP   see number 357

DELTA DELTA DELTA UNDERGRADUATE SCHOLARSHIP   see number 358

JOHN EDGAR THOMSON FOUNDATION

JOHN EDGAR THOMSON FOUNDATION GRANTS   • 371

Must be the daughter of a deceased railroad employee. Employee (mother/father) must have been actively employed at time of death. Recipients of disability, sick leave, workman's compensation are considered eligible. Monthly grant is available until the age of 22, as long as recipient is in college full-time, earning at least 12 credits. Termination at age 22 or upon graduation, whichever comes first. Recipient must remain unmarried. Based upon financial need. Submit birth certificate. *Award* Grant for use in freshman, sophomore, junior, or senior years; renewable.

Eligibility Requirements Applicant must be age 21 or under; enrolled or expecting to enroll full-time at a two-year or four-year or technical institution or university and single female. Applicant or parent of applicant must have employment or volunteer experience in railroad industry. Available to U.S. citizens.

Application Requirements Application, financial need analysis, interview, photo, references, transcript, birth certificate. *Deadline:* Continuous.

Contact: Sheila Cohen, Director
John Edgar Thomson Foundation
201 South 18th Street, Suite 318
Philadelphia, PA 19103
Phone: 215-545-6083
Fax: 215-545-6083

NATIONAL FEDERATION OF THE BLIND

HERMIONE GRANT CALHOUN SCHOLARSHIP • 372

Award for full-time female undergraduate and graduate students who are legally blind and planning to study for a degree. Need minimum 2.5 GPA. Must submit a letter from state officer of National Federation of the Blind with whom they have discussed their application. May reapply. Must attend school in the U.S. Award based on academic excellence, service to the community, and financial need. *Award* Scholarship for use in freshman, sophomore, junior, senior, or graduate years; not renewable. *Number:* 1. *Amount:* $3000.

Eligibility Requirements Applicant must be enrolled or expecting to enroll full-time at an institution or university and female. Applicant or parent of applicant must have employment or volunteer experience in community service. Applicant must be visually impaired. Applicant must have 2.5 GPA or higher. Available to U.S. and non-U.S. citizens.

Application Requirements Application, autobiography, essay, financial need analysis, references, transcript. *Deadline:* March 31.

World Wide Web: http://www.nfb.org

Contact: Peggy Elliot, Chairman, Scholarship Committee
National Federation of the Blind
805 Fifth Avenue
Grinnell, IA 50112
Phone: 641-236-3366

IMPAIRMENT

ETHEL LOUISE ARMSTRONG FOUNDATION

ETHEL LOUISE ARMSTRONG FOUNDATION SCHOLARSHIP • 373

Scholarship for any woman with a physical disability who is pursuing a graduate degree in a university in the U.S. We are especially interested in women who are involved in the disability movement in their community as well as nationwide. *Award* Scholarship for use in graduate years; not renewable. *Number:* 1–14. *Amount:* $500–$2000.

Eligibility Requirements Applicant must be enrolled or expecting to enroll full or part-time at an institution or university and female. Applicant must be physically disabled. Applicant must have 3.0 GPA or higher. Available to U.S. and non-U.S. citizens.

Application Requirements Application, essay, references, transcript, medical verification form. *Deadline:* June 1.

World Wide Web: http://www.ela.org

Ethel Louise Armstrong Foundation Scholarship (continued)

Contact: Ms. Deborah Lewis, Executive Director
Ethel Louise Armstrong Foundation
2460 North Lake Avenue
PMB 128
Altadena, CA 91001
Phone: 626-398-8840
Fax: 626-398-8843
E-mail: executivedirector@ela.org

NATIONAL FEDERATION OF THE BLIND

HERMIONE GRANT CALHOUN SCHOLARSHIP

see number 372

UTAH STATE BOARD OF REGENTS

UTAH EDUCATIONALLY DISADVANTAGED PROGRAM • 374

Renewable award for residents of Utah who are disadvantaged and attending an eligible institution in Utah. Must demonstrate need and satisfactory progress. Contact financial aid office of participating institution. *Award* Scholarship for use in freshman, sophomore, junior, or senior years; renewable.

Eligibility Requirements Applicant must be enrolled or expecting to enroll at a two-year or four-year institution; resident of Utah and studying in Utah. Applicant must be hearing impaired, learning disabled, physically disabled, or visually impaired.

Application Requirements Application. *Deadline:* Continuous.

World Wide Web: http://www.uheaa.org

Contact: Lynda Reid, Administrative Assistant
Utah State Board of Regents
60 South 400 West
The Board of Regents Building, The Gateway
Salt Lake City, UT 84101-1284
Phone: 801-321-7207
Fax: 801-321-7299

MILITARY SERVICE: AIR FORCE_____

DAUGHTERS OF THE CINCINNATI

DAUGHTERS OF THE CINCINNATI SCHOLARSHIP • 375

Need- and merit-based award available to graduating high school seniors. Minimum GPA of 3.0 required. Must be daughter of commissioned officer in regular Army, Navy, Coast Guard, Air Force, Marines (active, retired, or deceased). Must submit parent's rank and branch of service. *Award* Scholarship for use in freshman, sophomore, junior, or senior years; renewable. *Number:* up to 10. *Amount:* $1000–$3000.

Eligibility Requirements Applicant must be high school student; planning to enroll or expecting to enroll full-time at a four-year institution and female. Applicant must have 3.0 GPA or higher. Available to U.S. citizens. Applicant or parent must meet one or more of the following requirements: Air Force, Army, Coast Guard, Marine Corp, or Navy experience; retired from active duty; disabled or killed as a result of military service; prisoner of war; or missing in action.

Application Requirements Application, essay, financial need analysis, references, self-addressed stamped envelope, test scores, transcript. *Deadline:* March 15.

World Wide Web: http://fdncenter.org/grantmaker/cincinnati

Contact: Mrs. Robert Ducas, Scholarship Administrator
Daughters of the Cincinnati
122 East 58th Street
New York, NY 10022
Phone: 212-319-6915

MILITARY SERVICE: ARMY_____

DAUGHTERS OF THE CINCINNATI SCHOLARSHIP   see number 375

SOCIETY OF DAUGHTERS OF THE UNITED STATES ARMY

SOCIETY OF DAUGHTERS OF THE UNITED STATES ARMY SCHOLARSHIPS   • 376

Applicants for the Roberts, Wagner, Prickett, Simpson & DU.S.A scholarships must be a daughter or granddaughter (step or adopted) of a career warrant (WO 1-5) or commissioned (2nd & 1st LT, CPT, MAJ, LTC, COL, and BG, MG, LT or full General) officer in the U.S. Army who: (1) is currently on active duty; (2) retired from active duty after at least 20 years of service; (3) was medically retired before 20 years of active service; (4) died while on active duty; (5) died after retiring from active duty with 20 or more years of service. U.S. Army must have been the primary occupation. The officer's name, rank, component (Active, Reserve, Retired), social security number, and inclusive dates of active duty must be included in request for an application for these scholarships. Do not send birth certificates or original documents. Minimum GPA 3.0. Scholarship for undergraduate study only. Self-addressed, stamped business envelope required for reply. Must be postmarked between November 1 and March 1. *Award* Scholarship for use in freshman, sophomore, junior, or senior years; renewable. *Amount:* $1000.

Eligibility Requirements Applicant must be enrolled or expecting to enroll full-time at a two-year or four-year or technical institution or university; female and must have an interest in leadership. Applicant must have 3.0 GPA or higher. Available to U.S. citizens. Applicant or parent must meet one or more of the following requirements: Army experience; retired from active duty; disabled or killed as a result of military service; prisoner of war; or missing in action.

Application Requirements Application, essay, resume, references, self-addressed stamped envelope, test scores, transcript, proof of service of qualifying service member (state relationship to member). *Deadline:* March 1.

Contact: Mary P. Maroney, Chairman, Memorial and Scholarship Funds
Society of Daughters of the United States Army
11804 Grey Birch Place
Reston, VA 20191

MILITARY SERVICE: COAST GUARD_____

DAUGHTERS OF THE CINCINNATI

DAUGHTERS OF THE CINCINNATI SCHOLARSHIP   see number 375

LADIES AUXILIARY OF THE FLEET RESERVE ASSOCIATION

LADIES AUXILIARY OF THE FLEET RESERVE ASSOCIATION SCHOLARSHIP
see number 368

MILITARY SERVICE: GENERAL_____

AMERICAN LEGION AUXILIARY, DEPARTMENT OF COLORADO

AMERICAN LEGION AUXILIARY DEPARTMENT OF COLORADO DEPARTMENT PRESIDENT'S SCHOLARSHIP FOR JUNIOR MEMBERS   see number 346

AMERICAN LEGION AUXILIARY, DEPARTMENT OF KENTUCKY

MARY BARRETT MARSHALL SCHOLARSHIP   see number 348

AMERICAN LEGION AUXILIARY, DEPARTMENT OF MARYLAND

AMERICAN LEGION AUXILIARY DEPARTMENT OF MARYLAND CHILDREN AND YOUTH SCHOLARSHIPS   • 377

Nonrenewable scholarship for a daughter of a veteran to pursue full-time undergraduate study at accredited Maryland institution. Will need proof of enrollment in an approved program. Must be a U.S. citizen and Maryland resident pursuing an Arts and Science degree or medical degree other than nursing. Can reapply for up to four years. Contact for information. *Award* Scholarship for use in freshman, sophomore, junior, or senior years; not renewable. *Number:* 1. *Amount:* $2000.

Eligibility Requirements Applicant must be enrolled or expecting to enroll full-time at a two-year or four-year institution or university; female; resident of Maryland and studying in Maryland. Available to U.S. citizens. Applicant or parent must meet one or more of the following requirements: general military experience; retired from active duty; disabled or killed as a result of military service; prisoner of war; or missing in action.

Application Requirements Application, financial need analysis, references, transcript. *Deadline:* May 1.

Contact: Ms. Anna Thompson, Department Secretary
American Legion Auxiliary, Department of Maryland
1589 Sulphur Spring Road, Suite 105
Baltimore, MD 21227
Phone: 410-242-9519
Fax: 410-242-9553
E-mail: anna@alamd.org

AMERICAN LEGION AUXILIARY, DEPARTMENT OF MICHIGAN

AMERICAN LEGION AUXILIARY DEPARTMENT OF MICHIGAN MEMORIAL SCHOLARSHIP • 378

For daughters, granddaughters, and great-granddaughters of any honorably discharged or deceased veteran of U.S. wars or conflicts. Must be Michigan resident for minimum of one year, female ages 16 to 21, and attend college in Michigan. Include copy of discharge and copy of parent or guardian's IRS 1040 form. *Award* Scholarship for use in freshman, sophomore, junior, or senior years; not renewable. *Number:* 10–35. *Amount:* $500.

Eligibility Requirements Applicant must be age 16-21; enrolled or expecting to enroll full or part-time at a two-year or four-year or technical institution or university; female; resident of Michigan and studying in Michigan. Available to U.S. citizens. Applicant or parent must meet one or more of the following requirements: general military experience; retired from active duty; disabled or killed as a result of military service; prisoner of war; or missing in action.

Application Requirements Application, financial need analysis, references, transcript. *Deadline:* March 15.

World Wide Web: http://www.michalaux.org

Contact: Leisa Eldred, Scholarship Coordinator
American Legion Auxiliary, Department of Michigan
212 North Verlinden Avenue
Lansing, MI 48915
Phone: 517-371-4720 Ext. 19
Fax: 517-371-2401
E-mail: michalaux@voyager.net

AMERICAN LEGION AUXILIARY, DEPARTMENT OF MISSOURI

LELA MURPHY SCHOLARSHIP
see number 349

AMERICAN LEGION AUXILIARY, DEPARTMENT OF OREGON

AMERICAN LEGION AUXILIARY DEPARTMENT OF OREGON SPIRIT OF YOUTH SCHOLARSHIP
see number 351

AMERICAN LEGION AUXILIARY, DEPARTMENT OF SOUTH DAKOTA

AMERICAN LEGION AUXILIARY DEPARTMENT OF SOUTH DAKOTA THELMA FOSTER SCHOLARSHIP FOR SENIOR AUXILIARY MEMBERS
see number 352

AMERICAN LEGION AUXILIARY DEPARTMENT OF SOUTH DAKOTA THELMA FOSTER SCHOLARSHIPS FOR JUNIOR AUXILIARY MEMBERS   see number 353

AMERICAN LEGION AUXILIARY, DEPARTMENT OF SOUTH DAKOTA SENIOR SCHOLARSHIP   see number 354

MILITARY SERVICE: MARINES_____

DAUGHTERS OF THE CINCINNATI

DAUGHTERS OF THE CINCINNATI SCHOLARSHIP   see number 375

LADIES AUXILIARY OF THE FLEET RESERVE ASSOCIATION

LADIES AUXILIARY OF THE FLEET RESERVE ASSOCIATION SCHOLARSHIP   see number 368

MILITARY SERVICE: NAVY_____

DAUGHTERS OF THE CINCINNATI

DAUGHTERS OF THE CINCINNATI SCHOLARSHIP   see number 375

LADIES AUXILIARY OF THE FLEET RESERVE ASSOCIATION

LADIES AUXILIARY OF THE FLEET RESERVE ASSOCIATION SCHOLARSHIP   see number 368

NATIONALITY OR ETHNIC HERITAGE_____

AMERICAN ASSOCIATION OF COLLEGES OF OSTEOPATHIC MEDICINE

SHERRY R. ARNSTEIN MINORITY STUDENT SCHOLARSHIP   • 379

One award will be given to a current student and one award will be given to an incoming minority student pursuing research and/or a degree in osteopathic medicine. Must be a minority and a U.S. citizen. *Award* Scholarship for use in graduate, or postgraduate years; not renewable. *Number:* 2. *Amount:* $500–$1000.

Eligibility Requirements Applicant must be American Indian/Alaska Native, Asian/Pacific Islander, Black (non-Hispanic), or Hispanic and enrolled or expecting to enroll full-time at an institution or university. Available to U.S. citizens.
Application Requirements Application, essay. *Deadline:* May 1.
World Wide Web: http://www.aacom.org
Contact: Cathleen Kearns, Vice President, Communications and Member Services
American Association of Colleges of Osteopathic Medicine
5550 Friendship Boulevard, Suite 310
Chevy Chase, MD 20815-7231
Phone: 301-968-4174
Fax: 301-968-1554
E-mail: ckearns@aacom.org

AMERICAN FEDERATION OF STATE, COUNTY, AND MUNICIPAL EMPLOYEES

AFSCME/UNCF UNION SCHOLARS PROGRAM • 380

One-time award for a second semester sophomore or junior majoring in ethnic studies, women's studies, labor studies, American studies, sociology, anthropology, history, political science, psychology, social work or economics. Must be African-American, Hispanic-American, Asian Pacific Islander, or American-Indian/Alaskan Native. Minimum 3.0 GPA. Receipt of scholarship requires a ten-week internship. Application deadline is March 31. See Web site at http://www.afscme.org for further details. *Award* Scholarship for use in sophomore or junior years; not renewable. *Amount:* up to $5000.

Eligibility Requirements Applicant must be American Indian/Alaska Native, Asian/Pacific Islander, Black (non-Hispanic), or Hispanic and enrolled or expecting to enroll at a four-year institution. Applicant must have 3.0 GPA or higher. Available to U.S. citizens.
Application Requirements Application, essay, references, transcript. *Deadline:* March 31.
World Wide Web: http://www.afscme.org
Contact: Genevieve Marcus, Scholarship Coordinator
American Federation of State, County, and Municipal Employees
1625 L Street, NW
Washington, DC 20036
Phone: 202-429-1250
Fax: 202-429-1272

AMERICAN GEOLOGICAL INSTITUTE

AMERICAN GEOLOGICAL INSTITUTE MINORITY SCHOLARSHIP • 381

One-time award for minority geosciences majors, including the sub-disciplines of geophysics, geochemistry, hydrology, meteorology, physical oceanography, planetary geology, or earth science education. The program does not support students in other natural sciences, mathematics, or engineering. May apply for renewal. Application available at Web site http://www.agiweb.org. Deadline is March 1. *Award* Scholarship for use in freshman, sophomore, junior, senior, or graduate years; not renewable. *Amount:* $250–$1000.

Eligibility Requirements Applicant must be American Indian/Alaska Native, Asian/Pacific Islander, Black (non-Hispanic), or Hispanic and enrolled or expecting to enroll full-time at a four-year institution or university. Available to U.S. citizens.
Application Requirements Application, references, test scores, transcript. *Deadline:* March 1.
World Wide Web: http://www.agiweb.org

American Geological Institute Minority Scholarship (continued)

Contact: Geoscience Student Scholarship Coordinator
American Geological Institute
Attn: Government Affairs Program
4220 King Street
Alexandria, VA 22302-1507

AMERICAN INSTITUTE FOR FOREIGN STUDY

AMERICAN INSTITUTE FOR FOREIGN STUDY MINORITY SCHOLARSHIPS • 382

Applications will be accepted from African-Americans, Asian-Americans, Native-Americans, Hispanic-Americans and Pacific Islanders who are currently enrolled as undergraduates at a U.S. institution applying to an AIFS study abroad program. Applicants must demonstrate financial need, leadership ability, and academic accomplishment and meet program requirements. One full scholarship and three runners-up scholarships are awarded each semester. Submit application by April 15 for fall or October 15 for spring. Application fees are $75. *Award* Scholarship for use in sophomore, junior, or senior years; not renewable. *Number:* 8. *Amount:* $2000–$11,500.

Eligibility Requirements Applicant must be American Indian/Alaska Native, Asian/Pacific Islander, Black (non-Hispanic), or Hispanic; age 17; enrolled or expecting to enroll full-time at a two-year or four-year institution or university and must have an interest in leadership. Applicant must have 3.0 GPA or higher. Available to U.S. and non-U.S. citizens.

Application Requirements Application, essay, financial need analysis, photo, references, transcript. *Fee:* $75.

World Wide Web: http://www.aifsabroad.com

Contact: David Mauro, Admissions Counselor
American Institute for Foreign Study
River Plaza, 9 West Broad Street
Stamford, CT 06902-3788
Phone: 800-727-2437 Ext. 5163
Fax: 203-399-5598
E-mail: college.info@aifs.com

AMERICAN PLANNING ASSOCIATION

AMERICAN PLANNING ASSOCIATION FELLOWSHIP PROGRAM • 383

One-time award for first and second year graduate-level students studying urban planning. Fellowships are targeted to African-Americans, Hispanic-Americans and Native-Americans. Application deadline is April 30. *Award* Fellowship for use in graduate years; not renewable. *Amount:* $1000–$5000.

Eligibility Requirements Applicant must be American Indian/Alaska Native, Black (non-Hispanic), or Hispanic and enrolled or expecting to enroll full-time at an institution or university.

Application Requirements Application, financial need analysis, resume, references, test scores, transcript. *Deadline:* April 30.

World Wide Web: http://www.planning.org

Contact: Kriss Blank, Leadership Affairs Associate
American Planning Association
Minority Scholarship and Fellowship Programs
122 South Michigan Avenue, Suite 1600
Chicago, IL 60603-6107
Phone: 312-786-6722
Fax: 312-786-6727

AMERICAN SOCIETY OF SAFETY ENGINEERS (ASSE) FOUNDATION

UNITED PARCEL SERVICE DIVERSITY SCHOLARSHIP PROGRAM • 384

Two one-time awards available to minority ethnic or racial group students pursuing an undergraduate degree full-time in occupational safety, health, or environment. Must be an ASSE member, a U.S. citizen, and have a minimum 3.25 GPA. Recommendation by a safety faculty member required. Deadline is December 1. *Award* Scholarship for use in junior or senior years; not renewable. *Number:* 2. *Amount:* $3000–$4000.

Eligibility Requirements Applicant must be American Indian/Alaska Native, Asian/Pacific Islander, Black (non-Hispanic), or Hispanic and enrolled or expecting to enroll full-time at an institution or university. Available to U.S. citizens.

Application Requirements Application, essay, references, transcript. *Deadline:* December 1.

World Wide Web: http://www.asse.org/foundat.htm

Contact: Customer Service Department
American Society of Safety Engineers (ASSE) Foundation
1800 East Oakton Street
Des Plaines, IL 60018
Phone: 847-699-2929
Fax: 847-296-3769
E-mail: customerservice@asse.org

ARIZONA ASSOCIATION OF CHICANOS IN HIGHER EDUCATION (AACHE)

AACHE SCHOLARSHIP • 385

Scholarship available to students of Chicano/Hispanic/Latino heritage and identity who are residents of Arizona and enrolled full-time in a community college, 4-year college, or university. Application deadline is April 4. *Award* Scholarship for use in sophomore, junior, senior, or graduate years; not renewable. *Number:* 3. *Amount:* $300.

Eligibility Requirements Applicant must be Hispanic; enrolled or expecting to enroll full-time at a two-year or four-year institution or university and resident of Arizona. Available to U.S. citizens.

Application Requirements Application, autobiography, essay, transcript. *Deadline:* April 4.

World Wide Web: http://www.rio.maricopa.edu/ci/programs/aache

Contact: Silvia Serrata, Scholarship Coordinator, EMCC
Arizona Association of Chicanos in Higher Education (AACHE)
3000 North Dysart Road
Avondale, AZ 85323
Phone: 623-535-2787
E-mail: silvia.serrata@emcmail.maricopa.edu

ARKANSAS COMMUNITY FOUNDATION, INC.

SOUTHWESTERN BELL BATES SCHOLARSHIP FUND • 386

Award for outstanding minority high school seniors in Arkansas. Contact high school counselor's office for more information. *Award* Scholarship for use in freshman year; not renewable. *Amount:* $500–$5000.

Southwestern-Bell Bates Scholarship Fund (continued)

Eligibility Requirements Applicant must be American Indian/Alaska Native, Asian/Pacific Islander, Black (non-Hispanic), or Hispanic; high school student; planning to enroll or expecting to enroll at an institution or university and resident of Arkansas. Available to U.S. citizens.

Application Requirements Application. *Deadline:* March 15.

World Wide Web: http://www.arcf.org

Contact: Arkansas Community Foundation, Inc.
700 South Rock Street
Little Rock, AR 72202-2519

BECA FOUNDATION, INC.

DANIEL GUTIERREZ MEMORIAL GENERAL SCHOLARSHIP FUND • 387

Scholarships to full-time Latino students from San Diego County; high school graduate entering college in the fall of the same year. May pursue their education anywhere in the United States and pursue any profession. Financial need, scholastic determination, and community/cultural awareness are considered. *Award* Scholarship for use in freshman year; not renewable. *Amount:* $500–$1000.

Eligibility Requirements Applicant must be of Hispanic heritage; high school student; planning to enroll or expecting to enroll full-time at a four-year institution or university and resident of California. Applicant must have 2.5 GPA or higher. Available to U.S. citizens.

Application Requirements Application, essay, financial need analysis, references, transcript. *Deadline:* March 1.

Contact: Ana Garcia, Operations Manager
BECA Foundation, Inc.
830 East Grand Avenue
Suite B
Escondido, CA 92025
Phone: 760-741-8246

GENERAL SCHOLARSHIP FUND • 388

Scholarships to full-time Latino students from North San Diego County; high school graduate entering college in the fall of the same year. May pursue their education anywhere in the United States and pursue any profession. Financial need, scholastic determination, and community/cultural awareness are considered. *Award* Scholarship for use in freshman year; not renewable. *Amount:* $500–$1000.

Eligibility Requirements Applicant must be of Hispanic heritage; high school student; planning to enroll or expecting to enroll full-time at a four-year institution or university and resident of California. Applicant must have 2.5 GPA or higher. Available to U.S. citizens.

Application Requirements Application, essay, financial need analysis, references, transcript. *Deadline:* March 1.

Contact: Ana Garcia, Operations Manager
BECA Foundation, Inc.
830 East Grand Avenue
Suite B
Escondido, CA 92025
Phone: 760-741-8246

CANADIAN FEDERATION OF UNIVERSITY WOMEN

1989 POLYTECHNIQUE COMMEMORATIVE AWARD • 389

One-time award available to women who are Canadian citizens or have held landed immigrant status for at least one year for graduate studies in any field. Candidate must justify the relevance of her work to women. One award of CAN$2,800. Application fee of CAN$35. *Award* Scholarship for use in graduate years; not renewable. *Number:* 1. *Amount:* $2800.

Eligibility Requirements Applicant must be Canadian citizenship; enrolled or expecting to enroll full or part-time at an institution or university and female.

Application Requirements Application, autobiography, essay, references, transcript. *Fee:* $35. *Deadline:* November 1.

World Wide Web: http://www.cfuw.org

Contact: Betty Dunlop, Fellowships Program Manager
Canadian Federation of University Women
251 Bank Street, Suite 600
Ottawa, ON K2P 1X3
Canada
Phone: 613-234-2732
E-mail: cfuwfls@rogers.com

ALICE E. WILSON AWARD • 390

One-time award available to women who are Canadian citizens or have held landed immigrant status for at least one year and hold a bachelor's degree or equivalent. Students must have been accepted into their proposed programs and places of study. Special consideration for those returning after at least three years. Three awards of CAN$2500. Application fee is CAN$35. *Award* Scholarship for use in graduate years; not renewable. *Number:* 3. *Amount:* $2500.

Eligibility Requirements Applicant must be Canadian citizenship; enrolled or expecting to enroll full or part-time at an institution or university and female.

Application Requirements Application, autobiography, essay, references, transcript. *Fee:* $35. *Deadline:* November 1.

World Wide Web: http://www.cfuw.org

Contact: Betty Dunlop, Fellowships Program Manager
Canadian Federation of University Women
251 Bank Street, Suite 600
Ottawa, ON K2P 1X3
Canada
Phone: 613-234-2732
E-mail: cfuwfls@rogers.com

BEVERLEY JACKSON FELLOWSHIP • 391

One fellowship available to women who are Canadian citizens or have held landed immigrant status for at least one year. Applicants must be over the age of 35 and enrolled in graduate work at an Ontario university. One-time award of CAN$2,000. Application fee of CAN$35. *Award* Fellowship for use in graduate years; not renewable. *Number:* 1. *Amount:* $2000.

Eligibility Requirements Applicant must be Canadian citizenship; age 35; enrolled or expecting to enroll full or part-time at an institution or university; female and studying in Ontario.

Application Requirements Application, autobiography, essay, references, transcript. *Fee:* $35. *Deadline:* November 1.

World Wide Web: http://www.cfuw.org

Beverley Jackson Fellowship (continued)

Contact: Betty Dunlop, Fellowships Program Manager
Canadian Federation of University Women
251 Bank Street, Suite 600
Ottawa, ON K2P 1X3
Canada
Phone: 613-234-2732
E-mail: cfuwfls@rogers.com

BOURSE GEORGETTE LEMOYNE • 392

One-time award available to women who are Canadian citizens or have held landed immigrant status for at least one year for graduate study at a Canadian university where one of the languages of instruction and administration is French. Applicants must hold a bachelor's degree or equivalent. One award of CAN$2500. Application fee of CAN$35. *Award* Scholarship for use in graduate years; not renewable. *Number:* 1. *Amount:* $2500.

Eligibility Requirements Applicant must be Canadian citizenship; enrolled or expecting to enroll full or part-time at an institution or university and female.

Application Requirements Application, autobiography, essay, references, transcript. *Fee:* $35. *Deadline:* November 1.

World Wide Web: http://www.cfuw.org

Contact: Betty Dunlop, Fellowships Program Manager
Canadian Federation of University Women
251 Bank Street, Suite 600
Ottawa, ON K2P 1X3
Canada
Phone: 613-234-2732
E-mail: cfuwfls@rogers.com

DR. MARION ELDER GRANT FELLOWSHIP • 393

One fellowship available to women who are Canadian citizens or who have held landed immigrant status for at least one year. Award is non-renewable and for full-time study only. Application fee is CAN$35. *Award* Fellowship for use in graduate years; not renewable. *Number:* 1. *Amount:* $9000.

Eligibility Requirements Applicant must be Canadian citizenship; enrolled or expecting to enroll full-time at an institution or university and female.

Application Requirements Application, autobiography, essay, references, transcript. *Fee:* $35. *Deadline:* November 1.

World Wide Web: http://www.cfuw.org

Contact: Betty Dunlop, Fellowships Program Manager
Canadian Federation of University Women
251 Bank Street, Suite 600
Ottawa, ON K2P 1X3
Canada
Phone: 613-234-2732
E-mail: cfuwfls@rogers.com

MARGARET MCWILLIAMS PRE-DOCTORAL FELLOWSHIP • 394

One-time award available to women who have completed at least one full year of doctoral studies and are full-time students at time of application. Applicants may be studying abroad. One fellowship of CAN$10,000. Must be a Canadian citizen or have held landed immigrant status for at least one year at time of application. Application fee of CAN$35. *Award* Fellowship for use in graduate years; not renewable. *Number:* 1. *Amount:* $10,000.

Eligibility Requirements Applicant must be Canadian citizenship; enrolled or expecting to enroll full-time at an institution or university and female.

Application Requirements Application, autobiography, essay, references, transcript. *Fee:* $35. *Deadline:* November 1.

World Wide Web: http://www.cfuw.org

Contact: Betty Dunlop, Fellowships Program Manager
Canadian Federation of University Women
251 Bank Street, Suite 600
Ottawa, ON K2P 1X3
Canada
Phone: 613-234-2732
E-mail: cfuwfls@rogers.com

CITY COLLEGE OF SAN FRANCISCO LATINO EDUCATIONAL ASSOCIATION

LATINO EDUCATION ASSOCIATION SCHOLARSHIP • 395

Latina or Latino students with at least 60 transferable credits who have been accepted at any college or university will be evaluated for the scholarship based on financial need, academic excellence, community service, and student activism while at CCSF. Application deadline is first Friday in April. *Award* Scholarship for use in junior or senior years; not renewable. *Number:* 1-3. *Amount:* $500.

Eligibility Requirements Applicant must be Hispanic; enrolled or expecting to enroll at a four-year institution or university and resident of California. Applicant must have 3.0 GPA or higher. Available to U.S. citizens.

Application Requirements Application, autobiography, essay, references, transcript.

World Wide Web: http://www.ccsf.edu

Contact: City College of San Francisco Latino Educational Association
50 Phelan Avenue, Box L230
Scholarship Office, Batmale Hall, Room 366
San Francisco, CA 94112

COMMUNITY FOUNDATION FOR PALM BEACH AND MARTIN COUNTIES, INC.

COLONIAL BANK SCHOLARSHIP • 396

For minority student graduating from Palm Beach Lakes or Santaluces High Schools who has a 2.5 GPA or higher and demonstrates financial need. *Award* Scholarship for use in freshman year; not renewable. *Amount:* $750-$2500.

Eligibility Requirements Applicant must be American Indian/Alaska Native, Asian/Pacific Islander, Black (non-Hispanic), or Hispanic; high school student; planning to enroll or expecting to enroll full-time at a two-year or four-year or technical institution or university and resident of Florida. Applicant must have 2.5 GPA or higher. Available to U.S. citizens.

Application Requirements Application, financial need analysis, transcript. *Deadline:* March 1.

World Wide Web: http://www.cfpbmc.org

Colonial Bank Scholarship (continued)

Contact: Carolyn Jenco, Grants Manager/Scholarship Coordinator
Community Foundation for Palm Beach and Martin Counties, Inc.
700 South Dixie Highway
Suite 200
West Palm Beach, FL 33401

CONGRESSIONAL HISPANIC CAUCUS INSTITUTE

CONGRESSIONAL HISPANIC CAUCUS INSTITUTE PUBLIC POLICY FELLOWSHIPS • 397

Awards for Latinos from the United States, Puerto Rico, and Guam to gain hands-on experience at the federal level in the public policy area of their choice. Monthly stipend of $2061, round-trip transportation to Washington D.C., and health insurance. Fellows with a graduate degree receive $2500 per month. See Web site at http://www.chci.org for further information. *Award* Fellowship for use in graduate years; not renewable. *Number:* up to 20. *Amount:* up to $2500.

Eligibility Requirements Applicant must be Hispanic and enrolled or expecting to enroll at an institution or university. Available to U.S. citizens.

Application Requirements Application. *Deadline:* February 28.

World Wide Web: http://www.chciyouth.org

Contact: CHCI Fellowship Program
Congressional Hispanic Caucus Institute
504 C Street NE
Washington, DC 20002
Phone: 202-543-1771
Fax: 202-546-2143

CONGRESSIONAL HISPANIC CAUCUS INSTITUTE SCHOLARSHIP AWARDS • 398

One-time award for Latino students who have a history of public service-oriented activities. $5,000 to attend a four-year or graduate level institution; $1,500 to attend a two-year community college. Must be enrolled full time. See Web site at http://www.chci.org for further information. *Award* Scholarship for use in freshman, sophomore, junior, senior, or graduate years; not renewable. *Amount:* $1500–$5000.

Eligibility Requirements Applicant must be Hispanic and enrolled or expecting to enroll full-time at a two-year or four-year institution or university.

Application Requirements Application, essay, resume, references, transcript. *Deadline:* April 15.

World Wide Web: http://www.chciyouth.org

Contact: CHCI Scholarship Awards
Congressional Hispanic Caucus Institute
504 C Street NE
Washington, DC 20002
Phone: 202-543-1771

CONNECTICUT ASSOCIATION OF LATIN AMERICANS IN HIGHER EDUCATION (CALAHE)

CONNECTICUT ASSOCIATION OF LATIN AMERICANS IN HIGHER EDUCATION SCHOLARSHIPS
• 399

Must demonstrate involvement with, and commitment to, activities that promote Latino pursuit of education. Must be U.S. citizen or permanent resident. *Award* Scholarship for use in freshman, sophomore, junior, or senior years; not renewable. *Number:* 5. *Amount:* $500.

Eligibility Requirements Applicant must be Hispanic; enrolled or expecting to enroll full-time at a two-year or four-year or technical institution or university and resident of Connecticut. Applicant must have 3.0 GPA or higher. Available to U.S. citizens.

Application Requirements Application, essay, financial need analysis, transcript. *Deadline:* April 15.

World Wide Web: http://www.calahe.org

Contact: Dr. Wilson Luna, Gateway Community-Technical College
Connecticut Association of Latin Americans in Higher Education (CALAHE)
60 Sargent Drive
New Haven, CT 06511
Phone: 203-285-2210
Fax: 203-285-2211
E-mail: wluna@gwcc.commnet.edu

COUNCIL FOR INTERNATIONAL EDUCATIONAL EXCHANGE

ROBERT B. BAILEY III MINORITY SCHOLARSHIPS FOR EDUCATION ABROAD
• 400

One-time award for students from underrepresented groups in study abroad participating in Council for International Education Exchange-administered overseas study program. Application deadlines: March 15 and November 1. Applicant must be self-identified as belonging to an underrepresented group in study abroad. *Award* Scholarship for use in freshman, sophomore, junior, or senior years; not renewable. *Number:* 10. *Amount:* $500.

Eligibility Requirements Applicant must be American Indian/Alaska Native, Asian/Pacific Islander, Black (non-Hispanic), or Hispanic and enrolled or expecting to enroll full or part-time at an institution or university. Available to U.S. citizens.

Application Requirements Application, essay, financial need analysis, references, transcript.

World Wide Web: http://www.ciee.org/study

Contact: Janet Grunwald, Executive Assistant
Council for International Educational Exchange
205 East 42nd Street
New York, NY 10017
Phone: 212-822-2686
Fax: 212-822-2779
E-mail: jgrunwald@ciee.org

DOW JONES NEWSPAPER FUND

DOW JONES NEWSPAPER FUND MINORITY BUSINESS REPORTING PROGRAM
• 401

One-time paid business reporting internship and $1000 scholarship for minority college sophomores and juniors returning to undergraduate studies. Must submit application, essay,

Dow Jones Newspaper Fund Minority Business Reporting Program (continued)

transcript, clips, and resume; must take a test. Deadline is November 1. *Award* Scholarship for use in sophomore or junior years; not renewable. *Number:* 12. *Amount:* $1000.

Eligibility Requirements Applicant must be American Indian/Alaska Native, Asian/Pacific Islander, Black (non-Hispanic), or Hispanic and enrolled or expecting to enroll full-time at a two-year or four-year institution. Available to U.S. citizens.

Application Requirements Application, essay, portfolio, resume, references, transcript, test. *Deadline:* November 1.

World Wide Web: http://djnewspaperfund.dowjones.com

Contact: Jan Maressa, Office Manager
Dow Jones Newspaper Fund
PO Box 300
Princeton, NJ 08543-0300
Phone: 609-452-2820
Fax: 609-520-5804

EAST LOS ANGELES COMMUNITY UNION (TELACU) EDUCATION FOUNDATION

DAVID C. LIZARRAGA FELLOWSHIP • 402

Scholarships available for graduate or professional study to low-income applicants from the Greater East Side of Los Angeles. Must be U.S. citizen or permanent resident with Hispanic heritage. Must be a resident of one of the following communities: East Los Angeles, Bell Gardens, Commerce, Huntington Park, Montebello, Monterey Park, Pico Rivera, Santa Ana, South Gate, and the City of Los Angeles. Must be the first generation in their family to achieve a college degree. Must have a record of community service. Preference will be given to students who are in the last year of their program. *Award* Fellowship for use in graduate years; not renewable. *Number:* 4–5. *Amount:* $2500–$10,000.

Eligibility Requirements Applicant must be Hispanic; enrolled or expecting to enroll full-time at an institution or university and resident of California. Available to U.S. citizens.

Application Requirements Application, essay, financial need analysis, references, transcript. *Deadline:* April 6.

Contact: Michael A. Alvarado, Director
Phone: 323-721-1655

ESPERANZA, INC.

ESPERANZA SCHOLARSHIPS • 403

The Esperanza Scholarship is a one-year award valid only for full-time tuition and/or books at an accredited college or university. Recipients are eligible to apply yearly until they have completed their curriculum. *Award* Scholarship for use in freshman, sophomore, junior, senior, graduate, or postgraduate years; not renewable. *Number:* 45–60. *Amount:* $500–$1500.

Eligibility Requirements Applicant must be of Hispanic heritage; enrolled or expecting to enroll full-time at a two-year or four-year institution or university and resident of Ohio. Applicant must have 2.5 GPA or higher. Available to U.S. and non-U.S. citizens.

Application Requirements Application, essay, interview, references, test scores, transcript. *Deadline:* March 1.

World Wide Web: http://www.esperanzainc.com

Contact: Olga Ferrer, Office Assistant
Esperanza, Inc.
4115 Bridge Avenue
Room 108
Cleveland, OH 44113
Phone: 216-651-7178
Fax: 216-651-7183
E-mail: hope4ed@aol.com

FLORIDA BOARD OF EDUCATION, DIVISION OF COLLEGES AND UNIVERSITIES

DELORES A. AUZENNE FELLOWSHIP FOR GRADUATE STUDY • 404

Available for minority students pursuing full-time graduate study at one of the four-year public institutions in the Florida university system. Must have at least a 3.0 GPA. Renewable award. Contact the Equal Opportunity Office at each of the ten public state universities. *Award* Scholarship for use in graduate years; renewable. *Number:* 60. *Amount:* $2500–$5000.

Eligibility Requirements Applicant must be American Indian/Alaska Native, Asian/Pacific Islander, Black (non-Hispanic), or Hispanic; enrolled or expecting to enroll full-time at an institution or university and studying in Florida. Applicant must have 3.0 GPA or higher. Available to U.S. citizens.
Application Requirements Application, transcript. *Deadline:* May 31.
World Wide Web: http://www.fldcu.org
Contact: Equal Opportunity Office at university

FLORIDA DEPARTMENT OF EDUCATION

JOSE MARTI SCHOLARSHIP CHALLENGE GRANT FUND • 405

Award available to Hispanic-American students who were born in or whose parent was born in an Hispanic country. Must have lived in Florida for one year, be enrolled full-time in Florida at an eligible school, and have a GPA of 3.0 or above. Must be U.S. citizen or eligible non-citizen. Renewable award of $2000. Application must be postmarked by April 1. Free Application for Federal Student Aid must be processed by May 15. *Award* Scholarship for use in freshman, or graduate years; renewable. *Number:* 75. *Amount:* $2000.

Eligibility Requirements Applicant must be Hispanic; enrolled or expecting to enroll full-time at a two-year or four-year institution or university; resident of Florida and studying in Florida. Applicant must have 3.0 GPA or higher. Available to U.S. citizens.
Application Requirements Application, financial need analysis, FAFSA. *Deadline:* April 1.
World Wide Web: http://www.floridastudentfinancialaid.org
Contact: Scholarship Information
Florida Department of Education
Office of Student Financial Assistance
1940 North Monroe, Suite 70
Tallahassee, FL 32303-4759
Phone: 888-827-2004
E-mail: osfa@fldoe.org

ROSEWOOD FAMILY SCHOLARSHIP FUND • 406

Renewable award for eligible minority students to attend a Florida public postsecondary institution on a full-time basis. Preference given to direct descendants of African-American

Rosewood Family Scholarship Fund (continued)

Rosewood families affected by the incidents of January 1923. Must be Black, Hispanic, Asian, Pacific Islander, American-Indian, or Alaska Native. Free Application for Federal Student Aid (and Student Aid Report for nonresidents of Florida) must be processed by May 15. *Award* Scholarship for use in freshman, sophomore, junior, or senior years; renewable. *Number:* up to 25. *Amount:* up to $4000.

Eligibility Requirements Applicant must be American Indian/Alaska Native, Asian/Pacific Islander, Black (non-Hispanic), or Hispanic; enrolled or expecting to enroll full-time at a two-year or four-year or technical institution or university and studying in Florida. Available to U.S. citizens.

Application Requirements Application, financial need analysis. *Deadline:* April 1.

World Wide Web: http://www.floridastudentfinancialaid.org

Contact: Scholarship Information
Florida Department of Education
Office of Student Financial Assistance
1940 North Monroe, Suite 70
Tallahassee, FL 32303-4759
Phone: 888-827-2004
E-mail: osfa@fldoe.org

GENERAL BOARD OF GLOBAL MINISTRIES

NATIONAL LEADERSHIP DEVELOPMENT GRANTS • 407

Award for racial and ethnic minority members of the United Methodist Church who are pursuing undergraduate study. Must be U.S. citizen or resident alien or reside in U.S. as a refugee. Renewable award of $500 to $5000. Deadline: May 31. *Award* Grant for use in freshman, sophomore, junior, or senior years; renewable. *Number:* 75. *Amount:* $500–$5000.

Eligibility Requirements Applicant must be Methodist; American Indian/Alaska Native, Asian/Pacific Islander, Black (non-Hispanic), or Hispanic and enrolled or expecting to enroll full-time at a two-year or four-year or technical institution or university. Available to U.S. and non-U.S. citizens.

Application Requirements Application, essay, financial need analysis, photo, references, transcript. *Deadline:* May 31.

World Wide Web: http://www.gbgm-umc.org

Contact: Scholarship Office
General Board of Global Ministries
475 Riverside Drive
Room 1351
New York, NY 10115
Phone: 212-870-3787
Fax: 212-870-3932
E-mail: scholars@gbgm-umc.org

HBCU-CENTRAL.COM

HBCU-CENTRAL.COM MINORITY SCHOLARSHIP PROGRAM • 408

Targeted to minorities that choose to attend Historically Black Colleges and Universities. Recipients are selected based on essay submissions, grades, and financial need. *Award* Scholarship for use in freshman, sophomore, junior, or senior years; not renewable. *Number:* 3–10. *Amount:* $1000–$2500.

NATIONALITY OR ETHNIC HERITAGE

Eligibility Requirements Applicant must be American Indian/Alaska Native, Asian/Pacific Islander, Black (non-Hispanic), or Hispanic and enrolled or expecting to enroll full-time at a four-year institution or university. Available to U.S. citizens.

Application Requirements Application, autobiography, essay, interview, transcript. *Deadline:* Continuous.

World Wide Web: http://www.hbcu-central.com/

Contact: William Moss, Scholarship Administrator
        HBCU-Central.com
        7846 Grandlin Park
        Suite AA
        Blacklick, OH 43004
        Phone: 614-284-3007
        Fax: 215-893-5398
        E-mail: wrmoss@hbcu-central.com

HISPANIC ALLIANCE CAREER ENHANCEMENT

HISPANIC ALLIANCE FOR CAREER ENHANCEMENT NATIONAL SCHOLARSHIP PROGRAM   • 409

Provides financial support to encourage enrollment in and graduation from college by young Hispanic professionals. *Award* Scholarship for use in freshman, sophomore, junior, or senior years; not renewable. *Number:* 1–10. *Amount:* $500–$1000.

Eligibility Requirements Applicant must be Hispanic and enrolled or expecting to enroll full or part-time at a four-year institution or university. Applicant must have 3.0 GPA or higher. Available to U.S. citizens.

Application Requirements Application, autobiography, essay, resume. *Deadline:* March 31.

World Wide Web: http://www.hace-usa.org

Contact: Griselda Garibay, Program Officer
        Hispanic Alliance Career Enhancement
        25 East Washington Street
        Suite 1500
        Chicago, IL 60602
        Phone: 312-435-0498
        Fax: 312-435-1494
        E-mail: griselda@hace-usa.org

HISPANIC HERITAGE FOUNDATION AWARDS

HHAF CHASE AND MASTERCARD ACADEMIC EXCELLENCE YOUTH AWARD   • 410

Educational grants are awarded to two Hispanic students in each of twelve regions for demonstrated academic excellence. One student will receive $2000 and the other will receive $1000. One national winner will receive a $5000 educational grant from the pool of regional winners. For more details or an application see Web site: http://www.hispanicheritageawards.org. *Award* Grant for use in freshman year; not renewable. *Number:* 25. *Amount:* $1000–$5000.

Eligibility Requirements Applicant must be of Hispanic heritage; high school student and planning to enroll or expecting to enroll at an institution or university. Available to U.S. citizens.

Application Requirements Application. *Deadline:* March 6.

World Wide Web: http://www.hispanicheritageawards.org

Getting Money for College: Scholarships for Hispanic Students   www.petersons.com   **273**

Contact: application available at Web site

HHAF DR. PEPPER LEADERSHIP AND COMMUNITY SERVICE YOUTH AWARD • 411

Educational grants are awarded to two Hispanic students in each of twelve regions for demonstrated interest in leadership, community service and academic excellence in general. One student will receive $2000 and the other will receive $1000. One national winner will receive a $5000 educational grant from the pool of regional winners. For more details or an application see Web site: http://www.hispanicheritageawards.org. *Award* Grant for use in freshman year; not renewable. *Number:* 25. *Amount:* $1000–$5000.

Eligibility Requirements Applicant must be of Hispanic heritage; high school student and planning to enroll or expecting to enroll at an institution or university. Available to U.S. citizens.

Application Requirements Application. *Deadline:* March 6.

World Wide Web: http://www.hispanicheritageawards.org

Contact: application available at Web site

HHAF EXXON MOBIL MATHEMATICS YOUTH AWARD • 412

Educational grants are awarded to two Hispanic students in each of twelve regions for demonstrated interest in mathematics and academics excellence in general. One student will receive $2000 and the other will receive $1000. One national winner will receive a $5000 educational grant from the pool of regional winners. For more details or an application see Web site: http://www.hispanicheritageawards.org. *Award* Grant for use in freshman year; not renewable. *Number:* 25. *Amount:* $1000–$5000.

Eligibility Requirements Applicant must be of Hispanic heritage; high school student and planning to enroll or expecting to enroll at an institution or university. Available to U.S. citizens.

Application Requirements Application. *Deadline:* March 6.

World Wide Web: http://www.hispanicheritageawards.org

Contact: application available at Web site

HHAF GLAXO SMITH KLINE HEALTH AND SCIENCE YOUTH AWARD • 413

Educational grants are awarded to two Hispanic students in each of twelve regions for demonstrated interest in Health and Science and academic excellence in general. One student will receive $2000 and the other will receive $1000. One national winner will receive a $5000 educational grant from the pool of regional winners. For more details or an application see Web site: http://www.hispanicheritageawards.org. *Award* Grant for use in freshman year; not renewable. *Number:* 25. *Amount:* $1000–$5000.

Eligibility Requirements Applicant must be of Hispanic heritage; high school student and planning to enroll or expecting to enroll at an institution or university. Available to U.S. citizens.

Application Requirements Application. *Deadline:* March 6.

World Wide Web: http://www.hispanicheritageawards.org

Contact: application available at Web site

HHAF NBC JOURNALISM YOUTH AWARD • 414

Educational grants are awarded to two Hispanic students in each of twelve regions for demonstrated interest in journalism and academic excellence in general. One student will receive $2000 and the other will receive $1000. One national winner will receive a $5000 educational grant from the pool of regional winners. For more details or an application see Web site: http://www.hispanicheritageawards.org. *Award* Grant for use in freshman year; not renewable. *Number:* 25. *Amount:* $1000–$5000.

Eligibility Requirements Applicant must be of Hispanic heritage; high school student and planning to enroll or expecting to enroll at an institution or university. Available to U.S. citizens.

Application Requirements Application. *Deadline:* March 6.

World Wide Web: http://www.hispanicheritageawards.org

Contact: application available at Web site

HHAF SPORTS YOUTH AWARD • 415

Educational grants are awarded to two Hispanic students in each of twelve regions for demonstrated interest in sports and academic excellence in general. One student will receive $2000 and the other will receive $1000. One national winner will receive a $5000 educational grant from the pool of regional winners. For more details or an application see Web site: http://www.hispanicheritageawards.org. *Award* Grant for use in freshman year; not renewable. *Number:* 25. *Amount:* $1000–$5000.

Eligibility Requirements Applicant must be of Hispanic heritage; high school student and planning to enroll or expecting to enroll at an institution or university. Available to U.S. citizens.

Application Requirements Application. *Deadline:* March 6.

World Wide Web: http://www.hispanicheritageawards.org

Contact: application available at Web site

HISPANIC OUTLOOK IN HIGHER EDUCATION MAGAZINE

HISPANIC OUTLOOK IN HIGHER EDUCATION SCHOLARSHIP AWARD • 416

Renewable $1000 scholarship for graduating high school seniors entering a college or university on Hispanic Outlook Magazine's annual pick list published in November. Must be Hispanic, in upper quarter of class or have a minimum 3.5 GPA, and plan on studying full time. For information and an application, write to the PO Box and include a legal size, self-addressed, stamped envelope. Application deadline is May 1. *Award* Scholarship for use in freshman, sophomore, junior, or senior years; renewable. *Amount:* $1000.

Eligibility Requirements Applicant must be of Hispanic heritage; high school student and planning to enroll or expecting to enroll full-time at a two-year or four-year institution or university. Applicant must have 3.5 GPA or higher. Available to U.S. citizens.

Application Requirements Application, photo, references, self-addressed stamped envelope, transcript. *Deadline:* May 1.

World Wide Web: http://www.hispanicoutlook.com

Contact: Director
Hispanic Outlook in Higher Education Magazine
PO Box 68
Paramus, NJ 07652

HISPANIC PUBLIC RELATIONS ASSOCIATION

SCHOLARSHIP PROGRAM • 417

Scholarship open to California junior and senior students of Hispanic descent with at least a 2.7 cumulative GPA and 3.0 GPA in their major subject. Preference is given to students

Scholarship Program (continued)

majoring in public relations but students in communication studies, journalism, advertising and/or marketing will be considered. Students majoring in other disciplines who have a desire to work in public relations industry are invited to apply. *Award* Scholarship for use in junior or senior years. *Number:* 10. *Amount:* $1000.

Eligibility Requirements Applicant must be Hispanic; enrolled or expecting to enroll at a four-year institution or university and studying in California.

Application Requirements Application, resume, references, transcript. *Deadline:* May 30.

World Wide Web: http://www.hprala.org

Contact: Scholarship Committee
Hispanic Public Relations Association
660 South Figueroa Street, Suite 1140
Los Angeles, CA 90017

HISPANIC SCHOLARSHIP FUND

COLLEGE SCHOLARSHIP PROGRAM • 418

Awards available to full-time undergraduate or graduate students of Hispanic origin. Applicants must have 12 college units with a minimum 2.7 GPA before applying. Merit-based award for U.S. citizens or permanent residents. Must include financial aid award letter and SAR. *Award* Scholarship for use in sophomore, junior, senior, or graduate years; not renewable. *Number:* 2900–3500. *Amount:* $1000–$3000.

Eligibility Requirements Applicant must be of Latin American/Caribbean, Mexican, or Spanish heritage; Hispanic and enrolled or expecting to enroll full-time at a two-year or four-year institution or university. Available to U.S. citizens.

Application Requirements Application, essay, financial need analysis, references, self-addressed stamped envelope, transcript. *Deadline:* October 15.

World Wide Web: http://www.hsf.net

Contact: Art Taylor, Program Officer-College Scholarship
Hispanic Scholarship Fund
55 Second Street, Suite 1500
San Francisco, CA 94105
Phone: 415-808-2300
Fax: 415-808-2301
E-mail: info@hsf.net

COMMUNITY COLLEGE TRANSFER PROGRAMS • 419

Available to community college students in certain geographical areas transferring on a full-time basis to four-year institution in fall of following year. Must be of Hispanic descent, U.S. citizen or legal permanent resident with a minimum GPA of 3.0. *Award* Scholarship for use in freshman or sophomore years; not renewable. *Amount:* $1500–$2500.

Eligibility Requirements Applicant must be of Hispanic heritage and enrolled or expecting to enroll full-time at a two-year institution. Applicant must have 3.0 GPA or higher. Available to U.S. and non-Canadian citizens.

Application Requirements Application, essay, references, transcript. *Deadline:* February 15.

World Wide Web: http://www.hsf.net

Contact: Rita d'Escoto, Program Assistant
Hispanic Scholarship Fund
55 Second Street, Suite 1500
San Francisco, CA 94105
Phone: 415-808-2370
Fax: 415-808-2304
E-mail: rdescoto@hsf.net

GATES MILLENNIUM SCHOLARS PROGRAM • 420

Award enables Hispanic-American students to complete an undergraduate or graduate education. Must be entering a U.S.-accredited college or university as a full-time degree-seeking student. Minimum 3.3 GPA required. Must demonstrate leadership abilities. Must meet federal Pell Grant eligibility criteria. Visit Web site at http://www.gmsp.org. *Award* Scholarship for use in freshman, sophomore, junior, senior, or graduate years; renewable.

Eligibility Requirements Applicant must be Hispanic and enrolled or expecting to enroll full-time at a four-year institution or university. Available to U.S. citizens.

Application Requirements Application, financial need analysis, nomination packet. *Deadline:* February 1.

World Wide Web: http://www.hsf.net

Contact: GMS Representative
Hispanic Scholarship Fund
55 Second Street, Suite 1500
San Francisco, CA 94105
Phone: 415-217-5040
Fax: 415-217-5047
E-mail: gmsinfo@hsf.net

HIGH SCHOOL PROGRAM • 421

Designed to increase educational attainment of U.S. and Puerto Rico Hispanic high school students. Minimum 3.0 GPA required. Must be high school senior planning to attend accredited college or university the following fall semester after graduation. *Award* Scholarship for use in freshman year; not renewable. *Amount:* $1000–$2500.

Eligibility Requirements Applicant must be of Hispanic heritage; high school student and planning to enroll or expecting to enroll full-time at a two-year or four-year institution or university. Applicant must have 3.0 GPA or higher. Available to U.S. and non-Canadian citizens.

Application Requirements Application, essay, financial need analysis, references, self-addressed stamped envelope, transcript. *Deadline:* February 15.

World Wide Web: http://www.hsf.net

Contact: Sara Piredes, Program Office, High School Scholarship Program
Hispanic Scholarship Fund
55 Second Street, Suite 1500
San Francisco, CA 94105
Phone: 877-473-4636 Ext. 2372
Fax: 415-808-2304
E-mail: highschool@hsf.net

HSF/CLUB MUSICA LATINA SCHOLARSHIP • 422

Scholarships are available to Hispanic students entering their freshman or sophomore year at an accredited U.S. four-year college. Must be a member of Club Musica Latina. For more details, deadlines and an application see Web site: http://www.hsf.net. *Award* Scholarship for use in freshman or sophomore years; not renewable. *Amount:* $2500.

Eligibility Requirements Applicant must be Hispanic and enrolled or expecting to enroll full-time at a four-year institution or university. Applicant must have 3.0 GPA or higher. Available to U.S. citizens.

Application Requirements Application.

World Wide Web: http://www.hsf.net

Contact: application available at Web site

HSF/FORD MOTOR COMPANY CORPORATE SCHOLARSHIP PROGRAM • 423

Scholarships are available to Hispanic students entering their junior year at an accredited U.S. four-year college. For more details, deadlines and an application see Web site: http://www.hsf.net. *Award* Scholarship for use in junior year; not renewable. *Amount:* up to $15,000.

Eligibility Requirements Applicant must be Hispanic and enrolled or expecting to enroll full-time at a four-year institution or university. Applicant must have 3.0 GPA or higher. Available to U.S. citizens.

Application Requirements Application.

World Wide Web: http://www.hsf.net

Contact: application available at Web site

HSF/NHFA ENTERTAINMENT INDUSTRY SCHOLARSHIP PROGRAM • 424

Scholarships are available to Hispanic students pursuing their Master's degree in an entertainment-related field at an accredited U.S. university. For more details, deadlines and an application see Web site: http://www.hsf.net. *Award* Scholarship for use in graduate years; not renewable. *Amount:* $2500.

Eligibility Requirements Applicant must be Hispanic and enrolled or expecting to enroll full-time at a four-year institution or university. Applicant must have 3.0 GPA or higher. Available to U.S. citizens.

Application Requirements Application.

World Wide Web: http://www.hsf.net

Contact: application available at Web site

HSF/PFIZER, INC. FELLOWSHIP • 425

Fellowships are available to Hispanic graduate students. For more details, deadlines and an application see Web site: http://www.hsf.net. *Award* Fellowship for use in graduate years; renewable. *Amount:* $10,000.

Eligibility Requirements Applicant must be Hispanic and enrolled or expecting to enroll full-time at a four-year institution or university. Applicant must have 3.0 GPA or higher. Available to U.S. citizens.

Application Requirements Application.

World Wide Web: http://www.hsf.net

Contact: application available at Web site

HSF/SOUTH TEXAS SCHOLARSHIP • 426

Scholarships are available to undergraduate and graduate Hispanic students who have a permanent address in southern Texas. For more specifics, details, deadlines and an application see Web site: http://www.hsf.net. *Award* Scholarship for use in freshman, sophomore, junior, senior, or graduate years; not renewable. *Amount:* $1000–$2500.

Eligibility Requirements Applicant must be Hispanic; enrolled or expecting to enroll full-time at a two-year or four-year institution or university and resident of Texas. Applicant must have 3.0 GPA or higher. Available to U.S. citizens.
Application Requirements Application.
World Wide Web: http://www.hsf.net
Contact: application available at Web site

HSF/TOYOTA FOUNDATION SCHOLARSHIP PROGRAM-PUERTO RICO • 427
Scholarships are available to graduating high school seniors who are residents of Puerto Rico entering their freshman year at a Puerto Rican institution. For more details, deadlines and an application see Web site: http://www.hsf.net. *Award* Scholarship for use in freshman year; not renewable. *Amount:* $2500.

Eligibility Requirements Applicant must be Hispanic; high school student; planning to enroll or expecting to enroll full-time at a four-year institution or university; resident of Puerto Rico and studying in Puerto Rico. Applicant must have 3.0 GPA or higher. Available to U.S. citizens.
Application Requirements Application.
World Wide Web: http://www.hsf.net
Contact: application available at Web site

HSF/TOYOTA SCHOLARSHIP PROGRAM • 428
Scholarships are available to Hispanic students who are entering their freshman year. For more details, deadlines and an application see Web site: http://www.hsf.net. *Award* Scholarship for use in freshman year; not renewable.

Eligibility Requirements Applicant must be Hispanic; high school student and planning to enroll or expecting to enroll full-time at a two-year or four-year institution or university. Applicant must have 3.0 GPA or higher. Available to U.S. citizens.
Application Requirements Application.
World Wide Web: http://www.hsf.net
Contact: application available at Web site

NEW HORIZONS SCHOLARS PROGRAM • 429
Scholarships are available to Hispanic and African-American students who are infected with Hepatitis C or who are the dependent of someone infected with Hepatitis C. For more details, deadlines and an application see Web site: http://www.hsf.net. *Award* Scholarship for use in freshman, sophomore, junior, or senior years; not renewable.

Eligibility Requirements Applicant must be Black (non-Hispanic) or Hispanic and enrolled or expecting to enroll full-time at a two-year or four-year institution or university. Applicant must have 3.0 GPA or higher. Available to U.S. citizens.
Application Requirements Application.
World Wide Web: http://www.hsf.net
Contact: application available at Web site

IMGIP/ICEOP

ILLINOIS CONSORTIUM FOR EDUCATIONAL OPPORTUNITY PROGRAM FELLOWSHIP • 430
Overall intent of ICEOP is to increase the number of underrepresented faculty and staff at Illinois institutions of higher education and higher education governing boards. Requires

Illinois Consortium for Educational Opportunity Program Fellowship (continued)

minimum GPA of 2.75 in the last sixty hours of undergraduate work or over a 3.2 in at least 9 hours of graduate study. *Award* Fellowship for use in graduate years; renewable. *Number:* 160–170. *Amount:* $12,500.

Eligibility Requirements Applicant must be American Indian/Alaska Native, Asian/Pacific Islander, Black (non-Hispanic), or Hispanic; enrolled or expecting to enroll full or part-time at an institution or university; resident of Illinois and studying in Illinois. Available to U.S. citizens.

Application Requirements Application, essay, financial need analysis, references, test scores, transcript. *Deadline:* February 15.

World Wide Web: http://www.imgip.siu.edu

Contact: Ms. Jane Meuth, IMGIP/ICEOP Administrator
IMGIP/ICEOP
Woody Hall C-224, Southern Illinois University
Carbondale, IL 62901-4723
Phone: 618-453-4558
Fax: 618-453-1800
E-mail: fellows@siu.edu

JACKIE ROBINSON FOUNDATION

JACKIE ROBINSON SCHOLARSHIP   • 431

Scholarship for graduating minority high school seniors who have been accepted to accredited four-year colleges or universities. Must be U.S. citizen and show financial need, leadership potential and a high level of academic achievement. Application deadline: April 1. *Award* Scholarship for use in freshman year; renewable. *Number:* 50–60. *Amount:* up to $6000.

Eligibility Requirements Applicant must be American Indian/Alaska Native, Asian/Pacific Islander, Black (non-Hispanic), or Hispanic; high school student and planning to enroll or expecting to enroll full-time at a four-year institution. Available to U.S. citizens.

Application Requirements Application, essay, financial need analysis, references, test scores, transcript, school certification. *Deadline:* April 1.

World Wide Web: http://www.jackierobinson.org

Contact: Scholarship Program
Jackie Robinson Foundation
3 West 35th Street, 11th Floor
New York, NY 10001-2204
Phone: 212-290-8600
Fax: 212-290-8081

JOSE MARTI SCHOLARSHIP CHALLENGE GRANT FUND

JOSE MARTI SCHOLARSHIP CHALLENGE GRANT   • 432

Must apply as a senior in high school or as graduate student. Must be resident of Florida and study in Florida. Need-based, merit scholarship. Must be U.S. citizen or eligible non-citizen. Applicant must certify minimum 3.0 GPA and Hispanic origin. *Award* Scholarship for use in freshman, sophomore, junior, senior, or graduate years; renewable. *Number:* 50. *Amount:* $2000.

Eligibility Requirements Applicant must be of Hispanic heritage; enrolled or expecting to enroll full-time at a two-year or four-year institution or university; resident of Florida and studying in Florida. Applicant must have 3.0 GPA or higher. Available to U.S. citizens.

Application Requirements Application, financial need analysis. *Deadline:* April 1.

World Wide Web: http://www.floridastudentfinancialaid.org

Contact: Jose Marti Scholarship Challenge Grant Fund
1940 North Monroe Street, Suite 70
Tallahassee, FL 32303-4759
Phone: 888-827-2004

KANSAS BOARD OF REGENTS

ETHNIC MINORITY SCHOLARSHIP PROGRAM • 433

This program is designed to assist financially needy, academically competitive students who are identified as members of the following ethnic/racial groups: African-American; American-Indian or Alaskan Native; Asian or Pacific Islander; or Hispanic. Must be resident of Kansas and attend college in Kansas. Application fee is $10. Deadline: May 1. Minimum 3.0 GPA required. Must be U.S. citizen. *Award* Scholarship for use in freshman, sophomore, junior, or senior years; renewable. *Number:* 200–250. *Amount:* $1850.

Eligibility Requirements Applicant must be American Indian/Alaska Native, Asian/Pacific Islander, Black (non-Hispanic), or Hispanic; enrolled or expecting to enroll full-time at a two-year or four-year institution or university; resident of Kansas and studying in Kansas. Applicant must have 3.0 GPA or higher. Available to U.S. citizens.

Application Requirements Application, financial need analysis, test scores, transcript. *Fee:* $10. *Deadline:* May 1.

World Wide Web: http://www.kansasregents.org

Contact: Diane Lindeman, Director of Student Financial Assistance
Kansas Board of Regents
1000 Southwest Jackson, Suite 520
Topeka, KS 66612-1368
Phone: 785-296-3517
Fax: 785-296-0983
E-mail: dlindeman@ksbor.org

LATIN AMERICAN EDUCATIONAL FOUNDATION

LATIN AMERICAN EDUCATIONAL FOUNDATION SCHOLARSHIPS • 434

Scholarship award for Hispanic students or individuals actively involved in the Hispanic community who are Colorado residents planning to pursue postsecondary education. Must be a U.S. citizen with a minimum 3.0 GPA. Awards range from $500 to $3000. *Award* Scholarship for use in freshman, sophomore, junior, or senior years; not renewable. *Amount:* $500–$3000.

Eligibility Requirements Applicant must be Hispanic; enrolled or expecting to enroll full or part-time at a two-year or four-year or technical institution or university and resident of Colorado. Applicant must have 3.0 GPA or higher. Available to U.S. citizens.

Application Requirements Application, essay, financial need analysis, interview, references, self-addressed stamped envelope, test scores, transcript. *Deadline:* February 15.

World Wide Web: http://www.laef.org

Latin American Educational Foundation Scholarships (continued)

Contact: Scholarship Selection Committee
Latin American Educational Foundation
924 West Colfax Avenue, Suite 103
Denver, CO 80204-4417
Phone: 303-446-0541
Fax: 303-446-0526
E-mail: laef@uswest.net

LEAGUE OF UNITED LATIN AMERICAN CITIZENS NATIONAL EDUCATIONAL SERVICE CENTERS, INC.

LULAC NATIONAL SCHOLARSHIP FUND • 435

LULAC Councils will award scholarships to qualified Hispanic students who are enrolled or are planning to enroll in accredited colleges or universities in the United States. Applicants must be U.S. citizens or legal residents. Scholarships may be used for the payment of tuition, academic fees, room, board and the purchase of required educational materials. For additional information applicants should check LULAC Web site at http://www.lnesc.org to see a list of participating councils or send a self-addressed stamped envelope. *Award* Scholarship for use in freshman, sophomore, junior, senior, or graduate years; not renewable. *Number:* 1500–2000. *Amount:* $250–$1000.

Eligibility Requirements Applicant must be Hispanic and enrolled or expecting to enroll full-time at a two-year or four-year institution or university. Available to U.S. citizens.

Application Requirements Application, autobiography, essay, financial need analysis, interview, references, self-addressed stamped envelope, test scores, transcript. *Deadline:* March 31.

World Wide Web: http://www.lnesc.org

Contact: Scholarship Administrator
League of United Latin American Citizens National Educational Service Centers, Inc.
2000 L Street, NW
Suite 610
Washington, DC 20036

MCDONALD'S CORPORATION AND RMHC

RMHC/HISPANIC AMERICAN COMMITMENT TO EDUCATIONAL RESOURCES SCHOLARSHIP PROGRAM • 436

One-time award for graduating high school senior with at least one parent of Hispanic origin. Must attend a two-year or four-year college full time. Award is based on academic achievement, financial need, community involvement and personal qualities. Must be from a geographic area served by the program. See Web site at http://www.rmhc.org for list of geographic regions, further details, and scholarship application. *Award* Scholarship for use in freshman year; not renewable. *Amount:* up to $1000.

Eligibility Requirements Applicant must be Hispanic; high school student and planning to enroll or expecting to enroll full-time at a two-year or four-year institution.

Application Requirements Application, financial need analysis, references, transcript. *Deadline:* February 1.

World Wide Web: http://www.rmhc.org

Contact: application available at Web site

NATIONAL ACADEMIES

FORD FOUNDATION DISSERTATION FELLOWSHIPS FOR MINORITIES • 437

Applicants must be PhD or ScD degree candidates at U.S. institutions who aspire to a research and teaching career. Must be in designated minority group and a citizen or national of the U.S. Applicants strongly encouraged to use online application at: http://www.national-academies/osep/fo. *Award* Fellowship for use in graduate years; not renewable. *Number:* 35. *Amount:* $21,000.

Eligibility Requirements Applicant must be American Indian/Alaska Native, Asian/Pacific Islander, Black (non-Hispanic), or Hispanic and enrolled or expecting to enroll full-time at an institution or university. Available to U.S. citizens.
Application Requirements Application, references, transcript. *Deadline:* December 4.
World Wide Web: http://www.nationalacademies.org
Contact: Randy Higgins, Fellowship Office/GR 346A
National Academies
500 5th Street, NW
Washington, DC 20001
Phone: 202-334-2872
Fax: 202-334-3419
E-mail: infofell@nas.edu

NATIONAL ASSOCIATION FOR CAMPUS ACTIVITIES

MULTICULTURAL SCHOLARSHIP PROGRAM • 438

Scholarships will be given to applicants identified as African-American, Latina/Latino, Native-Americans, Asian-American or Pacific Islander ethnic minorities. A letter of recommendation affirming his/her ethnic minority status, his/her financial need and that he/she will be in the campus activity field at least one year following the program for which a scholarship is being sought should accompany applications. *Award* Scholarship for use in sophomore, junior, senior, or graduate years; not renewable.

Eligibility Requirements Applicant must be American Indian/Alaska Native, Asian/Pacific Islander, Black (non-Hispanic), or Hispanic; enrolled or expecting to enroll at a two-year or four-year institution or university and must have an interest in leadership. Available to U.S. citizens.
Application Requirements Application, essay, financial need analysis, references. *Deadline:* May 1.
World Wide Web: http://www.naca.org
Contact: application available at Web site

NATIONAL ASSOCIATION OF LATINO ELECTED AND APPOINTED OFFICIALS EDUCATION FUND

FORD MOTOR COMPANY FELLOWS PROGRAM • 439

One-time fellowship aimed at Latino recent graduates, college seniors and graduate students, 21 years of age and older, pursuing careers in public service. Fellows attend annual conference. Must be residents of select U.S. states and regions, including Puerto Rico. Application deadline is March 14. *Award* Fellowship for use in senior, or graduate years; not renewable. *Amount:* $1200.

Eligibility Requirements Applicant must be Hispanic; age 21; enrolled or expecting to enroll full-time at a four-year institution or university and resident of California, Florida, Illinois, Michigan, Puerto Rico, or Texas. Available to U.S. citizens.

Ford Motor Company Fellows Program (continued)

Application Requirements Application, resume, references, transcript, personal statement and legislative analysis. *Deadline:* March 14.

World Wide Web: http://www.naleo.org/

Contact: Lourdes Ferrer, Deputy Director of Constituency Services
National Association of Latino Elected and Appointed Officials Education Fund
1122 Washington Boulevard, 3rd Floor
Los Angeles, CA 90015
Phone: 213-747-7606 Ext. 127
Fax: 213-747-7664
E-mail: lferrer@naleo.org

NATIONAL ASSOCIATION OF SCHOOL PSYCHOLOGISTS-EDUCATION AND RESEARCH TRUST

NASP-ERT MINORITY SCHOLARSHIP PROGRAM   • 440

One-time scholarship of $5000 awarded to qualified and select minority graduate students. Must be U.S. Citizen. Minimum cumulative GPA of 3.0. Doctoral candidates will not be considered, only students enrolled in specialist level (or equivalent) school psychology training programs. Include transcripts, financial information (SAR), two letters of recommendation, statement of professional goals and personal accomplishments with your application. Deadline is February 1. *Award* Scholarship for use in graduate years; not renewable. *Number:* 2. *Amount:* $5000.

Eligibility Requirements Applicant must be American Indian/Alaska Native, Asian/Pacific Islander, Black (non-Hispanic), or Hispanic and enrolled or expecting to enroll full or part-time at an institution or university. Applicant must have 3.0 GPA or higher. Available to U.S. citizens.

Application Requirements Application, essay, financial need analysis, resume, references, transcript, statement of professional goals. *Deadline:* February 1.

World Wide Web: http://www.nasponline.org

Contact: Katie Britton, Manager, Special Projects
National Association of School Psychologists-Education and Research Trust
4340 East West Highway, Suite 402
Bethesda, MD 20814
Phone: 301-657-0270
Fax: 301-657-0275
E-mail: kbritton@naspweb.org

NATIONAL COUNCIL OF JEWISH WOMEN (GREATER BOSTON)

AMELIA GREENBAUM/RABBI MARSHAL LIPSON SCHOLARSHIP   • 441

Scholarships are available to aid Jewish women residing in the greater Boston area who attend a degree-granting undergraduate college in Massachusetts and whose studies are consistent with NCJW mission: to improve quality of life for women, children, and families and to ensure individual rights and freedom for all. Deadline varies. *Award* Scholarship for use in freshman, sophomore, junior, or senior years; not renewable. *Number:* 4. *Amount:* $500–$1000.

Eligibility Requirements Applicant must be Jewish; of Hebrew heritage; enrolled or expecting to enroll full or part-time at a two-year or four-year institution or university; female; resident of Massachusetts and studying in Massachusetts. Available to U.S. and non-U.S. citizens.

Application Requirements Application, essay, financial need analysis.
Contact: Laurie Ansorge Ball, Chair, Scholarship Committee, NCJW
National Council of Jewish Women (Greater Boston)
PO Box 1072
Framingham, MA 01701
Phone: 617-825-9191

NATIONAL MINORITY JUNIOR GOLF SCHOLARSHIP ASSOCIATION

NATIONAL MINORITY JUNIOR GOLF SCHOLARSHIP • 442

Awards for minority students based on academic achievement, financial need, evidence of community service, and golfing ability. Available to high school seniors who have entered information into the database located at http://www.nmjgsa.org, as well as to undergraduate students who previously received a scholarship as a freshman. Application deadline is April 15. *Award* Scholarship for use in freshman, sophomore, junior, or senior years; not renewable. *Amount:* $1000–$6000.

Eligibility Requirements Applicant must be American Indian/Alaska Native, Asian/Pacific Islander, Black (non-Hispanic), or Hispanic; enrolled or expecting to enroll at an institution or university and must have an interest in golf.
Application Requirements Application, essay, financial need analysis, references, test scores. *Deadline:* April 15.
World Wide Web: http://www.nmjgsa.org
Contact: application available at Web site

ORGANIZATION OF AMERICAN HISTORIANS

HUGGINS-QUARLES AWARD • 443

Annual one-time award for minority graduate students at the dissertation research stage of their PhD program in history. The student should submit a letter from the dissertation adviser, a two-page abstract of the dissertation project, and a budget. Application deadline December 1. *Award* Prize for use in graduate years; not renewable. *Amount:* up to $1000.

Eligibility Requirements Applicant must be American Indian/Alaska Native, Asian/Pacific Islander, Black (non-Hispanic), or Hispanic and enrolled or expecting to enroll at a four-year institution or university. Available to U.S. and non-U.S. citizens.
Application Requirements Application. *Deadline:* December 1.
World Wide Web: http://www.oah.org
Contact: Kara Hamm, Award and Prize Committee Coordinator
Organization of American Historians
112 North Bryan Avenue
Bloomington, IN 47408-4199
Phone: 812-855-9852
Fax: 812-855-0696
E-mail: awards@oah.org

PAGE EDUCATION FOUNDATION

PAGE EDUCATION FOUNDATION GRANT • 444

Grants are available to Minnesota students of color who attend Minnesota postsecondary institutions. Students must be willing to provide a minimum of 50 hours of service each year they accept a grant. This service is focused on K-8th grade children of color and encourages

Page Education Foundation Grant (continued)

the youngsters to value learning and education. Page scholars are tutors, mentors and role models. Mentors are also provided for the page scholars. *Award* Grant for use in freshman, sophomore, junior, or senior years; renewable. *Number:* 500–600. *Amount:* $900–$2500.

Eligibility Requirements Applicant must be American Indian/Alaska Native, Asian/Pacific Islander, Black (non-Hispanic), or Hispanic; enrolled or expecting to enroll full-time at a two-year or four-year or technical institution or university; resident of Minnesota and studying in Minnesota. Available to U.S. citizens.

Application Requirements Application, essay, financial need analysis, references, transcript. *Deadline:* May 1.

World Wide Web: http://www.page-ed.org

Contact: Ramona Harristhal, Administrative Director
Page Education Foundation
PO Box 581254
Minneapolis, MN 55458-1254
Phone: 612-332-0406
Fax: 612-332-0403
E-mail: pagemail@mtn.org

PRESBYTERIAN CHURCH (USA)

STUDENT OPPORTUNITY SCHOLARSHIP-PRESBYTERIAN CHURCH (U.S.A.) • 445

Available to graduating high school seniors. Applicants must be members of racial minority and be communicant members of the Presbyterian Church (U.S.A.). Renewable award based on academics and financial need. Must be a U.S. citizen. Minimum 2.5 GPA. *Award* Scholarship for use in freshman, sophomore, junior, or senior years; renewable. *Number:* up to 200. *Amount:* $100–$1000.

Eligibility Requirements Applicant must be Presbyterian; American Indian/Alaska Native, Asian/Pacific Islander, Black (non-Hispanic), or Hispanic; high school student and planning to enroll or expecting to enroll full-time at a two-year or four-year or technical institution or university. Applicant must have 2.5 GPA or higher. Available to U.S. citizens.

Application Requirements Application, autobiography, essay, financial need analysis, references, test scores, transcript. *Deadline:* May 1.

World Wide Web: http://www.pcusa.org/financialaid

Contact: Kathy Smith, Program Assistant, Undergraduate Grants
Presbyterian Church (USA)
100 Witherspoon Street
Louisville, KY 40202-1396
Phone: 888-728-7228 Ext. 5745
Fax: 502-569-8766
E-mail: ksmith@ctr.pcusa.org

RHODE ISLAND FOUNDATION

RAYMOND H. TROTT SCHOLARSHIP • 446

One-time scholarships of $1000 is awarded to a minority student, who is a Rhode Island resident entering his/her senior year at an accredited college. Must plan to pursue a career in banking. *Award* Scholarship for use in senior year; not renewable. *Number:* 1. *Amount:* $1000.

Eligibility Requirements Applicant must be American Indian/Alaska Native, Asian/Pacific Islander, Black (non-Hispanic), or Hispanic; enrolled or expecting to enroll full-time at a four-year institution or university and resident of Rhode Island. Available to U.S. citizens.

Application Requirements Application, essay, transcript. *Deadline:* June 13.

World Wide Web: http://www.rifoundation.org

Contact: Libby Monahan, Scholarship Coordinator
Rhode Island Foundation
One Union Station
Providence, RI 02903
Phone: 401-274-4564
Fax: 401-272-1359
E-mail: libbym@rifoundation.org

SALVADORAN AMERICAN LEADERSHIP AND EDUCATIONAL FUND

FULFILLING OUR DREAMS SCHOLARSHIP FUND ● 447

Up to sixty scholarships ranging from $500-$2500 will be awarded to students who come from a Hispanic heritage. Must have a 2.5 GPA. See Web site for more details: http://www.salef.org *Award* Scholarship for use in freshman, sophomore, junior, senior, graduate, or postgraduate years; not renewable. *Number:* 40–60. *Amount:* $500–$2500.

Eligibility Requirements Applicant must be of Hispanic or Latin American/Caribbean heritage and enrolled or expecting to enroll full-time at a four-year institution or university. Applicant must have 2.5 GPA or higher. Available to U.S. and non-Canadian citizens.

Application Requirements Application, essay, financial need analysis, interview, photo, resume, references, self-addressed stamped envelope, test scores, transcript. *Deadline:* June 28.

World Wide Web: http://www.salef.org

Contact: Mayra Soriano, Educational and Youth Programs Manager
Salvadoran American Leadership and Educational Fund
1625 West Olympic Boulevard, Suite 706
Los Angeles, CA 90015
Phone: 213-480-1052
Fax: 213-487-2530
E-mail: msoriano@salef.org

SOCIAL SCIENCE RESEARCH COUNCIL

SSRC-MELLON PRE-DOCTORAL RESEARCH GRANT ● 448

Awards for pre-doctoral research available only to participants in Mellon Minority Undergraduate Fellowships after they have graduated from a participating institution. For further information contact by email: mellonminority@ssrc.org. *Award* Grant for use in graduate years.

Eligibility Requirements Applicant must be American Indian/Alaska Native, Asian/Pacific Islander, Black (non-Hispanic), or Hispanic and enrolled or expecting to enroll full-time at an institution or university. Available to U.S. citizens.

Application Requirements Application.

World Wide Web: http://www.ssrc.org

SSRC-Mellon Pre-doctoral Research Grant (continued)

Contact: Patricia Bernard, Program Assistant
Social Science Research Council
810 Seventh Avenue
New York, NY 10019
Phone: 212-377-2700
Fax: 212-377-2727
E-mail: mellonminority@ssrc.org

SOCIETY FOR ADVANCEMENT OF CHICANOS AND NATIVE AMERICANS IN SCIENCE (SACNAS)

SACNAS FINANCIAL AID: LODGING AND TRAVEL AWARD • 449

Undergraduate and graduate students are encouraged to apply for lodging and travel to attend the SACNAS National Conference. The conference offers students the opportunity to be mentored, to present their research, attend scientific symposiums in all science disciplines, and professional development sessions to enhance their educational careers. *Award* Scholarship for use in freshman, sophomore, junior, or senior years; not renewable. *Number:* 400–550. *Amount:* $800–$1000.

Eligibility Requirements Applicant must be American Indian/Alaska Native, Asian/Pacific Islander, Black (non-Hispanic), or Hispanic and enrolled or expecting to enroll full or part-time at a two-year or four-year or technical institution or university. Applicant must have 2.5 GPA or higher. Available to U.S. citizens.

Application Requirements Application, essay, references, current enrollment verification. *Deadline:* June 3.

World Wide Web: http://www.sacnas.org

Contact: Rosalina Aranda, Student Program Manager
Society for Advancement of Chicanos and Native Americans in Science (SACNAS)
333 Front Street
Suite 104
Santa Cruz, CA 95060
Phone: 831-459-0170 Ext. 224
Fax: 831-459-0194
E-mail: rosalina@sacnas.org

SOCIETY OF ACTUARIES

ACTUARIAL SCHOLARSHIPS FOR MINORITY STUDENTS • 450

Award for minority students at the undergraduate or graduate level pursuing an actuarial career. Amount based on merit and individual need. Must be U.S. citizen or permanent resident. Recipients receive an additional $500 for each actuarial exam passed. Application deadline is May 1. See Web site at http://www.beanactuary.org for further details. *Award* Scholarship for use in freshman, sophomore, junior, senior, or graduate years; not renewable.

Eligibility Requirements Applicant must be American Indian/Alaska Native, Black (non-Hispanic), or Hispanic and enrolled or expecting to enroll at an institution or university. Available to U.S. citizens.

Application Requirements Application, financial need analysis, transcript. *Deadline:* May 1.

World Wide Web: http://www.soa.org

Getting Money for College: Scholarships for Hispanic Students

Contact: Minority Scholarship Coordinator
Society of Actuaries
475 North Martingale Road, Suite 800
Schaumberg, IL 60173-2226
Phone: 847-706-3500
E-mail: flupo@casct.org

SOCIETY OF PLASTICS ENGINEERS (SPE) FOUNDATION

FLEMING/BASZCAK SCHOLARSHIP ● 451

Award for full-time undergraduate or graduate student of Mexican heritage. Must have a demonstrated interest in the plastics industry. Must provide documentation of Mexican heritage. Application deadline is January 15. *Award* Scholarship for use in freshman, sophomore, junior, senior, or graduate years; not renewable. *Number:* 1. *Amount:* $2000.

Eligibility Requirements Applicant must be of Mexican heritage; Hispanic and enrolled or expecting to enroll full-time at a four-year institution or university.

Application Requirements Application, references, transcript. *Deadline:* January 15.

World Wide Web: http://www.4spe.org

Contact: Gail Bristol, Managing Director
Society of Plastics Engineers (SPE) Foundation
14 Fairfield Drive
Brookfield, CT 06804
Phone: 203-740-5447
Fax: 203-775-1157
E-mail: grbristol@4spe.org

SOUTHERN REGIONAL EDUCATION BOARD

SREB DISSERTATION YEAR FELLOWSHIP ● 452

Single-year fellowships are offered to minority students for support ($15,000/year plus tuition) while they write their dissertation. Eligible applicants will be those students who plan to become full-time faculty members upon completion of their doctoral program. For more details see Web site: http://www.sreb.org. *Award* Fellowship for use in graduate years; not renewable. *Amount:* $15,000.

Eligibility Requirements Applicant must be American Indian/Alaska Native, Asian/Pacific Islander, Black (non-Hispanic), or Hispanic and enrolled or expecting to enroll at an institution or university. Available to U.S. citizens.

Application Requirements Application, essay, references, transcript, curriculum vitae. *Deadline:* April 1.

World Wide Web: http://www.sreb.org

Contact: application available at Web site

SREB DOCTORAL SCHOLARS PROGRAM ● 453

Fellowship offers minority students a five-year package of support ($15,000/year plus tuition). For the first three years, each scholar is awarded a waiver of tuition and fees, an annual stipend and expenses associated with the program. Support for the final two years of the award is negotiated on an individual basis. For more details see Web site: http://www.sreb.org. *Award* Fellowship for use in graduate years; renewable. *Amount:* $15,000.

SREB Doctoral Scholars Program (continued)

Eligibility Requirements Applicant must be American Indian/Alaska Native, Asian/Pacific Islander, Black (non-Hispanic), or Hispanic and enrolled or expecting to enroll at an institution or university.

Application Requirements Application, transcript. *Deadline:* April 1.

World Wide Web: http://www.sreb.org

Contact: application available at Web site

UNITED METHODIST CHURCH

UNITED METHODIST CHURCH ETHNIC SCHOLARSHIP   • 454

Awards for minority students pursuing undergraduate degree. Must have been certified members of the United Methodist Church for one year. Proof of membership and pastor's statement required. One-time award but is renewable by application each year. Minimum 2.5 GPA required. *Award* Scholarship for use in freshman, sophomore, junior, or senior years; not renewable. *Number:* 430–500. *Amount:* $800–$1000.

Eligibility Requirements Applicant must be Methodist; American Indian/Alaska Native, Asian/Pacific Islander, Black (non-Hispanic), or Hispanic and enrolled or expecting to enroll full-time at a two-year or four-year institution or university. Applicant must have 2.5 GPA or higher. Available to U.S. and non-Canadian citizens.

Application Requirements Application, essay, references, transcript, membership proof, pastor's statement. *Deadline:* May 1.

World Wide Web: http://www.umc.org/

Contact: Patti J. Zimmerman, Scholarships Administrator
United Methodist Church
PO Box 340007
Nashville, TN 37203-0007
Phone: 615-340-7344
E-mail: pzimmer@gbhem.org

UNITED METHODIST CHURCH HISPANIC, ASIAN, AND NATIVE AMERICAN SCHOLARSHIP   • 455

Award for members of United Methodist Church who are Hispanic, Asian, Native-Americans, or Pacific Islander college juniors, seniors, or graduate students. Need membership proof and pastor's letter. Minimum 2.8 GPA required. *Award* Scholarship for use in junior, senior, or graduate years; not renewable. *Number:* 200–250. *Amount:* $1000–$3000.

Eligibility Requirements Applicant must be Methodist; American Indian/Alaska Native, Asian/Pacific Islander, or Hispanic and enrolled or expecting to enroll full-time at a four-year institution or university. Available to U.S. citizens.

Application Requirements Application, essay, references, transcript, membership proof, pastor's letter. *Deadline:* April 1.

World Wide Web: http://www.umc.org/

Contact: Patti J. Zimmerman, Scholarships Administrator
United Methodist Church
PO Box 340007
Nashville, TN 37203-0007
Phone: 615-340-7344
E-mail: pzimmer@gbhem.org

UNITED METHODIST YOUTH ORGANIZATION

RICHARD S. SMITH SCHOLARSHIP • 456

Open to racial/ethnic minority youth only. Must be a United Methodist Youth who has been active in his/her local church for at least one year prior to application. Must be a graduating senior in high school entering his/her first year of undergraduate study. Must be pursuing a "church-related" career. Must have maintained at least a "C" average throughout high school. *Award* Scholarship for use in freshman year; not renewable. *Amount:* up to $1000.

Eligibility Requirements Applicant must be Methodist; American Indian/Alaska Native, Asian/Pacific Islander, Black (non-Hispanic), or Hispanic; high school student and planning to enroll or expecting to enroll full-time at an institution or university. Available to U.S. citizens.

Application Requirements Application, essay, financial need analysis, transcript, certification of church membership. *Deadline:* June 1.

World Wide Web: http://www.umyouth.org

Contact: Bill Lizor, Office Assistant
United Methodist Youth Organization
PO Box 340003
Nashville, TN 37203-0003
Phone: 877-899-2780 Ext. 7184
Fax: 615-340-1764
E-mail: umyouthorg@gbod.org

VETERANS OF FOREIGN WARS

U.S. VFW MEXICAN ANCESTRY SCHOLARSHIP • 457

Scholarships for California Hispanic students through their local V.F.W. posts. Send letter requesting application and must include a self-addressed stamped envelope. *Award* Scholarship for use in freshman year. *Number:* 6. *Amount:* $3000.

Eligibility Requirements Applicant must be Hispanic; enrolled or expecting to enroll at an institution or university and resident of California. Available to U.S. citizens.

Application Requirements *Deadline:* March 15.

Contact: Emilio Holguin, Central Committee Chair
Veterans of Foreign Wars
651 Harrison Road
Monterrey Park, CA 91755-6732

WISCONSIN HIGHER EDUCATIONAL AID BOARD

MINORITY RETENTION GRANT-WISCONSIN • 458

Provides financial assistance to African-American, Native-Americans, Hispanic, and former citizens of Laos, Vietnam, and Cambodia, for study in Wisconsin. Must be Wisconsin resident, enrolled at least half-time in a two-year or four-year nonprofit college, and must show financial need. *Award* Grant for use in sophomore, junior, senior, or graduate years; not renewable. *Amount:* $250–$2500.

Eligibility Requirements Applicant must be American Indian/Alaska Native, Asian/Pacific Islander, Black (non-Hispanic), or Hispanic; enrolled or expecting to enroll full or part-time at a two-year or four-year or technical institution; resident of Wisconsin and studying in Wisconsin. Available to U.S. and non-U.S. citizens.

Application Requirements Application, financial need analysis. *Deadline:* Continuous.

World Wide Web: http://www.heab.state.wi.us

Minority Retention Grant-Wisconsin (continued)

Contact: Mary Lou Kuzdas, Program Coordinator
Wisconsin Higher Educational Aid Board
PO Box 7885
Madison, WI 53707-7885
Phone: 608-267-2212
Fax: 608-267-2808
E-mail: mary.kuzdas@heab.state.wi.us

WORLDSTUDIO FOUNDATION

SPECIAL ANIMATION AND ILLUSTRATION SCHOLARSHIP   • 459

Scholarships are for minority and economically disadvantaged students who are studying illustration, cartooning and animation in American colleges and universities. Scholarship recipients are selected not only for their ability and their need, but also for their demonstrated commitment to giving back to the larger community through their work. *Award* Scholarship for use in freshman, sophomore, junior, senior, or graduate years; not renewable. *Number:* 25. *Amount:* $1500.

Eligibility Requirements Applicant must be American Indian/Alaska Native, Asian/Pacific Islander, Black (non-Hispanic), or Hispanic and enrolled or expecting to enroll full-time at a two-year or four-year or technical institution or university. Applicant must have 2.5 GPA or higher. Available to U.S. and non-U.S. citizens.

Application Requirements Application, essay, financial need analysis, photo, portfolio, references, self-addressed stamped envelope, transcript. *Deadline:* February 14.

World Wide Web: http://www.worldstudio.org

Contact: Roben Stikeman, Associate Director
Worldstudio Foundation
200 Varick Street, Suite 507
New York, NY 10014
Phone: 212-366-1317 Ext. 18
Fax: 212-807-0024
E-mail: scholarships@worldstudio.org

YOUTH OPPORTUNITIES FOUNDATION

YOUTH OPPORTUNITIES FOUNDATION SCHOLARSHIPS   • 460

Scholarships for Hispanic/Latino high school students that rank in the top 10 of their class and score at least 1000 on the SATs. AP classes, leadership skills and community activities will be weighed toward consideration. Must be California resident. At least one parent must be of Hispanic descent. Students must write foundation for an application. *Award* Scholarship for use in freshman year; not renewable. *Number:* 100. *Amount:* $100–$500.

Eligibility Requirements Applicant must be Hispanic; high school student; planning to enroll or expecting to enroll full-time at a two-year or four-year institution or university; resident of California and must have an interest in leadership.

Application Requirements Application, test scores. *Deadline:* March 29.

Contact: Youth Opportunities Foundation
8820 South Sepulveda Boulevard, Suite 208
PO Box 45762
Los Angeles, CA 90045

RELIGIOUS AFFILIATION_____

GENERAL BOARD OF GLOBAL MINISTRIES
NATIONAL LEADERSHIP DEVELOPMENT GRANTS　　see number 407

JEWISH FOUNDATION FOR EDUCATION OF WOMEN
BILLER/JEWISH FOUNDATION FOR EDUCATION OF WOMEN　● **461**
This program provides scholarships to female Jewish permanent residents in the NY metropolitan area for undergraduate and graduate study. Financial need and reasonableness of course of study are the primary criteria. Must study full-time in NY. Check Web site for further details: http://www.jfew.org. *Award* Scholarship for use in freshman, sophomore, junior, senior, or graduate years; not renewable. *Amount:* $2000–$4000.

Eligibility Requirements Applicant must be Jewish; enrolled or expecting to enroll full-time at a two-year or four-year or technical institution or university; female; resident of New York and studying in New York. Available to U.S. and non-Canadian citizens.
Application Requirements Application, essay, financial need analysis. *Deadline:* May 1.
World Wide Web: http://www.jfew.org
Contact:　Marge Goldwater, Executive Director
　　　　　Jewish Foundation for Education of Women
　　　　　135 East 64th Street
　　　　　New York, NY 10021
　　　　　Phone: 212-288-3931
　　　　　Fax: 212-288-5798
　　　　　E-mail: fdnscholar@aol.com

NATIONAL COUNCIL OF JEWISH WOMEN (GREATER BOSTON)
AMELIA GREENBAUM/RABBI MARSHAL LIPSON SCHOLARSHIP　　see number 441

PRESBYTERIAN CHURCH (USA)
STUDENT OPPORTUNITY SCHOLARSHIP-PRESBYTERIAN CHURCH (U.S.A.)
　　see number 445

UNITED METHODIST CHURCH
UNITED METHODIST CHURCH ETHNIC SCHOLARSHIP　　see number 454

UNITED METHODIST CHURCH HISPANIC, ASIAN, AND NATIVE AMERICAN SCHOLARSHIP　　see number 455

UNITED METHODIST YOUTH ORGANIZATION
RICHARD S. SMITH SCHOLARSHIP　　see number 456

WOMEN OF THE EVANGELICAL LUTHERAN CHURCH IN AMERICA

ARNE ADMINISTRATIVE SCHOLARSHIP • 462

Scholarship provides assistance to women interested in reaching the top of their field as an administrator. Must hold membership in the ELCA and have at least a bachelor's degree. For more details see Web site: http://www.elca.org/wo. *Award* Scholarship for use in graduate years; not renewable. *Amount:* up to $450.

Eligibility Requirements Applicant must be Lutheran; enrolled or expecting to enroll full or part-time at an institution or university and female. Available to U.S. citizens.

Application Requirements *Deadline:* February 15.

World Wide Web: http://www.elca.org/wo

Contact: application available at Web site

BELMER/FLORA PRINCE SCHOLARSHIP • 463

Scholarships provided for ELCA women studying for ELCA service. Must be at least 21 years old and hold membership in the ELCA. Must have experienced an interruption in education of two or more years since the completion of high school. For more details see Web site: http://www.elca.org/wo. *Award* Scholarship for use in freshman, sophomore, junior, senior, or graduate years; not renewable. *Number:* 2. *Amount:* up to $1200.

Eligibility Requirements Applicant must be Lutheran; age 21; enrolled or expecting to enroll at an institution or university and female. Available to U.S. citizens.

Application Requirements *Deadline:* February 15.

World Wide Web: http://www.elca.org/wo

Contact: application available at Web site

ELCA SCHOLARSHIPS FOR WOMEN • 464

Several named scholarships provided for ELCA women in undergraduate, graduate, professional or vocational courses of study. Must be at least 21 years old and hold membership in the ELCA. Must have experienced an interruption in education of two or more years since the completion of high school. For more details see Web site: http://www.elca.org/wo. *Award* Scholarship for use in freshman, sophomore, junior, senior, or graduate years; not renewable. *Number:* 7. *Amount:* up to $1200.

Eligibility Requirements Applicant must be Lutheran; age 21; enrolled or expecting to enroll at a two-year or four-year or technical institution or university and female. Available to U.S. citizens.

Application Requirements *Deadline:* February 15.

World Wide Web: http://www.elca.org/wo

Contact: application available at Web site

STATE OF RESIDENCE

ALUMNAE PANHELLENIC ASSOCIATION OF WASHINGTON, D.C.

ALUMNAE PANHELLENIC ASSOCIATION OF WASHINGTON, D.C. SCHOLARSHIP • 465

One-time award for women pursuing postsecondary studies in Maryland, Virginia, or the District of Columbia. Application deadline is March 15. *Award* Scholarship for use in freshman, sophomore, junior, senior, graduate, or postgraduate years; not renewable. *Number:* 3. *Amount:* $500–$1000.

Eligibility Requirements Applicant must be enrolled or expecting to enroll full or part-time at a two-year or four-year institution or university; female and studying in District of Columbia, Maryland, or Virginia. Available to U.S. and non-U.S. citizens.

Application Requirements Application, essay. *Deadline:* March 15.

Contact: Victoria Lynn Barron, President Alumnae, Panhellenic Association of Washington, D.C.

Alumnae Panhellenic Association of Washington, D.C.
1253 Creek Drive
Annapolis, MD 21403
Phone: 240-305-5179
E-mail: victoria_barron@hotmail.com

AMARILLO AREA FOUNDATION

AMARILLO WOMEN'S NETWORK NANCY SAMPLE GARMS SCHOLARSHIP • 466

Scholarships are available to female residents of the 26 northernmost counties of the Texas Panhandle. Women who are single parents and married women who are attempting to complete their education will be given special consideration. For more details and an application see Web site: http://www.aaf-hf.org. *Award* Scholarship for use in freshman, sophomore, junior, or senior years; not renewable. *Amount:* $400.

Eligibility Requirements Applicant must be enrolled or expecting to enroll at an institution or university; female and resident of Texas. Applicant must have 2.5 GPA or higher. Available to U.S. citizens.

Application Requirements Application. *Deadline:* April 1.

World Wide Web: http://www.aaf-hf.org/

Contact: application available at Web site

AMERICAN LEGION AUXILIARY, DEPARTMENT OF COLORADO

AMERICAN LEGION AUXILIARY DEPARTMENT OF COLORADO DEPARTMENT PRESIDENT'S SCHOLARSHIP FOR JUNIOR MEMBERS   see number 346

AMERICAN LEGION AUXILIARY, DEPARTMENT OF FLORIDA

AMERICAN LEGION AUXILIARY DEPARTMENT OF FLORIDA MEMORIAL SCHOLARSHIP   see number 347

AMERICAN LEGION AUXILIARY, DEPARTMENT OF KENTUCKY

MARY BARRETT MARSHALL SCHOLARSHIP   see number 348

AMERICAN LEGION AUXILIARY, DEPARTMENT OF MARYLAND

AMERICAN LEGION AUXILIARY DEPARTMENT OF MARYLAND CHILDREN AND YOUTH SCHOLARSHIPS   see number 377

AMERICAN LEGION AUXILIARY, DEPARTMENT OF MICHIGAN

AMERICAN LEGION AUXILIARY DEPARTMENT OF MICHIGAN MEMORIAL SCHOLARSHIP   see number 378

AMERICAN LEGION AUXILIARY, DEPARTMENT OF MISSOURI

LELA MURPHY SCHOLARSHIP   see number 349

AMERICAN LEGION AUXILIARY, DEPARTMENT OF NEBRASKA

AMERICAN LEGION AUXILIARY DEPARTMENT OF NEBRASKA PRESIDENT'S SCHOLARSHIP FOR JUNIOR MEMBERS   see number 350

AMERICAN LEGION AUXILIARY, DEPARTMENT OF OREGON

AMERICAN LEGION AUXILIARY DEPARTMENT OF OREGON SPIRIT OF YOUTH SCHOLARSHIP   see number 351

AMERICAN LEGION AUXILIARY, DEPARTMENT OF SOUTH DAKOTA

AMERICAN LEGION AUXILIARY DEPARTMENT OF SOUTH DAKOTA THELMA FOSTER SCHOLARSHIP FOR SENIOR AUXILIARY MEMBERS   see number 352

AMERICAN LEGION AUXILIARY DEPARTMENT OF SOUTH DAKOTA THELMA FOSTER SCHOLARSHIPS FOR JUNIOR AUXILIARY MEMBERS   see number 353

AMERICAN LEGION AUXILIARY, DEPARTMENT OF SOUTH DAKOTA SENIOR SCHOLARSHIP   see number 354

AMERICAN LEGION AUXILIARY, DEPARTMENT OF WASHINGTON

AMERICAN LEGION AUXILIARY DEPARTMENT OF WASHINGTON SUSAN BURDETT SCHOLARSHIP   • 467

Applicant must be a former citizen of Evergreen Girls State. Applications must be obtained and processed through a Washington State American Legion Auxiliary Unit. One-time award of $500. *Award* Scholarship for use in freshman, sophomore, junior, or senior years; not renewable. *Number:* 1. *Amount:* $500.

Eligibility Requirements Applicant must be enrolled or expecting to enroll at an institution or university; female and resident of Washington. Available to U.S. citizens.

Application Requirements Application, essay, references, transcript. *Deadline:* April 1.

World Wide Web: http://www.walegion-aux.org
Contact: Education Chairman
American Legion Auxiliary, Department of Washington
PO Box 5867
Lacey, WA 98509-5867
Phone: 360-456-5995

ARIZONA ASSOCIATION OF CHICANOS IN HIGHER EDUCATION (AACHE)

AACHE SCHOLARSHIP
see number 385

ARKANSAS COMMUNITY FOUNDATION, INC.

SOUTHWESTERN BELL BATES SCHOLARSHIP FUND
see number 386

ASTRAEA LESBIAN ACTION FOUNDATION

MARGOT KARLE SCHOLARSHIP FOR CUNY WOMEN STUDENTS • 468
One-time award for full-time female undergraduate students enrolled at City University of New York system schools only. *Award* Scholarship for use in freshman, sophomore, junior, or senior years; not renewable. *Number:* 1. *Amount:* $1000.

Eligibility Requirements Applicant must be enrolled or expecting to enroll full-time at a four-year institution or university; female and studying in New York. Available to U.S. citizens.
Application Requirements Application, essay, references, transcript. *Deadline:* June 1.
World Wide Web: http://www.astraea.org
Contact: Astraea Lesbian Action Foundation
116 East 16th Street, Seventh Floor
New York, NY 10003
E-mail: grants@astraea.org

BARBARA ALICE MOWER MEMORIAL SCHOLARSHIP COMMITTEE

BARBARA ALICE MOWER MEMORIAL SCHOLARSHIP • 469
Award for women residents of Hawaii who are committed to using their education to help other women, especially women of Hawaii. Must be junior or senior level undergraduate. Graduate level also eligible. *Award* Scholarship for use in junior, senior, graduate, or postgraduate years; not renewable. *Number:* 1–25. *Amount:* $1000–$3500.

Eligibility Requirements Applicant must be enrolled or expecting to enroll full-time at a four-year institution or university; female and resident of Hawaii. Available to U.S. citizens.
Application Requirements Application, essay, references, transcript. *Deadline:* May 1.
Contact: Nancy Mower
Barbara Alice Mower Memorial Scholarship Committee
1536 Kamole Street
Honolulu, HI 96821
Phone: 808-373-2901
E-mail: nmower@hawaii.edu

BECA FOUNDATION, INC.

DANIEL GUTIERREZ MEMORIAL GENERAL SCHOLARSHIP FUND   see number 387

GENERAL SCHOLARSHIP FUND   see number 388

CALIFORNIA JUNIOR MISS SCHOLARSHIP PROGRAM

CALIFORNIA JUNIOR MISS SCHOLARSHIP PROGRAM   • 470

Scholarship program to recognize and reward outstanding high school junior girls in the areas of academics, leadership, athletics, public speaking and the arts. Must be single, female, a U.S. citizen, and resident of California. Minimum 3.0 GPA required. *Award* Scholarship for use in freshman year; not renewable. *Number:* 10–20. *Amount:* $300–$10,000.

Eligibility Requirements Applicant must be high school student; planning to enroll or expecting to enroll full-time at a two-year or four-year institution or university; single female; resident of California and must have an interest in leadership. Applicant must have 3.0 GPA or higher. Available to U.S. citizens.

Application Requirements Application, applicant must enter a contest, interview, test scores, transcript. *Deadline:* January 1.

World Wide Web: http://www.ajm.org/california

Contact: Becky Jo Peterson, California State Chairman
California Junior Miss Scholarship Program
3523 Glenbrook Lane
Napa, CA 94558
Phone: 707-224-5112
E-mail: caljrmiss@aol.com

CANADIAN FEDERATION OF UNIVERSITY WOMEN

BEVERLEY JACKSON FELLOWSHIP   see number 391

CENTRAL SCHOLARSHIP BUREAU

MARY RUBIN AND BENJAMIN M. RUBIN SCHOLARSHIP FUND   • 471

Renewable scholarship for tuition only to women who are attending a college, university or other institution of higher learning. Must be a resident of Maryland. Have a GPA of 3.0 or better and meet the financial requirements. Contact for application or download from Web site. *Award* Scholarship for use in freshman, sophomore, junior, senior, graduate, or postgraduate years; renewable. *Number:* 30–35. *Amount:* $500–$2500.

Eligibility Requirements Applicant must be enrolled or expecting to enroll full or part-time at a two-year or four-year or technical institution or university; female and resident of Maryland. Applicant must have 3.0 GPA or higher. Available to U.S. citizens.

Application Requirements Application, essay, financial need analysis, references, transcript. *Deadline:* March 1.

World Wide Web: http://www.centralsb.org

Contact: Roberta Goldman, Program Director
Central Scholarship Bureau
1700 Reisterstown Road
Suite 220
Baltimore, MD 21208-2903
Phone: 410-415-5558
Fax: 410-415-5501
E-mail: roberta@centralsb.org

CITY COLLEGE OF SAN FRANCISCO LATINO EDUCATIONAL ASSOCIATION

LATINO EDUCATION ASSOCIATION SCHOLARSHIP see number 395

COLORADO BUSINESS AND PROFESSIONAL WOMEN'S FOUNDATION SCHOLARSHIP

COLORADO BUSINESS AND PROFESSIONAL WOMEN'S FOUNDATION SCHOLARSHIP • 472

Ten to 20 scholarships awarded annually to women who are at least 26 years old and are Colorado residents attending an institution of higher education in Colorado. Scholarship program is designed to promote economic self-sufficiency for women. Recipients are generally low-income single mothers. Deadlines: March 31, June 30, October 31. Must be U.S. citizen. *Award* Scholarship for use in freshman, sophomore, junior, senior, graduate, or postgraduate years; not renewable. *Number:* 10–20. *Amount:* $300–$1000.

Eligibility Requirements Applicant must be age 26; enrolled or expecting to enroll full or part-time at a two-year or four-year or technical institution or university; female; resident of Colorado and studying in Colorado. Available to U.S. citizens.

Application Requirements Application, driver's license, essay, financial need analysis, references, transcript, proof of U.S. citizenship. *Deadline:* Continuous.

Contact: Scholarship Committee/CBPWF
Colorado Business and Professional Women's Foundation Scholarship
PO Box 1189
Boulder, CO 80306
Phone: 303-443-2573
Fax: 720-564-0397
E-mail: cbpwf@earthnet.net

COMMUNITY FOUNDATION FOR PALM BEACH AND MARTIN COUNTIES, INC.

CLAIRE B. SCHULTZ MEMORIAL SCHOLARSHIP • 473

Graduating seniors from a Palm Beach County High School. Based on financial need. Special preference to handicapped or minority students. *Award* Scholarship for use in freshman year; not renewable. *Amount:* $750–$2500.

Eligibility Requirements Applicant must be high school student; planning to enroll or expecting to enroll full-time at a two-year or four-year or technical institution or university and resident of Florida. Available to U.S. citizens.

Application Requirements Application, financial need analysis. *Deadline:* March 1.

World Wide Web: http://www.cfpbmc.org

Contact: Carolyn Jenco, Grants Manager/Scholarship Coordinator
Community Foundation for Palm Beach and Martin Counties, Inc.
700 South Dixie Highway
Suite 200
West Palm Beach, FL 33401

COLONIAL BANK SCHOLARSHIP see number 396

COURTLAND AND GINA MILLER SCHOLARSHIP FUND • 474

Graduating senior from Palm Beach or Martin Counties with preference to minority students. Consideration given for extra-ordinary circumstances, financial need. *Award* Scholarship for use in freshman year; not renewable. *Number:* 1. *Amount:* $750–$2500.

Eligibility Requirements Applicant must be high school student; planning to enroll or expecting to enroll full-time at a two-year or four-year or technical institution or university and resident of Florida. Available to U.S. citizens.

Application Requirements Application, financial need analysis. *Deadline:* March 1.

World Wide Web: http://www.cfpbmc.org

Contact: Carolyn Jenco, Grants Manager/Scholarship Coordinator
Community Foundation for Palm Beach and Martin Counties, Inc.
700 South Dixie Highway
Suite 200
West Palm Beach, FL 33401

DENISE LYNN PADGETT SCHOLARSHIP FUND • 475

Female graduating senior from Palm Beach or Martin Counties. Minimum of two years participation on high school/women's softball team; demonstrated financial aid. *Award* Scholarship for use in freshman year; not renewable. *Number:* 1. *Amount:* $750–$2500.

Eligibility Requirements Applicant must be high school student; planning to enroll or expecting to enroll full-time at a two-year or four-year or technical institution or university; female and resident of Florida. Available to U.S. citizens.

Application Requirements Application, financial need analysis. *Deadline:* March 1.

World Wide Web: http://www.cfpbmc.org

Contact: Carolyn Jenco, Grants Manager/Scholarship Coordinator
Community Foundation for Palm Beach and Martin Counties, Inc.
700 South Dixie Highway
Suite 200
West Palm Beach, FL 33401

GUBELMANN FAMILY FOUNDATION SCHOLARSHIP FUND • 476

For Palm Beach County and Martin County, Florida graduating high school seniors demonstrating financial need. Preference given to minority applicants. Maybe from public or private institutions. *Award* Scholarship for use in freshman year; not renewable. *Amount:* $750–$2500.

Eligibility Requirements Applicant must be high school student; planning to enroll or expecting to enroll full-time at a two-year or four-year or technical institution or university and resident of Florida. Available to U.S. citizens.

Application Requirements Application, financial need analysis. *Deadline:* March 1.

World Wide Web: http://www.cfpbmc.org

Contact: Carolyn Jenco, Grants Manager/Scholarship Coordinator
Community Foundation for Palm Beach and Martin Counties, Inc.
700 South Dixie Highway
Suite 200
West Palm Beach, FL 33401

HARRY AND BERTHA BRONSTEIN MEMORIAL SCHOLARSHIP • 477

For graduating high school seniors who are residents of Palm Beach and Martin Counties demonstrating financial need with special preference given to students who are either members of a minority group or handicapped. These may be two or four year scholarships but are restricted to undergraduate support. *Award* Scholarship for use in freshman, sophomore, junior, or senior years; renewable. *Amount:* $750–$2500.

Eligibility Requirements Applicant must be high school student; planning to enroll or expecting to enroll full-time at a two-year or four-year institution or university and resident of Florida. Available to U.S. citizens.

Application Requirements Application, financial need analysis. *Deadline:* March 1.

World Wide Web: http://www.cfpbmc.org

Contact: Carolyn Jenco, Grants Manager/Scholarship Coordinator
Community Foundation for Palm Beach and Martin Counties, Inc.
700 South Dixie Highway
Suite 200
West Palm Beach, FL 33401

MATTHEW "BUMP" MITCHELL /SUN-SENTINEL SCHOLARSHIP • 478

Graduating student from South Palm Beach County, Florida who excels in scholastics, demonstrates community service and has financial need. Preference given to minority students. *Award* Scholarship for use in freshman year; not renewable. *Number:* 1. *Amount:* $750–$2500.

Eligibility Requirements Applicant must be high school student; planning to enroll or expecting to enroll full-time at a two-year or four-year or technical institution or university and resident of Florida. Available to U.S. citizens.

Application Requirements Application, financial need analysis. *Deadline:* March 1.

World Wide Web: http://www.cfpbmc.org

Contact: Carolyn Jenco, Grants Manager/Scholarship Coordinator
Community Foundation for Palm Beach and Martin Counties, Inc.
700 South Dixie Highway
Suite 200
West Palm Beach, FL 33401

CONNECTICUT ASSOCIATION OF LATIN AMERICANS IN HIGHER EDUCATION (CALAHE)

CONNECTICUT ASSOCIATION OF LATIN AMERICANS IN HIGHER EDUCATION SCHOLARSHIPS
see number 399

CUBAN AMERICAN SCHOLARSHIP FUND

CUBAN AMERICAN SCHOLARSHIP FUND • 479

One-time award for California residents who were either born in Cuba or have parents or grandparents born in Cuba. Application dates are from January 1 to April 15. Mail an SASE for an application. *Award* Scholarship for use in freshman, sophomore, junior, senior, or graduate years; not renewable. *Number:* 8–15. *Amount:* $500–$1500.

Eligibility Requirements Applicant must be enrolled or expecting to enroll full-time at an institution or university and resident of California. Applicant must have 3.0 GPA or higher. Available to U.S. citizens.

Application Requirements Application, self-addressed stamped envelope. *Deadline:* April 15.

Contact: Cuban American Scholarship Fund
PO Box 6422
Santa Ana, CA 92706

DELAWARE HIGHER EDUCATION COMMISSION

AGENDA FOR DELAWARE WOMEN TRAILBLAZER SCHOLARSHIP • 480

Scholarships given to women residing in Delaware and enrolling in a public or private non-profit college in Delaware as an undergraduate student. Must have a 2.5 GPA. Deadline: April 15. *Award* Scholarship for use in freshman, sophomore, junior, or senior years; not renewable. *Amount:* $2500.

Eligibility Requirements Applicant must be enrolled or expecting to enroll at a two-year or four-year institution; female; resident of Delaware and studying in Delaware. Applicant must have 2.5 GPA or higher.

Application Requirements Financial need analysis. *Deadline:* April 15.

World Wide Web: http://www.doe.state.de.us/high-ed

Contact: Donna Myers, Higher Education Analyst
Delaware Higher Education Commission
820 North French Street
5th Floor
Wilmington, DE 19711-3509
Phone: 302-577-3240
Fax: 302-577-6765
E-mail: dhec@doe.k12.de.us

EAST LOS ANGELES COMMUNITY UNION (TELACU) EDUCATION FOUNDATION

DAVID C. LIZARRAGA FELLOWSHIP
see number 402

ESPERANZA, INC.

ESPERANZA SCHOLARSHIPS
see number 403

FAMILY CIRCLE CUP AND L'OREAL

L'OREAL /FAMILY CIRCLE CUP "PERSONAL BEST" SCHOLARSHIP • 481

Purpose of scholarship is to honor females who make a difference in the lives of others through role modeling, community involvement and services, volunteer experiences, and extracurricular activities. The scholarship will be applied towards college costs. Applicant must be a resident of Georgia, North Carolina or South Carolina. Open to high school students. *Award* Scholarship for use in freshman year; not renewable. *Number:* 3. *Amount:* $2500.

Eligibility Requirements Applicant must be high school student; planning to enroll or expecting to enroll full-time at a two-year or four-year or technical institution or university; female and resident of Georgia, North Carolina, or South Carolina. Available to U.S. and non-U.S. citizens.

Application Requirements Application, essay, references, transcript. *Deadline:* February 15.

World Wide Web: http://www.familycirclecup.com

Contact: Bryan Hutto, Sales Coordinator
Family Circle Cup and L'Oreal
161 Seven Farms Drive
Daniel Island
Charleston, SC 29492
Phone: 843-856-7900
Fax: 843-856-7901
E-mail: bhutto@gjusa.com

FLORIDA BOARD OF EDUCATION, DIVISION OF COLLEGES AND UNIVERSITIES

DELORES A. AUZENNE FELLOWSHIP FOR GRADUATE STUDY   see number 404

FLORIDA DEPARTMENT OF EDUCATION

JOSE MARTI SCHOLARSHIP CHALLENGE GRANT FUND   see number 405

ROSEWOOD FAMILY SCHOLARSHIP FUND   see number 406

FLORIDA WOMEN'S STATE GOLF ASSOCIATION

FLORIDA WOMEN'S STATE GOLF ASSOCIATION SCHOLARSHIP FUND   • 482

The FWSGA Scholarship Fund is designed to assist young women to whom golf is meaningful with their education. Applicants must be Florida residents, play golf, maintain a 3.0 GPA, attend a Florida college or university, and have a need for financial assistance. *Award* Scholarship for use in freshman, sophomore, junior, or senior years; renewable. *Amount:* $1000–$2000.

Eligibility Requirements Applicant must be age 18; enrolled or expecting to enroll full-time at a two-year or four-year institution or university; female; resident of Florida; studying in Florida and must have an interest in golf. Applicant must have 3.0 GPA or higher. Available to U.S. citizens.

Application Requirements Application, financial need analysis, interview, references, test scores, transcript. *Deadline:* February 28.

World Wide Web: http://www.fwsga.org

Contact: Judith Comella, Executive Director
Florida Women's State Golf Association
10,000 North US Highway 98, #107
Lakeland, FL 33809-1045
Phone: 863-815-1646
Fax: 863-816-9701
E-mail: fwsga@usga.org

FRESH START SCHOLARSHIP FOUNDATION, INC.

FRESH START SCHOLARSHIP   • 483

Scholarship offering a "fresh start" to women who are returning to school after a hiatus to better their life and opportunities. Must be entering an undergraduate program in Delaware. *Award* Scholarship for use in freshman, sophomore, junior, or senior years; not renewable. *Number:* up to 10. *Amount:* $750–$2000.

Eligibility Requirements Applicant must be age 20; enrolled or expecting to enroll full or part-time at a two-year or four-year institution or university; female and studying in Delaware. Available to U.S. and non-U.S. citizens.

Application Requirements Application, essay, financial need analysis, references, transcript. *Deadline:* May 30.

World Wide Web: http://www.wwb.org/fresh.htm

Fresh Start Scholarship (continued)

Contact: Cindy Cheyney, Secretary
Fresh Start Scholarship Foundation, Inc.
c/o Master, Sidlow & Associates, P.A.
2002 West 14th Street
Wilmington, DE 19806
Phone: 302-656-4411
Fax: 610-347-0438
E-mail: ccheyney@delanet.com

GENERAL FEDERATION OF WOMEN'S CLUBS IN WYOMING

MARY N. BROOKS DAUGHTER/GRANDDAUGHTER SCHOLARSHIP   see number 362

MARY N. BROOKS WYOMING GIRL SCHOLARSHIP   • 484

Award given yearly to any female high school graduate who will be attending any school of higher learning in the state of Wyoming. Must be a resident of Wyoming. Award is based on scholarship, community/school involvement, and financial need. Minimum 3.0 GPA required. Deadline: March 15. *Award* Scholarship for use in freshman, sophomore, junior, or senior years; not renewable. *Number:* 1. *Amount:* $500.

Eligibility Requirements Applicant must be enrolled or expecting to enroll full-time at a two-year or four-year or technical institution or university; female; resident of Wyoming and studying in Wyoming. Applicant must have 3.0 GPA or higher. Available to U.S. citizens.

Application Requirements Application, autobiography, financial need analysis, resume, references, transcript. *Deadline:* March 15.

Contact: Mrs. Norine Samuelson, Custodian, Scholarship Funds
General Federation of Women's Clubs in Wyoming
2005 Eagle Drive
Cheyenne, WY 82009
Phone: 307-638-9443
Fax: 307-433-1020
E-mail: samuelson63291@msn.com

RUTH CLARE YONKEE DISTRICT SCHOLARSHIP   • 485

Annual award given to a female high school graduate who will be attending a school of higher learning in Wyoming. Applicant must live in the geographic area of Wyoming designated for that year. For 2004, recipient must be from South District. Award is based on scholarship, community/school involvement, and financial need. Minimum 3.0 GPA required. *Award* Scholarship for use in freshman, sophomore, junior, or senior years; not renewable. *Number:* 1. *Amount:* $250.

Eligibility Requirements Applicant must be enrolled or expecting to enroll full-time at a two-year or four-year or technical institution or university; female; resident of Wyoming and studying in Wyoming. Applicant must have 3.0 GPA or higher. Available to U.S. citizens.

Application Requirements Application, autobiography, financial need analysis, resume, references, transcript. *Deadline:* March 15.

Contact: Mrs. Norine Samuelson, Custodian, Scholarship Funds
General Federation of Women's Clubs in Wyoming
2005 Eagle Drive
Cheyenne, WY 82009
Phone: 307-638-9443
Fax: 307-433-1020
E-mail: samuelson63291@msn.com

GENERAL FEDERATION OF WOMEN'S CLUBS OF MASSACHUSETTS

GENERAL FEDERATION OF WOMEN'S CLUBS OF MASSACHUSETTS MEMORIAL EDUCATION FELLOWSHIP • 486

Must be a female graduate student maintaining residence in Massachusetts for at least five years and must submit a letter of endorsement from president of the sponsoring General Federation of Women's Clubs of Massachusetts club. Applicable fields of study vary yearly. Submit a personal statement of no more than 500 words addressing professional goals and financial need. *Award* Fellowship for use in graduate years; not renewable. *Amount:* $3000.

Eligibility Requirements Applicant must be enrolled or expecting to enroll full-time at an institution or university; female and resident of Massachusetts.

Application Requirements Application, autobiography, interview, references, self-addressed stamped envelope, transcript. *Deadline:* March 1.

Contact: Shirley Gomes, Chairman of Trustees
General Federation of Women's Clubs of Massachusetts
PO Box 679
Sudbury, MA 01776-0679
Phone: 508-432-1431
E-mail: rickygomes@attbi.com

GENERAL FEDERATION OF WOMEN'S CLUBS OF VERMONT

BARBARA JEAN BARKER MEMORIAL SCHOLARSHIP FOR A DISPLACED HOMEMAKER • 487

A non-traditional scholarship designed for a woman who has been primarily a homemaker for 14-20 years and has lost her main means of support through divorce, separation or death of a spouse, and needs retraining for re-entry to the world of work. Must be a Vermont resident. *Award* Grant for use in freshman, sophomore, junior, senior, or graduate years; not renewable. *Number:* 1–3. *Amount:* $500–$1500.

Eligibility Requirements Applicant must be age 35; enrolled or expecting to enroll full or part-time at a two-year or four-year or technical institution or university; female and resident of Vermont. Available to U.S. citizens.

Application Requirements Application, autobiography, financial need analysis, interview, references. *Deadline:* March 15.

Contact: Marie Hall, Scholarship Chairman
General Federation of Women's Clubs of Vermont
PO Box 787
Milton, VT 05468
Phone: 802-893-2378

GIRL SCOUTS OF GULFCOAST FLORIDA, INC.

GULFCOAST COLLEGE SCHOLARSHIP AWARD
see number 363

HISPANIC PUBLIC RELATIONS ASSOCIATION

SCHOLARSHIP PROGRAM
see number 417

HISPANIC SCHOLARSHIP FUND

HSF/SOUTH TEXAS SCHOLARSHIP   see number 426

HSF/TOYOTA FOUNDATION SCHOLARSHIP PROGRAM-PUERTO RICO
                                                                   see number 427

IDAHO STATE BOARD OF EDUCATION

IDAHO MINORITY AND "AT RISK" STUDENT SCHOLARSHIP   • 488

Renewable award for Idaho residents who are disabled or members of a minority group and have financial need. Must attend one of eight postsecondary institutions in the state for undergraduate study. Deadlines vary by institution. Must be a U.S. citizen and be a graduate of an Idaho high school. Contact college financial aid office. *Award* Scholarship for use in freshman, sophomore, junior, or senior years; renewable. *Number:* 38–40. *Amount:* $3000.

Eligibility Requirements Applicant must be enrolled or expecting to enroll full-time at a two-year or four-year institution or university; resident of Idaho and studying in Idaho. Available to U.S. citizens.
Application Requirements Application, financial need analysis.
World Wide Web: http://www.idahoboardofed.org
Contact: Financial Aid Office

IMGIP/ICEOP

ILLINOIS CONSORTIUM FOR EDUCATIONAL OPPORTUNITY PROGRAM FELLOWSHIP   see number 430

JEWISH FOUNDATION FOR EDUCATION OF WOMEN

BILLER/JEWISH FOUNDATION FOR EDUCATION OF WOMEN   see number 461

JOSE MARTI SCHOLARSHIP CHALLENGE GRANT FUND

JOSE MARTI SCHOLARSHIP CHALLENGE GRANT   see number 432

KANSAS BOARD OF REGENTS

ETHNIC MINORITY SCHOLARSHIP PROGRAM   see number 433

LATIN AMERICAN EDUCATIONAL FOUNDATION

LATIN AMERICAN EDUCATIONAL FOUNDATION SCHOLARSHIPS   see number 434

MISS OUTSTANDING TEENAGER

MISS OUTSTANDING TEENAGER AND LEADERSHIP TRAINING PROGRAM • 489

Award program open to single girls age 13-18. Must be a resident of Montana, Hawaii, Idaho, Wyoming, Nevada or Utah. Minimum 3.25 GPA required. Judging based on teen image, scholastics, citizenship, personal projection and essay. Visit Web site for state registration fees and deadlines. *Award* Scholarship for use in freshman, sophomore, junior, or senior years; renewable. *Number:* 2–5. *Amount:* $500–$4000.

Eligibility Requirements Applicant must be age 13-18; enrolled or expecting to enroll full or part-time at a two-year or four-year or technical institution or university; single female; resident of Hawaii, Idaho, Montana, Nevada, Utah, or Wyoming and studying in Hawaii, Idaho, Montana, Nevada, Utah, or Wyoming. Available to U.S. citizens.

Application Requirements Application, applicant must enter a contest, essay, transcript.

World Wide Web: http://www.missoutstandingteen.com

Contact: Mark M. Budak, National Director/Founder
Miss Outstanding Teenager
Box 4388
Helena, MT 59604
Phone: 406-442-7035
Fax: 406-443-7322
E-mail: teenscholar@missoutstandingteen.com

NATIONAL ASSOCIATION OF LATINO ELECTED AND APPOINTED OFFICIALS EDUCATION FUND

FORD MOTOR COMPANY FELLOWS PROGRAM   see number 439

NATIONAL COUNCIL OF JEWISH WOMEN (GREATER BOSTON)

AMELIA GREENBAUM/RABBI MARSHAL LIPSON SCHOLARSHIP   see number 441

NEVADA WOMEN'S FUND

NEVADA WOMEN'S FUND SCHOLARSHIPS   • 490

Awards for women for a variety of academic and vocational training scholarships. Must be a resident of Nevada. Preference given to applicants from northern Nevada. Renewable award of $500 to $5000. Application deadline is the last Friday in February. Application can be downloaded from Web site (http://www.nevadawomensfund.org). *Award* Scholarship for use in freshman, sophomore, junior, or senior years; renewable. *Number:* 50–80. *Amount:* $500–$5000.

Eligibility Requirements Applicant must be enrolled or expecting to enroll full or part-time at a two-year or four-year or technical institution or university; female and resident of Nevada.

Application Requirements Application, financial need analysis, references, transcript.

World Wide Web: http://www.nevadawomensfund.org

Contact: Fritsi Ericson, President and CEO
Nevada Women's Fund
770 Smithridge Drive, Suite 300
Reno, NV 89502
Phone: 775-786-2335
Fax: 775-786-8152
E-mail: fritsi@nevadawomensfund.org

NEW JERSEY UTILITIES ASSOCIATION

NEW JERSEY UTILITIES ASSOCIATION SCHOLARSHIP • 491

Renewable award for minority, female, and disabled students pursuing a bachelor's degree in engineering, environmental science, chemistry, biology, business administration or accounting. Must be a New Jersey resident, academically excellent, with demonstrated financial need. Children of employees of any NJUA member company may not apply for this scholarship. Contact your high school guidance office for application information. *Award* Scholarship for use in freshman, sophomore, junior, or senior years; renewable. *Number:* 2. *Amount:* $1500.

Eligibility Requirements Applicant must be high school student; planning to enroll or expecting to enroll full-time at a four-year institution and resident of New Jersey.
Application Requirements Application. *Deadline:* April 1.
World Wide Web: http://www.njua.org
Contact: high school guidance office

NEW MEXICO COMMISSION ON HIGHER EDUCATION

MINORITY DOCTORAL ASSISTANCE LOAN-FOR-SERVICE PROGRAM • 492

Several loans available to increase the number of ethnic minorities and women available to teach in academic disciplines in which they are underrepresented. Must have a bachelor's or master's degree from New Mexico four-year public postsecondary institution and be accepted for enrollment as full-time doctoral student at eligible institution. As condition of the loan, recipient is required to teach at sponsoring New Mexico institution for a minimum of one year for each year loan is awarded. Several renewable loans for up to $25,000 per year. Deadline is in January. *Award* Forgivable loan for use in graduate years; renewable. *Amount:* up to $25,000.

Eligibility Requirements Applicant must be enrolled or expecting to enroll full-time at a four-year institution or university; resident of New Mexico and studying in New Mexico. Available to U.S. citizens.
Application Requirements Application, essay, references, transcript.
World Wide Web: http://www.nmche.org
Contact: Maria Barele, Financial Specialist
New Mexico Commission on Higher Education
PO Box 15910
Santa Fe, NM 87506-5910
Phone: 505-827-4026
Fax: 505-827-7392

NEW YORK STATE HIGHER EDUCATION SERVICES CORPORATION

REGENTS PROFESSIONAL OPPORTUNITY SCHOLARSHIPS • 493

Award for New York State residents pursuing career in certain licensed professions. Must attend New York State college. Priority given to economically disadvantaged members of minority group underrepresented in chosen profession and graduates of SEEK, College Discovery, EOP, and HEOP. Must work in New York State in chosen profession one year for each annual payment. *Award* Forgivable loan for use in freshman, sophomore, junior, senior, or graduate years; not renewable. *Amount:* $1000–$5000.

Eligibility Requirements Applicant must be enrolled or expecting to enroll full-time at a two-year or four-year institution or university; resident of New York and studying in New York. Available to U.S. citizens.

Application Requirements Application. *Deadline:* May 1.

World Wide Web: http://www.hesc.com

Contact: Scholarship Processing Unit-New York State Education Department
New York State Higher Education Services Corporation
EBA Room 1078
Albany, NY 12234
Phone: 518-486-1319

OREGON STUDENT ASSISTANCE COMMISSION

DOROTHY CAMPBELL MEMORIAL SCHOLARSHIP   • 494

Renewable award for female Oregon high school senior with a minimum 2.75 GPA. Must submit essay describing strong, continuing interest in golf and the contribution that sport has made to applicant's development. *Award* Scholarship for use in freshman, sophomore, junior, or senior years; renewable. *Number:* 2. *Amount:* $1500.

Eligibility Requirements Applicant must be high school student; planning to enroll or expecting to enroll at a four-year institution; female; resident of Oregon; studying in Oregon and must have an interest in golf. Available to U.S. citizens.

Application Requirements Application, essay, financial need analysis, test scores, transcript, activity chart. *Deadline:* March 1.

World Wide Web: http://www.osac.state.or.us

Contact: Director of Grant Programs
Oregon Student Assistance Commission
1500 Valley River Drive, Suite 100
Eugene, OR 97401-7020
Phone: 800-452-8807 Ext. 7395
E-mail: awardinfo@mercury.osac.state.or.us

PAGE EDUCATION FOUNDATION

PAGE EDUCATION FOUNDATION GRANT   see number 444

R.O.S.E. FUND

R.O.S.E. FUND SCHOLARSHIP PROGRAM   • 495

The R.O.S.E. scholarship program acknowledges women who are survivors of violence or abuse. Primarily awarded to women who have successfully completed one year of undergraduate studies. Scholarships are for tuition and expenses at any accredited college or university in New England. Must be U.S. residents. Deadlines are June 17 for the fall semester, December 3 for the spring semester. *Award* Scholarship for use in sophomore, junior, or senior years; renewable. *Number:* 10–15. *Amount:* $500–$10,000.

Eligibility Requirements Applicant must be age 18; enrolled or expecting to enroll full or part-time at a two-year or four-year institution or university; female and studying in Connecticut, Maine, Massachusetts, New Hampshire, Rhode Island, or Vermont. Applicant must have 2.5 GPA or higher. Available to U.S. and non-U.S. citizens.

Application Requirements Application, autobiography, essay, financial need analysis, interview, references, test scores, transcript.

World Wide Web: http://www.rosefund.org

R.O.S.E. Fund Scholarship Program (continued)

Contact: Alison Justus, Director of Programs
R.O.S.E. Fund
175 Federal Street, Suite 455
Boston, MA 02110
Phone: 617-482-5400 Ext. 11
Fax: 617-482-3443
E-mail: ajustus@rosefund.org

RAGDALE FOUNDATION

FRANCES SHAW FELLOWSHIP • 496

One-time award for a six-week residency at the Ragdale Foundation. Open to women writers, who began writing seriously after age 55. All expenses paid. No stipend. *Award* Fellowship for use in freshman, sophomore, junior, senior, graduate, or postgraduate years; not renewable. *Number:* 1. *Amount:* $7000.

Eligibility Requirements Applicant must be age 55; enrolled or expecting to enroll at an institution or university; female; studying in Illinois and must have an interest in writing. Available to U.S. and non-U.S. citizens.

Application Requirements Application, autobiography, portfolio, references, writing samples. *Deadline:* February 1.

World Wide Web: http://ragdale.org

Contact: Sylvia Brown, Director of Marketing and Programming
Ragdale Foundation
1260 North Green Bay Road
Lake Forest, IL 60045-1106
Phone: 847-234-1063 Ext. 205
Fax: 847-234-1063
E-mail: eventsragdale@aol.com

RHODE ISLAND FOUNDATION

RAYMOND H. TROTT SCHOLARSHIP see number 446

RHODE ISLAND COMMISSION ON WOMEN/FREDA GOLDMAN EDUCATION AWARD • 497

Renewable award to provide financial support for Rhode Island women to pursue their education or job training beyond high school. Can be used for transportation, child-care, tutoring, educational materials and/or other support services. Preference given to highly motivated, self-supported, low-income women. *Award* Scholarship for use in freshman, sophomore, junior, or senior years; renewable.

Eligibility Requirements Applicant must be enrolled or expecting to enroll at an institution or university; female and resident of Rhode Island.

Application Requirements Application, essay, self-addressed stamped envelope, transcript. *Deadline:* June 16.

World Wide Web: http://www.rifoundation.org

Contact: Libby Monahan, Scholarship Coordinator
Rhode Island Foundation
One Union Station
Providence, RI 02903
Phone: 401-274-4564
Fax: 401-272-1359
E-mail: libbym@rifoundation.org

UTAH STATE BOARD OF REGENTS

UTAH EDUCATIONALLY DISADVANTAGED PROGRAM
see number 374

VETERANS OF FOREIGN WARS

U.S. VFW MEXICAN ANCESTRY SCHOLARSHIP
see number 457

VIRGINIA BUSINESS AND PROFESSIONAL WOMEN'S FOUNDATION

BUENA M. CHESSHIR MEMORIAL WOMEN'S EDUCATIONAL SCHOLARSHIP
• 498

One-time award assists mature women seeking to complete or enhance their education. Its purposes are helping women who are employed or seeking employment, increasing the number of women qualified for promotion, and helping women achieve economic self-sufficiency. Award may be used for tuition, fees, books, transportation, living expenses, or dependent care. Must be a Virginia resident and studying in Virginia. *Award* Scholarship for use in junior, senior, or graduate years; not renewable. *Number:* 1–10. *Amount:* $100–$1000.

Eligibility Requirements Applicant must be age 25; enrolled or expecting to enroll at a four-year institution or university; female; resident of Virginia and studying in Virginia. Available to U.S. citizens.

Application Requirements Application, essay, financial need analysis, references, transcript. *Deadline:* April 1.

World Wide Web: http://www.bpwva.advocate.net/foundation.htm

Contact: Scholarship Chair
Virginia Business and Professional Women's Foundation
PO Box 4842
McLean, VA 22103-4842
E-mail: bpwva@advocate.net

KAREN B. LEWIS CAREER EDUCATION SCHOLARSHIP
• 499

This scholarship is offered to women pursuing postsecondary job-oriented career education, offering training in business, trade and industrial occupations (not to be used for education leading to a bachelor's or higher degree). This award may be used for tuition, fees, books, transportation, living expenses, or dependent care. Deadlines are January 1, April 1, and July 1. Must be a Virginia resident studying in Virginia. *Award* Scholarship for use in freshman or sophomore years; not renewable. *Number:* 1–10. *Amount:* $100–$1000.

Eligibility Requirements Applicant must be enrolled or expecting to enroll full or part-time at a two-year or technical institution; female; resident of Virginia and studying in Virginia. Available to U.S. citizens.

Application Requirements Application, essay, financial need analysis, references, transcript.

World Wide Web: http://www.bpwva.advocate.net/foundation.htm

Contact: Scholarship Chair
Virginia Business and Professional Women's Foundation
PO Box 4842
McLean, VA 22103-4842
E-mail: bpwva@advocate.net

WILLIAM F. COOPER SCHOLARSHIP TRUST

WILLIAM F. COOPER SCHOLARSHIP • 500

Scholarship trust to provide financial assistance to women living within the state of Georgia for undergraduate studies. Cannot be used for law, theology or medicine fields of study. Nursing is an approved area of study. *Award* Scholarship for use in freshman, sophomore, junior, or senior years; renewable.

Eligibility Requirements Applicant must be enrolled or expecting to enroll full or part-time at a four-year institution or university; female and resident of Georgia. Available to U.S. citizens.

Application Requirements Application, financial need analysis, test scores, transcript, tax info/W-2. *Deadline:* May 15.

Contact: R. Karesh, Vice President
William F. Cooper Scholarship Trust
Wachovia Bank CSG-GA8023
191 Peachtree Street, 24th Floor
Atlanta, GA 30303
Phone: 404-332-4987
Fax: 404-332-1389

WISCONSIN HIGHER EDUCATIONAL AID BOARD

MINORITY RETENTION GRANT-WISCONSIN see number 458

TALENT INCENTIVE PROGRAM-WISCONSIN • 501

Assists residents of Wisconsin who are attending a nonprofit institution in Wisconsin and have substantial financial need. Must meet income criteria, be considered economically and educationally disadvantaged and be enrolled at least half-time. *Award* Grant for use in freshman, sophomore, junior, or senior years; renewable. *Amount:* $600–$1800.

Eligibility Requirements Applicant must be enrolled or expecting to enroll full or part-time at a two-year or four-year or technical institution or university; resident of Wisconsin and studying in Wisconsin. Available to U.S. and non-U.S. citizens.

Application Requirements Application, financial need analysis. *Deadline:* Continuous.

World Wide Web: http://www.heab.state.wi.us

Contact: John Whitt, Program Coordinator
Wisconsin Higher Educational Aid Board
PO Box 7885
Madison, WI 53707-7885
Phone: 608-266-1665
Fax: 608-267-2808
E-mail: john.whitt@heab.state.wi.us

WOMEN'S RESEARCH AND EDUCATION INSTITUTE

CONGRESSIONAL FELLOWS PROGRAM • 502

One-time award for female graduate and post-graduate students to work for 8 months in a congressional office in Washington D.C. Contact for information on restrictions applicable to one of the fellowships. Application deadline is June 15. *Award* Fellowship for use in graduate, or postgraduate years; not renewable. *Number:* 5–10. *Amount:* $15,000.

Eligibility Requirements Applicant must be enrolled or expecting to enroll full or part-time at an institution or university; female and studying in District of Columbia. Available to U.S. citizens.

Application **Requirements** Application, essay, interview, references, self-addressed stamped envelope, transcript. *Deadline:* June 15.

Contact: Susan Scanlan, President
Women's Research and Education Institute
1750 New York Avenue NW
Suite 350
Washington, DC 20006
Phone: 202-628-0444 Ext. 12
Fax: 202-628-0458
E-mail: wrei@wrei.org

YOUTH OPPORTUNITIES FOUNDATION

YOUTH OPPORTUNITIES FOUNDATION SCHOLARSHIPS see number 460

TALENT

AMERICAN COED PAGEANTS, INC. -FLORIDA

MISS AMERICAN COED PAGEANT • 503

Award for women age 17 and under. Must be single and maintain a 3.0 GPA where applicable. Must submit transcripts with application. Application fee is $20 and is refunded to those not accepted into the competition. State level winners may compete at the national level. *Award* Prize for use in freshman year; not renewable. *Amount:* $500–$1000.

Eligibility Requirements Applicant must be age 17 or under; enrolled or expecting to enroll full or part-time at an institution or university; single female and must have an interest in beauty pageant. Applicant must have 3.0 GPA or higher.

Application Requirements Application, applicant must enter a contest, transcript. *Fee:* $20.

Contact: Mr. George Scarborough, National Director
American Coed Pageants, Inc. -Florida
3695 Wimbledon Drive
Pensacola, FL 32504-4555
Phone: 850-432-0069
Fax: 850-469-8841
E-mail: amerteen@aol.com

AMERICAN INSTITUTE FOR FOREIGN STUDY

AMERICAN INSTITUTE FOR FOREIGN STUDY MINORITY SCHOLARSHIPS
see number 382

CALIFORNIA JUNIOR MISS SCHOLARSHIP PROGRAM

CALIFORNIA JUNIOR MISS SCHOLARSHIP PROGRAM see number 470

FLORIDA WOMEN'S STATE GOLF ASSOCIATION

FLORIDA WOMEN'S STATE GOLF ASSOCIATION SCHOLARSHIP FUND
see number 482

HOSTESS COMMITTEE SCHOLARSHIPS/MISS AMERICA PAGEANT

MISS AMERICA ORGANIZATION COMPETITION SCHOLARSHIPS • 504

Scholarship competition open to 51 contestants, each serving as state representative. Women will be judged in Private Interview, Swimsuit, Evening Wear and Talent competition. Other awards may be based on points assessed by judges during competitions. Upon reaching the National level, award values range from $5000 to $50,000. Additional awards not affecting the competition can be won with values from $1000 to $10,000. Awards designed to provide contestants with the opportunity to enhance professional and educational goals. *Award* Scholarship for use in freshman, sophomore, junior, senior, or graduate years; not renewable. *Amount:* $1000–$50,000.

Eligibility Requirements Applicant must be enrolled or expecting to enroll at a two-year or four-year or technical institution or university; female and must have an interest in beauty pageant. Available to U.S. citizens.

Application Requirements Applicant must enter a contest.

World Wide Web: http://www.missamerica.org

Contact: Hostess Committee Scholarships/Miss America Pageant
Two Miss America Way, Suite 1000
Atlantic City, NJ 08401

LADIES AUXILIARY TO THE VETERANS OF FOREIGN WARS

JUNIOR GIRLS SCHOLARSHIP PROGRAM   see number 369

NATIONAL ASSOCIATION FOR CAMPUS ACTIVITIES

MULTICULTURAL SCHOLARSHIP PROGRAM   see number 438

NATIONAL LEAGUE OF AMERICAN PEN WOMEN, INC.

NLAPW VIRGINIA LIEBELER BIENNIAL GRANTS FOR MATURE WOMEN (LETTERS) • 505

One-time award given in even-numbered years to women ages 35 and older and who are U.S. citizens to be used to further creative purpose of applicant. Submit copies of work, statement of background, purpose of grant, and how applicant learned of grant. May submit in any or all categories, published or unpublished. Application fee: $8. Send self-addressed stamped envelope for entry requirements. Entry deadline is October 1 of odd-numbered year. *Award* Grant for use in freshman, sophomore, junior, senior, graduate, or postgraduate years; not renewable. *Number:* 1. *Amount:* $1000.

Eligibility Requirements Applicant must be age 35; enrolled or expecting to enroll at an institution or university; female and must have an interest in writing. Available to U.S. citizens.

Application Requirements Applicant must enter a contest, self-addressed stamped envelope, proof of U.S. citizenship. *Fee:* $8. *Deadline:* October 1.

Contact: Mary Jane Hillery, National Scholarship Chair
National League of American Pen Women, Inc.
66 Willow Road
Sudbury, MA 01776-2663
Phone: 978-443-2165
Fax: 978-443-2165
E-mail: nlapw1@juno.com

NLAPW VIRGINIA LIEBELER BIENNIAL GRANTS FOR MATURE WOMEN (MUSIC) • 506

Award offered in even-numbered years to women 35 years of age and over. Submit two scores of musical compositions, of which at least one must have been written in the past five years. Performance time should be at least 10 minutes. Neither score may have won a previous award. Must submit letter stating age, purpose, and how applicant learned of grant. Application fee is $8. One-time award of $1000. Send a self-addressed stamped envelope for entry requirements. Entry deadline is October 1 of odd-numbered year. *Award* Grant for use in freshman, sophomore, junior, senior, graduate, or postgraduate years; not renewable. *Number:* 1. *Amount:* $1000.

Eligibility Requirements Applicant must be age 35; enrolled or expecting to enroll at an institution or university; female and must have an interest in music/singing. Available to U.S. citizens.

Application Requirements Applicant must enter a contest, self-addressed stamped envelope, proof of U.S. citizenship. *Fee:* $8. *Deadline:* October 1.

Contact: Mary Jane Hillery, National Scholarship Chair
National League of American Pen Women, Inc.
66 Willow Road
Sudbury, MA 01776-2663
Phone: 978-443-2165
Fax: 978-443-2165
E-mail: nlapw1@juno.com

NATIONAL MINORITY JUNIOR GOLF SCHOLARSHIP ASSOCIATION

NATIONAL MINORITY JUNIOR GOLF SCHOLARSHIP see number 442

OREGON STUDENT ASSISTANCE COMMISSION

DOROTHY CAMPBELL MEMORIAL SCHOLARSHIP see number 494

RAGDALE FOUNDATION

FRANCES SHAW FELLOWSHIP see number 496

SOCIETY OF DAUGHTERS OF THE UNITED STATES ARMY

SOCIETY OF DAUGHTERS OF THE UNITED STATES ARMY SCHOLARSHIPS see number 376

SPINSTERS INK

SPINSTERS INK YOUNG FEMINIST SCHOLARSHIP • 507

Award for female student in last year of high school who submits best essay on feminism and what it means to her. Nonrenewable $1000 scholarship. Contact by e-mail only. More information is available on Web site. Application deadline is December 31. *Award* Scholarship for use in freshman year; not renewable. *Number:* 1. *Amount:* $1000.

Eligibility Requirements Applicant must be high school student; planning to enroll or expecting to enroll full-time at a two-year or four-year institution or university; female and must have an interest in writing. Available to U.S. citizens.

Spinsters Ink Young Feminist Scholarship (continued)

Application Requirements Essay. *Deadline:* December 31.

World Wide Web: http://www.spinsters-ink.com

Contact: Scholarship Information
Spinsters Ink
PO Box 22005
Denver, CO 80222
Phone: 303-762-7284
Fax: 303-761-5284
E-mail: spinster@spinsters-ink.com

WELLESLEY COLLEGE

ANNE LOUISE BARRETT FELLOWSHIP   • 508

Fellowships are available to graduating seniors and alumnae of Wellesley College only. Must be pursuing graduate research, preferably in music with emphasis on study or research in musical theory, composition, or the history of music abroad or in the United States. Merit and need will be considered. Information available by e-mail: cws-fellowships@wellesley.edu. *Award* Fellowship for use in graduate years; not renewable. *Amount:* up to $14,000.

Eligibility Requirements Applicant must be enrolled or expecting to enroll at an institution or university; female and must have an interest in music. Available to U.S. citizens.

Application Requirements Application, essay, financial need analysis, resume, references, transcript. *Deadline:* January 6.

World Wide Web: http://www.wellesley.edu/CWS/

Contact: Mary Beth Callery, Secretary to the Committee on Graduate Fellowships
Wellesley College
106 Central Avenue, Green Hall 441
Wellesley, MA 02481-8200
Phone: 781-283-3525
Fax: 781-283-3674
E-mail: cws-fellowships@wellesley.edu

WOMEN'S BASKETBALL COACHES ASSOCIATION

WBCA SCHOLARSHIP AWARD   • 509

One-time award for two women's basketball players who have demonstrated outstanding commitment to the sport of women's basketball and to academic excellence. Minimum 3.5 GPA required. Must be nominated by the head coach of women's basketball who is a member of the WBCA. *Award* Scholarship for use in freshman, sophomore, junior, senior, graduate, or postgraduate years; not renewable. *Number:* 2. *Amount:* $1000.

Eligibility Requirements Applicant must be enrolled or expecting to enroll full or part-time at a four-year or technical institution or university; female and must have an interest in athletics/sports. Applicant must have 3.5 GPA or higher. Available to U.S. and non-U.S. citizens.

Application Requirements Application, references, statistics. *Deadline:* February 7.

World Wide Web: http://www.wbca.org

Contact: Kristen Miller, Manager of Office Administration and Awards
Women's Basketball Coaches Association
4646 Lawrenceville Highway
Lilburn, GA 30247-3620
Phone: 770-279-8027 Ext. 102
Fax: 770-279-6290
E-mail: kmiller@wbca.org

WOMEN'S INTERNATIONAL BOWLING CONGRESS

ALBERTA E. CROWE STAR OF TOMORROW AWARD   see number 370

WOMEN'S SPORTS FOUNDATION

TRAVEL AND TRAINING FUND   • 510

Award to provide financial assistance to aspiring female athletes with successful competitive regional or national records who have the potential to achieve even higher performance levels and rankings. Must be a U.S. citizen or legal resident. *Award* Grant for use in freshman, sophomore, junior, or senior years; not renewable. *Number:* 90–100. *Amount:* $500–$2000.

Eligibility Requirements Applicant must be enrolled or expecting to enroll full or part-time at an institution or university; female and must have an interest in athletics/sports. Available to U.S. citizens.

Application Requirements Application, references. *Deadline:* December 31.

World Wide Web: http://www.womenssportsfoundation.org

Contact: Women's Sports Foundation
Eisenhower Park
East Meadow, NY 11554
Phone: 800-227-3988
E-mail: wosport@aol.com

WOMEN'S WESTERN GOLF FOUNDATION

WOMEN'S WESTERN GOLF FOUNDATION SCHOLARSHIP   • 511

Scholarships for female high school seniors for use at a four-year college or university. Based on academic record, financial need, character, and involvement in golf. (Golf skill not a criterion.) Twenty awards annually for incoming freshmen; approximately 60 scholarships renewed. Must maintain 2.5 GPA as freshman; 3.0 upperclassman GPA. Must continue to have financial need. Award is $2000 per student per year. Applicant must be 17-18 years of age. *Award* Scholarship for use in freshman, sophomore, junior, or senior years; renewable. *Number:* up to 80. *Amount:* $2000.

Eligibility Requirements Applicant must be high school student; age 17-18; planning to enroll or expecting to enroll full-time at a four-year institution or university; female and must have an interest in golf. Applicant must have 3.0 GPA or higher. Available to U.S. citizens.

Application Requirements Application, essay, financial need analysis, self-addressed stamped envelope, test scores, transcript. *Deadline:* April 5.

Contact: Mrs. Richard Willis, Scholarship Chairman
Women's Western Golf Foundation
393 Ramsay Road
Deerfield, IL 60015

YOUTH OPPORTUNITIES FOUNDATION

YOUTH OPPORTUNITIES FOUNDATION SCHOLARSHIPS   see number 460

MISCELLANEOUS CRITERIA

AMERICA'S JUNIOR MISS SCHOLARSHIP PROGRAM

AMERICA'S JUNIOR MISS SCHOLARSHIP PROGRAM • 512

Awards are given to contestants in local, regional and national levels of competition. Contestants must be female, high school juniors or seniors, U.S. citizens and legal residents of the county and state of competition. Contestants are evaluated on scholastics, interview, talent, fitness and poise. The number of awards and their size varies from year to year. For more information visit http://www.ajm.org. *Award* Scholarship for use in freshman, sophomore, junior, or senior years; not renewable.

Eligibility Requirements Applicant must be high school student; age 16-18; planning to enroll or expecting to enroll full-time at a two-year or four-year institution or university and single female. Available to U.S. citizens.

Application Requirements Application, applicant must enter a contest, test scores, transcript, birth certificate. *Deadline:* Continuous.

World Wide Web: http://www.ajm.org

Contact: Contestant Inquiries
America's Junior Miss Scholarship Program
751 Government Street
PO Box 2786
Mobile, AL 36652-2786

AMERICAN ASSOCIATION OF UNIVERSITY WOMEN (AAUW) EDUCATIONAL FOUNDATION

AAUW EDUCATIONAL FOUNDATION AMERICAN DISSERTATION FELLOWSHIP • 513

One-year dissertation fellowship for women who are U.S. citizens or permanent residents. Must submit proposal. Award for full-time study or research. Filing fee is $30. Winners must be in the final stages of dissertation writing at the time of the fellowship. *Award* Fellowship for use in graduate years; not renewable. *Number:* up to 51. *Amount:* $20,000.

Eligibility Requirements Applicant must be enrolled or expecting to enroll full-time at an institution or university and female. Available to U.S. citizens.

Application Requirements Application, references, transcript, proposal. *Fee:* $30. *Deadline:* November 15.

World Wide Web: http://www.aauw.org

Contact: Customer Service Center
American Association of University Women (AAUW) Educational Foundation
2201 North Dodge Street
Iowa City, IA 52243-4030
E-mail: aauw@act.org

AAUW EDUCATIONAL FOUNDATION AMERICAN POSTDOCTORAL FELLOWSHIP • 514

One-year nonrenewable postdoctoral fellowship for women who are U.S. citizens or permanent residents. Must submit proposal. Award for postdoctoral candidates completing dissertations or women scholars seeking funds for postdoctoral research leave from accredited institutions. Filing fee is $35. *Award* Fellowship for use in postgraduate years; not renewable. *Number:* up to 18. *Amount:* $30,000.

Eligibility Requirements Applicant must be enrolled or expecting to enroll full-time at an institution or university and female. Available to U.S. citizens.

Application Requirements Application, references, transcript, proposal. *Fee:* $35. *Deadline:* November 15.

World Wide Web: http://www.aauw.org

Contact: Customer Services Center
American Association of University Women (AAUW) Educational Foundation
2201 North Dodge Street
Iowa City, IA 52243-4030
E-mail: aauw@act.org

AAUW EDUCATIONAL FOUNDATION COMMUNITY ACTION GRANTS • 515

Community Action Grants provide seed money for innovative programs or non-degree research projects that promote education and equity for women and girls. Must be U.S. citizen or permanent resident. Projects must have direct public impact, be nonpartisan and take place within the United States or its territories. Preference given to AAUW branch and state projects that seek collaborative partners and to individual AAUW member applicants. Application fee is $25. *Award* Grant for use in ; renewable. *Number:* 20–30. *Amount:* $2000–$10,000.

Eligibility Requirements Applicant must be enrolled or expecting to enroll at an institution or university and female. Available to U.S. citizens.

Application Requirements Application. *Fee:* $25. *Deadline:* February 1.

World Wide Web: http://www.aauw.org

Contact: Program Manager
American Association of University Women (AAUW) Educational Foundation
2201 North Dodge Street
Iowa City, IA 52243-4030
Phone: 319-337-1716
E-mail: aauw@act.org

AAUW EDUCATIONAL FOUNDATION INTERNATIONAL FELLOWSHIPS • 516

Nonrenewable awards for international women (non-U.S. citizens and non-residents) to further their education at graduate and postgraduate level in the U.S. for one year. Must have strong commitment to cause of women and girls worldwide. Application fee is $20. *Award* Fellowship for use in graduate, or postgraduate years; not renewable. *Number:* up to 57. *Amount:* $18,000–$30,000.

Eligibility Requirements Applicant must be enrolled or expecting to enroll full-time at an institution or university and female. Available to Canadian and non-U.S. citizens.

Application Requirements Application, references, test scores, transcript, proposal. *Fee:* $20. *Deadline:* December 16.

World Wide Web: http://www.aauw.org

Contact: Customer Service Office
American Association of University Women (AAUW) Educational Foundation
2201 North Dodge Street
Iowa City, IA 52243-4030
E-mail: aauw@act.org

AAUW EDUCATIONAL FOUNDATION SUMMER/SHORT-TERM PUBLICATION GRANTS • 517

Six publication grants to fund women college and university faculty and independent researchers to prepare research for publication. Applicants may be tenure track, part-time, temporary faculty, or independent scholars and researchers, either new or established. Must be available for eight consecutive weeks of final writing, editing, and responding to issues raised in critical reviews. *Award* Fellowship for use in postgraduate years; not renewable. *Number:* up to 6. *Amount:* up to $6000.

Eligibility Requirements Applicant must be enrolled or expecting to enroll full-time at an institution or university and female. Available to U.S. citizens.

Application Requirements Application, references, transcript, proposal. *Fee:* $30. *Deadline:* November 15.

World Wide Web: http://www.aauw.org

Contact: Customer Service Center
American Association of University Women (AAUW) Educational Foundation
2201 North Dodge Street
Iowa City, IA 52243-4030
E-mail: aauw@act.org

AMERICAN ASSOCIATION OF UNIVERSITY WOMEN-HONOLULU BRANCH

AMERICAN ASSOCIATION OF UNIVERSITY WOMEN—AVIAETRIC FUND • 518

Scholarships for junior and senior undergraduate, graduate and post-graduate women. Must be studying full-time at a four-year college or university. *Award* Scholarship for use in junior, senior, graduate, or postgraduate years; not renewable. *Amount:* $100–$2500.

Eligibility Requirements Applicant must be enrolled or expecting to enroll full-time at a four-year institution or university and female. Available to U.S. and Canadian citizens.

Application Requirements Application, financial need analysis, references, self-addressed stamped envelope, test scores, transcript.

Contact: Dr. Sarah Vann
American Association of University Women-Honolulu Branch
1802 Keeaumoku Street
Honolulu, HI 96822

AMERICAN ASSOCIATION OF UNIVERSITY WOMEN—BLACKWELL FUND • 519

Scholarships for junior and senior undergraduate, graduate and post-graduate women. Must be studying full-time at a four-year college or university. *Award* Scholarship for use in junior, senior, graduate, or postgraduate years; not renewable. *Amount:* $100–$2500.

Eligibility Requirements Applicant must be enrolled or expecting to enroll full-time at a four-year institution or university and female. Available to U.S. and Canadian citizens.

Application Requirements Application, financial need analysis, references, self-addressed stamped envelope, test scores, transcript.

Contact: Dr. Sarah Vann
American Association of University Women-Honolulu Branch
1802 Keeaumoku Street
Honolulu, HI 96822

PACIFIC FELLOWSHIP FUND • 520

Scholarships for junior and senior undergraduate, graduate and post-graduate women. Must be studying full-time at a four-year college or university. *Award* Fellowship for use in junior, senior, graduate, or postgraduate years; renewable. *Amount:* $100–$2500.

Eligibility Requirements Applicant must be enrolled or expecting to enroll full-time at a four-year institution or university and female. Available to U.S. and Canadian citizens.

Application Requirements Application, financial need analysis, resume, references, self-addressed stamped envelope, test scores, transcript.

Contact: Dr. Sarah Vann
American Association of University Women-Honolulu Branch
1802 Keeaumoku Street
Honolulu, HI 96822

AMERICAN GI FORUM OF THE UNITED STATES

AMERICAN GI FORUM OF THE UNITED STATES HISPANIC EDUCATION FOUNDATION MATCHING SCHOLARSHIPS • 521

Renewable scholarship of up to $1000. Not restricted to, but priority given to Hispanics. Priority may be given to veterans and their families. Please contact local chapters for qualifications and deadline dates. *Award* Scholarship for use in freshman, sophomore, junior, senior, graduate, or postgraduate years; renewable. *Number:* 50–200. *Amount:* $250–$1000.

Eligibility Requirements Applicant must be enrolled or expecting to enroll full or part-time at a two-year or four-year or technical institution or university. Available to U.S. and non-U.S. citizens.

World Wide Web: http://www.agifnat.org

Contact: Local American GI Forum
American GI Forum of the United States
Attn: Hispanic Education Foundation
PO Box 952
Ulysses, KS 67880

AMERICAN SOCIETY OF SAFETY ENGINEERS (ASSE) FOUNDATION

ASSE-THOMPSON SCHOLARSHIP FOR WOMEN IN SAFETY • 522

This scholarship is for women pursuing post-baccalaureate education in safety engineering, safety management, occupational health nursing, occupational medicine, risk management, ergonomics, industrial hygiene, fire safety, environmental safety, environmental health or other safety related fields. Completion of at least 9 current semester hours and minimum GPA of 3.5 required. Deadline is December 1. *Award* Scholarship for use in graduate years; not renewable. *Number:* 1. *Amount:* $1000.

Eligibility Requirements Applicant must be enrolled or expecting to enroll full-time at an institution or university and female. Applicant must have 3.5 GPA or higher. Available to U.S. and non-U.S. citizens.

Application Requirements Application, essay, references, transcript. *Deadline:* December 1.

World Wide Web: http://www.asse.org/foundat.htm

ASSE-Thompson Scholarship for Women in Safety (continued)

Contact: Customer Service Department
American Society of Safety Engineers (ASSE) Foundation
1800 East Oakton Street
Des Plaines, IL 60018
Phone: 847-699-2929
Fax: 847-296-3769
E-mail: customerservice@asse.org

FORD MOTOR COMPANY SCHOLARSHIP-GRADUATE   • 523

Scholarships for women pursuing a graduate degree in occupational safety. Completion of 9 current semester hours and minimum GPA of 3.5 required. Deadline is December 1. *Award* Scholarship for use in graduate years; not renewable. *Number:* 1. *Amount:* $3375.

Eligibility Requirements Applicant must be enrolled or expecting to enroll full-time at an institution or university and female. Applicant must have 3.5 GPA or higher. Available to U.S. and non-U.S. citizens.

Application Requirements Application, essay, references, transcript. *Deadline:* December 1.

World Wide Web: http://www.asse.org/foundat.htm

Contact: Customer Service Department
American Society of Safety Engineers (ASSE) Foundation
1800 East Oakton Street
Des Plaines, IL 60018
Phone: 847-699-2929
Fax: 847-296-3769
E-mail: customerservice@asse.org

FORD MOTOR COMPANY SCHOLARSHIP-UNDERGRADUATE   • 524

For women pursuing an undergraduate degree in occupational safety. Completion of at least 60 current semester hours and minimum GPA of 3.0 required. Deadline is December 1. *Award* Scholarship for use in junior or senior years; not renewable. *Number:* 3. *Amount:* $3375.

Eligibility Requirements Applicant must be enrolled or expecting to enroll full-time at a four-year institution or university and female. Applicant must have 3.0 GPA or higher. Available to U.S. and non-U.S. citizens.

Application Requirements Application, essay, references, transcript. *Deadline:* December 1.

World Wide Web: http://www.asse.org/foundat.htm

Contact: Customer Service Department
American Society of Safety Engineers (ASSE) Foundation
1800 East Oakton Street
Des Plaines, IL 60018
Phone: 847-699-2929
Fax: 847-296-3769
E-mail: customerservice@asse.org

AMERICAN STATISTICAL ASSOCIATION

GERTRUDE COX SCHOLARSHIP FOR WOMEN IN STATISTICS   • 525

One-time awards to encourage women to enter statistically oriented professions. Must be a citizen or permanent resident of the U.S. or Canada and admitted to graduate statistical program by July 1. Women in or entering the early stages of graduate training in statistics are especially encouraged to apply. *Award* Scholarship for use in graduate years; not renewable. *Number:* 1–2. *Amount:* $500–$1000.

Eligibility Requirements Applicant must be enrolled or expecting to enroll full-time at an institution or university and female. Available to U.S. and Canadian citizens.

Application Requirements Application, autobiography, essay, references, transcript. *Deadline:* April 30.

World Wide Web: http://www.amstat.org

Contact: Holly B. Shulman, Cox Scholarship Committee Chair
American Statistical Association
205 College Avenue
Swarthmore, PA 19081
Phone: 610-690-7331
E-mail: hbs1@cdc.gov

BRITISH FEDERATION OF WOMEN GRADUATES (BFWG)

BFWG SCHOLARSHIPS • 526

Several scholarships are offered to final year women PhD students who are studying in an institution in Great Britain (England, Scotland or Wales). Awards typically range from £1000–£2500. Visit Web site for additional information and to download application. Application fee of £12. Deadline is April 11. *Award* Scholarship for use in postgraduate years; not renewable. *Number:* 1–8. *Amount:* $800.

Eligibility Requirements Applicant must be enrolled or expecting to enroll full or part-time at an institution or university and female. Available to U.S. and non-U.S. citizens.

Application Requirements Application, applicant must enter a contest, interview. *Fee:* $19. *Deadline:* April 11.

World Wide Web: http://www.bfwg.org.uk

Contact: Secretary
British Federation of Women Graduates (BFWG)
BFWG Scholarships
4 Mandeville Courtyard, 142 Battersea Park Road
London SW11 4N
United Kingdom
Phone: 44-20-74988037
Fax: 44-20-74985213
E-mail: awards@bfwg.demon.co.uk

CANADIAN FEDERATION OF UNIVERSITY WOMEN

1989 POLYTECHNIQUE COMMEMORATIVE AWARD see number 389

ALICE E. WILSON AWARD see number 390

BOURSE GEORGETTE LEMOYNE see number 392

DR. MARION ELDER GRANT FELLOWSHIP see number 393

MARGARET MCWILLIAMS PRE-DOCTORAL FELLOWSHIP see number 394

GLAMOUR

TOP TEN COLLEGE WOMEN COMPETITION • 527

Glamour is looking for female students with leadership experience on and off campus, excellence in field of study, and inspiring goals. Award is $1500 and a trip to New York City. Must be a junior studying full-time with a minimum GPA of 3.0. Non-U.S. citizens may apply if attending U.S. postsecondary institutions. Application deadline is January 31. See Web site at http://www.glamour.com from October to February for information. *Award* Prize for use in junior year; not renewable. *Number:* 10. *Amount:* $1500.

Eligibility Requirements Applicant must be enrolled or expecting to enroll full-time at a four-year institution or university and female. Applicant must have 3.0 GPA or higher. Available to U.S. and non-U.S. citizens.

Application Requirements Application, essay, photo, references, transcript, list of activities; signatures of faculty adviser and other college administrator. *Deadline:* January 31.

World Wide Web: http://www.glamour.com

Contact: Lynda Laux-Bachand, Reader Services Editor
Glamour
4 Times Square
16th Floor
New York, NY 10036-6593
Phone: 212-286-6667
Fax: 212-286-6922
E-mail: ttcw@glamour.com

GUARDIAN LIFE INSURANCE COMPANY OF AMERICA

GIRLS GOING PLACES SCHOLARSHIP PROGRAM • 528

Rewards the enterprising spirits of girls ages 12 to 16 who demonstrate budding entrepreneurship, are taking the first steps toward financial independence, and make a difference in their school and community. *Award* Prize for use in freshman year; not renewable. *Number:* 15. *Amount:* $1000–$10,000.

Eligibility Requirements Applicant must be high school student; age 12-16; planning to enroll or expecting to enroll full-time at a two-year or four-year or technical institution or university and single female. Available to U.S. citizens.

Application Requirements Application, essay. *Deadline:* February 28.

World Wide Web: http://www.girlsgoingplaces.com

Contact: Diana Acevedo, Project Manager
Guardian Life Insurance Company of America
7 Hanover Square 26-C
New York, NY 10004
Phone: 212-598-7881
Fax: 212-919-2586
E-mail: diana_acevedo@glic.com

INTERNATIONAL FEDERATION OF UNIVERSITY WOMEN

INTERNATIONAL FEDERATION OF UNIVERSITY WOMEN FELLOWSHIPS • 529

One-time award for members of the International Federation of University Women. Fellowships are intended to cover at least eight months of advanced scholarship and original research in any branch of learning, in the country of the applicant's choice. The next competition will be in 2005-2006. Application deadlines vary. See Web site at http://www.ifuw.org for more information. *Award* Fellowship for use in graduate, or postgraduate years; not renewable. *Number:* 15–25.

Eligibility Requirements Applicant must be enrolled or expecting to enroll at an institution or university and female.

Application Requirements Application.

World Wide Web: http://www.ifuw.org/i_fell.htm

Contact: International Federation of University Women
8 rue de l'Ancien-Port
Geneva CH-1201
Switzerland

JEANNETTE RANKIN FOUNDATION, INC.

JEANNETTE RANKIN FOUNDATION AWARDS   • 530

Applicants must be low-income women, age 35 or older, who are pursuing a technical/vocational degree, an associate's degree, or a first-time bachelor's degree. Applications are available November-February. Download materials from the Web site (http://www.rankinfoundation.org) or send a self-addressed stamped envelope to request an application by mail. *Award* Grant for use in freshman, sophomore, junior, or senior years; not renewable. *Number:* 25–40. *Amount:* $2000.

Eligibility Requirements Applicant must be age 35; enrolled or expecting to enroll full or part-time at a two-year or four-year or technical institution or university and female. Available to U.S. citizens.

Application Requirements Application, essay, financial need analysis, references, self-addressed stamped envelope, transcript. *Deadline:* March 1.

World Wide Web: http://www.rankinfoundation.org

Contact: Andrea Anderson, Program Coordinator
Jeannette Rankin Foundation, Inc.
PO Box 6653
Athens, GA 30604-6653
Phone: 706-208-1211
Fax: 706-208-1211
E-mail: info@rankinfoundation.org

MARGARET MCNAMARA MEMORIAL FUND

MARGARET MCNAMARA MEMORIAL FUND FELLOWSHIPS   • 531

One-time awards for female students from developing countries enrolled in accredited graduate programs relating to women and children. Must be attending an accredited institution in the U.S. Candidates must plan to return to their countries within two years. Must be over 25 years of age. U.S. citizens are not eligible. *Award* Grant for use in graduate, or postgraduate years; not renewable. *Number:* 5–6. *Amount:* $11,000.

Eligibility Requirements Applicant must be age 25; enrolled or expecting to enroll full-time at a four-year institution or university and female. Available to citizens of countries other than the U.S. or Canada.

Application Requirements Application, essay, financial need analysis, photo, references, transcript. *Deadline:* February 1.

World Wide Web: http://www.worldbank.org

Margaret McNamara Memorial Fund Fellowships (continued)

Contact: Chairman, M.M.M.F. Selection Committee
Margaret McNamara Memorial Fund
1818 H Street, NW, MSN-H2-204
Washington, DC 20433
Phone: 202-473-8751
Fax: 202-522-3142
E-mail: mmmf@worldbank.org

NATIONAL TEEN-AGER SCHOLARSHIP FOUNDATION

NATIONAL TEEN-AGER SCHOLARSHIP FOUNDATION • 532

One-time award for young women of leadership and intellect. Award based on school and community leadership, communication skills, academics and personal presentation. 3-5 awards per state. Awards come in the form of savings bonds from $500-1000 and in cash from $5000-10,000. Must be between the ages of 12-18 and be a U.S. citizen. Minimum 3.0 GPA required. $20 application fee. Deadline varies by state. For more details see Web site: http://www.nationalteen.com. *Award* Scholarship for use in freshman year; not renewable. *Number:* 250–1510. *Amount:* $1000–$10,000.

Eligibility Requirements Applicant must be age 12-18; enrolled or expecting to enroll full-time at a two-year or four-year institution or university and single female. Applicant must have 3.0 GPA or higher. Available to U.S. citizens.

Application Requirements Application, applicant must enter a contest, interview, photo, self-addressed stamped envelope, transcript. *Fee:* $20.

World Wide Web: http://www.nationalteen.com

Contact: Cheryl Snow, National Director
National Teen-Ager Scholarship Foundation
4708 Mill Crossing West
Colleyville, TX 76034
Phone: 817-577-2220
Fax: 817-428-7232
E-mail: csnow@dallas.net

NINETY-NINES, INC.

AMELIA EARHART MEMORIAL CAREER SCHOLARSHIP FUND • 533

Scholarships are awarded to members of The Ninety-Nines, Inc., who hold a current medical certificate appropriate for the use of the certificate sought. Applicants must meet the requirements for pilot currency (Flight Review or non-U.S. equivalent) and have financial need. Applicants must agree to complete the course, training and meet the requirements for ratings/certificates specific to the country where training will occur. *Award* Scholarship for use in freshman, sophomore, junior, or senior years; not renewable. *Number:* 15–18. *Amount:* $2000–$10,000.

Eligibility Requirements Applicant must be enrolled or expecting to enroll full-time at an institution or university and female. Available to U.S. and non-U.S. citizens.

Application Requirements Application, financial need analysis, photo, resume, references. *Deadline:* December 31.

World Wide Web: http://ninety-nines.org

Contact: Charlene H. Falkenberg, Chairman, Permanent Trustee
Ninety-Nines, Inc.
618 South Washington Street
Hobart, IN 46342-5026
Phone: 219-942-8887
Fax: 219-942-8887
E-mail: charf@prodigy.net

PEO INTERNATIONAL PEACE SCHOLARSHIP FUND
PEO INTERNATIONAL PEACE SCHOLARSHIP • 534
The International Peace Scholarship Fund is a program which provides scholarships for selected women from other countries for graduate study in the United States and Canada. An applicant must be qualified for admission to full-time graduate study, working toward a graduate degree in the college or university of her choice in the United States or Canada. *Award* Scholarship for use in graduate years; renewable. *Number:* 170–180. *Amount:* $6000.

Eligibility Requirements Applicant must be enrolled or expecting to enroll full-time at a four-year institution or university and female. Available to citizens of countries other than the U.S. or Canada.

Application Requirements Application, autobiography, financial need analysis, references, transcript. *Deadline:* December 15.

World Wide Web: http://www.peointernational.org

Contact: Project Supervisor/IPS
PEO International Peace Scholarship Fund
3700 Grand Avenue
Des Moines, IA 50312-2899
Phone: 515-255-3153
Fax: 515-255-3820

SOROPTIMIST INTERNATIONAL OF GREAT BRITAIN AND IRELAND
GOLDEN JUBILEE FELLOWSHIP • 535
Fellowships offered to assist women with education/training costs. Preference is given to women refurbishing their skills or acquiring new ones to return to employment after a career break or to improve their prospects of employment or achievement. *Award* Fellowship for use in freshman, sophomore, junior, senior, or graduate years. *Number:* up to 30. *Amount:* up to $500.

Eligibility Requirements Applicant must be enrolled or expecting to enroll at an institution or university and female. Available to U.S. and non-U.S. citizens.

Application Requirements Application, references. *Deadline:* April 30.

World Wide Web: http://www.soroptimist-gbi.org

Contact: Secretary
Soroptimist International of Great Britain and Ireland
127 Wellington Road South
Stockport SK1 3TS
United Kingdom
Phone: 44-161-4807686
Fax: 44-161-477 6152
E-mail: hq@soroptimistgbi.prestel.co.uk

SOROPTIMIST INTERNATIONAL OF THE AMERICAS

SOROPTIMIST WOMEN'S OPPORTUNITY AWARD • 536

Applicant must be a woman who is head of household and working toward vocational or undergraduate degree. Recipients are chosen on the basis of financial need as well as a statement of clear career goals. One-time award of $500-$10,000. Send a self addressed stamped business-size envelope with 60 cents postage for information. Must be a resident of SIA's member countries and territories. *Award* Prize for use in freshman, sophomore, junior, or senior years; not renewable. *Amount:* $500–$10,000.

Eligibility Requirements Applicant must be enrolled or expecting to enroll full or part-time at a two-year or four-year or technical institution or university and female. Available to U.S. and non-U.S. citizens.

Application Requirements Application, essay, financial need analysis, references, self-addressed stamped envelope. *Deadline:* December 1.

World Wide Web: http://www.soroptimist.org

Contact: Award Chairperson
Soroptimist International of the Americas
2 Penn Center Plaza, Suite 1000
Philadelphia, PA 19102
E-mail: siahg@soroptimist.org

SUNSHINE LADY FOUNDATION, INC.

WOMEN'S INDEPENDENCE SCHOLARSHIP PROGRAM • 537

Scholarship for female survivors of domestic violence (partner abuse) who are U.S. citizens or permanent legal residents with critical financial need to return to school to gain skills to become independent and self-sufficient. Requires sponsorship by non-profit domestic violence service agency. First priority candidates are single mothers with young children. *Award* Scholarship for use in freshman, sophomore, junior, or senior years; renewable. *Number:* 500. *Amount:* $250–$5000.

Eligibility Requirements Applicant must be enrolled or expecting to enroll full or part-time at a two-year or four-year or technical institution or university and female. Available to U.S. citizens.

Application Requirements Application, essay, financial need analysis, references, sponsor. *Deadline:* Continuous.

World Wide Web: http://www.sunshineladyfdn.org

Contact: Nancy Soward, Program Coordinator
Sunshine Lady Foundation, Inc.
4900 Randall Parkway
Suite H
Wilmington, NC 28403
Phone: 910-397-7742
Fax: 910-397-0023
E-mail: sunlady1@bellsouth.net

TAKE ME AWAY TO COLLEGE SCHOLARSHIP COMPETITION

CALGON, TAKE ME AWAY TO COLLEGE SCHOLARSHIP COMPETITION • 538

One-time award designed for students pursuing a degree at a 4-year accredited college or university. The award recognizes originality and expression as well as academic excellence, community involvement and overall achievement. Award designated for female applicants. Must be U.S. citizen or legal resident studying at an institution in the United States. Applications accepted only through Web site (http://www.takemeaway.com). *Award* Scholarship for use in freshman, sophomore, or junior years; not renewable. *Number:* 7. *Amount:* $2500.

Eligibility Requirements Applicant must be enrolled or expecting to enroll full-time at a four-year institution or university and female. Available to U.S. citizens.

Application Requirements Application, essay, transcript.

World Wide Web: http://www.takemeaway.com

Contact: application available at Web site
  E-mail: quickspritz@takemeaway.com

TALBOTS CHARITABLE FOUNDATION

TALBOTS WOMEN'S SCHOLARSHIP FUND • 539

One-time scholarship for women who earned their high school diploma or GED at least 10 years ago, and who are now seeking an undergraduate college degree. Deadline is March 3. *Award* Scholarship for use in freshman, sophomore, junior, or senior years; not renewable. *Number:* 5–50. *Amount:* $1000–$10,000.

Eligibility Requirements Applicant must be enrolled or expecting to enroll full or part-time at a two-year or four-year or technical institution or university and female. Available to U.S. citizens.

Application Requirements Application, essay, financial need analysis, references, transcript. *Deadline:* March 3.

World Wide Web: http://www.talbots.com

Contact: Deb Johnson, Citizens Scholarship Foundation
  Talbots Charitable Foundation
  1505 Riverview Road, PO Box 297
  Saint Peter, MN 56082
  Phone: 507-931-0452
  Fax: 507-931-9278
  E-mail: debj@csfa.org

THIRD WAVE FOUNDATION

SCHOLARSHIP FOR YOUNG WOMEN • 540

Our scholarship program is available to all full-time or part-time female students aged 17-30 who are enrolled in, or have been accepted to, an accredited university, college, or community college in the U.S. The primary criterion for funding is financial need. Students should also be involved as activists, artists, or cultural workers working on issues such as racism, homophobia, sexism, or other forms of inequality. Application available at Web site http://www.thirdwavefoundation.org. Application deadlines are April 1 and October 1. *Award* Scholarship for use in freshman, sophomore, junior, or senior years; not renewable. *Number:* 20–30. *Amount:* $500–$5000.

Eligibility Requirements Applicant must be age 17-30; enrolled or expecting to enroll full or part-time at a two-year or four-year or technical institution or university and female. Applicant must have 2.5 GPA or higher. Available to U.S. and non-U.S. citizens.

Application Requirements Application, essay, financial need analysis, resume, references, transcript.

World Wide Web: http://www.thirdwavefoundation.org

Scholarship for Young Women (continued)

Contact: Mia Herndon, Network Coordinator
Third Wave Foundation
511 West 25th Street, Suite 301
New York, NY 10001
Phone: 212-675-0700
Fax: 212-255-6653
E-mail: info@thirdwavefoundation.org

WELLESLEY COLLEGE

ALICE FREEMAN PALMER FELLOWSHIPS   • 541

One or more fellowships available to Wellesley alumnae for study or research abroad or in the United States. The holder must be no more than 26 years of age at the time of her appointment, and unmarried throughout the whole of her tenure. Fellowships awarded on basis of merit and need. Web site: http://www.wellesley.edu/cws contains guidelines and application. *Award* Fellowship for use in graduate years; not renewable. *Amount:* up to $25,000.

Eligibility Requirements Applicant must be age 26 or under; enrolled or expecting to enroll full-time at an institution or university and single female. Available to U.S. citizens.

Application Requirements Application, essay, financial need analysis, resume, references, transcript. *Deadline:* January 6.

World Wide Web: http://www.wellesley.edu/CWS/

Contact: Mary Beth Callery, Secretary to the Committee on Graduate Fellowships
Wellesley College
106 Central Avenue, Green Hall 441
Wellesley, MA 02481-8200
Phone: 781-283-3525
Fax: 781-283-3674
E-mail: cws-fellowships@wellesley.edu

FANNY BULLOCK WORKMAN FELLOWSHIP   • 542

One or more awards available to alumnae of Wellesley College for graduate study in any field. Recommendations and resume required. *Award* Fellowship for use in graduate years; not renewable. *Amount:* up to $15,000.

Eligibility Requirements Applicant must be enrolled or expecting to enroll full-time at an institution or university and female. Available to U.S. citizens.

Application Requirements Application, essay, financial need analysis, resume, references, transcript. *Deadline:* January 6.

World Wide Web: http://www.wellesley.edu/CWS/

Contact: Mary Beth Callery, Secretary to the Committee on Graduate Fellowships
Wellesley College
106 Central Avenue, Green Hall 441
Wellesley, MA 02481-8200
Phone: 781-283-3525
Fax: 781-283-3674
E-mail: cws-fellowships@wellesley.edu

HORTON-HALLOWELL FELLOWSHIP   • 543

One or more fellowships available to graduates of Wellesley College for study in any field. Preference given to applicants who are in the last two years of candidacy for PhD or equivalent or for private research. Based on need and merit. *Award* Fellowship for use in graduate, or postgraduate years; not renewable. *Amount:* up to $9000.

Eligibility Requirements Applicant must be enrolled or expecting to enroll full-time at an institution or university and female. Available to U.S. citizens.

Application Requirements Application, essay, financial need analysis, resume, references, transcript. *Deadline:* January 6.

World Wide Web: http://www.wellesley.edu/CWS/

Contact: Mary Beth Callery, Secretary to the Committee on Graduate Fellowships
Wellesley College
106 Central Avenue, Green Hall 441
Wellesley, MA 02481-8200
Phone: 781-283-3525
Fax: 781-283-3674
E-mail: cws-fellowships@wellesley.edu

MARY ELVIRA STEVEN TRAVELLING FELLOWSHIP • 544

One or more fellowships available to alumnae of Wellesley College for a full year of travel or study outside the United States. Any scholarly, artistic, or cultural purpose may be considered. Candidates must be at least 25 years of age in the year of application. Application forms may be obtained from the Alumnae Office. The application and supporting material should be returned by early December. *Award* Fellowship for use in graduate years; not renewable. *Amount:* up to $20,000.

Eligibility Requirements Applicant must be age 25; enrolled or expecting to enroll at an institution or university and female. Available to U.S. citizens.

Application Requirements Application, essay, financial need analysis, resume, references, transcript. *Deadline:* December 6.

World Wide Web: http://www.wellesley.edu/CWS/

Contact: Center for Work and Service
Wellesley College
106 Central Street
Wellesley, MA 02481-8201

WOMEN IN DEFENSE (WID), A NATIONAL SECURITY ORGANIZATION

HORIZONS FOUNDATION SCHOLARSHIP • 545

Scholarships are awarded to provide financial assistance to further educational objectives of women either employed or planning careers in defense or national security arenas (not law enforcement or criminal justice). Must be U.S. citizen. Minimum 3.5 GPA required. Deadlines are November 1 and July 1. *Award* Scholarship for use in junior, senior, graduate, or postgraduate years; renewable. *Number:* 5–10. *Amount:* $500–$1000.

Eligibility Requirements Applicant must be enrolled or expecting to enroll full or part-time at a four-year institution or university and female. Applicant must have 3.5 GPA or higher. Available to U.S. citizens.

Application Requirements Application, essay, financial need analysis, references, self-addressed stamped envelope, transcript.

World Wide Web: http://wid.ndia.org

Contact: application available at Web site

ZONTA INTERNATIONAL FOUNDATION

YOUNG WOMEN IN PUBLIC AFFAIRS AWARD • 546

One-time award for pre-college women with a commitment to the volunteer sector and evidence of volunteer leadership achievements. Must be 16-20 years of age with a career interest in public affairs, public policy and community organizations. Further information and application available at Web site http://www.zonta.org. *Award* Scholarship for use in freshman year; not renewable. *Amount:* $500–$1000.

Eligibility Requirements Applicant must be high school student; age 16-20; planning to enroll or expecting to enroll at a four-year institution or university and female.

Application Requirements Application, photo, references. *Deadline:* April 1.

World Wide Web: http://www.zonta.org

Contact: Ms. Ana Ubides, Foundation Assistant
Zonta International Foundation
557 West Randolph Street
Chicago, IL 60661-2206
Phone: 312-930-5848
Fax: 312-930-0951
E-mail: zontafdtn@zonta.org

Indexes

(Please note: The number reference found in these indexes is the sequence number of the award, not the number of the page on which it is found.)

Award Name Index 334

Sponsor Index 342

Academic Fields/Career Goals Index 347

Civic, Professional, Social, or Union Affiliation
Index 362

Employment Experience Index 364

Impairment Index 365

Military Service Index 366

Religious Affiliation Index 367

State of Residence Index 368

Talent Index 372

AWARD NAME INDEX

1989 Polytechnique Commemorative Award • 389

AACAP Jeanne Spurlock Minority Medical Student Clinical Fellowship in Child and Adolescent Psychiatry • 232

AACAP Jeanne Spurlock Research Fellowship in Drug Abuse and Addiction for Minority Medical Students • 233

AACHE Scholarship • 385

AALL and West Group George A. Strait Minority Scholarship Endowment • 279

AAUW Educational Foundation American Dissertation Fellowship • 513

AAUW Educational Foundation American Postdoctoral Fellowship • 514

AAUW Educational Foundation Community Action Grants • 515

AAUW Educational Foundation International Fellowships • 516

AAUW Educational Foundation Selected Professions Fellowships • 36

AAUW Educational Foundation Summer/ Short-Term Publication Grants • 517

ABB Lummis Global • 190

Actuarial Scholarships for Minority Students • 75

Actuarial Scholarships for Minority Students • 450

Adelante U.S. Education Leadership Fund • 34

Admiral Grace Murray Hopper Memorial Scholarship • 201

Adobe Systems Computer Science Scholarship • 202

AFSCME/UNCF Union Scholars Program • 380

Agenda For Delaware Women Trailblazer Scholarship • 480

Al-Ben Scholarship for Academic Incentive • 100

Al-Ben Scholarship for Professional Merit • 101

Al-Ben Scholarship for Scholastic Achievement • 102

Albert A. Marks, Jr. Scholarship for Teacher Education • 172

Albert W. Dent Graduate Student Scholarship • 227

Alberta E. Crowe Star of Tomorrow Award • 370

Alice E. Wilson Award • 390

Alice Freeman Palmer Fellowships • 541

Alice Newell Joslyn Medical Fund • 154

Alice T. Schafer Mathematics Prize for Excellence in Mathematics by an Undergraduate Woman • 318

Allfirst/ Hispanic College Fund Scholarship Program • 10

Alumnae Panhellenic Association of Washington, D.C. Scholarship • 465

Amarillo Women's Network Nancy Sample Garms Scholarship • 466

Amelia Earhart Fellowship Awards • 62

Amelia Earhart Memorial Career Scholarship Fund • 533

Amelia Greenbaum/Rabbi Marshal Lipson Scholarship • 441

America's Intercultural Magazine (AIM) Short Story Contest • 296

America's Junior Miss Scholarship Program • 512

American Association of University Women—Aviaetric Fund • 518

American Association of University Women—Blackwell Fund • 519

American Chemical Society Scholars Program • 94

American Dental Association Foundation Minority Dental Student Scholarship Program • 151

American Dental Hygienists' Association Institute Minority Scholarship • 152

American Gastroenterological Association Research Scholar Awards for Underrepresented Minorities • 231

American Gastroenterological Association Student Research Fellowship Underrepresented Minorities Award • 222

American Geological Institute Minority Scholarship • 381

American GI Forum of the United States Hispanic Education Foundation Matching Scholarships • 521

American Institute for Foreign Study Minority Scholarships • 382

American Institute of Architects Minority/ Disadvantaged Scholarship • 35

American Institute of Architects/American Architectural Foundation Minority/ Disadvantaged Scholarships • 37

American Legion Auxiliary Department of Colorado Department President's Scholarship for Junior Members • 346

American Legion Auxiliary Department of Florida Memorial Scholarship • 347

American Legion Auxiliary Department of
   Maryland Children and Youth
   Scholarships • 377
American Legion Auxiliary Department of
   Maryland Past President's Parley Nursing
   Scholarship • 311
American Legion Auxiliary Department of
   Michigan Memorial Scholarship • 378
American Legion Auxiliary Department of
   Nebraska President's Scholarship for
   Junior Members • 350
American Legion Auxiliary Department of
   Oregon Spirit of Youth Scholarship • 351
American Legion Auxiliary Department of
   South Dakota Thelma Foster Scholarship
   for Senior Auxiliary Members • 352
American Legion Auxiliary Department of
   South Dakota Thelma Foster Scholarships
   for Junior Auxiliary Members • 353
American Legion Auxiliary Department of
   Washington Susan Burdett Scholarship
   • 467
American Legion Auxiliary Girl Scout
   Achievement Award • 355
American Legion Auxiliary Spirit of Youth
   Scholarships for Junior Members • 356
American Legion Auxiliary, Department of
   South Dakota Senior Scholarship • 354
American Meteorological Society/Industry
   Minority Scholarships • 302
American Physiological Society Minority
   Travel Fellowships • 25
American Planning Association Fellowship
   Program • 383
American Political Science Association
   Minority Fellows Program • 321
American Psychiatric Association/Center for
   Mental Health Services Minority
   Fellowship Program • 234
Anne Louise Barrett Fellowship • 508
Anne Maureen Whitney Barrow Memorial
   Scholarship • 203
Appraisal Institute Educational Scholarship
   Program • 322
Arizona Section Scholarship • 191
Arkansas Minority Teacher Scholars Program
   • 167
Armed Forces Communications and
   Electronics Association Ralph W. Shrader
   Scholarships • 140
Arne Administrative Scholarship • 462
ASHF Graduate Student Scholarship for
   Minority Students • 117
Asian, Black, Hispanic, and Native American
   United Methodist History Research
   Awards • 261
ASM Minority Undergraduate Research
   Fellowship • 66
ASSE-Thompson Scholarship for Women in
   Safety • 522

Association for Women in Architecture
   Scholarship • 38
Association for Women in Mathematics
   Workshop for Graduate Students and
   Postdoctoral Mathematicians • 319
Association for Women in Science
   Pre-doctoral Fellowship • 32
Association for Women in Science
   Undergraduate Award • 26
B.J. Harrod Scholarship • 204
B.K. Krenzer Memorial Reentry Scholarship
   • 205
Bank of America Minority Scholarship • 77
Barbara Alice Mower Memorial Scholarship
   • 469
Barbara Jean Barker Memorial Scholarship
   for a Displaced Homemaker • 487
Bechtel Corporation Scholarship • 116
Belmer/Flora Prince Scholarship • 463
Beverley Jackson Fellowship • 391
BFWG Scholarships • 526
Biller/Jewish Foundation for Education of
   Women • 461
Block Dissertation Award • 335
Bobby McCallum Memorial Scholarship
   • 276
Bourse Georgette Lemoyne • 392
BPW Career Advancement Scholarship
   Program for Women • 68
Breakthrough to Nursing Scholarships for
   Racial/Ethnic Minorities • 312
Bristol-Myers Squibb Fellowship Program in
   Academic Medicine for Minority Students
   • 245
Brown Scholar • 169
Buena M. Chesshir Memorial Women's
   Educational Scholarship • 498
Burlington Northern Santa Fe Foundation/
   Hispanic College Fund Scholarship
   Program • 11
Cady McDonnell Memorial Scholarship • 342
CAHSEE Fellowship: Young Educators
   Program • 30
Calgon, Take Me Away to College
   Scholarship Competition • 538
California Adolescent Nutrition and Fitness
   (CANFit) Program Scholarship • 223
California Junior Miss Scholarship Program
   • 470
California Library Association Scholarship for
   Minority Students in Memory of Edna
   Yelland • 289
Canadian Federation of University Women
   Memorial Fellowship • 21
Carole Simpson Scholarship • 129
Caterpillar Scholars Award Fund • 198
Charles T. Stoner Law Scholarship Award
   • 288
Charlotte Observer Minority Scholarships
   • 76

Chevron Texaco Corporation Scholarships • 111

Chips Quinn Scholars Program • 270

Christian Services Graduate Study Scholarships for Women • 333

Cintas Fellowships Program • 41

Claire B. Schultz Memorial Scholarship • 473

Colgate "Bright Smiles, Bright Futures" Minority Scholarship • 153

Colin L. Powell Minority Postdoctoral Fellowship in Tropical Disease Research • 244

College Fund/Coca Cola Corporate Intern Program • 92

College Scholarship Program • 418

Colonial Bank Scholarship • 396

Colorado Business and Professional Women's Foundation Scholarship • 472

Community College Transfer Programs • 419

Compaq Computer Scholarship • 144

COMTO Boston/Garrett A. Morgan Scholarship • 40

Congressional Black Caucus Spouses Health Initiative • 226

Congressional Black Caucus Spouses Performing Arts Scholarship • 315

Congressional Fellows Program • 502

Congressional Hispanic Caucus Institute Public Policy Fellowships • 397

Congressional Hispanic Caucus Institute Scholarship Awards • 398

Connecticut Association of Latin Americans in Higher Education Scholarships • 399

Connecticut Special Education Teacher Incentive Grant • 337

Consortium Fellowship • 79

Corporate Sponsored Scholarships for Minority Undergraduate Students Who Major in Physics • 317

Council on Social Work Education/Mental Health Minority Research Fellowship • 240

Courtland and Gina Miller Scholarship Fund • 474

Cristina Saralegui Scholarship Program • 272

Cuban American Scholarship Fund • 479

Daimler Chrysler Corporation Scholarship • 188

Daniel Gutierrez Memorial General Scholarship Fund • 387

Daughters of the Cincinnati Scholarship • 375

David C. Lizarraga Fellowship • 402

David Sarnoff Research Center Scholarship • 145

Delayed Education for Women Scholarships • 192

Dell Computer Corporation Scholarships • 146

Delores A. Auzenne Fellowship for Graduate Study • 404

Delphi Scholarship • 206

Delta Delta Delta Graduate Scholarship • 357

Delta Delta Delta Undergraduate Scholarship • 358

Delta Gamma Foundation Fellowships • 359

Delta Gamma Foundation Scholarships • 360

Denise Lynn Padgett Scholarship Fund • 475

Denny's/Hispanic College Fund Scholarship • 12

Doctoral Fellowships in Social Work for Ethnic Minority Students Preparing for Leadership Roles in Mental Health and/or Substance Abuse • 241

Dorothy Campbell Memorial Scholarship • 494

Dorothy Harris Scholarship • 340

Dorothy Lemke Howarth Scholarships • 207

Dorothy M. and Earl S. Hoffman Scholarship • 208

Dow Jones Newspaper Fund Minority Business Reporting Program • 401

Dr. and Mrs. David B. Allman Medical Scholarships • 243

Dr. Juan D. Villarreal/ Hispanic Dental Association Foundation • 155

Dr. Marion Elder Grant Fellowship • 393

Dupont Company Scholarships • 112

Earl G. Graves NAACP Scholarship • 89

Eaton Corporation Multicultural Scholars Program • 141

Ed Bradley Scholarship • 130

Edna V. Moffett Fellowship • 263

Edward S. Roth Manufacturing Engineering Scholarship • 199

Edwin G. and Lauretta M. Michael Scholarship • 324

Elaine Osborne Jacobson Award for Women Working in Health Care Law • 229

ELCA Scholarships for Women • 464

Eleanor Roosevelt Teacher Fellowships • 166

Electronics for Imaging (EFI) Scholarships • 209

Elks National Foundation Gold Award Scholarships • 361

Emma L. Bowen Foundation for Minority Interests in Media • 345

Engineering Vanguard Program • 103

Esperanza Scholarships • 403

Ethel Louise Armstrong Foundation Scholarship • 373

Ethnic Diversity College and University Scholarships • 4

Ethnic Minority and Women's Enhancement Scholarship • 339

Ethnic Minority Scholarship Program • 433

Eugene L. Cox Fellowship • 264

Eugenia Vellner Fischer Award for Performing Arts • 316

Faculty Loan Repayment Program • 242

Fanny Bullock Workman Fellowship • 542

Felipe Rojas-Lombardi Scholarships • 224

Getting Money for College: Scholarships for Hispanic Students

Fellowship Program in AIDS Care for Minority Medical Students • 246

Fellowships for Minority Doctoral Students • 1

First in My Family Scholarship Program • 19

Fisher Broadcasting, Inc., Scholarship for Minorities • 122

Fleming/Baszcak Scholarship • 451

Florida Women's State Golf Association Scholarship Fund • 482

Foley & Lardner Minority Scholarship Program • 280

Ford Foundation Dissertation Fellowships for Minorities • 125

Ford Foundation Dissertation Fellowships for Minorities • 437

Ford Foundation Postdoctoral Fellowship for Minorities • 126

Ford Foundation Pre-doctoral Fellowships for Minorities • 127

Ford Motor Company Fellows Program • 439

Ford Motor Company Scholarship • 210

Ford Motor Company Scholarship-Graduate • 523

Ford Motor Company Scholarship-Undergraduate • 524

Frances Shaw Fellowship • 496

Franklin C. McLean Award • 247

Fredrikson and Byron Foundation Minority Scholarship • 281

Fresh Start Scholarship • 483

Fulfilling Our Dreams Scholarship Fund • 447

Future Journalists Scholarship Program • 121

Garth Reeves, Jr. Memorial Scholarships • 136

Gates Millennium Scholars Program • 420

GE/LULAC Scholarship • 87

GEM MS Engineering Fellowship • 22

GEM PhD Engineering Fellowship • 23

GEM PhD Science Fellowship • 70

General Electric Foundation Scholarship • 211

General Federation of Women's Clubs of Massachusetts Memorial Education Fellowship • 486

General Motors Foundation Graduate Scholarship • 113

General Motors Foundation Undergraduate Scholarships • 114

General Scholarship Fund • 388

George M. Brooker Collegiate Scholarship for Minorities • 323

Georgia Harkness Scholarships • 331

Gerber Fellowship in Pediatric Nutrition • 248

Gertrude Cox Scholarship for Women in Statistics • 525

Gina Auditore Boner Memorial Scholarship Fund • 78

Girls Going Places Scholarship Program • 528

Gladys Stone Wright Scholarship • 183

GM/LULAC Scholarship • 195

Golden Jubilee Fellowship • 535

Goldman Family Fund, New Leader Scholarship • 156

Governor's Opportunity Scholarship • 81

Graduate Fellowships • 161

Graduate Scholarship in Music Education • 176

GRE and Graduate Applications Waiver • 110

Gretchen L. Blechschmidt Award • 160

Gubelmann Family Foundation Scholarship Fund • 476

Gulfcoast College Scholarship Award • 363

Harriet A. Shaw Fellowship • 47

Harry and Bertha Bronstein Memorial Scholarship • 477

HBCU-Central.com Minority Scholarship Program • 408

Health Services Scholarship for Women Studying Abroad • 230

Helen May Butler Memorial Scholarship • 184

Herbert W. and Corinne Chilstrom Scholarship • 334

Hermione Grant Calhoun Scholarship • 372

HHAF Chase and Mastercard Academic Excellence Youth Award • 410

HHAF Dr. Pepper Leadership and Community Service Youth Award • 411

HHAF Exxon Mobil Mathematics Youth Award • 412

HHAF Glaxo Smith Kline Health and Science Youth Award • 413

HHAF NBC Journalism Youth Award • 414

HHAF Sports Youth Award • 415

High School Program • 421

Hispanic Alliance for Career Enhancement National Scholarship Program • 409

Hispanic College Fund Scholarship Program • 20

Hispanic College Fund/INROADS/Sprint Scholarship Program • 82

Hispanic Division Fellowships • 43

Hispanic Engineer National Achievement Awards Corporation Scholarship Program • 51

Hispanic Outlook in Higher Education Scholarship Award • 416

Hispanic Theological Initiative Dissertation Year Grant • 327

Hispanic Theological Initiative Doctoral Grant • 328

Hispanic Theological Initiative Special Mentoring Grant • 329

Historically Black Colleges and Universities Future Engineering Faculty Fellowship • 108

Holly A. Cornell Scholarship • 29
Horizons Foundation Scholarship • 545
Horton-Hallowell Fellowship • 543
Household International Corporate Scholars • 93
Howard Mayer Brown Fellowship • 303
HSF-ALPFA Scholarships • 3
HSF/Club Musica Latina Scholarship • 422
HSF/Ford Motor Company Corporate Scholarship Program • 423
HSF/General Motors Scholarship • 83
HSF/National Society of Hispanic MBA's Scholarship Program • 84
HSF/NHFA Entertainment Industry Scholarship Program • 424
HSF/Pfizer, Inc. Fellowship • 425
HSF/South Texas Scholarship • 426
HSF/Toyota Foundation Scholarship Program-Puerto Rico • 427
HSF/Toyota Scholarship Program • 428
Huggins-Quarles Award • 443
Hugh J. Andersen Memorial Scholarships • 249
Idaho Minority and "At Risk" Student Scholarship • 488
Illinois Consortium for Educational Opportunity Program Fellowship • 430
Illinois Minority Graduate Incentive Program Fellowship • 142
Indiana Minority Teacher and Special Education Services Scholarship Program • 180
Information Handling Services, Inc./SAE Women Engineers Committee Scholarship • 197
Institute for International Public Policy Fellowship Program • 44
Institute of Chinese Studies Awards • 45
Institute of Management Accountants Memorial Education Fund Diversity Scholarships • 13
Inter American Press Association Scholarships • 271
International Federation of University Women Fellowships • 529
International Society of Women Airline Pilots Airline Scholarships • 52
International Society of Women Airline Pilots Career Scholarship • 53
International Society of Women Airline Pilots Fiorenza de Bernardi Merit Scholarship • 54
International Society of Women Airline Pilots Grace McAdams Harris Scholarship • 55
International Society of Women Airline Pilots Holly Mullens Memorial Scholarship • 56
International Society of Women Airline Pilots North Carolina Career Scholarship • 57
International Teacher Education Scholarship • 165
Irving Graef Memorial Scholarship • 250

Ivy Parker Memorial Scholarship • 212
J. Frances Allen Scholarship Award • 63
Jackie Robinson Scholarship • 431
James Carlson Scholarship Program • 175
James H. Robinson M.D. Memorial Prize in Surgery • 251
Jeannette Rankin Foundation Awards • 530
Jennings Randolph Senior Fellow Award • 46
Jimmy A. Young Memorial Education Recognition Award • 237
Joel Garcia Memorial Scholarship • 120
John Edgar Thomson Foundation Grants • 371
Jose Marti Scholarship Challenge Grant • 432
Jose Marti Scholarship Challenge Grant Fund • 405
Joseph S. Adams Scholarship • 225
Judith L. Weidman Racial Ethnicity Minority Fellowship • 137
Judith Resnik Memorial Scholarship • 59
Junior Girls Scholarship Program • 369
Kala Singh Graduate Scholarship for International/Minority Students • 118
Kappa Alpha Theta Foundation Merit Based Scholarship Program • 364
Kappa Alpha Theta Foundation Named Trust Grant Program • 365
Kappa Kappa Gamma Foundation Graduate Scholarships • 366
Kappa Kappa Gamma Foundation Undergraduate Scholarship • 367
Karen B. Lewis Career Education Scholarship • 499
Karla Scherer Foundation Scholarships • 163
Katherine J. Shutze Memorial Scholarship • 325
Ken Inouye Scholarship • 277
Ken Kashiwahara Scholarship • 131
Kim Love Satory Scholarship • 5
Knight Ridder Minority Scholarship Program • 86
KPMG Minority Accounting Doctoral Scholarship • 14
L'Oreal /Family Circle Cup "Personal Best" Scholarship • 481
Ladies Auxiliary of the Fleet Reserve Association Scholarship • 368
Latin American Educational Foundation Scholarships • 434
Latino Education Association Scholarship • 395
Laurels Fund • 6
Leadership for Diversity Scholarship • 290
Lela Murphy Scholarship • 349
Leonard C. Horn Award for Legal Studies • 282
Leonard M. Perryman Communications Scholarship for Ethnic Minority Students • 138

Getting Money for College: Scholarships for Hispanic Students

Lexington Herald-Leader/Knight Ridder
Minority Scholarships • 88
Library and Information Technology
Association/LSSI Minority Scholarship
• 291
Library and Information Technology
Association/OCLC Minority Scholarship
• 292
Lilian Moller Gilbreth Scholarship • 213
Linda Riddle/SGMA Scholarship • 341
Lockheed Aeronautics Company
Scholarships • 189
Lockheed-Martin Corporation Scholarships
• 214
Lois McMillen Memorial Scholarship Fund
• 50
Lucille B. Kaufman Women's Scholarship
Fund • 200
Lucinda Todd Book Scholarship • 170
LULAC National Scholarship Fund • 435
Lydia I. Pickup Memorial Scholarship • 147
M.A. Cartland Shackford Medical Fellowship
• 258
MALDEF Law School Scholarship Program
• 283
Many Voices Residency Program • 297
Marby M. Noxon Scholarship Fund • 39
Margaret Dale Philp Biennial Award • 260
Margaret Freeman Bowers Fellowship • 287
Margaret McNamara Memorial Fund
Fellowships • 531
Margaret McWilliams Pre-doctoral Fellowship
• 394
Margot Karle Scholarship for CUNY Women
Students • 468
Maria Elena Salinas Scholarship • 273
Marlynne Graboys Wool Scholarship • 286
Martha Ann Stark Memorial Scholarship
• 185
Martin Luther King Physician/Dentist
Scholarships • 157
Martin Luther King, Jr. Memorial Scholarship
• 171
Martin Luther King, Jr. Scholarship Award
• 150
Mary Barrett Marshall Scholarship • 348
Mary Ellen Russell Memorial Scholarship
• 220
Mary Elvira Steven Travelling Fellowship
• 544
Mary Isabel Sibley Fellowship for Greek and
French Studies • 33
Mary McEwen Schimke Scholarship • 265
Mary N. Brooks Daughter/Granddaughter
Scholarship • 362
Mary N. Brooks Wyoming Girl Scholarship
• 484
Mary Rubin and Benjamin M. Rubin
Scholarship Fund • 471
Mas Family Scholarship Award • 85
Mas Family Scholarships • 80

MASWE Memorial Scholarship • 215
Matthew "Bump" Mitchell /Sun-Sentinel
Scholarship • 478
Medical Library Association Scholarship for
Minority Students • 293
Mentor Graphics Scholarship • 143
Meridith Thoms Memorial Scholarship • 216
Metropolitan Life Foundation Awards
Program for Academic Excellence in
Medicine • 252
Michele Clark Fellowship • 132
Microsoft Corporation Scholarships • 148
Mike Reynolds $1,000 Scholarship • 133
Mildred Richards Taylor Memorial
Scholarship • 298
Minorities in Government Finance
Scholarship • 9
Minority Affairs Committee Award for
Outstanding Scholastic Achievement • 95
Minority Doctoral Assistance
Loan-For-Service Program • 492
Minority Fellowship for HIV/AIDS Research
Training • 235
Minority Fellowship for Neuroscience
Training • 65
Minority Fellowship in Mental Health and
Substance Abuse Services • 236
Minority Fellowship Program • 239
Minority Master's Fellows Program • 168
Minority Research Awards • 262
Minority Retention Grant-Wisconsin • 458
Minority Scholarship Awards for College
Students • 96
Minority Scholarship Awards for Incoming
College Freshmen • 97
Minority Teachers of Illinois Scholarship
Program • 173
Minority Teaching Fellows Program/
Tennessee • 182
Minority Undergraduate Student Awards • 72
Miss America Organization Competition
Scholarships • 504
Miss American Coed Pageant • 503
Miss Outstanding Teenager and Leadership
Training Program • 489
Missouri Minority Teaching Scholarship
• 174
Multicultural Affairs Scholarship • 128
Multicultural Scholarship Program • 438
Music Technology Scholarship • 186
Music Therapy Scholarships (SAI) • 305
N.S. Bienstock Fellowship • 134
NACME Scholars Program • 196
NASP-ERT Minority Scholarship Program
• 440
National Association of Hispanic Journalists
Scholarship • 124
National Association of Minority Engineering
Program Administrators National
Scholarship Fund • 58

National Defense Science and Engineering Graduate Fellowship Program • 98

National Hispanic Explorers Scholarship Program • 31

National Leadership Development Grants • 407

National Medical Fellowships, Inc. General Need-Based Scholarship Programs • 253

National Minority Junior Golf Scholarship • 442

National Physical Science Consortium Graduate Fellowships in the Physical Sciences • 105

National Society of Professional Surveyors for Equal Opportunity/Mary Feindt Scholarship • 343

National Teen-Ager Scholarship Foundation • 532

Nellie Yeoh Whetten Award • 28

Nevada Women's Fund Scholarships • 490

New Horizons Scholars Program • 429

New Jersey Educational Opportunity Fund Grants • 158

New Jersey Scholarship • 217

New Jersey Utilities Association Scholarship • 491

NIH Undergraduate Scholarship for Individuals from Disadvantaged Backgrounds • 73

NIH Undergraduate Scholarship Program for Students from Disadvantaged Backgrounds • 71

NLAPW Virginia Liebeler Biennial Grants for Mature Women (Arts) • 48

NLAPW Virginia Liebeler Biennial Grants for Mature Women (Letters) • 505

NLAPW Virginia Liebeler Biennial Grants for Mature Women (Music) • 506

NOA Vocal Competition/ Legacy Award Program • 49

Norma Ross Walter Scholarship • 301

North American Doctoral Fellows Program • 326

Northwest Journalists of Color Scholarship • 119

Northwest Journalists of Color Scholarship • 274

NSPE Auxiliary Scholarship • 106

NSPE-Virginia D. Henry Memorial Scholarship • 107

Ohio Newspapers Foundation Minority Scholarship • 275

Olive Lynn Salembier Scholarship • 218

ONS Foundation Ethnic Minority Bachelor's Scholarship • 313

ONS Foundation Ethnic Minority Master's Scholarship • 314

ONS Foundation Ethnic Minority Researcher and Mentorship Grants • 257

Pacific Fellowship Fund • 520

Page Education Foundation Grant • 444

Past Presidents Scholarships • 219

Peggy Howard Fellowship in Economics • 164

PEO International Peace Scholarship • 534

Philanthrophy and the Nonprofit Sector Dissertation Fellowship • 90

Porter Physiology Fellowships • 64

Professor Elizabeth F. Fisher Fellowship • 162

Puerto Rican Bar Association Scholarship Award • 284

Puerto Rican Legal Defense and Education Fund Fr. Joseph Fitzpatrick Scholarship Program • 285

Puget Sound Chapter Scholarship • 159

R.O.S.E. Fund Scholarship Program • 495

Racial Ethnic Supplemental Grant • 330

Ralph W. Ellison Memorial Prize • 254

Raymond H. Trott Scholarship • 446

RDW Group, Inc. Minority Scholarship for Communications • 135

Regents Professional Opportunity Scholarships • 493

Rhode Island Commission on Women/Freda Goldman Education Award • 497

Richard S. Smith Scholarship • 456

RMHC/Hispanic American Commitment to Educational Resources Scholarship Program • 436

Robert B. Bailey III Minority Scholarships for Education Abroad • 400

Robert D. Watkins Minority Graduate Research Fellowship • 67

Robin Roberts/WBCA Sports Communications Scholarship Award • 139

Rosewood Family Scholarship Fund • 406

Royce Osborn Minority Student Scholarship • 238

Ruth Clare Yonkee District Scholarship • 485

Ruth Ingersoll Goldmark Fellowship • 299

SACNAS Financial Aid: Lodging and Travel Award • 449

Sarah Bradley Tyson Memorial Fellowship • 268

Sarah Bradley Tyson Memorial Fellowship • 24

Sarah Perry Wood Medical Fellowship • 259

Scholarship for Young Women • 540

Scholarship Program • 417

Scholarships for Minority Accounting Students • 2

Scotts Company Scholars Program • 267

Sevcik Scholarship • 221

Sexuality Research Fellowship Program • 336

Sherry R. Arnstein Minority Student Scholarship • 379

Sigma Alpha Iota Doctoral Grant • 177

Sigma Alpha Iota Graduate Performance Awards • 306

Sigma Alpha Iota Philanthropies Undergraduate Performance Scholarships • 307

Sigma Alpha Iota Philanthropies Undergraduate Scholarships • 178

Sigma Alpha Iota Scholarship for Conductors • 308

Sigma Alpha Iota Summer Music Scholarships in the U.S. or abroad • 309

Sigma Alpha Iota Visually Impaired Scholarship • 179

Sloan PhD Program • 104

Society of Daughters of the United States Army Scholarships • 376

Society of Hispanic Professional Engineers Foundation • 109

Society of Women Engineers-Rocky Mountain Section Scholarship Program • 149

Soroptimist Women's Opportunity Award • 536

Southwestern Bell Bates Scholarship Fund • 386

Special Animation and Illustration Scholarship • 459

Special Libraries Association Affirmative Action Scholarship • 294

Spectrum Scholarship • 295

Spinsters Ink Young Feminist Scholarship • 507

SREB Dissertation Year Fellowship • 452

SREB Doctoral Scholars Program • 453

SSRC-Mellon Pre-doctoral Research Grant • 448

Stan Beck Fellowship • 69

Student Council for Exceptional Children Ethnic Diversity Award • 338

Student Opportunity Scholarship-Presbyterian Church (U.S.A.) • 445

Susan Glover Hitchcock Scholarship • 304

Sylvia Lane Mentor Research Fellowship Fund • 18

Talbots Women's Scholarship Fund • 539

Talent Incentive Program-Wisconsin • 501

TEA Don Sahli-Kathy Woodall Minority Scholarship • 181

Technical Minority Scholarship • 115

TELACU Engineering Award • 99

Thomas Jefferson Fellowship • 266

Thomas R. Dargan Minority Scholarship • 123

Top Ten College Women Competition • 527

Transportation Clubs International Ginger and Fred Deines Mexico Scholarship • 60

Travel and Training Fund • 510

Travel Grants for Women in Mathematics • 320

Tyler Ward Minority Scholarship • 278

U.S. VFW Mexican Ancestry Scholarship • 457

UNCF/Pfizer Corporate Scholars Program • 27

United Methodist Church Ethnic Minority Scholarship • 332

United Methodist Church Ethnic Scholarship • 454

United Methodist Church Hispanic, Asian, and Native American Scholarship • 455

United Parcel Service Diversity Scholarship Program • 384

UPS Scholarship for Female Students • 193

UPS Scholarship for Minority Students • 194

Utah Educationally Disadvantaged Program • 374

Verna Ross Orndorff Career Performance Grant • 310

Vida Dutton Scudder Fellowship • 300

Virginia Society of CPAs Educational Foundation Minority Undergraduate Scholarship • 15

Volkwein Memorial Scholarship • 187

W.K. Kellogg Fellowship Program in Health Policy Research • 228

Walter Reed Smith Scholarship • 91

WBCA Scholarship Award • 509

Whirly Girls Scholarship Fund • 61

William and Charlotte Cadbury Award • 255

William F. Cooper Scholarship • 500

William Randolph Hearst Endowed Scholarship for Minority Students • 269

Women in Need Scholarship • 7

Women in Science and Technology Scholarship • 74

Women in Transition/Women in Need Scholarship • 8

Women's Independence Scholarship Program • 537

Women's Jewelry Association Scholarship Program • 344

Women's Western Golf Foundation Scholarship • 511

Worldstudio Foundation Scholarship Program • 42

WSCPA Fifth-Year Accounting Scholarships • 16

WSCPA Scholarships for Minority Accounting Majors • 17

Wyeth-Ayerst Laboratories Prize in Women's Health • 256

Young Women in Public Affairs Award • 546

Youth Opportunities Foundation Scholarships • 460

SPONSOR INDEX

Adelante! U.S. Education Leadership Fund
• 34
AGA Foundation for Digestive Health and
Nutrition • 222, 231
Aim Magazine Short Story Contest • 296
Alpha Delta Kappa Foundation • 165
Alumnae Panhellenic Association of
Washington, D.C. • 465
Amarillo Area Foundation • 466
America's Junior Miss Scholarship Program
• 512
American Academy of Child and Adolescent
Psychiatry (AACAP) • 232, 233
American Agricultural Economics
Association Foundation • 18
American Architectural Foundation • 35
American Association of Colleges of
Osteopathic Medicine • 379
American Association of Law Libraries • 279
American Association of University Women
(AAUW) Educational Foundation • 36,
166, 513, 514, 515, 516, 517
American Association of University
Women-Honolulu Branch • 518, 519, 520
American Chemical Society • 94
American Coed Pageants, Inc. -Florida • 503
American Congress on Surveying and
Mapping • 342, 343
American Correctional Association • 150
American Dental Association (ADA)
Foundation • 151
American Dental Hygienists' Association
(ADHA) Institute • 152, 153
American Federation of State, County, and
Municipal Employees • 380
American Fisheries Society • 63
American Geological Institute • 381
American GI Forum of the United States
• 521
American Institute for Foreign Study • 382
American Institute of Architects • 37
American Institute of Certified Public
Accountants • 1, 2
American Institute of Chemical Engineers
• 95, 96, 97
American Legion Auxiliary, Department of
Colorado • 346
American Legion Auxiliary, Department of
Florida • 347
American Legion Auxiliary, Department of
Kentucky • 348
American Legion Auxiliary, Department of
Maryland • 311, 377

American Legion Auxiliary, Department of
Michigan • 378
American Legion Auxiliary, Department of
Missouri • 349
American Legion Auxiliary, Department of
Nebraska • 350
American Legion Auxiliary, Department of
Oregon • 351
American Legion Auxiliary, Department of
South Dakota • 352, 353, 354
American Legion Auxiliary, Department of
Washington • 467
American Legion Auxiliary, National
Headquarters • 355, 356
American Meteorological Society • 302
American Musicological Society • 303
American Nuclear Society • 192
American Physical Society • 317
American Physiological Society • 25, 64
American Planning Association • 383
American Political Science Association • 321
American Psychiatric Association • 234
American Psychological Association • 65,
235, 236
American Respiratory Care Foundation • 237
American Society for Engineering Education
• 98
American Society for Microbiology • 66, 67
American Society of Radiologic
Technologists Education and Research
Foundation • 238
American Society of Safety Engineers (ASSE)
Foundation • 384, 522, 523, 524
American Sociological Association • 239
American Speech-Language-Hearing
Foundation • 117, 118
American Statistical Association • 525
American Vacuum Society • 28
American Water Works Association • 29
Appraisal Institute • 322
Arizona Association of Chicanos in Higher
Education (AACHE) • 385
Arkansas Community Foundation, Inc. • 386
Arkansas Department of Higher Education
• 167, 168
Armed Forces Communications and
Electronics Association, Educational
Foundation • 140
Asian American Journalists Association—
Seattle Chapter • 119
Aspen Institute • 269
Association for Women Geoscientists, Puget
Sound Chapter • 159

Association for Women in Architecture
Foundation • 38
Association for Women in Mathematics
• 318, 319, 320
Association for Women in Science
Educational Foundation • 26, 32
Association of Latino Professionals in
Finance and Accounting • 3
Astraea Lesbian Action Foundation • 468
Barbara Alice Mower Memorial Scholarship
Committee • 469
BECA Foundation, Inc. • 154, 387, 388
Bowen Foundation • 345
British Federation of Women Graduates
(BFWG) • 526
Brown Foundation for Educational Equity,
Excellence, and Research • 169, 170
Business and Professional Women's
Foundation • 68
California Adolescent Nutrition and Fitness
(CANFit) Program • 223
California Chicano News Media Association
(CCNMA) • 120
California Junior Miss Scholarship Program
• 470
California Library Association • 289
California School Library Association • 290
California Teachers Association (CTA) • 171
Canadian Federation of University Women
• 21, 260, 389, 390, 391, 392, 393, 394
Casualty Actuarial Society/Society of
Actuaries Joint Committee on Minority
Recruiting • 75
Center for the Advancement of Hispanics in
Science and Engineering Education
(CAHSEE) • 30
Central Scholarship Bureau • 471
Charlotte Observer • 76
City College of San Francisco Latino
Educational Association • 395
Colorado Business and Professional
Women's Foundation Scholarship • 472
Colorado Society of Certified Public
Accountants Educational Foundation • 4
Community Foundation for Palm Beach and
Martin Counties, Inc. • 5, 39, 77, 78, 396,
473, 474, 475, 476, 477, 478
COMTO-Boston Chapter • 40
Congressional Black Caucus Spouses
Program • 226, 315
Congressional Hispanic Caucus Institute
• 397, 398
Connecticut Association of Latin Americans
in Higher Education (CALAHE) • 399
Connecticut Department of Higher
Education • 337
Consortium for Graduate Study in
Management • 79
Council for Exceptional Children • 338
Council for International Educational
Exchange • 400

Council on Social Work Education • 240,
241
Cuban American National Foundation • 80
Cuban American Scholarship Fund • 479
Dallas-Fort Worth Association of Black
Communicators • 121
Daughters of the Cincinnati • 375
Delaware Higher Education Commission
• 480
Delta Delta Delta Foundation • 357, 358
Delta Gamma Foundation • 359, 360
Disciples of Christ Homeland Ministries
• 324, 325
Dow Jones Newspaper Fund • 401
East Los Angeles Community Union
(TELACU) Education Foundation • 99,
402
Eaton Corporation • 141
Educational Foundation for Women in
Accounting (EFWA) • 6, 7, 8
Elks Gold Award Scholarships/Girl Scouts of
the USA • 361
Entomological Foundation • 69
Esperanza, Inc. • 403
Ethel Louise Armstrong Foundation • 373
Family Circle Cup and L'Oreal • 481
Fisher Broadcasting Company • 122
Florida Board of Education, Division of
Colleges and Universities • 404
Florida Department of Education • 405, 406
Florida Women's State Golf Association
• 482
Foley and Lardner, Attorneys at Law • 280
Foundation of American College Healthcare
Executives • 227
Foundation of the National Student Nurses'
Association • 312
Fredrikson and Byron Foundation • 281
Freedom Forum • 270
Fresh Start Scholarship Foundation, Inc.
• 483
Fund for Theological Education, Inc. (FTE)
• 326
GEM Consortium • 22, 23, 70
General Board of Global Ministries • 407
General Commission on Archives and
History • 261
General Federation of Women's Clubs in
Wyoming • 362, 484, 485
General Federation of Women's Clubs of
Massachusetts • 486
General Federation of Women's Clubs of
Vermont • 487
Geological Society of America • 160
Girl Scouts of Gulfcoast Florida, Inc. • 363
Glamour • 527
Golf Course Superintendents Association of
America • 267
Government Finance Officers Association • 9
Governor's Office • 81

Guardian Life Insurance Company of America • 528

HBCU-Central.com • 408

Health Resources and Services Administration Division of Health Careers Diversity and Development (DHCDD) • 242

Hispanic Alliance Career Enhancement • 409

Hispanic College Fund, Inc. • 10, 11, 12, 19, 20, 31, 82

Hispanic Dental Association • 155

Hispanic Division, Library of Congress • 43

Hispanic Engineer National Achievement Awards Corporation (HENAAC) • 51

Hispanic Heritage Foundation Awards • 410, 411, 412, 413, 414, 415

Hispanic Outlook in Higher Education Magazine • 416

Hispanic Public Relations Association • 417

Hispanic Scholarship Fund • 83, 84, 418, 419, 420, 421, 422, 423, 424, 425, 426, 427, 428, 429

Hispanic Theological Initiative • 327, 328, 329

Hostess Committee Scholarships/Miss America Pageant • 172, 243, 282, 316, 504

Idaho State Board of Education • 488

Illinois Student Assistance Commission (ISAC) • 173

IMGIP/ICEOP • 142, 430

Institute for International Public Policy (IIPP) • 44

Institute of China Studies • 45

Institute of Industrial Engineers • 193, 194

Institute of Management Accountants • 13

Institute of Real Estate Management Foundation • 323

Inter American Press Association Scholarship Fund, Inc. • 271

International Federation of University Women • 529

International Society of Women Airline Pilots (ISA+21) • 52, 53, 54, 55, 56, 57

Jackie Robinson Foundation • 431

James Beard Foundation, Inc. • 224

Jeannette Rankin Foundation, Inc. • 530

Jewish Foundation for Education of Women • 461

John Edgar Thomson Foundation • 371

Jorge Mas Canosa Freedom Foundation • 85

Jose Marti Scholarship Challenge Grant Fund • 432

Kansas Board of Regents • 433

Kappa Alpha Theta Foundation • 364, 365

Kappa Kappa Gamma Foundation • 366, 367

Karla Scherer Foundation • 163

KATU Thomas R. Dargan Minority Scholarship • 123

Knight Ridder • 86

KPMG Foundation • 14

Ladies Auxiliary of the Fleet Reserve Association • 368

Ladies Auxiliary to the Veterans of Foreign Wars • 369

Latin American Educational Foundation • 434

League of United Latin American Citizens National Educational Service Centers, Inc. • 87, 195, 435

Lexington Herald-Leader • 88

Library and Information Technology Association • 291, 292

Los Angeles Council of Black Professional Engineers • 100, 101, 102

Margaret McNamara Memorial Fund • 531

Marin Education Fund • 156

McDonald's Corporation and RMHC • 436

Medical Library Association • 293

Mellon New England • 304

Mexican American Legal Defense and Educational Fund • 283

Miss Outstanding Teenager • 489

Missouri Department of Elementary and Secondary Education • 174

NAMEPA National Scholarship Foundation • 58

NASA New Hampshire Space Grant Consortium • 161

National Academies • 437

National Action Council for Minorities in Engineering-NACME, Inc. • 103, 104, 196

National Association for Campus Activities • 438

National Association for the Advancement of Colored People • 89

National Association of Hispanic Journalists (NAHJ) • 124, 272, 273

National Association of Latino Elected and Appointed Officials Education Fund • 439

National Association of School Psychologists-Education and Research Trust • 440

National Collegiate Athletic Association • 339

National Council of Jewish Women (Greater Boston) • 441

National Federation of the Blind • 372

National Foundation for Infectious Diseases • 244

National Institutes of Health • 71

National League of American Pen Women, Inc. • 48, 505, 506

National Medical Fellowships, Inc. • 228, 245, 246, 247, 248, 249, 250, 251, 252, 253, 254, 255, 256

National Minority Junior Golf Scholarship Association • 442

National Opera Association • 49

National Physical Science Consortium • 105

National Research Council • 125, 126, 127

National Teen-Ager Scholarship Foundation
• 532
Nevada Women's Fund • 490
New Jersey Utilities Association • 491
New Mexico Commission on Higher
Education • 492 .
New York State Higher Education Services
Corporation • 493
New York State Society of Professional
Engineers • 106, 107
Ninety-Nines, Inc. • 533
Northwest Journalists of Color • 274
Office of Naval Research • 108
Ohio Newspapers Foundation • 275
ONS Foundation • 257, 313, 314
Oregon Student Assistance Commission
• 143, 175, 494
Organization of American Historians • 443
Oscar B. Cintas Foundation, Inc. • 41
Page Education Foundation • 444
PEO International Peace Scholarship Fund
• 534
Phi Beta Kappa Society • 33
Playwrights' Center • 297
Presbyterian Church (USA) • 330, 445
Public Relations Student Society of America
• 128
Puerto Rican Legal Defense and Education
Fund • 284, 285
R.O.S.E. Fund • 495
Radcliffe Institute for Advanced
Study-Murray Research Center • 335
Radio-Television News Directors Association
and Foundation • 129, 130, 131, 132,
133, 134
Ragdale Foundation • 496
Rhode Island Foundation • 135, 286, 446,
497
Roscoe Pound Institute • 229
Salvadoran American Leadership and
Educational Fund • 447
Seattle Post-Intelligencer • 276
Sigma Alpha Iota Philanthropies, Inc. • 176,
177, 178, 179, 305, 306, 307, 308, 309,
310
Social Science Research Council • 90, 336,
448
Sociedad Honoraria Hispánica • 225
Society for Advancement of Chicanos and
Native Americans in Science (SACNAS)
• 449
Society of Actuaries • 450
Society of Automotive Engineers • 197
Society of Daughters of the United States
Army • 376
Society of Hispanic Professional Engineers
Foundation • 109
Society of Manufacturing Engineers
Education Foundation • 198, 199, 200
Society of Mexican American Engineers and
Scientists • 110

Society of Plastics Engineers (SPE)
Foundation • 451
Society of Professional Journalists, Los
Angeles Chapter • 277
Society of Professional Journalists-Mid-Florida
Chapter • 278
Society of Professional Journalists-South
Florida Chapter • 136
Society of Toxicology • 72
Society of Women Engineers • 59, 111, 112,
113, 114, 116, 144, 145, 146, 147, 148,
188, 189, 190, 191, 201, 202, 203, 204,
205, 206, 207, 208, 209, 210, 211, 212,
213, 214, 215, 216, 217, 218, 219
Society of Women Engineers-Pacific
Northwest Section • 220
Society of Women Engineers-Rocky
Mountain Section • 149
Soroptimist International of Great Britain
and Ireland • 535
Soroptimist International of the Americas
• 536
Southern Regional Education Board • 452,
453
Special Libraries Association • 294
Spinsters Ink • 507
State Student Assistance Commission of
Indiana (SSACI) • 180
Sunshine Lady Foundation, Inc. • 537
Take Me Away to College Scholarship
Competition • 538
Talbots Charitable Foundation • 539
Tennessee Education Association • 181
Tennessee Student Assistance Corporation
• 182
Texas Library Association • 295
Third Wave Foundation • 540
Transportation Clubs International • 60
Triangle Education Foundation • 221
United Daughters of the Confederacy • 91,
298
United Methodist Church • 331, 454, 455
United Methodist Church General
Commission on Archives and History
• 262
United Methodist Church-Iowa Annual
Conference • 332
United Methodist Communications • 137,
138
United Methodist Youth Organization • 456
United Negro College Fund • 27, 92, 93
United States Department of Health and
Human Services • 73
United States Institute of Peace • 46
University of Medicine and Dentistry of NJ
School of Osteopathic Medicine • 157,
158
Utah State Board of Regents • 374
Veterans of Foreign Wars • 457
Virginia Business and Professional Women's
Foundation • 74, 498, 499

Virginia Society of Certified Public
  Accountants Education Foundation • 15
Washington Society of Certified Public
  Accountants • 16, 17
Waterbury Foundation • 50
Wellesley College • 47, 162, 164, 258, 259,
  263, 264, 265, 266, 287, 299, 300, 508,
  541, 542, 543, 544
Whirly-Girls, Inc., International Women
  Helicopter Pilots • 61
Willa Cather Foundation • 301
William F. Cooper Scholarship Trust • 500
Wisconsin Higher Educational Aid Board
  • 458, 501
Woman's National Farm and Garden
  Association • 24
Women Band Directors International • 183,
  184, 185, 186, 187
Women in Defense (WID), A National
  Security Organization • 545

Women of the Evangelical Lutheran Church
  in America • 230, 333, 334, 462, 463,
  464
Women's Basketball Coaches Association
  • 139, 288, 509
Women's International Bowling Congress
  • 370
Women's Jewelry Association • 344
Women's National Farm and Garden
  Association • 268
Women's Research and Education Institute
  • 502
Women's Sports Foundation • 340, 341, 510
Women's Western Golf Foundation • 511
Worldstudio Foundation • 42, 459
Xerox • 115
Youth Opportunities Foundation • 460
Zonta International Foundation • 62, 546

ACADEMIC FIELDS/CAREER GOALS INDEX

Accounting

Allfirst/ Hispanic College Fund Scholarship Program • 10
Burlington Northern Santa Fe Foundation/ Hispanic College Fund Scholarship Program • 11
Denny's/Hispanic College Fund Scholarship • 12
Ethnic Diversity College and University Scholarships • 4
Fellowships for Minority Doctoral Students • 1
HSF-ALPFA Scholarships • 3
Institute of Management Accountants Memorial Education Fund Diversity Scholarships • 13
Kim Love Satory Scholarship • 5
KPMG Minority Accounting Doctoral Scholarship • 14
Laurels Fund • 6
Minorities in Government Finance Scholarship • 9
Scholarships for Minority Accounting Students • 2
Virginia Society of CPAs Educational Foundation Minority Undergraduate Scholarship • 15
Women in Need Scholarship • 7
Women in Transition/Women in Need Scholarship • 8
WSCPA Fifth-Year Accounting Scholarships • 16
WSCPA Scholarships for Minority Accounting Majors • 17

Agribusiness

First in My Family Scholarship Program • 19
Hispanic College Fund Scholarship Program • 20
Sylvia Lane Mentor Research Fellowship Fund • 18

Agriculture

Canadian Federation of University Women Memorial Fellowship • 21
GEM MS Engineering Fellowship • 22
GEM PhD Engineering Fellowship • 23
Sarah Bradley Tyson Memorial Fellowship • 24
Sylvia Lane Mentor Research Fellowship Fund • 18

Animal/Veterinary Sciences

American Physiological Society Minority Travel Fellowships • 25
Association for Women in Science Undergraduate Award • 26
UNCF/Pfizer Corporate Scholars Program • 27

Applied Sciences

CAHSEE Fellowship: Young Educators Program • 30
Canadian Federation of University Women Memorial Fellowship • 21
Holly A. Cornell Scholarship • 29
National Hispanic Explorers Scholarship Program • 31
Nellie Yeoh Whetten Award • 28

Archaeology

Association for Women in Science Pre-doctoral Fellowship • 32
Mary Isabel Sibley Fellowship for Greek and French Studies • 33

Architecture

AAUW Educational Foundation Selected Professions Fellowships • 36
Adelante U.S. Education Leadership Fund • 34
American Institute of Architects Minority/ Disadvantaged Scholarship • 35
American Institute of Architects/American Architectural Foundation Minority/ Disadvantaged Scholarships • 37
Association for Women in Architecture Scholarship • 38
Cintas Fellowships Program • 41
COMTO Boston/Garrett A. Morgan Scholarship • 40
Denny's/Hispanic College Fund Scholarship • 12
GEM MS Engineering Fellowship • 22
GEM PhD Engineering Fellowship • 23
Marby M. Noxon Scholarship Fund • 39
Worldstudio Foundation Scholarship Program • 42

Area/Ethnic Studies

Hispanic Division Fellowships • 43
Institute for International Public Policy Fellowship Program • 44
Institute of Chinese Studies Awards • 45
Jennings Randolph Senior Fellow Award • 46

Area/Ethnic Studies (continued)

Mary Isabel Sibley Fellowship for Greek and French Studies • 33

Art History
Harriet A. Shaw Fellowship • 47
Mary Isabel Sibley Fellowship for Greek and French Studies • 33

Arts
Cintas Fellowships Program • 41
Harriet A. Shaw Fellowship • 47
Lois McMillen Memorial Scholarship Fund • 50
Mary Isabel Sibley Fellowship for Greek and French Studies • 33
NLAPW Virginia Liebeler Biennial Grants for Mature Women (Arts) • 48
NOA Vocal Competition/ Legacy Award Program • 49
Worldstudio Foundation Scholarship Program • 42

Aviation/Aerospace
Amelia Earhart Fellowship Awards • 62
CAHSEE Fellowship: Young Educators Program • 30
Hispanic Engineer National Achievement Awards Corporation Scholarship Program • 51
International Society of Women Airline Pilots Airline Scholarships • 52
International Society of Women Airline Pilots Career Scholarship • 53
International Society of Women Airline Pilots Fiorenza de Bernardi Merit Scholarship • 54
International Society of Women Airline Pilots Grace McAdams Harris Scholarship • 55
International Society of Women Airline Pilots Holly Mullens Memorial Scholarship • 56
International Society of Women Airline Pilots North Carolina Career Scholarship • 57
Judith Resnik Memorial Scholarship • 59
National Association of Minority Engineering Program Administrators National Scholarship Fund • 58
National Hispanic Explorers Scholarship Program • 31
Transportation Clubs International Ginger and Fred Deines Mexico Scholarship • 60
Whirly Girls Scholarship Fund • 61

Biology
American Physiological Society Minority Travel Fellowships • 25
ASM Minority Undergraduate Research Fellowship • 66
Association for Women in Science Pre-doctoral Fellowship • 32
Association for Women in Science Undergraduate Award • 26
BPW Career Advancement Scholarship Program for Women • 68

CAHSEE Fellowship: Young Educators Program • 30
Canadian Federation of University Women Memorial Fellowship • 21
GEM MS Engineering Fellowship • 22
GEM PhD Engineering Fellowship • 23
GEM PhD Science Fellowship • 70
Hispanic Engineer National Achievement Awards Corporation Scholarship Program • 51
Holly A. Cornell Scholarship • 29
J. Frances Allen Scholarship Award • 63
Minority Fellowship for Neuroscience Training • 65
Minority Undergraduate Student Awards • 72
National Hispanic Explorers Scholarship Program • 31
NIH Undergraduate Scholarship for Individuals from Disadvantaged Backgrounds • 73
NIH Undergraduate Scholarship Program for Students from Disadvantaged Backgrounds • 71
Porter Physiology Fellowships • 64
Robert D. Watkins Minority Graduate Research Fellowship • 67
Stan Beck Fellowship • 69
UNCF/Pfizer Corporate Scholars Program • 27
Women in Science and Technology Scholarship • 74

Business/Consumer Services
AAUW Educational Foundation Selected Professions Fellowships • 36
Actuarial Scholarships for Minority Students • 75
Allfirst/ Hispanic College Fund Scholarship Program • 10
Bank of America Minority Scholarship • 77
Burlington Northern Santa Fe Foundation/ Hispanic College Fund Scholarship Program • 11
Charlotte Observer Minority Scholarships • 76
College Fund/Coca Cola Corporate Intern Program • 92
Consortium Fellowship • 79
Denny's/Hispanic College Fund Scholarship • 12
Earl G. Graves NAACP Scholarship • 89
First in My Family Scholarship Program • 19
GE/LULAC Scholarship • 87
Gina Auditore Boner Memorial Scholarship Fund • 78
Governor's Opportunity Scholarship • 81
Hispanic College Fund Scholarship Program • 20
Hispanic College Fund/INROADS/Sprint Scholarship Program • 82
Household International Corporate Scholars • 93

Getting Money for College: Scholarships for Hispanic Students

HSF-ALPFA Scholarships • 3
HSF/General Motors Scholarship • 83
HSF/National Society of Hispanic MBA's Scholarship Program • 84
Knight Ridder Minority Scholarship Program • 86
Lexington Herald-Leader/Knight Ridder Minority Scholarships • 88
Marby M. Noxon Scholarship Fund • 39
Mas Family Scholarship Award • 85
Mas Family Scholarships • 80
Minorities in Government Finance Scholarship • 9
Philanthrophy and the Nonprofit Sector Dissertation Fellowship • 90
UNCF/Pfizer Corporate Scholars Program • 27
Walter Reed Smith Scholarship • 91
WSCPA Fifth-Year Accounting Scholarships • 16

Chemical Engineering
Al-Ben Scholarship for Academic Incentive • 100
Al-Ben Scholarship for Professional Merit • 101
Al-Ben Scholarship for Scholastic Achievement • 102
American Chemical Society Scholars Program • 94
Association for Women in Science Undergraduate Award • 26
CAHSEE Fellowship: Young Educators Program • 30
Canadian Federation of University Women Memorial Fellowship • 21
Chevron Texaco Corporation Scholarships • 111
Denny's/Hispanic College Fund Scholarship • 12
Dupont Company Scholarships • 112
Engineering Vanguard Program • 103
First in My Family Scholarship Program • 19
General Motors Foundation Graduate Scholarship • 113
General Motors Foundation Undergraduate Scholarships • 114
GRE and Graduate Applications Waiver • 110
Hispanic College Fund Scholarship Program • 20
Hispanic Engineer National Achievement Awards Corporation Scholarship Program • 51
Historically Black Colleges and Universities Future Engineering Faculty Fellowship • 108
HSF/General Motors Scholarship • 83
Mas Family Scholarship Award • 85
Mas Family Scholarships • 80
Minority Affairs Committee Award for Outstanding Scholastic Achievement • 95

Minority Scholarship Awards for College Students • 96
Minority Scholarship Awards for Incoming College Freshmen • 97
National Association of Minority Engineering Program Administrators National Scholarship Fund • 58
National Defense Science and Engineering Graduate Fellowship Program • 98
National Hispanic Explorers Scholarship Program • 31
National Physical Science Consortium Graduate Fellowships in the Physical Sciences • 105
NSPE Auxiliary Scholarship • 106
NSPE-Virginia D. Henry Memorial Scholarship • 107
Sloan PhD Program • 104
Society of Hispanic Professional Engineers Foundation • 109
Technical Minority Scholarship • 115
TELACU Engineering Award • 99
UNCF/Pfizer Corporate Scholars Program • 27

Civil Engineering
Al-Ben Scholarship for Academic Incentive • 100
Al-Ben Scholarship for Professional Merit • 101
Al-Ben Scholarship for Scholastic Achievement • 102
Bechtel Corporation Scholarship • 116
CAHSEE Fellowship: Young Educators Program • 30
Canadian Federation of University Women Memorial Fellowship • 21
Chevron Texaco Corporation Scholarships • 111
COMTO Boston/Garrett A. Morgan Scholarship • 40
Engineering Vanguard Program • 103
GEM MS Engineering Fellowship • 22
GEM PhD Engineering Fellowship • 23
GRE and Graduate Applications Waiver • 110
Hispanic Engineer National Achievement Awards Corporation Scholarship Program • 51
Historically Black Colleges and Universities Future Engineering Faculty Fellowship • 108
HSF/General Motors Scholarship • 83
Mas Family Scholarship Award • 85
National Association of Minority Engineering Program Administrators National Scholarship Fund • 58
National Defense Science and Engineering Graduate Fellowship Program • 98
National Hispanic Explorers Scholarship Program • 31
NSPE Auxiliary Scholarship • 106

Civil Engineering (continued)

NSPE-Virginia D. Henry Memorial
    Scholarship • 107
Sloan PhD Program • 104
Society of Hispanic Professional Engineers
    Foundation • 109

Communications

ASHF Graduate Student Scholarship for
    Minority Students • 117
Carole Simpson Scholarship • 129
College Fund/Coca Cola Corporate Intern
    Program • 92
Denny's/Hispanic College Fund Scholarship
    • 12
Ed Bradley Scholarship • 130
First in My Family Scholarship Program • 19
Fisher Broadcasting, Inc., Scholarship for
    Minorities • 122
Ford Foundation Dissertation Fellowships for
    Minorities • 125
Ford Foundation Postdoctoral Fellowship for
    Minorities • 126
Ford Foundation Pre-doctoral Fellowships
    for Minorities • 127
Future Journalists Scholarship Program • 121
Garth Reeves, Jr. Memorial Scholarships
    • 136
Hispanic College Fund Scholarship Program
    • 20
Hispanic College Fund/INROADS/Sprint
    Scholarship Program • 82
Joel Garcia Memorial Scholarship • 120
Judith L. Weidman Racial Ethnicity Minority
    Fellowship • 137
Kala Singh Graduate Scholarship for
    International/Minority Students • 118
Ken Kashiwahara Scholarship • 131
Leonard M. Perryman Communications
    Scholarship for Ethnic Minority Students
    • 138
Mas Family Scholarship Award • 85
Mas Family Scholarships • 80
Michele Clark Fellowship • 132
Mike Reynolds $1,000 Scholarship • 133
Multicultural Affairs Scholarship • 128
N.S. Bienstock Fellowship • 134
National Association of Hispanic Journalists
    Scholarship • 124
National Hispanic Explorers Scholarship
    Program • 31
Northwest Journalists of Color Scholarship
    • 119
RDW Group, Inc. Minority Scholarship for
    Communications • 135
Robin Roberts/WBCA Sports
    Communications Scholarship Award
    • 139
Thomas R. Dargan Minority Scholarship
    • 123

Computer Science/Data Processing

AAUW Educational Foundation Selected
    Professions Fellowships • 36
Al-Ben Scholarship for Academic Incentive
    • 100
Al-Ben Scholarship for Professional Merit
    • 101
Al-Ben Scholarship for Scholastic
    Achievement • 102
Allfirst/ Hispanic College Fund Scholarship
    Program • 10
Armed Forces Communications and
    Electronics Association Ralph W. Shrader
    Scholarships • 140
Association for Women in Science
    Pre-doctoral Fellowship • 32
Association for Women in Science
    Undergraduate Award • 26
BPW Career Advancement Scholarship
    Program for Women • 68
CAHSEE Fellowship: Young Educators
    Program • 30
Canadian Federation of University Women
    Memorial Fellowship • 21
College Fund/Coca Cola Corporate Intern
    Program • 92
Compaq Computer Scholarship • 144
David Sarnoff Research Center Scholarship
    • 145
Dell Computer Corporation Scholarships
    • 146
Denny's/Hispanic College Fund Scholarship
    • 12
Eaton Corporation Multicultural Scholars
    Program • 141
Engineering Vanguard Program • 103
First in My Family Scholarship Program • 19
Ford Foundation Pre-doctoral Fellowships
    for Minorities • 127
GEM MS Engineering Fellowship • 22
GEM PhD Engineering Fellowship • 23
Hispanic College Fund Scholarship Program
    • 20
Hispanic College Fund/INROADS/Sprint
    Scholarship Program • 82
Hispanic Engineer National Achievement
    Awards Corporation Scholarship Program
    • 51
Household International Corporate Scholars
    • 93
Illinois Minority Graduate Incentive Program
    Fellowship • 142
Lydia I. Pickup Memorial Scholarship • 147
Mentor Graphics Scholarship • 143
Microsoft Corporation Scholarships • 148
National Association of Minority Engineering
    Program Administrators National
    Scholarship Fund • 58
National Hispanic Explorers Scholarship
    Program • 31

National Physical Science Consortium
Graduate Fellowships in the Physical
Sciences • 105
Northwest Journalists of Color Scholarship
• 119
Sloan PhD Program • 104
Society of Women Engineers-Rocky
Mountain Section Scholarship Program
• 149
Technical Minority Scholarship • 115
TELACU Engineering Award • 99
Walter Reed Smith Scholarship • 91
Women in Science and Technology
Scholarship • 74

Criminal Justice/Criminology
Martin Luther King, Jr. Scholarship Award
• 150

Dental Health/Services
Alice Newell Joslyn Medical Fund • 154
American Dental Association Foundation
Minority Dental Student Scholarship
Program • 151
American Dental Hygienists' Association
Institute Minority Scholarship • 152
BPW Career Advancement Scholarship
Program for Women • 68
Colgate "Bright Smiles, Bright Futures"
Minority Scholarship • 153
Dr. Juan D. Villarreal/ Hispanic Dental
Association Foundation • 155
Goldman Family Fund, New Leader
Scholarship • 156
Martin Luther King Physician/Dentist
Scholarships • 157
New Jersey Educational Opportunity Fund
Grants • 158
Women in Science and Technology
Scholarship • 74

Drafting
COMTO Boston/Garrett A. Morgan
Scholarship • 40
First in My Family Scholarship Program • 19
Hispanic College Fund Scholarship Program
• 20

Earth Science
Association for Women in Science
Pre-doctoral Fellowship • 32
Association for Women in Science
Undergraduate Award • 26
Canadian Federation of University Women
Memorial Fellowship • 21
GEM MS Engineering Fellowship • 22
GEM PhD Engineering Fellowship • 23
GEM PhD Science Fellowship • 70
Graduate Fellowships • 161
Gretchen L. Blechschmidt Award • 160
National Hispanic Explorers Scholarship
Program • 31

National Physical Science Consortium
Graduate Fellowships in the Physical
Sciences • 105
Professor Elizabeth F. Fisher Fellowship
• 162
Puget Sound Chapter Scholarship • 159
Sarah Bradley Tyson Memorial Fellowship
• 24

Economics
Allfirst/ Hispanic College Fund Scholarship
Program • 10
Denny's/Hispanic College Fund Scholarship
• 12
First in My Family Scholarship Program • 19
Hispanic College Fund Scholarship Program
• 20
Hispanic College Fund/INROADS/Sprint
Scholarship Program • 82
Institute for International Public Policy
Fellowship Program • 44
Jennings Randolph Senior Fellow Award
• 46
Karla Scherer Foundation Scholarships • 163
Mas Family Scholarship Award • 85
Mas Family Scholarships • 80
Minorities in Government Finance
Scholarship • 9
Peggy Howard Fellowship in Economics
• 164
Sloan PhD Program • 104
Sylvia Lane Mentor Research Fellowship
Fund • 18

Education
Albert A. Marks, Jr. Scholarship for Teacher
Education • 172
Arkansas Minority Teacher Scholars Program
• 167
BPW Career Advancement Scholarship
Program for Women • 68
Brown Scholar • 169
COMTO Boston/Garrett A. Morgan
Scholarship • 40
Eleanor Roosevelt Teacher Fellowships • 166
Gladys Stone Wright Scholarship • 183
Governor's Opportunity Scholarship • 81
Graduate Scholarship in Music Education
• 176
Helen May Bulter Memorial Scholarship
• 184
Indiana Minority Teacher and Special
Education Services Scholarship Program
• 180
International Teacher Education Scholarship
• 165
James Carlson Scholarship Program • 175
Lucinda Todd Book Scholarship • 170
Martha Ann Stark Memorial Scholarship
• 185
Martin Luther King, Jr. Memorial Scholarship
• 171
Minority Master's Fellows Program • 168

Education (continued)

Minority Teachers of Illinois Scholarship
Program • 173

Minority Teaching Fellows Program/
Tennessee • 182

Missouri Minority Teaching Scholarship
• 174

Music Technology Scholarship • 186

Sigma Alpha Iota Doctoral Grant • 177

Sigma Alpha Iota Philanthropies
Undergraduate Scholarships • 178

Sigma Alpha Iota Visually Impaired
Scholarship • 179

TEA Don Sahli-Kathy Woodall Minority
Scholarship • 181

Volkwein Memorial Scholarship • 187

Electrical Engineering/Electronics

AAUW Educational Foundation Selected
Professions Fellowships • 36

Al-Ben Scholarship for Academic Incentive
• 100

Al-Ben Scholarship for Professional Merit
• 101

Al-Ben Scholarship for Scholastic
Achievement • 102

Armed Forces Communications and
Electronics Association Ralph W. Shrader
Scholarships • 140

Bechtel Corporation Scholarship • 116

CAHSEE Fellowship: Young Educators
Program • 30

COMTO Boston/Garrett A. Morgan
Scholarship • 40

Daimler Chrysler Corporation Scholarship
• 188

Dell Computer Corporation Scholarships
• 146

Denny's/Hispanic College Fund Scholarship
• 12

Eaton Corporation Multicultural Scholars
Program • 141

Engineering Vanguard Program • 103

First in My Family Scholarship Program • 19

GEM MS Engineering Fellowship • 22

GEM PhD Engineering Fellowship • 23

General Motors Foundation Undergraduate
Scholarships • 114

Hispanic College Fund Scholarship Program
• 20

Hispanic College Fund/INROADS/Sprint
Scholarship Program • 82

Hispanic Engineer National Achievement
Awards Corporation Scholarship Program
• 51

HSF/General Motors Scholarship • 83

Illinois Minority Graduate Incentive Program
Fellowship • 142

Lockheed Aeronautics Company
Scholarships • 189

Mas Family Scholarship Award • 85

Mas Family Scholarships • 80

Mentor Graphics Scholarship • 143

National Association of Minority Engineering
Program Administrators National
Scholarship Fund • 58

National Defense Science and Engineering
Graduate Fellowship Program • 98

National Hispanic Explorers Scholarship
Program • 31

National Physical Science Consortium
Graduate Fellowships in the Physical
Sciences • 105

NSPE Auxiliary Scholarship • 106

NSPE-Virginia D. Henry Memorial
Scholarship • 107

Sloan PhD Program • 104

Society of Hispanic Professional Engineers
Foundation • 109

Technical Minority Scholarship • 115

TELACU Engineering Award • 99

Engineering-Related Technologies

AAUW Educational Foundation Selected
Professions Fellowships • 36

ABB Lummis Global • 190

Al-Ben Scholarship for Academic Incentive
• 100

Al-Ben Scholarship for Professional Merit
• 101

Al-Ben Scholarship for Scholastic
Achievement • 102

Allfirst/ Hispanic College Fund Scholarship
Program • 10

Arizona Section Scholarship • 191

BPW Career Advancement Scholarship
Program for Women • 68

CAHSEE Fellowship: Young Educators
Program • 30

Compaq Computer Scholarship • 144

COMTO Boston/Garrett A. Morgan
Scholarship • 40

Denny's/Hispanic College Fund Scholarship
• 12

Eaton Corporation Multicultural Scholars
Program • 141

Engineering Vanguard Program • 103

First in My Family Scholarship Program • 19

Ford Foundation Dissertation Fellowships for
Minorities • 125

Ford Foundation Postdoctoral Fellowship for
Minorities • 126

Ford Foundation Pre-doctoral Fellowships
for Minorities • 127

General Motors Foundation Undergraduate
Scholarships • 114

GRE and Graduate Applications Waiver
• 110

Hispanic College Fund Scholarship Program
• 20

Hispanic College Fund/INROADS/Sprint
Scholarship Program • 82

Getting Money for College: Scholarships for Hispanic Students

Historically Black Colleges and Universities Future Engineering Faculty Fellowship • 108
HSF/General Motors Scholarship • 83
Illinois Minority Graduate Incentive Program Fellowship • 142
Mas Family Scholarship Award • 85
Mas Family Scholarships • 80
National Association of Minority Engineering Program Administrators National Scholarship Fund • 58
National Defense Science and Engineering Graduate Fellowship Program • 98
National Hispanic Explorers Scholarship Program • 31
NSPE Auxiliary Scholarship • 106
NSPE-Virginia D. Henry Memorial Scholarship • 107
Sloan PhD Program • 104
Society of Hispanic Professional Engineers Foundation • 109
Technical Minority Scholarship • 115
TELACU Engineering Award • 99

Engineering/Technology

AAUW Educational Foundation Selected Professions Fellowships • 36
ABB Lummis Global • 190
Admiral Grace Murray Hopper Memorial Scholarship • 201
Adobe Systems Computer Science Scholarship • 202
Al-Ben Scholarship for Academic Incentive • 100
Al-Ben Scholarship for Professional Merit • 101
Al-Ben Scholarship for Scholastic Achievement • 102
Allfirst/ Hispanic College Fund Scholarship Program • 10
Anne Maureen Whitney Barrow Memorial Scholarship • 203
Arizona Section Scholarship • 191
Armed Forces Communications and Electronics Association Ralph W. Shrader Scholarships • 140
Association for Women in Science Pre-doctoral Fellowship • 32
Association for Women in Science Undergraduate Award • 26
B.J. Harrod Scholarship • 204
B.K. Krenzer Memorial Reentry Scholarship • 205
Bechtel Corporation Scholarship • 116
BPW Career Advancement Scholarship Program for Women • 68
Burlington Northern Santa Fe Foundation/ Hispanic College Fund Scholarship Program • 11
CAHSEE Fellowship: Young Educators Program • 30
Caterpillar Scholars Award Fund • 198

Chevron Texaco Corporation Scholarships • 111
College Fund/Coca Cola Corporate Intern Program • 92
Compaq Computer Scholarship • 144
COMTO Boston/Garrett A. Morgan Scholarship • 40
David Sarnoff Research Center Scholarship • 145
Delayed Education for Women Scholarships • 192
Dell Computer Corporation Scholarships • 146
Delphi Scholarship • 206
Denny's/Hispanic College Fund Scholarship • 12
Dorothy Lemke Howarth Scholarships • 207
Dorothy M. and Earl S. Hoffman Scholarship • 208
Eaton Corporation Multicultural Scholars Program • 141
Edward S. Roth Manufacturing Engineering Scholarship • 199
Electronics for Imaging (EFI) Scholarships • 209
Engineering Vanguard Program • 103
First in My Family Scholarship Program • 19
Fisher Broadcasting, Inc., Scholarship for Minorities • 122
Ford Motor Company Scholarship • 210
GE/LULAC Scholarship • 87
GEM MS Engineering Fellowship • 22
GEM PhD Engineering Fellowship • 23
General Electric Foundation Scholarship • 211
General Motors Foundation Graduate Scholarship • 113
General Motors Foundation Undergraduate Scholarships • 114
GM/LULAC Scholarship • 195
Graduate Fellowships • 161
GRE and Graduate Applications Waiver • 110
Hispanic College Fund Scholarship Program • 20
Hispanic College Fund/INROADS/Sprint Scholarship Program • 82
Hispanic Engineer National Achievement Awards Corporation Scholarship Program • 51
Historically Black Colleges and Universities Future Engineering Faculty Fellowship • 108
Holly A. Cornell Scholarship • 29
HSF/General Motors Scholarship • 83
Illinois Minority Graduate Incentive Program Fellowship • 142
Information Handling Services, Inc./SAE Women Engineers Committee Scholarship • 197
Ivy Parker Memorial Scholarship • 212

Engineering/Technology (continued)
Judith Resnik Memorial Scholarship • 59
Lilian Moller Gilbreth Scholarship • 213
Lockheed-Martin Corporation Scholarships
   • 214
Lucille B. Kaufman Women's Scholarship
   Fund • 200
Lydia I. Pickup Memorial Scholarship • 147
Mary Ellen Russell Memorial Scholarship
   • 220
Mas Family Scholarships • 80
MASWE Memorial Scholarship • 215
Meridith Thoms Memorial Scholarship • 216
NACME Scholars Program • 196
National Association of Minority Engineering
   Program Administrators National
   Scholarship Fund • 58
National Defense Science and Engineering
   Graduate Fellowship Program • 98
National Hispanic Explorers Scholarship
   Program • 31
Nellie Yeoh Whetten Award • 28
New Jersey Scholarship • 217
NSPE Auxiliary Scholarship • 106
NSPE-Virginia D. Henry Memorial
   Scholarship • 107
Olive Lynn Salembier Scholarship • 218
Past Presidents Scholarships • 219
Sevcik Scholarship • 221
Sloan PhD Program • 104
Society of Hispanic Professional Engineers
   Foundation • 109
Society of Women Engineers-Rocky
   Mountain Section Scholarship Program
   • 149
Technical Minority Scholarship • 115
TELACU Engineering Award • 99
UPS Scholarship for Female Students • 193
UPS Scholarship for Minority Students • 194
Women in Science and Technology
   Scholarship • 74

Fashion Design
Worldstudio Foundation Scholarship
   Program • 42

Filmmaking/Video
Worldstudio Foundation Scholarship
   Program • 42

Food Science/Nutrition
American Gastroenterological Association
   Student Research Fellowship
   Underrepresented Minorities Award • 222
California Adolescent Nutrition and Fitness
   (CANFit) Program Scholarship • 223
Felipe Rojas-Lombardi Scholarships • 224
Goldman Family Fund, New Leader
   Scholarship • 156
National Hispanic Explorers Scholarship
   Program • 31
Walter Reed Smith Scholarship • 91

Food Service/Hospitality
California Adolescent Nutrition and Fitness
   (CANFit) Program Scholarship • 223

Foreign Language
Ford Foundation Dissertation Fellowships for
   Minorities • 125
Ford Foundation Postdoctoral Fellowship for
   Minorities • 126
Ford Foundation Pre-doctoral Fellowships
   for Minorities • 127
Hispanic Division Fellowships • 43
Institute for International Public Policy
   Fellowship Program • 44
Joseph S. Adams Scholarship • 225
Mary Isabel Sibley Fellowship for Greek and
   French Studies • 33
Minority Master's Fellows Program • 168

Geography
Association for Women in Science
   Pre-doctoral Fellowship • 32
Graduate Fellowships • 161
Hispanic Division Fellowships • 43

Graphics/Graphic Arts/Printing
Denny's/Hispanic College Fund Scholarship
   • 12
First in My Family Scholarship Program • 19
Future Journalists Scholarship Program • 121
Gina Auditore Boner Memorial Scholarship
   Fund • 78
Hispanic College Fund Scholarship Program
   • 20
Knight Ridder Minority Scholarship Program
   • 86
Worldstudio Foundation Scholarship
   Program • 42

Health Administration
Albert W. Dent Graduate Student
   Scholarship • 227
Congressional Black Caucus Spouses Health
   Initiative • 226
Elaine Osborne Jacobson Award for Women
   Working in Health Care Law • 229
Goldman Family Fund, New Leader
   Scholarship • 156
Health Services Scholarship for Women
   Studying Abroad • 230
W.K. Kellogg Fellowship Program in Health
   Policy Research • 228

Health and Medical Sciences
AACAP Jeanne Spurlock Minority Medical
   Student Clinical Fellowship in Child and
   Adolescent Psychiatry • 232
AACAP Jeanne Spurlock Research
   Fellowship in Drug Abuse and Addiction
   for Minority Medical Students • 233
AAUW Educational Foundation Selected
   Professions Fellowships • 36
Alice Newell Joslyn Medical Fund • 154

American Gastroenterological Association Research Scholar Awards for Underrepresented Minorities • 231

American Gastroenterological Association Student Research Fellowship Underrepresented Minorities Award • 222

American Physiological Society Minority Travel Fellowships • 25

American Psychiatric Association/Center for Mental Health Services Minority Fellowship Program • 234

ASHF Graduate Student Scholarship for Minority Students • 117

BPW Career Advancement Scholarship Program for Women • 68

Bristol-Myers Squibb Fellowship Program in Academic Medicine for Minority Students • 245

California Adolescent Nutrition and Fitness (CANFit) Program Scholarship • 223

Canadian Federation of University Women Memorial Fellowship • 21

Colin L. Powell Minority Postdoctoral Fellowship in Tropical Disease Research • 244

Congressional Black Caucus Spouses Health Initiative • 226

Council on Social Work Education/Mental Health Minority Research Fellowship • 240

Doctoral Fellowships in Social Work for Ethnic Minority Students Preparing for Leadership Roles in Mental Health and/or Substance Abuse • 241

Dr. and Mrs. David B. Allman Medical Scholarships • 243

Elaine Osborne Jacobson Award for Women Working in Health Care Law • 229

Faculty Loan Repayment Program • 242

Fellowship Program in AIDS Care for Minority Medical Students • 246

Franklin C. McLean Award • 247

Gerber Fellowship in Pediatric Nutrition • 248

Goldman Family Fund, New Leader Scholarship • 156

Governor's Opportunity Scholarship • 81

Health Services Scholarship for Women Studying Abroad • 230

Hugh J. Andersen Memorial Scholarships • 249

Irving Graef Memorial Scholarship • 250

James H. Robinson M.D. Memorial Prize in Surgery • 251

Jimmy A. Young Memorial Education Recognition Award • 237

Kala Singh Graduate Scholarship for International/Minority Students • 118

M.A. Cartland Shackford Medical Fellowship • 258

Martin Luther King Physician/Dentist Scholarships • 157

Metropolitan Life Foundation Awards Program for Academic Excellence in Medicine • 252

Minority Fellowship for HIV/AIDS Research Training • 235

Minority Fellowship for Neuroscience Training • 65

Minority Fellowship in Mental Health and Substance Abuse Services • 236

Minority Fellowship Program • 239

Minority Undergraduate Student Awards • 72

National Medical Fellowships, Inc. General Need-Based Scholarship Programs • 253

New Jersey Educational Opportunity Fund Grants • 158

NIH Undergraduate Scholarship for Individuals from Disadvantaged Backgrounds • 73

NIH Undergraduate Scholarship Program for Students from Disadvantaged Backgrounds • 71

ONS Foundation Ethnic Minority Researcher and Mentorship Grants • 257

Porter Physiology Fellowships • 64

Ralph W. Ellison Memorial Prize • 254

Royce Osborn Minority Student Scholarship • 238

Sarah Perry Wood Medical Fellowship • 259

W.K. Kellogg Fellowship Program in Health Policy Research • 228

William and Charlotte Cadbury Award • 255

Women in Science and Technology Scholarship • 74

Wyeth-Ayerst Laboratories Prize in Women's Health • 256

Health Information Management/ Technology

Albert W. Dent Graduate Student Scholarship • 227

Congressional Black Caucus Spouses Health Initiative • 226

Goldman Family Fund, New Leader Scholarship • 156

Health Services Scholarship for Women Studying Abroad • 230

W.K. Kellogg Fellowship Program in Health Policy Research • 228

History

Asian, Black, Hispanic, and Native American United Methodist History Research Awards • 261

Edna V. Moffett Fellowship • 263

Eugene L. Cox Fellowship • 264

Ford Foundation Dissertation Fellowships for Minorities • 125

Ford Foundation Postdoctoral Fellowship for Minorities • 126

Ford Foundation Pre-doctoral Fellowships for Minorities • 127

History (continued)

Hispanic Division Fellowships • 43
Jennings Randolph Senior Fellow Award
• 46
Margaret Dale Philp Biennial Award • 260
Mary Isabel Sibley Fellowship for Greek and
French Studies • 33
Mary McEwen Schimke Scholarship • 265
Minority Research Awards • 262
Philanthrophy and the Nonprofit Sector
Dissertation Fellowship • 90
Thomas Jefferson Fellowship • 266

Home Economics
Walter Reed Smith Scholarship • 91

Horticulture/Floriculture
Sarah Bradley Tyson Memorial Fellowship
• 268
Sarah Bradley Tyson Memorial Fellowship
• 24
Scotts Company Scholars Program • 267

Hospitality Management
Denny's/Hispanic College Fund Scholarship
• 12

Humanities
BPW Career Advancement Scholarship
Program for Women • 68
Hispanic Division Fellowships • 43
Institute for International Public Policy
Fellowship Program • 44
Margaret Dale Philp Biennial Award • 260
Mary Isabel Sibley Fellowship for Greek and
French Studies • 33
William Randolph Hearst Endowed
Scholarship for Minority Students • 269

Interior Design
Association for Women in Architecture
Scholarship • 38
Worldstudio Foundation Scholarship
Program • 42

International Migration
Hispanic Division Fellowships • 43
Jennings Randolph Senior Fellow Award
• 46

International Studies
Hispanic Division Fellowships • 43
Institute for International Public Policy
Fellowship Program • 44
Jennings Randolph Senior Fellow Award
• 46

Journalism
Bobby McCallum Memorial Scholarship
• 276
Carole Simpson Scholarship • 129
Charlotte Observer Minority Scholarships
• 76
Chips Quinn Scholars Program • 270
Cristina Saralegui Scholarship Program • 272

Ed Bradley Scholarship • 130
Fisher Broadcasting, Inc., Scholarship for
Minorities • 122
Future Journalists Scholarship Program • 121
Garth Reeves, Jr. Memorial Scholarships
• 136
Gina Auditore Boner Memorial Scholarship
Fund • 78
Inter American Press Association
Scholarships • 271
Jennings Randolph Senior Fellow Award
• 46
Joel Garcia Memorial Scholarship • 120
Judith L. Weidman Racial Ethnicity Minority
Fellowship • 137
Ken Inouye Scholarship • 277
Ken Kashiwahara Scholarship • 131
Knight Ridder Minority Scholarship Program
• 86
Leonard M. Perryman Communications
Scholarship for Ethnic Minority Students
• 138
Lexington Herald-Leader/Knight Ridder
Minority Scholarships • 88
Maria Elena Salinas Scholarship • 273
Mas Family Scholarship Award • 85
Mas Family Scholarships • 80
Michele Clark Fellowship • 132
Mike Reynolds $1,000 Scholarship • 133
N.S. Bienstock Fellowship • 134
National Association of Hispanic Journalists
Scholarship • 124
Northwest Journalists of Color Scholarship
• 119
Northwest Journalists of Color Scholarship
• 274
Ohio Newspapers Foundation Minority
Scholarship • 275
Tyler Ward Minority Scholarship • 278

Landscape Architecture
Association for Women in Architecture
Scholarship • 38
Sarah Bradley Tyson Memorial Fellowship
• 268

*Law Enforcement/Police
Administration*
Governor's Opportunity Scholarship • 81

Law/Legal Services
AALL and West Group George A. Strait
Minority Scholarship Endowment • 279
AAUW Educational Foundation Selected
Professions Fellowships • 36
BPW Career Advancement Scholarship
Program for Women • 68
Charles T. Stoner Law Scholarship Award
• 288
Elaine Osborne Jacobson Award for Women
Working in Health Care Law • 229
Foley & Lardner Minority Scholarship
Program • 280

Fredrikson and Byron Foundation Minority Scholarship • 281

Jennings Randolph Senior Fellow Award • 46

Leonard C. Horn Award for Legal Studies • 282

MALDEF Law School Scholarship Program • 283

Margaret Freeman Bowers Fellowship • 287

Marlynne Graboys Wool Scholarship • 286

Puerto Rican Bar Association Scholarship Award • 284

Puerto Rican Legal Defense and Education Fund Fr. Joseph Fitzpatrick Scholarship Program • 285

UNCF/Pfizer Corporate Scholars Program • 27

Library and Information Sciences

AALL and West Group George A. Strait Minority Scholarship Endowment • 279

California Library Association Scholarship for Minority Students in Memory of Edna Yelland • 289

Hispanic Division Fellowships • 43

Leadership for Diversity Scholarship • 290

Library and Information Technology Association/LSSI Minority Scholarship • 291

Library and Information Technology Association/OCLC Minority Scholarship • 292

Medical Library Association Scholarship for Minority Students • 293

Special Libraries Association Affirmative Action Scholarship • 294

Spectrum Scholarship • 295

Literature/English/Writing

America's Intercultural Magazine (AIM) Short Story Contest • 296

Cintas Fellowships Program • 41

Ford Foundation Dissertation Fellowships for Minorities • 125

Ford Foundation Postdoctoral Fellowship for Minorities • 126

Ford Foundation Pre-doctoral Fellowships for Minorities • 127

Many Voices Residency Program • 297

Mary Isabel Sibley Fellowship for Greek and French Studies • 33

Mary McEwen Schimke Scholarship • 265

Mildred Richards Taylor Memorial Scholarship • 298

Norma Ross Walter Scholarship • 301

Ruth Ingersoll Goldmark Fellowship • 299

Vida Dutton Scudder Fellowship • 300

Materials Science, Engineering, and Metallurgy

Al-Ben Scholarship for Academic Incentive • 100

Al-Ben Scholarship for Professional Merit • 101

Al-Ben Scholarship for Scholastic Achievement • 102

American Chemical Society Scholars Program • 94

Association for Women in Science Pre-doctoral Fellowship • 32

Association for Women in Science Undergraduate Award • 26

Engineering Vanguard Program • 103

GEM MS Engineering Fellowship • 22

GEM PhD Engineering Fellowship • 23

General Motors Foundation Graduate Scholarship • 113

Hispanic Engineer National Achievement Awards Corporation Scholarship Program • 51

Historically Black Colleges and Universities Future Engineering Faculty Fellowship • 108

Mas Family Scholarship Award • 85

National Association of Minority Engineering Program Administrators National Scholarship Fund • 58

National Defense Science and Engineering Graduate Fellowship Program • 98

National Physical Science Consortium Graduate Fellowships in the Physical Sciences • 105

NSPE Auxiliary Scholarship • 106

NSPE-Virginia D. Henry Memorial Scholarship • 107

Sloan PhD Program • 104

Society of Hispanic Professional Engineers Foundation • 109

Technical Minority Scholarship • 115

Mechanical Engineering

Al-Ben Scholarship for Academic Incentive • 100

Al-Ben Scholarship for Professional Merit • 101

Al-Ben Scholarship for Scholastic Achievement • 102

Association for Women in Science Undergraduate Award • 26

Bechtel Corporation Scholarship • 116

CAHSEE Fellowship: Young Educators Program • 30

Chevron Texaco Corporation Scholarships • 111

COMTO Boston/Garrett A. Morgan Scholarship • 40

Daimler Chrysler Corporation Scholarship • 188

Dell Computer Corporation Scholarships • 146

Dupont Company Scholarships • 112

Eaton Corporation Multicultural Scholars Program • 141

First in My Family Scholarship Program • 19

Mechanical Engineering (continued)

GEM MS Engineering Fellowship • 22
GEM PhD Engineering Fellowship • 23
General Motors Foundation Graduate
    Scholarship • 113
General Motors Foundation Undergraduate
    Scholarships • 114
Hispanic College Fund Scholarship Program
    • 20
Hispanic College Fund/INROADS/Sprint
    Scholarship Program • 82
Hispanic Engineer National Achievement
    Awards Corporation Scholarship Program
    • 51
HSF/General Motors Scholarship • 83
Lockheed Aeronautics Company
    Scholarships • 189
Mas Family Scholarship Award • 85
Mas Family Scholarships • 80
National Association of Minority Engineering
    Program Administrators National
    Scholarship Fund • 58
National Defense Science and Engineering
    Graduate Fellowship Program • 98
National Physical Science Consortium
    Graduate Fellowships in the Physical
    Sciences • 105
NSPE Auxiliary Scholarship • 106
NSPE-Virginia D. Henry Memorial
    Scholarship • 107
Society of Hispanic Professional Engineers
    Foundation • 109
Technical Minority Scholarship • 115
TELACU Engineering Award • 99

Meteorology/Atmospheric Science

American Meteorological Society/Industry
    Minority Scholarships • 302
Association for Women in Science
    Pre-doctoral Fellowship • 32
Association for Women in Science
    Undergraduate Award • 26
CAHSEE Fellowship: Young Educators
    Program • 30
Canadian Federation of University Women
    Memorial Fellowship • 21
Engineering Vanguard Program • 103
GEM PhD Science Fellowship • 70
Graduate Fellowships • 161
National Physical Science Consortium
    Graduate Fellowships in the Physical
    Sciences • 105
Sloan PhD Program • 104

Museum Studies

Harriet A. Shaw Fellowship • 47

Music

Gladys Stone Wright Scholarship • 183
Graduate Scholarship in Music Education
    • 176
Helen May Butler Memorial Scholarship
    • 184

Howard Mayer Brown Fellowship • 303
Martha Ann Stark Memorial Scholarship
    • 185
Music Technology Scholarship • 186
Music Therapy Scholarships (SAI) • 305
Sigma Alpha Iota Doctoral Grant • 177
Sigma Alpha Iota Graduate Performance
    Awards • 306
Sigma Alpha Iota Philanthropies
    Undergraduate Performance Scholarships
    • 307
Sigma Alpha Iota Scholarship for Conductors
    • 308
Sigma Alpha Iota Summer Music
    Scholarships in the U.S. or abroad • 309
Sigma Alpha Iota Visually Impaired
    Scholarship • 179
Susan Glover Hitchcock Scholarship • 304
Verna Ross Orndorff Career Performance
    Grant • 310
Volkwein Memorial Scholarship • 187

Natural Resources

Holly A. Cornell Scholarship • 29
J. Frances Allen Scholarship Award • 63
Sarah Bradley Tyson Memorial Fellowship
    • 268
Sylvia Lane Mentor Research Fellowship
    Fund • 18

Natural Sciences

American Chemical Society Scholars
    Program • 94
Association for Women in Science
    Pre-doctoral Fellowship • 32
Association for Women in Science
    Undergraduate Award • 26
Graduate Fellowships • 161
J. Frances Allen Scholarship Award • 63
Sarah Bradley Tyson Memorial Fellowship
    • 268
Society of Hispanic Professional Engineers
    Foundation • 109

Nuclear Science

Association for Women in Science
    Undergraduate Award • 26
Delayed Education for Women Scholarships
    • 192
Engineering Vanguard Program • 103
GEM MS Engineering Fellowship • 22
GEM PhD Engineering Fellowship • 23
Hispanic Engineer National Achievement
    Awards Corporation Scholarship Program
    • 51
National Defense Science and Engineering
    Graduate Fellowship Program • 98
Sloan PhD Program • 104
Society of Hispanic Professional Engineers
    Foundation • 109

Nursing

Alice Newell Joslyn Medical Fund • 154

American Legion Auxiliary Department of Maryland Past President's Parley Nursing Scholarship • 311

Breakthrough to Nursing Scholarships for Racial/Ethnic Minorities • 312

Goldman Family Fund, New Leader Scholarship • 156

Governor's Opportunity Scholarship • 81

ONS Foundation Ethnic Minority Bachelor's Scholarship • 313

ONS Foundation Ethnic Minority Master's Scholarship • 314

ONS Foundation Ethnic Minority Researcher and Mentorship Grants • 257

Walter Reed Smith Scholarship • 91

Peace and Conflict Studies

Institute for International Public Policy Fellowship Program • 44

Jennings Randolph Senior Fellow Award • 46

Performing Arts

Congressional Black Caucus Spouses Performing Arts Scholarship • 315

Eugenia Vellner Fischer Award for Performing Arts • 316

Gladys Stone Wright Scholarship • 183

Graduate Scholarship in Music Education • 176

Helen May Bulter Memorial Scholarship • 184

Martha Ann Stark Memorial Scholarship • 185

Music Technology Scholarship • 186

NOA Vocal Competition/ Legacy Award Program • 49

Sigma Alpha Iota Doctoral Grant • 177

Sigma Alpha Iota Graduate Performance Awards • 306

Sigma Alpha Iota Philanthropies Undergraduate Performance Scholarships • 307

Sigma Alpha Iota Philanthropies Undergraduate Scholarships • 178

Sigma Alpha Iota Scholarship for Conductors • 308

Sigma Alpha Iota Summer Music Scholarships in the U.S. or abroad • 309

Sigma Alpha Iota Visually Impaired Scholarship • 179

Verna Ross Orndorff Career Performance Grant • 310

Volkwein Memorial Scholarship • 187

Photojournalism/Photography

Fisher Broadcasting, Inc., Scholarship for Minorities • 122

Future Journalists Scholarship Program • 121

Joel Garcia Memorial Scholarship • 120

Judith L. Weidman Racial Ethnicity Minority Fellowship • 137

Leonard M. Perryman Communications Scholarship for Ethnic Minority Students • 138

National Association of Hispanic Journalists Scholarship • 124

Northwest Journalists of Color Scholarship • 119

Physical Sciences and Math

AAUW Educational Foundation Selected Professions Fellowships • 36

Al-Ben Scholarship for Academic Incentive • 100

Al-Ben Scholarship for Professional Merit • 101

Al-Ben Scholarship for Scholastic Achievement • 102

Alice T. Schafer Mathematics Prize for Excellence in Mathematics by an Undergraduate Woman • 318

American Physiological Society Minority Travel Fellowships • 25

Armed Forces Communications and Electronics Association Ralph W. Shrader Scholarships • 140

Association for Women in Mathematics Workshop for Graduate Students and Postdoctoral Mathematicians • 319

Association for Women in Science Pre-doctoral Fellowship • 32

Association for Women in Science Undergraduate Award • 26

BPW Career Advancement Scholarship Program for Women • 68

CAHSEE Fellowship: Young Educators Program • 30

Canadian Federation of University Women Memorial Fellowship • 21

Corporate Sponsored Scholarships for Minority Undergraduate Students Who Major in Physics • 317

Eleanor Roosevelt Teacher Fellowships • 166

Engineering Vanguard Program • 103

Ford Foundation Dissertation Fellowships for Minorities • 125

Ford Foundation Postdoctoral Fellowship for Minorities • 126

Ford Foundation Pre-doctoral Fellowships for Minorities • 127

GEM PhD Science Fellowship • 70

Graduate Fellowships • 161

Illinois Minority Graduate Incentive Program Fellowship • 142

Minority Master's Fellows Program • 168

National Defense Science and Engineering Graduate Fellowship Program • 98

National Physical Science Consortium Graduate Fellowships in the Physical Sciences • 105

Nellie Yeoh Whetten Award • 28

Physical Sciences and Math (continued)

NIH Undergraduate Scholarship for Individuals from Disadvantaged Backgrounds • 73

Porter Physiology Fellowships • 64

Puget Sound Chapter Scholarship • 159

Sloan PhD Program • 104

Travel Grants for Women in Mathematics • 320

Women in Science and Technology Scholarship • 74

Political Science

American Political Science Association Minority Fellows Program • 321

Association for Women in Science Pre-doctoral Fellowship • 32

Ford Foundation Dissertation Fellowships for Minorities • 125

Ford Foundation Postdoctoral Fellowship for Minorities • 126

Ford Foundation Pre-doctoral Fellowships for Minorities • 127

Governor's Opportunity Scholarship • 81

Hispanic Division Fellowships • 43

Institute for International Public Policy Fellowship Program • 44

Jennings Randolph Senior Fellow Award • 46

Mas Family Scholarships • 80

Minorities in Government Finance Scholarship • 9

Vida Dutton Scudder Fellowship • 300

Real Estate

Appraisal Institute Educational Scholarship Program • 322

George M. Brooker Collegiate Scholarship for Minorities • 323

Religion/Theology

Asian, Black, Hispanic, and Native American United Methodist History Research Awards • 261

Christian Services Graduate Study Scholarships for Women • 333

Edwin G. and Lauretta M. Michael Scholarship • 324

Ford Foundation Dissertation Fellowships for Minorities • 125

Ford Foundation Postdoctoral Fellowship for Minorities • 126

Ford Foundation Pre-doctoral Fellowships for Minorities • 127

Georgia Harkness Scholarships • 331

Herbert W. and Corinne Chilstrom Scholarship • 334

Hispanic Theological Initiative Dissertation Year Grant • 327

Hispanic Theological Initiative Doctoral Grant • 328

Hispanic Theological Initiative Special Mentoring Grant • 329

Judith L. Weidman Racial Ethnicity Minority Fellowship • 137

Katherine J. Shutze Memorial Scholarship • 325

Leonard M. Perryman Communications Scholarship for Ethnic Minority Students • 138

Mary Isabel Sibley Fellowship for Greek and French Studies • 33

North American Doctoral Fellows Program • 326

Racial Ethnic Supplemental Grant • 330

United Methodist Church Ethnic Minority Scholarship • 332

Science, Technology, and Society

Eleanor Roosevelt Teacher Fellowships • 166

Engineering Vanguard Program • 103

Governor's Opportunity Scholarship • 81

GRE and Graduate Applications Waiver • 110

Illinois Minority Graduate Incentive Program Fellowship • 142

Jennings Randolph Senior Fellow Award • 46

Minority Master's Fellows Program • 168

Sloan PhD Program • 104

Society of Hispanic Professional Engineers Foundation • 109

Sylvia Lane Mentor Research Fellowship Fund • 18

Women in Science and Technology Scholarship • 74

Social Sciences

Association for Women in Science Pre-doctoral Fellowship • 32

Block Dissertation Award • 335

BPW Career Advancement Scholarship Program for Women • 68

Council on Social Work Education/Mental Health Minority Research Fellowship • 240

Doctoral Fellowships in Social Work for Ethnic Minority Students Preparing for Leadership Roles in Mental Health and/or Substance Abuse • 241

Ford Foundation Dissertation Fellowships for Minorities • 125

Ford Foundation Postdoctoral Fellowship for Minorities • 126

Ford Foundation Pre-doctoral Fellowships for Minorities • 127

Goldman Family Fund, New Leader Scholarship • 156

Institute for International Public Policy Fellowship Program • 44

Jennings Randolph Senior Fellow Award • 46

Margaret Dale Philp Biennial Award • 260

Mary Isabel Sibley Fellowship for Greek and French Studies • 33

Minority Fellowship for HIV/AIDS Research Training • 235

Minority Fellowship in Mental Health and Substance Abuse Services • 236

Minority Fellowship Program • 239

NIH Undergraduate Scholarship Program for Students from Disadvantaged Backgrounds • 71

Sexuality Research Fellowship Program • 336

Sylvia Lane Mentor Research Fellowship Fund • 18

Vida Dutton Scudder Fellowship • 300

William Randolph Hearst Endowed Scholarship for Minority Students • 269

Social Services

ASHF Graduate Student Scholarship for Minority Students • 117

Council on Social Work Education/Mental Health Minority Research Fellowship • 240

Doctoral Fellowships in Social Work for Ethnic Minority Students Preparing for Leadership Roles in Mental Health and/or Substance Abuse • 241

Goldman Family Fund, New Leader Scholarship • 156

Kala Singh Graduate Scholarship for International/Minority Students • 118

Margaret Freeman Bowers Fellowship • 287

Special Education

Connecticut Special Education Teacher Incentive Grant • 337

Indiana Minority Teacher and Special Education Services Scholarship Program • 180

James Carlson Scholarship Program • 175

Minority Teachers of Illinois Scholarship Program • 173

Minority Teaching Fellows Program/ Tennessee • 182

Student Council for Exceptional Children Ethnic Diversity Award • 338

Sports-Related

California Adolescent Nutrition and Fitness (CANFit) Program Scholarship • 223

Dorothy Harris Scholarship • 340

Ethnic Minority and Women's Enhancement Scholarship • 339

Linda Riddle/SGMA Scholarship • 341

Surveying; Surveying Technology, Cartography, or Geographic Information Science

Cady McDonnell Memorial Scholarship • 342

COMTO Boston/Garrett A. Morgan Scholarship • 40

Graduate Fellowships • 161

National Society of Professional Surveyors for Equal Opportunity/Mary Feindt Scholarship • 343

Therapy/Rehabilitation

Alice Newell Joslyn Medical Fund • 154

ASHF Graduate Student Scholarship for Minority Students • 117

Goldman Family Fund, New Leader Scholarship • 156

Indiana Minority Teacher and Special Education Services Scholarship Program • 180

Jimmy A. Young Memorial Education Recognition Award • 237

Kala Singh Graduate Scholarship for International/Minority Students • 118

Music Therapy Scholarships (SAI) • 305

Sigma Alpha Iota Doctoral Grant • 177

Trade/Technical Specialties

General Motors Foundation Graduate Scholarship • 113

Women's Jewelry Association Scholarship Program • 344

Transportation

COMTO Boston/Garrett A. Morgan Scholarship • 40

Transportation Clubs International Ginger and Fred Deines Mexico Scholarship • 60

TV/Radio Broadcasting

Carole Simpson Scholarship • 129

Cristina Saralegui Scholarship Program • 272

Ed Bradley Scholarship • 130

Emma L. Bowen Foundation for Minority Interests in Media • 345

Fisher Broadcasting, Inc., Scholarship for Minorities • 122

Future Journalists Scholarship Program • 121

Joel Garcia Memorial Scholarship • 120

Judith L. Weidman Racial Ethnicity Minority Fellowship • 137

Ken Kashiwahara Scholarship • 131

Leonard M. Perryman Communications Scholarship for Ethnic Minority Students • 138

Maria Elena Salinas Scholarship • 273

Michele Clark Fellowship • 132

Mike Reynolds $1,000 Scholarship • 133

N.S. Bienstock Fellowship • 134

National Association of Hispanic Journalists Scholarship • 124

Northwest Journalists of Color Scholarship • 119

Thomas R. Dargan Minority Scholarship • 123

CIVIC, PROFESSIONAL, SOCIAL, OR UNION AFFILIATION INDEX

American Congress on Surveying and Mapping
Cady McDonnell Memorial Scholarship • 342
National Society of Professional Surveyors for Equal Opportunity/Mary Feindt Scholarship • 343

American Dental Hygienist's Association
American Dental Hygienists' Association Institute Minority Scholarship • 152
Colgate "Bright Smiles, Bright Futures" Minority Scholarship • 153

American Legion or Auxiliary
American Legion Auxiliary Department of Colorado Department President's Scholarship for Junior Members • 346
American Legion Auxiliary Department of Florida Memorial Scholarship • 347
American Legion Auxiliary Department of Nebraska President's Scholarship for Junior Members • 350
American Legion Auxiliary Department of Oregon Spirit of Youth Scholarship • 351
American Legion Auxiliary Department of South Dakota Thelma Foster Scholarship for Senior Auxiliary Members • 352
American Legion Auxiliary Department of South Dakota Thelma Foster Scholarships for Junior Auxiliary Members • 353
American Legion Auxiliary Spirit of Youth Scholarships for Junior Members • 356
American Legion Auxiliary, Department of South Dakota Senior Scholarship • 354
Lela Murphy Scholarship • 349
Mary Barrett Marshall Scholarship • 348

American Physiological Society
American Physiological Society Minority Travel Fellowships • 25

American Society for Microbiology
Robert D. Watkins Minority Graduate Research Fellowship • 67

California Teachers Association
Martin Luther King, Jr. Memorial Scholarship • 171

Fleet Reserve Association/Auxiliary
Ladies Auxiliary of the Fleet Reserve Association Scholarship • 368

General Federation of Women's Clubs in Wyoming
Mary N. Brooks Daughter/Granddaughter Scholarship • 362

Geological Society of America
Gretchen L. Blechschmidt Award • 160

Girl Scouts
American Legion Auxiliary Girl Scout Achievement Award • 355
Elks National Foundation Gold Award Scholarships • 361
Gulfcoast College Scholarship Award • 363

Greek Organization
Delta Delta Delta Graduate Scholarship • 357
Delta Delta Delta Undergraduate Scholarship • 358
Delta Gamma Foundation Fellowships • 359
Delta Gamma Foundation Scholarships • 360
Kappa Alpha Theta Foundation Merit Based Scholarship Program • 364
Kappa Alpha Theta Foundation Named Trust Grant Program • 365
Kappa Kappa Gamma Foundation Graduate Scholarships • 366
Kappa Kappa Gamma Foundation Undergraduate Scholarship • 367

Institute of Industrial Engineers
UPS Scholarship for Female Students • 193
UPS Scholarship for Minority Students • 194

Other Student Academic Clubs
Graduate Scholarship in Music Education • 176
Music Therapy Scholarships (SAI) • 305
Sigma Alpha Iota Doctoral Grant • 177
Sigma Alpha Iota Graduate Performance Awards • 306
Sigma Alpha Iota Philanthropies Undergraduate Performance Scholarships • 307
Sigma Alpha Iota Philanthropies Undergraduate Scholarships • 178
Sigma Alpha Iota Scholarship for Conductors • 308
Sigma Alpha Iota Summer Music Scholarships in the U.S. or abroad • 309
Sigma Alpha Iota Visually Impaired Scholarship • 179
Verna Ross Orndorff Career Performance Grant • 310

Society of Women Engineers

Bechtel Corporation Scholarship • 116

Chevron Texaco Corporation Scholarships
• 111

Daimler Chrysler Corporation Scholarship
• 188

Judith Resnik Memorial Scholarship • 59

United Daughters of the Confederacy

Mildred Richards Taylor Memorial
  Scholarship • 298

Walter Reed Smith Scholarship • 91

Veterans of Foreign Wars or Auxiliary

Junior Girls Scholarship Program • 369

Young American Bowling Alliance

Alberta E. Crowe Star of Tomorrow Award
• 370

EMPLOYMENT EXPERIENCE INDEX

Community service
American Legion Auxiliary Girl Scout
  Achievement Award • 355
Delta Delta Delta Graduate Scholarship • 357
Delta Delta Delta Undergraduate Scholarship
  • 358
Hermione Grant Calhoun Scholarship • 372
Hugh J. Andersen Memorial Scholarships
  • 249
Puerto Rican Legal Defense and Education
  Fund Fr. Joseph Fitzpatrick Scholarship
  Program • 285

Designated career field
Michele Clark Fellowship • 132

ONS Foundation Ethnic Minority Bachelor's
  Scholarship • 313
ONS Foundation Ethnic Minority Master's
  Scholarship • 314
Journalism
Michele Clark Fellowship • 132
Railroad industry
John Edgar Thomson Foundation Grants
  • 371
Teaching
American Gastroenterological Association
  Research Scholar Awards for
  Underrepresented Minorities • 231
Eleanor Roosevelt Teacher Fellowships • 166
Faculty Loan Repayment Program • 242

IMPAIRMENT INDEX

Hearing Impaired
Utah Educationally Disadvantaged Program
• 374

Learning Disabled
Utah Educationally Disadvantaged Program
• 374

Physically Disabled
Ethel Louise Armstrong Foundation
Scholarship • 373

Utah Educationally Disadvantaged Program
• 374

Visually Impaired
Hermione Grant Calhoun Scholarship • 372
Sigma Alpha Iota Visually Impaired
Scholarship • 179
Utah Educationally Disadvantaged Program
• 374

MILITARY SERVICE INDEX

Air Force
Daughters of the Cincinnati Scholarship
• 375

Army
Daughters of the Cincinnati Scholarship
• 375
Society of Daughters of the United States
Army Scholarships • 376

Coast Guard
Daughters of the Cincinnati Scholarship
• 375
Ladies Auxiliary of the Fleet Reserve
Association Scholarship • 368

General
American Legion Auxiliary Department of
Colorado Department President's
Scholarship for Junior Members • 346
American Legion Auxiliary Department of
Maryland Children and Youth
Scholarships • 377
American Legion Auxiliary Department of
Maryland Past President's Parley Nursing
Scholarship • 311

American Legion Auxiliary Department of
Michigan Memorial Scholarship • 378
American Legion Auxiliary Department of
Oregon Spirit of Youth Scholarship • 351
American Legion Auxiliary Department of
South Dakota Thelma Foster Scholarship
for Senior Auxiliary Members • 352
American Legion Auxiliary Department of
South Dakota Thelma Foster Scholarships
for Junior Auxiliary Members • 353
American Legion Auxiliary, Department of
South Dakota Senior Scholarship • 354
Lela Murphy Scholarship • 349
Mary Barrett Marshall Scholarship • 348

Marine Corp
Daughters of the Cincinnati Scholarship
• 375
Ladies Auxiliary of the Fleet Reserve
Association Scholarship • 368

Navy
Daughters of the Cincinnati Scholarship
• 375
Ladies Auxiliary of the Fleet Reserve
Association Scholarship • 368

RELIGIOUS AFFILIATION INDEX

Christian
Hispanic Theological Initiative Dissertation
  Year Grant • 327
Hispanic Theological Initiative Doctoral
  Grant • 328
Hispanic Theological Initiative Special
  Mentoring Grant • 329
North American Doctoral Fellows Program
  • 326

Disciple of Christ
Edwin G. and Lauretta M. Michael
  Scholarship • 324
Katherine J. Shutze Memorial Scholarship
  • 325

Jewish
Amelia Greenbaum/Rabbi Marshal Lipson
  Scholarship • 441
Biller/Jewish Foundation for Education of
  Women • 461

Lutheran
Arne Administrative Scholarship • 462
Belmer/Flora Prince Scholarship • 463

Christian Services Graduate Study
  Scholarships for Women • 333
ELCA Scholarships for Women • 464
Health Services Scholarship for Women
  Studying Abroad • 230
Herbert W. and Corinne Chilstrom
  Scholarship • 334

Methodist
Georgia Harkness Scholarships • 331
Minority Research Awards • 262
National Leadership Development Grants
  • 407
Richard S. Smith Scholarship • 456
United Methodist Church Ethnic Minority
  Scholarship • 332
United Methodist Church Ethnic Scholarship
  • 454
United Methodist Church Hispanic, Asian,
  and Native American Scholarship • 455

Presbyterian
Racial Ethnic Supplemental Grant • 330
Student Opportunity
  Scholarship-Presbyterian Church (U.S.A.)
  • 445

STATE OF RESIDENCE INDEX

Alaska
Cady McDonnell Memorial Scholarship • 342

Arizona
AACHE Scholarship • 385
Burlington Northern Santa Fe Foundation/
Hispanic College Fund Scholarship
Program • 11
Cady McDonnell Memorial Scholarship • 342
Metropolitan Life Foundation Awards
Program for Academic Excellence in
Medicine • 252

Arkansas
Arkansas Minority Teacher Scholars Program
• 167
Minority Master's Fellows Program • 168
Southwestern Bell Bates Scholarship Fund
• 386

California
ABB Lummis Global • 190
Burlington Northern Santa Fe Foundation/
Hispanic College Fund Scholarship
Program • 11
Cady McDonnell Memorial Scholarship • 342
California Adolescent Nutrition and Fitness
(CANFit) Program Scholarship • 223
California Junior Miss Scholarship Program
• 470
California Library Association Scholarship for
Minority Students in Memory of Edna
Yelland • 289
Cuban American Scholarship Fund • 479
Daniel Gutierrez Memorial General
Scholarship Fund • 387
David C. Lizarraga Fellowship • 402
Ford Motor Company Fellows Program • 439
General Scholarship Fund • 388
Governor's Opportunity Scholarship • 81
Joel Garcia Memorial Scholarship • 120
Latino Education Association Scholarship
• 395
Metropolitan Life Foundation Awards
Program for Academic Excellence in
Medicine • 252
TELACU Engineering Award • 99
U.S. VFW Mexican Ancestry Scholarship
• 457
Youth Opportunities Foundation
Scholarships • 460

Colorado
American Legion Auxiliary Department of
Colorado Department President's
Scholarship for Junior Members • 346
Burlington Northern Santa Fe Foundation/
Hispanic College Fund Scholarship
Program • 11
Cady McDonnell Memorial Scholarship • 342
Colorado Business and Professional
Women's Foundation Scholarship • 472
Ethnic Diversity College and University
Scholarships • 4
Latin American Educational Foundation
Scholarships • 434
Metropolitan Life Foundation Awards
Program for Academic Excellence in
Medicine • 252
Society of Women Engineers-Rocky
Mountain Section Scholarship Program
• 149

Connecticut
Connecticut Association of Latin Americans
in Higher Education Scholarships • 399
Lois McMillen Memorial Scholarship Fund
• 50
UNCF/Pfizer Corporate Scholars Program
• 27

Delaware
Agenda For Delaware Women Trailblazer
Scholarship • 480

District of Columbia
Metropolitan Life Foundation Awards
Program for Academic Excellence in
Medicine • 252

Florida
American Legion Auxiliary Department of
Florida Memorial Scholarship • 347
Bank of America Minority Scholarship • 77
Claire B. Schultz Memorial Scholarship • 473
Colonial Bank Scholarship • 396
Courtland and Gina Miller Scholarship Fund
• 474
Denise Lynn Padgett Scholarship Fund • 475
Florida Women's State Golf Association
Scholarship Fund • 482
Ford Motor Company Fellows Program • 439
Garth Reeves, Jr. Memorial Scholarships
• 136
Gina Auditore Boner Memorial Scholarship
Fund • 78
Gubelmann Family Foundation Scholarship
Fund • 476
Gulfcoast College Scholarship Award • 363
Harry and Bertha Bronstein Memorial
Scholarship • 477
Jose Marti Scholarship Challenge Grant • 432

Jose Marti Scholarship Challenge Grant Fund • 405

Kim Love Satory Scholarship • 5

Marby M. Noxon Scholarship Fund • 39

Matthew "Bump" Mitchell /Sun-Sentinel Scholarship • 478

Metropolitan Life Foundation Awards Program for Academic Excellence in Medicine • 252

Georgia
ABB Lummis Global • 190

L'Oreal /Family Circle Cup "Personal Best" Scholarship • 481

Metropolitan Life Foundation Awards Program for Academic Excellence in Medicine • 252

William F. Cooper Scholarship • 500

Hawaii
Barbara Alice Mower Memorial Scholarship • 469

Cady McDonnell Memorial Scholarship • 342

Miss Outstanding Teenager and Leadership Training Program • 489

Idaho
Cady McDonnell Memorial Scholarship • 342

Idaho Minority and "At Risk" Student Scholarship • 488

Miss Outstanding Teenager and Leadership Training Program • 489

Illinois
Burlington Northern Santa Fe Foundation/ Hispanic College Fund Scholarship Program • 11

Ford Motor Company Fellows Program • 439

Illinois Consortium for Educational Opportunity Program Fellowship • 430

Metropolitan Life Foundation Awards Program for Academic Excellence in Medicine • 252

Minority Teachers of Illinois Scholarship Program • 173

Indiana
Indiana Minority Teacher and Special Education Services Scholarship Program • 180

Iowa
United Methodist Church Ethnic Minority Scholarship • 332

Kansas
Ethnic Minority Scholarship Program • 433

Kentucky
Lexington Herald-Leader/Knight Ridder Minority Scholarships • 88

Mary Barrett Marshall Scholarship • 348

Maryland
Allfirst/ Hispanic College Fund Scholarship Program • 10

American Legion Auxiliary Department of Maryland Children and Youth Scholarships • 377

American Legion Auxiliary Department of Maryland Past President's Parley Nursing Scholarship • 311

Mary Rubin and Benjamin M. Rubin Scholarship Fund • 471

Massachusetts
Amelia Greenbaum/Rabbi Marshal Lipson Scholarship • 441

General Federation of Women's Clubs of Massachusetts Memorial Education Fellowship • 486

Metropolitan Life Foundation Awards Program for Academic Excellence in Medicine • 252

Susan Glover Hitchcock Scholarship • 304

Michigan
American Legion Auxiliary Department of Michigan Memorial Scholarship • 378

Ford Motor Company Fellows Program • 439

UNCF/Pfizer Corporate Scholars Program • 27

Minnesota
Many Voices Residency Program • 297

Page Education Foundation Grant • 444

Missouri
Burlington Northern Santa Fe Foundation/ Hispanic College Fund Scholarship Program • 11

Lela Murphy Scholarship • 349

Missouri Minority Teaching Scholarship • 174

Montana
Cady McDonnell Memorial Scholarship • 342

Mary Ellen Russell Memorial Scholarship • 220

Miss Outstanding Teenager and Leadership Training Program • 489

Nebraska
American Legion Auxiliary Department of Nebraska President's Scholarship for Junior Members • 350

Norma Ross Walter Scholarship • 301

Nevada
Cady McDonnell Memorial Scholarship • 342

Miss Outstanding Teenager and Leadership Training Program • 489

Nevada Women's Fund Scholarships • 490

New Jersey
Martin Luther King Physician/Dentist Scholarships • 157

New Jersey Educational Opportunity Fund Grants • 158

New Jersey Scholarship • 217

New Jersey (continued)

New Jersey Utilities Association Scholarship • 491

UNCF/Pfizer Corporate Scholars Program • 27

New Mexico

Burlington Northern Santa Fe Foundation/ Hispanic College Fund Scholarship Program • 11

Cady McDonnell Memorial Scholarship • 342

Minority Doctoral Assistance Loan-For-Service Program • 492

New York

Biller/Jewish Foundation for Education of Women • 461

Metropolitan Life Foundation Awards Program for Academic Excellence in Medicine • 252

Regents Professional Opportunity Scholarships • 493

UNCF/Pfizer Corporate Scholars Program • 27

North Carolina

ABB Lummis Global • 190

Charlotte Observer Minority Scholarships • 76

International Society of Women Airline Pilots North Carolina Career Scholarship • 57

L'Oreal /Family Circle Cup "Personal Best" Scholarship • 481

Ohio

ABB Lummis Global • 190

Esperanza Scholarships • 403

Metropolitan Life Foundation Awards Program for Academic Excellence in Medicine • 252

Ohio Newspapers Foundation Minority Scholarship • 275

Oklahoma

Metropolitan Life Foundation Awards Program for Academic Excellence in Medicine • 252

Oregon

American Legion Auxiliary Department of Oregon Spirit of Youth Scholarship • 351

Cady McDonnell Memorial Scholarship • 342

Dorothy Campbell Memorial Scholarship • 494

James Carlson Scholarship Program • 175

Mentor Graphics Scholarship • 143

Pennsylvania

ABB Lummis Global • 190

Allfirst/ Hispanic College Fund Scholarship Program • 10

Metropolitan Life Foundation Awards Program for Academic Excellence in Medicine • 252

Puerto Rico

Ford Motor Company Fellows Program • 439

HSF/Toyota Foundation Scholarship Program-Puerto Rico • 427

Rhode Island

Marlynne Graboys Wool Scholarship • 286

Metropolitan Life Foundation Awards Program for Academic Excellence in Medicine • 252

Raymond H. Trott Scholarship • 446

RDW Group, Inc. Minority Scholarship for Communications • 135

Rhode Island Commission on Women/Freda Goldman Education Award • 497

South Carolina

Charlotte Observer Minority Scholarships • 76

L'Oreal /Family Circle Cup "Personal Best" Scholarship • 481

Metropolitan Life Foundation Awards Program for Academic Excellence in Medicine • 252

South Dakota

American Legion Auxiliary Department of South Dakota Thelma Foster Scholarship for Senior Auxiliary Members • 352

American Legion Auxiliary Department of South Dakota Thelma Foster Scholarships for Junior Auxiliary Members • 353

American Legion Auxiliary, Department of South Dakota Senior Scholarship • 354

Tennessee

Minority Teaching Fellows Program/ Tennessee • 182

TEA Don Sahli-Kathy Woodall Minority Scholarship • 181

Texas

ABB Lummis Global • 190

Amarillo Women's Network Nancy Sample Garms Scholarship • 466

Burlington Northern Santa Fe Foundation/ Hispanic College Fund Scholarship Program • 11

Dr. Juan D. Villarreal/ Hispanic Dental Association Foundation • 155

Ford Motor Company Fellows Program • 439

Future Journalists Scholarship Program • 121

HSF/South Texas Scholarship • 426

Metropolitan Life Foundation Awards Program for Academic Excellence in Medicine • 252

Utah

Cady McDonnell Memorial Scholarship • 342

Miss Outstanding Teenager and Leadership Training Program • 489

Utah Educationally Disadvantaged Program • 374

Vermont
Barbara Jean Barker Memorial Scholarship
  for a Displaced Homemaker • 487

Virginia
Allfirst/ Hispanic College Fund Scholarship
  Program • 10
Buena M. Chesshir Memorial Women's
  Educational Scholarship • 498
Karen B. Lewis Career Education Scholarship
  • 499
Women in Science and Technology
  Scholarship • 74

Washington
American Legion Auxiliary Department of
  Washington Susan Burdett Scholarship
  • 467
Bobby McCallum Memorial Scholarship
  • 276
Cady McDonnell Memorial Scholarship • 342
Mary Ellen Russell Memorial Scholarship
  • 220

Northwest Journalists of Color Scholarship
  • 119
Northwest Journalists of Color Scholarship
  • 274

Wisconsin
Minority Retention Grant-Wisconsin • 458
Talent Incentive Program-Wisconsin • 501

Wyoming
Cady McDonnell Memorial Scholarship • 342
Mary N. Brooks Daughter/Granddaughter
  Scholarship • 362
Mary N. Brooks Wyoming Girl Scholarship
  • 484
Miss Outstanding Teenager and Leadership
  Training Program • 489
Ruth Clare Yonkee District Scholarship
  • 485
Society of Women Engineers-Rocky
  Mountain Section Scholarship Program
  • 149

TALENT INDEX

Art
Cintas Fellowships Program • 41
NLAPW Virginia Liebeler Biennial Grants for
Mature Women (Arts) • 48

Athletics/sports
Charles T. Stoner Law Scholarship Award
• 288
Ethnic Minority and Women's Enhancement
Scholarship • 339
Linda Riddle/SGMA Scholarship • 341
Robin Roberts/WBCA Sports
Communications Scholarship Award
• 139
Travel and Training Fund • 510
WBCA Scholarship Award • 509

Beauty pageant
Albert A. Marks, Jr. Scholarship for Teacher
Education • 172
Dr. and Mrs. David B. Allman Medical
Scholarships • 243
Eugenia Vellner Fischer Award for
Performing Arts • 316
Leonard C. Horn Award for Legal Studies
• 282
Miss America Organization Competition
Scholarships • 504
Miss American Coed Pageant • 503

Bowling
Alberta E. Crowe Star of Tomorrow Award
• 370

Designated field specified by sponsor
Garth Reeves, Jr. Memorial Scholarships
• 136
Women's Jewelry Association Scholarship
Program • 344

English language
Gina Auditore Boner Memorial Scholarship
Fund • 78
Inter American Press Association
Scholarships • 271
Kim Love Satory Scholarship • 5

French language
Inter American Press Association
Scholarships • 271
Mary Isabel Sibley Fellowship for Greek and
French Studies • 33

Golf
Dorothy Campbell Memorial Scholarship
• 494
Florida Women's State Golf Association
Scholarship Fund • 482

National Minority Junior Golf Scholarship
• 442
Women's Western Golf Foundation
Scholarship • 511

Greek language
Mary Isabel Sibley Fellowship for Greek and
French Studies • 33

Leadership
American Institute for Foreign Study
Minority Scholarships • 382
California Junior Miss Scholarship Program
• 470
Fellowship Program in AIDS Care for
Minority Medical Students • 246
Ford Motor Company Scholarship • 210
Franklin C. McLean Award • 247
General Motors Foundation Graduate
Scholarship • 113
General Motors Foundation Undergraduate
Scholarships • 114
Gerber Fellowship in Pediatric Nutrition
• 248
Hugh J. Andersen Memorial Scholarships
• 249
Irving Graef Memorial Scholarship • 250
Junior Girls Scholarship Program • 369
Kim Love Satory Scholarship • 5
Mas Family Scholarships • 80
Multicultural Scholarship Program • 438
Ralph W. Ellison Memorial Prize • 254
Society of Daughters of the United States
Army Scholarships • 376
William and Charlotte Cadbury Award • 255
Wyeth-Ayerst Laboratories Prize in Women's
Health • 256
Youth Opportunities Foundation
Scholarships • 460

Music
Anne Louise Barrett Fellowship • 508
Cintas Fellowships Program • 41
NOA Vocal Competition/ Legacy Award
Program • 49

Music/singing
Gladys Stone Wright Scholarship • 183
Graduate Scholarship in Music Education
• 176
Helen May Bulter Memorial Scholarship
• 184
Martha Ann Stark Memorial Scholarship
• 185
Music Technology Scholarship • 186
Music Therapy Scholarships (SAI) • 305

NLAPW Virginia Liebeler Biennial Grants for Mature Women (Music) • 506

NOA Vocal Competition/ Legacy Award Program • 49

Sigma Alpha Iota Doctoral Grant • 177

Sigma Alpha Iota Graduate Performance Awards • 306

Sigma Alpha Iota Philanthropies Undergraduate Performance Scholarships • 307

Sigma Alpha Iota Philanthropies Undergraduate Scholarships • 178

Sigma Alpha Iota Scholarship for Conductors • 308

Sigma Alpha Iota Summer Music Scholarships in the U.S. or abroad • 309

Sigma Alpha Iota Visually Impaired Scholarship • 179

Verna Ross Orndorff Career Performance Grant • 310

Volkwein Memorial Scholarship • 187

Photography/photogrammetry/ filmmaking
Carole Simpson Scholarship • 129

Cintas Fellowships Program • 41

National Association of Hispanic Journalists Scholarship • 124

NLAPW Virginia Liebeler Biennial Grants for Mature Women (Arts) • 48

Portuguese language
Inter American Press Association Scholarships • 271

Joseph S. Adams Scholarship • 225

Spanish language
Cristina Saralegui Scholarship Program • 272

Inter American Press Association Scholarships • 271

Joseph S. Adams Scholarship • 225

Maria Elena Salinas Scholarship • 273

Writing
Carole Simpson Scholarship • 129

Cintas Fellowships Program • 41

Frances Shaw Fellowship • 496

Many Voices Residency Program • 297

National Association of Hispanic Journalists Scholarship • 124

NLAPW Virginia Liebeler Biennial Grants for Mature Women (Letters) • 505

Spinsters Ink Young Feminist Scholarship • 507

Give Your Admissions Essay An Edge At...

EssayEdge✒.com

Put Harvard-Educated Editors To Work For You

As the largest and most critically acclaimed admissions essay service, EssayEdge.com has assisted countless college, graduate, business, law, and medical program applicants gain acceptance to their first choice schools. With more than 250 Harvard-educated editors on staff, EssayEdge.com provides superior editing and admissions consulting, giving you an edge over hundreds of applicants with comparable academic credentials.

Visit **www.essayedge.com today,**
and take your admissions essay to a new level.

"One of the Best Essay Services on the Internet"
—*The Washington Post*

"The World's Premier Application Essay Editing Service"
—*The New York Times Learning Network*

THOMSON
PETERSON'S